ORIGI

HOLY WAR

To Jenny

Best Wishes !

Phillip Day

Origins II – Holy War

Copyright © 2014
Phillip Day

ISBN 1-904015-31-X

Manufactured in Great Britain and distributed globally by:

Credence Publications
PO Box 3
TONBRIDGE
Kent TN12 9ZY UK
www.credence.org

1st ed.

TABLE OF CONTENTS

AUTHOR'S NOTE

The book you are about to read is a compendium of research material and commentary compiled on a complex but enthralling series of subjects. During the course of my travels and teachings over the past 30 years, I resolved to do some leg-work and gather some principal sources, drawing together the raw data, differing opinions, research and commentaries and present them to you in some sort of cohesive form. Now you can sit back in your armchair with more than a few facts at your fingertips, the hard slog is done. And if you want to investigate a particular point further, adequate sources and recommendations are given in the text and footnotes.

Often, seemingly meaningless information takes on a new significance when placed in context with other pieces of the overall jigsaw. This is the excitement of working the information puzzle. For instance, putting together different events in history known to have occurred at the same time gives a greater clue as to why historical characters acted the way they did and why the world is as we find it today. Many personalities have spoken out and commented on one or more of the subjects covered in the following pages. It has been my aim to quote them as accurately as I can and scour book and article releases to reflect the most up-to-date positions on these issues for your consideration.

I have included sources that do not necessarily reflect my own views but enhance the subject matter, and quoted much source material verbatim with adequate references where possible. Where newspapers are cited, those selected are typically publications representing the wider readerships. Biblical commentaries are from a wide spectrum of denominational camps and quotes are from the Authorised King James Version (KJV), unless otherwise indicated (e.g. NKJV, NIV, ASB, ISV, etc.). Forgive me for underlining sections of quotes to draw the reader's attention to something specific.

You will notice in places that I have labelled quotes from 'John's gospel' as 'Fourth Gospel' (i.e. FG 3:16). The later attribution of the fourth gospel to John Zebedee of Galilee is purely ex-Biblical tradition and, I believe, in error. This in no way detracts from the inspired nature of the book, and we'll discover the anonymity of the gospel and its uniqueness from the Synoptics was intentioned and necessary. So please bear with this labelling in *Origins 1, 2 and 3* and I will present the full case and evidence for this intriguing enigma, together with the most surprising candidate for its authorship, in *Origins 4 – Tetelestai.*

The *Origins* series is designed to be a study resource. Due to the copious themes explored in this project, footnotes are given detailing sources which can be employed for further study. The purpose here is not to compel the reader into any one interpretation, but to broaden appreciation of the subject as a whole. As usual, you will get my opinion on everything, but this is less to influence than to inform!

I have added Google Earth co-ordinates where appropriate to enable the reader to view the locations under discussion. Just enter the co-ordinates into Google Earth exactly as given and hit your <Enter> key. This is probably the best resource to use to gain an appreciation of the geography of the story.

Lastly, scientific and medical data are indexed where appropriate and intended for educational purposes only. Specialists in certain of the subjects covered are quoted and their opinions discussed.

The reader must, of course, appreciate that no source is 100% accurate or unbiased, not even this one! However, neither should a particular source be discounted because the position held is contentious. As always, it is up to you, the reader, to do your own research and come to your own conclusions.

Bon voyage!

Phillip Day

INTRODUCTION

"We are all atheists about most of the gods that societies have ever believed in. Some of us just go one god further." – **Richard Dawkins**

"For the invisible things of Him from the Creation of the world are clearly seen, being understood by the things that are made, even His eternal power and Godhead; so that they are without excuse." (Rom 1:20)

Welcome to *Origins 2 – Holy War.*

So, here we all are. By blind, random chance or part of a far larger plan being rolled out? Is there a God who created the universe and all within it, or did the universe make itself? Or perhaps we were seeded here by some extraterrestrial progenitors – a popular view today known as panspermia. Is life essentially meaningless or can we attach any ultimate significance to our existence? And if so, on what grounds? Has the Universal Mind (God) ever made contact? If so, how do we know?

Even today all this is a hot topic. In the comments section of the British *Daily Mail,* Alistair H M wrote:

"No atheist I have asked can answer this question. 'If there is no God, what is the point of the universe?'"

He got the following replies:

"That's because it is an illogical question. Like asking, 'If there is no tooth fairy, what is the point of teeth?'"

"Simple, let me put you out of your misery. There is no point. Religion was invented by 'leaders' in order to frighten and control the proletariat. It has now got so out of hand among the gullible and insane that it is the #1 threat to peace on this planet..."

"Every atheist you ask has probably told you the answer, you just didn't want to hear it. There is no point. Why must there be a point? We don't exist for billions of years, then we live for less than a hundred years, and then cease to exist once more. There is no 'point' however much you want there to be one. Why must there be a point to enjoy life?"

"You're making quite an assumption there. Why does there have to be a point?"

"And no God-fearer I have asked has been able to answer this question: 'If there IS a God, what is the point of the universe?'"

Such philosophical arguments are not new. They have tested the best minds for the past three thousand years. The truth of our origins bears extraordinary implications for us as individuals, and not least society, for if life is ultimately meaningless and there is no big plan, then you are living without any ultimate hope or a future. So why not do what you want, free of any eventual responsibility or reckoning? Why bother working when the do-gooders can pay your benefits? Who cares if you rape, murder, lie, cheat and steal your way to the top of the evolutionary pile if there's no ultimate accountability? After all, it's survival of the fittest on the Serengeti, according to David Attenborough. Aren't human animals just the same?

And if there's no design, no Creator, no accountability, the universe doesn't have us in mind and Earth made itself, then why not start genetically modifying everything with our newfound brilliance to improve our environment, even ourselves, if, in the end, nothing really matters?

And what about religion – man's attempt to cover himself before an ultimate Creator? Is religion a dangerous fake or is there something to it? If so, which religion is valid and which is fake? They can't all be right. Indeed, why do any need to be right? Why do we have to take some book's word for it? How can we know for sure?

Evolution has slaughtered millions in the name of humanism, but what about religion? When we hear the term 'Holy War', perhaps Joshua's ethnic cleansing of the Canaanites comes to mind. What about the onward march of Islam from the 7th century, swords glinting in the sun? The Crusader wars between Muslims and Christians; the Crusader massacres of the Jews, Cathars, Waldensians and Albigenses in the 11th - 13th centuries; the appalling behaviour of the medieval popes; wars between

Catholics and Protestants; Cromwell's Protestant slaughter of Catholic Drogheda; my God is better than your God; today's Islamic extremism, even at the expense of moderate Muslim lives. Sunni versus Shi'ite, the 1,400-year simmering war no-one wants to talk about. Which God? Who's wrong? Who's to say who's right? How do we know what we know? What happens when I press this?

What a fantastic subject, one that has enthralled me my entire life. One tool I've always used to get to the heart of thorny subjects like this is to imagine myself rising up to stare down at the overall shape of the conundrum *from outside the system*. First, get a bird's eye view – a completely different perspective to the problem. How do you do this? You start by examining, not suppositions or theories, but what actually is. In other words, the evidence. If you don't do this, you'll find one's views and conclusions will tend towards what makes us comfortable rather than any uncomfortable truths we might trip across that don't fit with our preconceived bias. This is certainly the case with the notorious subject of human origins. And we all come to the project with prejudices. Yes, even me.

Betwixt the miracle of our origins and mystery of our destiny lies the messy business of life, and life really needs some explaining… *or does it?* Should we really attach any meaning to this journey called 'life' or should we be content living life in the natural for eighty years, following the underpinning evolutionary ethos of our age that it's all one big, glorious accident but ultimately meaningless and therefore not worthy of comment? That's what they teach the kids in the classroom today. You're nothing but an evolved monkey. You got here by a bewildering chain of billions of 'beneficial', random mistakes. Quell your interrogatory spirit and make the most of the playground you've fallen into, but don't dare ascribe any ultimate meaning to the experience of 'life' or you're a religious nut.

But *is* there something more out there, something wondrous, incredible, knowable, tantalisingly just out of reach? If so, how can we *really* know?

Well, we know what religion says, and we know what atheists believe, but let's try another approach. Look around and examine the reality that cocoons you – who you are, what surrounds you physically; what eventually becomes of you – and there are major clues. You're born, you live, you die and nothing can halt or reverse that process. In fact, *you're born to die*. In the incredible 21st century where we have legions of scientific experts pontificating on just about any subject, there's one on which they all fall silent. "What's going to happen to me when I die?" "My life. Do I have the right to ask, 'What on Earth was the point?'"

They've got nothing to say scientifically about what lies beyond death, I've asked them. A few mumble about how you're just chemicals which go back into the earth after they bury you and the bacteria have done their thing. You're part of *The Lion King's* great Circle of Life. According to Wallace McRae's excellent cowboy poem, *Reincarnation*, you become a flower which is then eaten by a horse for its sustenance…

"But some is left that he can't use
And so it passes through,
And finally lays upon the ground
This thing that once wuz you." [1]

In *Origins I*, I demonstrate how our sophisticated, space-age culture has underpinned itself with the greatest lie of all – evolution – which is the idea that, via undirected processes, our universe, world and all the creatures and systems within somehow *made themselves*, as did the 'natural' phenomena which govern the whole, such as the weak nuclear force, strong nuclear force, Boltzmann's Constant, proton and electron mass, atomic mass, speed of light, gravity, Planck's Constant, and so on. Evolution means, philosophically, that your life is ultimately meaningless; that what you do or think doesn't matter; that all the skills you learnt and 'I love you's' whispered are laughably pointless, and your ultimate destination may well not be back to stardust but out the back end of Wallace McRae's steed to start the whole tedious process all over again. *Sheesh*, it's enough to turn you to religion.

---

[1] **McRae, W** *Reincarnation*, www.cowboypoetry.com/mcrae.htm#Rein

The trouble is, aside from mockery, renowned British evolutionary biologist and atheist Richard Dawkins has yet to devise an effective means of stopping you from reaching for something more. Man, it seems, has been blessed or cursed with an innate craving to ascribe some meaning to his existence, to give his adulation to a higher power. Whether our worship goes to 'God', to another person, to a national leader such as Tony Blair, Stalin or Hitler (unintended juxtaposition), or even to ourselves or a Porsche, there exists 'a God-shaped vacuum in every heart', and a cursory examination of history will reveal that man's restless search for the spiritual – a cogent explanation for his destiny - has shaped and often blighted his chequered history upon this planet. Are there some people looking for God in all the wrong places? Jim Jones did. Even today, those like Richard Dawkins, who profess no spiritual belief whatsoever, have to *believe* in no God, since it is a logical impossibility to prove beyond doubt the *non-existence* of something unless you are omniscient, omnipresent and omnipotent, three attributes of the God they hate. More than a few atheists slink off to a medium or tarot reader from time to time in the hope of finding – well, answers. Is it better to hope or to have no hope? Man is naturally predisposed to *belief* to explain what he does not know. Belief need not be a disease but a profound hope. What will play at your funeral: Sinatra's *My Way* or *Nearer My God to Thee?*

So what do we know for sure? On the one hand we are constrained by our biology. We are mortal and death holds the ultimate Sword of Damocles over us. We know we will age, grow infirm, suffer tragedy and the inevitable loss, not only of teeth, but of those who mean the most to us. But there's another part of us which soars beyond the physical, disdaining to accept the effluent fate of Wallace McRae's nag. The wondrous complexity and sheer order of the world around us begs even the dullest to imagine that there could be some ultimate plan. So people turn to religion to explain the unexplainable. And someone called 'God' appears to be smack in the middle of it all.

The *Origins* series is an attempt to get to the bottom of the big questions. *Who are we? Where do we come from? What are we doing here? And what's going to happen to us when this life is over?* In tackling such a monumental project, the first challenge is in finding source material that can be trusted. Who's the ultimate authority we consult to explain the unexplainable and give us the answers? *God?* Which God? Whose God? Isn't God the last jacket you throw on when all other rational options have flown out of the window?

God's definitely a problem. Richard Dawkins bemoans God's reluctance to make Himself known, likening the odds of an all-powerful Deity existing to those of fairies dancing up his garden path. The Hebrew/Christian God, if He exists at all, must be a *"petty, unjust, unforgiving control freak; a vindictive, racist, infanticidal, genocidal, filicidal, malevolent bully."*[2] The Bible could even harm schoolchildren. Dawkins feels strongly enough about the 'con' of religion to have shaped an extension to his sterling scientific career by championing the cause of atheism. God is dangerous. What about all those slaughters carried out by popes, kings, ayatollahs, imams and zealots in the name of religion? Creationists are deluded saps. *Real* scientists hold to the evolutionary view of our origins. This is proper science, not sanctimonious sophistry.

Proper science? We examined the scam of evolution in *Origins I – The Greatest Scientific Discovery*. We learned that even from a scientific standpoint, evolution is a wretched attempt to ignore what's staring us in the face. That we live in a designed system wherein every primal scientific ratio, calibration and constant has been set just so to ensure the genesis and propagation of complex life systems on Earth. Many have accepted evolution because it is all they have ever heard. Evolution is taught as established fact by credentialed experts in classrooms, museums, on television and in glossy periodicals. For the unwary, or those unwilling either to question what they are fed or face the militant bigotry provoked by denial, evolution seems as good an explanation as any for man's origins; a merciful, no-blame hypothesis since the alternative is God and all the judgment He brings. Evolution spells freedom from any scintilla of universal justice. You are a glorious accident but ever an accident. You are born, you live, then that's your lot.

---

[2] **Dawkins Richard** *The God Delusion*, Bantam, London, 2006

All you accomplish during the short time you are here means nothing. Right and wrong are old religious concepts to enslave and control the masses and should be discarded. You are nothing but the product of a cosmic burp, the end-game of billions of random mutations, so enjoy life while you've got it. You are the bird which flies into a party hall from the dark, enjoys the brief sensation of light, warmth and comfort as you traverse the festivities, then out you zoom into the dark once more, never to return. You are a fleeting dream in the great sea of Know Nothingness. Endless oblivion awaits you after a pointless life.

Richard Dawkins et al. championed an advertising campaign in January 2009, in which red buses drove around London proclaiming on their sides,

"There is probably no God. Now stop worrying and enjoy your life."[3]

But the public *is* worried. We have a sneaky sense all is not what it seems. Two years later, when Dawkins ducked a debate at Oxford with America's leading Christian apologist, the analytic philosopher and theologian William Lane Craig, another advert appeared on the buses:

"There is probably no Dawkins. Now stop worrying and enjoy Oct 25th at the Sheldonian Theatre."[4]

Paul Vallely writes:

The erstwhile Professor for Public Understanding of Science [Dawkins] was stung into a response in a newspaper article. Craig, he said, was a "deplorable apologist for genocide", with whom he would not share a platform. The genocide in question is that of the Canaanites in the Old Testament Book of Deuteronomy, which you might have expected our top atheist to point out is of dubious historical accuracy. But then any stick will do to beat a dogma."[5]

---

[3] *Daily Mail,* 22nd January 2009
[4] *Independent,* 23rd October 2011
[5] Ibid.

But Dawkins is not in tune with the general population he claims to represent. A 2006 poll revealed that only 48% of Britons accept evolution as an explanation of our origins in spite of all the brainwashing.[6] A whopping 92% of Americans believe in God or a universal spirit, but some say 'that's America'.[7] The fact is, religion's embarrassing, especially in Britain. The Anglican state churches lie bare, the lead stripped off their roofs, war memorials vandalised for their copper and bronze. Most don't want to talk about religion ("Marjorie will think I've joined a cult."). Some hedge their bets, attempting to balance the freedom to do what they want with 'a good life' just in case there's a reckoning. Dr Dawkins is frustrated by such gullibility:

"It is completely right to say that since the evidence for evolution is so absolutely, totally overwhelming, nobody who looks at it could possibly doubt that if they were sane and not stupid, so the only remaining possibility is that they're ignorant. And most people who don't believe in evolution are ignorant.... Evolution is a fact. It's a fact which is established as securely, essentially, as any other fact that we have in science." [8]

Then he selects his Target with care, presumably to avoid a fatwa:

"I am an atheist with respect to the Judeo-Christian God, because there is not a shred of evidence in favour of the Judeo-Christian God."[9]

We'll get to all sorts of gods in a minute – just hold your horses, Professor. As a student at one of England's premier establishments of private learning – Charterhouse – I studied your Darwinism at tedious length and my first reaction was hilarity; my second complete bafflement as to how such lettered scions like you

---

[6] *Weekend* magazine, *Daily Mail,* 24th January 2009, p.12

[7] Washington Post, 24th June 2008, p.A02

[8] *Expelled – No Intelligence Allowed,* documentary, Premise Media Corporation, 2008, www.credence.org

[9] *Expelled – No Intelligence Allowed* DVD, Premise Media Corporation, 2008. Available via www.credence.org

could buy into such tommyrot, even if you hate God. Forget religion, consider Charlie's theory for what it is. The Earth's population at the time I was at college was five billion, far too small to have resulted from countless sexual acts over millions of years. And how did those sexual organs evolve during the time when they were all floppy and no good for procreation, eh? And where are all those transitional/intermediate forms that must exist to prove monkeys turned into men, reptiles grew feathers and flew, whales became cows, rats morphed into bats, and fish grew legs, crawled up onto dry land, shed their scales and breathed air? I mean, if we're talking *facts*, Dr Dawkins, *you don't preach any*. The few 'missing links' you still parade have long been exposed as frauds or mere human or animal remains, yet they still show up in our children's textbooks.

Dig deeper and the Oprah moment comes upon you when you realise arguments about human origins aren't really about science at all but *belief*. Richard Lewontin, Professor of Zoology and Biology at Harvard University, paints the scandal this way:

"Our willingness to accept scientific claims that are against common sense is the key to an understanding of the real struggle between science and the supernatural. We take the side of science in spite of the patent absurdity of some of its constructs, in spite of its failure to fulfill many of its extravagant promises of health and life, in spite of the tolerance of the scientific community for unsubstantiated just-so stories, because we have a prior commitment, a commitment to materialism. It is not that the methods and institutions of science somehow compel us to accept a material explanation of the phenomenal world, but, on the contrary, that we are forced by our *a priori* adherence to material causes to create an apparatus of investigation and a set of concepts that produce material explanations, no matter how counter-intuitive, no matter how mystifying to the uninitiated. Moreover, that materialism is absolute, for we cannot allow a Divine Foot in the door."[10]

---

[10] **Lewontin R C** "Billions and Billions of Demons", Review of **Sagan, Carl** *The Demon-Haunted World: Science as a Candle in the Dark*, New York Review, 9th January 1997

In other words, many scientists know evolution is a crock but believe in it anyway because a) it produces a pay-cheque and b) under no circumstances can 'God' ever be permitted to crash the party.

I named the first book in this series *Origins – The Greatest Scientific Discovery*. That discovery is that humans are provably taking part in an intricate, spacetime digital simulation on a multi-dimensional/galactic scale, wherein we are meant to discover the deeper truths to our existence and ultimate destiny. In other words, huge effort has been spent crafting the Creation and everything in it *for our benefit*, so it must have been done for a reason. What is that purpose? Can we ever know? What is our role in that purpose? Where/who do we turn to for guidance? *What is the source material?*

In *Origins I*, I cover the extraordinary, undeniable evidence that man, the Earth, the planets, galaxies and universe have been exquisitely designed with attention's every detail right down to the cell, DNA, proteins, molecules, atoms and sub-atomic particles. In fact, below the scale of the indivisible quantum particle, matter loses locality and dissolves into a heaving sea of infinite energy that has come to be known as the Zero Point Field. *The Field has mind.* Scientists now wonder whether the reality you and I experience is but a highly elaborate digital simulation/projection from this quantum energy or Infinite Mind. Here's the kicker. The world is literally bursting with *information*. And *information* is the product of *intelligence*. And *intelligence* means a *mind*, which means a *person*. Science cannot explain the origin of life because it cannot explain the origin of the information which underpins life. So where does that leave us?

The story so far

In *Origins I*, I covered the tools scientists are now using to uncover an astonishing new picture of human existence. Contrary to popular belief, the great discoveries of the 20th century were not the atomic bomb, Simon Cowell or the iPod. What has been found has been so controversial that even today newspapers studiously avoid the subject for fear of ridicule, and few scientists discuss them openly for fear of losing their jobs or worse. These discoveries can be summarised as follows:

1. We've discovered the boundaries to our reality. There is a limit to the macro structure ('bigness'). The universe is *finite* (Hubble).

2. And the micro universe is *finite*. You cannot split a quantum particle or it loses locality and goes everywhere at once. The micro system is also *quantised* (digital). The study of these indivisible phenomena (Planck length, Planck time, Planck mass, etc.) is known as quantum physics.

3. With size limits set at either end, the conclusion is that mankind is part of a highly elaborate digital simulation, wherein the Earth, planets and entire cosmos appear to have been crafted as a backdrop to the human experience. The reality we experience is but a subset of a much larger reality involving dimensions to which we don't yet have access.[11]

4. Information is found everywhere in our Creation, coded into the very DNA of every organism on the planet. It has been calculated that the sum total of all the A, T, G, C DNA bases *in one human* would fill books which would fill Grand Canyon 50 times. Conclusion: Someone's gone to a lot of trouble to code you up.

5. Information weighs nothing, yet conveys everything. True information is anomalous. When we find information, its source is intelligent, i.e. a mind, a person. You cannot have information without intelligence. Natural selection cannot compile genetic information; by its very operation natural selection *reduces* genetic information. That we find our Creation so ordered and orchestrated by *laws* is the giveaway.

6. The current (evolutionary) scientific paradigm is known as the Copernican or Mediocrity Principle. This holds that Planet Earth is not unique, is nothing special, the universe does not have us in mind, and we have no preferred place in the cosmos. Yet scientists are finding the opposite. From the complexity of

---

[11] *Scientific American*, June 1985; www.templetonprize.org/esprelease.html

the cell, to the forces operating within an atom, to the laws governing gravity, the tides, planets and galaxies, the sheer *ordered* nature of the universe and our planet refutes this utterly and demands an explanation, however unpopular and unwelcome.

7. The miracle of Earth's existence is reflected in the many precise conditions that must exist for the planet, let alone humankind, to survive. Over 100 finely tuned constants must exist for a planet to be habitable and a further 30 for complex life to be possible, and this still does not get you life from non-living matter in the first place.[12] Some of these constants are so finely calibrated that a scale-variance of just 10^{-55} would render life impossible (Meyer, Dembski, McDowell, Missler).

8. Despite his evolutionary stance, co-discoverer of DNA, Francis Crick, remarked:

"An honest man, armed with all the knowledge available to us now, could only state that in some sense, the origin of life appears at the moment to be almost a miracle, so many are the conditions which would have had to have been satisfied to get it going."[13]

9. Though the universe has been designed to be *knowable*, it appears to have been crafted in such a way that you have to search for it. i.e. Earth has been positioned between two spiral arms of the Milky Way galaxy in such a way as to form an ideal platform from which to make scientific discoveries, not only within our own solar system (unique transparent atmosphere, solar system location, anthropic constants, etc.), but into deep space due to our specific, dust-free, galactic location (Gonzalez, Richards).

10. A solar eclipse is only possible because the moon fits precisely over the sun in such a way so as not to blind the observer, yet reveal the sun's chromosphere. From this we observed the electromagnetic 'flash' spectrum and modern astrophysics was born. The obvious conclusion? We were meant to discover this.

---

[12] www.reasons.org/articles/design-and-the-anthropic-principle

[13] **Crick, F** *Life Itself: Its Origin and Nature,* Simon and Schuster, New York, 1981, p.88

11. The 'fit' of a solar eclipse is perfect for this discovery. What are the chances that our sun is 400 times larger than the moon but just so happens to be 400 times further away? Astronomer Guillermo Gonzalez calculated that of the 70-odd planets and moons in our solar system, the best platform from which to observe a total solar eclipse is from the surface of the only planet hosting complex life capable of knowing what it's looking at.

12. Within the vast band of solar radiation emitted by our sun, which ranges from gamma through x-ray to ultraviolet to infrared, microwave and radio, there exists an impossibly narrow zone of visible light in the middle by which all things live and can be seen. This visible spectrum comprises only *1 trillion of a trillionth* of the entire range of the universe's electromagnetic emissions, which just so happens to be the light spectrum our sun emits in abundance. This light penetrates our wafer-thin atmosphere in precise amounts to be used by plants, animals and humans for life. *And it's the only part of the spectrum detectable by the human eye.*

13. Physics now believes there are at least ten dimensions, four of which are knowable ('spacetime': x, y, z and time). The other six are believed to be curled into less than 10^{-33} cm (below the quantum limit) and are not knowable but can be inferred (sometimes referred to as 'the metacosm' or 'spiritual realm').

14. Time is a physical dimension which can change according to mass, acceleration and gravity (Einstein). Identical atomic clocks located at the National Institute of Standards and Technology (NIST), Boulder, Colorado and Royal Observatory, Greenwich, England *keep different time* due to variance in altitude and therefore gravity.

15. The universe gives the impression of having been 'wound up' and is now 'unwinding' (Second Law of Thermodynamics - entropy). Universal constants such as the speed of light are also slowing down (Setterfield), as is the rotational period of the Earth and the planet's magnetic field. Who/what originally wound everything up?

16. Far from man and all creatures having evolved from a primordial pollywog in Darwinian fashion, the work of Crick, Wilson and Watkins reveals that DNA in all living creatures contains the same source code of *digital information* in a one-dimensional form, from which three dimensional proteins are constructed for every creature. Some of these codings are even layered over other codings! When we find *information,* this means *intelligence*, which means a *mind*, which means a *designer*

17. Even simple proteins are far too complex to have been formed by natural selection acting on random variations, since information is required not only to construct but *sustain* them. Darwinian evolution *denies* the existence of organisational intelligence as an explanation for man's origins, so actually denies the information coded on the bases of the DNA molecule, one of the great discoveries of the 20th century.

18. Did it all happen by chance? If the odds of a single event or combination of events occurring by chance are smaller than 1 in 10^{50}, Borel's Law holds that chance as an explanation for the occurrence is 'absurd'.

19. Mathematician William Dembski sets the Universal Probability Bound for chance at a far larger figure. He calculates the outside limit to chance as the number of physical events that could have happened in the universe since its inception. He takes the number of atoms in the observable universe (10^{80}), multiplies them by the maximum rate per second at which physical particles can react (10^{45}), then multiplies this by the number of seconds estimated for the generally accepted age of the universe (10^{17}). He then increases this figure a billion times (American billion) to be on the safe side (10^{25}). The final product of this calculation is 10^{150}. To Dembski, any odds exceeding this figure assume *"a degree of improbability, below which a specified event of that probability cannot reasonably be attributed to chance regardless of whatever probabilitistic resources from the known universe are factored in."* [14]

---

[14] www.iscid.org/encyclopedia/Universal_Probability_Bound

20. Now consider haemoglobin, the oxygen-carrying truck in your blood, which is formed from a protein chain 574 amino acids long. Working from an available proteinaceous alphabet of 20 amino acids, what is the chance that haemoglobin occurred by natural selection acting on random variations according to Darwinian evolution? Zero, because natural selection only selects from *beneficial* precursors, and anything leading up to haemoglobin won't be haemoglobin until all the bits are in place and the protein folds, locks and launches.

21. So what are the chances that haemoglobin got it right by accident? 1 chance in 10^{650}. That's one chance in 10 with 649 zeroes after it, or roughly equal to the same person winning the California Super Lotto Jackpot 92 times. Out of that *staggering* number of possible permutations of amino acids, only one is haemoglobin with an error-rate of zero or *you're dead*. Compare haemoglobin's 10^{650} with the maximum number of particulate reactions that could have occurred since the start of the universe (10^{150}), and the conclusion is that I am 4.33 times more certain that haemoglobin was purposefully *designed* by a transcendent intelligence than I am about the fact of my own existence.

22. And that's just haemoglobin. Now you've got to account for a further 33,000 proteins forming in like random fashion, and 2,000-odd enzymes, and then all the fats, vitamins, minerals, hormones and substrates happening by accident to build 1,000,000 species of insects in all their multiplicity, 20,000 species of fish in all their size and assortment, over 350,000 plant species of incredible variety, 9,000 species of bird from the minute to the magnificent, and 5,400 species of mammal, from rabbits to meerkats to rhinos and everything in between. Oh, and us. And everything looks and is finished. There's no creature on its way to becoming anything else. And all within a timeframe of 10^{17} seconds, the evolutionist's age for the universe which, it turns out, is hopelessly wrong.

23. Why is evolution not possible even for one protein? Not nearly enough time and nowhere near enough stuff.

24. Many structures in nature are 'irreducibly complex', meaning that all the components of the system must be assembled at the same time and often in a unique order to achieve function. This is irrefutable evidence of design. Take the eye with its numerous sub-systems of lens, iris, retina, optic nerve, etc. Such systems could never have evolved by natural selection since there was no *functioning* precursor from which to select. No one sub-system can work on its own, so would not have survived natural selection. So what, for instance, was the iris doing for 400,000 years flopping about in a mud swamp before it found the eye and achieved function? The liver, brain, pancreas and ear are examples of other systems within systems.

25. Even evolution's most outspoken advocate, Dr Richard Dawkins, author of *The God Delusion* and *The Greatest Show on Earth*, admits that the signature of a designer can be found in the details of molecular biology.[15] However, he attributes any design to an alien civilisation which may have designed a form of life which it seeded onto Earth. This view, known as 'panspermia', has become popular among evolutionary scientists who can no longer plausibly deny the discovery of design. Far from explaining anything, panspermia merely kicks the problem into outer space. Who/what made the aliens?

26. The other problem with panspermia is that the design found across the macro, medial and micro structures of the universe is provably the same, which means that one Designer accomplished the lot. So, no aliens running up human pond-slime in a lab somewhere. Whoever the Designer is, he/she created a billion galaxies and is daily maintaining them at the sub-atomic level while renewing the trillions of cells in your body, creating your tears, extending the nose of the aardvark, and dusting the powder on butterfly wings.

27. All life on Earth appears to have come from the same software house, since all species' DNA is coded the same way, using an alphabet of four nucleotide bases, A, T, G and C. Put another way, the digital instructions to build the amoeba, horse, fly,

---

[15] Stein, Ben, *Expelled – No Intelligence Allowed* DVD, op. cit. Available at www.credence.org

elephant, kangaroo and duck-billed platypus all came from the same mind (software house), and it wasn't Ray Kurzweil and Google. DNA is a three-out-of-four, error-correcting *digital* code containing stop and start bits to parse the assembly instructions of every protein on Earth.

28. Design attributes of the cell are identical across the whole gamut of species. Professor of Biochemistry, Michael Behe, writes:

"At the very basis of life where molecules and cells run the show, we've discovered machines, literally molecular machines... There are little molecular trucks that carry supplies from one end of the cell to the other. There are machines which capture the energy from sunlight and turn it into usable energy.... When we look at these machines, we ask ourselves, where do they come from? And the standard answer – Darwinian evolution – is very inadequate in my view."[16]

Kinesins are two-legged machines that actually walk along microtubules transporting cargo! The flagellum (whippy tail), for example, which propels the *E. coli* bacterium, is essentially an outboard motor. Next time you throw Domestos down the loo to kill all those germs, consider that the design of *E. coli's* flagellum comprises a hook with filament or propeller rotating up to 100,000 rpm, a rotor, stator, drive shaft, U-joint, bushings and engine casing (inner and outer membranes). Its assembly defies any notion of a functional precursor in the evolutionary process. If just one of 40 structural components of the engine is missing, it does not work and the bacterium dies. How could the flagellum have evolved? Darwin seemed to anticipate the problem when he wrote,

"If it could be demonstrated that any complex organ existed which could not possibly have been formed by numerous, successive, slight modifications, my theory would absolutely break down."[17]

Well, guess what, Charlie?

---

[16] Ibid.

[17] Darwin, Charles, *Origin of Species,* op. cit., p.154

29. The Designer is dwelling both within and outside spacetime to get the job done.
30. All systems have not just been created, they are being *minutely sustained* at the sub-atomic level.
31. All matter is highly organised energy at its fundamental level. Something/someone has to do the organising. Humans are packets of quantum energy exchanging information with an inexhaustible energy sea known as the Zero Point Field (Pribram, Sheldrake, Backster, etc.).
32. The ZPF has intelligence and contains an imprint of everything that has ever happened (McTaggart).
33. What we believe, think, say and do is universally known and imprints the ZPF for all time (McTaggart).
34. The Field knows when we lie, deceive, cheat or don't mean it (Placebo, Primary Perception, Backster).
35. Our soul/spirit/ethereal has zero mass, is outside spacetime and therefore eternal, whether we like it or not. So are our thoughts. The very best of news for some is that we are going to live forever. The very worst of news for others is that we are going to live forever. The conclusion is that we are eternal spiritual beings having a temporary human experience, whether we like it or not. *For what reason?*
36. A current world population of 7.25 billion (01/08/2014) means that mankind has been in the procreation business for no more than 4,400 – 6,000 years, give or take a plague or war or three. If mankind has been evolving for 300,000 – 1 million years (standard evolutionary theory), where is everyone? No *genuine* transitional forms proving evolution from monkeys to humans have ever been found.
37. There is abundant evidence that Earth was destroyed at one point by a universal flood. This event can be dated to around 2345 BC by a number of methods.[18] Today's world population is consistent with the generative rates calculated for both Jews

---

[18] Day, Phillip, *Origins I – The Greatest Scientific Discovery*, op. cit.

and Muslims since their faiths' inception representing the expansion rate of the population in general.[19]

38. Around 200 cultures still have legends of the Flood. The stories seem to be describing the same event and substantially agree on story details.

39. The ecology of the pre-Flood Earth was very different from what we know today. Humans, animals, insects and vegetation grew prolifically and enjoyed pronounced longevity prior to the Flood. The remains of pre-Flood vegetation and animals are regularly excavated and a picture emerges of a pre-Flood 'Edenic' paradise.

40. Evidence of massive flood damage abounds in the canyons, hills and mountains of the Earth. Weird anomalies such as the dinosaur graveyards, a higher global sea-level, fossils on mountain-tops, Bryce Canyon, the Sahara Desert, highways under the sea and those Siberian mammoths are best explained by the effects of catastrophic flood processes, other examples of which we will examine in the *Origins* series.

41. The fossil record resoundingly endorses the Flood. Billions of clam and shell fossils are found around the world in unusually high locations in the closed position, indicating that they were buried alive. The uniformitarianism of evolutionary theory cannot account for either the fossils or hydrologically sorted sedimentary (flood) layers in which they are found.

42. Most dinosaurs were destroyed in the Inundation but a few survived and some may even be alive today. Many cultures have legends of human and animal giants, dragons and dinosaur-like creatures. More about this lot later.

43. Properly organised, recorded history is generally accepted to have commenced around the 5th century BC, approximately 1,700 years after the best estimates for the Inundation. If evolving mankind had been around hundreds of thousands of years before that, how come we only attained a state of recorded civilisation around the time of Herodotus?

---

[19] Ibid.

44. If everything is evolving from simple to complex with no informational/organisational input (a scientifically impossible feat), why do we still have 'simple' lifeforms like the amoeba? If monkeys turned into man, why do we still have monkeys?

45. If we all started from the same primordial pollywog, how come man is the only animal which evolved so inordinately further in intelligence than any other life-form? Why don't we have dogs that do calculus? Where are the budgies muscling ahead of us to place sell-orders on the stock markets? Why has not one rhino written a more arresting soliloquy than Shakespeare?

46. We're the only species with language. The only species that understands the concept of the past and can plan for the future. We're the only species that marvels at art and beauty, creates music, and is drawn to a Creator. *Only one species alone* made it this far out of 1,000,000 species of insects, 20,000 species of fish, 350,000 plant species of incredible variety, 9,000 species of bird, and 5,400 species of mammal, from rabbits to rhinos! Why don't we have some of our smart, near relative, gorilla-kin beating us at chess and chiding us in iambic pentameters, as evolution, mathematical probability and sound reason should have it?

47. The logical conclusion is that the world and everything within and beyond have been designed with attention's every detail and are daily sustained by some quantum intelligence (Neh 9:6; Col 1:17). So the next questions must be:
   1. Who is the Designer?
   2. If a Designer has the technology to create us, he has the technology to get a message to us. Has he done so?
   3. If he has, how would we validate that message to be certain it was from the Designer and not an impostor?
   4. Are we justified in using a properly validated Message System as source material to stride out into the unknown? To determine where mankind and the planet are heading from here?
   5. Why not a She?

Extraterrestrial contact

Could Dawkins be right? Perhaps mankind could have been seeded on Earth by an alien race which periodically revisits the planet to ensure we haven't yet detonated ourselves to Kingdom Come. These questions, many may be surprised to learn, are being taken seriously by governments, the Vatican and other organisations around the world, and there is an expectation among many that a disclosure-type event of some kind regarding the existence of ETs is in our near future.

One of the most popular fields of entertainment these days is alien science fiction. Into this you can toss the whole smorgasbord of werewolves, zombies, vampires, trolls, sylphs, fairies, monsters, giants and miscellaneous demonic ne'er-do-wells that have traditionally dominated cinema theatres since the 1950's, and lately iTunes, Lovefilm and Netflix. This genre has softened up the world to the idea that Earth has been, and is being regularly visited by aliens – a concept that has been hinted at by three US presidents, leading Vatican spokesmen, and numerous astronaut and air force personnel.[20] Today a sizeable chunk of the population now believes that we came from the star people, and religion was a control mechanism given to us by our space brethren to keep us in line.

In any event, as we'll discover later, serious preparations have been made by religions and governments for just such an announcement. Science programmes like SETI (The Search for Extraterrestrial Intelligence) spend fortunes scanning space for some signal or message from beyond, though millions are convinced contact has long since been made with extraterrestrial intelligence and our governments are keeping quiet because of the chaos and panic disclosure might cause. Consider what the global impact on existing religious belief systems might be if such an announcement were made. Consider also that any message received from 'out there' would have to give unequivocal proof of its authenticity as an intelligent source.

One movie, atheist Carl Sagan's *Contact!* starring Jodie Foster and Matthew McConaughey, explores this very theme. The plot

---

[20] **Horn T and Putnam C** *Exo-Vaticana*, Defender Pub, Crane, MO, USA, 2013

goes that one day, just before her SETI funding runs out, Jodie Foster's astrophysicist character Dr Ellie Arroway comes upon a powerful signal emitting an unmistakable sequence of prime numbers from the distant star Vega. Notice that she receives what she interprets as *information,* which means *an intelligence,* which means *a mind,* which means *a person.*

Sciences author Dr Chuck Missler believes we are solidly in the realm of the information sciences here, specifically teleology (the study of purpose or design), epistemology (the study of knowledge, its scopes and limits), and hermeneutics (the theory of information interpretation). Missler reasons that any genuine Designer wishing to authenticate His message to Earth would do so in such a way as to demonstrate an unequivocally transcendent/extra-dimensional intelligence, in contradistinction to human authorship, which is characteristically flawed. Several methods could be used to get our attention in such a message, each revealing an attribute only the Designer possesses.

- He could place improbably intricate design patterns in the words and letters passed to us in the message system (code).
- He could tell us things that have not happened yet to demonstrate he exists outside of time (transcendency).
- He might reveal advanced knowledge unknown in ancient times only to be discerned in the future (prophecy).
- And, of course, if he wanted, there is nothing stopping the Creator of the Universe from very publicly announcing his existence to even atheists by starting each new day with the following words etched across our skies: "I AM GOD AND THERE IS NONE LIKE ME!" (revelation). That he has so far failed to do so actually does tell us something, as we'll discover.

We might reasonably expect a celestial message replete with design – after all, the Designer is a mathematical prodigy. In the movie *Contact,* the message Dr Arroway receives has 60,000 pages of technical drawings encoded within it. Dr Missler is not the first to examine whether quantum design can be detected in any of the

Earth's great religious books; he has written and lectured extensively on the subject.[21] Professor M Montiero-Williams, former Boden professor of Sanskrit, spent forty-two years studying the religious books of the East and came to the same conclusion. In summing up the wealth of his findings, he stated:

"Pile them [the Eastern books], if you will, on the left side of your study table; but place your own Holy Bible on the right side - all by itself, all alone - and with a wide gap between them. For... there is a gulf between it and the so-called sacred books of the East which severs one from the other utterly, hopelessly and forever.... a veritable gulf which cannot be bridged over by any science of religious thought."[22]

Why should the Designer be the God of the Bible? Why not Allah of the Koran, the god of the Mormons, aliens from a distant galaxy, the Flying Spaghetti Monster or even someone we don't know about yet? How can we know? Why couldn't the Bible have been manipulated for nefarious gain to con people into thinking it was God's book when it wasn't? The simple answer is, none of the other great religious books on Earth hang themselves on the hook with such extensive *prophetic* writings for self-verification. Dr Missler writes:

"The Bible is the only book on Planet Earth that will stake its credibility on its track record in prophecy. You will not find that true of the Koran of Islam, or the Vedas of the Hindus, or the Bhagavad Gita of India, or the Book of Mormon or [even] Nostradamus's *Centuries*... [which has] many known failures. Occultic mediums, channelers and New Age spirit guides may make claims of this sort of thing but they will not stand up under investigation, certainly not with a 20/20 unbroken track record."[23]

One third of the Bible is prophecy in the form of pre-written history of the twelve tribes of Israel, God's chosen people. Most of this prophecy has been discharged, giving us a unique view of how

[21] www.khouse.org
[22] **Collett, Sidney** *All About the Bible,* Old Tappan: Revell, pp.314-315
[23] **Missler, Chuck** *Macrocodes: 'Past',* www.khouse.org

well the Judaeo-Christian God has done. The remaining prophecies cover key events of worldwide significance in the 'last days' before Jesus Christ's return. In total, the Bible contains over 8,000 predictive verses with 1,817 specific prophecies on over 700 matters, dwarfing the attempts of Michel de Nostradame, Edgar Cayce and Gordon Michael Scallion to peek behind the veil and get it right ten out of ten. This should get the attention of any serious, unbiased researcher. It got mine. I believe an extraterrestrial intelligence has long since made contact with us – the Designer, in fact - but He's been largely ignored in recent times because we don't like His tone. I believe we are also in possession of His extensive, transcendent, self-authenticating Message System that more or less clears up any queries we might ever have on who we are, where we came from, what we're doing here, and what will happen to us when this life is over. The trouble is, we don't like what that tells us either. Why? Because if what that book says is true, then we're all in trouble.

Put your sandals where your mouth is

There's another phenomenon, says author Josh McDowell. Many religions claim 'to know God', but only one has a God who actually shows up one time. Such a performance is worthy of detailed study, if only to unhorse an imposter. Thomas Schulz writes:

"Not one recognised religious leader, not Moses, Paul, Buddha, Mohammed, Confucius, etc., has ever claimed to be God; that is, with the exception of Jesus Christ. Christ is the only religious leader who has ever claimed to be Deity, and the only individual ever who has convinced a great portion of the world that He is God." [24]

In the Bible, three hundred specific prophecies, written hundreds of years in advance, and committed to the official Koine Greek Septuagint translation between 295 – 275 BC, tell in detail of the Designer coming to Earth as a man. All three hundred predictions were fulfilled by the life of Jesus of Nazareth in very

---

[24] **Schultz, Thomas** *The Doctrine of the Purpose of Christ with an Emphasis upon the Hypostatic Union,* Dallas Theological Seminary, May 1962

specific ways. Statisticians have calculated that the cumulative odds of just sixteen of these prophecies coming true by chance for one life vastly exceed the odds calculated for the law of gravity to fail. Could Jesus have deliberately fulfilled all these prophecies? Could the Messiah have had human control over the place of his birth? Over the timing of it? How about arranging for his mother to be a virgin? Could he have engineered his own crucifixion and burial in a rich man's tomb? That not a bone of his would be broken when it was standard practice for Roman soldiers, if required, to shatter the shin-bones of crucifixion victims with clubs to hasten death? What about the last words Jesus spoke on Earth? Would it not take a lunatic of quantum proportions to think of organising something like that? Did Jesus set up his own betrayal at the hands of Judas and somehow arrange for 30 pieces of silver to be the blood money? How could Jesus have arranged for Judas to become remorseful and throw the money into the Temple? How could he coerce the priests into using the money to buy a potter's field after his death? Did Jesus orchestrate his own mocking, the spitting and wagging of heads and beatings just to fit the prophetic jacket of Messiah the Jews were expecting? There's a curious passage written by the disciple Peter which most people miss:

"And this voice which came from heaven we heard, when we were with Him [Yeshua/Jesus] **in the holy mount. We have also a more sure word of prophecy; whereunto ye do well that ye take heed, as unto a light that shineth in a dark place, until the day dawn, and the day star arise in your hearts."** (2 Peter 1: 18-19)

Here Peter, who lived, ate and worked with Yeshua (עושי)[25] during the three years of his ministry, states that witnessing all the miracles Yeshua performed, hearing his teaching, watching his final hours and later Christ's ascension into heaven before his very eyes; all that is one thing. But we have *a more sure word of prophecy* in the scriptures, Peter states, which proves beyond doubt Yeshua was God made flesh on the Earth for the salvation of men.

Many authors have written extensively on the quantum phenomenon the Bible displays in prophecy which defies secular

---

[25] This is the Hebrew name the disciples would have used to address Jesus.

explanation, and we'll examine examples as we proceed. Such spooky architecture should not be dismissed. It is markedly absent from any other 'holy' book the world has seen. Says Dr Missler:

"There are a number of... incredible discoveries of hidden designs in the Biblical text. Our exploration of the genealogy of Noah in Genesis 5 should be well-known to our readers.[26] The remarkable acrostics on the names of God in the Book of Esther are also well known in the Talmudic literature.[27] Also remarkable are the discoveries of Ivan Panin who, without the aid of a computer, spent 50 years and 43,000 handwritten pages of calculations to give us his incredible discoveries.[28] Perhaps less well known, except to serious students of cryptography, are the encryptions hidden in the texts of both Isaiah and Jeremiah."[29]

That the Bible comprises 66 books written by 40 authors over 1,500 years, which agree in the smallest part across dozens of controversial subjects with no errors or contradictions, is surprise enough. But the individual science, history, detailed genealogies, prophecy and supernatural acrostics contained in this work pale before the astonishing whole, which has been spread across the entire transmission/bandwidth of publication, **precept upon precept, line upon line, here a little, there a little** (Isa 28:10,13). This has been done in such a way that if one part of the message is lost, the key message survives. Missler, who has a background in cryptography and the defence industry, believes the Bible is a classic example of a message system which has been carefully compiled to anticipate hostile jamming. There is no one chapter on baptism, nor one on salvation. Each theme the Bible deals with has

---

[26] **Missler, Chuck** *Personal UPDATE,* February 1996, pp.19-23; *Footprints of the Messiah,* p.3; *Flood of Noah,* p.2; *The Christmas Story,* pp.13-14; *Countdown to Eternity,* pp.103-106
[27] *Personal UPDATE,* March 1996, pp.5-9; *Beyond Coincidence,* pp.15-21
[28] *Personal UPDATE,* February 1995, pp.12-15; Also, in *Expositional Commentary on Matthew,* vol.3, pp.47-54
[29] **Missler, Chuck** Discussed in *Expositional Commentary on Isaiah,* vol.1, pp.15-16; from **David Kahn** *The Code-Breakers: the Story of Secret Writing,* Macmillan, New York, 1967

been spread throughout the whole using a patterning format we will examine as we go.

Hebrew

Ninety percent of the Bible was originally written in Hebrew. Most think the New Testament writings came to us from an original Greek version, but this is not true. John Klein and Adam Spears explain:

"What most scholars now call the Mattityahu Document (i.e. the Matthew Document), containing Matthew, Mark, Luke and Acts 1:1-15:35, was originally written on one scroll, in Hebrew. Later on, these were broken out into separate scrolls. It's difficult to be as certain about the other New Testament books, but many signs also indicate that the original text of Revelation, if not written in Hebrew, might have been recorded first in Aramaic, an ancient dialect of Hebrew. Beyond all that, "Revelation's 404 verses contain as many as 278 quotes, or allusions to the Old Testament (Tanakh), especially Psalms, Isaiah, Ezekiel, Daniel and Zechariah".[30] In other words, 68.2 percent of Revelation either is or contains Hebrew Scripture, and the rest probably is or does the same!" [31]

Researchers David Bivin and Roy Blizzard write:

"We tend to forget that the Old Testament comprises approximately 78% of the biblical text, and the New Testament only 22 percent. When we add the highly Hebraic portions of the New Testament (Matthew, Mark, Luke and Acts 1:1-15:35, approximately 43 percent of the New Testament) to the Old Testament, the percentage of the biblical material originally written in Hebrew rises to 88 percent (or 87% if we omit the portions of Ezra and Daniel – less than 1 percent of the Old Testament – composed in Aramaic). Not more than 12 percent of the entire Bible was originally written in Greek. When we subtract from that 12 percent the 176 quotations

---

[30] www.baonline.com, click on 'Study the Books of the Bible', select rev.pdf
[31] **Klein, J & A Spears** *Devils, Demons and the Return of the Nephilim*, Xulon Press, 2005, p.14

from the Old Testament... the percentage of the Bible originally composed in Hebrew rises to over 90 percent." [32]

Why is this important? Because to process the astonishing world we're about to visit, we need to have some understanding of the cultural context into which the Message System was sent. The language itself is a good start.

Hebrew is a remarkable, other-worldly tongue whose strange characters convey not only words and meaning like any language, but also *numbers* and *concepts*. Hebrew is phonetic, numeric and pictographic – each letter having a range of meanings of its own. Hebrew contains no vowels and is therefore an extremely 'dense' language, which makes maximum use of available bandwidth for transmission.[33] Hebrew is also remarkable for the unique attribute of having been the only language to have passed into history only to be resurrected for use by an entire nation in the modern age. What a tremendous metaphor for the journey we're about to take.

Hebrew is such a remarkable communications medium, it is deserving of our further study for these reasons alone. That Earth's most popular, bestselling book of all time, which self-verifies with buckets of prophecy and purports to have come from God, was almost entirely compiled in this language should make even the hardened sceptic sit up and take note. Even on a superficial level we have something weird going on. With letters which can be replaced with numbers and concepts, the multi-dimensional properties of Hebrew are matched only by the most extraordinary concepts it describes in the Message System. The whole work quickly leaves the superficial and soars to unfathomable heights when you start delving deeper. The ancients knew it, and today an increasing number of scientists are loosening up to the evidence that the black book in our hands might be far more extraordinary than just a collection of quaint tales of moral rectitude that used to amuse or scare our children at bedtime. The Old and New

---

[32] **Bivin, David and Roy Blizzard** *Understanding the Difficult Words of Jesus: New Insights From a Hebraic Perspective,* Destiny Image, 1995, pp.4-5
[33] i.e. fewer letters/words are required to convey the same meaning, a little like text-speak.

Testament writings, in their original, linguistic form, *appear to be an integrated message system delivered from outside spacetime,* having been given to the authors to write down, with every letter, word, phrase, number and name there by supernatural design.

The purpose of *Origins 2 – Holy War* is not only to examine some of these incredible claims in more detail and see how they stack up against science, history and logic, but to discover whether these ancient writings are valid to use as source material for shedding light on mankind's ultimate destiny, and what the Designer expects of us in the first place. Many make this intensely personal quest through faith alone, and yet intriguingly, the God of the Bible encourages us **to prove that these things are so** and to **study to show ourselves approved** so we won't be deceived.[34]

That the existence of God is a mathematical certainty will come as a shock to many, though probably not to UK bookmakers Paddy Power, who slashed the odds on proof being found of God's existence to just 4-1.[35] For you the reader, however, you should steel yourself or shut this book now. In the movie *The Matrix,* the lead character Neo is offered a red pill or a blue pill. The red pill will cause Neo to witness the unveiling of the true reality – like hitting the Reveal Codes button on your word-processing programme. Once the red pill's down the hatch you can never go back. The blue pill leaves you in blissful ignorance, none the wiser. In our world most people are gobbling down 'blue pills' and believing the sanitised untruths fed to them by the mainstream media. The reason? Laziness, dependency, apathy, and above all, fear.

This book will compel you to rethink and restructure your priorities for the future. Over time, you will see the scenario described in this book unfolding in the newspapers and on TV. You already are. What I am going to reveal in the coming chapters is going to affect you both personally and profoundly, so you are now at *The Matrix's* red pill, blue pill moment. Forget Dan Brown's *The Da Vinci Code* or *Angels and Demons,* the journey we are about

---

[34] Rom 12:2; 1 Thess 5:21; 1 John 4:1; Acts 17:11. But NB Deut 6:16.
[35] *Daily Telegraph,* 3rd November 2008

to take will make your hair stand on end, yet also provide an astounding, heart-warming perspective on an incredible hope. Who you are, why what you do matters, why you're alive at this point in the Earth's history, what the Designer has in store for you in the months and years ahead, and the proof behind all of it. *Nothing has happened to you by accident.* The extent to which this is *literally* true will curl those toes in your slippers. So put on the kettle, plump up the cushions in your favourite chair, and let's find out if these things are so.

IN THE BEGINNING WAS THE WORD

"Have not I commanded thee? Be strong and of a good courage. Be not afraid, neither be thou dismayed, for the LORD thy God is with thee whithersoever thou goest." (Josh 1:9)

"Men occasionally stumble over the truth, but most of them pick themselves up and hurry off as if nothing has happened."
— **Winston Churchill**

The Bible is the most terrifying book ever written. Firmly hung on the hook of its hyperdimensional pedigree, it must either self-authenticate its otherworldly authorship or be exposed as a fraud.

The Bible is a book of action describing the Holy War between good and evil. The players in this conflict may surprise you. They are not God versus Satan, nor Jew versus Muslim, nor even Republican versus Democrat. In a nutshell, God's good and *we're evil*, so God's going to put the Bad Lad's Army through boot camp to see if He can make something of us. We will be confronted with evil in all its forms and we're supposed to overcome it. Most won't.

What is the Bible about? In one word: redemption. In another word: Yeshua. Jesus Christ. The name that is above every name: God's book given to man to show man how to get back to God via His Son, the long-awaited *Mashiach* (Messiah). It's about paradise lost and paradise regained. One researcher describes it as a love story written in blood on a wooden cross 2,000 years ago in Judaea.[36] The Bible claims the Creator made everything. It claims the Creator went to the extremes of despatching his Son to Earth in human form to suffer death so that sinful man could be reconciled with a perfect Creator after the Holy War was won. It's the ultimate script. There's love, betrayal, sex, battles, sacrifice, incest, royal court life, palace plots, stunning beauties, ordinary heroes, drugs, drunkenness, gruesome executions, gay rights, fantastic penances, miracles, plot-twists, deception, giants, demons, aliens,

---

[36] www.khouse.org

an arch villain, natural disasters, extreme weather, super-volcanoes, space wars and superhuman champions. In fact, about the only the thing the Bible doesn't feature is football. And through it all, the leading personality, God, aka YHWH[37] ('Yahweh'), aka Yeshua aka Jesus Christ, aka the Father of Creation walks with you through every page of the greatest story ever told. Your Maker. The entire panoply of history - His Story – is rolled out and we are its witness. Turn to the back of the book and you can see who wins. We are told that each of us needs to be on that winning side before we die because the implications either way are eternal. Right now, most aren't.

The Bible is an extraordinary book which provokes extraordinary reactions; indeed we are told it can only be unlocked and understood under the light of God's Holy Spirit, which God gives to whom He pleases. That does not mean any Joe in the street can't pick up the scriptures and have a thumb-through – they're more than welcome - but they won't unless God prompts them (Rom 8:7; 1 Cor 2:12-14). To these the Bible will have no form or comeliness that they should desire it until it is illuminated with God's Spirit, then it makes the most blazing sense in the world. I know, I've been on both sides of the fence.

A sampling of comments on the Bible by atheists is revealing:

"Nobody questions that the Bible possibly contains some elements of historical fact. It is the concept of the existence of a supernatural deity that many people have problems with." - grayle, London, United Kingdom

"The holy bible has already been proven wrong multiple times. Just read Genesis. The universe and the earth were not created in 6 days around 6000 years ago and we can prove it, end of debate, easy...."

And:

"I'm not saying that what the bible teaches doesn't have some value, only that it is not a literal historically accurate document, and shouldn't be used as fact. If taken metaphorically, some of it teaches

---

[37] God's name in Hebrew. God's holy name 'Yahweh' is represented by the Tetragrammaton 'YHWH'. It is sometimes extrapolated as 'JeHoVaH'.

some decent lessons about morality (although it also teaches some pretty horrible stuff as well). The point is, it is a book of fables and should be treated as such." - milesp, wigan, United Kingdom

"If the bible was ever 'accurate like a newspaper', then isn't that enough to tell us it's complete rubbish?! I like the one where Moses definitely parted the sea - pretty sure that happened." - John Dough, London, United Kingdom

"My favorite is the talking snake, why take the apple? I would have grabbed the snake and said to Adam check out this talking snake. The first Dr Doolittle moment recorded. Or how about 20 million varieties of wildlife on the Ark – that's another good one. Trouble is there are so many comedy events it's hard to just pick one." - Roger, Guildford, United Kingdom

"How do you know [the Bible is] true? Before you answer that - go away and think about it for a minute and ask yourself HONESTLY how you actually know it's true? Like most historical documents, it is likely to be based on a mixture of truth, mis-remembered content and downright untruths, generally recorded for political expediency. But how do we know which is true and which isn't? You think it's all true because you have convinced yourself that some deity inspired its writing, but you have not grounded that belief on any solid evidence. You believe it because you choose to believe it." - Stu, Laholm, Sweden

"Some day in the distant future ... I foresee some being picking up a copy of Harry Potter and realising that thousands of years ago the ancient people travelled by brooms." - just me, pluto

Atheists suppose that exposure of the Bible as a fake scripture has long been accomplished. *It hasn't.* They pour scorn on a young Earth, claiming this too has been exposed by science as a ridiculous falsehood. *It hasn't.* In claiming the Bible has been 'discredited' thousands of times, they do so not *à propos* of their own study, which they have not undertaken, but on the hearsay of others. Many also state – like Stu above – that a believer's faith is not based on any solid evidence. This too is a myth.

On the other hand, when smart people reject God and His Word, just sit back and watch what nonsense they start believing instead. Why? Because man is programmed to believe in

41

something, even if it's believing that there's nothing to believe in and that life is essentially hopeless. Many reject the Bible because of a deep spiritual antagonism they can neither rationalise nor identify. In fact, not only is atheism a belief, it's actually the classic definition of Satanism, defined here by none other than American occultist Anton LaVey, who founded the worldwide Church of Satan in San Francisco:

"And he must, as a Satanist, knowing this, realising what his human potential is, eventually, and here is one of the essential points of Satanism, attaining his own godhood in accordance with his own potential. Therefore, each man, each woman, is a god or goddess in Satanism."[38]

Peter Gilmore, who took over as 'high priest' after LaVey's death in 1997, elaborates:

"Satanists do not believe in the supernatural, in neither God nor the Devil. To the Satanist, he is his own God. Satan is a symbol of Man living as his prideful, carnal nature dictates. The reality behind Satan is simply the dark evolutionary force of entropy that permeates all of nature and provides the drive for survival and propagation inherent in all living things. Satan is not a conscious entity to be worshipped, rather a reservoir of power inside each human to be tapped at will. Thus any concept of sacrifice is rejected as a Christian aberration—in Satanism there's no deity to which one can sacrifice."[39]

As opposed to *theistic* Satanism, which is the worshiping of the Devil as God, involving the practice of magic(k), arcane ritual and sometimes animal and child sacrifice.

Atheistic Satanism then, according to LaVey and Gilmore who should know, is not worshiping the Devil at all. It is egotism (pride), acknowledging no higher power above you, not even Satan. It's spirit-led; the serpent's hiss in the Garden; the Devil's desire to **'be like the Most High'**; man liberated to become his own god; to be who he wants to be and do what he wants to do with no singeing of the conscience. Aleister Crowley's *"Do what thou wilt*

---

[38] **Holmberg, Eric** *The Allure of Rock* DVD, Amercian Portrait Films, 1999
[39] http://www.churchofsatan.com/Pages/Feared.html

shall be the whole of the law" is the endgame, along with *"Life is the great indulgence. Death is the great abstinence. Therefore make the most of life here and now."* (Book of Satan 1:4). God knows all about atheists:

"For the wrath of God is revealed from heaven against all ungodliness and unrighteousness of men, who hold the truth in unrighteousness. Because that which may be known of God is manifest in them, for God hath shewed it unto them. For the invisible things of Him from the creation of the world are clearly seen, being understood by the things that are made, even His eternal power and Godhead, so that they are without excuse.

Because that, when they knew God, they glorified Him not as God, neither were thankful, but became vain in their imaginations, and their foolish heart was darkened.

Professing themselves to be wise, they became fools, and changed the glory of the incorruptible God into an image made like to corruptible man, and to birds, and four-footed beasts and creeping things [evolution]. <u>Wherefore God also gave them up to</u> [notice God's giving them up to.... – they're not deciding to do it themselves...] uncleanness through the lusts of their own hearts, to dishonour their own bodies between themselves. Who changed the truth of God into a lie, and worshipped and served the creature [evolution] more than the Creator, who is blessed for ever. Amen." (Rom 1:18-25)

The fool hath said in his heart, 'There is no God.' (Psa 53:1)

The Designer throws down the gauntlet for scoffers to match his unbeaten track record of prognostication, a unique challenge that sets the Bible apart from all those other 'holy' books on Earth:

"Present your case," says the LORD. "Set forth your arguments," says Jacob's King. "Bring in your idols to tell us what is going to happen. Tell us what the former things were, so that we may consider them and know their final outcome. Or declare to us the things to come, tell us what the future holds, so we may know that you are gods. Yes, do good or do evil, that we may be dismayed and see it together. Indeed you are nothing, and your work is nothing. <u>He who chooses you is an abomination</u>." (Isa 41:21-24)

"I am God and there is none like Me, declaring the end from the beginning, and from ancient times the things that are not yet done, saying, 'My counsel shall stand and I will do all My pleasure.'" (Isa 46:9-10)

"I have declared the former things from the beginning; and they went forth out of My mouth, and I shewed them. Suddenly I did them and they came to pass. I have even from the beginning declared it to thee; before it came to pass I shewed it thee: lest thou shouldest say, 'Mine idol hath done them, and my graven image, and my molten image, hath commanded them'." (Isa 48:3,5)

Yeshua: "Now I tell you before it come, that, when it is come to pass, ye may believe that I am He." (FG 13:19)

Josh McDowell writes:

"The purpose of prophecy is to let us know that God exists and that He has a plan for this world. By the foretelling of persons, places and events hundreds of years before their occurrence, the Bible demonstrates a knowledge of the future that is too specific to be labelled a good guess. By giving examples of fulfilled prophecy, the Scriptures give a strong testimony to their own inspiration."[40]

The Bible is plainly not the sort of book a man would have written. It tells us things about ourselves we do not like. It deals with even its most beloved characters in warts-and-all fashion. It claims we are pawns in an extraterrestrial, spiritual war of hyperdimensional proportions with real devils and angels taking advantage of our own twisted nature which has been set at enmity with God. The Message System claims we are eternal spirit beings having a temporary human experience in order to exercise the free will we were given either to make peace with God or reject Him. In effect, the Bible describes the Earth Programme as a time-limited boot-camp experience; on-the-job training under live-fire conditions to determine our job description and destiny for eternity.[41] It claims to hold the secrets to our ultimate fate. It speaks

---

[40] **McDowell, Josh & Don Stewart** *Answers to Tough Questions,* Here's Life Publishers, Inc., 1980, pp.22-23

[41] Psa 82:6; 2 Cor 4:16-18; FG 10:34; 17:11

of a coming Earthly Millennial Kingdom of peace and order ruled physically by Jesus Christ Himself, but only after the most terrifying period of time ever to befall Earth – the Great Tribulation of God's wrath poured out upon men. It speaks of a beatific Heaven with God, and an unimaginable Hell eternally separated from Him. It demands we take these concepts literally, not for God's benefit but for our own. The Bible tells us a lot of things we should and should not be doing. Clearly a book claiming authority over such matters must be one of the following:

1. Completely deluded.
2. A hoax of pure wickedness.
3. What it says it is.

Validating the source material

For a researcher wishing to learn more about such unfathomable subjects, an unimpeachable information source is vital. If you're visiting Botswana, you need a reliable guide familiar with the territory, whom you can validate with multiple references. When venturing into territory unfamiliar to our frame of reference with the *Origins* project, multiple validations to a source should ideally be secured before heeding what that source has to tell us. The question is, what criteria should we use to secure the credibility of a book dealing with such incredible subjects? What is the source material for where *we're* headed?

Firstly, it is not unreasonable to make certain assumptions about a book purporting to have come from God. We would expect it to exhibit some otherworldly attributes. It should be bullet-proof in terms of its survival. It should be self-authenticating by revealing unique attributes about its Author. It should be error-free in its original form. It should not demand that we take it on trust alone as the aforementioned Stu seems to believe. How does the Message System stack up?

The Bible is the most read, the most popular and bestselling book of all time. That alone is not a validation but a curiosity. Its survival throughout the ages, though, has been a miracle. Scholars have never been able to come up with any other rational explanation for the origin and *survival* of this extraordinary work beyond what the Bible says it is. God-breathed. People have fought, murdered, loved, willingly gone to their deaths, been roasted alive and sawn in two over its contents, but so they have over other religious books. Around the world today the Bible is still scorned, mocked, burned, banned and ignored as a bygone irrelevance, yet in all the years scholars have studied its pages, an utter conviction has gripped many that they are in the presence of unfathomable greatness. Yet such emotional rather than scientific appeals do not a God-Book make. What is the Bible? Is it, as Dawkins and his atheists presume, the ultimate guilt trip, or is it a genuine divine revelation? How can we tell?

Has God ever got a message to us? If He has, *no mistakes* would be a starter. I was able to discount virtually all the world's 'holy books' in this study for one straightforward reason. They bottled out and did not demonstrate transcendency.[42] Some had flat-out errors – geographical, historical, scientific – or did not put themselves on the hook in any verifiable fashion. There was nothing about these books which indicated divine authorship beyond what others said of them, and what these works said of themselves. There were no otherworldly qualities intrinsic to the text; no outstanding revelation of an attribute only God would possess that would shout loud and clear that we had something special in our hands. If God made everything, He's certainly capable of communicating an error-free message to catch our attention, and at the same time reveal an attribute only God possesses to authenticate the work – namely transcendency. That He is without error, ubiquitous, omniscient, omnipotent. That He exists outside of time.

Which means that He knows the end from the beginning because He made time. Which means that He knows what's going to happen in advance (Amos 3:7), and can let us know so we know it's Him doing the talking and not some cave-dwelling fruitcake

---

[42] Transcendency – surpassing others; existing beyond the ordinary range of perception; being above and independent of the material universe; *spec.* the ability to transmit information beyond the constraints of time.

looking to jump-start a cult. There's only one book for which all this is true, and that's the 66 books comprising the Judaeo-Christian Bible *in their original Hebrew/Aramaic/Greek forms* (i.e. before the translators got hold of them). Those other 'holy' relics out there, while curious, are the work of mere men, admittedly like the Bible, but unlike the Bible, they cannot prove divinely inspired, transcendent authorship.

The very nature of how the Bible is compiled seems in itself provocative and extraordinary. We have 66 books written by 40 authors under the power of the Holy Spirit agreeing on a whole raft of topics down to the smallest detail. *Do not dismiss this phenomenon lightly.* Not only do such themes run consistently through dozens of books but so do the codes we've heard so much about. Most of the Bible's authors did not know each other personally, nor were even contemporaries. Though written by kings, priests, herdsmen, fishermen, musicians, warriors and generals, the overall content of the Bible's books is stunningly congruent in continuity, a unique attribute in itself. Try getting 40 authors these days to agree on *anything,* let alone the dozens of controversial subjects the Bible tackles with glee.

In their original form, the books of the Bible were written over a fifteen-hundred-year span variously in Hebrew, Aramaic[43] or Greek. Hebrew and Aramaic are extraordinary since the letters of the language are also regarded as *numbers* and *pictorial concepts.* Today we can number-crunch the alpha-numeric properties of Hebrew using sophisticated computers. Some researchers are even plotting the Torah in different dimensions and interrogating the cuboid grid to see what they find. Christians are aware that God is referred to as the Word (Gr. *Logos*), that He entered His creation (spacetime) as a man (Yeshua/Jesus) to dwell among us, and that

---

[43] Aramaic is the longest surviving language on Earth. It originated in the Patriarchal Period (*c.* 1900 – 1700 BC), and is still being spoken by some people today. Linguistically very similar in structure and form to Hebrew, Aramaic is more comprehensive in terms of tense use, loan words and connectives, rendering it a vehicle of exact expression, similar to Greek.

this Jesus, at the same time fully human and fully divine,[44] is referred to as the Word made Flesh (FG (Fourth Gospel) 1:1-14). Further, that God's name may be holy, but there is something God has magnified even above His own name: His Word (His Son) (Psa 138:2).

This Word or Message System the Creator has provided is incredibly literal. Dr Chuck Missler, a Bible specialist for fifty years, is not alone in contending that every number, place-name and feature in the Bible is there by deliberate design and nothing is included *or omitted* without reason. Though this 'fundamentalist' approach to the Bible makes liberal theologians wince, the scriptures themselves declare that they have been purified, as with silver, seven times in the fire, and are completely trustworthy (Prov 30:5-6; Psa 12:6). After decades of my own critical Bible study, I cannot dispute its authenticity. The quality of scholarship brought to bear on this Book of books over the centuries by the top minds ever to walk the planet is unprecedented. The unbiased researcher should rightly stand in awe of the Bible's uniqueness and singular precision.

The genealogy of King David is predicted in Genesis 38 centuries before Israel's famous king ascended the throne. The scriptures predicted across five centuries *the very day* the Messiah would enter Jerusalem and proclaim himself King of the Jews. Hundreds of Messianic prophecies subsequently came true for Yeshua (Jesus). The scriptures predicted across 1900 years *the very day* the Jews went back into Israel in May 1948. The opening genealogy of Christ in the book of Matthew contains mathematically impossible heptadic structures that could not have been contrived by human hand. And on and on. We'll examine these as we proceed and the reader can make up their own mind.

Notice the high view the scriptures have of their own inspiration:

---

[44] This was foreseen in the Old Testament. Isaiah 9:6 states: **For unto us a child is born** [his human side, accomplished at Bethlehem], **unto us a Son is given** [the divine side, accomplished at Golgotha]: **and the government shall be upon His shoulder: and His name shall be called Wonderful, Counsellor, The mighty God, The everlasting Father, The Prince of Peace.**

48

"The words of the LORD are pure words: as silver tried in a furnace of earth, purified seven times. Thou shalt keep them, O LORD, Thou shalt preserve them from this generation forever." (Psa 12:6-7)

"Thy Word is true from the beginning: and every one of Thy righteous judgments endureth for ever." (Psa 119:160)

"I know that, whatsoever God doeth, it shall be forever: Nothing can be put to it, nor any thing taken from it: and God doeth it, that men should fear before Him." (Ecc 3:14)

"The grass withereth, the flower fadeth: but the Word of our God shall stand forever." (Isa 40:8)

"For verily I say unto you, Till Heaven and Earth pass, one jot or one tittle shall in no wise pass from the law till all be fulfilled." (Matt 5:18)

"Heaven and Earth shall pass away but My words shall not pass away." (Matt 24:35)

"And it is easier for Heaven and Earth to pass than one tittle of the law to fail." (Luke 16:17)

"Being born again, not of corruptible seed but of incorruptible, by the Word of God, which liveth and abideth for ever. For all flesh is as grass, and all the glory of man as the flower of grass. The grass withereth, and the flower thereof falleth away: But the Word of the LORD endureth forever. And this is the Word which by the gospel is preached unto you." (1 Pet 1:23-25)

Scholar Josh McDowell proclaims the Bible unique in its continuity, unique in its circulation, unique in its translation and manuscript evidence, unique in its survival, unique in its teachings, unique in its influence on literature, and in its influence on civilisation.[45] Historian Wilbur M Smith comments:

"Whatever one may think of the authority of, and the message presented in the book we call the Bible, there is worldwide agreement that, in more ways than one, it is the most remarkable volume that has ever been produced in these some five thousand years of writing on the part of the human race.

---

[45] **McDowell, J** *The New Evidence That Demands a Verdict,* Thomas Nelson Inc., 1999

It is the only volume ever produced by man or a group of men, in which is to be found a large body of prophecies relating to individual nations, to Israel, to all the peoples of the Earth, to certain cities, and to the coming of the One who was to be the Messiah.... Mohammedism cannot point to any prophecies of the coming of Mohammed uttered hundreds of years before his birth. Neither can the founders of any cult in this country rightly identify any ancient text specifically foretelling their appearance." [46]

Norman Geisler and William Nix agree:

"Other books claim divine inspiration, such as the Koran, the Book of Mormon, and parts of the [Hindu] Veda, but none of these books contain predictive prophecy. As a result, fulfilled prophecy is a strong indication of the unique, divine authority of the Bible."[47]

These are fighting words but we must eschew the offence they cause to get to the heart of what it means to be 'God-breathed'. God's Word, if it exists, will stand on its own, human offence notwithstanding, and if it doesn't, it's not God's Word. The Bible does not escape unscathed. Log on to www.biblegateway.com to appreciate how many translations of the Old and New Testaments exist just in English. Often these versions are produced and copyrighted to make money – the Bible's the bestselling book of all time after all. The only serious, free, public-domain Bible is the 'authorised' King James Version (KJV), which happens to be the most error-free English translation, though the 17th century language is a tad chewy. Great effort has gone into many of these translations but they are not the original language versions which display the startling traits we'll examine. They suffer from subjectivism. For instance, Catholic scholars translated the Greek word for 'synagogue' as 'church' in some passages of the New Testament to convey the false premise that Paul and the other apostles renounced traditional Jewish worship in favour of 'the way' (cf: Acts 15; 18:25-26). Ethnocentrism has also skewed the mix.

---

[46] **Smith W M** *The Incomparable Book,* Beacon Publications, Minneapolis, USA: 1961, pp.9-10

[47] **Geisler, N L and W E Nix** *A General Introduction to the Bible,* Moody Press, Chicao: 1986, p.196

This is the translator's prejudice to interpret foreign writings within the framework of his own beliefs, culture and experiences. Want an example of how fatal even one mistranslated word can be? Consider the following from a 1953 article in *Harper's* magazine:

MOKUSATSU

A Japanese word, *mokusatsu*, may have changed all our lives. It has two meanings:

1) to ignore
2) to refrain from comment

The release of a press statement using the second meaning in July 1945 might have ended the war at this point. The Japanese emperor was ready to end it and had the power to do so. The Japanese cabinet was preparing to accede to the Potsdam ultimatum of the Allies – 'surrender or be crushed' – but wanted more time to discuss the terms.

The press release was prepared announcing a policy of *mokusatsu* with the <u>no-comment</u> implication. But it got on the wires with the <u>ignore</u> implication due to a mix-up in translation:

'The cabinet ignores the demand to surrender.'

To recall the release would have entailed an unthinkable loss of face. Had the intended meaning been publicized, the cabinet might have backed the emperor's decision to surrender. If this had been the case, it is unlikely that the two atomic bombs would have been dropped by the Americans on the Japanese cities of Hiroshima and Nagasaki, resulting in the catastrophic loss of life that followed. Possibly even following these events, the subsequent Russian invasion of Manchuria and the Korean War may have had vastly different outcomes if indeed they would have occurred at all. The lives of countless thousands of Japanese and American boys could have been saved.

One word, misinterpreted.

To understand the Bible, we must accept that it comprises a collection of 66 Jewish documents written by 40 authors over some 1,500 years in the context of their culture and age. For that reason we will zero in on curious aspects of Hebrew culture which shed great light on the extraordinary stories which follow. Moreover, as we proceed through its history, we'll see types, models or macrocodes of events repeating themselves with extraordinary precision. These are among the most provocative proofs of divine ordination and paint an extraordinary picture of what's in store for mankind's immediate future.

Without error?

The Bible's bold claims to inerrancy and God's breath are a potential deal-breaker and should be resolved first. The Apostle Paul writes:

"All scripture is given by inspiration of God, and is profitable for doctrine, for reproof, for correction, for instruction in righteousness." (2 Tim 3:16).

Exodus 32:16, Leviticus 1:1, Numbers 1:1 and Deuteronomy 31:24-26 all claim that God spoke the words of the Torah (first five books) and Moses wrote them down letter by letter. Psalms 19:8; 119:140,160, Proverbs 30:5 and James 3:17 specifically state that God's word is pure. Yeshua himself made a telling remark:

"For verily I say unto you, till Heaven and Earth pass, one jot or one tittle shall in no wise pass from the law till all be fulfilled." (Matt 5:18)

What is being said here? Jesus Himself is saying that the Law of Moses, which is generally recognised by scholars as the Torah, though more specifically the regulations and edicts contained across the first five books of the Bible, are so firmly anchored in Truth that Heaven and Earth will pass before the smallest incidentals of the Hebrew text (jot and tittle) are found to be wrong. In other words, this is a clarion call to take the text very seriously.

But is the Bible really infallible and without error? Vincent McCann has made a detailed study. He summarises the problem thus:

"How can you believe a Bible that is full of errors and contradictions?" Questions like this are asked of Christians every day by people all over the world. But it is incredible to find that in most cases those who ask such a question don't even have a particular error in mind but are rather making this assertion because they have heard somebody else say it. It appears that the idea that the Bible is full of discrepancies is something which is circulated from person to person as a kind of gossip without any real substance. But be that as it may, the question assumes that the Bible is filled with so many discrepancies that it is impossible to believe that it is of Divine origin."[48]

It can be stated with scholarly certainty that all apparent anomalies in the scriptures have been resolved if you 'wear the jacket' of the culture doing the writing and understand the context in which they were written. Here are some examples:

THE REMEZ ('a hint of something deeper')

There are occasions in the Bible where the attentive reader's eye is drawn to an apparent mistake/anomaly in the text, only to dig deeper to find a startling insight. One such example is 1 Kings 7:23. Here, Hiram the bronze-worker is crafting a huge bath ('laver', 'molten sea') the priests will use in the Temple for ceremonial purification purposes. The passage reads:

And he [Hiram] **made a molten sea** [brass wash basin]**, ten cubits from the one brim to the other: it was round all about, and its height was five cubits: and a line of thirty cubits did compass it round about.**

A standard cubit is approximately 18 inches – the span from a man's middle fingertip to his elbow. The problem is, any schoolboy will tell you that if the diameter of a circle is 10 cubits, its circumference will be approximately 3.141509 x 10 cubits (i.e. πd) or 31. 41509 cubits round, *not 30 cubits* as the Bible states. It's an obvious mistake, not a huge one, but atheists gleefully leap on it as a decisive rebuttal to the notion of scriptural inerrancy. "Can't God get his basic maths right?" Chuck Missler enlightens:

"In the Hebrew Bible, the scribes never altered any text which they felt had been previously copied incorrectly. Rather, they noted in the margin what they thought the written text should be. The written

---

[48] www.spotlightministries.org.uk/inner.htm

[original] variation is called a *kethiv* (here as וקוה); and the marginal annotation is called the *qere* (here, וקו)."[49]

It seems a *heh* has been inexplicably added to the usual word for 'circumference' – *qav* – rendering it *qaveh*. The *heh* is regarded by some Jewish scholars as 'God's breath', and was added by God to the names of two Biblical protagonists to bless them. Thus Abram is changed to Abra̲h̲am in the Hebrew and Sarai to Sara̲h̲ (Gen 17:5,15) to imply both were now 'God-breathed' or full of God's Spirit.

Hebrew letters also have a numerical value. If you calculate the value of the correct word for circumference – *qav* – it comes to 106. If you calculate the actual word used for circumference in the above 1 Kings 7:23 passage – *qaveh* - it comes to 111. This implies a ratio of 111/106. If this is applied to the 30 cubits given in the text as the circumference of the basin, you get (30 x 111)/106, which is 31.4150943396 cubits circumference – true with an error of less than 15 thousands of an inch!

We'll look at other *remez* examples as we proceed. They don't teach doctrine, you have to dig for them, but they are the Author's unique watermark, at times startling, astonishing, always correct, and for His glorification.

THE 'WAIT AND SEE' APPROACH

Many apparent discrepancies in the Bible have been cleared up through the 'wait and see' approach inherent in archaeology and document discovery. In other words, if the answer to a problem is not immediately forthcoming, it sometimes crops up as time passes, i.e. dig discoveries, the Dead Sea Scrolls, and so on. Palestinian archaeologist Nelson Gluek was constrained to declare in *Rivers in the Desert* in 1959, p.31:

"…it may be stated categorically that no archaeological discovery has ever controverted a Biblical reference…"

Vincent McCann writes:

---

[49] **Missler, Chuck** *Hidden Treasures*, Koinonia House, Coeur d'Alene, ID, p.35

"Some scholars assumed that Luke's use of the word 'politarchs' in Acts 17:6, as a title for civil authorities in Thessalonica, was thought to be an inaccurate description, since the word was not known to exist in classical literature. However, more recent discoveries have shown Luke to be perfectly accurate in his use of this word, since some nineteen inscriptions were discovered that make use of the title, five of which are used in specific reference to Thessalonica." [50]

ETHNIC CUSTOMS, FIGURES OF SPEECH AND EVERYDAY LANGUAGE

Believe it or not, some leap upon Biblically-quoted casualty numbers in a battle as being too rounded, not accurate, incorrect, and therefore proof of the 'flawed' nature of the Bible. This attitude is to be ignorant of the effects of ethnocentricity – i.e. judging another's culture solely by the values and standards of one's own. The Hebrew culture, like ours, is not out of step by professing 22,000 dead in a battle when the exact toll might be 21,823 or 22,138. Or how about the scientific inaccuracy of stating that the sun 'rises and sets'? This is the experience of the human observer and entirely in accordance with Hebrew culture.

Similarly, when Psalms 91:4 states that God **shall cover thee with His feathers, and under His wings shalt thou trust...** this does not mean that God is a big chicken. We are told in Hosea 12:10 that God uses similitudes; actually E W Bullinger's exhaustive study reveals over 200 different figures of speech used in the Bible, from alliteration, allegory, acrostics and asyndeton to epanalepsis, meiosis, metaphor, repetition and zeugma. No serious scholar has a problem with these ancient, poetic styles except those bent on mischief.

LOOSE OR FREE QUOTATIONS

Vincent McCann writes:

"It should be recognised that the procedures that people use when quoting others differ from culture to culture. In the modern Western world we are used to quoting a person's exact words. In New Testament times, however, when people quoted others, it was more

---

[50] http://www.spotlightministries.org.uk/inner.htm

common just to give an accurate representation of the content of what a person had said, and not necessarily quote them word for word. Inerrancy is therefore consistent with loose or free quotations of the Old Testament in New Testament passages as long as the content is truthful."[51]

VARIANCE IN DETAIL EXPLAINING THE SAME EVENT

In the four Gospels, there are several occasions where the same event is described differently. For instance, there is one angel attending at the tomb of Jesus in the accounts of Matthew and Mark, yet two in the Luke text, and none mentioned in the fourth gospel.

Another example is the case of the blind men at Jericho. Matthew says only one man met Jesus, while Mark and Luke both describe two. McCann comments:

"When dealing with [such events] it should be noted that different accounts of the same incidents can differ from each other without being contradictory. For example, with regards to the issue of whether the Gospel accounts speak of there being one or two angels at the tomb of Jesus. The answer to this is that there were two. This can be illustrated with the following story:

Suppose I met President Clinton and his advisor, who both tell me to work on a project. I then meet you and tell you that I met President Clinton who had given me a job to do. Later I meet your friend and tell him/her of the meeting, but this time mention that it was both the president 'and' his advisor whom I had met. You and your friend meet and talk about how privileged I am to be given a job by the president. However, when you compare notes you discover that I have told you that I only met the president, whereas I tell your friend that I met his the president 'and' his advisor. There is an 'apparent' contradiction, but not an irreconcilable one."[52]

In fact, far from being a problem, police officials will tell you that minor variations to descriptions of the same event lend more credence to the authenticity of these accounts.

---

[51] www.spotlightministries.org.uk/inner.htm
[52] Ibid.

Can the Bible be trusted?

Sceptics who have never done their homework are happy to bandy about the following accusations:

1. The Bible can't be trusted because the text has been changed, corrupted and tampered with down through the ages
2. You can prove the Bible is false because it teaches a flat Earth and geocentric universe
3. The Bible's so-called prophetic record was written after the fact
4. Christian zealots can twist scripture to make it say whatever they want it to say

The old saying goes, "The only barrier to truth is the presumption you already have it." Though a convinced atheist might be immune to arguments overturning his position, the facts will speak for themselves. Once again, it is necessary to be certain of, trust and have confidence in our source material as our guide into the strange territory into which we shall be venturing in our examination of the Holy War.

So let's briefly review where our modern Bible came from. Today we see an Old and New Testament. The Old Testament deals with the history of God's holy line from the Creation up to a few hundred years BC. The New Testament comprises, among other books, the four Gospels of Jesus (Matthew, Mark, Luke and the Fourth Gospel),[53] the Acts of the Apostles, the Epistles (a series of letters written to various church groups), and the Revelation of St John the Apostle. Both Old and New Testament writings have been collated into their respective 'canons' or compilations, which are considered inspired and genuine due to transcendent content, as opposed to the OT and NT Apochryphas, which are ex-Biblical writings considered flawed.

---

[53] Only church tradition holds that the Galilean fisherman John Zebedee authored the inspired Fourth Gospel – there is no textual evidence that this is the case. The disputed real author of the Fourth Gospel is a real surprise, a definite *remez*, proof of which will be provided later in the *Origins* series.

The scriptures Jesus and the disciples/apostles used comprised the same Old Testament we have today, but were available back then in their original Hebrew/Aramaic and also the Koine Greek translation – the Septuagint – completed around 250 years before Yeshua's birth. OT quotes in the New Testament are almost all from the Septuagint. The OT writings were divided into the Law (the TORAH – first five books of the Bible), The Prophets, the Poetical Books, the Five Rolls and Historical Books. Unusually, the Old Testament 'canon' did not come about until after the destruction of the Second Temple by Titus 37 years after the crucifixion.[54] Josh McDowell explains:

"The Jewish sacrificial system was ended by the destruction of Jerusalem and the temple in 70 AD. Even though the Old Testament canon was settled in the Jewish mind long before 70 AD, there was a need for something more definitive. The Jews were scattered and they needed to determine which books were the authoritative Word of God because of the many extra-scriptural writings and the decentralization. The Jews became a people of one Book and it was this Book which kept them together. Christianity started to blossom and many writings of the Christians were beginning to be circulated. The Jews needed to expose them vividly and exclude them from their writings and use in the synagogues."[55]

Why were the books of the Old Testament Apocrypha rejected? Unger's Bible Dictionary states that they contain verifiable historical and geographical inaccuracies as well as anachronisms, proving they are not inspired. They promote doctrines at variance with accepted scripture, do not contain the signature of prophecy, and are written in styles dissimilar to traditional scripture.[56] Jesus and the apostles never quoted from them, neither did the Church Fathers and extra-Biblical sources such as Philo or Josephus.

The New Testament canon was compiled along similar lines. The writings must not contradict anything in the Old Testament;

---

[54] From the Hebrew word 'ganeh' and Greek 'Kanon' meaning 'reed' or standard.
[55] **McDowell, Josh** *Evidence That Demands a Verdict*, Here's Life Publishers, 1972, p.30
[56] **Unger, Merrill F** *Unger's Bible Dictionary*, Moody Press, Chicago, 1971, p.70

must be historically and geographically correct; must not contradict any other writings within the New Testament canon; must be inspired, and must hold Jesus Christ as their supreme authority (a feature known as apostolicity). The writings which fail these standards go into the New Testament Apocrypha. All of which begs the question: Who had the final say in determining what was the true word of God in the New Testament?

Constantine's Roman Catholic Church in the 4th century AD.

Anathasius of Alexandria provided the earliest list of New Testament books identical to our own around 367 AD.[57] Jerome and Augustine confirmed the official canon shortly thereafter.[58] Copies of the gospels had been in circulation within a few decades of the death of Christ. The earliest extant copy dates from 125 AD, within as little as 25 years of the original (40 AD – 100 AD), according to best estimates.[59] The conformity of successive texts is impressive, says Josh McDowell:

> "The bibliographical test is an examination of the textual transmission by which documents reach us. In other words, since we do not have the original documents, how reliable are the copies we have in regards to the number of manuscripts and the time interval between the original ['the autograph'] and extant copy?... There are now more than 5,300 known Greek manuscripts of the New Testament. Add over 10,000 Latin Vulgate and at least 9,300 other early versions and we have more than 24,000 manuscript copies of portions of the New Testament in existence today. No other document of antiquity even begins to approach such numbers and attestation. In comparison, the Iliad by Homer is second only with 643 manuscripts that still survive. The first complete preserved text of Homer dates from the 13th century."[60]

---

[57] McDowell, Josh, *Evidence That Demands a Verdict,* op. cit. p.37

[58] **Bruce F F** *The Books and the Parchments,* Revell Co, 1963, p.112

[59] For an exhaustive study of this subject, together with sources, **McDowell, Josh** *Evidence That Demands a Verdict,* Here's Life Publishers, 1972

[60] Ibid. p.39; also, **Leach, Charles** *Our Bible. How We Got It,* Moody Press, 1898, p.145

Something other-worldly is going on. When we examine the manuscript evidence for, say Caesar's *Commentarii de Bello Gallico (Gallic Wars)* (composed between 58 and 50 BC), or the works of Tacitus or Livy, we find the number of surviving manuscripts (MSS) in low double digits. Ten versions of Caesar's *Commentarii de Bello Gallico* have survived of any worth, and these date from 900 years after the original. Of the 142 books of the Roman history of Livy, only 35 survive, derived from no more than 20 MSS of any quality, the earliest dated in the 4th century.[61] The deciding factors on reliability include: the number of surviving MSS, their condition and readability, their text variance, and length of time between the autograph and earliest surviving manuscript. David Holdaway writes:

"The procedure for assessing the reliability of the New Testament is the same as for any other important ancient document when the original no longer exists. There are three vital factors. First, the bibliographical test – have the original manuscripts been handed down faithfully? Then there is the internal evidence test – what the Gospels tell us about themselves. Finally there is the external evidence test – an examination of other sources that shed light, such as contemporary ancient literature. Following this process, which is the one used to check the authenticity of all ancient writings, we can come to an accurate decision regarding the accuracy of modern belief based upon ancient manuscripts. When we find several copies which are basically similar and fairly near in time to the original author, we are able to build a case for the reliability of their trustworthiness."[62]

No historical scholar would dare quibble over the veracity of the *Annals* of Tacitus, yet only 20 copies remain, *the earliest of which is dated a thousand years after the autograph.* How about Herodotus's *History?* Eight copies remain, of which the earliest is dated 1,300 years after the autograph. In comparison, we have 24,633 surviving

[61] **Bruce, FF** *The New Testament Documents: Are They Reliable?* Inter-Varsity Press, 1964, pp.16,17
[62] **Holdaway, David** *The Life of Jesus,* Sovereign World Ltd, Tonbridge, UK, 1997, pp.76-77

MSS of the New Testament, of which the earliest is within 100 years of the autograph which makes up the NT books.

Philip Schaff carried out an in-depth comparison between the Greek New Testament texts and the English translations. He concluded that:

"...only 400 of the 15,000 variant readings caused doubt about the textual meaning, and only 50 of these were of great significance. Not one of the variations altered an article of faith or a precept of duty which is not abundantly sustained by other and undoubted passages, or by the whole tenor of Scripture teaching."[63]

In other words, what has come down to us in the King James Version is as close to what was originally written as it is possible to get in English. Geisler and Nix believe the sum total of research into New Testament manuscript veracity reveals that:

"...only about one-eighth of all the variants had any weight, as most of them are merely mechanical matters such as spelling or style. Of the whole, then, only about one-sixtieth rise above 'trivialities' or can in any sense be called 'substantial variations'. Mathematically, this would compute to a text that is 98.33 percent pure."[64]

A stunning verification came with the discovery of the Dead Sea Scrolls by a Bedouin shepherd boy and his two companions in a cave in Qumran in March 1947. Searching for a lost goat, young Muhammed Edh-Dhib tossed a stone into a hole in a cliff and the boys were surprised to hear the sound of shattering pottery. The 40,000-odd inscribed fragments subsequently recovered from eleven caves between 1947 and 1956 were entombed around 68 AD. The authorship is traditionally thought to be of the Essenes, a Jewish religious sect. Significantly, excerpts of all the Biblical books except Esther are represented in the Scrolls, including a complete scroll of Isaiah, predating the earliest extant manuscript (Masoretic

---

[63] McDowell, Josh, *Evidence That Demands a Verdict*, op. cit. p.44; see also **Schaff, Philip** *Companion to the Greek Testament and the English Version*, Harper Brothers, New York, 1883, p.177

[64] **Geisler, Norman L & William E Nix** *A General Introduction to the Bible*, Moody Press, Chicago, 1968, p.365

Text – 916 AD) *by a thousand years.* This is highly significant when assessing the reliability and accuracy of transmission of not only this key Biblical book but others featured in the historic find. The result?

Dr Chuck Missler:

"The gap between the last prophet Malachi and extant manuscripts was narrowed from 1,400 years to as little as 150 years." [65]

Prof Millar Burrows, Dead Sea Scrolls expert:

"Of the 166 words in Isaiah 53, there are only seventeen letters in question. Ten of these letters are simply a matter of spelling, which does not affect the sense. Four more letters are stylistic changes, such as conjunctions. The remaining three letters comprise the word 'light' which is added in verse 11, and does not affect the meaning greatly. Furthermore, this word is supported by the LXX [Septuagint translation] and IQ Is (one of the Isaiah scrolls found in the Dead Sea caves). Thus, in one chapter of 166 words, there is only one word (three letters) in question after a thousand years of transmission – and this word does not significantly change the meaning of the passage."[66]

Garry K Brantley:

"Interestingly, when scholars compared the [Masoretic Text - 9th century AD] of Isaiah to the Isaiah scroll of Qumran, the correspondence was astounding. The texts from Qumran proved to be word-for-word identical to our standard Hebrew Bible in more than 95 percent of the text. The 5 percent of variation consisted primarily of obvious slips of the pen and spelling alterations (Archer, 1974, p. 25). Further, there were no major doctrinal differences between the accepted and Qumran texts. This forcibly demonstrates the accuracy with which scribes copied sacred texts, and bolstered our confidence in the Bible's textual integrity (Yamauchi, 1972, p. 130). The Dead Sea

---

[65] **Missler, Chuck** *An Extraterrestrial Message* audio commentary, www.khouse.org, p.9
[66] **Burrows, M** *The Dead Sea Scrolls,* p.304, per McDowell, J, *More Evidence that Demands a Verdict,* op. cit., p.79

62

Scrolls have increased our confidence that faithful scribal transcription substantially has preserved the original content of Isaiah." [67]

No serious scholar disputes the singular accuracy employed by the Jewish scribal system, which faithfully copied OT manuscripts for the benefit of future generations using a numerical 'lock' for supreme accuracy.[68] The New Testament is even more impressive. The early Church Fathers quoted so extensively from the New Testament that Sir David Dalrymple and J Harold Greenlee independently calculated that the entire NT canon could be reconstructed from their writings alone bar eleven verses.

Some liberal scholars, generally hostile to an early dating of the NT (most ascribed them to the 2nd century AD), have since revised their positions, most notably Dr John A Robinson in his book, *Redating the New Testament.* Dating of the Synoptic Gospels (Matthew, Mark and Luke) is now generally agreed to be prior to the commencement of the Jewish revolt in 66 AD; Paul's letters are dated to between 50-66 AD, and the Fourth Gospel between 80 – 100 AD. No mention is made in NT writings of Yeshua's step-brother James's famous martyrdom in 62 AD, nor of the Christian persecutions under Nero, nor of the commencement of the Jewish revolt against Roman rule in 66 AD, nor even of the total destruction of Jerusalem and the Second Temple in 70 AD by Titus and his legions, resulting in the slaughter of over a million and a half Jewish inhabitants.

Paul alludes to eyewitnesses to Christ's ministry *still being alive* at the time of his own writings, who certainly would have had something to say if the earliest circulating gospels were incorrect in any way.

Similarly, an underlying theme in Luke's Acts of the Apostles is that the religious unrest after the crucifixion was not being caused by Christians, but by the Jewish authorities stirring up trouble against the new Christian sect. The Romans throughout

---

[67] **Brantley, Garry K** *The Dead Sea Scrolls and Biblical Integrity,* www.apologeticspress.org/articles/266

[68] Since Hebrew letters also have a numerical value, the content of pages or passages can be calculated numerically to compare them with the new copies to ascertain any variance in the text.

Acts are actually portrayed as good guys, which clearly would not be the case if Rome were tossing Christians to the lions or burning them alive, as Nero subsequently ordered, or if Titus's four legions had just got through slaughtering a million and a half Jews in the appalling immolation of Jerusalem in 70 AD. These omissions are telling date-stamps for the originality of the NT. The obvious conclusion is that these momentous events are not mentioned in NT writings because the latter had been completed before the events in question occurred. Biblical archaeological scholar William Foxwell Albright summarises:

"We can say emphatically that there is no longer any solid basis for dating any book of the New Testament after about 80 AD, two full generations before the date between 130 – 150 AD given by the most radical New Testament critics of today." [69]

And in *Christianity Today*, 18th January 1963, he writes:

"In my opinion, every book of the New Testament was written by a baptised Jew between the forties and eighties of the first century AD (very probably some time between about 50 AD and 75 AD)."

The sceptics' assertion, therefore, that the Bible, either OT or NT, has been somehow edited, changed or distorted down through the ages is a lie put about by those who bank on their listeners' ignorance, compliance or apathy not to be found out. A spiritual agenda is, of course, abroad whose goal is to cast doubt upon and discredit God's *Logos* (the Son). For instance, there have been notable tamperings with some of the translations, and we'll examine examples of this aspect of the Holy War as we proceed.

Archaeological verification

Major corroboration of the Bible's unique track record for accuracy is also given by the archaeological record. As previously mentioned, Palestinian archaeologist Dr Nelson Glueck famously stated back in 1959 that:

---

[69] **Albright, W F** *Recent Discoveries in Biblical Lands,* Funk & Wagnalls, New York: 1955, p.136

"...it may be stated categorically that no archaeological discovery has ever controverted a Biblical reference." [70]

A wealth of finds has come to light supporting the Biblical text since Dr Gluek made his assertion over half a century ago. Discoveries across Syria, Israel, Egypt and Iraq reveal a stunning congruence with bold statements made in the Biblical record that shed light on our origins. Some of this proof comes in the form of confirmation of events portrayed in the Bible; for instance, evidence for the destructions at Jericho, Sodom and Gomorrah, proofs for the record of Kings Saul, David and Solomon, Biblical towns, Biblical names, religious practices, ancient Hebrew words, the Flood, Babel, the Patriarchs, the Roman census to which Mary and Joseph responded, accurate dating and naming of governors, high priests and monarchs, the court where Jesus was tried by Pilate ('the Pavement' – FG 19:13, now known to be the court of the Tower of Antonia), the Pool of Bethesda, details of the process and medical effects of crucifixion, evidence of the existence of Pontius Pilate, and so on. As these finds and their implications are so extensive, we'll examine examples as we proceed.

The scoffers, however, will never be satisfied. Theirs is a spiritual antagonism compelling them to press attacks at every quarter. Why? Wasn't British Christianity consigned to the dustbins from the 1970s onwards? Since the bottom has progressively dropped out of Anglican church attendance in my country, Christianity has become a social irrelevance in Britain – a quaint throwback to an earlier age. Critics talk of the post-Christian era, of our new Secular Society. Today militant Islam is always in the news with its attacks, bombs, bullets and marches in Parliament Square calling for various British people to be beheaded, yet editors studiously avoid giving Muslims the critical bashing dished out to Jesus, presumably to avoid a *fatwa*. Instead *Daily Mail* columnist Andrew Alexander sharpens his talons on an old enemy:

---

[70] **Gluek, N** *Rivers in the Desert,* Jewish Publication Society of America, 1st ed., p.31

"The sad truth is that Christianity claims to reveal the greatest truth of our existence, yet the Church's attitude to facts has always been remarkably cavalier. You do not need Darwin to show it. Christian scholars acknowledge that of the four evangelists – Matthew, Mark, Luke and John – only the third is a truthful attribution. And he wrote long after Jesus's death, inspired by Paul, who never even met Jesus. Misattributions are not a good start. Then we come to the Virgin Birth tales in Matthew and Luke. The texts have clearly been tampered with later, as Biblical scholars also concede, to produce a miracle. No biography in history has ever started with a lengthy bloodline of a stepfather."[71]

Firstly, Biblical scholars concede no such thing. And Paul said he met Jesus on the road to Damascus and went on years later to die for his faith. Paul/Saul was a feared Jewish persecutor of Christians following Christ's crucifixion. He held the coats of those who illegally stoned Stephen, then soon after converted to Christianity! What's going on? Was Paul *mad?* Dig deeper and you discover Saul of Tarsus was arguably one of the most brilliant minds ever to have walked the Earth. His texts are studied in universities today as the highest standard of literature. Paul was trained in the top Greek schools, spoke Greek, Latin and Hebrew fluently, was tutored by the legendary Jewish sage, Gamaliel, and was a Roman citizen. Paul's New Testament writings, passed down intact, reveal a man of profound learning and humility in inspired control of his senses.

Secondly, Andrew Alexander accuses the Gospels themselves of being faked for ignominious gain. He does so in breathtaking disregard of the textual evidence, the archaeological evidence, the thousands of citizens who saw Jesus personally, knew what He did and said, and survived long enough to pass this information on to others.

Is it important to know who wrote the gospels? It was obviously not a point of interest among the writers to identify themselves in their work. The one exception is the author of the Fourth Gospel, who reveals himself mysteriously only as 'the

---

[71] *Daily Mail,* 5th February 2009

disciple whom Jesus loved' (Fourth Gospel 21:20-24). The Fourth Gospel is now known to have been misattributed to the Galilean fisherman John Zebedee via church tradition.[72] And why four Gospels when surely one would have done? Watch what happens when you lay the Gospels on top of one another and align them chronologically. They dovetail into a four-camera-angled eyewitness view of the life, ministry and death of Jesus of Nazareth, passed down to us intact in the face of insuperable odds. No errors. No contradictions. Now that's inspired.

Thirdly, Alexander mocks the genealogy of Jesus Christ, which significantly opens the New Testament (Matthew's Gospel). Alexander writes, *"No biography in history has ever started with a lengthy bloodline of a stepfather."* I mentioned earlier that many scholars have been compelled to revise their hermeneutics to a surprisingly higher/literal interpretation of the Bible since, time after time, it becomes clear supposedly incongruous names, places, statements and phrases have been installed in the text only to emerge later in an astonishing light. Matthew's genealogy of Yeshua is one such example, missed by almost everyone not bothered enough to study it (most don't). Alexander won't have been made privy to the supernatural architecture behind Matthew's list of generations. By way of an example, Chuck Missler challenges anyone to construct a genealogy, *even a fictitious one,* on the basis of God's number (7) with the following attributes in Greek the way they are found in the first chapter of Matthew's Gospel:

"The number of words must be divisible by 7, evenly. The number of letters must also be divisible by 7, evenly. The number of vowels and number of consonants must also be divisible by 7. The number of words that begin with a vowel must be divisible by 7. The number of words that begin with a consonant must be divisible by 7. The number of words that occur more than once must be divisible by 7. Those that occur in more than one form must be divisible by 7. Those that occur in only one form must be divisible by 7. The number

---

[72] The surprising mystery of the Fourth Gospel authorship is revealed later in the *Origins* series.

of nouns must be divisible by 7. Only 7 words shall not be nouns. The number of names shall be divisible by 7. Only 7 other kinds of nouns are permitted. The number of male names must be divisible by 7. The number of generations shall be divisible by 7 (21)."[73]

Another scholar writes:

"The second chapter of Matthew tells of the childhood of the Christ. Its vocabulary has 161 words, or 23 sevens, with 896 letters, or 128 sevens, and 238 forms, or 34 sevens; the numeric value of the vocabulary is 123,529, or 17,647 sevens; of the forms, 166,985, or 23,855 sevens; and so on through pages of enumeration. This chapter has at least four logical divisions, and each division shows alone the same phenomena found in the chapter as a whole. Thus the first six verses have a vocabulary of 56 words, or 8 sevens, etc. There are some speeches here: Herod speaks, the Magi speak, the angel speaks. But so pronounced are the numeric phenomena here, that though there are as it were numerous rings within rings, and wheels within wheels, each is perfect in itself, though forming all the while only part of the rest." [74]

These gametrical signatures run throughout the New Testament. It can also be demonstrated that Matthew had to have been written last:

"In [Matthew's] very first section, the genealogy discussed above, the words found nowhere else in the New Testament occur 42 times, 7 x 6; and have 126 letters, 7 x 6 x 3, each number a multiple not only of seven, but of 6 sevens, to name only two of the many numeric features of these words. But how did Matthew know, when designing this scheme for these words (whose sole characteristic is that they are found nowhere else in the New Testament), that they would not be found in the other 26 books? That they would not be used by the other 7 New Testament writers? Unless we assume the impossible hypothesis that he had an agreement with them to that effect, he must

---

[73] **Missler, Chuck** *Cosmic Codes,* vol.2, www.khouse.org
[74] Panin, I, "The Inspiration of the Scriptures Scientifically Demonstrated", http://www.biblebelievers.org.au/panin.htm

have had the rest of the New Testament before him when he wrote his book. **The Gospel of Matthew, then, was written last."** [75]

The problem is, Mark, Luke, the Fourth Gospel, Peter, the epistles of Paul, James, Jude and John's work all exhibit the same transcendent characteristics *and can all be shown to have been authored last!*

"The phenomena are there and there is no human way of explaining them.... There remains only to be added that by precisely the same kind of evidence the Hebrew Old Testament is proved to be equally inspired. Thus the very first verse of Genesis has seven words, 28 letters, or 4 sevens: to name only two out of the dozens of numeric features of this one verse of only seven words." [76]

But Andrew Alexander is not interested. He dismisses with a wave of the hand the painstaking research conducted into the origins and veracity of NT documents over the past century, including archaeology, manuscript evidence, gematria/codes and corroborative verification of extra-Biblical authors. Some of the atheist researchers caught up in their study were even converted. Alexander cocks a snook at the overarching evidence of changed lives in Christ and withdraws instead into Darwin, who won't judge him as a writer or sinner because Charlie is dead and still in his grave. Alexander won't even consider the apostles themselves who had every chance to flee and live out peaceful lives in distant lands, but chose instead the way of the Master. Were they mad and deluded to have died as they did? I've always sensed something more going on here - timeless, pressing, imperative, forcing itself to the surface to be discovered before the clock of our own mortality ticks down to its inevitable date with destiny.

So why could the apostles see it, yet Andrew Alexander, Dawkins and millions of others to this day cannot? The answer will both surprise and offend some who have read even this far.

---

[75] Ibid.
[76] Ibid.

The Word is God

The Bible states that Jesus Himself is the Word and that all the scriptures testify of Him (FG 1:1; 5:39; Rev 19:13). The idea that the Bible, even in its original Hebrew, Greek and Aramaic forms, could be the actual Word (*Gr: Logos*) of God without error is visibly scoffed at today and mocked *with great feeling* as fundamentalist rubbish even by religionists, yet it's worth taking a look at the issue from a different angle – one which uses a key research axiom when studying historical/ancient documents, bringing us into better congruence with the ethnocentric dynamic. Ask this question: What did the Biblical participants themselves believe the scriptures they wrote represented?

There's a simple answer. The Old Testament contributors claimed their message was directly from God.[77] So did the New Testament writers.[78] Moreover, inspired writers of the Bible claimed the offerings of other contributors were also directly from God.[79] Today it's fashionable, even convenient for many to believe that the writers of the Bible made up their stories, so all we may have been left is a concatenation of man-centred angst with possibly some God-breathed guidance buried in there somewhere. In other words, you can choose what to believe. You have your truth, I have mine. This is utterly rejected by the Biblical authors who carried out their missions in deadly earnest, many perishing for their belief. These writers go much further. They even state that anyone who says they are speaking a word/gospel from God when they're not is a false prophet and thereafter under God's curse. The book of Revelation even promises that the plagues of that

---

[77] Isa 1:2; Jer 10:1,2; Ezekiel 1:3; Hosea 1:1,2; Jon 1:1; Micah 1:1; Zech. 1:1; Joel 1:2; Amos 1:3,6, etc; Obad 1:1; Zeph 1:1; Hab. 2:2; Deut 30:10; Num 12:6-8; 23:5,12,16,19, etc.

[78] 1 Cor 14:37; Eph 3:3-5; 1 Tim 4:1; FG 12:48-50; Acts 16:32; Rom 1:16; 1 Thess 1:5; 4:15; 2 Thess 3:12

[79] 2 Chron 34:14-19; Isa 2:1-3; Matt 1:22; 2:15; 15:4; 19:4-6; 22:29-32, 43; FG 10:35; 16:13; Acts 1:16; 4:24f; 28:25; Rom 1:1,2; Heb 1:1,2; 3:7; 1 Pet 1:10-12; 2 Pet 1:20f; 3:15f

frightening tome will be added to anyone who adds to Revelation.[80]

Moreover, the Bible writers state that the compilation of scripture is so pure in terms of God's Word, the reader is left with a simple choice: accept it all or reject it all. No alternatives are left open, at least in the scripture writers' eyes. They state that God's word is perfect, right and true. All God's precepts are right. The words written are true and faithful. If one claims the Bible errs, then he must either utterly reject the Bible as God's will, or call God a liar or worse. The Bible states that it is all from God with no extra bits. You get the picture.[81] Here's the uncomfortable bit. There is a selection process underway based on what *you* think the Bible is or isn't. And since the Word of God is Jesus Himself, God's Son is asking each of us, **"But whom say ye that I am?"** (Mark 8:29) [82]

So if we buy the view of the liberals that parts of the Bible are flawed, contain mistakes, and the whole is not literally God's *Logos,* which parts should we revere and which get the chop? Many Christian ministers don't believe in a literal Creation, the Flood, Moses and the Exodus, David, Solomon or even that Jesus was born of a virgin and performed miracles, let alone died on a cross for our sins and was resurrected to the right hand of God. Journalist Stephen Glover writes:

"Last Friday, at a party in Oxford, I found myself talking to the biologist and atheist Richard Dawkins and a very senior Anglican clergyman. I asked this cleric, whom I know and like, whether he believed in the Resurrection. He said that he did not. He added that he 'didn't think for a moment' that he 'would survive after death'. A senior clergyman in our Established Church publicly and shamelessly professing such disbelief makes one despair.... What was so painful was this clergyman's easy denial of a cornerstone of his faith in front

---

[80] For a study on this, see Num 22:35; Deut 18:18-22; Jer 14:14; 23:16,26; Eze 3:26,27;13:2-7,17; Matt 10:19,20; 15:9; Rom 10:17; 1 Cor 2:4,5; Galatians 1:8-12; 1 Thess 2:13; 2 Peter 1:20,21; Rev 22:18,19

[81] Num 22:35,38; 23:5,12,16,19,20; Deut 18:18-22; Psa 19:7-9; 33:4; 119:128,142,160; 147:4,5; FG 10:35; 17:17; Rom 3:4; Titus 1:2,3; Heb 6:18; Gal 1:20; Jam 1:25; Rev 19:9; 21:5

[82] FG 1:1, 14; 1 Pet 1:23; Rev 19:13, etc.

of the most notable and militant atheist of our age. In effect he was saying to Mr Dawkins: 'You're right, and the Church is wrong.'" [83]

You may well ask what on earth they are doing as ministers. The answer is, they're pulling a pay-cheque and there's a recession on. And they do like editing God. And after what I've found out, I would not do that if I were them, for God puts His Word (His Son) even above His own name (Psa 138:2). The spiritual enemy is at work, doing what he does best, casting doubt on God's Word and sowing deception and apostasy among God's ministers. It's all part of your training programme.

Elsewhere in this extraordinary work, God's Word is given a name: In the Greek: *IHCOY XPICTOY*. In Hebrew: *Yeshua ha-Mashiach*. In English: Jesus the Messiah/Christ:

In the beginning was the Word, and the Word was with God, and the Word was God. The same was in the beginning with God. All things were made by Him; and without Him was not any thing made that was made.... And the Word was made flesh and dwelt [*lit.* 'tabernacled'] among us, (and we beheld His glory, the glory as of the only begotten of the Father) full of grace and truth.... For the law was given by Moses, but grace and truth came by Jesus Christ. (FG 1:1-3, 14,17).

The name and nature of God

Ecumenical liberals like to claim that all the religions of the world are worshiping the same god. This is expressly refuted in scripture, as we shall see. For instance, the God of the Judaeo-Christian Bible is not the 'Allah' of Islam, who is described in Muslim writings as 'unknowable', 'capricious'.[84] By contrast, the God of the Bible, whose name is given as the tetragrammaton YHWH ('Yahweh') in the OT (Exo 3:13-14), and *IHCOY XPICTOY* (Jesus Christ) in the NT (Heb: *Yeshua – cf.* FG 8:58), desires not only

---

[83] *Daily Mail*, "God help us when Girl Guides ditch religion for the shallow cult of the individual", 19th June 2013

[84] Indeed, it is tantamount to blasphemy to assert that one can know the Muslim god intimately or claim any sort of close, personal relationship with him. See www.studytoanswer.net/myths_ch3.html

to be known in detail by all mankind, the Kinsman-Redeemer (*goel*) role God Himself must play to redeem not only mankind but the entire Creation from the Holy War necessitates that He must be made flesh as the 'Seed of the woman' (*cf*: Gen 3:15). This is the first messianic prophecy given in Genesis. YHWH delights in making and keeping His promises. No clearer examples of God's uniqueness and transcendence can be seen than in the following passages. Watch carefully again as God lays it down:

"Present your case," says the LORD. **"Set forth your arguments,"** says Jacob's King. **"Tell us, you idols, what is going to happen. Tell us what the former things were, so that we may consider them and know their final outcome. <u>Or declare to us the things to come, tell us what the future holds, so that we may know you are gods</u>. Do something, whether good or bad, so that we will be dismayed and filled with fear. But you are less than nothing and your works are utterly worthless; whoever chooses you is detestable."** (Isa 41:21-24, NIV UK)

I am always amused when people say there's no proof of God. Most maintain this because they've heard someone else say it, so assume it's correct. It isn't. When you show them the proof, they reject it. What is the proof? Notice in the above passage that YHWH reveals a unique attribute about Himself – that of precogniscence – and uses it to set a challenge to anything else that might claim to be god. i.e. "You claim to be god? Fine. Tell us what's going to happen. Make some prophecies." As already noted, the rest of the world's gods and their books are conspicuously silent on successful prophecy. YHWH, on the other hand, goes for it across 66 books and there's no stopping Him. The Bible is literally stuffed with prophecy, along with micro and macro codes that authenticate YHWH's authorship of His Message System.

"I am God <u>and there is none like Me</u>, declaring the end from the beginning, and from ancient times the things that are not yet done, saying, "My counsel shall stand and I will do all My pleasure."' (Isa 46:9-10)

"I have declared the former things from the beginning. They went forth from My mouth and I caused them to hear it. Suddenly I did them and they came to pass.... Even from the

beginning I have declared it to you. Before it came to pass I proclaimed it to you, lest you should say, 'My idol has done them, and my carved image and my moulded image have commanded them'." (Isa 48:3,5, NKJV)

Notice God rolling out one of many unique attributes to His nature, namely His ability to dwell outside of time and therefore predict the future. He puts Himself on the hook for us now, daring us to see if these things are so. Very well, let's dare Him. Imagine the incongruity of a carpenter telling his friends 2,000 years ago: **"Heaven and Earth shall pass away, but My words will by no means pass away"** (Matt 24:35), and that statement being true to this day.

The above verses certainly sound like the sorts of things God might say, yet the reality is that they were words spoken by men and written down by men in what we understand to be the Bible today. *God-breathed* is a stumbling block for many, who view it as a fanciful crutch for the gullible who so want to believe God decreed what people wrote that they'll grab at anything. But hold your horses a moment. If it's not God's book, we'll find mistakes in the original form. If it *is* God's book, He can compile it however He likes, for He's God whether we like it or not. If a group of greybeards made it all up, why do we have such startling cohesion in the 66 books across such a wide variety of subjects spanning centuries of cultural upheaval, when most of these authors never even met each other, let alone read what the others wrote? [85]

So the most common complaint you'll hear against the Bible is that it's just a book and should not be taken seriously since it's obviously written by men and full of errors. When pressed to come up with inconsistencies, however, the accusers will always falter. When asked whether they are aware of the astonishing accuracy of Bible prophecy thus far across 2,700 years and what a phenomenon it is, they try to change the subject. I don't let them. When pushed, they maintain the Bible is in error because other people have said so. Wendy Wallace writes:

---

[85] The various books comprising the 'Old Testament' today were put together in the days of Ezra, c. 450 BC., though most were written centuries earlier.

God has promised His people increasing clarity as the time of the end approaches. **"But ye, brethren, are not in darkness, that that day should overtake you as a thief…"** (1 Thess 5:4). **"Behold, the former things are come to pass, and new things do I declare: before they spring forth I tell you of them."** (Isa 42:9). **"Surely the LORD God will do nothing, but He revealeth His secret to His servants, the prophets."** (Amos 3:7). And God keeps His promises: **"God is not a man that He should lie."** (Num 23:19)[86]

We're repeatedly drawn back to a more literal interpretation of the Message System. The incredible prophecies of the Bible were never given off-handedly by the righteous seers of old. If you were a prophet in ancient times who dished up a prophecy beginning, *"Thus saith the LORD…"* which later turned out to be utter bunk, you could be taken outside the city walls and stoned to death for blasphemy. A prophet's life expectancy in Old Testament times was generally poor due to the prophet's unpopularity for telling the truth which, as history repeatedly demonstrates, most don't want to hear. Of course, we don't kill God's prophets any more these days – at least not yet – but who on earth *is* God? Can we get any closer to finding out? What is His personality? What does He like? What does He hate? Moreover, what does He expect of us so we don't fall foul of Him? Is He the sum total of everything that ever was, is and shall be? Can there really be an all-powerful being out there who spoke Creation into existence and is daily sustaining us (Col 1:15-17)? Science is certainly spitting tacks over the intelligent design movement, as we found out in *Origins I*. Perhaps the best place to start with God is to examine another unique attribute of His nature – His perfection, His holiness. And that's a question of Truth with a capital 'T', reckons Dr Stuart Crane.

The definition of Truth

In his Montreal conferences, Dr Crane defines Truth as:

"An <u>accurate</u> representation of that under consideration <u>and its relationship to all other things</u> as it always has been in the past, is

---

[86] **Wallace, Wendy** *The Four Horsemen of the Apocalypse and The New World Order*, Prescott, AZ, USA, 1994

universally so in the present, and will hold <u>without a single exception</u> in the entire future. Anything less than this is error."

It's worth reading the above definition a few times to get the full meaning out of how transcendent Truth really is. Truth can only be understood in conjunction *with its relationship to ALL things*. This is known as cause and effect. Every cause has an effect and every effect is a cause. This property is recognised in the field of quantum physics, which holds that all things in the universe are inter-relational and all-knowing at the sub-atomic level. Therefore anything I wish to know about, says Dr Crane, if I wish to know the Truth about it, I need to know about its relationship *with all other things in the universe*. Truth will never have an exception in the past, will never have one on-going in the present, and can never have an exception in the future. It will always stand alone as the Truth. All else is error.

Crane makes the point that if he is to tell you the Truth, he must know all of the above to be absolutely certain, otherwise he is giving you an opinion. Yeshua said, **"I am the truth."** He did not say, *"I am telling the truth,"* He said *He was the Truth.* In other words, Jesus was saying that He knew all things in the past, present and future and their intermeshed relationships with each other throughout eternity (FG 8:58). Christ also stated, while walking the Earth, *that He had the same mind as the Father* (FG 10:15). Jesus was declaring His Deity.

Truth with a capital 'T' is impossible to the finite/human mind, says Crane. Truth is only possible to an infinite mind, one without limitations. The only way Truth could exist in the universe is if there were an Infinite Mind. And even if there were an Infinite Mind in the universe, then Truth would only be possible to humankind if that Infinite Mind chose to reveal it to us. Has this in fact occurred? We cannot get Truth on our own by discovery, by work or by diligence. Truth is only possible through revelation by the Infinite Mind if the Infinite Mind so chooses to tell us. The only way we can keep from error *is blindly to follow the Infinite Mind.* This trust is known as *faith.* Faith is a belief which taps into the intermeshed quantum Truth of the Infinite Mind, says Crane. Those who sincerely seek Truth will ultimately be led into a study of God's Word, for contained therein is the provable revelation of the Infinite Mind.

Hmmm. This does not deter people from trying to imagine what God looks like. A child sits at the kitchen table drawing a picture.

"What are you doing?" Mum asks.

"I'm drawing a picture of God," replies the boy.

"Don't be silly, darling, no one knows what God looks like."

"They will when I've finished my picture."

In the Bible, instead of revealing to us that He looks like Jim Caviezel, God reveals something far more earth-shattering. His Will. What He wants us to do, and what He's going to do for us. He reveals His character and a love for us that is so multi-dimensional, it bathes us even in the harshest of His acts. God instructs us through His Word (Son). God's reality is so far beyond our comprehension that His will demands our humility before Him. How many people are humble before the God of Abraham, Isaac and Jacob today? Not many. But keep watching and they soon will be.

Bible codes

In *Origins I,* I briefly covered the phenomenon of equidistant letter sequences (ELS), the so-called Bible codes, popularized by Michael Drosnin's bestselling eponymous book. Though Drosnin's work was for the most part contrived, the book stirred up enormous interest worldwide and loosened up many to the possibility that the Bible might have God's signature all over it, authenticating it as the Book of books. After all, only God could do immeasurably clever things with words while maintaining the integrity of the surface text. It would be one of the great proofs of His existence that God could spin wonders with words, even prophecies, only to be uncovered in the modern age of computers and burgeoning knowledge at the time of the end when such things could be understood (Dan 12:4). Has this in fact happened? Yes. Let's look at some examples.

Here a little, there a little

The Equidistant Letter Sequence phenomenon works by taking the original Masoretic Hebrew Text of the Tanakh – the Old Testament (OT) – and skipping a set number of letters through the text to make new words or phrases. The concept of doing this is not new and many rabbis down through the centuries gave hints that the Torah was not just the God-given Law of Moses but could be the very executable for the Creation itself, hence the meticulous methods by which it was copied. A view is also held by many Christians that the Bible, in its original, linguistic form, could be the mysterious Book of Life, wherein the name of every saved person is encoded in the hyperdimensional matrix of the Word. If Jesus Christ is both Saviour and Word, it can be argued that all believers are known and recorded in Him.

A Slovak rabbi, Chaim Michael Dov Weissmandl, popularised the informational properties of ELS when he revealed codes in the first five books of the Bible – the Torah.[87] He found that if you take the first Hebrew 't' in Genesis and then skip 49 letters (7 x 7), you find an 'o', then another 49 letters you find an 'r' and lastly an 'h', spelling TORH. This also works for the book of Exodus, but not for Leviticus, the central book of the Law. In Deuteronomy, the fifth book of the Torah, it works backwards – namely, you find the last 't' and work back every 49th letter to spell HROT. This also works for the Book of Numbers. A closer look at Leviticus reveals that every seventh letter (God's number), commencing with the first 'Y' spells out the tetragammatron YHWH (Yahweh), the Hebrew name for God. To Rabbi Weissmandl, the Torah always pointed to God.

TORH	->	TORH	->	YHWH	<-	HROT	<-	HROT
Genesis		Exodus		Leviticus		Numbers		Deuteronomy

Weissmandl's story is a heart-wrenching one. Prior to 1939, his fascination with ancient documents led him to examine ancient rabbinical claims that the Torah contained significant data in skip-sequences within the plain text. He transcribed all 304,805

---

[87] Genesis, Exodus, Leviticus, Numbers, Deuteronomy.

consonantal letters in a 10 x 10 array and made some surprising discoveries. The war interrupted his studies, abruptly plunging him into the horrors of Nazi Europe where, for the next six years, this brilliant Czech scholar helped run 'The Working Group', an underground organisation which sought to bribe Nazi officials to delay transportation of Slovak Jews to the concentration camps.

Weissmandl was one of the first to entreat the allies to bomb the railway leading to Auschwitz, and even the camp itself, to halt the exterminations. He even wrote to Churchill, Roosevelt and the Pope warning them of the progressive genocide of European Jewry. Then in 1944, Weissmandl and his family found themselves on a train bound for Auschwitz. Weissmandl managed to escape during the journey by sawing through the lock of the carriage with an emery wire hidden in some bread. His subsequent jump from the train broke his leg but he managed to hide out in Bratislava until assisted to Switzerland by two repentant Nazi sympathizers.

Ultimately Weissmandl was unable to save either Slovak Jewry or his loved ones. Following his emigration to America, he suffered frequent bouts of depression over what the Holocaust had done to his family and people. He remarried and had five further children but never forgot the fate of his first family in Europe. He died in 1957 from a heart attack, never having seriously reprised his pre-war research on the Torah codes.

God's watermark

Ironically, it was probably a burgeoning interest in the codes between the wars which led to the development of more advanced cryptographic techniques, which led to Alan Turing's cracking of the German Enigma Code at Bletchley Park, which led to the development of the modern computer, which today is used to investigate highly complex arrays within the Torah! The codes are not without controversy but there is a phenomenon here, and the more you dig, the stranger it gets.

How we're supposed to respond to the presence of the codes is another issue hotly dividing experts. Atheist Drosnin unabashedly presents them as some sort of cosmic Ouija board from which predictions can be made. His book, *The Bible Code*, is overly contrived in this regard and, in my view, misses the whole point. Many competent Christian scholars want nothing to do with the whole subject as, to them, the codes smack of divination. In my view, they're missing the point too.

If the codes exist beyond mathematical certainty, and they do, and if their ubiquity points to a supernatural authorship, and it does, then it's quite clear how we should interpret them. The Bible forbids divination or any forms of sorcery, so that leaves one option. God put the codes into His Holy Word to authenticate His authorship. He's also done it in such a way that the extent of the coding would only come to light at a pivotal point in mankind's technological development when computers using advanced cryptographic techniques could unlock the puzzle.

The codes do not impart doctrine. They don't tell us anything in themselves. They are not the path to salvation. They are better understood as God's validation and watermark of His particular Word over any other given to man on the Earth. In the majority of cases, the codes always point to His Son, Yeshua. This has led to accusations that the four-letter Hebrew word for Jesus (*Joshua* or *Yehoshua*, *lit.* 'Yahweh is salvation', written יהשע) could statistically crop up in any large body of text a number of times, especially in Hebrew – a stripped-down, consonantal tongue ideally suited to broad bandwidth. No-one disputes the mathematics of this but that's not the phenomenon. It's the context of *where* the name crops up in relation to the plain/surface text, and what words are coded around it that's the revelation. Another strange property of the codes is that they are usually appreciated *after* the event occurs to which they relate, if applicable, and we'll look at examples as we proceed.

In my opinion, the codes are in the Bible for God's glory and for the edification of those who seek them out. Draw close to God and He'll draw close to you (Jam 4:8). There's actually a Bible verse which states, **"It is the glory of God to conceal a thing, but the honour of kings is to search out a matter."** (Prov 25:2). We'll be doing a fair amount of kingly research in the coming chapters and the results will astound you.

Where two or more are gathered in My Name

Before we launch into this rollercoaster of what the Message System says about the Holy War, there are some simple guidelines which make understanding how the Bible works far more rewarding.

1) In all the years I've studied it, one conclusion I've come to is that the Bible can be taken far more literally than most people imagine. I believe God says what He means and means what He says. It's clear when idioms and figures of speech are being used.

2) The best interpreter of the Bible is the Word (Yeshua) itself *read by you* under revelation of the Holy Spirit. That's not to say that pastors, ministers and teachers don't have a lot to impart – of course they do – but God speaks to individuals through His Word, so *you* have to read it. For those who can't be bothered with God's Son (the Word), a spirit of slumber appears to ensure the revelations are sealed and not disparaged (Matt 7:6; Rom 11:8; Isa 29:10-11). The Bible is the only book where you get to take the Author home. It is the Holy Spirit's job to point things out to you as you read, for God has promised you that He will reveal, not some things, nor more things than usual, but *all things* (FG 14:26).

3) A particular doctrinal issue will be repeated somewhere else in the Bible if valid (Deut 19:15). The basis of the Mosaic legal system is 'in the presence of two or more witnesses let a thing be established'. For instance, when we read in the Book of Revelation that the number of the coming Antichrist (pseudo-Christ) world leader will be 666 (Rev 13:18), we need to find where else this number appears in the Bible for more information. There is only one other place it appears, and in a rather surprising context.[88]

4) If you are not sure what something means, the Bible usually interprets itself, so keep reading.

5) If you come across what appears to be a contradiction, this is a jewel God wants you to investigate further. The rabbis call this a *remez*, a clue to something profound to be revealed. Contrary to

---

[88] In fact, some modern scholars are now questioning that Revelation's original language actually means '666' at all. Another, more alarming interpretation has come to light, which will be covered later in the *Origins* series.

some reports, there are no mistakes or unresolved contradictions in the Bible in its original format.

6) According Amos 3:7, God will do nothing unless He has revealed it to His prophets in advance. Which means that we have God's battleplan in advance, all written down and ready for our study.

7) God is the ultimate mathematician. On average, one in every five verses in the Bible contains a number. Before you groan and tell me you only got a 'D' in maths, be aware that specific numbers have a relevance and you'll find them cropping up time and again as we proceed. For instance, 7 is the number of completion - God's number. This 'heptadic' (7's) structure is not only all over the plain text, it's hidden away in numerous codes and prophecy too. I am indebted to Michael Hunt for the following brief summary of numbers 1 to 10:

ONE: Uniqueness, sovereignty, unity and the one God (Deut 6:4).

TWO: Difference, division or double portion. Two items/events/pharaohs/brothers compared. On the second day, God created light and darkness. The Ten Commandments were on two tablets of stone. The second person of the Trinity, Yeshua/Jesus, fully God and fully human.

THREE: Represents an announcement of something significant to follow. *cf.* Isa 6:3; Rev 4:8; the three sons of Noah who survived the Flood. The three days Jonah spent in the whale, which prefigured the three days and nights Yeshua would spend in the tomb before His resurrection. Three disciples were taken onto the mount of transfiguration. The third person of the Trinity, the Holy Spirit.

FOUR: represents the Creation. Four cardinal quadrants of the Earth (see also Rev 7:1). The four letters of God's unpronounceable name, YHWH. Four seasons. Four rivers out of Eden, etc.

FIVE: Divine grace. Five books of the Torah (the Pentateuch).

SIX: The number of man, sin and rebellion. One interpretation of the revelation number of the beast – 666 – is the ultimate expression of human pride. The Sixth Commandment deals with the sin of murder. Jesus was on the cross for six hours and died at the beginning of the seventh (divine perfection). The world turned dark at the sixth hour, symbolising the judgment on sin. Six days a week of human labour, and on the seventh (perfection), rest.

SEVEN: Rest, perfection, completion, God's number. Covenant. Holy Spirit. Seven seals of Revelation. Seven trumpets. Seven bowls. Seven days of the week. Seven holy feasts in the Sinai Covenant. Seven gifts of the Holy Spirit. The heptadic structure of the Bible acts as a type of authentication lock throughout, and even crosses over between the Old and New Testaments. The gestation period for mammals is always a multiple of seven: mouse 21 days (3 x 7), cat 56 days (8 x 7), sheep 147 days (21 x 7), dog 63 days (9 x 7), lion 98 days (14 x 7); duck 42 days (6 x 7), human 280 days (40 x 7), etc. Seven colours of the spectrum. Man's pulse beats faster six days of the week and slower on the seventh (rest)!

EIGHT: Salvation, regeneration, new birth, new beginnings. The first perfect cube (2 x 2 x 2). Eight people saved in the Ark, including Noah. Circumcision is always on the eighth day (new beginnings). Eight classes of furniture in the Temple/Tabernacle. The gematria of Jesus's name in Greek ('Iesous') is 888.

NINE: The number of finality and judgment.

TEN: Divine Law, order, testimony and witness. Noah was the tenth generation from Adam when the Flood came. Abraham was the tenth generation from Shem, son of Noah, for the next covenant. King David was the tenth generation from Pharez, the bastard son of Judah and his daughter-in-law Tamar (*cf.* Gen 38:6-29; Deut 23:2). We have the Ten Commandments. Ten clauses in the LORD's Prayer. Ten plagues on Egypt. Ten virgins in Yeshua's parable. 10 times Yeshua uses the words *"I Am"* (YHWH) in the Fourth Gospel.[89]

TWELVE: The Kingdom *from* Heaven number. 12 disciples. 12 tribes. 12 apostles. 12 kingdom parables. 12,000 sealed from each of the 12 tribes in the book of Revelation. The New Jerusalem has 12

---

[89] For a fuller exposition on this subject, see Michael E. Hunt, "The Significance of Numbers in Scripture", AgapeBibleStudy.com, 1998, Revised 2007. http://www.agapebiblestudy.com/documents/The%20Significance%20of%20Nu mbers%20in%20Scripture.htm

gates and 12 foundation stones and its dimensions are 12,000 x 12,000 x 12,000 furlongs.

TWENTY-FOUR: Symbolic of the priesthood.

FORTY: God's period of testing and judgment. The rains fell on the Earth forty days and forty nights, symbolising judgment (Gen 7:4,12). The Hebrews ate manna in the wilderness for forty years – a period of testing (Exo 16:35). The three periods of Moses' life, forty years each, symbolising testing both on Moses and the Israelites. forty stripes was the maximum whipping penalty (Deut 25:3). Saul, David and Solomon each reigned for forty years. God gave Nineveh forty days to repent (Jonah 3:4). Jesus fasted forty days and nights (Matt 4:2). Jesus was tempted forty days (Luke 4:2, Mark 1:13). Jesus remained on earth forty days after resurrection (Acts 1:3). Women are pregnant for forty weeks.

THE PREDICAMENT OF MAN

"It could be that the purpose of your life
is only to serve as a warning to others." - **Anon**

"Why does God have a gender? Does he have a penis? A 'Y'
chromosome? Is there a lady god? Or is it because he was invented
by MISOGYNISTIC MEN?" – **Facebook post**

**The natural man receiveth not the things of the Spirit of God, for
they are foolishness unto him. Neither can he know them,
because they are spiritually discerned.** (1 Cor 2:14)

Are we really accountable after death for what we do in life?
What really lies beyond death?
Is what the Bible tells us verifiable?
What is the true predicament of man?

Ask anyone these questions and prepare for some strange
responses, ranging from anger to being completely ignored. Many
people won't process life and death in a meaningful way since they
have been taught evolution, which holds as its basic tenet the lie
that life is meaningless, that anything you ultimately accomplish
doesn't mean anything. Death, therefore, is the ultimate sword of
Damocles hanging over our heads – a mindless oblivion after a
pointless life. Best ignored until we are forced to confront it.

I did it *My Way*

In the materialistic, post-Christian, liberal society of the 21st
century, we've adopted 'Eat, drink, fornicate, do drugs and
anything else you like today if it feels good, for tomorrow we die'.
Or put another way: *"Life is the great indulgence. Death is the great
abstinence. Therefore make the most of life here and now."* A direct quote
from the Book of Satan, chapter 4, verse 1.

What do they teach in schools and universities? Evolution. As
we'll discover, evolution is a creed Satanists take very seriously.
It's sugar-coated for public consumption and goes like this. Be nice.

Don't moralise. Don't judge. Don't call anything sin. Be a good person and all will pan out. You are merely the product of genetics and environment so there's no God, no judgments, and definitely no Lake of Fire. There, feel better already, don't you? Any urges you may experience – including thoughts of lust, hatred, murder, lies, rape, pillage, stealing or fiddling thy Parliamentary expenses – are those of the primitive form from which you evolved. Relax, you're not responsible for any of it. It's your genes. You have blanket moral freedom from all accountability because there are no moral absolutes and you're nothing but animal – a human resource. Sounds great, right? Put another way: *"Do what thou wilt shall be the whole of the law."* A direct quote from the world's most famous Satanist, Aleister Crowley. In other words, there's only one law. Do what you want.

There's Death, which is scary. Everyone thinks about it often, even when they say they don't. It's the not knowing. Death the one-way door through which each of us must pass alone, and no-one ever comes back. No comfort there, or perhaps there is if the lights just go out. Meaningless oblivion after pointless life. Who gives a tinker's? The best you can do to cock a snook at Death, the Reaper, and the God Who Never Was, is to play Sinatra's *My Way* at your funeral. "Take that, life! Up yours! I was always in control! Took what I wanted and bailed!" Sounds good when you say it in front of your friends, especially with music to it:

For what is a man, what has he got?
If not himself, then he has naught
To say the things he truly feels
And not the words of one who kneels
The record shows I took the blows and did it my way! [90]

It's a different matter when we're facing The End alone. That's when many start wondering if anything does lie beyond. We can believe and say what we want during the heady business of life, but that won't change what actually is after death. It would take someone to rise from the dead and come back from the grave to tell us the details for us to know for certain. If that ever did happen, would we even listen?

---

[90] **Sinatra F** *My Way,* Universal Music Publishing Group

Welcome to the Holy War. The Predicament of Man. What the Bible's all about. Your Creator, Yeshua *ha-Mashiach* (FG 1:1-3), and the eternal relationship He wants with *you*. The official Bible trailer goes something like this: God has an extraordinary redemptive plan for your predicament in the Holy War raging between good and evil. The book's about His eventual visits to Earth firstly as a man to pay for your redemption for eternity (already accomplished, you just have to claim it), and secondly as avenging Creator of the Universe to destroy the wicked and reclaim the Earth from the usurper, the god of this world, *ha-Satan* (yet future). As an author, let me tell you that's quite a book plot.

The Bible can be described as the tale of two seeds – the seed of the Woman (the good seed) and the seed of the serpent (the evil seed) (Gen 3:15). The Bible can also be described as a tale of two cities: Jerusalem, idiomatically the city of God, and Babel (Babylon), the city of man/sin. The Bible can be described as the war between the visible (spacetime) and invisible (metacosmic/'spiritual') realms. Above all, the Bible is about mankind's redemption from the penalty of sin at the hand of a loving Creator, and the incredible, eternal destiny God has promised those He redeems after physical death. My question is, why would God go to all the bother? Sounds exhausting. Couldn't He just wave a wand? If you study the Bible from Genesis to Revelation, another uncomfortable thought strikes you. *God doesn't get what He wants out of the whole programme.* (1 Tim 2:3-4; 2 Pet 3:9)

The spiritual predicament of man is an extraordinary concept completely absent in the mind of today's secular culture, let alone many denominational churches. In the pages of the daily newspapers we read of evil in our midst, we know sin when we commit or learn about it, yet via tacit consent we have permitted our atheist rulers to call evil good and good evil (Isa 5:20), manufacturing a raft of psychiatric diagnoses instead, complete with drugs as the cure and a social worker to stop by to see how we're coping. Atheists have a problem with the existence of evil in our world, so they simply unname it. They have a problem with the existence of free will in our world too, so they unname that one also.

In contrast, the Bible gets right to it. Man is in a fallen, spiritual condition. His heart is incurably wicked, who can know it? Man will always tend towards sin and cannot fix himself (Jer 17:9; Matt 7:9-11; Mark 7:20-23; Rom 3:10-18). History shows this to be true. We are not improving our behaviour as the centuries pass. Instead, we have dug ourselves into an unholy predicament from which the Bible says only God Himself can extricate us. Not a popular view in today's man-centred, right-on, hand-wringing, prize-giving, God-abhorring, values-relativist world where the sovereignty of man rules. You have your truth and I have mine. It's not sin, just sickness. There's no such thing as love, just chemicals. Apparently we're all evolving our clogs off to a higher spiritual plane, though not so you'd notice. I agree with Wendy Wallace. I think the observable evidence shows that we're devolving back into pond scum, and our minds are so far along in the process we can't figure it out.[91]

So how did we get in such a mess in the first place? In two words, *free will*. The Bible states that God created man and gave him the ability to choose good from evil. He did this to enjoy genuine fellowship with His creations. He did not want robots. Ultimately there are several things God cannot do - actions which violate His holy nature. He cannot sin. He cannot excuse sin. He cannot lie. He cannot learn or be surprised. And He cannot force you to love Him. Love's not worth a sou if it's not freely given, and God wants you to love Him – that's the point of the whole programme and what He wants out of the deal (1 Tim 2:3-4; 2 Pet 3:9).

He wants an eternal relationship with *friends,* not grovelling servants or cyborgs (FG 15:14-16). Free will is the only mechanism by which this can be accomplished. He's given each of us the right to choose, free of coercion or pressure, whether to accept or reject Him. Every day I can choose to live God's ways or my own, He's left that choice up to me. Every day people deny or reject God, blaspheme the One who made them, blame their hideous actions on others or nothing, and it all grieves God. (Did you know God

---

[91] **Wallace, Wendy** *The Four Horsemen of the Apocalypse and The New World Order,* op. cit.

can be grieved?) Yet most of us, if we're honest, have a sneaking suspicion we humans are not absolved from the ultimate consequences of our actions. Is there such a thing as universal justice? Did Hitler and Stalin really get away with it? One atheist writes:

"True atheists have nothing to worry about on their deathbed. To quote Mark Twain – "I do not fear death. I had been dead for billions and billions of years before I was born, and had not suffered the slightest inconvenience from it." - milesp, Wigan, UK

That's quite a sound bite. So the lights just go out, Miles? Is that based on any evidence *at all* or just your wishful, default position? US President Thomas Jefferson, not noted for his orthodox Christian views, was more uncomfortable:

"I tremble for my country when I reflect that God is just; that his justice cannot sleep forever."

The Bible states there will certainly be a universal judgment of the unsaved. Even the saved/elect/chosen/redeemed will go before Christ's 'bema seat' judgment for debriefing and have their works assessed for inheritance and rewards in the Eternal Kingdom (2 Cor 5:10; 1 Cor 3:12-15). Everything we do on Earth is being meticulously recorded for later presentation before the Judge of All Things – Jesus Christ. And all that dirty laundry we thought we handled in secret? Verily it shall be pegged out on thy rooftops, flapping abroad for all to behold:

"For God shall bring every work into judgment, with every secret thing, whether it be good or whether it be evil." (Ecc 12:14)

"I the LORD search the heart, I try the reins, even to give every man according to his ways, and according to the fruit of his doings." (Jer 17:10)

"But I say unto you, that every idle word that men shall speak, they shall give account thereof in the day of judgment. For by thy words thou shalt be justified, and by thy words thou shalt be condemned." (Matt 12:36-37)

"For there is nothing covered that shall not be revealed; neither hid, that shall not be known. Therefore whatsoever ye have spoken in darkness shall be heard in the light; and that

which ye have spoken in the ear in closets shall be proclaimed upon the housetops." (Luke 12:2-3)

"And I saw the dead, small and great, stand before God; and the books were opened: and another book was opened, which is the Book of Life: and the dead were judged out of those things which were written in the books, according to their works. And the sea gave up the dead which were in it; and Death and Hades delivered up the dead which were in them: and they were judged every man according to their works. And death and Hades were cast into the Lake of Fire. This is the second death. And whosoever was not found written in the Book of Life was cast into the Lake of Fire." (Rev 20:12-15)

"But I'm a good person! I led a good life!" goes the cry. "Why would a righteous God punish *me?*" Depends on what yardstick you're using for 'righteous'. On a human level, you may not have been Reinhard Heydrich's favourite henchman, nor a Janjaweed mass murderer of Sudanese villages, neither slave-trader nor medieval Crusader vying with his mates to see how many Jewish babies he could get on a sword. But did I ever tell a lie? Yes, hundreds, probably thousands. Then I'm a liar. Did I ever steal anything that wasn't mine? Of course. Many times. Then I'm a thief. Did I ever lust after a woman who was not my wife? Blimey, do I *have* to answer that? Then I'm a fornicating adulterer. Did I ever think angry thoughts towards my parents? Of course. Then I'm a parent-hater. Did I ever do anything inappropriate on a Saturday, God's Day of Rest? *Strewth, every week!* Then I'm a Sabbath-breaker. Did I ever take God's name in vain? Well, I had several dogs who thought their names were Jesus Christ. In that case, I'm a blasphemer. Did I ever love any material thing more than God? Yes, my Mitsubishi 3000GT VR4. Then I'm an idolater.

So here's Phillip Day. I'm a lying, thieving, adulterous, parent-hating fornicator who blasphemes God on a regular basis – every Saturday, in fact. What does God have to say to that?

Know ye not that the unrighteous shall not inherit the kingdom of God? Be not deceived: neither fornicators, nor idolaters, nor adulterers, nor effeminate, nor abusers of themselves with mankind, nor thieves, nor covetous, nor

drunkards, nor revilers, nor extortioners, shall inherit the kingdom of God. (1 Cor 6:9-10)

This from the book that's never been wrong. Which means I'm finished.

Gulp.

"But I've been a good person!"

You may merely have trundled through life on beatific autopilot, tossing the odd fiver into the poor box to feel good about yourself, smiling at babes, sponsoring an African kid, being nice to gays and Muslims, joining Greenpeace, enjoying a good buzz. But on God's level of perfection *we're all finished*. God is a perfect God of universal justice and no-one gets away with anything – *ever*. Did you sin just once? During the Sermon on the Mount, Jesus summarises to His baffled disciples, **"Be ye therefore perfect, even as your Father which is in heaven is perfect."** (Matt 5:48) Most believers take that as referring to the imputed righteousness of Christ after the covering of His blood after being 'born again', and it certainly does mean that in the post-crucifixion sense. But this statement was made by Jesus not only pre-crucifixion (obviously), but as a summary of His extraordinary, preceding statements. Read Matthew 5 straight off, no interruptions, ending at verse 48 and a more sinister, unsettling interpretation emerges.

The Sermon on the Mount is taken by Christians to be the highest ethical teaching in the Bible, and it is, yet if you read it, the listener is left broken by condemnation before a perfect Creator's coming judgment with no visible means of reprieve. The unsettling truth is the Sermon on the Mount doesn't offer a way out. Believe me, don't cry to God for justice, beg for mercy. The Sermon on the Mount was not given to unbelievers *but to those Christ had already selected.* In effect, the Creator is stating that if you thought living by the Ten Commandments was difficult, try this: Even *thinking* of hurting or killing your enemy, even *imagining* ravishing your neighbour's wife, *even entertaining the notion of* lying, cheating, stealing paperclips from the office cupboard or saying a naughty word, *and you're finished.* With the Commandments jacked to the metacosmic n'th degree, Yeshua is demonstrating how you would have to live and die without God's help to make it to Heaven *Your*

Way. You won't understand the solution if you don't understand the problem. You're dealing with the uncompromising moral perfection and justice of an infinite Creator. According to the book that's never been wrong, God has chosen that the entire world will be judged, condemned or redeemed purely on the basis of our attitude towards what happened to His Son on a wooden cross erected in Judaea 2,000 years ago. How astonishing is that if you think about it? In other words, there is a judgment coming which will finish you utterly unless you claim the free pardon purchased by the Son to give God the legal right to pronounce you 'not guilty' at your judgment bar and dismiss your case. You can even elect for the Judge to become your defence attorney. He's never lost a case. What does this 'Get out of Hell Free card' cost? Nothing. Everything. Wild doesn't even cut it.

Stand back from the scriptures as a whole and you notice something significant. The Bible spends just a few chapters on how everything was made (the Creation), then the rest of the book is given over to the predicament of man and its resolution (the Redemption). We spent *Origins I* examining the creation-evolution saga, but that's not really where God wants our attention. The Message System states that *all* have sinned and come short of the glory of God (Rom 3:23). There is none righteous, no, not one (Rom 3:10). The gulf that exists between the purity of a universal, transcendent God of Justice and the utter filth and degradation of us lot on Earth cannot even begin to be comprehended by the degenerate mind. Our very best acts are but filthy rags in God's sight (Isa 64:6). The losing side of the Holy War is our default position. *In fact we're born losers.* If we have committed one sin – *just one,* we won't make it to Heaven *My Way* and God knows it, which is why He went to such extremes to pay the penalty for our imperfections *Himself,* not only to satisfy His eternal justice and uncompromising perfection, but so He could dismiss the handwriting of ordinances pinned against us, and redeem us to become *joint heirs and friends* to rule a new Heaven and a new Earth with Him throughout eternity (Psa 82:6; FG 1:10-13; 10:34; Rom 8:14-17). That's the Bible's position on your fate. God wants you to make peace with Him so He can move you to the next level – the extraordinary destiny He's had in store for you from before the foundation of the world. And it won't be sitting on some cloud strumming *My Way* on a harp either. How utterly unproductive.

"Come now and let us reason together," saith the LORD. "Though your sins be as scarlet, they shall be as white as snow. Though they be red like crimson, they shall be as wool. If ye be willing and obedient, ye shall eat the good of the land. But if ye refuse and rebel, ye shall be devoured with the sword, for the mouth of the LORD hath spoken." (Isa 1:18-20)

The fear of the LORD is the beginning of wisdom: and the knowledge of the holy is understanding. (Prov 9:10)

The current Earth programme is our training ground, the selection process for that astonishing eternal destiny. Everyone has an equal chance to dodge the judgment and qualify for eternal life in God's eyes since the pardon *is a free gift* and ours for the asking. We can't work for it, we cannot earn it with good works – in fact to attempt to do so is blasphemy. No gift is a gift unless it is free. The question is, will we repent and surrender? Can we quell our insufferable pride enough to control our free will and voluntarily bring it in line with God's own? Do we even want to? Millions couldn't care less.

It's a common bleat today that the wicked get away with everything. In fact, *the horror is* that the unsaved wicked will get away with nothing. The only thing anyone can do now to avoid a horrendous solitary fate in eternal separation from God is to surrender and switch sides. And since our toes are hanging over the edge of eternity and tomorrow is never promised to anyone, now would be better time to capitulate than a week next Tuesday. The pardon is free and there for the asking but pride, ignorance and apathy will keep millions from claiming it. So a few seconds after their heart stops beating, or the truck hits them on the highway, or they finally expire with cancer or Alzheimer's in some death clinic in Switzerland, they're done for. I'm not making this up. This comes right out of the very Message System whose pronouncements and prophetic record have never failed.

Here it is, right from the Messiah Himself:

"For God so loved the world that He gave His only begotten Son, that whosoever believeth in Him should not perish but have everlasting life. For God sent not His Son into the world to condemn the world, but that the world through Him might be saved.

He that believeth on Him is not condemned: but he that believeth not is condemned already, because he hath not believed in the name of the only begotten Son of God.

And this is the condemnation, that light is come into the world, and men loved darkness rather than light because their deeds were evil.

For every one that doeth evil hateth the light, neither cometh to the light, lest his deeds should be reproved. But he that doeth truth cometh to the light, that his deeds may be made manifest, that they are wrought in God." (FG 3:16-21)

And:

"I am the way, the truth and the life: no man cometh unto the Father but by Me. If ye had known Me, ye should have known My Father also: and from henceforth ye know Him and have seen Him." (FG 14:6-7)

And:

"I said therefore unto you, that ye shall die in your sins. For if ye believe not that I am He [i.e. God come in the flesh], ye shall die in your sins." (FG 8:24)

And:

"Except ye repent, ye shall all likewise perish." (Luke 13:3,5)

So, the Bible is pretty clear. The God of the Bible states that there are no other stairways to Heaven. Not via Led Zeppelin, not Buddha, not Mohammed, crystals, Gaia, David Icke, aliens, the Virgin Mary, Pope Francis, Frank Sinatra, nor some cockamamie, man-centred, pride-filled, Masonic, Kabbalistic, Illuminist, Rosicrucian, occult, salvation-by-works tommyrot. It's Jesus Christ, the Name that is above every name, who is the only gate, the narrow way that leads to life, the gift of grace which you could not possibly earn, which frees you from God's eternal justice, the absence of which will sentence millions to the second death. (Luke 16:19-31).

Frightening proofs of this are all around us in astonishing forms and we'll examine these as we proceed. Christ Himself tells us the Crazy Days are coming, and so is His wrath, after which His eternal kingdom will be set up, the Kingdom *from* Heaven, wherein dwelleth righteousness.[92] That's what you are praying for when you intone: "Hallowed be Thy name. Thy Will be done. *Thy Kingdom come on Earth as it is in Heaven....*" If you are not praying, you've got bigger problems in your future than who's going to set up the Millennial Kingdom, and God's going to labour the importance of your salvation with you, at the risk of riling your *Guardian*-induced PC sentiments, right up until your dying nanosecond *so you get it,* because if you don't get it, you shall surely get it. And God won't get what He wants out of the whole programme, *which is you* (1 Tim 2:3-4; 2 Pet 3:9).

Free will is, thus, the greatest blessing and most deadly curse to mankind due to the pride it generates - the same sin that condemned *ha-Satan,* as we'll see. Yet God must have free will to determine who will love Him of their own accord and who won't. And here's something else. Incredible though it might be, obtaining our 'Get Out of Hell Free' card *is just the beginning* (known as 'justification' – i.e. coming to Christ - being 'saved' from the judgment – 'born again'). We have also been selected to undergo bootcamp training in the Earth Project under live-fire conditions to determine our eligibility for a position in Christ's coming *physical* Millennial Kingdom on Earth,[93] and later *the Eternal Kingdom.*[94] During our time on Earth we will be forced to confront *Ha-Satan* and his considerable resources, as well as our fallen nature and the evil of others, *and we are expected to overcome.* We will mess up. Often. Welcome to Sanctification, the process by which we progressively de-filth ourselves with Christ's help and move

---

[92] Isa 9:6-7; Luke 1:30-33; Rev 19:11-16

[93] ...to be ruled by Christ Himself from Jerusalem after the Great Tribulation with a resurrected David as His vice-regent (Eze 37:24-25; Jer 30:9; Hos 3:5). Hundreds of as yet unfulfilled Biblical prophecies give details of this thousand-year reign of Christ's on Earth ruling the nations with a rod of iron from the Jewish throne in Jerusalem. His kingdom will have no end.

[94] Psa 82:6; 2 Cor 4:16-18; FG 10:34; 17:11

towards God's nature. Atheist Earth-dwellers scorn this process, labelling those who undertake it 'holier than thou', 'do-gooders' and 'self-righteous'. For these who flinch at, and cannot tolerate even the words 'God', 'Jesus' or 'Born Again', they will get the desires of their hearts and never be bothered by God again. Ever. This most terrifying of fates will confront millions at the Great White Throne Judgment, before which they will stand without excuse, resurrected in their Earthly bodies. The Second Death is eternal separation from the Father – every physical cell, molecule, atom and electrical impulse blasted apart, then God's Spirit cleaved from the carnal soul, leaving it conjoined with its raw sin for eternity. There is no appeal, not even at the European Court of Human Rights. Jesus gone for good just like you wanted. God doesn't punish forever to be cussed. His realm *is* eternity. Time's exception was Earth. Eternal separation from the Father apparently feels like burning. I don't believe mankind possesses even the vaguest capacity to comprehend the horror of what this truly entails. Every feeling, sensation and any good thing an atheist ever experienced during their time on Earth *came from Him*. Now He's gone, there's nothing but *My Way*. Forever. As the old saying goes, nobody will end up in Hell because of their sin. They'll end up in Hell for refusing the provision God made for their sin, which was the free pardon they never bothered to claim, which cost them nothing, but which cost God His only Son.

So there's the Bible's summary. Just wild, religious nonsense? Or the way things really are *out there,* whether we like it or not?

"Man, look how far we've come!"

So how have we done as a race? Not good. History teaches us that man doesn't learn the lessons of history. History teaches us that man is incapable of ruling himself. History teaches us that man has never yet made a weapon he hasn't used. As the centuries pass, the bodycount increases: 262 million killed by democide (government) in the 20th century alone.[95] We're not on the path to evolving into anything, quite the opposite. Today we live in an

---

[95] http://www.hawaii.edu/powerkills/20TH.HTM

insane society. We murder the unborn by the million in the holy of holies of a mother's womb and call it the right to choose. We kill the elderly with state-sanctioned euthanasia on programmes like the Liverpool Care Pathway and call it mercy. Instead of eating the natural food God intended, we take nature's bounty and drench it with man-made pesticides, fungicides, genetically modified weedkillers that cause Alzheimer's, Parkinson's and cancer, then strip all the goodness out of it, process it, irradiate it, add carcinogenic additives, then cremate it and poison ourselves and our children with it before processing its 'digestion' with medication. God's food isn't good enough, apparently. Man's food rules – just walk into any supermarket and look at all the packaging. God's water isn't good enough either. We have to poison it with grade A carcinogenic fluoride additives like H_2SiF_4 which not only *don't* stop the cavities you got from eating Man's Food, they make you thick and give you bone cancer.[96] We've urinated and dumped so many estrogenic chemicals and mind-altering substances into the English Channel, you have to say 'please' before the tide will come in. Perversion is now an alternative lifestyle, gay used to be happy, murder's still the right to choose. You can practise how to murder all day long with *Call of Duty* and *Grand Theft Auto* on Playstation and Xbox.

Today our religion is the religion of 'me' and our god is gold. We're working hard at our naughtiness. We're proud of our lawlessness. We celebrate them in our mindless soaps. We lift them up in our toe-curling pop videos. We idolise them in the zoo media and those mawkish, camp celebrity quiz shows. Surely we deserve some reward for all the abhorrence we've honed into fine art. An effigy of Jesus Christ in a bowl of urine? Why stop there? As the posters for British comedian Dennis Pennis proudly proclaim above his gravestone, *"Rest in P*ss."*

Once we had churches, now we have glass cathedral malls decked out with all the latest retail outlets to satisfy that spiritual yearning. Once we went to church on Sundays to worship with the family. Today on Sundays we take the family to worship at B & Q

---

[96] www.fluoridealert.org

or Bluewater. Instead of being given a song sheet at the door, we're given a loyalty card application. Instead of lining up at the rail for communion, we queue impatiently at the checkout. Instead of leaving our sins at the feet of Christ, we heave our shopping into the Volvo. We worship our Harley Davidsons instead of our heavenly David's Son. We celebrate our greed with our sons instead of confessing it before the Son. We cry in anger at the cost of spirits instead of weeping in thanks for what we cost the Spirit.

Today you no longer need to watch TV, you can date one. You no longer have to drink Coke, you can snort it. You no longer marry the heroine, you can freebase her. When we contemplate divorce, we're so hardened, our only definition of 'a crying shame' is a plane full of lawyers crashing and burning with two empty seats.

Forget the kids. Our teenage boyz don't know whether to lead or follow on the dance-floor. Our teenage gurlz are obscene and not heard. With divorce proceedings going out at £100 an hour and half their worldly estate, have married men come to the conclusion that the cheapest sex is the sex they can pay for?

Rupert Murdoch, thank you for your digital TV revolution. Now we have a porn channel for every psalm:

THE TWENTY-THIRD CHANNEL
The TV is my shepherd,
I shall not want,
It makes me lie down on the sofa,
It leads me away from the faith,
It destroys my soul,
It leads me in the path of sex and violence
For the sponsor's sake.
Yea, though I walk
In the shadow of Christian responsibilities,
There will be no interruption,
For the TV is with me,
Its cable and remote,
They comfort me.
It prepares a commercial for me

In the presence of all my worldliness.
It anoints my head with
Humanism and consumerism,
My coveting runneth over.
Surely laziness and ignorance
Shall follow me
All the days of my life.
And I shall dwell in the house
Watching TV forever.

A newspaper cartoon depicts a man arriving in Hell, faced with the Devil and a TV.

"Wow!" exclaims the man. "I didn't know there'd be TV down here!"

The Devil replies, "There's nothing but TV down here."

Stand by your beds, men....

I remember when I was undergoing my education at Charterhouse, I joined the Army cadet force (CCF), for which the school is famous, especially in providing suitable cannon fodder for the British armed forces. I qualified for Wingate Squad, the inner élite, and obtained my rifle marksman certificate. Teenage boys playing soldiers with real weapons – what could possibly go wrong? The problem was, every now and then the sadistic officers who ran Wingate dreamt up some special exercise to test us and hone our skills. These occasions were always terrifying. On one exercise, I remember, we were shipped out in army trucks to Hankley Common in bitter mid-winter and told that elements of the British Army's Parachute Regiment would be pitted against us. This involved us Wingate trainees defending some pitiful outpost in the woods during the frigid night with rifles, blanks and thunderflash grenades, having been told that at some point in the wee hours the Paras were coming for us.

Now there's nothing average about your hard-as-nails peak-trained British Para. Many hail from pretty deprived areas of Britain, so they probably did their first bank job at eight. They're killing machines at the best of times, but how much more terrifying in the dead of a frosty, windblown night with only your teenage mates for company when you know what's coming? We were certain to be given a royal drubbing, being posh public schoolboys and all.

Anyway, we had to come up with a plan to defend our charge, so our NCO decided to set up ambushes to the approaches to our outpost, working on the reasonable principle that Paras wouldn't be thick enough to crash cross-country through bracken and bush, announcing their approach to all and sundry, but instead would take the forest paths to ensure a stealthy attack. We were wrong. They came cross-country like they would later in the Falklands. We never heard a thing.

One minute, all is black save the orange glows of our illegal, hand-rolled cigarettes, the next, the whole world explodes. Everywhere is fire and thunderous detonations. Guns firing blanks at us, deafening, blinding and bowel-loosening. I experience what every defeated enemy must have felt down through the ages; utter disorientation, not knowing where to run or what to do next. We duly surrender and quell our thrashing tickers, after which we are most impressed with the Paras' understated professionalism at the debrief. Their sergeant gathers us around and repeats snippets of conversations and jokes Wingate Squad had bandied about in hushed tones while waiting for the attack. The Paras had got that close to us undetected through the bracken, they had heard and seen everything.

We learned loads. All army training is about practice so the behaviour becomes second nature, and it struck me a while back that so is the training programme God has set up, complete with an opposing force dead set on our destruction, and other helpers to assist us when the going gets tough.

The ABCs of the unseen reality

Microcosm – the reality smaller than man

Macrocosm – the reality larger than man

Metacosm – encompassing the above two, plus hyperdimensions which interpenetrate man but cannot be directly experienced by him

We have Albert Einstein to thank for his breakthrough theories on Special Relativity (1905) and General Relativity (1915). Currently, physics believes that there are four physical dimensions – three spatial: length, width and height – and one non-spatial: time (x, y, z, t). By combining space and time into spacetime, scientists have been able to simplify the understanding of many systems at work in the macro universe and micro, sub-atomic world. Yet other dimensions can be inferred but not directly known, as covered in *Origins I*. Similar to how we can observe a fishbowl from all dimensions and even stick our hands in, the metacosmic or spiritual dimensions intersect, interpenetrate and surround our own physical reality yet we – 'the fish' - cannot experience them directly.

The best scientific guess these days to explain everything is called Superstring Theory, sometimes referred to as Unified Field Theory. This holds that both the physical and non-physical universe comprise one-dimensional superstrings vibrating in ten dimensions. Now if that doesn't mean anything to you, relax, it didn't to me either. Don't worry about specifics for now – just get the concept. Marty Rosenblatt holds a BA and MS in physics from University of California at Los Angeles (UCLA), and he writes:

"Remember, physical theories are mathematical systems of equations that permit accurate predictions of the real world. The complexities of our universe require rather complex mathematics to predict the measurements observed on the very small (sub-atomic), the very large (cosmology, black holes) and the very fast (near the speed of light). These measurements do not agree with 'common sense', so, it is unrealistic to expect the mathematical models to be simple and easy to explain in words.

The General Theory of Relativity and Quantum Mechanics are accurate theories for predicting our physical universe. Relativity already introduced the intimate coupling of a 4th 'dimension' (time) with the 3 spatial dimensions. Hey, so what's another 6 dimensions if a unified theory can be developed? These additional dimensions are 'curled up' in a fashion that makes them unobservable directly. What you observe are the effects... a reflection, if you will, of a more complex reality. For example, the reflection of the sun on the ocean surface only hints at the complexity of the sun itself." [97]

The Flats

Let me give you an example of the beauty of additional dimensions and how they change everything. Take a sheet of paper and draw two stick figures on it. Let's name them Mr and Mrs Flat. Draw them holding hands and gazing lovingly into each other's eyes if you wish, it'll add drama to what's coming in a minute.

Now examine your handiwork. You've just drawn a couple of two-dimensional figures. In other words, Mr and Mrs Flat have a length and width but no depth. They're flat! Now take the tip of your finger and hover it over Mrs Flat and see how close you can get to the paper without actually touching it. Notice that you enjoy an extra dimension denied to the Flats - depth – but if you don't touch that paper, they will never be aware of your presence. You can enjoy a closeness and intimacy with Mrs Flat that even her husband cannot experience, yet she won't be aware of your presence until you choose to touch the paper and enter her realm with the tip of your finger.

When you do touch the paper, Mr and Mrs F will only see you as a dot quickly expanding to a small circle as you press the tip of your finger onto the paper. In other words, they will only be aware of the two-dimensional cross-section of your finger.

Mrs Flat turns to her husband, exclaiming: "I've just seen Phillip!"

Mr Flat: "Coots, what did he look like?"

Mrs Flat, triumphant: "He's a circle!"

Do either of them have the slightest idea what I really look like? No, because they don't have my dimensionality. As with the skit where a group of blind men feel different parts of an elephant and conclude that the beast looks like the bodypart they are holding, none have a total picture of what an elephant looks like. Notice, in the case of the Flats, that I can surround their realm – above them, below them, to one side or the other – witnessing everything they do and say, and they'll never have the slightest

[97] http://p-i-a.com/Magazine/Issue6/Physics_6.htm

idea I'm right with them until I choose to reveal myself by touching their dimensionality.

Now cut out a circular section of the paper above their heads, hold the paper up horizontally and drop a marble through the hole. All Mr and Mrs Flat will fleetingly glimpse is a dot expanding to a circle, going back to a dot before disappearing. Remember this example as it has amazing relevance when we get to the ministry of Yeshua later.

So, to summarise: We have millions of people today who are atheists because it suits them not to believe in God but to remain in the natural to escape an ultimate accountability and judgment which the Book of books says is coming upon them anyway. I always think an atheist is like a bacterium inside a lion which says to his companions, "You deluded saps, there's no such thing as a lion! Have you ever seen one? Thought not. Who knows why we are here? Do what you want!" Atheists reject God with their toes hanging over the edge of eternity. God continues to divide their cells and digest their lunches while providing ample opportunity to seek Him while He yet may be found.[98] Sometimes God cheats. Often what it takes to get an atheist to repent is to put his rear-end into a position of such utter dire peril that he's compelled to cry out to God for relief. Then again, more than a few go to their deaths cursing the God they never believed in anyway. Go figure.

It gets even more interesting when you discover that these additional dimensions are home to sophisticated, sentient, knowledgeable, hyperdimensional creatures, a third of which do not have your best interests at heart; indeed are dead set on your destruction. We're back to the Paras pitched against us to test our mettle. (Not that Paras are demons, I hasten to add, though the Taliban probably thought so.) I used to think the whole notion of angelic beings was fanciful rubbish sucked up by deluded saps until personal experience and my own research turned me into a deluded sap. Today I have absolutely no doubt that the physical world you and I inhabit is but a subset of a far larger, extremely active, hyperdimensional reality. Science supports this conclusion,

---

[98] Deut 4:19; 1 Chron 28:9; Psa 34:8, 18; Jer 29:12-14; Joel 2:32; Isa 55:6-7; Jam 4:8; FG 3:19-21, etc.

as covered in *Origins I,* and this is the Bible's position. We'll examine the metacosm and hyperdimensional beings more fully as we proceed. They influence a great deal of what you do and think even if you think they don't.

Batten down the hatches

The observable evidence indicates that mankind is historically capable of the most depraved acts of cruelty, and also of soaring compassion and self-sacrifice. We're a complex mix. To what extent is our behaviour our own or influenced by external dynamics? Go back through history and you'll see mankind's schizophrenic nature has enthralled and puzzled philosophers the world over. A baby is born innocent but as he or she grows and increases in self-awareness, the parents don't have to teach them how to be bad! Laws are required to control the darker angels of our human nature. If it were not so, we would not need laws. Lending the lie to atheist contention that man's behaviour can be wholly laid at the door of genetics and environment, we find both extremes of human behaviour across *all* ages, cultures, belief systems, demographic groups and walks of life. From the primitive in the Amazonian rainforest to the Harvard intellectual, all have equally appalled and excelled if you take the trouble to study them. Those who tuned in to the *Origins* series in the hope of finding, as evidence of religious depravity, Christian, Jewish and Islamic atrocities will not be disappointed, but what about everyone else? If you have an honest desire to get to the heart of the Holy War, you are left with one unsavoury conclusion. As Dr Missler puts it, all humans are born SIN-positive, and the condition is genetic and completely incurable by man.

Four-year-old Daniel Pelka from Coventry, England was imprisoned, starved and eventually beaten to death by his stepfather, egged on by his mother. Weeks before he was killed, Daniel had been spotted by his teachers rifling school rubbish bins for scraps to eat. Describing him as looking like a concentration camp victim, the teachers notified social service authorities who did nothing. The sustained programme of cruelty against Daniel finally ended when he was killed by a massive blow to the head.

One of the final, haunting CCTV pictures is of Daniel innocently hurrying after the mother who would later betray and kill him. The stepfather, Polish army veteran Mariusz Krezolek, demonstrated not one shred of remorse during his 17 hours in the witness box. [99]

STRAIGHT-A SCHOOLBOY, 16, JAILED FOR ATTEMPTING TO 'GUT 12-YEAR-OLD GIRL LIKE A PIG' AFTER SHE SPURNED HIS ADVANCES:

Cameron Cleland, from Bradford, put on surgical gloves before luring his victim to a secluded lane and attempting to stab her to death with a blunt penknife.[100]

SADISTIC FATHER BEAT HIS NEWBORN DAUGHTER, HELD A PILLOW OVER HER FACE AND FORCED HER HEAD UNDERWATER BECAUSE HE 'WANTED TO CAUSE HER PAIN'

Joshua Stephens, 22, of Mirfield, West Yorkshire, was violent to the baby from her being born until she was six weeks old. He was told by a judge that he posed a significant risk to the public after hearing that he had slapped the girl 'as hard as you would hit a man'. [101]

PARENTS' HORROR AS CHINESE BOY, 6, HAS HIS EYES GOUGED OUT AFTER BEING 'KIDNAPPED BY ORGAN TRAFFICKER WHO STOLE BOTH HIS CORNEAS'

The youngster was playing alone outside his home in Linfen, Shanxi Province, when he was allegedly snatched on Monday evening. His parents began a frantic search with other relatives and eventually found him in a nearby field with blood covering his face. The child's eyes were found nearby but the corneas were missing, implying that an organ trafficker was behind the harrowing attack. The boy's father said: "We didn't notice his eyes were gone when we discovered him. We thought he fell down from high and smashed his face." [102]

POLICE ARREST US MOTHER, 26, FOR MURDER AFTER SHE 'GAVE BIRTH IN BATHROOM OF SPORTS BAR AND

---

[99] *Daily Mail,* 1st August 2013
[100] *Daily Mail,* 14th August 2013
[101] *Daily Mail,* 22nd August 2013
[102] *Daily Mail,* 27th August 2013

DUMPED LIVE BABY IN TOILET CISTERN BEFORE RETURNING TO WATCH A WRESTLING MATCH'

Amanda Catherine Hein, 26, allegedly killed her baby at Starters Pub near Bethlehem, Pennsylvania, in between watching pay-per-view wrestling with three friends. Police say Amanda Catherine Hein, 26, of Allentown, admitted to giving birth to a live baby and suffocating it. After allegedly killing her baby, Hein smoked a cigarette and continued watching pay-per-view wrestling for an hour until she went home. [103]

ORADOUR-SUR-GLANE, 10TH JUNE 1944: Four days after the Allied landings on D-Day, a German Waffen-SS company comprising around 200 soldiers arrives in trucks at this sleepy French village. The soldiers disembark, officers barking orders. The women and children are separated from the men, and the systematic massacre of the village population commences. The men are herded into three barns, two garages, a warehouse and a hangar. They are deliberately machine-gunned in the legs. Those who die are fortunate. Those still conscious look on in horror as the SS soldiers, calmly chatting to each other, cover their victims' bodies with straw, hay, wood and anything else that burns, set fire to the tinder and move away. The mortally wounded are burned alive in the subsequent conflagrations.

The women and children are taken to the church as the shots ring out around the village, murdering their menfolk. They are locked in, and incendiary devices are triggered. When some try to escape into the sacristy, choking and screaming, the SS are waiting outside and fire their machine pistols through the windows, scything down their victims. The rest are burnt alive in the church. A mother with her baby escapes out of a church window but both are shot down as they attempt to escape to the garden in the presbytery. The oldest victims of the massacre are in their nineties. The youngest, one week.

All 328 buildings in the village are torched. All night long the German soldiers eat, drink and sing as the flames roar into the sky. Many of the houses have well stocked cellars which are looted

---

[103] Ibid.

before being set on fire. The SS company leaves Oradour the following morning to head north to meet the Allied invasion. Most of the perpetrators of this crime will themselves be dead within three weeks in the subsequent Battle of Normandy. Today, Oradour-sur-Glane remains exactly as the Germans left it 70 years ago as testament to the inhumanity of man.

Can we blame such atrocities on a God who controls everything? Perhaps so but for one technicality. Man was given free will and the ability to choose good from evil. Was it God who beat Daniel Pelka to death, or was it not his stepfather and mother, both of whom had a free choice to engage or withhold their cruelty? Was it God who murdered the 642 men, women and children of Oradour-sur-Glane, or was it not General Lammerding who gave the order, and Commandant Diekmann, Captain Kahn and Leutnant Barth who ensured the Waffen-SS company under their control carried out the atrocity with Teutonic efficiency?

While we may be familiar with such stories, we may never get used to the levels of evil they exhibit. There's an otherworldly influence to all this, as we'll discover, dead set on the destruction of humans in general, and certain demographic groups in particular. We'll cover this phenomenon as we proceed.

Truth and the counterfeit

I'll show you something else that's right before your eyes, though you may not notice it unless it's pointed out. Lift the corner of your reality, peek under the blanket and you notice something strange in this Holy War. Across a whole raft of subjects there's the true way - God's way – and the counterfeit – man's way. You have the explanation for our origins, Creation, and man's counterfeit – evolution, or creation without God. You have God's Law and man's counterfeit laws, a whole slew of them, in fact, passed every year to control aberrant human behaviour. You have Passover and man's counterfeit, Easter. You have Christ and man's counterfeit, Xmas ('X' marks the spot where Christ used to be). You have God's natural way of giving birth and man's counterfeit, Caesarian section (once a lifesaving operation, now an alternative birth choice). You have God's love and man's lust. God's intended sex act and man's pornographic perversions. God's decree of one man with one woman, and man's alternative: one man with anything with a pulse. You have God's holy matrimony and man's living in sin. You have God's way of making a baby and man's artificial insemination. You have God creating and man faking creation (cloning). You have 'Just Say No', and man's counterfeit, 'Just Say Yes' followed by murder by abortion if you 'fall victim' to inconvenient consequences. You have God's natural food and man's processed, denatured, GMO'd, pesticide-ridden counterfeit. You have God's wisdom and man's counterfeit – pride. God's medicine – sensible diet and lifestyle choices – and man's counterfeit: live any way you want, then take man-made drugs when you get sick.

Notice how in each case man refuses to yield his own will to God's. Indeed every effort is made to remove God from the picture altogether. The media teaches nutrition is useless for therapeutics and man-made prescription medications are the only cure for disease. It is now a criminal offence in the EU, punishable by two years in prison, to claim that water can cure dehydration.[104] Psychiatry just invents diseases with no science to back up any diagnosis, then prescribes dangerous, mind-altering drugs in an attempt at a cure. Today you can suffer from Lottery Stress Disorder. Caffeine Addiction Disorder. ADHD. PMS. Disagreeing with your psychiatrist is even a mental disease.[105] The most doctor-popular treatments for cancer – chemotherapy and radiation – um, cause cancer. We've known for 80 years that the cure for cancer is the immune system, the very thing these toxic, man-centred treatments devastate. Perhaps that's why, despite the billions spent, the five-year or better survival rates for almost all forms of cancer remain unchanged over the past 40 years. You can't cure people of cancer by poisoning them with carcinogens.

---

[104] *Daily Mail,* "Now barmy EU says you can't claim drinking water cures dehydration", 18th November 2011

[105] **Day, Phillip** *The Mind Game,* Credence, 2004, available at www.credence.org

Take cover - the coming time of trouble

Welcome to the lead-up to the Crazy Days. If you think they're crazy now, the Bible states there is some full-tilt, barking mayhem on the horizon God Himself has labelled 'Great Tribulation' (Matt 24:21). The Trib is an unprecedented, future period of such intense apocalyptic terror and slaughter, Jesus Himself states that unless He comes back to stop it all ('the Second Coming'), no flesh on Earth will be saved. The Trib will be the climax of the Holy War on Earth between man and God. Guess who wins? Guess who treads the winepress of His wrath so the blood rises to the horses' bridles? Guess whose side we need to be on if we know what's good for us?

The LORD does not break His promises but delights in making and keeping them. And God's promised He's going to turn up the heat under everyone's backsides to such an extent that many will repent. Others will gnaw their tongue from the pain of the Trib judgments, yet still blaspheme God (Rev 16:10-11). The Trib will actually be God's climactic dealings with His holy nation of Israel, against which the whole world will have turned its weapons and hate. Sound familiar? In the metacosmic realm, the Bible states that Satan will be loosed during this time, unrestrained by the Holy Spirit, to wreak havoc as the human 'Antichrist' – this coming world leader given 33 titles in the Old Testament and 13 in the New. The term 'Antichrist' is actually more accurately translated 'pseudo-Christ'. Yes, there's even going to be a pseudo John the Baptist-type false prophet character assisting him who, like the coming world leader, will also be brilliant and charismatic; able to do miracles; directing all worship to his leader.

The Satanic world leader will seem to be the answer to all the world's catastrophic problems at that time, and will be the most accomplished politician and peacemaker the world will have ever seen. Almost everyone will be taken in, accept and worship him, for he will exalt himself above all that is called God (2 Thess 2:4), and show by many signs and wonders that he is God. We'll discover later in the *Origins* series that today's world is very ready for a saviour, given the serious problems facing the planet. When this man is revealed, Catholicism will be taken in; so will Islam; Judaism too worldwide, as prophesied by Jesus Himself in FG 5:43:

"I am come in my Father's name and ye receive Me not. If another shall come in his own name, him ye will receive."

The big mistake this man of sin will make, however, is guaranteeing Israel's safety from her enemies, then walking into the Holy of Holies of the recently rebuilt Jewish temple in Jerusalem and proclaiming himself to be God. At this point, God goes toxic and His Great Tribulation begins. Jesus Himself warns that when you see the abomination of desolation, spoken of by the prophet Daniel, standing in the holy place, you need to jettison fast, right now, split, flee, sling your hook, and don't even go back in the house for your iPad.

Later in the *Origins* series we will study this period and notice how precise the Bible is with its prophetic insights. The Great Tribulation will last three and a half years, or 42 months, or 1,260 days, from the moment the Antichrist declares himself to be God in the Temple to the Second Coming of Jesus Christ to stop it all (God uses a 360-day year and 30-day month for prophecy). In other words, unlike the *harpazo* ('Rapture'), which we'll also examine later, those who have these prophecies but find themselves in the middle of the Trib can set their watch by them and predict the very day Christ will return to call a halt to the slaughter.[106] Those who love God will never be left in the dark (Amos 3:7; 1 Thess 5:3-4). Even more surprising, the scriptures have more to say prophetically on this 'end-days' period *than any other,* and that includes the extremely detailed accounts of Yeshua's life on Earth. For every prophecy detailing the circumstances of Christ's First Coming (over 300 of which were fulfilled to the letter by His life), there are around *eight* detailing the final years of the Holy War, which culminate in the infamous Armageddon and Christ's Second Coming to set up His Millennial Kingdom to rule Planet Earth from Jerusalem with His prince, the Old Testament icon, King David.[107]

We often hear people saying that Armageddon will be the end of the world. While it will be for many who perish during this time

---

[106] Matt 24:22 even hints that the Trib could be cut short for the sake of the elect, or no flesh would be saved.

[107] Eze 37:24-25; Jer 30:9; Hos 3:5

of unprecedented global upheaval, the planet itself will survive the horrors, be made clean again, and Christ Himself will rule Planet Earth with a rod of iron in a highly visible fashion from Israel for 1,000 years. All anti-Semites and Israel-haters take heed. The Creator of the universe and future king of the world will be a Jewish king of Israel ruling the planet from the ancient throne of David in Jerusalem.[108] This was promised to Mary by the archangel Gabriel at the Annunciation:

And the angel said unto her, "Fear not, Mary, for thou hast found favour with God. And, behold, thou shalt conceive in thy womb, and bring forth a son, and shalt call His name Jesus. He shall be great and shall be called the Son of the Highest, and the Lord God shall give unto Him the throne of His father [lit. 'forefather'] **David, and He shall reign over the house of Jacob forever, and of His kingdom there shall be no end."** (Luke 1:30-33)

This would be the same Gabriel who, five centuries before, gave the prophet Daniel a vision of the end times and predicted *to the very day* when Jesus would present Himself to Israel as their Messiah (Dan 9:24-27). Is he likely to be wrong over this? Daniel describes the Trib as a time of trouble, the like of which Earth has never seen since there was a nation, nor ever shall again. We'll examine this period in detail as we proceed. God's Great Tribulation will be His wrath poured out on the God-haters without measure, the *denouement* of the Holy War, at least for this century. This won't be Cuddly Jesus this time around but Vengeful Deity tramping those who hate Him in the winepress of His wrath (Matt 26:64; Rev 19:11-16).

And I saw the beast ['Antichrist'], **and the kings of the earth, and their armies, gathered together to make war against Him that sat on the horse** [Yeshua], **and against His army. And the beast was taken, and with him the false prophet that wrought miracles before him, with which he deceived them that had received the mark of the beast, and them that worshipped his image. These both were cast alive into a lake of fire burning with brimstone.**

---

[108] Isa 2:1-3; 9:7; 11:4; Zech 2:10-13;8:2-3; 14:8ff; Eze 43:1-8; Dan 7:13-14

And the remnant were slain with the sword of Him that sat upon the horse, which sword proceeded out of His mouth. And all the fowls were filled with their flesh. (Rev 19:19-21)

Think of the worst, most terrifying time in all history, multiply that by 1,000 and you're still not there. It's going to be bad. Nuclear war plays a big part, so do demons, aliens, celestial catastrophes, famine, disease, and a global tyranny run by Satan himself that will make Hitler and Stalin look like beginners. The good news? God is giving us the chance of being spared *from the very time* of the Tribulation (Luke 21:35-36; Rev 3:10). Alternatively, we can scoff, be a God-hater and go right through it. What we won't be able to say is that we weren't told. God wrote it all down beforehand precisely so we would know what was coming and how to avoid it. Though the outcome of the Holy War is never in doubt, God's not going to get what He wants – namely 100% repentance – but He will save enough to call His own and take them into eternity to rule with Him (1 Tim 2:3-4; 2 Pet 3:9).

Baby Jesus, the wrath of God?

Most people have no idea who Yeshua/Jesus really is. When pushed they'll say he was a great prophet, a humble, holy man, a hippie peacenik spreading love and rainbows everywhere. Most have little idea that the New Testament baby Jesus is the same God of the Old Testament who created everything, killed the planet's original population in a global flood, organised genocide after the Exodus among the tribes of Canaan to rid the planet of human/demon chimeras, and carried out countless executions among His own people, the Jews. While He walked the Earth, Yeshua claimed to be God Almighty, the Creator Himself come to Earth in human form. **"He that hath seen Me hath seen the Father."** (FG 14:9) We'll look at other passages as we proceed. Those who maintain that Jesus never said He was God either haven't done their homework or they've spent too much time in Kingdom Hall. The Pharisees certainly had no trouble understanding where He was coming from. Yeshua was condemned to an agonising death for blasphemy on the basis that He said He was the voice of the Burning Bush, and thus the Creator of the universe.[109] In other words, He was crucified for telling the Jews that He was their God and the long-awaited Messiah (*cf.* Dan 9:24-27; Luke 19:41-44).[110]

The source of all evil

But all this, of course, is nonsense to the highly intelligent, rational atheist. Here's an article that appeared in the press in August 2013:

ATHEISTS 'HAVE HIGHER IQS': THEIR INTELLIGENCE 'MAKES THEM MORE LIKELY TO DISMISS RELIGION AS IRRATIONAL AND UNSCIENTIFIC':
People with higher IQs were more likely to dismiss religious beliefs as irrational and unscientific, scientists from the University of Rochester found.... Study co-author Jordan Silberman, a graduate student of neuroeconomics at the University of Rochester, said: 'Intelligence may lead to greater self-control ability, self-esteem, perceived control over life events, and supportive relationships, obviating some of the benefits that religion sometimes provides [emphasis mine].' [111]

Ray Comfort is a New Zealander who knows how to make trouble. He interviewed 'rational and scientific' atheists and their professors at two of America's leading educational establishments: University of California Los Angeles (UCLA) and University of Southern California (USC). The video is on YouTube, has provoked 1.5 million views and 105,000 comments at the time of writing, and is an experience to watch.[112] Pastor Comfort asks all these rational and scientific atheists, one after the other, if they can provide any evidence for evolution – any at all – that can be *observed* today, according to the scientific method, without having to take the 'millions and billions of years' thing on faith. Of course they can't.

---

[109] Compare Exo 3:13-15 with FG 8:58

[110] See also Fourth Gospel (FG) 8:58; FG 10:30-33; FG 8:24; FG 4:26; FG 13:13; Mark 14:61-62; Luke 5:20-24; FG 14:9; FG 17:5; (*cf.* Matt 1:23; Isa 9:6; Luke 7:16; FG 20:28; Col 1:14-17; Phil 2:6; Titus 2:13; Rev 19:16)

[111] *Daily Mail*, 17th August 2013

[112] http://youtu.be/U0u3-2CGOMQ

Confusion clouds furrowed brows. "Well that's what I was taught at this fantastic learning institution that costs me so much. But I'm going to believe my tutors, not some 4,000-year old book!" Most of the comments on Ray Comfort's video (and do take a look) come from the outraged. Welcome to the Holy War.

In denying God's existence, atheists fall, not at the first hurdle, but before they even leave the starting gate. Before I explain, let me confess that I do know something of what the above study, reported in the British press, is getting at. I did extremely well at college, was trained in evolution, came out in the top percentiles of my year across a whole raft of subjects, succeeded at everything to which I turned my hand, and my achievements caused me all the usual afflictions of pride and arrogance. I knew better and wouldn't hear differently; indeed, people who disagreed with me were ignorant, stupid trolls. I was not a nice person. These days when I research atheist websites, the language I see there reminds me so much of myself in those early days.

Unrestrained free will breeds pride, the source of all evil, and so does intelligence and success in many people. Being smart in itself is not wrong; you can be intelligent and humble. Those who are intelligent, but prideful and arrogant, perceive that they have a greater self-control ability, self-esteem, perceived control over life events, and supportive relationships, to paraphrase the above article. In other words, they have need of nothing outside themselves and scorn the weakness and convictions they see in others.

God hates pride. The Bible has much to say on the subject:

This know also, that in the last days perilous times shall come [the Crazy Days]. **For men shall be lovers of their own selves, covetous, boasters, proud, blasphemers, disobedient to parents, unthankful, unholy, without natural affection, trucebreakers, false accusers, incontinent, fierce, despisers of those that are good, traitors, heady, high-minded, lovers of pleasures more than lovers of God; having a form of godliness, but denying the power thereof: from such turn away.**

For of this sort are they which creep into houses and lead captive silly women laden with sins, led away with divers lusts,

ever learning and never able to come to the knowledge of the truth.

Now as Jannes and Jambres withstood Moses, so do these also resist the truth; men of corrupt minds, reprobate concerning the faith. But they shall proceed no further: for their folly shall be manifest unto all men, as theirs also was. (2 Tim 3:1-9)

But God hath chosen the foolish things of the world to confound the wise; and God hath chosen the weak things of the world to confound the things which are mighty. And base things of the world, and things which are despised, hath God chosen, yea, and things which are not, to bring to nought things that are, that no flesh should glory in his presence. (1 Cor 1:27-29)

Every one that is proud in heart is an abomination to the LORD: though hand join in hand [i.e. though they join forces...], he shall not be unpunished. (Prov 16:5)

When pride cometh, then cometh shame, but with the lowly is wisdom. (Prov 11:2)

Do you see a man wise in his own conceit? There is more hope for a fool than for him. (Prov 26:12, NKJV)

There is a generation that is pure in its own eyes, and yet is not washed of its filth. (Prov 30:12, NKJV)

The fear of the LORD is to hate evil: pride, and arrogancy, and the evil way, and the froward mouth [perverted speech], do I hate. (Prov 8:13)

Thou sayest, 'I am rich, and increased with goods, and have need of nothing', and knowest not that thou art wretched, miserable, poor, blind and naked. I counsel thee to buy of Me gold tried in the fire, that thou mayest be rich; and white raiment, that thou mayest be clothed, and that the shame of thy nakedness does not appear; and anoint thine eyes with eyesalve, that thou mayest see. (Rev 3:17-18)

But the natural man receiveth not the things of the Spirit of God, for they are foolishness unto him. Neither can he know them, for they are spiritually discerned. (1 Cor 2:14)

The apostle Paul, arguably one of the most learned and intelligent men of his age, knew something of pride too. He wrote to an assistant:

"O Timothy, keep that which is committed to thy trust, avoiding profane and vain babblings, and oppositions of science falsely so called, which some professing have erred concerning the faith." (1 Tim 6:20)

Is God good?

I wrote the following piece after listening to a lecture by Dr Stuart Crane on truth and duality. The concept is his, the words mine. To my surprise, *Is God Good* went viral after I posted it online, and now appears on sites all over the world, including a Harvard University web-page! Google any few words of the following and you'll see. Other religions and even atheists have modified it for their own purposes. You know what that tells me? Lots of people want answers, but not at any price.

*　*　*　*　*

"Let me explain the problem science has with Jesus Christ."

The atheist professor of philosophy pauses before his class and then asks one of his new students to stand.

"You're a Christian, aren't you, son?"

"Yes, sir."

"So you believe in God?"

"Absolutely."

"Is God good?"

"Yes, God is good."

"Is God all-powerful? Can God do anything?"

"Yes."

"Are you good or evil?"

"The Bible says I'm evil."

The professor grins knowingly. "Ahh! THE BIBLE!" He considers for a moment. "Here's one for you. Let's say there's a sick person over here and you can cure him. You can do it. Would you help them? Would you try?"

"Yes, sir, I would."

"So you're good...!"

"I wouldn't say that."

"Why *not* say that? You would help a sick and maimed person if you could... in fact most of us would if we could, wouldn't we?"

"Yes, sir."

"God doesn't."

No answer.

"He doesn't, does he? My brother was a Christian who died of cancer even though he prayed to Jesus to heal him. How is this Jesus good? Hmmm? Can you answer that one?"

No answer.

The elderly man is sympathetic.

"No, you can't, can you?" The professor takes a sip of water from a glass on his desk to give the student time to relax. In philosophy, you have to go easy with the new ones. "Let's start again. Is God good?"

"Er... Yes."

"Is Satan good?"

"No."

"Where does Satan come from?"

The student falters. "From... God..."

"That's right. God made Satan, didn't he?" The elderly man runs his bony fingers through his thinning hair and turns to the smirking student audience. "I think we're going to have a lot of fun this term, ladies and gentlemen." He turns back to the Christian. "Tell me, son. Is there evil in this world?"

"Yes, sir."

"Evil's everywhere, isn't it? Did God make everything?"

"Yes."

"Who created evil?"

No answer.

"Is there sickness in this world? Immorality? Hatred? Ugliness. All the terrible things - do they exist in this world?"

The student squirms on his feet.

"Yes."

"Who created them?"

No answer.

The professor suddenly shouts at his student. "WHO CREATED THEM? TELL ME, PLEASE!"

The professor closes for the kill and climbs into the Christian's face. In a still, small voice he whispers, "God created all evil, didn't He, son?"

No answer. The student tries to hold the steady, experienced gaze but fails. Suddenly the lecturer breaks away to pace the front of the classroom like an ageing panther. The class is mesmerised.

"Tell me," he continues, "How is it that this God is good if He created all evil throughout all time, hmmm?" The professor swishes his arms around to encompass all the wickedness of the world. "All the hatred, the brutality, all the pain, all the torture, all the death and ugliness and all the suffering created by this good God is all over the world, isn't it?"

No answer.

"Don't you see it all over the place?" Pause. "Don't you?" The professor leans into the student's face again and whispers, "Is God good?"

No answer.

"Do you believe in Jesus Christ, son?"

The student's voice betrays him and cracks. "Yes, professor. I do."

The old man shakes his head sadly. "Science says you have five senses you use to identify and observe the world around you. Have you ever seen your Jesus?"

"No, sir. I've never seen him."

"Then tell us if you've ever heard your Jesus?"

"No, sir. I have not."

"Have you ever felt your Jesus, tasted your Jesus or smelt your Jesus... in fact, do you have any sensory perception of your God whatsoever?"

No answer.

"Answer me, please."

"No, sir, I'm afraid I haven't."

"You're AFRAID... you haven't?"

"No, sir."

"Yet you still believe in him?"

"...yes..."

118

"That takes FAITH!" The professor smiles sagely at the underling. "According to the rules of empirical, testable, demonstrable protocol, because you've had no sensory perception of Him, science says your God doesn't exist. What do you say to that, son? Where is your Jesus now?"

The student doesn't answer.

"Sit down, please."

The Christian sits...

Defeated.

Another Christian raises his hand. "Professor, may I address the class?"

The professor turns and smiles. "Ah, another Christian in the vanguard! Come, come, young man. Speak some proper wisdom to the gathering."

The Christian looks around the room. "Some interesting points you are making, sir. Got a question for you. Is there such thing as heat?"

"Yes," the professor replies. "There's heat."

"Is there such a thing as cold?"

"Yes, son, there's cold too."

"No, sir, there isn't."

The professor's grin freezes. The room suddenly goes very cold.

The second Christian continues. "You can have lots of heat, even more heat, super-heat, mega-heat, white heat, a little heat or no heat but we don't have anything called 'cold'. We can hit 459.67 degrees below zero Fahrenheit, which is absolute zero or no heat, but we can't go further than that. There is no such thing as cold, otherwise we would be able to go colder than minus 459 - You see, sir, cold is only a word we use to describe the absence of heat. We cannot measure cold. Heat we can measure in thermal units because heat is energy. Cold is not the opposite of heat, sir, just the absence of it."

Silence.

A pin drops somewhere in the classroom.

"Is there such a thing as darkness, professor?"

119

"That's a dumb question, son. What is night if it isn't darkness? What are you getting at...?"

"So you say there *is* such a thing as darkness?"

"Yes..."

"You're wrong again, sir. Darkness is not something, it is the absence of something. You can have low light, normal light, bright light, flashing light but if you have no light constantly you have nothing and it's called darkness. That's the meaning we use to define the word. In reality, Darkness isn't. If it were, you would be able to make darkness darker and give me a jar of it. Can you... give me a jar of darker darkness, professor?"

Despite himself, the professor smiles at the young effrontery before him. This will indeed be a good semester.

"Would you mind telling us what your point is?"

"Yes, professor. My point is, your philosophical premise is flawed to start with, your argument is *accurate*, so your conclusion must be in error."

The professor goes toxic. "Flawed...? How dare you...!"

"Sir, may I explain what I mean?"

The class is all ears. Explain... oh, explain...

The professor makes an effort to regain control. Suddenly he is affability itself. He waves his hand to silence the class. For the student to continue.

"You are working on the premise of duality," the Christian explains. "That for example there is life and then there's death. A good God and a bad God. You are viewing the concept of God as something finite, something we can measure. Sir, science cannot even explain a thought. It uses electricity and magnetism but has never seen, much less fully understood them. To view death as the opposite of life is to be ignorant of the fact that death cannot exist as a substantive thing. Death is not the opposite of life, merely the absence of it." The young man holds up a newspaper he takes from the desk of a neighbour who has been reading it.

"Here is one of the most disgusting tabloids this country hosts, professor. Is there such a thing as immorality?"

"Of course there is, now look..."

"Wrong again, sir. You see, immorality is merely the absence of morality. Is there such thing as injustice? No. Injustice is the absence of justice. Is there such a thing as evil?" The Christian pauses. "Isn't evil just the absence of good?"

The professor's face has turned an alarming colour. He is so angry he is temporarily speechless. The Christian continues.

"If there is evil in the world, professor - and we all agree there is - then God, if he exists, must be accomplishing a work through the absence of good. What is that work God is accomplishing? The Bible tells us it is to see if each one of us will, of our own free will, choose to be good - or no good."

The professor bridles. "As a philosophical scientist, I don't view this matter as having anything to do with any choice. As a realist, I absolutely do not recognize the concept of God or any other theological factor as being part of the world equation because God is not observable."

"I would have thought that the absence of God's moral code in this world is probably one of the most observable phenomena going," the Christian replies. "Newspapers make millions of dollars reporting it every week! Tell me, professor. Do you teach your students that they evolved from a monkey?"

"If you are referring to the natural evolutionary process, young man, yes, of course I do."

"Have you ever observed evolution with your own eyes, sir?"

The professor makes a sucking sound with his teeth and gives his student a stony stare.

"Professor. Since you have never observed the process of evolution at work, cannot show me any transitional forms and cannot even prove that this process is an ongoing endeavour with one kind changing into another, are you not teaching your belief, sir? Are you now not a scientist, but a priest?"

"I'll overlook your impudence in the light of our philosophical discussion," the professor hisses. "Now, have you quite finished?"

"So you don't accept God's moral code to do what is right?"

"I believe in what is - that's science!"

"Ahh! SCIENCE!" the student's face splits into a grin. "Sir, you rightly state that science is the study of *observed* phenomena. Science too is a premise which is flawed...."

"SCIENCE IS FLAWED..?" the professor splutters. The class is in uproar.

The Christian remains standing until the commotion has subsided.

"To continue the point you were making earlier to the other student, may I give you an example of what I mean?"

The professor wisely keeps silent. The Christian looks around the room.

"Is there anyone in the class who has ever seen the professor's brain?"

The class breaks out in laughter. The Christian points towards his elderly, crumbling tutor.

"Is there anyone here who has ever heard the professor's brain... felt the professor's brain, touched or smelt the professor's brain?"

No one appears to have done so.

The Christian shakes his head. "It appears no one here has had any sensory perception of your brain whatsoever, sir. Well, according to the rules of empirical, testable, demonstrable protocol, science says you have no brain."

The class is chaos.

The Christian sits...

"It's truth, Jim, but not as we know it...."

Sorry, but atheism is the illogical religion of the ignorant. Permit me to explain. Atheists forever wax large on how intelligent, rational and logical they are compared with the thick, medieval trogs who need Christ for a crutch. The problem is, the atheist position fails from the outset. How can we know for sure there is no God? We can't. *It's a philosophical impossibility to prove the non-existence of something,* since to do so would require omnipresence, omniscience and therefore omnipotence – three attributes of the God atheists are foaming to debunk. You can never logically say, *from inside the system,* God does not exist, for the one rock you don't look behind might be the very one God's using to conceal Himself. "So what does that tell you about God then?" crows the atheist. It tells me a) God might have a sense of humour and b) *might only reveal Himself to those whom He chooses.* The last is the spookiest of all, for the scriptures state clearly that God's personally calling some people and He's not calling others.[113]

And then we have the ones who can't be bothered, who call themselves agnostics. Agnostics throw up their hands and attempt to duck the issue by believing that since the matter isn't settled, why bother engaging in the debate in the first place. The lawn needs mowing. The hedge needs clipping. The word 'agnostic' is derived from the Greek *gnōsis,* meaning 'knowledge'. Pop an 'a' in front and you amend the meaning to 'without knowledge'. So agnostics are people without knowledge. The Latin equivalent of *agnōsis* is *ignoramus.* Lee Strobel states that 'a'theism ('without a belief in God') is also a faith which draws conclusions far beyond the available evidence.[114] Wait... *So Christianity, Judaism and Islam don't?*

Forgive me for not speaking up for modern, Talmudic Judaism or Islam, but Christians most certainly can prove the legitimacy of their beliefs from the Bible. Many like myself are happy to do so. That doesn't mean I'm in the business of forcing my beliefs on you. God doesn't want robots, He wants you to get it. Information sciences expert Dr Chuck Missler states that you can ascertain the Bible's transcendent integrity by verifying the extraordinary design of the complete package throughout the 66 books written by 40 authors, and you most certainly can. Throughout the *Origins* series, we will examine the astonishing prophetic record, look at the unique manuscript evidence, scrutinise the Book of books for its scientific accuracy, scientific foreknowledge, gematrical and code evidence (heptadic structure, inter-Testament heptadic bridges, etc.); also its archaeological verification. We'll also take a trip through history and examine the real Holy War raging across the dimensions in ways that will astonish you. In so doing, we will

---

[113] Eph 1:4-5; FG 6:44; FG 6:64; FG 15:16; 17:2, 9; 2 Tim 2:19; 2 Thess 2:13; Rom 1:7; Isa 49:1,5; Jer 1:5; Gal 1:15; Acts 13:48
[114] **Strobel, L** *The Case for a Creator,* Zondervan, 2004, p.286

establish the identity of Jesus Christ not only as God and Creator of everything, but Author of this unique and matchless Message System which was crafted by Him precisely for you.

LET THERE BE LIGHT

"My thoughts are not your thoughts, nor are your ways My ways," saith the LORD. (Isa 55:8)

I remember a colleague of mine confronting a famous Christian pastor one time in Texas. He showed him the first verse of his Bible: **"In the beginning, God created the heavens and the Earth."** He asked the minister, "Do you believe that?" A troubled look came over the fellow's face: "You know, it's really not that simple...."

We're going to hear a lot of that as we proceed. Authenticating the Bible as God's Word – as the extraterrestrial, hyperdimensional Message System we've all been waiting for – allows us to experience a margin of security and confidence in analysing what God has to say about matters hopelessly beyond our own experience and frame of reference. We are about to discover that God's realm and environment are more extraordinary than anything the writers of *The Matrix* or *Inception* could ever have dreamt up. Since this is our future if we so choose, it might behove us to become familiar with our future home and employment. Closing the validation loop is the testimony given by God's Son come to Earth in human form, and the astonishing events that surrounded His ministry, miracles, teachings, six trials, a very public execution and subsequent resurrection from the dead, all set in real history, recorded by even the secular scribes of the age, witnessed by thousands.

The Biblical genealogies and dates imply that the Creation took place a mere 6,000 years ago (around 4004 BC) and that around 4,400 years ago (*c.* 2345 BC) there was a global flood which destroyed the surface of the planet, and all air-breathing creatures apart from eight humans perished. This is usually too much for modern, sophisticated Christians to believe, let alone everyone else. In *Origins I,* I explained the reasons why I and 10,000 scientists in the US alone[115] believe that the Genesis account is not only

---

[115] www.trueorigin.org/edupolls.asp

plausible scientifically, but correct in every respect. In this chapter I'd like to examine some of the supernatural architecture of God's enigmatic first book, Genesis, and see what it tells us about the Holy War.

The extraordinary (by today's standards) assertion of a young creation is unfamiliar to most, so brainwashed have we become with the 'billions and billions of years' mantra pushed out by *National Geographic, The Discovery Channel* and David Attenborough on TV every night. Yet the idea of an ancient Earth is a relatively new phenomenon which came about in the early to mid-19th century as a new secular age was launched following the French Revolution. The belief that the Earth was young was the constant opinion of antiquity. Ancient scholars from Alexandria, Greece and Rome took it for granted. Isaac Newton believed it. And when the famous Irish prelate Bishop James Ussher carefully examined the genealogies in the Bible and pronounced that the Creation occurred on the night preceding 23rd October 4004 BC according to the proleptic Julian calendar, few in the Church had any problem with it.

In fact, Ussher had done a huge amount of research to arrive at this figure. If you plot the ages given for the Bible patriarchs in Genesis 5, it's possible to produce a chart with an unbroken genealogy from Adam down to the dawn of recorded history, generally taken as the building of Solomon's temple. Things are made somewhat easier by the astonishingly precise periods God uses to span history. This, of course, presents serious ramifications for the 'accepted' dating of Egyptian dynasties, and even secular historians admit we're in a pickle over those. Let's examine the evidence as we proceed.

Never mind atheists, a 6,000-year-old Earth so outrages evolutionist Christians to this day that they torture the text to force billions of years into Genesis. Interestingly, as covered in *Origins I*, there is compelling evidence that the Earth is young. The accumulation of dust on the surface of the moon; the salinity of the oceans; erosion of the continents; the sedimentation volume of the Mississippi River Delta and its accumulation rate; the half-life decay of Earth's magnetic field; today's human population – all point to a radically different explanation from that given in your standard biology textbook. There are estimated to be over 75 young-Earth chronometers. Only one has to be correct for the Earth to be young.

Then there's the issue of *information* being found in the cell, perhaps the most compelling evidence for design so far. The utter complexity of the cell baffles even evolutionists, so Richard Dawkins must cast up his hands and find another explanation, as he already has done. The debate is on the move again, forcing both sides to shore up their data and discipline their battlegroups accordingly.

We have to consider the lens through which we examine the reality in which we find ourselves. French physicist Bernard d'Espagnat was awarded the Templeton Prize in May 2009 for his work in quantum mechanics. The Templeton site explains:

"D'Espagnat, Professor Emeritus of Theoretical Physics at the University of Paris-Sud… understood the philosophical importance of these new physics-based insights into the nature of reality. Much of it centers on what he calls 'veiled reality', a hidden yet ultimate reality beyond time, space, matter and energy – concepts challenged by quantum physics as possibly mere appearances. Since then, his writings and lectures on fundamental questions such as "What information does science really give us?" have provoked debate among scientists and philosophers."[116]

Very heated debate. Science has discovered the limits to largeness in the universe and smallness in quantum physics, so the unsettling but enthralling conclusion is that the universe, Earth and all of us are but a subset of d'Espagnat's far larger reality. We are part of a highly elaborate digital simulation wrought for the benefit of the human experience, wherein the rules have all been laid out in advance – a common theme throughout the Bible – which pushes us to the ultimate question of why. What is it all for? Why has God gone to such extremes to insert us into what amounts to a magnificently accurate, stunningly beautiful, highly structured,

---

[116] www.templetonprize.org/espielease.html

127

convoluted and, yes, violent video game? The *Origins* series aims to find the answers.

Genesis 1:1

There are two Creation accounts in the Bible, one in the Old Testament (OT) at Gen 1:1 and one in the New (NT) commencing Fourth Gospel 1:1. The first line of the Old Testament reads: **"In the beginning, God created the heavens and the Earth."** (Gen 1:1) Hebrew letters have numeric equivalents. If you take the product of the Hebrew letters in Genesis 1:1 multiplied by the number of letters there, then divide that by the product of Hebrew words multiplied by the number of words, you get the mathematical constant pi (π) to four decimal places (3.1415).[117] Pi is the universal constant relating the diameter of a circle to its circumference (circ = π x diameter). What does this prove? Nothing. It's a curiosity. God's signature. Carry out the same exercise with the Creation account in the NT, commencing with FG 1:1 in the Greek, and you get the mathematical (logarithmic) constant *e*, again to four decimal places. Hmmm.

Rabbi Yacov Rambsel writes:

"The number seven and its multiples play an important role in the Creation. Seven has unique meanings such as fullness, completion, perfection. There are seven words and 28 (4 x 7) letters that form the first verse in the Hebrew text. The 434 words of chapter 1 equal 7 x 62."[118]

Rabbi Rambsel devoted himself to uncovering hidden codes behind the Genesis texts. Just in the first few verses of the Torah, we find the following equidistant letter sequences (ELS) encoded in Hebrew: *Yeshua is able* (Gen 1:1), *the light, the speed, the glory of Yah seen.* The Hebrew phrase *and God saw* appears seven times in the account of the first six days of Creation. The Hebrew for *good* also appears in the same place and frequency.

---

[117] http://homepage.virgin.net/vernon.jenkins/Pi_File.htm
[118] **Rambsel, Yacov** *The Genesis Factor,* Lions Head Publishing, 2000, p.44

Fifty is the number of the Hebrew Jubilee (Lev 25:9). Every fifty years in ancient Israel, the Jubilee was celebrated as a particular outpouring of God's grace for the remission of sins, wherein slaves and prisoners were freed, debts forgiven, and leased land reverted to its owner. One of the codes in this 50-letter matrix which caught Rambsel's attention was the Hebrew phrase, *ha aohav aba*, which translates *Behold, the love of the Father*. No matter who we are or whatever our circumstances, says Rambsel, our Creator loves us if we are obedient to Him.

So, **"In the beginning God created the heaven and the Earth"** - we're all familiar with it. Missler states that if you believe that first verse, you'll have no other problem with the rest of the book. The Hebrew for this verse contains seven words, with one two-character word standing on its own which is not translated. Here's the Hebrew for Genesis 1:1 *from right to left* with the word underlined. If you ever wondered what an extraterrestrial language looks like, here it is:

בְּרֵאשִׁית, בָּרָא אֱלֹהִים, אֵת הַשָּׁמַיִם, וְאֵת הָאָרֶץ

The two underlined letters are *aleph-tau*. In English they would translate AZ, or in Greek, the Alpha and Omega, the First and the Last – a perfect description of our God who inhabits eternity. Another thing you won't pick up in the English is that the Hebrew word for God in Gen 1:1 is plural, *Elohim*. This has provoked all manner of theories that 'Gods' might refer to a race of aliens who seeded us onto Earth (panspermia again), and they return from time to time to see how we're doing - a favourite with the Dawkins brigade who can no longer deny design in the cell. In fact, there *are* aliens in the Bible – proper Sigourney Weaver ones – and we'll get to them in a little bit. For our part here, the generally accepted, non-hysterical, scholastic view of *Elohim* is that it collectively refers to the triune godhead of Father, Son and Holy Spirit, expounded in the OT and NT (*cf.* Psa 2).

Genesis 1:1-2

Relax, we won't be going through the Bible verse by verse, but these first two are classics and hold some great clues. Together they read:

(1)In the beginning God created the heaven and the Earth. (2)And the Earth was without form and void; and darkness was upon the face of the deep. And the Spirit of God moved upon the face of the waters.

These verses seem to contradict Isaiah 45:18, which reads:

For thus saith the LORD that created the heavens; God himself that formed the Earth and made it; He hath established it, He created it not in vain, He formed it to be inhabited: I am the LORD, and there is none else.

So here is our first *remez*, a clue to a nugget. A quick look at the Hebrew and we note three interesting factors. The 'And' commencing verse 2 is actually an aversive conjunction translated 'but' elsewhere in the scriptures, and the Hebrew word for 'was' is 'became' from היתה *hâyâh* – 'actioned' (Strongs 1961). And the Spirit of God 'moved' is מרחפת *râchaph* – 'brooded' (Strongs 7363) over the face of the water. In other words, you are quite within your rights to translate these first two verses as follows:

(1) In the beginning God created the heaven and the Earth. (2) But the Earth became without form and void, and darkness was upon the face of the deep. And the Spirit of God brooded upon the face of the waters.

What is the relevance of this? From the Biblical text, it seems that the Earth was in existence but unformed *prior to the formation of the sun, moon and stars*. Some scholars imply a gap between the two verses, either reasoning that millions of years could account for evolution in between, or more intriguingly, suggesting that perhaps a war occurred between Gen 1:1 and 1:2, resulting in God's most beloved angel, erroneously named 'Lucifer' by some, being kicked out of Heaven for his attempted *coup d'état*. I agree the language in Gen 1:2 is provocative, implying that destruction could have occurred. Some theorists point to Jeremiah 4:23, where **'without form and void'** occurs again – in fact, the only other place in scripture where it does. The Jeremiah passage describes an apocalyptic judgment levelled by God on the planet – and I mean apocalyptic – but God says He won't make a full end of it (Jer 4:27). Interesting. And I'd go along with the Gen 1:2/Satan war theory if not for some problems.

Firstly, to put to bed the 'millions of years of evolution' between Gen 1:1-2, the Creator Himself, Yeshua, states that Adam and Eve were created *in the beginning* (Matt 19:4; Mark 10:6). It doesn't sound like millions of years preceded those two events. Secondly, with regard to the 'Satan war' theory, after the six days of creation, God pronounced it all **'very good'** in Gen 1:31, which would hardly be the case if Lucifer had been attacking the Creation since Gen 1:2 with a third of the angelic realm as his henchmen.

Notice when the foundations of the Earth were laid in Gen 1:1, *all* the 'sons of God' (angels; *B'ni ha-Elohim*) cried out for joy (Job 38:4-7), including a still pristine 'Lucifer' at this time. Perhaps a few hundred years passed until Genesis 3:1, when Satan approaches Eve in Eden in his slithering duplicity as the *nachash*/serpent (he has fallen at this point). *Yet he was apparently in Eden beforehand, pristine, ornate and still favoured,* according to Ezekiel 28:13,14-16, which means that he can't have been disgraced between Gen 1:1-2. In summary then: we know that God created <u>everything</u> in six literal days (Exodus 20:11), including the angelic realm and the spirit being often referred to as 'Lucifer', and that 'Lucifer' was in the Garden of Eden, pristine, until he sinned (Eze 28:15), and that the Garden of Eden was planted after day 7 (Genesis 2:8). This does to death the gap theory between Gen 1:1-2.

As for the Satan war, we know from what's coming up that Satan's attempted hostile *coup* fails, and he will be thrown out of Heaven with a third of the angelic realm who followed him in his revolt (*cf.* Luke 10:18; Rev 12:7-10). Satan's fate is something God should expound upon in more detail, and He does, but you have to dig for it. I'm intrigued, though, that we've got two appearances of **'without form and void'** with more description in Jeremiah. I'm also intrigued that Yeshua decides to comment, past tense: **"I beheld Satan like lightning fall from Heaven"** in Luke 10:18. The question is, does the Jeremiah 4:23 obliteration passage refer to the 'end times' Great Tribulation or to some other mysterious judgment? Why does God appear to fight shy of covering the circumstances and timing of Satan's fall openly? [119] More clues to follow.

Project Earth

Richard Dawkins says you're on Earth for a lifetime, then that's your lot, none of it meant anything. You're the result of billions of years of *mistakes.*

"Be thankful that you have a life, and forsake your vain and presumptuous desire for a second one."[120]

Here by chance? Imagine I brought over a Monet masterpiece to your place and told you Monet didn't paint it. What really happened was that there was this big explosion in a paint shop one day and this picture was the result. How insulting would that be to Monsieur Monet? You can see it from God's standpoint. Of all the false gods man ever concocted, Darwin's monkey god must be the most offensive, consigning the wonders of our existence to random processes entirely without organisation or purpose. The No-God of Creation. Chance. Happenstance. The Creator cut out of the process. No meaning to life. A Christian god of know-nothing relegated to the garden shed of childish superstition along with the tooth fairy. Today, YHWH is hated with a passion. Richard Dawkins writes:

---

[119] There is confusion among some scholars as to when Satan is ultimately cast out of Heaven, since Jesus appears to be talking about this event in the past tense during His ministry (Luke 10:18). Yet Rev 12:7-10 unequivocally reveals that Satan's ultimate fall from Heaven with his angels occurs in the end times immediately prior to the Great Tribulation. It's another *remez*, a hint of something deeper. Jesus speaks prophetically in the past tense, since He has already seen this event in the metacosm. He is providing an explanation to His disciples as to why the demons are submitting to them in His name (Luke 10:17-20). Today, however, the rebellious cherub still has access to God's throne, even as he did in Job's day (Job 1:6 ff.), accusing the brethren before the Almighty at every opportunity (Rev 12:10). And Yeshua is there at God's right hand to make intercession on the believer's behalf (Rom 8:34). Welcome to the Earth Training Programme!

[120] www.goodreads.com/author/quotes/1194.Richard_Dawkins

"The God of the Old Testament is arguably the most unpleasant character in all fiction: jealous and proud of it; a petty, unjust, unforgiving control-freak; a vindictive, bloodthirsty ethnic cleanser; a misogynistic, homophobic, racist, infanticidal, genocidal, filicidal, pestilential, megalomaniacal, sadomasochistic, capriciously malevolent bully."[121]

When asked what he might say if he ran into the Almighty after he died, Richard Dawkins quotes atheist Bertrand Russell:

"Sir, why did You take such pains to hide Yourself?"[122]

Hide Himself? I'm looking out of my home study window into the garden as I write this and the flowers are in full bloom. Have you ever stopped to study the awesome complexity of a lupin? Then watch how a bee interacts with it – I won't spoil the surprise. If you stop and ponder the unfathomable processes necessary to make nature possible, you should be struck dumb with amazement. Forget it. Most of us are too busy sexting or listening to *The Kings of Leon* on our iPhones. The Designer intends holding each of us to account for His very *visible* power in the Creation alone, and He's said so in advance. How scary is that? In fact, Richard Dawkins is in the Bible:

For the wrath of God is revealed from heaven against all ungodliness and unrighteousness of men, who hold the truth in unrighteousness. Because that which may be known of God is manifest in them; for God hath shewed it unto them. For the invisible things of Him from the creation of the world are clearly seen, being understood by the things that are made [us!], even His eternal power and Godhead; <u>so that they</u> [that's us!] <u>are without excuse</u>. Because that, when they knew God, they glorified Him not as God, neither were thankful, but became vain in their imaginations, and their foolish heart was darkened. <u>Professing themselves to be wise, they became fools, and changed the glory of the uncorruptible God into an image made like to corruptible man, and to birds, and fourfooted beasts, and creeping things</u> [monkeys, amoebas, etc.]. (Rom 1:18-23)

---

[121] **Dawkins, Richard** *The God Delusion*, Bantam, London, 2006
[122] Ibid.

The Bible says that God (Yeshua) made us for His glory (Isa 43:7), not because He had to, but because He desired to. Project Earth is on-the-job training; apparently the proving ground to find out who will rule Earth's Millennial Kingdom with Yeshua for 1,000 years, and thereafter the greater Creation (universe) with God *for eternity* (Dan: 7:18; Heb 2:7-8; Rev 2:26). Oh, *and who won't* (Matt 7:21-23). This present life is a tactical review of our obedience capability under live-fire conditions and the pressure is on. You can learn a lot about a man when you see him in situations he would rather not have you see him in. Character is who you are when no-one's looking. It's about refining free will – learning to control and harness what we are literally capable of in God (Gen 11:6). No-one will be able to claim after death that they weren't told what this was about. The Christian gospel has penetrated to the furthest points of the planet. The Bible's in every hotel bedroom drawer. Today, everyone's heard of Jesus, but who cares? "You have your truth and I have mine." Really? The only man to have died and provably come back from the grave stated: **"I am the way, the truth and the life. No man cometh unto the Father but by Me."** (FG 14:6) Are you willing to pick and choose the theology that's right for you in the light of that statement? God intends to hold every being accountable. There's a war on and you're on enemy turf.

Russell Howard and Andy Parsons insult YHWH and His Son in *Mock the Week*. *The Vicar of Dibley, QI, The Daily Show* and a hundred other programmes all vie to get laughs at the Creator's expense. I wouldn't do that if I were them. God won't be mocked. **Whatsoever a man soweth, that shall he also reap**, and the universe is taking detailed notes (Gal 6:7, Matt 12:36). Nothing is happening by chance. Dawkins has been put on Earth to test you to see if you will fail. As we'll see, all this is rather more serious than most people imagine.

In the beginning....

Project Earth begins in a blaze of Shekinah light at Creation. YHWH creates time and space and fills it with lots of stuff. It's all for our benefit and God has put man in charge (Psa 8:5-9). The

Kepler spacecraft/satellite, named after the Renaissance astronomer, has discovered 132 confirmed exoplanets[123] across 76 stellar systems at the time of writing. Astronomers at the Harvard-Smithsonian Center for Astrophysics have extrapolated the existing Kepler data to calculate that there could be as many as 17 billion exoplanets of Earth size in the Milky Way alone.

Consider the immensity of the universe, then ponder the implications of that one for a moment. In the Hollywood movie *Contact,* released in 1997, the film opens with a father encouraging his young daughter, Ellie, in her hobby of astronomy on the lawn outside her home at night with her telescope. The conversation turns to whether or not there might be other beings in the universe. The father replies with a paternal, "Well if not, it's an awful waste of space."

It's a common viewpoint among Mediocrity Principle ufologists and even astronomer-theologians in the Vatican.[124] Why would God waste his resources only creating and populating *one world?* The answer lies in the very first verse of the Bible that's been under their noses for centuries. **In the beginning God created the heaven and the Earth** (Gen 1:1). In other words, the Earth is extraordinary right from the start, set apart from the rest of the heavens for special mention. Completely *un*mediocre. Central to God's programme. If you don't get the first verse, the rest of the book won't make much sense to you either. The early Christian scholar Origen (185 – 253 AD) was certainly puzzled.

"If the world had its beginning in time, what was God doing before the world began? For it is at once impious and absurd to say that the nature of God is inactive and immovable." [125]

People like Origen decline to consider another angle. Namely, that God's resources are not limited but infinite. That He's chosen to do it this way to confound people like Origen, Dawkins, Andy

---

[123] Planets outside our own Solar System.

[124] **Putnam C and T Horn** *Exo-Vaticana,* Defencer, Crane, MO, USA, 2013, pp.175-210

[125] **Schaff, Philip** *The Nicene and Post-Nicene Fathers,* vol.2, Logos Research, Oak Harbour, USA, 1997, p.207

Parsons and Russell Howard. We're being told it's all been for us and we are to glorify Him. In return, God will show the exceeding riches of His grace in the ages to come in His kindness to man through His Son (Psa 19; Eph 2:4-10). In other words, a far more expansive future programme for the universe hoves into view, though Earth has not yet received *that* briefing. We recall Earth started out without form and void before the Creator spoke (Gen 1:2-3). Perhaps all those planets are awaiting a future make-over similar to Earth's past and future for those God has decided will rule with Him in eternity (*cf.* Isa 65:17; 66:22; 2 Pet 3:13; Rev 21:1).

Professor Stephen C Meyer is director of the Discovery Institute's Center for the Renewal of Science and Culture. He writes:

"Imagine that you are a cosmic explorer who has just stumbled into the control room of the whole universe. There you discover an elaborate 'universe-creating machine' with rows and rows of dials, each with many possible settings. As you investigate, you learn that each dial represents some particular parameter that has to be calibrated with a precise value in order to create a universe in which life can exist. One dial represents the possible settings for the strong nuclear force, one for the gravitational constant, one for Planck's constant, one for the ratio of the neutron mass to the proton mass, one for the strength of electromagnetic attraction, and so on. As you, the cosmic explorer, examine the dials, you find that they could easily have been turned to different settings. Moreover, you determine by careful calculation that if any of the dial settings were even slightly altered, life would cease to exist. Yet for some reason, each dial is set at just the exact value necessary to keep the universe running. What do you infer about the origin of these finely tuned dial settings?"[126]

Er, *design?* King David wrote:

"When I consider Thy heavens, the work of Thy fingers, the moon and the stars, which Thou hast ordained; what is man, that Thou art mindful of him? And the son of man, that Thou visitest him?" (Psa 8:3-4)

---

[126] Behe, Michael, Dembski, William A, Meyer, Stephen C, *Science and Evidence for Design in the Universe,* op. cit., p.55-56

The Creation is a model for what God wants for each of us. He wants us with Him forever, dwelling in His light, not basking in our own (pride) which leads to outer darkness. He makes it clear we are eternal spirits having a human experience, and He'll set tests in the training programme and help us overcome them (1 Cor 10:13). We are comprised of software (mind - eternal) and hardware (body - subject to death and decay at the appointed time). Science supports this. If you were awake in Physics 101, you'll recall from the Mass-Distance-Time (MDT) cube that when mass = 0, time is eternal. Your thoughts, love, anger – the entire software package – weighs nothing, so you are eternal whether you like it or not (Matt 10:28). Whether you are saved or not. We're in the game, we cannot escape, we don't control the play for even a nano-second, and we're certainly not making the rules. In such circumstances, a smart person might ask what God wants.

A literal account

The traditional scientific belief used to be that the universe had always existed (steady state model). This was overturned once we had a proper understanding of the first three laws of thermodynamics:

1) Conservation of Energy - matter cannot be created or destroyed
2) Entropy - all systems in the observable universe are winding down (which means they used to be wound up)
3) Zero Point - if the temperature of an empty container is lowered to absolute zero (−273.15°C), there still remains a residual amount of thermal energy that cannot be removed. This is known as 'zero-point energy'

Dr Chuck Missler writes:

"Heat always flows from hot bodies to cold bodies. If the universe were infinitely old, then the temperature throughout the universe would be uniform. It's obviously not, so the universe cannot be infinitely old. This is a simple demonstration that the universe had a beginning." [127]

In other words, the universe cannot be eternal since it would have suffered ultimate heat death long before now and be of a uniform temperature. The universe is not only not a uniform temperature, it gives every appearance of still expanding and stabilising, pointing to a far more recent origin.[128] Astronomer Edwin Hubble clarified the picture when he discovered other galaxies outside our own Milky Way. He noticed that the degree of redshift observed in the light emitting from these celestial bodies increased in proportion to their distance from the observer (Hubble's Law). The impact of this discovery on science cannot be overstated. Einstein tried to reconcile the steady state model with his 'Cosmological Constant', which he later admitted was the biggest blunder of his career. Hubble's research was showing that the universe was expanding and therefore had to have had a beginning. Interestingly, the Bible states this on numerous occasions, among which:

[God] **which alone spreadeth out the heavens, and treadeth upon the waves of the sea.** (Job 9:8)

Bless the LORD, O my soul. O LORD my God, Thou art very great. Thou art clothed with honour and majesty. Who coverest Thyself with light as with a garment. Who stretchest out the heavens like a curtain... (Psa 104:1-2)

It is He that sitteth upon the circle of the Earth, and the inhabitants thereof are as grasshoppers; that stretcheth out the heavens as a curtain, and spreadeth them out as a tent to dwell in... (Isa 40:22)

Thus saith God the LORD, He that created the heavens, and stretched them out... (Isa 42:5)

Thus saith the LORD, thy Redeemer, and He that formed thee from the womb, "I am the LORD that maketh all things; that stretcheth forth the heavens alone; that spreadeth abroad the earth by Myself..." (Isa 44:24)

---

[127] www.khouse.org, the Genesis commentary
[128] **Day, Phillip** *Origins – The Greatest Scientific Discovery*, Credence, 2012

138

"I have made the Earth and created man upon it: I, even My hands, <u>have stretched out the heavens,</u> and all their host have I commanded." (Isa 45:12)

Here we see God explaining an expanding, stretching universe and a spherical Earth. After Hubble's bombshell, a combination of models was proposed to explain how the universe could have come into existence. These have collectively come to be known as the Big Bang Theory which, in a nutshell, states that first there was nothing and then it exploded, and from that we got the sun, moon and stars, all highly organised by blind random chance, and everything after that too the same way, and I mean everything – newts, amoebas, rhinos, bumblebees, swans and Lady Gaga. All this stuff came from nowhere, violating Law No.1, and then evolved from simple to incredibly complex by blind, random, chance *mistakes*, violating Law No. 2. And here we are today and everything somehow just *works*. Good luck with that theory.

How about Job 26:7, a verse from arguably the oldest book in the Bible (an authorship accepted by many to be around 2000 BC):

He stretcheth out the north over the empty place and hangeth the Earth upon nothing.

God literally hangs the Earth upon nothing? That's not what the most scientifically advanced cultures believed for centuries. The Greeks believed the Earth sat on Atlas's shoulders. The Hindus believed the Earth stood on the back of an elephant, which stood on a huge turtle. Turtles seem to be figure prominently in this regard, don't ask me why. Robert Anton Wilson writes in his *Prometheus Rising:*

William James, father of American psychology, tells of meeting an old lady who told him the Earth rested on the back of a huge turtle. "But, my dear lady", Professor James asked as politely as possible, "what holds up the turtle?" "Ah", she said, "that's easy. He is standing on the back of another turtle." "Oh, I see," said Professor James, still being polite. "But would you be so good as to tell me what holds up the second turtle?" "It's no use, Professor," said the old lady, realizing he was trying to lead her into a logical trap. "It's turtles-turtles-turtles, all the way down!"[129]

Well, come the 20th century, we go into space and lo, we find no turtles propping up the planet. The Earth literally hangs upon nothing. As covered in *Origins I*, the Bible has quite a lot to say about science centuries before scientists figured it out for themselves. Dr Missler lists out some ready examples:

Time, space and matter are finite: Gen 1:1; 2 Tim 1:9; Titus 1:2
Conservation of mass and energy: Ecc 1:9; 3:14-15
The water cycle: Ecc 1:7; Isa 55:10
Gravity: Job 26:7; 38:31-33
Effects of emotions on physical health: Prov 16:24; 17:22
Control of contagious diseases: Lev 13:45-46
Importance of sanitation on health: Lev; Num 19; Deut 23:12-13
Expanding universe: Psa 104:1-2; *cf.* Isa 40:22; 42:5; 45:12
Stars cannot be numbered: Jer 33:22
Cell replacement/remission from cancer: Job 33:25
Matter is made of invisible units: Heb 11:3
Stars make sounds: Job 38:7
Light in motion: Job 38:19-20
Sunlight causing wind patterns: Job 38:24
Electricity carrying information: Job 38:35
Winds blowing in cyclones: Ecc 1:6
Blood as the source of life and healing: Lev 17:11
The weight of air: Job 28:25 [130]

Dr Missler lists further examples as:
Modern weapons technology: Matt 24:22
Oceanic currents/pathways in the sea: Psa 8:8; Isa 43:16
Ocean-floor mountains : Jon: 2:5-6
Medical hygiene: Ex 15:26; Deut 23:12,13
Circumcision: Gen 17:10-12

---

[129] **Wilson, RA** *Prometheus Rising,* New Falcon, Phoenix, AZ, 1997, p.25
[130] **Ross, Hugh** *A Scientist's Search for Truth,* www.reasons.org

Weapons of mass destruction: Zech 14:12; Eze 38,39; Matt 24:21-22

Radioactive fallout: Eze 39:11-16

Nuclear physics: 2 Pet 3:10

Smart weapons: Jer 50:9

Global TV coverage: Matt 24:15; 27,30; Rev 11:8-10

Meteorological cycle: Eccl 1:6,7; Job 36:27,28

Electronic funds transfer: Rev 13:17

Spherical Earth: Job 26:10; Isa 40:22; Luke 17:34-36

The Earth hangs in space supported by nothing: Job 26:7

Animation: Rev 13:15

Cloning: Daniel 2:43

The language of life, digitally defined: Gen 1:25 [131]

Information revealed outside of time

How could Biblical authors have known any of this unless it was knowledge revealed to them? And what about the literally mountains of Creation evidence covered in *Origins I?* Today there is a war going on across the sciences – chance versus design, evolution versus creation, signal versus cacophony, call it what you will. You won't find any of this featured in your atheist newspapers, yet the Holy War is important to understand, and not just for religious reasons, for it not only controls the type of information we get from the myriad sources we rely on for 'the truth', but also reveals a cogent explanation for the utter weirdness soon to present itself in the planet's not too distant future.

The Creation account in Genesis contains thirteen steps which are described in the correct order geologically, logically and have been proven archeologically.[132] The odds of the writer, traditionally Moses, getting these steps in the correct order by chance are calculated at *one chance in six trillion.* Yet many ministers want to be man-pleasers. They've lost their faith in God's inerrancy because of secular hectoring, so evolution gets shoe-horned in. The days of Creation become long periods of time (Day-Age Theory). There

[131] **Missler, Chuck** *Technology and the Bible,* notes, www.khouse.org

[132] Day, Phillip, *Origins I,* op. cit. See also forthcoming text under 'Turn It On'.

was a pre-Adamic civilisation between Genesis 1:1 and 1:2, which accounts for man's evolution (Gap Theory). Perhaps the first question to ask is not what we think Genesis says, but what its Author intended His readers to believe. Jack Heyford writes:

"Jewish tradition lists Moses as the author of Genesis and of the next four books. Together these books are called the Pentateuch. Jesus said, "If you believed Moses, you would believe Me, for He wrote about Me." (John 5:46) The Pentateuch itself depicts Moses as having written extensively. Acts 7:22 tells us that "Moses was learned in all the wisdom of the Egyptians".... We observe a number of loanwords from Egyptian that are found in Genesis, a fact which suggests that the original author had his roots in Egypt, as did Moses."[133]

The style of Genesis is unabashed and to the point. Nothing leads us to believe that we should be interpreting the Creation text as anything other than *literal narrative*. In fact, as Genesis 2:4 states:

This is the <u>history</u> of the heavens and the Earth when they were created, in the day that the LORD God made the Earth and the heavens. (NKJV)

Bodie Hodge writes:

"The Bible gives us principles of interpretation in 2 Corinthians 4:2 and Proverbs 8:8–9: **Rather, we have renounced secret and shameful ways; we do not use deception, nor do we distort the word of God. On the contrary, by setting forth the truth plainly, we commend ourselves to every man's conscience in the sight of God** (2 Cor 4:2 NIV).

All the utterances of my mouth are in righteousness; there is nothing crooked or perverted in them. They are all straightforward to him who understands and right to those who find knowledge (Prov 8:8–9 NIV).

In other words, we are to read and understand the Bible in a *plain* or *straightforward* manner. This is usually what people mean when they say 'literal interpretation of the Bible' (this phrase is common among those not well-versed in hermeneutics).... Reading the Bible 'plainly' means understanding that literal history is literal history, metaphors are

---

[133] **Heyford, Jack** editor *The Spirit-Filled Bible,* Thomas Nelson Inc., Nashville, USA, 1991

142

metaphors, poetry is poetry, etc. The Bible is written in many different literary styles and should be read accordingly. This is why we understand that Genesis records actual historical events. It was written as historical narrative."[134]

Professor James Barr, Regius Professor of Hebrew at the University of Oxford, writes:

"Probably, so far as I know, there is no professor of Hebrew or Old Testament at any world-class university who does not believe that the writer(s) of Genesis 1-11 intended to convey to their readers the ideas that:

(a) creation took place in a series of six days which were the same as the days of 24 hours we now experience

(b) the figures contained in the Genesis genealogies provided by simple addition a chronology from the beginning of the world up to later stages in the biblical story

(c) Noah's flood was understood to be worldwide and extinguished all human and animal life except for those in the ark.

Or, to put it negatively, the apologetic arguments which suppose the 'days' of creation to be long eras of time, the figures of years not to be chronological, and the flood to be a merely local Mesopotamian flood, are not taken seriously by any such professors, as far as I know.""[135]

www.christiananswers.net writes:

"The principal people mentioned in Genesis chapters 1-11 are referred to as real – historical, not mythical – people in the rest of the Bible, often many times. For example, Adam, Eve, Cain, Abel, and Noah are referred to in 15 other books of the Bible.

The Lord Jesus Christ referred to the Creation of Adam and Eve as a real historical event by quoting Genesis 1:27 and 2:24 in His teaching about divorce (Matthew 19:3-6; Mark 10:2-9), and by referring to Noah as a real historical person and the Flood as a real

---

[134] www.answersingenesis.org

[135] Letter from Professor James Barr to David Watson of the UK, dated 23rd April 1984

143

historical event, in His teaching about the 'coming of the Son of man'. (Matthew 24:37-39; Luke 17:26-27)."

Turn it on

Genesis 1:3 says:

And God said, "Let there be light", and there was light. And God saw the light, that it was good. And God divided the light from the darkness. And God called the light Day, and the darkness he called Night. And the evening and the morning were the first day.

This is interesting because the sun, moon and stars don't get made until day four! In other words, according to God, the Earth was around, albeit without form and void, *before the universe was created*. And what was this light? Here we have the first of many models or types. God manifests Himself as the Light in all glory. The Fourth Gospel (FG) 1:9 refers to Yeshua the Creator as the True Light. Malachi 4:2 calls Him the Sun of Righteousness and this theme will endure throughout the Bible until the end. In the New Testament, the Creator enters time and comes to Earth as a man to walk among us. He accomplishes His will as Light and Truth, and we are to walk in the light as He is the light: **"Let your light so shine before men, that they may see your good works and glorify your Father which is in Heaven."** (Matt 5:16). Yeshua makes it clear that our physical existence is not where our allegiance should lie; it is not the 'real' world as He sees it (Matt 6:19-21). How about that for making the haughty humble?

Genesis 1:7 codes

Rabbi Rambsel reports that, commencing behind the text of Genesis 1:7, the following phrases are found encrypted in Hebrew (letter skips are in brackets; '–' for backwards, '+' for forwards):

equidistant sequences (-14)

the codes of truth (+3)

This startled the rabbi as this portrayed the very method he was using! Mathematical analysis reveals that the odds of the phrase *the codes of truth* occurring by chance in Genesis 1 are less than 10 billion to one. What does this mean? It's God's watermark on His work. His signature.

Tree codes

From Genesis 1:29 to Genesis 2:9 - a matter of 12 verses - the following trees are encoded in equidistant letter sequences (ELS) in Hebrew behind the plain text. The positive numbers represent the tree being spelled forward and the negative backwards. The numerical value corresponds to the number of letters skipped.

1) Tamarisk: +2
2) Terebinth: -2
3) Thicket: -3
4) Citron: -3
5) Acacia: -3
6) Almond: +5
7) Wheat: +5
8) Date Palm: +5
9) Cedar: -5
10) Aloe: +6
11) Grape: -6
12) Boxthorn or Bramble: +7
13) Cassia: +7
14) Pomegranate: +8
15) Gopherwood or fir: +8
16) Thornbush: +9
17) Olive: -9
18) Pistachio Nut: +13
19) Hazel: -13
20) Fig: +14
21) Willow: -15
22) Oak: +17
23) Vine: -18
24) Barley: -28
25) Chestnut: +44
26) Poplar: -85

This phenomenon is all the more extraordinary for the surface text within which these trees are clustered. It describes trees, ending in v.9 with the fabled Tree of Life and the Tree of the Knowledge of Good and Evil, which will cause all the trouble in a minute.

The above 'tree' example was reported in a *Daily Mail* article on Bible codes dated 4th August 1985. Rabbi David Ordman, an Israeli researcher, and 19 other rabbis used one of the most sophisticated computers of the 1980s, installed at the Hebrew University in Jerusalem. Ordman summarised:

"To plan this kind of thing would take years. And they had to prepare a text as well, with perfect grammar, a message and no contradictions. We are not trying to prove the divinity of the Torah here, but that the statistical odds against it being humanly written are impossible."

Genesis 1:22 codes

A further startling phenomenon is pointed out by Rabbi Rambsel:

"Genesis 1:22: **And God blessed them, saying, "Be fruitful, and multiply, and fill the waters in the seas, and let fowl multiply in the earth."** From this scripture we have a prophetic picture of God's ultimate purpose for the patriarch Abraham.

Starting with the first letter in the third word [of Genesis 1:22], counting forward every 50th letter spells *Abraham; Avraham;* אברהם. Abraham was chosen by God to be the father of many nations. Not only is Abraham encoded at 50-ELS [the Jubilee number] but Sarah; שרה, his wife as well.

An analysis was done on this code, and the percentages of this happening by chance in the first chapter of Genesis are less than .004 to 1,000,000 (one million)." [136]

Created in God's image

Genesis 1:26-28 reads: **"And God said, "Let Us make man in <u>Our image, after Our likeness:</u> and let them have dominion over the fish of the sea, and over the fowl of the air, and over the cattle, and over all the Earth, and over every creeping thing that creepeth upon the Earth." So God created man in His own image, in the image of God created He him, male and female created He them. And God blessed them, and God said unto them, "Be**

---

[136] **Rambsel, Yacov** *The Genesis Factor,* Lions Head, USA, 2000, pp.60-61

fruitful, and multiply, and replenish the Earth and subdue it, and have dominion over the fish of the sea, and over the fowl of the air, and over every living thing that moveth upon the Earth."

Several points here. First, the Us is intriguing. **"Let Us make man in <u>Our image</u>, after <u>Our likeness</u>** might allude to God discussing the issue with the angelic host. A closer appreciation of the language, however, reveals that the 'Us' is doing the creating, so scholars maintain this to be the Bible's first insinuation of the creative Trinity, an assertion often attacked by Bible detractors who protest, "There's no mention of the Trinity in the Bible!" (*cf.* Matt 28:18-20) Daniel B Wallace Ph.D is a professor of New Testament Studies at Dallas Theological Seminary and one of the world's great experts on textual criticism and Biblical exegesis. He disagrees:

"The Bible clearly contains these four truths: the Father is God, Jesus is God, the Holy Spirit is God, and there is only one God... And that's the Trinity." [137]

Secondly, UFO-ers maintain that if God is actually an alien who made us, then He's talking here with fellow aliens (**"Let Us...."**) in their discussions on running up a few human prototypes. One problem among many with this popular view is that most of the aliens reported by contactees are appearing decidedly inhuman in appearance (Greys, Reptilians, etc.) with the exception of the kind known as Nordics. Third, the Creator wants man, in the form of the first man, Adam, (whose name means 'man'), to have dominion over Earth and all its creatures. Man created in God's image as his proxy ruler of Earth, therefore, makes congruent sense. Jack Heyford comments that, apart from our physical similarity to God, as manifested in Jesus (who looked so decidedly unalien-like that Judas had to point him out to the soldiers when the Messiah was arrested in Gethsemane), other attributes of God would pass muster in the human image ideologue:

---

[137] **Strobel, Lee** *The Case for the Real Jesus,* Zondervan, 2007, p.94

"God was speaking, not only to what the New Testament reveals to be the rest of the Trinity, but to the entire host of heaven, the angels, as well. 'Our image' likely refers to such qualities as reason, personality and intellect, and to the capacity to relate, to hear, to see and to speak. All of these are characteristics of God, which he chose to reproduce in mankind."[138]

Put another way, we are very familiar to God and He to us because of shared, not alien attributes. This becomes important in a minute. This is not a hands-off Creator. No impersonal godforce He. This is the LORD who divides every one of our cells, blinks our eyes, digests our food and knows our most intimate thoughts before we think them, *yet we have free will*. The free will/predestination paradox disappears when we understand that God is outside of time and inhabits eternity. He alone knows the end from the beginning.

The three billion-plus bits of information on the human DNA strand contained in the nucleus of every cell in our body comprise combinations of a four-letter alphabet: A, T, G, C. The same goes for an elephant, crocodile, kitten, eagle, shark, mosquito, meerkat, lion and aardvark. In fact, the DNA for all creatures provably originates from the same software house. Only one of these creatures – man – possesses the intelligence to discover and comprehend this wonder. Which means that we were meant to find out that these creatures were made for our enjoyment, benefit, instruction, caution and chastisement. And who made them.

The Bible states that God has a people He has chosen from the beginning. If you are being drawn by His Spirit, you were not only planned before you were a twinkle in your Daddy's eye; God had your eternal salvation on His mind from the foundation of the world.[139] You were created for His glory (Isa 43:7).

"For You formed my inward parts; You covered me in my mother's womb. I will praise You, for I am fearfully and wonderfully made. Marvellous are Your works, and that my soul

[138] Heyford, Jack, *Spirit Filled Bible,* op. cit., notes, p.5

[139] Eph 1:4-5; FG 6:44; FG 6:64; FG 15:16; FG 17:2, 9; 2 Tim 2:19; 2 Thess 2:13; Rom 1:7; Isa 49:1,5; Jer 1:5; Gal 1:15; Acts 13:48

knows very well. My frame was not hidden from You when I was made in secret, and skilfully wrought in the lowest parts of the Earth. Your eyes saw my substance, being yet unformed. And in Your book they all were written, the days fashioned for me, when as yet there were none of them." (Psa 139:13-16, NKJV)

This puts abortion in the starkest light. Murder is abhorrent to YHWH, the greatest insult possible to His creative love and sovereignty. *Yet God is the biggest killer in the Bible.* Since He is omnipotent, *He must permit every atrocity.* How to reconcile? Let's find out.

The Edenic paradise

Adam is placed into the leafy paradise of Eden, a fabulous garden which God grows for Adam's home. **And out of the ground the LORD God made every tree grow that is pleasant to the sight and good for food** (NKJV). Then an interesting thing happens, which most people miss. God creates every land-dwelling animal and bird *again,* but this time specifically for Adam in Eden, separate and distinct from those he created in Gen 1:20-25 for the wider world. What's going on here? God creates each creature, shows it to Adam, and Adam names each species because God has made Adam the boss of all creatures on Earth (Gen 2:19).

Notice Adam witnesses God's creative ability firsthand. No-one will be able to tell Adam's progeny later that God was not the Creator. Adam saw Him do it. And Adam will live long enough to tell Noah's father, Lamech. And Noah's eldest son Shem will survive the Flood and live long enough to tell Abraham, and so on.

Where was Eden? Does it still exist? Googling that question kept me up until the wee hours one night tracking down research that placed Eden everywhere from India to Ethiopia, from Turkey to the Nile Delta and the Mediterranean Atlantis. After the Americans invaded Iraq, a common story ran the rounds in US newspapers that the Marines were tramping over the Garden of Eden, since Eden is described in the Bible as being 'eastward', and most scholars take this to mean somewhere in 'Mesopotamia' (*lit.* 'land between two rivers', i.e. Euphrates and Tigris), since Biblical geography is usually oriented from Israel. The Bible describes a river running out of Eden which splits into four riverheads, two of which are directly identified as the Euphrates and Hiddekel (Tigris), hence the headlines.

So where was Eden? Everyone's missed the right answer except our friends at *Answers in Genesis*. Eden is buried under piles and piles of sedimentary mud, having been utterly destroyed in the catastrophic global upheaval of the Flood.

"If Christians would accept the straightforward historical account of a worldwide Flood (Genesis 6-8), they could not say that the Tigris/Euphrates Rivers and the Garden were located in the current Mesopotamian region of Iraq. The global Flood would have been so catastrophic that the world before the Flood would have been completely torn apart and reworked, with massive amounts of erosion and tremendous thicknesses of sediment laid down. The pre-Flood world, and thus the Garden, ceased to exist—it perished, as 2 Peter 3:6 confirms. Neither river could have possibly survived such a cataclysmic event.

After the Flood, Genesis 10:10 records that Noah's family and descendants moved from the region of Ararat to the plain of Shinar (the area known as Sumeria/Babylonia), which has two rivers, the Tigris and Euphrates. These rivers, however, cannot be the same as those in Genesis 2. These newer rivers, then and now, run on top of huge thicknesses of Flood-deposited layers of rock."[140]

Though we can in no way presume upon Eden's geography in the light of the apocalyptic *global* upheaval of the Flood, there are tantalising hints that Eden was a radically different eco-system from what we observe today. Evidence shows the pre-Flood world contained a higher oxygen content, double atmospheric pressure and a radiation shield to filter out harmful solar radiation. There was no rain pre-Flood, but a mist **went up from the earth and watered the whole face of the ground.** (Gen 2:6, NKJV) Archaeological finds paint an extraordinary picture:

"Fossil ferns have been discovered the size of trees and horsetails once shot up over thirty feet tall. There were cockroaches about two

---

[140] www.answersingenesis.org/docs2003/1021eden.asp

feet long, as well as crickets, grasshoppers and monstrous spiders that thrived in a land of endless summer. Dragonflies with a three-foot wingspan skimmed over swamps in which eight-foot beavers and sixty-foot cattails flourished. Beetles once grew to be the size of a baseball mitt and climbed up conifers that towered a hundred feet high. The fossil record is replete with examples of immense creatures that flourished in the past. Fossil hunters in Uruguay uncovered the remains of a one-ton rat. The rodent would have been roughly the size of an economy car and its head alone would have been larger than a cow! Huge rodents like the giant guinea pig grew as big as a modern rhinoceros while the ancient rhino grew as big as a two-story building (there is an 18 foot tall rhino in the University of Nebraska Museum.)"[141]

Humans lived stupendous lifespans – 900 years was common (Adam lived 930 years). In *Origins I*, I cover the canopy theory which some scientists believe may account for the longevity, fabled size of pre-Flood humans and creatures, extreme proliferation of vegetation discovered, and one of the destructive forces of the Flood we'll discover later. When lush vegetation and abundant animals and humans are buried and compressed, they turn into… oil! This is one cryptic clue to where Eden might have been. All that iconic footage during the Iraq War of those oil wells burning off… Think about it. For the past one hundred years we've been running the global economy off the ancient sins of our ancestors. And now scientists have discovered huge shale gas deposits on virtually every continent, which some say could keep the global economy going for another 400 years, if the 'fracking' process to extract the gas doesn't do us a mischief first.[142]

The tale of two trees

Among the luscious flora and fauna abounding in Eden, God places two trees that will cause trouble. Do you think God knows they will? Of course He does. These are the Tree of Life and the

---

[141] www.genesispark.com/genpark/large/large.htm

[142] http://www.justmeans.com/Fracking-Finance-Pros-Cons-of-New-Fossil-Fuel-Energy/55972.html

Tree of the Knowledge of Good and Evil. The Tree of Life makes you immortal if you are allowed to eat of it. The Tree of the Knowledge of Good and Evil is an entirely different ball of wax. It's *The Matrix* moment when you must choose between the red and blue pill. God proceeds to give the first ordinance (law) of the Message System to humankind, which goes like this: **"Of every tree of the garden you may freely eat, but of the tree of the knowledge of good and evil you shall not eat, for in the day that you eat of it you shall surely die."** (Gen 2:16-17, NKJV)

Implying there is no death up to this point.

Adam is immortal. So I can't help imagining our first ancestor a little non-plussed by this strange new rule. "Death, LORD? What's that?" But God moves Adam swiftly along, making all the animals in the garden and getting Adam to name them. Adam finds none he would call a pal, so God puts Adam into a deep sleep and creates Eve out of Adam's rib-bone to be his mate. Yes, really. God takes Adam's bride out of his body in the same way Christ will take His bride out of His body. Notice God creates *Eve* from the rib-bone, not *Steve*. God's holy ordination of the male-female relationship is incepted here and built upon as the epic proceeds. Other unions, such as male-male, female-female, male-animal, female-animal, male-smurf, female-smurf are all condemned in the strongest possible terms, and will later be punishable by death.

WHO IS THE DEVIL?
Peeking behind the spiritual veil

The 'Lucifer' hoax

In Genesis 3, the Bible narrative shifts gears into one of the most pivotal chapters, wherein we are confronted by a character in the shape of the *nachash* – the shining one – *aka* the serpent. Today, most mainstream churches are wary of mentioning the Devil for fear of upsetting the Flower Group. The red god has all but been excised out of the apple-blossom seminaries of the Anglicans and rarely makes it to the pulpit in most parishes. When he does, he's allegorical or has a walk-on part in the temptations of Jesus or the slithery snake in Eden.

The Devil is most commonly known as Satan or Lucifer. The problem is, neither of these are his name. *Ha-Satan* is a Hebrew *title,* meaning 'the adversary'. The name 'Lucifer' does not appear anywhere in the original OT Hebrew text - it's actually a *Latin* name. The only place where 'Lucifer' is usually translated is Isaiah 14:12, which reads in the King James Version (KJV):

How art thou fallen from heaven, O Lucifer, son of the morning! How art thou cut down to the ground, which didst weaken the nations!

The Hebrew word translated 'Lucifer' is הֵילֵל – *heylel,* from Strongs 1984, 'a sense of brightness'. It's not a proper name but refers to 'the morning star'. The word 'Lucifer' (*lit.* 'Light-Bearer') was inserted by Jerome into his 4th century translation of the Bible (known as the Latin Vulgate), since in Jerome's view the 'son of the dawn' was the planet Venus, *aka* the morning star, which was known at the time as Lucifer, the Bringer of Light. Unfortunately, Lucifer was morphed into a proper name in demonology by Christians during the Dark Ages to scare the parishioners, and even Luciferians and Mormons were later fooled.

If you step outside Christianity where this hoax has been perpetrated, Hebrew scriptures – the originals for the OT – translate the verse as follows:

How art thou fallen from heaven, O *day-star*, son of the morning! How art thou cut down to the ground, that didst cast lots over the nations!

If you read the passage in context, Isaiah 14:12 ostensibly refers to a lamentation against the pagan king of Babylon, who is a type or model of wickedness, so the analogy with 'Satan' is not bankrupt. The point is that 'Satan' – and we'll use this 'name' for convenience on and off throughout the *Origins* series – *appears to have had his real identity erased because of his rebellion.* Nowhere in the Bible, OT or NT, is this covering cherub given *a name*, whereas Michael and Gabriel are. In the NT, 'Satan' is rendered in the Greek either *diabolos* (meaning false accuser, slanderer, devil), *satana* (the same meaning) or the Hebrew equivalent, אֶל-הַשָּׂטָן, *ha-Satan*. But his theology is intact, so don't go thinking there's no Devil in the Bible. God put him in there and knew he would rebel, and indeed uses him to accomplish His purposes. *God knows and controls everything*, even the horrid bits. Satan and his fallen host are part of our job interview and work experience in preparation for the eternal kingdom. Good cop, bad cop. They're *supposed* to come after us and we're *supposed* to resist and overcome them so God can see how we do. (1 Cor 10:13) Call it character-building.

No, Mavis! ...*The Devil?*

While Satan's frankly an embarrassment to modern powder-puff Churchianity, millions of pagans today accept the existence of super-dimensional wicked entities but transmogrify them into 'wise ones', 'ascended masters', ancient astronauts, aliens, poltergeists or dead old Uncle Bert who 'comes up' in a Ouija session. The common feature of these interpretations is no accountability, no judgment. Thanks to *Harry Potter*, the *Twilight* vampire movies, *Buffy the Vampire Slayer* and a thousand similar Hollywood offerings, agnostics and even atheists are quite comfortable with witches, zombies, ghosts, aliens, werewolves, demons and vampires, but a personal Biblical Devil is a rarity. To the left-wing, *Guardian*-toting, atheist, gay, hip and trendy liberal *chatterati*, Satan is only acceptable *as a person* if he's Jack Nicholson in *The Witches of Eastwick* or Al Pacino in *The Devil's Advocate,* and

154

then he must be lethally suave and snappily dressed with a Samuel Jackson edge on cool. Or else *ha-Satan* is the cartoon imp in the red pyjamas, a will o' the wisp at Halloween, or a mask you can don yourself with which to scare the kids. No judgment, though. And *definitely* no Lake of Fire.

Many theologians cringe that the observational science and history in Genesis should be stirred in with a healthy dollop of demonology, but let that not deter our quest. We're learning that God puts everything in for a reason. It's His pleasure to hide a thing, and a kingly, noble pursuit for us to unearth it, remember? (Prov 25:2). Let's examine the story as originally written, for it yields God's explanation of the manifestation of evil in our society. Moreover, lest we forget, the tale comes from the very Message System that bears the supernatural hallmarks of authorship outside of time, so God expects us to take Adam and Eve and what happens to them *literally,* for our present life and the eternal state to which we shall be consigned will depend upon it.

Hostile takeover – the spirit realm

The greatest being God ever created was a beloved angel with timbrels and pipes in his very being for use in the worship of God. His name has been excised from the record; we don't know what it was. The passage to examine in this regard is Ezekiel 28:11-19, which we'll get to in a minute. Notice that the aforementioned 'Lucifer' passage in Isaiah is ostensibly a lamentation against the king of Babylon but, deeper, a type of Satan, the power behind the kingdom of Babylon. This 'onion peel' effect of Hebrew exegesis (an interpretation discipline known as 'Pardes') is what Biblical hermeneutics is all about, say John Klein and Adam Spears:

"When the ancient Greek philosophers translated Hebrew writings, of both the Old and New Testament, they believed that the text 'worked' on one of two levels only, the *literal* and the *allegorical* – and never both at the same time…. By contrast, Hebrew hermeneutics… recognizes that about 98% of those scriptures operate on four levels simultaneously [emphasis mine]: 1) *p'shat* – direct, simple; 2) *remez* – hinting; 3) *darash* – commentary, comparison; and 4) *sod* – deep, hidden. Hebrew hermeneutics also require the interpreter to agree to a moral standard of unbiased translation. Nothing can be added or subtracted; to the Hebrew mind, scripture is 100 percent true, exactly as written. The goal is to recognize and understand that truth, wherever the hunt might lead."[143]

In other words, the *p'shat* plain text is talking about the wicked king of Babylon in the earlier 'Lucifer' example, but the *remez* and *sod* inferences go far deeper. This multi-layered style of interpretation occurs throughout the Bible, not only via types and models, but through the existence of the ELS (equidistant letter sequence) codes beneath the surface text. Our physical existence on Earth is similar. From the macro structures of the universe to the galaxies, to the Earth realm, down into the minimal and micro structures of the cells, molecules, the nucleotide information on DNA, atoms and sub-atomic particles which comprise everything (Heb 11:3), it's 'turtles-turtles-turtles all the way down', wheels within wheels, until we hit the bounds of our existence, the Planck limits, and that's just the physical stuff. As previously mentioned, quantum physics now believes that our physical reality is but a subset of a far larger reality comprising ten dimensions, maybe more.[144] In effect, we are living in a digital simulation wherein everything has been crafted just so for the human condition. The apostle Paul clarifies with his famous Ephesians passage, wherein he states that there are extra-dimensional creatures and powers behind the scenes manipulating us at every level. He lists out an interesting hierarchy of infernal spirits:

"Finally, my brethren, be strong in the LORD, and in the power of his might. Put on the whole armour of God, that ye may be able to stand against the wiles of the Devil [*diabolou*]. For we wrestle not against flesh and blood, but against <u>principalities, against powers, against the rulers of the darkness of this world, against spiritual wickedness in high places</u>. Wherefore take unto you the whole armour of God, that ye may be able to withstand in the evil day, and having done all, to stand." (Eph 6:10-13)

---

[143] **Klein, J & A Spears** *Devils and Demons and the Return of the Nephilim*, Xulon Press, 2005, pp.13-14
[144] *Scientific American*, June 2005

Living life in the physical in today's scientifically sophisticated 21st century causes many these days to scoff at the merest notion that sentient, intelligent spirits even exist, let alone could be manipulating mankind with supportive or malevolent interventions. Yet from ancient times man has believed such entities inhabited his own reality, possessing the capability of materialising or disappearing at will via portals or spirit 'stargates'. These beings have been described as gods, demigods, watchers, angels, aliens, Titans, Nephilim and the like. Every culture on Earth, past and present, can table a veritable cast of second-division elementals too, such as goblins, faeries, gnomes, trolls, sylphs, werewolves, leprechauns and miscellaneous will-o'er-the-wisps both in their mythology and real-world experience. If none of these exist, then explain the phenomenon. No smoke without fire? Mere ancient superstition? What accounts for similar legends around the globe?

The majority of citizens on Planet Earth today believe in a spirit God or gods. Are we all delusional as Dawkins and his disciples would have us believe? 'Ghost Hunter' specials run continuously on TV. There are 6,000 professional publications on UFOs, 2,000 non-English publications and 1,350 UFO-related periodicals. Fifty-seven percent of Americans believe in UFOs. Fifteen percent believe they have seen a UFO. About 5% of Americans believe they have had an alien abduction experience of some kind, a phenomenon not exclusive to our sometimes hyper-sensitive Atlantic cousins. These days, up to 60% of us complain of a bizarre condition called Sleep paralysis (SP) that strikes at least once a lifetime. Five percent of the population report they suffer regular attacks:

I WOKE UP TO FIND A DEMON AT THE END OF MY BED: ONE WOMAN'S TERRIFYING ACCOUNT OF A SLEEP DISORDER THAT AFFLICTS MILLIONS

Hannah Foster was lying in bed with her eyes open. She could see by the clock that it was 3am, but something was very wrong - she couldn't move a muscle of her body. Even worse, she could sense something pressing down on her and she was struggling to breathe.

Consumed by panic, she tried to scream, but nothing happened. It felt like a nightmare, but she knew that it wasn't, because she was too alert and she recognised her green flowery duvet and the wooden floor of her room.

Being unable to move is disturbing enough in itself, but around 5 per cent of people can also experience horrific visual hallucinations of dark shadows, lights or monstrous figures; a sense of something or someone else in the room; a feeling of pressure on your chest; and difficulty breathing or hearing footsteps or voices.

Some suffers can have hallucinations about movement - such as being touched or dragged down the bed. It has even been suggested as a real cause, due to reports of alien abduction in the U.S.[145]

WAKING NIGHTMARES: HEART POUNDING. FROZEN WITH FEAR. UNABLE TO EVEN SCREAM. THE LITTLE-KNOWN CONDITION MILLIONS ARE SUFFERING FROM

Lying in her bed in the middle of the night, Elizabeth Earle woke with a start to see a menacing dark shadow in the corner of her room. Heart pounding in her ears, she tried to scream. But when she tried to open her mouth, it was impossible.

She was unable to utter a sound — in fact, to her horror she found herself paralysed and unable to move. Finally after what seemed an eternity, but was probably no more than a few minutes, she found herself able to move again. When she looked, the menacing dark shadow had disappeared.

Elizabeth is one of millions who suffer from a terrifying sleep disorder called sleep paralysis, which causes you to partially wake up during a dream, while your body is still 'asleep'. It's also dubbed Old Hag syndrome — because, according to folklore, an old hag would sit on a sleeper's chest, causing shortness of breath and an inability to move, sending nightmares to him or her. [146]

Something's going on and the Bible unabashedly fills us in. Demons, angels and even the Devil inhabit the secret realms of our subconscious in dimensions beyond those we can sense and observe. Throughout the Biblical narrative, numerous apparitions,

---

[145] *Daily Mail,* 8th December 2009
[146] *Daily Mail,* 30th July 2012

spooky events and miracle phenomena are described in plain language and attributed to the spirit realm, such as Isaiah's king of Babylon passage, viewed as one of two major passages on the Devil:

"**Thy pomp** [the king of Babylon's] **is brought down to the grave, and the noise of thy viols** [lyres]**: the worm is spread under thee and the worms cover thee. How art thou fallen from heaven, O day-star, son of the morning! How art thou cut down to the ground, which didst weaken the nations! <u>For thou hast said in thine heart</u>, I will ascend into Heaven, I will exalt my throne above the stars of God: I will sit also upon the mount of the congregation, in the sides of the north: I will ascend above the heights of the clouds; I will be like the most High. Yet thou shalt be brought down to Hell, to the sides of the pit. They that see thee shall narrowly look upon thee and consider thee, saying, 'Is this the man that made the Earth to tremble, that did shake kingdoms; <u>that made the world as a wilderness, and destroyed the cities thereof</u>; that opened not the house of his prisoners?'"** (Isa 14:11-17, Hebrew)

Whoa! However powerful the king of Babylon became, he did not make the world a wilderness. In fact, when was the world ever made a wilderness and the cities brought to nought? Another allusion to that Jeremiah apocalypse? The above text is working on different levels as the language soars. The *p'shat* (direct) interpretation of this passage is that the king of Babylon is wicked because of his unbridled, personal ambition. The *remez* (hinting) interpretation is that, like all wicked rulers, he is a model of the rebellious cherub (Satan) challenging God's holy order. The *darash* (commentary/comparison) is that this type of behaviour has only one end and it's not good. And the *sod* (deep, hidden) revelation is that the king of Babylon is in fact being controlled and manipulated by the rulers of darkness of this world and spiritual wickedness in high places for their own ends.

God says in Malachi 3:6: "**For I am the LORD, I do not change** (NKJV)." Numbers 23:19 states: **God is not a man that He should lie, neither the son of man that He should repent. Hath He said, and shall He not do it? Or hath He spoken, and shall He not make it good?** Another confirming verse can be found in James

159

1:17: "Every good gift and every perfect gift is from above, and cometh down from the Father of lights, <u>with whom is no variableness</u>, neither shadow of turning."

Ha-Satan also does not change. His primary goal is to deceive every human into deserting God, and thus their chance of salvation, by convincing man that there is no ultimate accountability. And *ha-Satan* has resources. A third of the angelic realm followed him in his attempted putsch (Rev 12:4) and all are hard at work sowing deceptions into the Earth realm. God has decreed there will be no repentance for the 'covering cherub' and his hordes, no absolution (Isa 14:15; Eze 28:16-19, Rev 20:10). Yet if they can thwart God's plan, can their own hideous destiny be averted? Is this all fanciful nonsense or hideous truth? We'll uncover unsettling answers to this as we proceed.

Many believers credit Satan with more clout than the Bible infers he actually has, putting him on a par with God. Yet Satan is described as a created being, a person with locality and without the power of omnipresence (Matt 4:11). Neither is *ha-Satan* omniscient nor omnipotent. Yeshua, who made Satan, says he was a liar and murderer from the beginning (FG 8:44).[147] *Ha-Satan's* fall from God's grace through *pride,* the original sin, will thus be the same as the king of Babylon's. The Devil's pride is summarised by those five 'I will' statements:

I will ascend into heaven...

I will exalt my throne above the stars of God...

I will sit also upon the mount of the congregation, in the sides of the north...

I will ascend above the heights of the clouds...

I will be like the most High.

Notice all this comes from the heart (Isa 14:13). Today it's fashionable to tell people, "Hey, just follow your heart". Many pops songs feature "Listen to your heart" encouragements. Then again, guess who was the angel of music? The Creator cautions the opposite, **for the heart is deceitful above all things and desperately wicked: who can know it?** (Jer 17:9) Following your heart is *pride,* the serpent's hiss, *I Did It My Way,* that which

---

[147] Satan's first murders were Adam and Eve.

160

unhorsed Satan from his privileged position in the first place. God abhors pride and will punish those who replace the eternal need for Him with their own temporal self-deification.

The King of Tyrus

Now let's examine the first part of the Ezekiel 28 passage, another which yields some information about Satan. It's a fabulous piece for its language alone, and starts as a lamentation to the king of Tyrus (Tyre), who has much the same problem with pride as the king of Babylon:

Son of man, say unto the prince of Tyrus, Thus saith the Lord GOD; Because thine heart is lifted up and thou hast said, I am a God, I sit in the seat of God, in the midst of the seas, yet thou art a man and not God, though thou set thine heart as the heart of God. Behold, thou art wiser than Daniel; there is no secret that they can hide from thee. With thy wisdom and with thine understanding thou hast gotten thee riches, and hast gotten gold and silver into thy treasures.

By thy great wisdom and by thy traffick hast thou increased thy riches, and thine heart is lifted up because of thy riches. Therefore, thus saith the Lord GOD; Because thou hast set thine heart as the heart of God, behold, therefore I will bring strangers upon thee, the terrible of the nations: and they shall draw their swords against the beauty of thy wisdom, and they shall defile thy brightness.

They shall bring thee down to the pit, and thou shalt die the deaths of them that are slain in the midst of the seas. Wilt thou yet say before him that slayeth thee, I am God? But thou shalt be a man and no God, in the hand of him that slayeth thee. Thou shalt die the deaths of the uncircumcised by the hand of strangers, for I have spoken it, saith the LORD God. (Eze 28: 1-10)

Now notice how the language changes:

Moreover the word of the LORD came unto me, saying, Son of man, take up a lamentation upon the king of Tyrus, and say unto him, Thus saith the LORD God; <u>Thou sealest up the sum, full of wisdom and perfect in beauty</u>. <u>Thou hast been in Eden the garden of God</u>; every precious stone was thy covering, the sardius, topaz, and the diamond, the beryl, the onyx, and the

jasper, the sapphire, the emerald, and the carbuncle, and gold: the workmanship of thy tabrets and of thy pipes was prepared in thee in the day that thou wast created.

Thou art the anointed cherub that covereth; and I have set thee so: thou wast upon the holy mountain of God; thou hast walked up and down in the midst of the stones of fire.

By the multitude of thy merchandise they have filled the midst of thee with violence, and thou hast sinned: therefore I will cast thee as profane out of the mountain of God: and I will destroy thee, O covering cherub, from the midst of the stones of fire.

Thou wast perfect in thy ways from the day that thou wast created, till iniquity was found in thee.

Thine heart was lifted up because of thy beauty, thou hast corrupted thy wisdom by reason of thy brightness: I will cast thee to the ground, I will lay thee before kings, that they may behold thee.

Thou hast defiled thy sanctuaries by the multitude of thine iniquities, by the iniquity of thy traffick; therefore will I bring forth a fire from the midst of thee, it shall devour thee, and I will bring thee to ashes upon the Earth in the sight of all them that behold thee. All they that know thee among the people shall be astonished at thee: thou shalt be a terror, and never shalt thou be any more. (Eze 28:11-19)

There's a lot of information here. Obviously the king of Tyre was not perfect in beauty, neither was he in Eden, but there *was* a perfect cherub who dwelt there until he fell. *Ha-Satan.* The two Ezekiel passages complement one another in that both targets of God's anger are similar, though human and angel. Both are full of wisdom and pride, seeking to elevate themselves above God's rule. We get a rare insight into how Satan must have been before he rebelled. Apparently he was the most beautiful creature Yeshua ever created (*cf.* FG 1:1-3). His very being was studded with priceless stones and musical instruments. Popular tradition holds that he led the worship of God (for '**he defiled his sanctuaries**'). The phrase **Thou art the anointed cherub that covereth** is clumsy King James for a cherub who was granted the highest rank of the heavenly host and given special access by God **into the midst of** the stones of fire, the Holy of Holies in the third heaven, into the very presence of God Himself. Throughout the Bible and popular literature, 'Lucifer' is linked not just with music, mischief and evil, but *false light*. The apostle Paul writes:

"For such are false apostles, deceitful workers, transforming themselves into the apostles of Christ. And no marvel, for Satan himself is transformed into an angel of light. Therefore it is no great thing if his ministers also be transformed as the ministers of righteousness, whose end shall be according to their works." (2 Cor 11:13-15)

Notice the Devil is not light but has to transform himself into an angel of light (*nachash*) in contradistinction to the **true light** of the world, Yeshua *ha Mashiach,* Jesus the Messiah (FG 1:9), the Creator come to Earth in human form to sacrifice Himself for the redemption of mankind (*Immanuel* – lit. 'God is with us'). Bible passages link *ha-Satan* to the reptile which tempts Eve in the Garden. The Devil also crops up as the accuser of the righteous (Rev 12:10), the terrible power behind the Antichrist (Rev 13), **the secret power of lawlessness** (2 Thess 2:7, NIV), and the dragon in Revelation. As you link these passages together, you build up an enthralling picture of the spirit realm behind our own reality and what went wrong from the start.

Quick Angel Q & A

Why did God create angels?

They are hyperdimensional, heavenly messengers who help administer God's creation (Psalms 103:20-22).

What powers do angels have?

The Bible states that humans were created a little lower than the angels (Psa 8:3-5). Angels have access to dimensions beyond our own. They can appear like humans (Acts 12:7-11), eat like humans (Gen 18:8; 19:3; Psa 78:24-25), and take humans by the hand (Gen 19:16). Angels have locality and are not omnipresent. Angels appear capable of possessing emotions like our own. Apparently they walk among us and we have unwittingly entertained them, believing them human (Heb 13:2).

Is it true that humans will judge angels?

Yes, the apostle Paul makes the following fascinating statement:

Do ye not know that the saints shall judge the world? And if the world shall be judged by you, are ye unworthy to judge the smallest matters? Know ye not that we shall judge angels? How much more things that pertain to this life? (1 Cor 6:2-3)

Got Questions has this to say:

"We know that the Greek word for 'judge', *krino*, also means 'to rule or govern'. This strongly implies that we will have authority over the holy angels, for they have no sin for which to be 'judged' in the sense of 'condemned'. Most likely, the meaning of this passage is that believers in Heaven will take part in the judgment of the fallen angels and exercise some authority over the holy angels. Christ has been exalted above all the angels (Eph 1:20-23), and it seems reasonable that those who are in Him and made in His likeness (Rom 8:29; 1 Cor 15:49; Eph 4:24; 1 John 3:2) will share in His authority, including His authority over the angels (Matt 19:28; 2 Tim 2:12; Rev 20:4)." [148]

Here is further scriptural proof that God's elect is being prepared and trained under live-fire conditions in the current Earth Programme for their eventual rule as joint heirs with Christ in the Eternal Kingdom. So they will share His powers. Notice that angels are not made in the image of God and are not redeemed by Christ's sacrifice (Heb 1:14; 2:16).

Do humans have guardian angels?

Some draw an inference from the following statement made by the Creator Himself in Matthew 18:10 that children, and therefore adults, have at least two:

"Take heed that ye despise not one of these little ones; for I say unto you, that in Heaven <u>their angels</u> do always behold the face of my Father which is in Heaven."

An analysis of the pertinent verses on this subject in scripture, however, appears to indicate that God has not assigned specific angels to children or faithful believers, but rather provides angels as a resource to protect and deliver those who fear Him (the

---

[148] http://www.gotquestions.org/judge-angels.html

'chosen' or 'elect') from evil. In this regard, angels are always 'beholding the face of the Father' in readiness for further orders.[149]

How are angels organised?

There are different ranks of angels (see next section). Demons are not the same as fallen angels. Demons appear to be disembodied spirits which take possession of a human or animal only if granted permission to do so by the host (an act of volition/free will). Demons know their time is short and are desperate to escape their fate. They, along with Satan's fallen host, play an extremely active role in today's world in ways that will astonish you.

Who is the mightiest angel?

One stands out above the rest, the enigmatic Angel of the LORD, thought to be the pre-incarnate Yeshua. The Angel of the LORD slew 185,000 Assyrians in one night to stop them attacking Jerusalem (Isa 37:36). Many times in the Bible the Angel of the LORD speaks of Himself as God in the first person, even receiving worship and sacrifice as if unto God.[150] Regular (good) angels go out of their way not to receive worship (Rev 22:8-9).

Did God know the covering cherub would rebel?

Yes, God knows the end from the beginning. He's the only one who does.

So why didn't God just snuff Satan out?

The Earth programme is a proving ground and work experience under live-fire conditions. God wants to train us up to rule with Him as immortals for eternity.[151] Eternity is not a lot of time, it's the absence of time. God created this temporal subset of His much larger reality, gave us a world comprising free will and the keys to it. To the degree that we allow evil in and court it, our world changes. For instance, it's no use blaming God for the Boxing Day tsunami. Seismic activity still results from the

---

[149] Psa 34:7; 91:11-12; Dan 6:22; Zech 1:10; Matt 4:11; 18:10; Luke 16:22; Heb 1:14; 13:2

[150] Gen 16:7-14; Gen 22:11-15; Gen 31:11-13; Exo 3:2-4; Num 22:22-38; Judg 2:1-3; Judg 6:11-23; Judg 13:3-22, etc.

[151] Psa 82:6; 2 Cor 4:16-18; FG 10:34; 17:11

catastrophic upheaval of the Flood, and the Flood was God's judgment on sin. Satan is currently accomplishing God's will in seeing who will rebel and who will stay loyal.

What has Satan got to do with the king of Tyre?

He's the power behind the king of Tyre. As we progress through history, we'll see powerful elemental spirits behind all human empires and powers, good and bad, past and present in this Holy War. Once again, Project Earth is a pale reflection of the true reality. God wants to put us under pressure to discipline us for the purpose of godliness. Under such conditions a man can be trained and measured.

Why did Satan go bad?

God made angels and humans with free will – He did not make robots. The covering cherub had free will and tremendous power and *chose* to abuse it. Choice of pride was Satan's downfall and it came from the heart. **Thou wast perfect in thy ways from the day that thou wast created, till iniquity was found in thee** (Eze 28:15). Many endue Satan with powers on a par or even superior to those of God (Yeshua), but Satan is a created being himself with no powers to create, only deceive. One of his titles is 'the prince of the power of the air' (Eph 2:2). Some theologians surmise that the ancients' belief that demons inhabited the air/atmosphere may not be so wide of the mark in view of a growing realisation that a great delusion is currently being foisted upon the planet *via the air*. More on the UFO/EBE[152] phenomenon later.

A third of the angelic realm followed *ha-Satan* in his attempted *coup* (Rev 12:4). The rebellion failed. Vain, dangerous and Machiavellian, Satan is also known as the 'god of this world' (2 Cor 4:4) and you're on his turf. In Revelation 9:1, his casting out of the 'second heaven' to Earth by God triggers the Great Tribulation. His Earthly rule will come to an end when Yeshua returns to reclaim and enforce His title to the Earth at the Second Coming (Rev 5). Charles Ryrie writes:

---

[152] Unidentified flying object/extra-biological entity

"Satan has been judged by God for his sins, and will be further judged for his sins. There are at least six judgments associated with Satan:

1) He was barred from his original privileged position in Heaven (Ezekiel 28:16)

2) Judgment for his temptation of Adam and Eve (Genesis 3:14-15)

3) At the cross of Calvary (John 12:31)

4) Satan will be barred from Heaven during the tribulation period (Revelation 12:13)

5) Satan will be confined to the abyss during the millennium (Revelation 20:2)

6) At the conclusion of the millennium, Satan will be cast into the lake of fire for all eternity (Revelation 20:10)."[153]

The Bible expects us to take this invisible realm very seriously. Today, in their ruthless quest to thwart God and save themselves, we are told the fallen creatures in the metacosm are counterfeiting all the ways of God to damn Creation and the LORD's redemptive plan for mankind. *Ha-Satan* is the anti-human seeking to destroy all beings made in God's image, especially the most vulnerable among us - babies and children, the sick and depressed, and the elderly. Jews and Christians have also come in for a special type of creepy, inhuman, unreasoning hatred and persecution down through the centuries into our modern age, particularly from those who profess to follow the same beliefs: the Pharisees' persecution of Christ, the apostles and early church; Catholics against Protestants and vice versa. We'll see numerous examples of this particular aspect of the Holy War as we proceed through the *Origins* series.

The Message System tells us the Devil and his angels are destined for the Lake of Fire, which God has prepared in advance for them (Matt 25:41; Jude 6-7). Humans who rebel against Yeshua and fail to repent and accept His pardon will share the same fate. All humans have sinned and come short of the glory of God, so there are none righteous, at least on the scale of purity and perfection God demands for those who will be in His presence for eternity. And that's the whole point. Again, humans will not find

---

[153] **Ryrie, CC** *A Survey of Bible Doctrine,* Moody Press, 1995

themselves in Hell because of their sin, they will find themselves in Hell because they rejected God's provision for their sin. The Creator's offer of amnesty and restoration through the shed blood of His Son provides for this, but only for humans, not for other classes of beings we will shortly examine. God is slow to anger and unwilling that any human should perish (FG 3:14-16). That the LORD is dead serious about this is seen in what the redemption of mankind cost Him: His only Son. God has known from the foundation of the world who are His,[154] who will repent and who won't, yet on Earth time every day, each of us has the free will to choose our ultimate destiny, so the selection process continues.

Angels, angels

Let's fill in a little background, since the spirit/metacosmic realm will figure prominently in what we'll be covering. These days, angels are very popular and seem to be everywhere, pulling people from car wrecks, speaking great wisdoms through human channellers, appearing at shrines, abducting people into UFOs. Hollywood's infested with them. In the New Age movement, you can have your own personal spirit-angel assigned and a little badge to put on your coat in any one of fifteen different angel belief systems, or you make up your own (Col 2:18). Wendy Wallace writes:

"Inundated with the media's ecstatic accounts of angels fluttering everywhere — saving lives, bringing people through crises, escorting them through heavenly realms of wisdom in near-death experiences, tooting their trumpets while hitching rides, manifesting in unplugged TV sets, etc., one might reasonably ask, "Well, what about the good angels?" [155]

What we originally know about angels comes from the Bible, so it serves us to examine the source and do our homework carefully. Apparently angels are ranked in a celestial hierarchy. The apostle Paul writes:

---

[154] Eph 1:4-5; FG 6:44; FG 6:64; FG 15:16; FG 17:2, 9; 2 Tim 2:19; 2 Thess 2:13; Rom 1:7; Isa 49:1,5; Jer 1:5; Gal 1:15; Acts 13:48
[155] Wallace, Wendy, *The Four Horsemen of the Apocalypse*, op. cit.

"**For by him** [Yeshua] **were all things created, that are in Heaven, and that are in Earth, visible and invisible, whether** [they be] <u>**thrones**</u> **or** <u>**dominions**</u> **or** <u>**principalities**</u> **or** <u>**powers**</u>**: all things were created by Him, and for Him, and He is before all things, and by Him all things consist** [are sustained]." (Col 1:16-17; see also Neh 9:6)

Clues are given in both Biblical and Apocryphal literature as to the various kinds: Cherubim, Seraphim, Teraphim, Ophanim. The first two are given in the main scriptures, the other two in ex-canonical works, most notably the discredited Book of Enoch.[156] In their book, *Devils, Demons and the Return of the Nephilim,* John Klein and Adam Spears list out what they believe are the three main types:

Cherubim: also called archangels, are angels of the highest and most powerful order. They literally surround the throne of God. Cherubim have six wings, four faces, and are quite large. The four faces (Rev 4:7, Eze 1:10) are a man's face, a lion's face, a bull's face and an eagle's face. They are also covered with eyes.[157]

Klein and Spears cite six cherubim in total. While these authors make it clear it is only conjecture that *a third of each class* fell, there is equally no evidence that they didn't. The loyal ones are named as follows, only two of which are cited in canonical scripture:

Michael – the Prince of Israel (Dan 10:13, 21; Dan 12:1; Jude 9; Rev 12:7)

Gabriel – the Redeemer of God (Dan 8:16; 9:21; Luke 1:19; Luke 1:26)

Raphael – Healer of God (Talmud, Mishnah, and Apocrypha)

Uriel – Bringer of God's light (Talmud, Mishnah, and Apocrypha)

And the two who fell:

---

[156] Some say the Book of Enoch was considered canon in Yeshua's day and referred to by two of the apostles, though this need not be the case. There is no connection between Enoch and 'his book'. In addition, there are scriptural and form problems with the Book of Enoch which have been widely exposed.

[157] Klein, J & A Spears, *Devils and Demons and the Return of the Nephilim*, op. cit., p.79

169

Ha-Satan – Unnamed, the title means 'The Adversary'. God's Covering Cherub, now 'the Devil' (scripture)

Abaddon – the Angel of Life, now Death (Rev 9:11)

There are various interpretations of the names, role, identities, form and missions of the above, and we'll examine these as we proceed. They can, apparently, transform themselves into human-like figures, albeit with a stunning presence (Luke 1:11-19).

Seraphim: The middle order of angels, sometimes known as the 'Burning Ones' or 'Healing Angels'. According to the scriptures, these angels burn with fire…. As messengers of God, they race back and forth between Heaven and Earth, doing His will.[158]

It is possible that Daniel met a seraph by the banks of the Tigris in Dan 10:5-9:

"Then I lifted up mine eyes, and looked, and behold a certain man clothed in linen, whose loins were girded with fine gold of Uphaz. His body also was like the beryl, and his face as the appearance of lightning, and his eyes as lamps of fire, and his arms and his feet like in colour to polished brass, and the voice of his words like the voice of a multitude. And I, Daniel, alone saw the vision, for the men that were with me saw not the vision, but a great quaking fell upon them, so that they fled to hide themselves. Therefore I was left alone and saw this great vision, and there remained no strength in me, for my comeliness was turned in me into corruption, and I retained no strength. Yet heard I the voice of his words, and when I heard the voice of his words, then was I in a deep sleep on my face, and my face toward the ground."

Ophanim: The word *ophan* means 'wheel' in Hebrew, so the Ophanim have been associated with the description in Ezekiel 1:15-21 and possibly again in the Daniel 7:9 (mentioned as *gagal*, traditionally 'the wheels of gagallin', in 'fiery flame' and 'burning fire') of the four, eye-covered wheels (each composed of two nested wheels), that move next to the winged Cherubim, beneath the throne of God. The four wheels move with the Cherubim because the spirit of the Cherubim is

---

[158] Klein, J & A Spears, *Devils and Demons and the Return of the Nephilim,* op. cit., p.82

in them. These are also referred to as the 'many-eyed ones' in the Second Book of Enoch.[159]

Teraphim: The lowest order of angels. They are the only ones who can take on human form and maintain it for extended periods. You may even entertain them unawares, as indicated in Hebrews 13:2. In addition, teraphim are also denoted by the Hebrew word, *ayir,* which means 'watcher'. Daniel 4:17-18 refers to angels that watch over us and serve as protectors and custodians of men's souls.

Jack Wellman writes:

"Luke 16:22 indicates that when the believer dies, angels bring their spirit to heaven in the presence of God. The word 'angels' in Luke 16:22 is plural, so this gives some indication that more than one angel is involved, just as children have more than one angel (also plural) watching over them (Matt. 18:10). Angels are actually commanded by God to "encamp all around us" and keep us from falling, getting hurt, who have been with us and will be with us "...from this time forth and forever to be with us"... and even strengthen us, and minister to us (Psa 34:7, 91:10-13, 103:21). The angels are also messengers of ours to God and sometimes from God to us (Dan 10, Matt 18:10). And it appears that there are particular angels for particular churches or church ages too (Rev. 1:20)." [160]

The Fall – trouble at the tree

Exactly when Satan's rebellion occurs against God is not clear, though we can logically surmise that it happens sometime between all the angels crying for joy at Creation and the famous incident at the Tree of Knowledge, perhaps several hundred years later. Here, Eve is approached by the cunning serpent who remarks, **"Yea, hath God said, you shall not eat of every tree in the garden?"**(Gen 3:1)

This is a clumsy 1611 King James translation. The New King James records: **"Has God indeed said, You shall not eat of every tree in the garden?"** It's an expression of disbelief. In today's vernacular, this might read, "No way! God never said you couldn't help yourself to every tree in the garden, did He?"

---

[159] http://en.wikipedia.org/wiki/Ophan
[160] www.whatchristianswanttoknow.com/are-guardian-angels-biblical/

Eve replies that this is indeed so, except for the Tree of the Knowledge of Good and Evil, which is off-limits to scrumpers under penalty of death. The *nachash* scoffs: **"Ye shall not surely die! For God doth know that in the day ye eat thereof, then your eyes shall be opened <u>and ye shall be as gods</u>, knowing good and evil."** (Gen 3:4-5)

Notice that the first words out of the serpent's mouth (**"Yea, hath God said...?"**) encourage Eve to doubt God's Word. Satan then tempts her to become as God through disobedience, the same temptation which resulted in Satan's initial expulsion from God's place ('third heaven') to the Devil's realm 'in the air' (outer space - 'second heaven' (*cf.* Isa 14:12-14; Eze 28:12-15; Eph 6:10-12).[161]

The serpent's second statement implies that God is keeping Adam and Eve in a state of ignorance in order to be more powerful than they, but if they eat of the tree they will gain wisdom, discernment and be like God. Eve does not yet comprehend evil, but wisdom seems desirable to her so she eats the forbidden fruit in the hope of having her eyes opened and gets her husband to do the same.

The consequences of betraying God are sin and death – two concepts alien at that time to our two human progenitors – and a loss of man's title to the Earth. Note that the decision to sin is a deliberate act of human will. Adam and Eve had been created in a sinless state (God's image) but now their eyes are opened to their own nakedness and shame, and in what seems a huge overreaction, God curses Creation with the Second Law of Thermodynamics and sin enters the world through Adam's line.

The implications of the Tree of the Knowledge of Good and Evil are more than just about fruit, *they're fascinating*. God must have known Adam and Eve would disobey Him and defer to the serpent. Did God fail to understand the possible consequences of giving His created beings free will, that this might happen? Hardly.

---

[161] The first heaven – Earth's atmosphere where the birds fly (Deut 11:17; Deut 28:12; Judg 5:4; Acts 14:17). The second heaven – outside the confines of Earth in inner and outer space (Psa 19:4,6; Jer 8:2; Isa 13:10). The third heaven – 'Paradise'. God's dwelling place, where the apostle Paul was caught up to (Deut 10:14; 1 Kings 8:27, 30; Psa 2:4; Matt 5:16; 2 Cor 12:2-4).

The Designer knows all things. It had to be in line with His agenda for Project Earth, the entire programme of which occurs within spacetime, but a blink on God's watch. Clearly, if you tell a child there's a tree in the garden and 'Don't touch it if you know what's good for you', the first thing the child will do is... you guessed it. God certainly lamented Adam and Eve's actions but was not surprised. In fact, God can never be surprised – it's another attribute of His perfect nature. If you think it through, it's blessed news for us that our Creator can never be surprised by anything we do.

There's another insight into the Fall. Adam knew the ramifications of eating from the tree; he had no reason to doubt God's word. Adam and Eve were under the law not to eat of the tree. They only had one rule to keep and they broke it. But notice that Adam himself was not deceived (1 Tim 2:14). He knew Eve was going to die for her transgression, *and yet he ate the fruit anyway to share her fate*. He could quite easily have said, "You ate of the tree, Eve. Your problem, honey. No way am I going the same way! Hey, I'll pray for you." Adam didn't. *He made a conscious, voluntary decision (free will!) to share Eve's fate*, no matter the consequences. In fact, Adam loved Eve so much that he deliberately made himself sinful and died for her *when he didn't need to*. Remind you of Anyone? To the ancient Greeks and modern Christians, prophecy is all about prediction and fulfilment. To the Jews, both ancient and modern, prophecy is not only prediction and fulfilment, *it's also pattern*. The Fall of Man is a pattern, a model, a type, of Yeshua to follow. Eve is a type of the Church. Notice also that the First Adam, a servant created to tend God's garden, voluntarily breaks the law in his desire to become as God (the transgression). Jesus, **the Last Adam** (1 Cor 15:45), is God voluntarily becoming a servant to keep the Law and restore man (the redemption).

Declaration of Holy War

So what was the Fall exactly? It appears Satan gains dominion over the Earth ('the prince of this world') in leading Adam and Eve into sin against God. One theory is that the four spacetime dimensions (length, width, height and time) were fractured from at least another six and thereafter subjected to entropy (decay). Interestingly, God curses *the ground* for Adam's sake; now man will have to work. God also curses the serpent for his slithering duplicity; upon his belly shall he go *henceforth*, implying that the serpent had been moving about differently hitherto – sheesh, *upright?*

"And I will put enmity between thee and the woman, and between thy seed and her seed; it shall bruise thy head, and thou shalt bruise his heel." (Gen 3:15)

This is *the* pivotal verse in the entire scriptures and the first prophecy of the coming Redeemer who shall be bruised by this enmity (*cf.* Isa 53:10). Read the verse a few times and see if you spot the detail – most don't. This is the declaration of Holy War by God on *ha-Satan,* (not the other way round!), wherein mankind's Kinsman-Redeemer – God made human/flesh – will be born of the 'woman's seed' (virgin birth) precisely to remain free of God's curse down the male line to qualify as the unblemished sacrifice for sin. *Ha-Satan* will do everything possible to destroy the bloodline of the Messiah to prevent this Seed from being born, an event which will set in motion the rebellious cherub's own fate and eventual destruction in the Lake of Fire. There's another important insight here. God's God, so He could equally have mashed up the snake, tossed it in the bin, restored Adam and Eve to His good graces, and everyone lives happily ever after. *God doesn't.* Because all this is part of our on-the-job training (Rom 15:4).

Did you spot the detail in the above Gen 3:15 verse? *There are two seeds mentioned.* The other seed is *Ha-Satan's seed.* This Holy War is between two seeds at enmity: the Seed of the woman (Messiah and His antecedents) and the seed of the serpent (Antichrist and his antecedents). When Satan rebelled, desiring to usurp God's creation and **'be like the Most High'** (and once again notice his rebellion was the result of God's incredible gift of free will), he took a third of an innumerable host of angelic superbeings with him in his revolt and subsequent banishment (*cf.* Heb 12:22; Rev 12:3-9). *So he is outnumbered two to one.* He intends making up the numbers *by producing from his own seed.* How on earth do bad angels – even wicked cherubim – do that? We'll find out.

This book you are reading is entitled *Origins 2 - Holy War*. Shortly, in the future – could be next week, next year, or in a decade's time – there will be an official disclosure announcement made by governments and organised religion around the world as to the 'truth' of our origins. The 'proof' they will provide will be extraordinary and immensely compelling to the unwary, accompanied by all lying signs and wonders. Extraordinary preparations have already been, and are being made behind the scenes for this clarion event, the revealing of what scripture terms 'The Lie'[162] (2 Thess 2:5-12). This will be a delusion so powerful and convincing, that even those people of God, if possible, will be taken in and deceived. More about this as we go.

On so many levels, Genesis 3:15 sums up the central theme which runs throughout God's Message System, from the ancient dawn of Adam's genesis down the centuries of bloody history to modern conflicts which splash onto newspaper front pages and TV newsflashes today. A Holy War fought between the misguided human righteous and wicked in the physical Earth realm with knives, swords and bullets on the one hand, but in the spiritual realm (i.e. metacosm: hyperdimensional first and second heavens and the Earth), where the real conflict rages, the warriors are superhuman and their weaponry comprises far more destructive ordnance. The Holy War declared by God will see repeated attempts by the seed of the serpent (descendants/spiritual followers of evil) to wipe out God's people. From Nimrod to Haman to Rome's Caligula, Titus, Vespasian and Hadrian, to the Vikings, to the medieval church's Inquisition, to Stalin and Hitler, to modern-day Iran, radical ISIS-style Islam and Hamas, the Holy War plays out not only in the metacosm, not only in the geopolitical arena, *but also in our personal lives*. The Seed of the woman will eventually feature God Himself entering the physical realm as a human to assure the righteous of victory. History is therefore His Story, a hefty chunk of which God has written in advance for our benefit to advise us of the War and its outcome *for*

---

[162] Most translations unfortunately render this 'a lie'. The Greek is very specific. It's THE Lie.

eternity. God takes His Word extremely seriously, placing it even above His own name (Psa 138:2). Will we read it or scoff?

The Bible actually states that in the last days scoffers will come, and describes their behaviour in very specific ways (2 Peter 3:3-7) Atheists have always scoffed at God with zero understanding of what death is, what will happen to them when their heart stops beating, what lies beyond the veil, or who controls their software forever (Matt 16:26). When each of us is but a single heartbeat from that forever, and we have already been served notice that *we are without excuse* (Rom 1:20), might we trouble ourselves to examine God's extraordinary Word for the gameplan, if only to save each of us a sorry "Oh God, I had NO IDEA!" moment just the other side of death's door? Thomas à Kempis puts it like this:

"Very soon it will be over with you here, then see how things stand. Today we are, and tomorrow we are gone. And when we are taken out of sight, we soon pass out of mind. Oh, the dullness and hardness of our hearts that only think of the present and do not look forward more to the future. This being the case, you ought to master yourself in every act and thought as if you were to die today. If you had a good conscience, you would not fear death so much. It would be better to guard against sins than to run away from death. If you are not prepared today, how will you be ready tomorrow? …When that final hour does come, you will begin to think quite differently about all your past life, and you will be exceedingly sorry that you were so careless and remiss.

The present time is very precious. Now are the safe days. Now is the acceptable time. But how sad that you do not spend this time well while you have the strength to gather the merit, which will allow you to live forever! The time will come when you will wish for one day or one hour for changing your ways, and I do not know whether you will get it." [163]

Consequences of the Fall

Unto the woman [God] said, "I will greatly multiply thy sorrow and thy conception; in sorrow thou shalt bring forth

---

[163] **Kempis, Thomas à** *The Imitation of Christ,* translated by William C Casey, Ave Maria Press, 1989

children; and thy desire shall be to thy husband, and he shall rule over thee."

And unto Adam He said, "Because thou hast hearkened unto the voice of thy wife, and hast eaten of the tree, of which I commanded thee, saying, 'Thou shalt not eat of it': cursed is the ground for thy sake; in sorrow shalt thou eat of it all the days of thy life. Thorns also and thistles shall it bring forth to thee; and thou shalt eat the herb of the field. In the sweat of thy face shalt thou eat bread, till thou return unto the ground; for out of it wast thou taken: for dust thou art, and unto dust shalt thou return." (Gen 3:16-19)

The above verses immediately follow the pivotal Gen 3:15 declaration of war by God on Satan. God is now addressing the consequences that will befall Adam and Eve for their disobedience. Richard Ritenbaugh comments:

"A human female is unique among mammalian creatures in this respect [of childbirth]. Animal females generally bear their young without pain and rarely sicken and die during or from the experience. Women, on the other hand, always experience pain and grief throughout their pregnancies – from morning sickness to contractions – and have historically had a very high mortality rate from childbirth. Better nutrition and hygiene have cut the numbers of deaths dramatically, but the pain and grief remain." [164]

The Creator now curses the Earth because of Adam's failure to obey simple orders. Here we are introduced to the thorns and thistles idiom as a type of sin. This model will be used throughout the Message System in association with 'snares' even up to God Himself bearing mankind's sin on the cross in the form of a crown of thorns (Matt 27:29). God's judgment on Adam and Eve has been viewed by some scholars as harsh, yet from God's perspective the ramifications of sin are more grievous than we can possibly imagine. The Creation is now visibly skewed in a way that would have been immediately evident to our two human progenitors. The shock of their predicament would have been disorientating. Bewildering. Total.

---

[164] www.theberean.org: Genesis-3:16 note

Aware for the first time of their 'nakedness', Adam and Eve sew together coverings of fig leaves and hide from God in the Garden. God, being omniscient, finds them anyway after calling out, **"Where are you?"** (Gen 3:9, NIV).[165] My personal suspicion is that the traditional picture conjured up by this scene of Adam and his missus clasping hands over genitals in mortal shame at their disobedience masks a far more profound event occurring. Some scholars speculate that Adam and Eve's original immortal and hyperdimensional state clothed them in light, and now bereft of it, they realised something was seriously wrong.

Now, confronting them with their own "Oh God, I had NO IDEA!" moment, the Creator does something most people miss. He *personally* makes Adam and his wife two tunics of skin to clothe them (Gen 3:21), thus carrying out the first animal sacrifice to atone for man's sin. *Notice God does all the work.* The two new mortals doubtless just stand there and gawp. Perhaps the animal was a lamb, sacrificed for the sins of man (and woman) - we're not told. Author Grant Jeffrey records that what *has* been found ELS-encoded behind the Hebrew text, commencing with the last Hebrew letter *heh* (ה) in the previous verse (Gen 3:20) and counting forward every ninth letter, is *Yoshiah* – "He will save" (*cf:* Matt 1:21).[166]

Here is God's predicament. The Designer's nature is perfection. God's reconciliation with man henceforth will be via substitutionary atonement with the shedding of an unblemished animal's *innocent blood*, necessitating 'judgment upon the innocent to provide a covering for the guilty'.[167] God will not violate His perfect nature by nodding at imperfection or acquitting the guilty. His nature of perfection demands justice to vindicate His righteousness and to defend the moral order of His Creation against sin. The punishment for sin is death. Most today don't even give sin a second thought, much less recognise the concept after society's wildly successful unnaming of evil. Today, if it feels good Just Do It. But God does not change (Mal 3:6). God has decreed that

---

[165] i.e."Where is your heart at?"
[166] **Jeffrey, Grant R** *The Signature of God,* Waterbrook Press, 2002, p.266
[167] Heyford, Jack, *Spirit-Filled Life Bible,* op. cit., p.10

each of our sins must be paid for in the heavy coin of *innocent blood*. The scriptures declare that without the shedding of innocent blood there is no remission of sins (Heb 9:22). It's a tough concept for us to relate to in this day and age of PETA and animal rights, yet if God's the boss then He's free to do what He wants with His creation. We are not in possession of the big picture about the eternal consequences of sin. I have little doubt that if we were, we'd be horrified. And while animal activists abhor the abuse of innocent animals like all right-thinking people, most are curiously silent about the millions of innocent babies murdered in the holy of holies of their mother's womb since 1973 through abortion. Conclusion? God's not looking for any input from us on how to run His universe, and He's dead serious about justice and His offer of mercy. Once again, what did the Creation cost the Creator? Six days. What did the redemption of mankind cost Him? His only Son.

Sent packing

Adam and Eve are banished from Eden – here is the reason: **And the LORD God said, "Behold, the man is become <u>as one of Us</u>, to know good and evil. And now, lest he put forth his hand and take also of the Tree of Life, and eat, and live forever –"** (Gen 3:22).... God does not finish the sentence in His haste to get as much distance between Adam and Eve and the Tree of Life as possible. If they eat of the Tree of Life they will become immortal in a sinful state. It is of paramount importance to God that this does not happen. He banishes the pair from Eden and posts cherubim with a flaming sword at the east of the Garden to block access to the Tree of Life. One is tempted to ask why super-angels are required to stop Adam and Eve gaining the tree when any old angel would do. The answer could be: Perhaps you use super-angels to stop another super-angel from accessing the Tree to gain immortality in a sinful state. Jack Heyford comments:

"Beyond the tragedy of man's loss, two other facts unfold. First, through his disobedience to God and submission to the Serpent's suggestions, man's rule has been forfeited to the Serpent. Rev 12:9 [cf. 20:2] verifies that the spirit employing the snake's form was Satan himself. The domain originally delegated to man now falls to Satan, who becomes administrator of this now-cursed realm. The Serpent's 'seed' and 'head' indicate a continual line (seed) of evil offspring extending Satan's rule (head). However, a second fact offers hope. Amid the tragedy of this sequence of events, God begins to move redemptively, and a plan for recovering man's lost estate is promised (Gen 3:15) and set in motion with the first sacrifice."[168]

Satan now has rule over the Earth after man's fall. In the Bible, the 'god of a thousand names' is variously referred to as **the old serpent, the dragon, the prince of this world, god of this world, prince of power of the air** and **the ruler of darkness of this world.**[169]

In the temptation of Christ in Matthew 4, Satan offers Yeshua all the kingdoms of the world in return for His worship. There are a couple of observations to note here. Firstly, this is a confrontation between a created being in superhuman form, *ha-Satan*, and Satan's Creator, Yeshua, in human form. Most miss the irony of the occasion. Secondly, notice that Jesus never disputes that the kingdoms of the Earth are Satan's to give away – the Devil's offer makes no sense if the claim is false. If God is omnipotent, and He is, then *God has allowed* Satan control of the Earth to deceive the unwary and propel the righteous to Himself. Once again, this is clear evidence of the training programme underway.

S A Cranfill wonders why Satan would be made **prince of this world** *after* he had sinned unless he was **prince of the world** *before* he sinned. The traditional atheist/agnostic argument that 'if there were a God, he wouldn't allow two world wars' is done to death since man has free will in a world under control of the Anti-Human, who is dead set on providing us with every technological advantage to create more efficient weapons with which to kill not only ourselves but everyone else created in the image of God. Daily each of us must make the choice to imitate God's ways and be a good man/woman or not. Unseen forces in the metacosm attempt to manipulate each of us via our volition – our choices. You know

---

[168] Ibid.
[169] FG 12:31; 14:30; 2 Cor 4:4; Eph 2:2; 6:12; Rev 20:2

they do. You do have those thoughts. Do you take every evil one into captivity to stop it blooming, or do you play around with it for a while to see where it takes you? Holy versus unholy. Pure versus profane. Welcome to the Holy War. And you're in it up to your eyeballs.

Death in the fields

After the Fall in Eden it all starts to unravel. Destined for eventual death, Adam and Eve move away and have their first two children, named Cain and Abel.[170] Each child of Adam and Eve will be born with Adam's fallen nature – a predilection to rebel against God and do evil. Of course, the idea that man's nature is inherently wicked is challenged by the modern atheist/materialist, yet who has to teach a child to be naughty? They have that down from the start. We're not spiritually evolving into anything better by ourselves. History clearly reveals this, as do the volumes of laws on the statute books of nations around the world to keep our unruly nature in order. If we were evolving into better beings as time passed, we should be seeing fewer laws to control us, not more!

Anyway, Cain becomes a tiller of the ground while Abel keeps sheep. In presenting their atonement offerings to the LORD for their sin one day, watch what happens. Abel's gift of the firstborn of his flock is accepted by God while Cain's gift of fruit is rejected on the grounds that it is not *bloodworthy*.

And the LORD said unto Cain, "Why art thou wroth? And why is thy countenance fallen? If thou doest well, shalt thou not be accepted? And if thou doest not well, sin lieth at the door.

---

[170] "All we are told about Adam's offspring is that the first son was named Cain, the second Abel [Genesis 4:1-2], then after Abel's murder, another son named Seth was 'begotten when Adam was 130 years old'. After that, Adam 'begat sons and daughters' [Genesis 5:3-4]. This same passage also tells us that Adam lived for 930 years [Genesis 5:5]. Therefore, according to Scripture, Adam and Eve's family consisted of sons Cain, Abel and Seth, plus a minimum of two other sons and two daughters, giving a total of seven children. However, accepting that Adam, and likely Eve, lived for 930 years, seven children would be the minimum number, but does this seem reasonable?" - http://www.creationmoments.com/content/how-many-children-did-adam-and-eve-have

And unto thee shall be his desire, <u>and thou shalt rule over him</u>." (Gen 4:6-7) [God is telling Cain to overcome!]

There are two essential points being made by God here. Cain's gift is rejected on the grounds that it came from the cursed ground and comprised the fruits of his own labour, which can never atone (pay the penalty) for sin. So the first message is this: man cannot *atone* for his own sin by works, it must be paid for by the shed blood of an innocent. And God Himself will provide the Lamb.

Yet, in the previous verses, God is also telling Cain to *overcome* (not atone for) sin in his own life by doing good. The (sometimes forceful) application by the believer of good works to drive out sinful behaviour in his day-to-day strivings is a common theme throughout the Message System.[171] Do not confuse this with *atoning* for sin by works. Religion is man's attempt to cover his sin by works before a sinless Creator – the most futile endeavour. God will offer a paid redemption for man's sin as a free gift, *but only for those who claim it as a free gift by faith.* By just believing. Attempting to add to God's gift of redemption by working the dirt off ourselves is actually *blasphemy,* but our inward change (repentance) should be reflected by our outward desire henceforth to do good for others. Notice how God (Jesus) models the eventual sacrifice of Himself, the Lamb of God, on the *firstborn* of Abel's flock.

Here also is the first of many passages on the theme of 'overcoming'. God knows we will be tempted by sin, but we must overcome our fallen nature – that's part of the job interview and training programme; the test of life. We can only do this with God's help by asking Him. *This forges a relationship between man and God.* Cain doesn't do this. Later in the fields, he kills his brother in a fit of jealousy. When God finds out, Cain's punishment is to wander the Earth. The condemned man is mortified:

"**Behold, thou hast driven me out this day from the face of the Earth, and from Thy face shall I be hid. And I shall be a fugitive and a vagabond in the Earth. And it shall come to pass, <u>that every one</u> that findeth me shall slay me.**" (Gen 4:14)

---

[171] Gen 4:7; Psa 34:14; Psa 37:27; Dan 4:27; Matt 3:8-10; Luke 13:3,5; Acts 26:20; Rom 12:21; Gal 5:24; Eph 5:1; Titus 1:16; 1 Pet 3:10; 2 Pet 3:9; Rev 2:26

Adam and Eve's reaction to this nightmare goes unrecorded, but we can imagine how they felt. Their secondborn is murdered. Their firstborn is a fugitive killer. God sets his mark upon Cain to protect him and makes known that whoever kills Cain will suffer vengeance sevenfold (notice the above underlined phrase implies that Adam and Eve fathered other children). Cain flees eastward and thereafter disappears from the record, multiplying his descendants. These become tent-dwellers and herdsmen and one even builds a city. Where did Cain get his wife from? He married his sister. No genetic load. Once again, Adam had sons and daughters other than Cain and Abel.

Bronze and iron technology are mentioned in Gen 4:22, so Earth's early civilization is already advanced, having benefited from direct interaction with the Designer and angelic realm. *Ha-Satan* also follows Cain and his descendants, whose cultures later degenerate into slayings, pride and immorality.

Longevity of the patriarchs

Then Adam and Eve have another son, Seth. **"For God hath appointed me another seed instead of Abel, whom Cain slew."** (Gen 4:25). This time the seed 'takes'. Seth's descendants become the lineage through which mankind's hope for the future Seed of the woman and mankind's own redemption lie. Satan has his eye on this lot and will play havoc with them. There are ten patriarchs prior to the Flood and their lifespans are immense. They beget numerous sons and daughters. The patriarchs, and the meaning of their Hebrew names, are listed as:

Adam ('man') lives 930 years
Seth ('appointed') lives 912 years
Enosh ('mortal') lives 905 years
Cainan ('sorrow') lives 910 years
Mahalalel ('the blessed God') lives 895 years
Jared ('shall come down') lives 962 years
Enoch ('teaching') lives 365 years
Methuselah ('his death shall bring') lives 969 years
Lamech ('the despairing') lives 777 years (Gen 5:1-31)
Noah ('rest') lives 950 years (Gen 9:28)

Many Jews and Christians alike are frankly embarrassed about the lifespans, believing the Bible to be in error at this point. However, scientific evidence indicates that the pre-Flood era was a radically different eco-system to today's, in which such lifespans may well have been possible. In *Origins I*, I cover the research behind why some scientists believe that that not only was the Earth pressurised to two atmospheres prior to the Flood, but that the planet may have had some sort of crystalline hydrogen shield/canopy to protect it from solar radiation. Certainly many archaeological finds reveal improbable tropical forests under today's tundra, inexplicably large fossils and animal remains, and huge skeletal remains, not only of dinosaurs but of humans.

When you plot these lifespans given in Genesis, you discover that Noah almost got to know Adam. In fact Noah's father, Lamech, was a contemporary of Adam's. *The Bible expects us to take this information literally*, and Jesus, Moses and Abraham did so, in spite of modern efforts to allegorise Genesis. What were those pre-Flood campfire chats like? How much knowledge could one man amass in a nine-hundred-year lifespan, especially one instructed by God and the angelic realm personally?

Notice the comparatively short lifespan of Enoch, the *seventh* patriarch (God's number). Not much is known about him. There is a 'Book of Enoch' kicking around today but there is no evidence this was penned by the pre-Flood patriarch and, as previously mentioned, is not considered inspired scripture due to a number of formatting and content issues. It is useful, however, for vocabulary contemporary with the second century BC, so scholars do refer to it, and it does give an insight into what was believed by some at that time.

Anyway, back to the real Enoch. In the NT, the apostle Paul writes: **"By faith, Enoch was taken away so that he did not see death, 'and was not found because God had taken him'; for before he was taken he had this testimony, that he pleased God."** (Heb 11:5, NKJV). That's it. In Genesis, nothing else is known of Enoch other than he **"walked with God; and he was not, for God**

took him." (Gen 5:24)[172] In other words, one minute there is righteous Enoch, the next, he's gone. Translated. Morphed into the Field's energy flux. Raptured. The good sometimes go young, if you can call three hundred and sixty-five years old 'young'. The prevailing view is that, because of his righteousness, Enoch was spared what Earth was rapidly degenerating into, and whisked off to destinations unknown. This 'rapture' phenomenon (Lat. *rapiere* – 'stealing away', 'carry off', 'snatch away') is hyperdimensional in its description and crops up every so often with Biblical figures as we proceed. Again, it becomes a type throughout the scriptures - a strange concept not often taught in the denominational churches but entirely Biblical and a blessed necessity as we'll see. Enoch's rapture is thus the first type or foreshadowing of the main rapture (Gr. *harpazo*) of the Church covered in the New Testament (NT), where millions of believers, just before the Great Tribulation, are taken off the surface of the Earth in the last days 'in the twinkling of an eye' to 'meet the LORD in the air' (triumphing over Satan's aerial domain), doubtless leaving global chaos behind them. Theologians uncomfortable with this bizarre but fully scriptural teaching attempt to undermine the *harpazo* by complaining that there's no mention of it in the Old Testament (OT). They would be wrong.[173]

Back to the pre-Flood patriarchs. The name-roots of these ten, when linked together, spell out the Designer's plan in the form of the Christian Gospel, squirreled away in the names of the first ten patriarchs of the Jewish Torah! **Man appointed mortal sorrow. The blessed God shall come down teaching that His death shall bring the despairing rest.**[174] Chuck Missler comments:

---

[172] There are also two curious verses in Jude 14-15 in the NT attributed to Enoch, amounting to the first chronological prophecy of the Second Coming of Christ in history.

[173] Some say the word 'rapture' does not appear in the English Bible and they'd be right. It's actually found in the Latin Vulgate translation of 1 Thess 4:13-18. See also Matt 16:27 and 1 Cor 15:51-53. A full treatment of the *harpazo* and its foreshadowing in the OT is covered later in the *Origins* series.

[174] www.khouse.org, *Beyond Coincidence*, audio presentation

"There is no way you will ever convince me that a group of Jewish rabbis contrived to hide a summary of the Christian gospel in a geneaology in the Torah…. This is evidence of design and an anticipation of what's coming…. The New Testament is in the Old Testament concealed, and the Old Testament is in the New Testament revealed. The Bible is an integrated message system… every detail, every number, every place-name is there by deliberate design. If that can be demonstrated, then the conclusion is that the origin of this message is outside our dimensions of time and space."[175]

The above name-roots are a surprising *remez* which prefigures what the central character in the Bible is all about: God coming to Earth as a man, fully human, fully God, to pay the price for sin so *He* can know *us* for eternity.

What? All because Adam and Eve ate some apples?

Actually apples aren't mentioned at all in Genesis 3. And by the time you get to Noah's life a thousand years after the Creation, there's a lot more wickedness staining Planet Earth than just a fruit fetish. Despairing these venerable patriarchs must have grown as they gazed about at the perfect world God had created, which was now being frothed into hate as Satan pursued his goal to thwart God and **'become like the Most High'**.

And it all ends in tears.

---

[175] www.khouse.org, "The Creation and the Fall of Man", *Learn the Bible in 24 Hours.*

THE DOOMED EARTH
Why did God do it?

"And it came to pass, when men began to multiply on the face of the Earth and daughters were born unto them, that the sons of God saw the daughters of men that they were fair; and they took them wives of all which they chose.... There were giants [Heb: *Nephilim*] in the Earth in those days, and also after that, when the sons of God came in unto the daughters of men, and they bare children to them, the same became mighty men [Heb: *ha-Gibborim*] which were of old, men of renown." (Gen 6:1...4)

Welcome to some of the stickiest verses in the Bible. To the conservative Christian ladies of the Sunday Bible group, these verses mean that the godly sons of Seth grabbed wives of the wicked daughters of Cain and had kids with them (known as the 'Lines of Seth' or 'Sethite' theory). Nothing particularly controversial about that, apart from the fact that this isn't what the Bible teaches.

The Sethite explanation is preferred today because the other view, the one held by the apostles, early church fathers and antiquity, is frankly *appalling*. The above four verses are crucial to understand, so it's worth re-reading them several times to get the full meaning, for in them lies the reason for the worldwide destruction of the Flood, and why God does some strange, unsettling things later in the Bible. Some scholars go further and state that an incomplete understanding of these verses in Genesis 6 leaves much of the Old Testament and most of the New completely baffling to the reader, especially in relation to the Creator's judgment on sin. I don't disagree with that assessment.

Read the above passage again and something more sinister emerges when you learn that 'sons of God' is translated from *B'ni ha-Elohim* (בְּנֵי הָאֱלֹהִים), which *always* refers to direct creations of God, i.e. angels (*cf.* Job 1:6, 2:1 38:7), or in this case, *fallen* angels finding the daughters of men to be beautiful, coming down and having sex with them.

The ensuing progeny is impressive, described as 'giants, men of renown, mighty'. The Hebrew word for the giants (Gen 6:4) is *ha-nephiylim* הַנְּפִלִים which comes from the Hebrew root, *naphal,* or 'fallen ones'. The Greek Septuagint translation is *gigantes,* which actually means 'earth-born' though they are really big too. Notice another term used. The Earth-born giants became the mighty ones – *ha-Gibborim.*

The expression 'sons of God' (Gen 6:2) is reminiscent of the Creation account in Job 38:1-7 when all the *B'ni ha-Elohim* cried out for joy. Clearly the 'sons of God' mentioned at the Creation could not have been humans since Adam had not been created yet. *B'ni ha-Elohim* almost always refers to the angelic realm in the sense of direct creations of God. Of course, Adam and Eve were direct creation of God too, whereas we are the sons and daughters of Adam.

In the NT, Jesus's brother Jude tells us about wicked **angels which kept not their first estate, but left their own habitation** [*oiketerion*], **He hath reserved in everlasting chains under darkness unto the judgment of the great day. Even as Sodom and Gomorrah, and the cities about them in like manner, giving themselves over to fornication, and going after strange flesh, are set forth for an example, suffering the vengeance of eternal fire.** (Jude 6-7).

Notice this word *oiketerion.* The only other place in the NT where *oiketerion* appears is in 2 Cor 5:2. Here Paul uses it to describe the heavenly body all believers will be clothed in for eternity. The unsavoury view of Genesis 6, therefore, when coupled with Jude 6-7, tells of fallen angels who discarded their heavenly bodies expressly to come down to Earth, steal those wives of humankind whom they found beautiful, and have sex with them. The resultant human/angel hybrids were giants, 'men of renown', 'Nephilim' before the Flood, and afterwards referred to as Nephilim ('fallen ones'), Rephaim ('the dead ones'), Emim ('the fearsome ones') or the giants of Anak, or Anakim ('the long-necked ones'), who so terrified the spies Moses sent into Canaan prior to Israel's invasion centuries later. On this latter occasion, these scouts return to their commander ashen-faced:

"The land, through which we have gone to search it, is a land that eateth up the inhabitants thereof; and all the people that we saw in it are men of a great stature. And there we saw the giants, the sons of Anak, which come of the giants [Nephilim]: and we were in our own sight as grasshoppers, and so we were in their sight." (Num 13:32-33)

These were huge humanoid creatures, the spawn of the serpent's seed. There are legends everywhere of giant men and their remains, some of which I covered in *Origins I*. We are also told in Genesis 6:4 that, although the Flood wiped out all but eight people,[176] this weird, angelic intermarriage with humans continued after the Inundation (**'and also after that...'** (Gen 6:4; Num 13:28,33; Deut 2:20-21). At the risk of labouring the point: since all previous, air-breathing giants had been destroyed in the Flood, Gen 6:4 is evidence that Satan reinitiated the Nephilim programme post-Flood, and more angels 'came down' to do their dirty deeds among 'the daughters of men'.

In effect, Satan's ploy appears to kill two birds with one stone: firstly to create more soldiers to even up the numbers for the Holy War against God and His loyal angelic realm, and secondly to pollute the human gene-pool, take over mankind and thwart the birth of the Seed of the woman.

Angels, fallen or otherwise, cannot 'marry' in heaven according to the Creator Himself (Matt 22:29-30), though they can apparently have sex if they cast off their heavenly bodies (*oiketerion*). I have no idea what this involves. The sin described in Jude 6-7 is clearly sexual in nature and, judging by the severity of the penalty, more than 'mere' human fornication. Though there is resistance to this interpretation today among those who eschew the spiritual warfare aspects of the Bible, a lot of what follows can be clearly understood in the light of the Angels Theory of Genesis 6 which, it must be said, was the widely-held view of early church fathers such as Irenaeus, Athenagoras, Justin and Quintus Tertullian. All were clear that this demonic sexual pollution of the human race was Satan's attempted *coup-de-grace* of God's new creatures (humans)

---

[176] Noah and his wife, plus their three sons and their wives.

189

using the *B'ni ha-Elohim*,[177] and also the singular reason why God took the fateful, unique decision to bring down the Flood to exterminate all air-breathing flesh, apart from those creatures and humans kept safe on the Ark.

Dirty genes

Genesis 6:9-12 tells us that Satan's corruption of humanity was so far advanced that only Noah remained **'perfect in his generations'** (Gen 6:9). We know from what happened after the Flood that Noah was not perfect; the phrase must refer to his biological purity. Sure enough, the Hebrew word employed is תמים – *tamiym* – 'without blemish', 'undefiled'. The logical conclusion, therefore, is that *ha-Satan* was attempting to thwart God's attempt to produce the Messiah figure foretold in Genesis 3:15, ever mindful his forces were outnumbered two to one in the angelic realm (Rev 12:4). Perhaps creating hybrids on Earth would go some way to addressing the shortfall.

Did the Nephilim have souls or spirits? Some theologians believe demons are the spirits of the Nephilim killed in the Flood, unable to attain a spiritual resurrection:

O LORD our God, other lords beside thee have had dominion over us, but by Thee only will we make mention of Thy name. They are dead, they shall not live; they are deceased, they shall not rise: therefore hast Thou visited and destroyed them, and made all their memory to perish. (Isa 26:13-14)

The 'lords' mentioned cannot have been human since all humans, both righteous and wicked, will rise in the resurrection, some to everlasting life and the rest to damnation (Dan 12:2; FG 5:28-29). The picture, therefore, could be one of dead bodies of the Nephilim in the Flood and their disembodied spirits, desperately seeking embodiment, compassion, restitution and salvation, yet knowing they are already judged. Demons appear not to be the same as 'fallen angels'. Demons can only possess humans or animals with the host's, or God's, *permission*. They seem to yearn for this possessive state, as seen when Yeshua confronts the

---

[177] **Thomas, I D E** *The Omega Conspiracy,* Hearthstone, 1991, passim.

demoniac among the tombs at Gadara. Here the 'legion' of demons infesting the unfortunate *ask* to be sent into a herd of two thousand pigs, which promptly hurl themselves down the hill and drown in Lake Galilee.[178] These days, demonic possession is explained away with a raft of psychiatric diagnoses, yet underlying the actions of the possessed, as we'll see, is often a desire for human destruction at any cost, even to their own immolation.

'The Ancients'

The Nephilim, *ha-Gibborim* and the 'wise gods' (fallen angels) who descended to spawn them are very popular with New Agers today who channel spirits, ETs, aliens, ancient astronauts, ascended masters and dead old Uncle Bert, all promising to impart transcendent, esoteric knowledge and wisdom so you can be 'as gods'. Yet invoking demons and fallen angels, inviting them into your life, is inviting demon possession and is roundly condemned by God.[179] Celebrated as the 'Old Ones', 'Wise Ones' or 'The Ancients', the existence of such hybrids may explain hundreds of legends across Earth's cultures involving titans, demi-gods, half-human/half reptilian monsters, aliens, giants and other less wholesome entities. For example, Hercules was the result of the intermarriage between Zeus (god) and Alcmena (human female). Zeus fathered many hybrids in legend. Was Goliath one of the last of the Anakim? Was the reason the shepherd David took five stones from the brook that historic day (1 Sam 17:40), not because he believed he would miss something as big as Goliath with God's help, *but because Goliath had four brothers?* (2 Sam 21:18-22) Certainly God becomes unsettlingly slaughterous when Joshua takes the Israelites against the wicked tribes of Canaan centuries later, as author Joe Kovacs describes:

"When God exacted revenge against the Midianites who fought against His people, Moses was surprised to see women and children alive. So he ordered the slaughter of all non-virgin women and male children. **"Now therefore kill every male among the little ones,**

---

[178] Matt 8:28-34; Mark 5:1-20; Luke 8:26-39
[179] Deut 18:10, 14; 2 Kings 17:17; Rev 9:21; 18:23; 21:8; 22:15

and kill every woman that hath known man by lying with him."
(Num 31:17)[180]

This systematic programme of destruction on God's part leaves
a bad taste in the mouth of Christians taught the Sethite view of
Genesis 6. Those who have connected the dots with the Angel view
see in God's slaughter of the Canaanite races a hefty dose of bleach
being added to the Devil's gene pool. More about that later in the
Origins series.

The Sethite versus Angels argument

Most churches I've been to steer clear of the whole sticky
problem of Genesis 6 altogether. In fact, some churches I've been to
don't even teach the Old Testament. Those who do merely hold the
view that there's nothing more controversial occurring in Genesis 6
than the righteous sons of Seth having it away with the wicked
daughters of Cain. There are problems with this interpretation.

1) *B'ni ha-Elohim* always refers to direct creations of God and
   is never used in the Bible to refer to human believers.[181]
2) How could this fornication have caused God to take the
   extreme action of virtually wiping out the planet? Malachi
   3:6 says God does not change, so if regular human
   wickedness was the reason for the Flood, why hasn't God
   re-flooded the world in the time of Nero, Pope Innocent III,
   Stalin and Hitler, or, come to think of it, Tony and Cherie
   Blair?
3) Genesis 6:12 makes it pretty clear that all flesh had *corrupted*
   itself upon Earth.
4) There is no evidence that the Sethites were godly. In fact,
   Seth's son was Enos, in whose days men began to profane
   the name of the LORD.[182]

---

[180] **Kovacs, J** *Shocked by the Bible,* Thomas Nelson, Tennessee, USA, 2008, p.126

[181] Apart from Adam and Eve, the only humans who were ever direct creations of
God.

[182] Your English translation may say 'then men began to call upon the name of the
LORD.' (Gen 4:26). Most scholars, together with the Jewish Targums of Onkelos
and Jonathan, not to mention the Rabbi Maimonides, maintain that the literal

192

5) If Seth's lineage were righteous, why were almost all destroyed in the Flood?
6) There was no explicit command on God's part to keep any lines separate until after Genesis 11.
7) The text is quite clear that the *B'ni ha-Elohim* helped themselves to the women with scant regard for any female say in the matter. Not really godly.

Chuck Missler comments:

"Procreation by parents of differing religious views do not produce unnatural offspring! It was this unnatural procreation and the resulting abnormal creatures that were designated as a principal reason for the judgment of the Flood. The very absence of any such adulteration of the human genealogy in Noah's case is also documented in Genesis 6:9: Noah's family tree was distinctively unblemished. The term used, *tamiym*, is used for *physical* blemishes. A further difficulty seems to be that the offspring were only *men*; no 'women of renown' are mentioned. Was there a chromosome deficiency among the Sethites? Were there *only* 'Y' chromosomes available in this line?"[183]

Further, passages in the NT corroborate the Angel view. In the second epistle of Peter, the apostle writes:

"For if God spared not the angels that sinned, but cast them down to Hell [*lit:* Tartarus]**, and delivered them into chains of darkness to be reserved unto judgment; And spared not the old world, but saved Noah the eighth person** [eight - the number of new beginnings]**, a preacher of righteousness, bringing in the flood upon the world of the ungodly..."** (2 Pet 2:4-5)

Peter uses the word Tartarus, which is Greek for 'the dark abode of woe', a most scary region separate from other compartments of 'Hell' we'll examine in the series as we proceed. Homer described Tartarus in the *Iliad*: "*...as far beneath Hades as the Earth is below Heaven.*"[184] This was the place where God threw the

---

translation here is 'profane'; that this represented the point at which mankind began to err and move into idolatry.
[183] www.khouse.org/articles/1997/110/
[184] **Homer** *Iliad*, viii, 16

fallen angels who 'went after strange flesh'. Missler ties this in with the legends of Greece:

"Some of the demigods, Chronos and the rebel Titans, were said to have rebelled against their father, Uranus, and after a prolonged contest were defeated by Zeus and condemned to Tartarus."[185]

The Creator's own half-brother, Jude, writes:

"And the angels which kept not their first estate, but left their own habitation [*oiketerion*], he hath reserved in everlasting chains under darkness unto the judgment of the great day. Even as Sodom and Gomorrah, and the cities about them <u>in like manner</u>, giving themselves over to fornication, <u>and going after strange flesh</u>, are set forth for an example, suffering the vengeance of eternal fire." (Jude 6-7)

The happenings of Genesis 6 are compared **in like manner** to the **going after strange flesh** in Sodom and Gomorrah to make the point that these were not just any old sexual shenanigans. Alien creatures were coming down, having sex with human females and populating the planet with a bastardised, male-only race of half-angel, half-human hybrid *gigantes* - *aka* the Nephilim, or 'fallen ones'. The situation was beyond redemption. Dr Missler speculates:

"It is remarkable that these same notions populate the legends of every ancient cultural tradition on Earth: Sumer, Assyria, Incas, Mayan, Gilgamesh, etc. Who built the ancient monuments? The Great Pyramid at Giza? Stonehenge? The 'face' on the planet Mars? There are many scholars who believe these are linked to the Nephilim of old."[186]

And there were giants in those days...

Every ancient culture on Earth has its legends of giants. Did they really all read *Jack and the Beanstalk* or was there a germ of truth in the stories that were subsequently embellished?

In Gympie, Queensland, a portion of jawbone was discovered which still possessed the hollow for a missing lower back molar tooth. The owner of the tooth would have stood 10 feet tall.

---

[185] www.khouse.org/articles/1997/110/
[186] **Missler, Chuck** *Return of the Nephilim*, www.khouse.org

In 1936, two French archaeologists, Lebeuf and Griaule, dug up several egg-shaped funeral jars on an expedition to Chad, Africa, which contained the remains of gigantic humans, along with pieces of their jewellery and works of art. The giants, according to the natives, were called the Saos.

Cornwall, UK: The Cornish giants were a six-toed, six-fingered race, some known to be 'gentle'. Another report reads:

"A skeleton found in 1692 in a tomb near Angers, France, measured seventeen feet four inches. In his *De Gigantibus*, J Cassanio relates that while in Bordeaux, Francis I of France (1494-1547) saw a giant of such height that he immediately enlisted him as one of his guards. It is said that the giant, who subsequently became an archer, stood so tall that a man of ordinary size could walk between his legs."[187]

Gary Varner writes:

"In both Old World and New World mythology, the giants reportedly were destroyed when they dared to challenge the gods. In Beowulf, the giants are drowned after they had attacked the gods, and in Tarascan (Mexico) lore, the giants are destroyed "when God decided to bless the world", or in the mythology of Honduras they are simply changed into animals "during God's conquest."[188] In Inca lore, the first human race created by the creator god Viracocha was the race of giants. These giant men and women, who were not evil, lived in a world of darkness as the sun had not yet been made. According to legend, Viracocha was unhappy with his creation and destroyed the giants in a world-wide flood."[189]

Glen Kimball writes:

"Reaveneau de Lussan reported contact with natives of Chile who were of enormous bulk and stature. Frezier also relates that natives of the coast of Chile told him that some of the Indians living inland stood nine feet high.... Captain George Shelvock, on his voyage in

---

[187] www.bibleufo.com/humanphenom90.htm

[188] **Bierhorst, J** *The Mythology of Mexico and Central America,* New York: William Morrow and Company, Inc. 1990, p.172

[189] www.authorsden.com/visit/viewarticle.asp?AuthorID=1215&id=18794

1719 to the Island of Chiloe off the coast of Chile, saw Indians who stood nine to ten feet high."[190]

Wild West showman 'Buffalo' Bill Cody wrote in his *Buffalo Bill's Story:*

"While we were in the sandhills scouting the Niobrara country, the Pawnee Indians brought into camp some very large bones, one of which the surgeon of the expedition pronounced to be the thigh bone of a human being. The Indians said the bones were those of a race of people who long ago had lived in that country. They said these people were three times the size of a man of the present day, that they were so swift and strong that they could run by the side of a buffalo and, taking the animal in one arm, could tear off a leg and eat it as they ran.

These giants, said the Indians, denied the existence of a Great Spirit. When they heard the thunder or saw the lightning, they laughed and declared that they were greater than either. This so displeased the Great Spirit that he caused a deluge. The water rose higher and higher till it drove these proud giants from the low grounds to the hills and thence to the mountains. At last even the mountain-tops were submerged and the mammoth men were drowned. After the flood subsided, the Great Spirit came to the conclusion that he had made men too large and powerful. He therefore corrected his mistake by creating a race of the size and strength of the men of the present day. This is the reason, the Indians told us, that the man of modern times is small and not like the giants of old. The story has been handed down among the Pawnees for generations, but what is its origin no man can say."[191]

I can say. The disparate legends of giants around the world may reflect the passing down of oral history from one generation to the next. By the way, it is said that the old Indian greeting, where the hand is held up ('How!' in Hollywood) was originally to reveal whether the approaching stranger was one of the devilish six-fingered ones.

The *Journal Litteraire of the Abbé Nazari* reports that the skeleton of a huge giant exhumed in Calabria, Italy, measured 'eighteen

[190] www.stevequayle.com/Giants/articles/giants.Kimball.html
[191] **Cody, William F** *Buffalo Bill's Story,* Skyhorse Publishing, 2010, ch.6

Roman feet'. The fellow's teeth weighed at least an ounce each. Peter Kolosimo reports that at Agadir, Morocco, the French Captain Lafanechere:

"...discovered a complete arsenal of hunting weapons, including five hundred double-edged axes weighing seventeen and a half pounds, which were twenty times as heavy as would be convenient for modern man. To handle the axe at all one would need to have hands of a size appropriate to a giant with a stature of at least 13 feet."[192]

In the late 1950's, during road construction in the Euphrates Valley of south-east Turkey, many tombs containing the remains of giants were uncovered. At the sites, the leg bones were measured to be 120 cm (47.24 inches). Joe Taylor, Director of Mt. Blanco Fossil Museum, was commissioned to sculpt the human femur. This giant stood some 14-16 feet tall.

And, of course, we'll meet Goliath of Gath later, reputed to be nine feet tall. He is part of a family of giants David and his mighty men later confront and slay. These giants were trained, professional warriors who truly terrified their enemies. One of these, slaughtered by Elhanan of Bethlehem, **"was a man of great stature, that had on every hand six fingers, and on every foot six toes, four and twenty in number; and he also was born to the giant."** (2 Sam 21:20)

So, to sum up, we have fallen angels throwing off their heavenly bodies, coming down and having sex with human women to produce strange, male-only, human/angel hybrid *gigantes* which God wipes out in the Flood. Unfortunately, this state of affairs persists afterwards (Gen 6:4) and you are going to have a problem understanding the motives behind God's slaughterous actions in the OT, and the agenda behind today's UFO/EBE conundrum and the future alien disclosure announcement, unless you do your homework on the Nephilim. Satan fully intends to attack the 'man created in God's image' type too by creating grotesque creatures in the Nephilim, already popularised in a thousand TV programmes and films such as *Star Wars* (featuring Anakin Skywalker as Darth Vader), *Stargate,*

---

[192] www.bibleufo.com/humanphenom90.htm

Contact, The Abyss, Avatar, Battle: Los Angeles, Close Encounters of the Third Kind, Communion, Independence Day, E.T – The Extraterrestrial, and so on.

Here follows a small selection of 'giant' passages from the Bible:

And in the fourteenth year came Chedorlaomer, and the kings that were with him, and smote the Rephaims [giants] in Ashteroth Karnaim, and the Zuzims [giants] in Ham, and the Emims [giants] in Shaveh Kiriathaim... (Gen 14:5)

And Caleb stilled the people before Moses, and said, "Let us go up at once and possess it, for we are well able to overcome it." But the men that went up with him said, "We be not able to go up against the people; for they are stronger than we." And they brought up an evil report of the land which they had searched unto the children of Israel, saying, "The land, through which we have gone to search it, is a land that eateth up the inhabitants thereof, and all the people that we saw in it are men of a great stature. And there we saw the giants, the sons of Anak, which come of the giants [Nephilim]: and we were in our own sight as grasshoppers, and so we were in their sight." (Num 13:30-33)

And ye murmured in your tents and said, "Because the LORD hated us, he hath brought us forth out of the land of Egypt to deliver us into the hand of the Amorites to destroy us. Whither shall we go up? Our brethren have discouraged our heart, saying, 'The people are greater and taller than we; the cities are great and walled up to Heaven, and moreover we have seen the sons of the Anakim [giants] there'." Then I said unto you, "Dread not, neither be afraid of them. The LORD your God which goeth before you, He shall fight for you, according to all that He did for you in Egypt before your eyes." (Deut 1:27-30)

And the LORD said unto me, "Distress not the Moabites, neither contend with them in battle, for I will not give thee of their land for a possession, because I have given Ar unto the children of Lot for a possession. The Emim [giants] dwelt therein in times past, a people great and many, and tall, as the Anakim, which also were accounted giants as the Anakim, but the Moabites called them Emim." (Deut 2:9-11)

For only Og, king of Bashan, remained of the remnant of giants. Behold his bedstead was a bedstead of iron; is it not in Rabbath of the children of Ammon? Nine cubits was the length thereof, and four cubits the breadth of it, after the cubit of a man. (Deut 3:11) This makes King Og's bed 6 feet wide and 14 feet long. King Og's height is estimated at over 12 feet.

And it's not over

In the NT, Yeshua grants his inner core of disciples a confidential briefing on the Mount of Olives ('the Olivet Discourse'). The four fishermen James, John, Peter and Andrew ask the Messiah about the signs which will immediately precede His Second Coming at the end of the age (Matt 24:3). Jesus opens his reply with **"Take heed that no man deceive you..."** implying that deception will be the major risk. Further into his reply comes the unusual statement: **"But as the days of Noah were, so shall also the coming of the Son of man be.'** (Matt 24:37-38, NKJV). This is also confirmed by Yeshua on a separate occasion at the Jerusalem temple in Luke 17:26-27. In other words, a particular characteristic of Noah's age will be prevalent in the Crazy Days before Christ's return to set up His Millennial Kingdom.

What could He be referring to? Wickedness? Noah's day didn't have the monopoly on evil – look at Stalin, Hitler, Pol Pot and a thousand tin-pot dictatorships over the past two hundred years. Perhaps Yeshua is referring to the reason why God took the stern action of wiping out all air-breathing creatures and wrecking the Earth while He did it. What about *ha-Satan's* Nephilim and *ha-Gibborim* transgenic breeding programme? Notice Jesus also cross-references the conditions prior to His return with the fate of Sodom and Gomorrah, just so we get the message that sexual wickedness between humans and strange flesh will be re-occurring prior to his return – something more than homosexuality condoned in macro societies, as was the case during the Roman and Greek empires. S A Cranfill writes:

"William Whiston, the 17th/18th century mathemetician, theologian and translator of the works of Josephus, notes the belief that the fallen angels were fathers to the giants was 'the constant

199

opinion of antiquity'.[193] Also to be considered are the widespread persistent pagan 'mythologies' of the half-god/half-man beings, found not only in Greece but all over the world, including the Americas. A man who was half-angel would not be half-divine as only God is divine, but would certainly be supernaturally superior to a normal man. TV films and dramas about angels and demons explore this theme routinely. Believers in the occult recognise beings they call incubus (male demons) and succubus (female demons) who mate with humans."[194]

In both Deuteronomy 30:4 and Nehemiah 1:9, God appears to reassure us that even if we are abducted **unto the furthest parts of heaven,** He will rescue and return us if we keep his commandments. Underground and undersea bases aren't hidden from God either. He'll punish the wicked, angel or human, whatever hole they crawl into (Amos 9:1-4).[195] The scriptures declare that if mankind wants delusions, God will make them available. If we seek after 'Wise Ones', 'Ascended Masters', demons, astrology, divination, familiar spirits, aliens, 'extraterrestrial' contact, Ashtar (Satan), Ashtoreth (1 Kin 11:5,33; 2 Kin 23:13) and other Nephilic invocations, we will find them.

Well, we're still watching *The X Files, Men in Black, Predator, Skyline, Species, Starship Troopers, Thor, War of the Worlds* and a hundred other half-man/space-beast depictions of reptilian aliens coming down to interact with mankind. Millions these days crave a UFO experience – social societies devote their time to tracking down ghosts, aliens, chupacabras, vampires and the like. A popular teaching is that God Himself is an alien who returns from time to time to check on His creations, hence Elijah's wheels-within-wheels imagery and various celestial abduction ('rapture') goings-on throughout the Bible. Few outside the Biblically literate are aware or give any credence to the demonic potential of the 'star people' and their future relevance to both the Days of Noah and

---

[193] **Whiston, William** (translator), *Antiquities of the Jews* by Flavius Josephus, Complete Works, Grand Rapids: Kregel Publications, 1960

[194] Cranfill, S A, *They Came From Babel,* op. cit. p.34; also **Drury, Nevill** *Dictionary of Mysticism and the Occult,* San Francisco, Harper & Row, 1985

[195] Wallace, Wendy, *The Four Horsemen of the Apocalypse,* op. cit.

Christ's Second Coming, as expounded by Jesus in the aforementioned Matt 24:37-38 and other New Testament texts we'll examine. Everyone is talking about aliens – even the Roman Catholic Church. You know the seeds for a huge origins deception are being sown when a spokesman of Monsignor Corrado Balducci's calibre (theologian, member of the Vatican Curia (papal government) and personal friend of the Pope) – goes public on numerous occasions testifying that extraterrestrials are not only already known to Earth governments, but are freely interacting with them:

"[They] are not demonic, there are not due to psychological impairment, and they are not a case of entity attachment, but these encounters deserve to be studied carefully." [196]

Researchers Putnam and Horn comment:

"[Monsieur Balducci] even disclosed how the Vatican itself has been closely following the phenomenon and quietly compiling material evidence from Vatican embassies (nunciatures) around the world on the extraterrestrials and their mission. For example, at a forum concerning the enormous UFO flap in Mexico, he stated, 'I always wish to be the spokesman for these star peoples who also are part of God's glory, and I will continue to bring it to the attention of the Holy Mother Church.'" [197]

Dubbed 'The Greatest Secret of All Time', has there ever been a subject more discussed, more maligned, more misunderstood and misrepresented than the UAP/EBE phenomenon?[198] Most are still willing to giggle about UFOs and little green critters without recognising the unusually intricate conditioning programme underway. Despite all the scepticism, it is a fact that among the millions - and you did read that right, MILLIONS - of people who have reported abduction experiences or sightings of weird,

---

[196] **Boylan, Richard** "Vatican declares extraterrestrial contact is real", *UFO Digest,* 4th December 2012

[197] **Putnam and Horn** *Exo-Vaticana,* Zondevan, USA, 2013, p.20

[198] Unidentified Aerial Phenomenon/Extra-Biological Entity possessed of ETI (Extraterrestrial Intelligence)

aeronautical phenomena, there have been scientists, law enforcement officers, engineers, airline pilots, military personnel, NASA astronauts, senators, MPs and at least three American presidents who have gone on record. It is an indication of how seriously the American and British governments are taking the UFO phenomenon that many documents pertaining to abductions and sightings are routinely classified above Top Secret.[199] The options naturally present themselves to the curious: Is it all nonsense? Is there a legitimate, extraterrestrial element to what we are hearing, or is there a conspiracy of gargantuan proportions currently being orchestrated for some hitherto unrevealed purpose?

The smoke-screen hiding the facts is actually a point of discussion in itself since, to even the half-energised researcher, it seems abundantly clear that there is mischief afoot, and mischief no-one in official government circles is about to come clean about. A cursory trip around your local Barnes and Noble or Waterstones bookstores will satisfy the casual observer that much is being written about this enigmatic subject. And not only by interested researchers.

Ronald Reagan, while president of the United States in the 1980s, made the following comment in front of 176 delegates at the United Nations:

"What if we discovered we were being threatened by a power from outer space? Wouldn't we find out that we are all human beings on this planet?" [200]

Naturally this is not the sort of statement a president would want to make in a re-election year unless compelled to do so. Compelled by whom? A reluctant Reagan looked extremely uncomfortable as he spoke these words before an astonished audience, words no doubt given to him for public dissemination and stupefaction. Reagan has probably been the most vociferous but certainly not the only high-profile politician to have claimed a

---

[199] **Good, Timothy** *Beyond Top Secret,* Sidgwick & Jackson, 1996
[200] You can view Ronald Reagan's various ET disclosures on YouTube. Another example is at: http://www.youtube.com/watch?v=CfejBpD_wm4

personal experience with UFOs (his plane was buzzed by several 'lights' over Bakersfield, California). Jimmy Carter also filed a report based on an event which made a deep impression on him while governor of Georgia in 1969. Curiously, nuclear science graduate Carter took the risk and made a similar comment to Reagan's while running for the presidency:

"If I become president, I'll make every piece of information this country has about UFOs available to the public and the scientists." [201]

Well, history shows that Jimmy got to be president, but did we get any clandestine information on space aliens released to us? No. When pushed by Ben Stein on a design inference for the origin of life on Earth, even our old friend Richard Dawkins has changed his tune:

"It could come about in the following way. It could be that at some earlier time, somewhere in the universe, a civilisation evolved by probably some kind of Darwinian means to a very, very high level of technology, and designed a form of life that they seeded onto, perhaps, this planet. Now that is a possibility, and an intriguing possibility. And I suppose it's possible that you might find evidence for that if you look at the details of biochemistry, molecular biology, you might find a signature of some sort of designer...." [202]

Panspermia

What seems at first glance a glorious *faux pas* by the high priest of atheism actually is a calculated change of direction in line with the official wisdom. Unable to deny the notorious evidence for design in the cell, the latest *volte face* by humanists like Dawkins is that we were seeded on Earth by extraterrestrial beings, then we evolved by some Darwinian means into the splendid creatures we are today (in spite of the Second Law of Thermodynamics) with an alien Matron returning now and then in a shining spaceship to see how we're doing. 'Proof of this' will be punted by government 'experts' and world-religion advocates like the Vatican when the

---

[201] See also: http://www.youtube.com/watch?v=kBRpIdpJZh8
[202] Stein, Ben, *Expelled – No Intelligence Allowed*, op. cit.

global disclosure announcement on ETs/UFOs is finally made. If this is in fact 'The Lie' prophesied in scripture (2 Thess 2:11) – and I believe it is – the effect such a disclosure will have on unwary Judaism and Christianity will be catastrophic. Witness Father Giuseppe Tanzella-Nitti, Vatican astronomer, member of Opus Dei and professor of theology at the University of the Holy Cross in Rome:

"...It seems important to note that a believer who is respectful of the requirements of scientific reasoning would not be obliged to renounce his own faith in God simply on the basis of the reception of new, unexpected information of a religious character from extraterrestrial civilisations.... However, once the religious content originating from outside the Earth has been verified, they will have to conduct a re-reading [of the Gospel] inclusive of the new data...." [203]

Even the elect, if possible, will be deceived, so powerful and convincing will be the delusion (Matt 24:24; 2 Thess 2:3-12). Which could imply that this momentous public disclosure will be made prior to the *harpazo* ('Rapture') of the Gentile elect ('Body of Christ', 'Church').[204] Researchers suspect that the rapture of the faithful will be attributed to the new alien presence, who have taken steps to remove recalcitrant troublemakers from the Earth to pave the way for mankind's next quantum leap in spiritual and physical evolution.

---

[203] **Tanzella-Nitti, G** "Extraterrestrial Life", *Interdisciplinary Encyclopaedia of Religion and Science,* www.disf.org/en/Voci/65.asp

[204] Further to my previous note on this subject, the *harpazo* (*Gr.*) or rapture (*Lat.*) of the Body of Christ has been scorned as 'the most preposterous doctrine in the Bible' by atheists – an event when millions of staunch believers or 'elect' in Christ are snatched off the Earth, literally vanishing in their millions in the twinkling of an eye. The Holy Spirit thus removed, the revealing of the Antichrist is permitted by God – Satan's brief but disastrous global rule, which triggers God's wrath (the Great Tribulation) to be poured out without measure on Planet Earth. Christian theologians have debated for centuries whether the faithful in Christ will be forced to endure the infamous Trib with all its horrors, or whether they will be taken out of the way before the action starts. The matter is easily resolved using scripture, and we'll examine some astonishing additional evidence as we proceed. The main 'Rapture' verses in the NT can be found at Matt 24:30-36; 40-41; FG 14:1-3; 1 Cor 15:51-52; 1 Thess 4:16-17; Phil 3:20-21.

Preposterous? We haven't even got to the juicy bits yet. At a time of global fiscal instability and recession, there are currently two scientific rovers on the surface of Mars as well as three orbiters currently scouring the red planet's surface. And India's just launched a Mars mission. Two questions. *Why?* And *Looking for what?* If you've taken the red pill, you'll wish you didn't know. The planet Mars will feature significantly as the story unfolds. Mars is the Roman god of war. Unholy War.

The Bible is quite clear. Satan's strategy prior to the Flood involved the demonic pollution of Adam's seed to thwart the coming of the Seed of the woman.[205] This was carried out by fallen angels coming down and having sex with human women to produce the hybridised Nephilim – the product of the serpent's seed – huge, powerful and frightening creatures that roamed the Earth before and after the Flood. Yeshua said, **"As it was in the Days of Noah, so shall it be also in the days of the Son of Man."** (Luke 17:26) With millions across the world these days claiming an abduction experience linked to all manner of bestial sexual shenanigans with Sigourney Weaver aliens; mutilated cattle with their private parts excised so precisely experts have no idea of the technology used; scholars are suspecting the Bible may have called the conspiracy with uncanny accuracy. We'll explore more as we proceed.

It's worth noting that part of the motivation for scientists developing panspermia as a 'viable hypothesis' for man's origins has been the complete lack of evidence for abiogenesis on the Earth.[206] Putnam and Horn explain that panspermia is hardly a new idea. The theory that 'life had always been' and could conduct itself about the universe by various means had been around since the 5th century BC with Anaxagoras. When Darwinism became

---

[205] Notice that the Bible validates any important doctrine in at least two other places in the scriptures (*cf.* Matt 18:16; Deut 17:6; 19:15; 2 Cor 13:1, etc.). Those who still dispute the 'Angel View' of Genesis 6 might consider the following passages corroborating fallen angel mischief in connection with sexual acts, the Flood of Noah, and their current incarceration in the blackest depths of Tartarus awaiting judgment: Jude 6-7; 2 Pet 2:4-8.

[206] Abiogenesis: Life arising spontaneously from simple organic compounds with no organising principle.

fashionable but failed to explain the origin of the first cell, scientists such as William Thompson Kelvin, Hermann von Helmholtz, Jöns Jacob Berzelius and later Svante Arrhenius speculated about panspermia in their writings but produced no evidence. Darwin was not against the idea; indeed panspermia got Charlie off the hook with regard to the improbable complexities of Earthly abiogenesis.

Various theories were offered to provide the mechanism by which life could whiz around a terminally hostile universe. Meteorites could carry extremophiles – organisms capable of suviving and even thriving in extreme conditions hostile to other life. Spores could always hitch a ride – unicellular reproductive units able to give rise to a new individual unit without sexual fusion. It all sounds plausible, but it just sounds that way. Most unbiased scientists cite insurmountable problems with deep-space ultraviolet radiation or intense heat on atmospheric entry in getting life to Earth by these means, leaving God, aliens or some hitherto unknown progenitor system as the agency for the origin of life. And if so, who made God or the aliens? German physicist Hermann von Helmholtz had an interesting take on the issue:

"It seems to me perfectly just scientific procedure, if we, after the failure of all our attempts to produce organisms from lifeless matter, put the question whether life has had a beginning at all, or whether it is not as old as matter, and whether seeds have not been carried from one planet to another and have developed everywhere that they have fallen on fertile soil." [207]

In other words, life has always been, so its origin needs no comment, so get a life and move on. Brilliant.

The Bible plainly describes cosmic mischief afoot, though not extraterrestrial but hyperdimensional. In the opening chapters of Genesis, the Holy War is underway. By Genesis 6, the genetic pollution of Adam's seed and the rampant mischief and violence done on Earth has pushed the Creator to the end of His tether. Only one option remains. Reboot.

---

[207] **Helmholtz** *Populare Wissenschaftliche Vortrage*, vol.iii, Braunschweig, 1876

Then the LORD saw that the wickedness of man was great in the Earth, and that every intent of the thoughts of his heart was only evil continually. And the LORD was sorry that He had made man on the Earth, and He was grieved in His heart [God can have regrets and be grieved!]. So the LORD said, "I will destroy man, whom I have created from the face of the Earth, both man and beast, creeping thing and birds of the air, for I am sorry that I have made them." But Noah found grace in the eyes of the LORD. This is the genealogy of Noah. Noah was a just man, perfect in his generations. Noah walked with God. And Noah begot three sons, Shem, Ham and Japheth. (Gen 6:5-10, NKJV)

Perhaps to drive home the reason for the Flood, the above verses come directly after those describing those 'sons of God' having sex with humans and producing the 'mighty' offspring, which are most definitely NOT created in God's image. Events are so serious that God sets the hourglass in motion. No fear of Him remains before the eyes of those on Earth (Rom 3:18), a situation the LORD is about to remedy.

"And God said to Noah, "The end of all flesh has come before Me, for the Earth is filled with violence through them [bad angels and Nephilim]; and behold, I will destroy them from the Earth. Make yourself an ark of gopherwood; make rooms in the ark, and cover it inside and outside with pitch. And this is how you shall make it: the length of the ark shall be three hundred cubits, its width fifty cubits, and its height thirty cubits." (Gen 6:13-15, NKJV)

The name of one of the ten pre-Flood patriarchs, Methuselah, means 'his death shall bring'. When Methuselah dies, that's going to be it. *Yet the legendary Methuselah will be the longest surviving human of all,* living an awesome 969 years, a model of God's extreme forbearance and mercy. Yet even legends must die, and as old Methuselah breathes his last and the light in his eyes fades on a terminally lawless planet, events are set in motion to bring about the fulfilment of God's wrath upon a degenerate Earth.

GROUND ZERO

Some scientists believe that the Flood was a local event (the Black Sea theory). In that case, why instruct Noah to build the Ark if the Flood will be regional? Why not just tell Noah and his family to move to a different location? God does not. Also, God promises never to flood the world again. If the Noahic Flood were local, then God has broken His promise numerous times. There are floods all over the world – routinely. Ask the inhabitants of Queensland.

Noah's Flood is going to be a global, extinction-level event and the blueprints for the Ark's monumental construction are passed to Noah, who is told he has a grace period in which to build it, during which he must attempt, surprisingly, to persuade the hybrid population to clean up its act and repent (1 Peter 3:18-20). The inference is that Noah preached on the Flood for 120 years (Gen 6:3; Jasher 5:11), so the idea of a flood judgment was, by no stretch of the imagination, *unknown* to the wicked. They were doubtless *staggered* when it started to happen.

Repent!

Consider Enoch. As close as he came to God, it is evident that he received an insight into the coming judgment to name his son 'Methuselah': 'his death shall bring'. Enoch is also credited with being given the earliest Messianic prophecy, alluded to in Jude 14-15.

Consider that Noah was required to preach on the Flood for four generations to lead the wicked to repentance, yet fails to turn any hearts *because God had already made up His mind to kill the lot*. The question is, if Noah alone was **perfect in his generations** while the rest were contaminated by this weird Nephilic human/angel hybridisation, why did God imagine *any* would repent? And why would He even want them to? The answer to both questions is, God didn't. YHWH knew beforehand that the wicked were doomed and there would be no resurrection for them (Isa 26:13-

14),[208] but He wished to demonstrate the quality of forbearance to Noah. One wonders what would have happened if one of the Nephilim had fallen on his huge face, wept his heart out with remorse and begged God for forgiveness and mercy. None are recorded doing so. Only Noah's family is on the last bus – and God goes along also, as it happens, to ensure no unwelcome additions make it onto the manifest. The lesson? Repentance is verily for today, for tomorrow ye will be chopped.

And while we're at it, what is repentance? One of the most fascinating aspects of the Holy War is the requirement by the Creator that we surrender on His terms or suffer the penalty. Most think repentance means, *"Oh God, I'm so sorry. I didn't mean to kick the dog and treat my mother-in-law in such a beastly fashion."* How many tell God they're sorry when they're not? How many 'repent', then go out and do the same thing all over again? Sin persisted in. Common sense tells us such insincerity cuts no ice with the Almighty, who requires less *words* of repentance than *actions* and *overcoming*. It's the whole point of the training. Repentance by each of us is a conscious act of free will, of volition on our part, which declares to all which side we're on in the Holy War. Notice that a human's default allegiance in the Holy War is self-pride; on the side of evil; the wrong side; the side that eventually loses.

God states: **But unless you repent, you will all likewise perish** [that's Hell, by the way: into the Pit with you]. (Luke 13:3, NKJV). Then He repeats the same thing two verses later so we get it. **But unless you repent, you will all likewise perish.** (Luke 13:5, NKJV)

The Bible teaches that the visible outworkings and evidence of repentance in a person's life are good works. God wants changed lives, not excuses. A believer must learn to do good and *practise* righteousness, not because he is trying to work his way into God's

---

[208] We are told all humans, both righteous and wicked, will be resurrected, the saved to glory, the rest to damnation (Dan 12:2; FG 5:28-29; Acts 24:15). But Isaiah 26:13-14 mentions a third class which will not be resurrected at all. Some scholars believe this refers to the Nephilim; that that their disembodied souls after the Flood are synonymous with the demons who constantly seek embodiment, but are destined for eternal separation from God and Hell (*cf.* Matt 8:28-29).

kingdom (you can't), but because good works are the fruits of a repentant person's life *and required by God* (*cf.* 1 John 3:10; Rev 22:11). Secondly, we are taught that doing good for God is the method by which we begin overcoming evil in our lives. God desires to see us living clean, simple and holy lives, doing good and serving others, as this behaviour demonstrates we are trying to imitate God by living as He lives.[209]

Note that in the following passages the message of the prophets and apostles is entirely the message of God Himself:

(God speaks to Cain) **"If you do well, will you not be accepted? And if you do not do well, sin lies at the door. And its desire is for you, but you shall rule over it [**God is telling Cain to overcome!]." (Gen 4:7, NKJV)

(John the Baptist speaks) **"Therefore bear fruits worthy of repentance, and do not think to say to yourselves, 'We have Abraham as our father.' For I say to you that God is able to raise up children to Abraham from these stones. And even now the axe is laid to the root of the trees. Therefore every tree which does not bear good fruit is cut down and thrown into the fire."** (Matt 3:8-10, NKJV)

(The Apostle Peter speaks) **"He who would love life and see good days, let him refrain his tongue from evil, and his lips from speaking deceit. Let him turn away from evil and do good** [this is repentance]...." (1 Pet 3:10-11, NKJV)

(The Apostle Paul speaks) **"Therefore King Agrippa, I was not disobedient to the heavenly vision, but declared first to those in Damascus and in Jerusalem, and throughout all the region of Judaea, and then to the Gentiles, that they should repent, turn to God, and do works befitting repentance."** (Acts 26:19-20, NKJV)

(Daniel addressing Nebuchadnezzar) **"Therefore, O King, let my advice be acceptable to you; break off your sins by being righteous** [this is repentance], **and your iniquities by showing mercy to the poor** [so is this!]. **Perhaps there may be a lengthening of your prosperity."** (Dan 4:27, NKJV)

Depart from evil and do good [Repent!]; **seek peace and pursue it.** (Psa 34:14, NKJV)

---

[209] Eph 5:1; Matt 3:8; Luke 3:8; Acts 26:20; Eph 2:8-10

Depart from evil and do good [Repent!]; **and dwell forevermore** [have eternal life]. (Psa 37:27, NKJV)

Do not be overcome by evil, but overcome evil with good [Repent and do good]. (Rom 12:21, NKJV)

Let him turn away from evil and do good. (1 Peter 3:11, NKJV)

The LORD is not slack concerning His promises, as some count slackness, but is longsuffering towards us, unwilling that any should perish, <u>but that all should come to repentance.</u> (2 Pet 3:9, NKJV)

"And he who overcomes <u>and keeps My works until the end,</u> to him will I give power over the nations...." (Rev 2:26, NKJV)

And who is he who will harm you <u>if you become followers of what is good?</u> (1 Peter 3:13, NKJV)

"Therefore be imitators of God as dear children." (Eph 5:1, NKJV)

These passages demonstrate the following:

➢ If we do not repent, we will perish.
➢ God requires good deeds *from the heart* to demonstrate repentance. No faking. Don't be a 'tare' (Matt 13:24-30)
➢ Good deeds for others are how we overcome evil, both around us and in our own lives
➢ If we overcome the evil in our lives and keep Yeshua's works until the end, we will rule with Him over nations *forever* (the Eternal Kingdom)
➢ We are to imitate God's ways, which are all righteous
➢ God requires a person to believe that His Son, Yeshua (Jesus), died for their sins *according to the scriptures*, was buried and then rose again from the dead on the third day *according to the scriptures* (this is 'the Gospel' – 1 Cor 15:3-4).
➢ God requires repentance for salvation
➢ Good works without repentance are dead ('works of the law'). For instance, "I don't believe in God but I'm a good person..."
➢ There can be no repentance without a believer doing works befitting repentance

> Notice God is unwilling that any should perish, but that all should come to repentance. However, we later learn that millions harden their hearts and scorn God, so are damned.

> *So God doesn't get what He wants out of the programme.*

Actually He does. The Creator has had a people picked out from all nations from the foundation of the world who will repent and become joint heirs with Him for eternity (Psa 37:11; Matt 5:5; Rom 8:16-17; Heb 2:8). The rest of humankind won't. God knows who His people are. The elect or chosen don't know they are chosen until they repent.[210]

Which means repentance is *granted by the Creator Himself;* it is not a favour we do for God. Repentance is not even entered into unilaterally by the believer as most might imagine:

The God of our fathers raised up Jesus, whom ye slew and hanged on a tree. Him hath God exalted with His right hand to be a Prince and Saviour, <u>for to give repentance to Israel and forgiveness of sins</u>. (Acts 5:30-31)

When they heard these things, they held their peace and glorified God, saying, "<u>Then hath God also to the Gentiles granted repentance unto life</u>." (Acts 11:18)

Yeshua: "I came not to call the righteous, but sinners to repentance." (Luke 5:32)

In meekness instructing those that oppose themselves; <u>if God peradventure will give them repentance</u> to the acknowledging of the truth... (2 Tim 2:25)

For it is impossible for those who were once enlightened, and have tasted of the heavenly gift, and were made partakers of the Holy Ghost, and have tasted the good word of God, and the powers of the world to come, <u>if they shall fall away, to renew them again unto repentance</u>; seeing they crucify to themselves the Son of God afresh, and put him to an open shame. (Heb 6:4-6)

It's God's programme and he knows what you'll decide anyway. The free-will-versus-predestination paradox is resolved once you understand that God is outside the time dimension

---

[210] Eph 1:4-5; FG 6:44; FG 6:64; FG 15:16; 17:2, 9; 2 Tim 2:19; 2 Thess 2:13; Rom 1:7; Isa 49:1,5; Jer 1:5; Gal 1:15; Acts 13:48

altogether and inhabits eternity. He alone sees the end from the beginning.

Two by two

Back to the Flood. Noah's evangelism fails but his engineering project does not. The Ark standing before him now is enormous: 450 feet long, 75 feet wide and 45 feet high with a capacity exceeding 500 railroad stock cars. The barge-like shape of the vessel will make it difficult to capsize in what's coming.[211] The very sight of the thing must have engendered hoots of derision from the godless bystanders. "Hey Noah! You're as mad as a box of frogs!" Now put yourself in Noah's shoes, knowing beyond doubt that the Deluge is coming. A surreal predicament.

"Then the LORD said to Noah, "<u>Come into the Ark</u>, you and all your household, because I have seen that you are righteous before Me in this generation. You shall take with you <u>seven each of every clean animal</u>, a male and his female; <u>two each of animals that are unclean</u>, a male and his female; also seven each of birds of the air, male and female, to keep the species alive on the face of all the Earth. <u>For after seven more days I will cause it to rain</u> on the earth forty days and forty nights, and I will destroy from the face of the Earth all living things that I have made." And Noah did according to all that God commanded him. <u>Noah was six hundred years old</u> when the floodwaters were on the Earth." (Gen 7:1-6, NKJV)

These are some of the most fascinating verses in Genesis for the information they yield. Notice God says **"<u>Come</u> into the Ark..."** God's in there already and going with them, perhaps to ensure no Nephilim attempt to crash the party at the last moment. Who closes the door to the Ark? God does (Gen 7:16). At that point, all speculative theology goes out of the window. The only way you could be saved from the coming judgment was to walk through that door. God's forbearance lasts just so long and then the door closes and that's it. We'll see this model repeated throughout the scriptures. God does not change (Mal 3:6). Who is the door?

---

[211] **Heyford, Jack** *Spirit-Filled Bible* (NKJV), Thomas Nelson, 1991, p.15

Yeshua: **"I am the door. By Me if any man enter in, he shall be saved...."** (FG 10:9)

John Sears is upbeat:

"At last! After 100 years of boat-building, God calls to Noah – apparently from inside the ark – "Come into the ark" and find safety with Him. This resonates with the call of Jesus nearly 2,000 years ago: "Come to Me, all you who labor and are heavy laden, and I will give you **rest**." "Take My yoke upon you and learn from Me, for I am gentle and lowly in heart, and you will find **rest** for your souls." (Matt 11:28-29) Remember that the name 'Noah' means 'rest' in Hebrew, and Jesus' Hebrew listeners surely recognized the connection."[212]

Now, what about those animals? *Answers in Genesis* writes:

"In the book, *Noah's Ark: A Feasibility Study:* ...creationist researcher John Woodmorappe suggests that, at most, 16,000 animals were all that were needed to preserve the created kinds that God brought into the Ark. The ark did not need to carry every kind of animal – nor did God command it. It carried only air-breathing, land-dwelling animals, creeping things, and winged animals such as birds. Aquatic life (fish, whales, etc.) and many amphibious creatures could have survived in sufficient numbers outside the Ark. This cuts down significantly the total number of animals that needed to be on-board.

"Another factor which greatly reduces the space requirements is the fact that the tremendous variety in species we see today did not exist in the days of Noah. Only the parent 'kinds' of these species were required to be on-board in order to repopulate the Earth. For example, only two dogs were needed to give rise to all the dog species that exist today."[213]

Children are taught in Sunday school that the animals went in two by two. Actually, that's not strictly true. If you study the above scripture, one pair of each parent species of <u>unclean</u> animals and seven pairs of each parent species of <u>clean</u> animals and birds were saved by Noah and his sons (Gen 6:20; 7:2). This implies that by Noah's time, a type of sacrificial law code had been given to Earth's

---

[212] www.biblrytr.com/noah2.htm
[213] www.answersingenesis.org/articles/nab/really-a-flood-and-ark

214

inhabitants by God to distinguish what was acceptable to God ('clean') and what wasn't. Notice previously that Cain did not plead ignorance when his 'non-bloodworthy' offering was rejected, so this implies that the first law code was given at least as far back as Cain, and most likely to Adam and Eve immediately after their banishment from Eden as a result of the Fall.

There's another fascinating insight usually missed in the above scripture. John Sears explains:

"When I was a kid, I couldn't figure out how Noah managed to gather up all the animals and get them on-board in just seven days. The truth is, he could not possibly have managed such a task. Instead, the Scripture says they came to Noah. Some animals must have come a long distance, so they doubtless began the migration *before* God gave one week's notice to Noah. The boarding process itself took a full week. This migration should not surprise you. If God can create animals, He can direct them to report in pairs (and sevens!) to the loading ramp. The animals obeyed God. Noah's neighbors did not."[214]

Self-gathering, self-loading animals?

And Noah went in, and his sons, and his wife, and his sons' wives with him into the Ark, because of the waters of the flood. Of clean beasts, and of beasts that are not clean, and of fowls, and of every thing that creepeth upon the Earth, <u>there went in two and two unto Noah into the Ark</u>, the male and the female, as God had commanded Noah. And it came to pass after seven days, that the waters of the flood were upon the Earth. (Gen 7:7-10)

These animals would include the land- and air-dwelling dinosaurs too. Obviously Noah took babies or young ones; there were no fully grown T-rexes rousting the antelope and munching the piglets. One can imagine the stick Noah got during the final loading phase. "Hey, Noah! Hurry that aardvark, there's a flood coming!!" "Ha! Ha! Ha! Ha! Ha! Ha! Ha! Ha! Ha!" "Here, take my wife! Glad to be rid of her!"

These were not very nice people.

And they were soon to be very dead people.

---

[214] www.biblrytr.com/noah2.htm

A radically different ecosystem

The scriptures state that Noah was six hundred years old when the Flood came upon the Earth (Gen 7:6). In that respect, his longevity is consistent with the other patriarchs of the period. This always raises eyebrows. *Could humans really have lived such lifespans?* I know many Christians who become embarrassed at so obvious a flaw. It doesn't seem possible, not by today's standards at any rate, with what we think we know of genetics and longevity. One hundred years and that's pushing it, right? "The Bible is clearly in error!"

In *Origins I,* I examined the case for extreme lifespans based on compelling evidence that the world Adam, Eve and Noah knew *was very different* from the one we live in today. Science is unearthing a unique ecology prior to the Flood. There is some dissent among creationists over the canopy theory, but it's worth taking a short detour here to examine the concept, because it fits a great deal of the evidence.

A few verses into the Genesis creative process at the beginning of the Bible, we read: **"Then God said, "Let there be a <u>firmament in the midst of the waters, <u>and let it divide the waters from the waters</u>.</u>" Thus God made the firmament, and divided the waters which were under the firmament from the waters which were above the firmament, and it was so."** (Gen 1:6-7, NKJV)

This section has been argued over for centuries. What is a firmament? Usually where the birds fly – the atmosphere or 'first heaven'. There were waters *above* the atmosphere? In the original Hebrew, the word 'firmament' is translated from הָרָקִיעַ (*ha-râqîya'*), which implies thin layers hammered into strips. Later in the New Testament (NT), the apostle Peter highlights man's attitudes in the last days before Yeshua's Second Coming, giving more information on the subject:

"Knowing this first, that there shall come in the last days scoffers, walking after their own lusts, and saying, 'Where is the promise of his coming? for since the fathers fell asleep, all things continue as they were from the beginning of the creation.' For this <u>they will be willingly ignorant</u>: that by the word of God the heavens were of old, <u>and the Earth standing out of the water and</u>

216

in the water, by which the world that then existed perished, **being flooded with water."** (2 Peter 3:3-7)

The above states that:

- Scoffers in the last days will be walking according to their own lusts (doing what they want).
- These scoffers will believe in uniformitarianism, in other words, "As the world was yesterday, so it will be tomorrow".
- They will be 'willingly ignorant' of the fact that God created the heaven and the Earth. In other words, creation evidence will be deliberately ignored.
- They will be 'willingly ignorant' of the fact that the Earth stood out of the water and in the water…
- <u>By which</u> **the world that then existed perished, being flooded with water.**
- In other words, they will be wilfully ignorant of the Flood.

Not a bad summary of current scientific/evolutionary attitudes. Genesis 1:7 and Psalms 148:4 seem to imply that a canopy of water existed above the atmosphere (the first heaven) prior to the Flood. There is abundant scientific evidence to suggest that at some point the planet had a type of atmospheric shield causing a radically different eco-structure, one not dissimilar to a modern-day tropical terrarium at a tourist attraction. The Bible states that there was no rain as we know it prior to the Flood, **but a mist went up from the Earth and watered the whole face of the ground** (Gen 2:6, NKJV). *Genesis Park* reports:

"Dan Carlson was inspired by this verse to experiment with 'misting' plants. He also incorporated the music of birds with certain oscillating frequencies that open the plants' stomata. While these pores are open, the leaves are sprayed with a plant nutrient enzyme through mist. The results are amazing. A purple passion plant, which normally grows to about 18 inches, has grown to a Guinness World Record 1,300 feet. Carlson grows 10-inch-long potatoes and cantaloupes the size of soccer balls. His system was dubbed 'Sonic Bloom'. The patented process was used to treat apple orchards in Wisconsin. In a state averaging 290 bushels/acre, the mist and song-bird music helped trees yield over 500 bushels/acre and the fruit has a shelf life of five months instead of the normal 30 days. Cucumbers, soybeans, cabbages, tomatoes, cauliflower, and even redwood trees have been greatly impacted by this revolutionary agricultural system."[215]

Dr Henry Morris believes a planetary canopy pronounced 'very good' by God would have filtered out the sun's harmful ultra-violet and gamma rays and allowed a sympathetic greenhouse-type ecosystem to produce ideal conditions for growth and longevity. Some scientists surmise that the Earth could have been pressurised up to two atmospheres (29.4 lbs/in²), double today's pressure of 14.7 lbs/in². Unusual metal and halogen combinations can be compounded under such conditions, as borne out by archaeological finds covered in *Origins I*. Because of the increased pressure, the atmosphere would have been thicker prior to the Flood, making it easier to breathe the air (more O_2 saturation of blood cells) and for larger birds to fly. Experiments done in using radiation filtration and increased pressure reveal that organic material grows prolifically. *Genesis Park* again:

"Particularly interesting experiments were conducted by the late Dr Kei Mori of Keio University in Tokyo. Dr Mori raised plants under special light that filtered out IR and UV radiation. His unique process of fiberoptic sunlight collection and transmission, called 'Himawari sunlighting', is now marketed worldwide. At first, Mori feared the filtered light would be detrimental. But after extensive experiments he claimed it could promote healing and "because the ultraviolet is blocked, this sunlight does not fade fabrics or damage skin." (Gilmore, Elaine, "sunflower over Tokyo", *Popular Science*, May 1988, p.75.) One long-lived tomato plant was grown in a special nutrient-rich solution to be exhibited at the Japan Expo '85. Under piped sunlight and controlled atmosphere, this tomato tree grew over 30 ft high and yielded more than 13,000 ripe tomatoes during the six months of the Expo! (Hiroshi, Koichibara, "Tomatomation", *UNESCO Courier*, March 1987.) Could Mori's environment of filtered sunlight, enhanced

---

[215] www.genesispark.com/genpark/exper/exper.htm
"Sonic Bloom", *Creation Illustrated*, Vol. 7 No. 2, 2000, pp.24-31

carbon dioxide, and nutrient-rich liquids mirror the conditions on the early Earth?"[216]

More oxygen in the atmosphere would have had a dramatic effect on organic life. The February 1988 edition of *Discover* recounts how two researchers analysed air bubbles caught in amber believed to be 'some 80 million years old'.

"The researchers clamped the amber into a vacuum chamber of a quadrupole mass spectrometer, a device that identifies the chemical composition of a substance. As the machine slowly crushed the sample, the microscopic bubbles were released, exhaling up to 100 billion molecules. These breaths disclosed some surprising evidence: the ancient air contained 50 percent more oxygen than the air today."

Such factors, combined with double atmospheric pressure, an unloaded gene pool (prior to hybrid contamination), and an absence of harmful solar energies filtered out by the canopy would have dramatically increased the size and lifespans of humans and animals. As we've seen, the Bible is unabashed. Some humans lived over 900 years before the Flood.

Dinosaurs in pre-Flood Eden

Dinosaurs are even mentioned in the Bible, though there are not referred to as such, since the term was only coined by Sir Richard Owen in 1841. Over three dozen verses in the Message System are given over to describing two beasts in some detail (Job 40:15-24; 41:1-34). Read the descriptions of 'behemoth' and 'leviathan' carefully. Clearly these animals are not 'hippos', 'elephants' or other animals researchers have claimed – they can only be dinosaurs. Job in his day was obviously quite familiar with them (Job 38-41). Ask yourself how the writer of the book of Job could have known how to describe a dinosaur this accurately if they all died out 65 million years before he was born.

Many sea-dwelling dinosaurs would have survived the Flood, such as whales, sharks and plesiosaurs. Those air-breathing dinosaurs not saved by Noah would have drowned. Their bodies

---

[216] Ibid.

were buried in sedimentary mud where they collectively solidified and fossilised into the huge graveyards one can view today in Vernal (Utah), the Badlands (South Dakota) and elsewhere. From the lack of damage to their remains, it is evident these animals were not hunted or killed by other animals, their carcasses rotted apart. Bones of dinosaurs in certain areas are so numerous they have to be removed by bulldozers.

Evolutionists still cannot work out how dinosaurs did not starve because of their metabolic rates, nor can they explain how a 52-foot wingspan Pterodactyl could ever have flown in today's atmospheric pressure.[217] The answer is, it couldn't. Dr Carl Baugh contends that in the proposed thicker air of the Eden era, these great flying beasts would have had little trouble lifting off the ground. How does an 80-foot Apatosaurus breathe with nostrils the size of a horse's? It couldn't today, but back then it would have been a different matter.

After the Flood, the reduced pressure, lower oxygen content (from 35% to 21%) and increased solar radiation would have eventually proved disastrous for the descendants of the air-breathing dinosaur babies Noah took with him on the Ark.[218] Once fully grown, these great reptiles would have experienced trouble eating quickly enough to feed themselves, and so would have been in a state of perpetual hunger and therefore a danger to humans. As time passed, it is reasonable to suppose that the physical size of these animals would have greatly diminished over successive generations.

Flood evidence

The exotic pre-Flood conditions would have had a remarkable impact on the environment, abundant evidence of which is still with us today. The additional pressure would produce a hyperbaric effect, causing all organic matter to grow prolifically (including plants, humans, insects and animals). How tall humans

---

[217] **Anderson, Ian** "Dinosaurs Breathed Air Rich in Oxygen", *New Scientist,* vol. 116, 1987, p.25
[218] **Baugh, Carl** *Dinosaur,* Promise Publishing, CA, USA, 1987

like Adam were, we can only surmise from uncovered skeletons. As we've seen, Genesis 6:4 states: **There were giants in those days, and also afterward...** and we know where that led.

Biblical Creation writes:

IN 2011, THE REMAINS OF 80 WHALES WERE FOUND IN THE CHILEAN DESERT

"How would whales have become stranded in the middle of a desert? Researchers were quick to explain that it must have happened over a long period of time. However, a more logical explanation is that these whales swam together and were stranded as the waters subsided after Noah's flood. They are found in sedimentary sandstone in the same layers and some of the whales even overlap: meaning this did not happen over a long stretch of time. They were buried rapidly and preserved, as the skeletons are complete and fossilized." [219]

A tropical forest has been discovered deep below the tundra in Alaska.[220] One tree alone was 300 feet in height and had actually been drilled down into before being brought to the surface.[221] A metal hammer comprising iron and chlorine has been found compounded without the presence of silicon, a feat impossible to achieve in today's 14.7 lbs/in² pressure.[222]

We can have no concept today of this different Earth: only fragments remain. I have been intrigued to see, though, how much of the picture can be put together with a patient weighing of the evidence. The existence of continental shelves under the oceans today argues for the seas being shallower prior to the Inundation. Evidence of the Flood remains in every mountain, hillside, fossil, barrel of oil and stratum of shale gas.

---

[219] *Daily Mail*, 21st November 2011

[220] www.cbc.ca/health/story/2002/03/21/arcticwood020321.html

[221] Hovind, Kent, *Creation Seminars*, op. cit.

[222] "The London Artefact, discovered in June 1934 by Frank and Emma Hahn near London, Texas. This artefact is a metal hammer in Cretaceous rock. The hammer is composed of 96.6% iron, 0.74% sulphur, and 2.6% chlorine. This chlorine composition in compound with metallic iron renders this artefact irreproducible by modern scientific methods." – www.creationevidence.org

I can only wince at the terror that must have overtaken the inhabitants when it dawned on them that something of lethal significance was underway. At what point did the wicked realise this would be an extinction-level event? Did a meteor really strike the Earth resulting in the evolutionist's destruction of the dinosaurs? The worldwide geological evidence indicates that the formation of mountains, deep oceans and almost all current geological phenomena is best explained by flood processes arising from a global, cataclysmic event (Psa 104:5-9). The Earth's crust is only 3 miles thick in certain places under the sea. That's the same relative thickness as the skin of an apple to the fruit. Certainly, trillions of tons of water hitting the Earth over a forty-day period would have appalling effects on both geology and climate. At the same time, **'the <u>fountains</u> of the deep'** were broken up, blasting super-heated magma, water and roiling steam up from the Earth's massive subterranean chasms and out into the oceans and sky.

In *Origins I,* I cover the theories I believe hold the best scientific merit for what happened. I have collected Flood evidence for the past thirty years and believe it is possible to get close to the truth. We have colossal and very bizarre phenomena, some of which we looked at in the previous book. We have those mammoths and 'dragons' (dinosaurs) buried in compromising positions by the thousand. A whale on its tail at Lompoc. Billions of clams found in the closed position indicating that they were buried alive, even on mountains. Giant dragonflies, cockroaches, flies and other insects found fossilised. Flood legends all over the world. A population of just 7.4 billion today, pointing to only 4,000–5,000 years' growth. A 50% higher oxygen content on the pre-Flood Earth and a uniform, warm climate.[223] Followed by the Flood. An Ice Age. Ice covering

---

[223] "Many Arctic dinosaurs have been found. The bones of at least three dinosaur species and two other reptiles have been recovered from a site in the Alaskan tundra by researchers from the University of California at Berkeley. The dinosaur bones were first discovered at the site by Shell Oil Company in 1961, but Shell did not reveal the find until last year. Researchers say the fossil finds indicate both young and old dinosaurs were at the Alaska site in great numbers, and represent the first find of dinosaurs at such high, cold altitudes. This adds further weight to the idea that the Earth has had a period of time which was far more uniform in

lush, semi-tropical vegetation. The ice caps. A wandering magnetic pole. The Earth tilted over at 23.5°, beset with Chandler's Wobble, suggesting something hit the planet. Damage all over the moon, and yet no-one has ever seen a major impact on the moon. Damage on Mars and Mercury. The rings of Saturn still separating in the Poynting-Robertson effect, indicating they are not billions of years old but still stabilising. Dozens of anthropic indicators pointing to a young Earth. Huge forests and coal deposits found under hundreds of feet of ice in Alaska and Antarctica. And on and on and on.

How many died?

I was living in Sherman Oaks, northern Los Angeles, on the morning of 17th January 1994 when the big earthquake hit. Sherman Oaks was just a few miles from the temblor's epicentre at Chatsworth in the San Fernando Valley. You take for granted the solid ground beneath your feet, or should I say the bed, since the quake struck at 4:31 am while I was asleep. One minute, there I was in the land of Nod, the next, the world went crazy as if someone had flown a 747 into the building. I remember jerking awake in a state of shock, wondering what on Earth was going on. The din was tremendous and didn't stop - a deep roaring and the sound of smashing, splintering, screaming – and I mean, *screaming*. People were in terror of their lives and fled into the streets, those who were able. I remember the barely concealed panic on the faces of those who gathered outside, wondering when the next shock would hit. Which park or patch of land was safest? Were all the family members accounted for? Was the house completely ruined? How much more terrifying do you imagine the Flood was to the world at that time when it eventually came?

The effect the Flood had on the Earth's population could only have been catastrophic. Estimates vary wildly on how many people actually perished. I asked the question on some Internet sites and got 7 billion, 32.9 million, 500 million, 1.5 billion - take your pick. A

warm tropical-like conditions than it is at the present." (*Science News*, 31st August 1985)

223

few websites lost no opportunity to castigate God for this cruelty in the strongest terms. There were no opinions on *why* God did it.

Working out the lifespans of the patriarchs, though, the Bible states that the Flood occurred 1656 years after Creation (4004 BC), so circa 2345 BC. At the time of writing, we have just over 7.4 billion people on the planet, which came from eight people surviving the Flood just under 4,400 years ago. The Berlin census report of 1922 put the world's population at 1.8 billion. The estimates of world population around the birth of Christ vary between 170 and 400 million.[224] If one plots known census figures to form a parabola, our current world population appears to begin 4,400-5,000 years ago, when the Bible states eight people survived a worldwide Flood, so not bad so far.

William Williams takes the Berlin census figure of 1,804,187,000 for the global population in 1922 and calculates that man's numbers would have to have doubled 30.75 times from his original ancestors. Based on Bible chronology, one can quite reasonably arrive at today's population from eight people surviving the Flood 4,400-5,000 years ago. With these figures, it requires 168.3 years each time for the population to double.

Williams quotes the Jewish yearbook's population of Jews to be 15,393,815 in 1922. He calculates the Jewish population must have doubled its numbers 23.8758 times from the days of its patriarch Jacob (3,850 years since Jacob's marriage to Leah), or once every 161.251 years. This is a stunning, independent correlation with the Berlin census for the planet's population rate. Furthermore, a calculation of Muslims alive in 1922 (25,000,000) from the birth of Abraham's illegitimate son, Ishmael, (3,988 years) produces an aggregate population doubling every 162.275 years. Williams exults:

"We would not expect the figures to be exactly the same, nor be greatly surprised if one period were twice the other. But their correspondence singularly corroborates the age of the human race and

[224] http://www.census.gov/ipc/www/worldhis.html

of the Jewish people, as gleaned from the word of God by the most proficient chronologists." [225]

So if the population doubled, on average, every 168 years *after* the Flood, can we reasonably apply the same rate to calculate the aggregate of population during the 1656 years *prior* to the Flood? If you do, you get around 2,048 people from two common ancestors. The inference is that the early families were extensive and lived massive lifespans, so if we allow a doubling of the population every 80 years – twice the post-Flood rate – the figure you get by the time the Flood strikes is around a million. It's a better guess to say, therefore, that probably over a million perished in the Flood, all of whom were contaminated with the Nephilic hybridisation covered earlier. Tas Walker writes:

"Compare [the Indonesian tsunami] with the disaster documented in the Bible. Noah's Flood would have begun with massive earthquakes when the fountains of the great deep burst open (Genesis 7:11). But Noah's Flood also involved heavy rain (Genesis 7:12) and a continual increase in sea-level (Genesis 7:17–20). The disaster was not over in an hour or two, but continued to worsen day after day for five whole months (Genesis 7:24).

"...Massive movements in the Earth's crust would have caused huge tsunamis and destruction on a global scale. The Indonesian quakes and resulting waves would have been tiny by comparison to the events at the time of the great Flood. Billions of creatures, including dinosaurs, were killed and buried in sediments as the entire Earth became flooded. Fossils frequently show creatures suddenly killed and buried. To stay alive at sea for eight days is exceptional. But, without anyone to rescue them, the people in Noah's day — people who managed to cling to floating vegetation — would have perished of exposure and starvation in the months that followed. Their remains would never have been found." [226]

[225] **Williams, William** *The Evolution of Man Scientifically Disproved,* Bibliobazaar, 2007
[226] http://creation.com/tsunami-tragedy

The greatest catastrophe in history

The Flood is the first macro destruction event since God pronounced the Creation 'very good', so it's not implausible that whatever came through the solar system at that time wrought the destruction we see today on the moon, Mars, Venus, Mercury and Earth, triggering the Flood. Some scientists think they know what was responsible. Don Patton Ph.D's research reveals an altogether more apocalyptic scenario we'll examine in the next chapter. He writes:

"Fifty years ago virtually all academic astronomers and geologists classified themselves as millions of years 'gradualists'. However, times do change. Photographic evidence has come in showing heavy catastrophism of the surfaces of Mercury, Venus, the moon, Mars, Deimos, Phobos, Io, Europa, Ganymede, Callisto, Titan, the Rings of Saturn and other satellites more distant."[227]

Comet/bolide remnants would have brought down the canopy, accounting for forty days and nights of rain, halving the atmospheric pressure of the planet. Impacts across the Earth would have broken up the crust, releasing the **'fountains of the deep'**, those huge, subterranean chambers containing trillions of tons of water which were blasted up and into the atmosphere to fall as more rain. But Patton believes a comet alone would not have caused the type of evidence left to us today:

"A single asteroid collision with the Earth cannot create a spin axis shift, an orbital shift, a geomagnetic field dynamo (or generator), a fragmentation (icy or rocky), or a paleomagnetic polarity reversal, much less sudden crustal tears and up-thrusts, a hemispheric-sized flash flood and sudden sedimentary strata. Our planet, the Earth, has experienced all of these. Evidence indicates the timing thereof has been 'recent'."[228]

The Flood with which God judged the Earth was a tectonic event of enormous dimensions, says Tas Walker, and the destruction wrought on life would have been terminal. Massive

---

[227] **Patton D W & S R Windsor** *The Mars-Earth Wars*, Pacific Meridian Pub., 2003
[228] Ibid.

damage to the Earth's crust would have resulted, releasing the power of continental super-quakes, huge tsunamis and constant volcanic activity from the Earth's furious energies. Today the planet is still settling, as evidenced by moving tectonic plates and continued earthquakes, volcanic eruptions and tsunamis. In *Origins I*, I cover the sequence of events which explain the frozen mammoths of Siberia, the forming of Grand Canyon, Meteor Crater and Niagara Falls, and the evidence left to us today of such a catastrophe.

The first the human/hybrid inhabitants would have known of the disaster would have been sudden and inexplicable rain, an unknown phenomenon up to that point (Gen 2:5-6). It seems likely that as the deluge progressed, groups of families would have panicked as they made their way to whatever higher ground was available. The effects of the ruptured fountains of the deep would have been felt in an alarming increase in water coverage. Perhaps some even made an attempt to get into the Ark, recalling Noah's warnings of the catastrophe, but the boat would have towered above them battened down, an unassailable fortress.

Some geologists who have studied the Flood and its after-effects believe the pre-Flood Earth comprised mostly shallow seas and gentle, insignificant hills/mountains. The jagged mountains and ocean trenches we know today, they state, were formed as a result of the catastrophe. That being the case, it would not have taken long for all the dry land to become covered. Where is all the Flood water today? In the seas and oceans. It's instructive to note that if you flatten Earth's mountains and lift up the ocean trenches and basins to level ground, today's water would cover the entire planet to a depth of around 2.7 km (1.62 miles).

I believe God gave Noah just seven days warning of the calamity so *ha-Satan* and his dread angels would have no time to save their hybrid offspring. This will be a recurring model with God as we proceed in our study of the Holy War. *Ha-Satan* manoeuvres according to intelligence received, but in the case of the Flood, God has the drop. Notice the Flood story comprises three groups of people:

    1.   Those who perish (the Nephilim and 'wicked')

2. Those God preserves through the ordeal (Noah and his family)
3. Those who died or are taken out before it happens (Lamech, Enoch (raptured), Methuselah and previous patriarchs)

This is the type or model for all tribulations God visits upon the Earth, and we'll see this pattern repeated into our modern age.

Panic. Fear. Grief. Despair. Anger. These would have been the final emotions of the inhabitants fleeing the inexorable rising waters until there was no high ground left to flee to. There is abundant evidence the animals did the same. The Victoria Cave in Yorkshire, England, was found to contain the bones of grizzly bear, bison, reindeer, mammoth, hyena, hare, hippopotamus and fox all packed in together.[229] This cave is 1,450 feet above sea level. The Elbolton Cave is 800 feet up and contained bears, reindeer and mammoths. The Raygill Quarries at 750 feet, excavated in 1880, contained the remains of bear, lion, hippo and slender-nosed rhinoceros. None of these remains show signs that the animals perished in combat. And what are lions and hippos doing in Yorkshire? Could it be that this area, along with the rest of the planet, had a radically different eco-structure prior to the Flood? What are these types of animals doing together in a cave in the first place? What circumstances drove them to seek shelter together *before being buried in sediment?*

What *caused* the Flood?

---

[229] www.capra.group.shef.ac.uk/4/bonecavechamberlain.html

THE RED GOD

There are two kinds of Earth scientists: those who believe in uniformitarianism and those who subscribe to catastrophism. A uniformitarian believes that all Earth's features were formed gradually over billions of years through endless erosion and evolutionary processes. In other words, as things are today, so they have always been, and will be tomorrow. By contrast, the catastrophist sees evidence for sudden, calamitous events, which have wrought epoch-shaping effects on the planet. There are those who believe in a little of both. I am not one of those people. I am a dyed-in-the-wool catastrophist. On my global travels, I see a young Earth with flood evidence by the bulldozer-load all over our planet. And if I grab my binoculars and turn them on the moon, a pale, pockmarked world greets my widened eyes. In fact, an hour on the Internet studying the other planets and moons in our solar system reveals something you don't notice unless it's pointed out to you.

Not only does the solar system no longer look 'very good' by God's standards, our celestial neighbourhood has taken a complete bashing. The Earth goes through Chandler's Wobble, indicating something hit it. We have over one hundred serious craters and thousands of minor impacts on Earth, testifying to a calamitous past. Someone's really done for the moon. It's riddled with craters, yet during the four hundred years we've had telescopes, we've never seen anything sizeable hit the moon. Dr Jamie Love disagrees:

"It would be unfair to say that nothing happens on the moon. There are occasional reports of localized 'glows' and 'brightenings' that are called Lunar Transient Phenomena (LTP). We suspect these are caused by the release of gas from below the moon's surface or the impact of something against the moon. Some amateur astronomers specialize in looking for and recording LTPs. Of course, these folks have first become experts on lunar features and geography." [230]

---

[230] http://www.synapses.co.uk/astro/moon3.html

'Glows' and 'brightenings' are not what we're talking about, Jamie. We're talking major trauma. Take Venus. Naming it after the Roman goddess of love seems fatuous. It's a volcanic hell-hole covered with craters and clouds of carbon dioxide, which heats up to 460ºC and rains sulphuric acid. Mercury? The sun's closest planet is a toasty 500ºC by day, a frigid -140ºC at night, and each day lasts three Earth months. Astronomer Percival Lowell described it as *"the bleached bones of a world."*

Mars? Blasted. Inhospitable. Mars hosts over 43,000 craters over 5km in diameter.[231] 93% of Mars' craters *are on one side*, 80% of which landed within half an hour. I'd say that's a catastrophe. Mars terrified the ancients. Why? Astronomically I'm fairly literate, but I can't find Mars in the night sky without help, and neither can you. Yet early civilisations went in mind-numbing fear of the planet. Dr Donald Patton writes:

"Ancient Chinese knew Mars as 'the fire star'. Sumerians thought Enlil (Mars) was the cause of the Great Flood. [emphasis mine]. Classical Greeks indicted Ares (Mars) as the 'bane of mortals'. And the Romans saw Mars as the God of War. *Why?*"[232]

Too close for comfort

Such fear would indicate that Mars, the god of war, somehow intervened in the lives of those on Earth. A group of scientists went back to re-examine the data and what they found astonished them. In their book, *The Mars-Earth Wars*, Drs. Donald Patton and Samuel Windsor lay out the science behind why they believe Mars was on an eccentric orbit in ancient times and did near fly-bys of Earth every 108 years, resulting in catastrophic events. Dr Chuck Missler points out that the ancient calendars of the Chaldeans, Egyptians, Romans, Hebrews, Greeks, Phoenicians, Chinese, Mayans and Etruscans were all calibrated on 30-day months, 360-day years. In 701 BC, apparently, all these changed to the 365.25 days per year we know today. In other words, the problem resolved itself and, coincidentally or otherwise, Mars doesn't visit anymore. And

---

[231] **Wright, Shawn** "Infrared Analyses of Small Impact Craters on Earth and Mars", University of Pittsburgh, 4th April 2003
[232] Patton D W & S R Windsor, *The Mars-Earth Wars,* op. cit.

judging by the evidence we're about to examine, I'd count our lucky corn chips it doesn't.

Ancient literature positively shudders with exotic passages of macro events and celestial obliterations, chief among them the Bible's Old Testament, or Jewish Tanakh. The more genteel scholars assume that God is employing violent imagery to embellish His anger rather than describing actual disasters, but I see no reason to treat these passages allegorically. They plainly describe a world in chaos, and other cultures around the world appear to have made similar, independent observations. Patton gives an example:

"The Innuit (Alaskan Eskimos) have an account, when once a living was easily made by their distant ancestors. Then the earth quaked, volcanoes erupted and the path of the sun in the sky suddenly went low. A cold, harsh climate ensured that a living became difficult to achieve…. There is an organization, AISES, the American Indian Society for Engineering and Science (Boulder, Colo.), which addresses the need for American Indian elders to preserve their various ancient traditions from all over the North American continent, from Alaska to Mexico, and from Labrador to California…. Based on data presented in the 1995 AISES convention, Boulder, Colo., it is clear that numerous Indian tribes have heritages of ancient, catastrophic times when the path of the sun in the sky changed, when they lived longer, and when they fought larger animals…. It is predicted that when research is completed among the Indian tribes of North America and collated, no less than thirty different Indian tribes will be found with stories of ancient, catastrophic ages, interrupted by catastrophes featuring a change in the sun's path across the sky."[233]

A change in the sun's path means an axial change or pole shift with all the trauma that entails. Could this really have happened?

Take cover

It is no secret that Earth is under constant bombardment. Anywhere from 60 to 100 tons of interplanetary material fall onto

---

[233] Ibid.

our planet's surface each day, though the finer particles burn up as they abrase the atmosphere and decelerate. Every so often larger bits get through – much larger bits. Those who maintain a uniformitarian view of Earth's history would do well to revisit what happened at the Podkamennaya Tunguska River at 7:14 am local time on 30th June 1908. An explosion rated at 10-15 megatons flattened an estimated 80 million trees across 830 square miles. The force of the explosion was estimated to be around 1,000 times the magnitude of 'Little Boy', which destroyed Hiroshima. The cause is believed to have been a bolide, which detonated 5-10 km above the Earth's surface, radiating its power out in a colossal cone.[234] Tunguska is unwelcome evidence that our planet is vulnerable to interstellar assault, and these events are more common than most people imagine. *Discovery News* reported on 13th January 2010:

"A near-Earth object hurtled past us on Wednesday, just two days after its discovery was announced. Orbital projections indicated that the object called 2010 AL30 flew by Earth at a distance of just 80,000 miles (130,000 kilometers). That's only one-third of the way from here to the moon."[235]

Sky News reported another close encounter nine months earlier:

EARTH-ASTEROID NEAR MISS

"The Earth has had a near miss this week when a huge asteroid whizzed past, less than 50,000 miles away. The asteroid - about the size of a 10-storey building - flew past the Earth at roughly twice the distance of the highest Earth-orbiting satellites, according to website space.com. It is similar in size to a rock that exploded above Siberia in 1908, flattening 80 million trees across an 800 square-mile area. The impact had the force of a thousand atomic bombs, astronomers say."[236]

---

[234] Bolide - a celestial fireball, 'impactor' or flaming, crater-forming projectile attaining a magnitude of -14 or brighter.
[235] www.msnbc.msn.com/id/34826596/ns/technology_and_science-space/
[236] *Sky News*, 4th March 2009

A tenth planet?

Most of these projectiles originate from the asteroid belt – a conglomeration of small bodies which orbit our sun. Some scientists believe this debris is the result of a tenth solar system planet which disintegrated after 'an event'. A small body approaching a larger body will accelerate according to the inverse square law (halve the distance, quadruple the attraction). When the smaller body reaches the Roche limit of the larger planet, usually 2.44 x the radius of the larger body, the smaller body disintegrates when the larger's tidal forces exceed the smaller's own gravitational ability to maintain cohesion. Patton and Windsor believe such a thing happened between Mars and a tenth planet they name Astra. Their published evidence argues that:

"…if the tenth planet, Astra, once in the solar system, wasn't already apparent from the spread of asteroids, it would have to be invented because of the spread of craters on Mars."[237]

Patton and Windsor aren't the only ones interested in Mars' apocalyptic history. The mainstream press has also been reporting renewed interest in the Red Planet's chequered past.

LIFE ON MARS? THE RED PLANET'S ATMOSPHERE ONCE CONTAINED MORE OXYGEN THAN EARTH UNTIL IT WAS DAMAGED IN A CATASTROPHIC COLLISION WITH ANOTHER WORLD THE SIZE OF PLUTO

"The atmosphere on Mars was once thicker, warmer and wetter than it is today until it was damaged in a 'catastrophic collision' with a planet the size of Pluto, scientists claim.

"Data collected by Nasa's Curiosity rover suggests the Red Planet's atmosphere once had more oxygen in it than Earth, giving serious weight to the theory it could have previously harboured alien life.

"Yet a major upheaval, thought to have been caused when a Pluto-sized planet collided into Mars billions of years ago, created a shift in gases that led the atmosphere around it to shrink." [238]

---

[237] www.creationism.org/Patton/PattonMarsEarthWars/PattonMEW01.htm

Patten and his colleagues believe Astra fragmented on its approach to Mars and showered the Red Planet with lethal debris. Most of the remains which missed Mars went on to become the asteroid belt, while Mars picked up two moons. Extrapolating the asteroids, Dr Patton estimates the diameter of Astra at 1,600 miles, plus or minus 100 miles, making it 26% smaller than the moon and 15% larger than Pluto. Using established orbital mechanics, Patton and Windsor calculated the perihelions[239] of the asteroids, which would indicate the distance from the sun where the collision might have occurred. The answer is surprising. If Mars was involved, it was not even within *50 million miles* of its modern orbit, which means the red planet had a different, more eccentric circuit in prehistory, which took it out up to 250 million miles from the sun.[240] That being the case, how far *inward* did this eccentric orbit bring the Red Planet?

Damage assessment

Patton's examination of Mars involves an erudite cataloguing of the red planet's craters 20 miles or larger in diameter. There is indeed a 'Clobbered Hemisphere' where all the action occurred, and a Serene Hemisphere, largely unscathed. To view this yourself, log onto Google, select 'Images', and type in the names of the following craters.

Close to the centre of the Clobbered Hemisphere is the largest dent in the solar system – the giant Hellas Crater. If a myriad of Astra fragments impacted Mars (which one would expect from a Roche-limit disintegration), Patton argues that the damage is consistent with what we observe on the planet:

"There is an abrupt edge, or 'rim' for a dramatic drop off of the density of craters on Mars. This rim is where 'the buckshot ends'. It is where the red planet's Serene Hemisphere begins. This rim is obvious to anyone who is thinking 'fragmentation' on the Roche limit of

---

[238] *Daily Mail*, 19th July 2013

[239] Perihelion - That point in a body's orbit when it is closest to the sun.

[240] Today, Mars's aphelion (furthest point from the sun) is 154.80 million miles.

Mars. So far, astronomers who fail to think 'planetary catastrophism' also have failed to see the obvious."[241]

When the sizes of the largest asteroid bodies were compared with the craters in the Clobbered Hemisphere, Patton and Windsor noticed two things. Firstly, 15 of the largest craters on Mars are in the Clobbered Hemisphere. Secondly, twice as many asteroids missed Mars than hit it. The most spectacular hit in the solar system - the Hellas Fragment - produced a crater 990 miles in diameter on Mars, or 2.66 times the size of Texas. In European terms, the Hellas Crater is equal to the combined areas of Great Britain, Ireland, France, Belgium, Luxembourg, the Netherlands, Switzerland, Germany, Denmark, Switzerland, Austria, Italy, Monaco, San Marino, Liechtenstein and half of Hungary combined. Remember, this occurred on a planet only 28% the size of Earth. I'd call that a catastrophe. The Hellas Fragment was estimated to be 600 to 625 miles in diameter and struck Mars at 25,000 mph, or 7 miles per second. Though the devastation would have been unimaginable, *Hellas was by no means the only major impact on Mars that day.*

Bulging in all the right places

The 'H' fragment was accompanied by a second rock, the Isidis asteroid, which produced a crater 684 miles in diameter. And yet a third projectile, which caused the Argyre Crater, 481 miles across. And yet a fourth, Cassini, 291 miles across. In all, 15 asteroids over 95 miles in diameter ploughed into the Clobbered Hemisphere, the larger smashing through the 20 miles of Mars crust, while the heaviest three penetrated deep into the 4,000 miles of molten magma, causing bulges to appear on the opposite side of the planet an hour later. These asteroids would have been *rotating* when they hit, adding considerable angular momentum to the impact. Any one of these strikes would have been an extinction level event on Earth. Interestingly, there's strong evidence that what happened to Mars would play a key role in some fascinating observations made by the ancients we'll get to in a minute. Today in our sophisticated

---

[241] Patton D W & S R Windsor, *The Mars-Earth Wars,* op. cit.

world of cosmology, Mars screams a *recent*, catastrophic history, but few are listening, and fewer still find themselves willing to go where the evidence leads them.

Patton and Windsor challenge us to observe the shocking features on Mars and draw our own conclusions. Mars has been really bashed and today is a planet of superlatives. If Astra were responsible, absorbing the impact of her pieces would cause Mars to increase its mass by up to 1.5%. To accommodate this expansion, the crust split into the greatest rift complex in the solar system. The Tharsis and Elysium Bulges can in no sense be termed gradual uplifts. Patton believes the Hellas Fragment was eventually forestalled by the crustal underside of the Serene Hemisphere on the opposite side of the planet. Is it coincidence that Tharsis hosts the largest volcano in the solar system? Olympus Mons at 27 km is three times the size of Everest, Earth's highest mountain. Patton believes this monster was one of several forced into existence as a result of the magma pressure from the collisions.

Researchers Luchitta and Rosanova record that the length of Valles Marineris, the largest canyon in the solar system, is equivalent to the length of Europe, extending across one-fifth of the Martian circumference, and goes down up to 7 km. In other words, Mars *split*. By comparison, Earth's Grand Canyon is only 446 km long and nearly 2 km deep. These scientists conclude that Valles Marineris was formed due to the swelling of the Tharsis area which caused the crust to collapse.[242]

Patton gets into the thermal emission systems such impacts would provoke. The incredible rifting across the surface of Mars was required to relieve the enormous pressures of such a catastrophe. The authors conclude:

"…between 30% and 33% of the fragments of Astra hit Mars in its Clobbered Hemisphere. Between 65% and 68% missed Mars and began to orbit the sun. Also, a small percent, perhaps almost 2%, missed Mars but began to orbit around Mars instead of the sun.

---

[242] **Lucchitta, B K, Rosanova, C E** "Valles Marineris; The Grand Canyon of Mars", USGS. http://astrogeology.usgs.gov/Projects/VallesMarineris/. Retrieved 26th August 2003

Evidence of this… is the foundation of an ancient ring system of Mars."[243]

Fear and panic

Professor Asaph Hall made astronomy history in August 1877 when, using the US Naval Observatory's recent, state-of-the-art, 66 cm telescope, he discovered that Mars had two moons. The revelation was all the more extraordinary given that these celestial bodies are tiny and among the least reflective in our solar system. The moons were named Phobos and Deimos ('fear' and 'panic') by the science master of Eton, Henry Madan, who thought the names appropriate considering Ares ('Mars', the Roman god of war) summoned them in Homer's *Iliad*, book XV.

The larger moon, Phobos, measures a mere 27 x 22 x 18 km and has a highly irregular shape featuring the large Stickney crater towards the leading apex. Phobos has horizontal striations from impacts and is pocked with strikes, though the Stickney hit came close to destroying it. Phobos orbits very close to Mars and crosses the Martian sky in a little over four hours, twice a day. It has an albedo (reflectivity) of only 3%, making it the darkest body in our solar system.

The smaller moon, Deimos, is further out and measures 15 x 12.2 x 10.4 km. It also bears collision damage and its two largest craters were named Swift and Voltaire. Both moons are generally thought to be captured asteroids. Patton and Windsor maintain they are remnants of the Astra collision brought into the Martian influence by the larger planet's tidal forces. The authors believe that a close scrutiny of the orbit above the Martian equator should yield evidence of fine particles left over from the ancient ring system that once circled the planet. This would make the case for the Astra collision as compelling, if not more so, than the extraordinary evidence we are about to examine. Patton writes:

"In Greek cosmology, Phobos was one of the two orbiting 'steeds' seen pulling the chariot of Mars across the cosmos. In Greek, 'phobos' meant fear, or a phobia to flee to some safe place from the

---

[243] Patton D W & S R Windsor, *The Mars-Earth Wars*, op. cit.

approaching Ares and its bolts of cosmic lightning.... However, if Mars has always orbited 35,000,000 miles or more from the Earth, as gradualists assume, why did the Greeks claim to see this tiny satellite and its partner, littler Deimos?"[244]

All the ancient attention and emotion paid out to a distant planet raises questions. Why was Cairo named after the Arabic word for Mars? Why is Tuesday named after the Old English god of war, Tiw, or, as he is known in the Greek, Ares, or Roman Mars? Wikipedia records:

"In the Greek world, Tuesday (the day of the week of the Fall of Constantinople) is considered an unlucky day. The same is true in the Spanish-speaking world, where a proverb runs: *En martes, ni te cases ni te embarques*, meaning, "On Tuesday, neither get married nor begin a journey"... In the Thai solar calendar, the day is named for the Pali word for the planet Mars, which also means 'Ashes of the Dead'; the color associated with Tuesday is pink." [245]

Dr Missler agrees with Patton and Windsor in believing that the previous eccentric orbit of Mars caused it to do terrifyingly close fly-bys of Earth. All through the Old Testament there are catastrophes described in the most stunning language. When you try to date them, says Missler, they are separated by 54 years or multiples thereof. The pertinent dates of the fly-bys were 20/21st March and the 25th of October, just before Halloween. The Ides of March in Rome were on 15th March – a day made infamous by the assassination of Julius Caesar. But Shakespeare's immortal words, "Beware the Ides of March" may have possessed more sinister overtones for those unlucky enough to have been caught in their thrall. Missler writes:

"The recent space age discovery of 'orbital resonance' – the tendency of orbits to synchronize on a multiple of one another – has led to a fascinating conjecture that the orbits of Earth and Mars were once on resonant orbits of 360 days and 720 days respectively. A computer analysis has suggested that this could yield orbital

---

[244] Ibid.
[245] http://en.wikipedia.org/wiki/Mars

interactions that would include a near pass-by on a multiple of 54 years, and this would occur on either March 25 or October 25. Such near pass-bys would transfer energy, altering the orbits of each."[246]

Patton refers to these interactions as the Mars-Earth Wars, of which there were several hundred. He believes the Martian moons hold the key to unravelling whether Mars, in fact, was Earth's most fearsome predator:

"The explanation for Deimos and Phobos orbiting Mars is simple: they are fragments of Astra that became Mars asteroids, and they remained Mars asteroids throughout the Mars-Earth Wars era. Hence the ancient Greeks have accounts of them, the 'steeds of Ares', accompanying Ares, the 'bane of mortals'. The blind bard Homer some 2,860 years ago was both profound and precisely correct."[247]

That Mars could have passed so close to Earth that even its tiny moons could be glimpsed with the naked eye is terrifying but by no means the whole story. Patton's model puts the pass-bys at 100,000 miles, even down to 70,000 miles, centre to centre. The catastrophic exchange of energy between Mars and Earth would have produced ample Biblical effects. Rising off the horizon an angry red, fifty times the size of the moon, the god of war would have unleashed a flux tube of lightning and storms of bolides arcing in at terrific speeds to explode across Earth's landscape. Immense tidal forces generated by the gravitational proximity of the planets would have ripped up Earth's soil in terrifying crustal tides 85 metres high. On Mars, the largest volcanoes in the solar system would have burst forth in liquid flame, led by Olympus Mons, towering 82,500 feet high with 525,000 cubic miles of ejecta materials, mostly lava. Then Ascraeus Mons at 50,000 feet, followed by Arsia and Pavonis Mons, both 40,000 feet high - the third and fourth largest volcanoes in the solar system. We can only surmise how the internal distress of Mars must have appeared from Earth, blasting out white-hot effluent from these super-vents, changing to

---

[246] **Missler, Chuck** *Signs in the Heavens,* www.khouse.org

[247] Patton D W & S R Windsor, *The Mars-Earth Wars,* op. cit.

yellow, orange and red. The ancients were under no illusions though, writes Dr Patton:

"The ancient, magnificent cometary tail of Mars was called by the Greeks 'The Golden Fleece of Ares', and it was for several reasons. First, Ares was Mars. Second its cometary tail was in full bloom as it swept across the face of the Earth, in the month of Ares.

It was this glistening gauze that trailed the chariot of Mars, wheels rotating, pulled by its [his] two trusty steeds, Phobos and Deimos. Those close Mars fly-bys were fearful, inflicting mass damage by fire, flood and earthquake, throwing out high voltage lightning toward the Earth, causing volcanoes to erupt, causing earthquakes, causing radical tides and tidal waves at the seaside.

Dreadful as the occasions were, destructive as they were, ugly as the face of Mars was, its long, glistening cometary tail threatened to sweep across the face of the Earth. To a neutral observer in space, it must have been a scintillating sight. To an Earth-dweller, the sight was far from funny. Such was the terror of the ancient authors who saw the 'fleece of Ares' and its associated nucleus, Mars." [248]

And passing before this astonishing picture? Mars's two moons, Phobos and Deimos, black against the fiery backdrop, presiding over the type of chaos best left to James Cameron, Peter Berg and other Hollywood directors with a flair to emulate. Or even the Bible itself:

Behold, the LORD maketh the Earth empty, and maketh it waste, and turneth it upside down, and scattereth abroad the inhabitants thereof. And it shall be, as with the people, so with the priest; as with the servant, so with his master; as with the maid, so with her mistress; as with the buyer, so with the seller; as with the lender, so with the borrower; as with the taker of usury, so with the giver of usury to him. The land shall be utterly emptied and utterly spoiled, for the LORD hath spoken this word.

The Earth mourneth and fadeth away, the world languisheth and fadeth away, the haughty people of the Earth do languish. The Earth also is defiled under the inhabitants thereof because

---

[248] Patton D W & S R Windsor, *The Mars-Earth Wars*, op. cit.

they have transgressed the laws, changed the ordinance, broken the everlasting covenant. Therefore hath the curse devoured the Earth and they that dwell therein are desolate. Therefore the inhabitants of the Earth are burned, and few men left....

In the city is left desolation, and the gate is smitten with destruction. When thus it shall be in the midst of the land among the people, there shall be as the shaking of an olive tree, and as the gleaning grapes when the vintage is done.... Wherefore glorify ye the LORD in the fires, even the name of the LORD God of Israel in the isles of the sea....

Fear, and the pit, and the snare, are upon thee, O inhabitant of the Earth. And it shall come to pass that he who fleeth from the noise of the fear shall fall into the pit; and he that cometh up out of the midst of the pit shall be taken in the snare: for the windows from on high are open, and the foundations of the Earth do shake. The Earth is utterly broken down, the Earth is clean dissolved, the Earth is moved exceedingly. The Earth shall reel to and fro like a drunkard and shall be removed like a cottage; and the transgression thereof shall be heavy upon it; and it shall fall, and not rise again. (Isa 24:1...20)

Or this passage from the Psalms:

In my distress I called upon the LORD and cried unto my God. He heard my voice out of His temple, and my cry came before Him, even into His ears. Then the earth shook and trembled. The foundations also of the hills moved and were shaken because He was wroth. There went up a smoke out of His nostrils and fire out of his mouth devoured; coals were kindled by it. He bowed the heavens also and came down, and darkness was under his feet.

And He rode upon a cherub and did fly: yea, He did fly upon the wings of the wind. He made darkness His secret place; His pavilion round about Him were dark waters and thick clouds of the skies. At the brightness that was before Him His thick clouds passed, hailstones and coals of fire. The LORD also thundered in the heavens, and the Highest gave His voice; hailstones and coals of fire. Yea, He sent out His arrows and scattered the foe. And He shot out lightnings and discomfited them. Then the channels of waters were seen, and the foundations of the world were

discovered at Thy rebuke, O LORD, at the blast of the breath of Thy nostrils. (Psa 18:6-15)

Missler draws our attention to the fact that Troy was rebuilt seven times from its own rubble. Early cities like Rome were not built on the coast but well inland to protect from tsunamis.

"...Such pass-bys would be accompanied by meteors, severe land tides, earthquakes, etc., and this would help explain why all the ancient cultures were so terrified by the Planet Mars and why calendars tended to reflect either March or October. A series of such pass-bys could also explain a number of the 'catastrophes' of ancient history, including the famous 'long day of Joshua' and several other Biblical episodes. Stability appears to have been attained during the last near pass-by in 701 BC, resulting in Earth's and Mars' present orbits of 365 1/4 days and 687 days, respectively. Provocative, but where's the evidence?"[249]

The word from Laputa

Could all this have really happened? A surprising corroboration may be found in the writings of renowned Irish satirist and clergyman Jonathan Swift. Swift lived and worked in England and Ireland through the period of Catholic displacement in the Glorious Revolution (1688), and after, when England went under the rule of protestants William and Mary, and later the Hanoverians. Swift was an accomplished wit and intellectual who counted Isaac Newton, Edmund Halley and William Whiston among his friends – all accomplished astonomers. The Irish Swift was a member of London's John Bull Club and relished sending up stuffy English academia in his novels, essays and poems. Writing in the third book of *Gulliver's Travels* (1726), Swift has his eponymous protagonist, Lemuel Gulliver, declare that the astronomers of the 'flying island of Laputa' have an extraordinary boast:

"They [the Laputans] have likewise discovered two lesser stars, or satellites, which revolve about Mars, whereof the innermost is distant from the center of the primary planet exactly three of its diameters,

---

[249] www.khouse.org, "Signs in the heavens" briefing pack

and the outermost five; the former revolves in the space of ten hours, and the latter in twenty-one and a half; so that the squares of their periodical times are very near the same proportion with the cubes of their distance from the center of Mars, which evidently shows them to be governed by the same law of gravitation that influences the other heavenly bodies."

This information appeared in a book *150 years before* Asaph Hall discovered Phobos and Deimos in 1877, and *that* feat only possible with the latest of telescopes. Even more intriguing, Swift's Laputan information is remarkably accurate, beyond statistical chance, so begs the questions: a) how could Swift know Mars had two moons and b) what was the source of his information? A sub-culture has grown up around this enigma and the battlelines between catastrophists and gradualists are clearly demarked. Flippant conjecturists maintain Swift himself was a Martian. Others that he followed Voltaire and Kepler's reasoning that since Mercury and Venus were the closest planets to the sun and had no moons, and the planets further out had many (and Earth had one moon), it seemed a fair guess that Mars was in line for probably two.

But how did Swift get the details of their rotational speeds and sizes so accurate? As previously mentioned, Phobos and Deimos are not moons in the classic sense (far too small) but putative, captured asteroids. Most scientists are embarrassed and baffled by Jonathan Swift's information, doubtless the satirist's every intent. Science forums put the Gulliver phenomenon down to a lucky guess on Swift's part and his penchant for mathematical malarkey – a wholly unsatisfactory explanation. Others surmise that Newton and Halley might have had a hand in the mathematics. Patton believes there's another possibility few dare to consider:

"At that time, in 1725 and 1726, astronomers did not know the diameter of Mars. Laputans disclosed the distance of Phobos and Deimos from Mars not in English miles but rather in Mars diameters. Astronomers in the early 1700's did not know the accurate value for the length of the astronomical unit, or how far the Earth is from the sun. And they didn't know how far Mars was from the sun. This unit of measurement in the satire suggests a very ancient sketch was involved, or a copy thereof from the Catastrophic Era.

This floats two questions. (1) Where did the sketch come from and what was on it? (2) Who, then, did Swift's calculations for him? Swift was an Irishman, a satirist and a wit. A mathematician he was not."[250]

It might be that Swift's greatest clue is the location of his fictional island – off the coast of China. The Catholic Church was very active in missionary work in China in the seventeenth and eighteenth centuries. One of the great concords of Eastern and Western thought was astronomy, and the Chinese were much taken with Keplerian theory, in which there was an avid exchange of ideas. Chinese astronomical knowledge was made available to the Jesuits, and among that data, Patton believes, there would have been diagrams of the heavens charted by China's ancient astronomers sequestered in Peking's archives.

"If such sketches existed, very possibly one of the Jesuit missionaries seeing such a sketch of the ancient 'Fire Star' would be puzzled by Mars with two tiny satellites. Perhaps a copy of the copied original sketch arrived in Europe by the early 18th century. Swift's close friend, a Catholic [poet], Alexander Pope, had Jesuit contacts…. If such a sketch was there, the Jesuit fathers in Peking would have been puzzled, and the Jesuit fathers in Paris… would not have known what to make of such a sketch.

But if a copy of such a sketch fell into the hands of Swift, Newton or Whiston, perhaps at the John Bull Club, some interesting interpretations could have resulted, and laughs also. A scenario like this, it is suspected, is where Swift got his 'inspiration' about the Laputan astronomers and their understanding of Mars with satellites.

To Swift, at the very least, such a sketch could provide the basis for an excellent satire on the 'backwardness' of English academia. They weren't as intelligent as they thought they were. They needed to have some fun poked at them.

Charles McDowell has researched this subject, and he suspects that the transmission of a Mars-Deimos-Phobos sketch, or sketches,

---

[250] Patton D W & S R Windsor, *The Mars-Earth Wars*, op. cit.

came from Peking via a Dr. Cunningham to Dr. Hans Sloane. Sloane gathered samples of thousands of new plants from newly explored lands for his greenhouse and herbarium. Sloane's personal collection of 50,000 books was purchased by parliament in 1753, and became the core of the British Museum.[251]

McDowell thinks 'Lemuel Gulliver' was a cryptic name for Sloane, Queen Anne's physician. 'Lemuel' in Proverbs [31:1,4] was a wise man, one close to publishers and to the royal family." [252]

Jonathan Swift could have little idea whether the Mars information was true or not, much less the resources to confirm if the moons of Mars existed firsthand. The information was a bagatelle, a trifle to insert in his novel, but one which reasonably may have had its origins in eye-witness accounts of Mars from the Catastrophic Era. For the moons of Mars to have been observed by naked eye from the Earth's surface at all, Mars would have to have been close. Very close.

'Monuments' on Mars
S A Cranfill writes:

"In the summer of 1976, NASA's Viking I spacecraft established an orbit around the planet Mars. In July it captured and relayed an image of what looked to be a massive human face carved out of a 'knob' (large hill), but the single frame was viewed and dismissed without further analysis as a trick of light and shadow. Several years later, Vincent DiPietro and Gregory Molenar, two engineers working at NASA's Goddard Space Flight Center, found another very recognizable image of the face, taken 35 orbits later, proving that the image was not merely a fleeting trick of light and shadow. The face is about 1.55 miles long, 1.25 miles wide, and 1,312 feet high. If a building storey was 10 feet, the Face would be some 131 stories tall. It has eyes below bilaterally crossed lines, a ridge-like nose, a mouth with fine structure that some have called teeth, and some sort of headpiece or helmet with regularly spaced lateral stripes. These same features

[251] **McDowell, C** "Catastrophism and Puritan Thought," Symposium on Creation VI. 1977, Seattle, Pacific Meridian, pp.57-60
[252] Patton D W & S R Windsor, *The Mars-Earth Wars*, op. cit.

appear in both images, 35 orbits apart. The right side of the Face is either degraded or was never completed, though it also shows an eye and part of the mouth." [253]

Meta Research believes:

"...a natural origin is ruled out by legitimate *a priori* tests at highly significant levels. The most reasonable remaining possibility is that the object exists on Mars and was built by an intelligent species in the distant past." [254]

The area where the Face is located on Mars is known as Cydonia. Other anomalies have been reported in this area; pyramidal structures known as the 'City', whose 'Fortress',

"...appears to include several wall-like sections, including two straight sides enclosing an inner space." [255]

The symmetry is intimidating, for natural features are by their nature anomalous. The D & M pyramid is similar to the Giza structures in Egypt, say researchers, displaying,

"...hexagonal symmetry, pentagonal symmetry and a Golden Section (phi or 1.618)." [256] Meta Research reports Cydonia also displays up to "five embedded, congruent, equi-spaced triangles, whose sides end in sharp vertices almost unknown in nature." 'Glass tubes' are also visible, showing highly ordered structure with perpendicular intersections unknown in nature. Suggestions include water pipes or an environmentally protected underground rapid transit system. Taken together, Meta Research concludes from the evidence "the natural origin hypothesis of the features displayed at Cydonia is disproved at odds of 1000 billion billion to one." [257]

[253] **Cranfill, S A** *They Came From Babel,* Write House, 1994, p.35

[254] www.metaresearch.org

[255] **Carlotto, M J** *The Martian Enigmas, A Closer Look,* North Atlantic Books, USA, 1991; also **Carlotto, M J** "Digital Imagery Analysis of Unusual Martian Surface Features", *Applied Optics* 27, 1926-1933, 1988

[256] Cranfill, S A, *They Came From Babel,* op. cit.

[257] www.metaresearch.org/solar%20system/cydonia / asom / artefact_html / default.htm – photos for reference

Dr Mark J Carlotto has a Ph.D in Electrical Engineering from Carnegie-Mellon University. He spent five years examining the Viking I pictures using advanced digital computer analysis. His conclusion is that the Cydonia phenomenon exhibits "non-fractal modelling indicative of design".

NASA cries conspiracy, a hoax, a trick of the light. Today, though, Mars currently sports three orbiting spacecraft – *Mars Odyssey, Mars Express* and *Mars Reconnaissance Orbiter,* as well as two ground-crawling rovers beaming back pictures, *Curiosity* and *Opportunity.* Conclusion? In today's austere times, someone is interested enough in Mars to splash out *billions* at a time when budgets are being severely curtailed or cut altogether. *Suppressed Science* reports:

"The turning point came in 1993 when Professor Emeritus of Philosophy, Stanley McDaniel, made NASA's failure to acknowledge and act on the new evidence the subject of a scientific study of the sociology of science, titled The McDaniel Report: On the Failure of Executive, Congressional and Scientific Responsibility in Investigating Possible Evidence of Artificial Structures on the Surface of Mars and in Setting Mission Priorities for NASA's Mars Exploration Program. In his report, Professor McDaniel states:

'As my study of the work done by the independent investigators and NASA's response to their research continued, I became aware not only of the relatively high quality of the independent research, but also of glaring mistakes in the arguments used by NASA to reject this research. With each new NASA document I encountered, I became more and more appalled by the impossibly bad quality of the reasoning used. It grew more and more difficult to believe that educated scientists could engage in such faulty reasoning unless they were following some sort of hidden agenda aimed at suppressing the true nature of the data.'

"The McDaniel Report was instrumental in forcing NASA to re-image Cydonia using the Mars Global Surveyor in 1998. The pictures obtained by MGS strengthened the case for artificiality, but NASA did everything it could to discourage this conclusion. On April 6, 1998, only hours after the first new data on the formation for 22 years had been acquired, NASA released a doctored image to the mass media that had virtually all three-dimensional information removed by inappropriate filtering and showed what seemed like scratches on a flat plain. This image has become known as the 'Catbox'."[258]

This from NASA contractor, Lan Fleming:

"The 'Catbox' is undoubtedly the shoddiest piece of image-processing work released in the 40-year history of the space program. Why did they do it? Unless JPL permitted complete incompetents to run loose in their lab, the only reasonable conclusion is that the MGS image was deliberately doctored for public consumption in order to kill public interest in the subject of planetary SETI in general and Cydonia in particular. The rapid and broad distribution of the Catbox to the media would seem to confirm that interpretation of events. It was displayed on CNN, in local newspapers, *US News and World Report*, *Astronomy* magazine, and most shamefully, in *Scientific American* (June, 1998, page 18)."[259]

A hoax? Spielberg's extraterrestrials? A resurgent malevolence, long ago suppressed? These days, there's a different Mars conspiracy doing the rounds. Michael Brooks, consultant for *New Scientist* and author of *13 Things That Don't Make Sense*, wonders:

"Have attempts to explore Mars been secretly scuppered by religious scientists keen to keep planet Earth 'special'? Have they been hiding their sabotage under a veil of incompetence? Or is it that scientists really can be astonishingly incompetent without any outside help? Only Dan Brown's next novel can tell us." [260]

Mission to Mars – Why?

In fact, this scenario was featured in the movie, *Mission to Mars*, released in 2000. The Brian de Palma movie recounts how a NASA mission to Mars results in the discovery of artificial structures, within which the astronauts discover a holographic image revealing that Mars once used to be a beautiful paradise covered with water until struck by a large asteroid which ruined the planet.

---

[258] www.suppressedscience.net/mars.html
[259] www.vgl.org
[260] "Is There a Life on Mars Conspiracy?" *Times Online*, 11th June 2009

The Martians evacuated from Mars via spacecraft and left the solar system. On their way out, one of the spaceships visits Earth, unformed as yet, and deposits something in the ocean. The holographic presentation then fast-forwards millions of years to reveal panspermian life coming about on the previously barren Earth via Darwinian evolution – i.e. fish, amphibians, birds, reptiles, mammals – one day resulting in humans with the capability to visit their Martian forebears on their long dead red planet. Putnam and Horn write:

"A staple doctrine among many ufologists is that such a discovery on any exoplanet would confirm that the hero myths of antideluvian history, as well as the sudden appearance of man himself, were the direct result of ancient, intelligent, extraterrestrial activity. The Great Sphinx in Giza, pyramidal structures around the world, and legends of early cultures would be seen as but trace evidence of this encounter when ET astronauts arrived in our galaxy and on our planet a long time ago and genetically upgraded *Homo sapiens* from primates like apes.

Such theorists also claim primitive man would have recorded their arrival, experiments, and departure in steles and stone tablets as a supernatural encounter between gods and men. Having engineering help from the flying geniuses, the same men likely would have modelled the temples and holy sites they built on Earth in dedication to those 'deities' based on designs they had been led to believe reflected similar configurations on the home planets of their creators. Thus, pyramids, monuments, mounds, and sphinx-like formations not only dot the ancient Earth, but similar buildings could be (or have been) found on Mars or elsewhere, and would be the 'loaded gun' that New Age unfologists have been waiting for." [261]

Tom van Flandern Ph.D, former celestial mechanics expert from Yale University and professor of physics at the University of Maryland, is well known for his outspoken assertions that such artificial structures have already been found on Mars, and that the US government and interested parties are continuing their

---

[261] Putnam and Horn, *Exo-Vaticana,* op. cit., p.468

investigations to see what they reveal. He stated in a 2007 interview with Thomas Horn:

"The biggest surprise of the space program to date has been the finding of several categories of anomalies on the surface of Mars that, if seen on Earth, would certainly be attributed to human activity. These include an abundance of special shapes not normally found in nature, such as closed triangles and pyramids; vehicle-like tracks and trails across otherwise featureless desert terrain; mostly underground networks of 'glassy tubes' apparently extending for hundreds of miles, visible in places where the surface is cracked, and seeming to connect interesting surface places; odd patterns and symbols; and an abundance of large-scale 'artistic' imagery such as the five known faces on Mars and some geoglyphs reminiscent of those on the plains of Nazca in Peru." [262]

Prof. van Flandern spent 21 years at the US Naval Observatory in Washington DC, where he became chief of the Celestial Mechanics Branch of the National Almanac Office. No slouch in orbital mechanics and a dedicated scientist, he spent decades mulling over the enigmatic evidence Mars presented. Van Flandern states that NASA conducted a number of authentication tests covertly to confirm the teleology (design) of the Cydonian anomalies. Cydonia is currently located at latitude 41 degrees north, which to the scientists favoured a natural origin for the phenomena. However when the pole shift was examined, it was discovered Cydonia had originally been located at the old equator, which changed the game significantly. All eight authentication tests eventually favoured an artificial origin for the anomalies at Cydonia. Everyone knew the implications. They were huge and would have profound implications for the theory of human origins on Earth.

Van Flandern made it clear he did not believe Mars was ever a host planet to a civilisation as such, but a large moon serving a former tenth solar system 'water-world' planet which no longer exists, having met a violent end similar to Patten, Steinhauer and Hatch's Astra. There is so far no evidence for an extended

---

[262] Ibid, p.474

250

civilisation on Mars beyond the 'artistic' anomalies found, van Flandern states. He suggests a further planet [Astra] was most likely the host, whose fragmentation terminated that civilisation. Van Flandern further suggests that a technically advanced, spacefaring civilisation based on [Astra] would have colonised its moon(s) – in [Astra's] case Mars (similar to NASA hopes to colonise Earth's moon). A natural further step, van Flandern states, would have been to construct surface exhibits on the Martian surface to be viewed from either the host planet or an orbiting space-station.[263]

Pick your theory or choose none. If you don't believe any of it, it doesn't matter because NASA, the Vatican. and a large chunk of the worldwide space-oriented scientific community do. Here are four typical articles, among many, that have appeared in the press over the past twelve months:

OUR GALAXY COULD CONTAIN 60 BILLION ALIEN PLANETS CAPABLEOF SUPPORTING LIFE - DOUBLE THE NUMBER THOUGHT BEFORE

Scientists believe our galaxy could contain a staggering 60 billion planets that might be capable of supporting life. Based on data from NASA's Kepler spacecraft, scientists had predicted there should be one Earth-size planet in the habitable zone of each red dwarf, the most common type of star. But a group of researchers has now doubled that estimate after considering how cloud cover might help an alien planet support life. Cloud cover is crucial for life, as clouds not only reflect sunlight to cool things off - they keep the planet warm enough to sustain life.[264]

SEARCHING FOR ET: HOW BRITISH ASTRONOMERS ARE JOINING FORCES TO EXPLORE WHETHER WE'RE ALONE IN THE UNIVERSE

---

[263] Ibid, p.479
[264] *Daily Mail,* 6th July 2013

Are we alone in the universe? We could be closer to finding out. British astronomers are joining forces to hunt for ET – or at least signs of his existence. Scientists from 11 institutions, including the renowned Jodrell Bank observatory, have launched a network that will help those working in different fields of research to share their expertise. Telescopes will listen in for radio and light 'broadcasts' beamed out by TVs, radios, satellites, radar and lasers from other worlds.[265]

ALIENS ALREADY WALK AMONG US BUT THEY'RE REFUSING TO SHARE THEIR TECHNOLOGY UNTIL WE CHANGE OUR WARRING AND POLLUTING WAYS, CLAIMS FORMER CANADIAN DEFENCE MINISTER

Former Canadian defense minister Paul Hellyer, 90, declared on Russian TV on Saturday that there are 80 different species of aliens and that most are benevolent toward humanity….

In a bizarre interview, Hellyer made a series of pronouncements about aliens which grew increasingly outlandish and sounded closer to the plot of Star Trek than what is officially known about ETs.

'We have a long history of UFOs and of course there has been a lot more activity in the last few decades since we invented the atomic bomb,' he said.[266]

'ON A GREAT THRESHOLD OF SPACE EXPLORATION': EVIDENCE OF ALIEN LIFE WILL BE FOUND IN THE NEXT 20 YEARS, CLAIMS SCIENTIST

Astronomers are standing on a 'great threshold' of space exploration that could see evidence of extra-terrestrial life being discovered in the next 20 years, an expert has claimed. Life beyond the Earth seems 'inevitable', given the immensity of the universe, according to planetary scientist Dr Sara Seager. In the coming decades, chemical fingerprints of life written in the atmospheres of planets

---

[265] Ibid.

[266] *Daily Mail*, 8th January 2014

orbiting nearby stars could be found by the next generation of space telescopes.[267]

As the old saying goes, it doesn't matter if you don't believe it, they do. In fact, science has articulated three new interdisciplinary areas of study in anticipation:

Astrobiology: the search for habitable planets beyond our own, including lifeforms that may exist there. As yet this is the only science in existence for which there is no evidence to study.

Xenoarchaeology: The study and cataloguing of extraterrestrial, artificial structures.

Exobiology: The search for life beyond Earth and the effects of extraterrestrial environments on life.

And just a reminder: At a time of global fiscal instability and recession today, huge amounts of money are being spent funding two scientific rovers scouring the surface of Mars, while three orbiters minutely search and record the red planet's surface. India launched a mission to Mars on 5th November 2013. Everyone's interested in Mars. *Looking for what?*

The coming Great Deception

People ask, why not *genuine* extraterrestrials? Who's to say that all these UFOs and astronaut reports we'll summarise in a later treatment on the subject, and abduction goings-on are not as the movies like *Close Encounters* make out; that we are witnessing the coming of our benevolent space brethren? After all, as the headlines proclaim, the law of averages states there has to be other life out there among the billions of galaxies that must exist, otherwise it's an awful waste of space. It's the most popular position that almost everyone takes in their enthusiasm to reach for something bigger than Earth. The problem is, it doesn't come close to fitting what we know of the evidence.

Unsettlingly, a third interdisciplinary area – demonology – was initiated by some scientists, including two of the foremost experts in UFOs – Dr Jacques Vallée and government analyst Professor J Allen Hynek. Perplexed and not a little unnerved by the

---

[267] *Daily Mail,* 4th August 2014

extraordinary, disturbing evidence surfacing across thousands of UFO sightings, EBE[268] contacts and abductions, Vallée and Hynek detected an ulterior agenda unfolding, that of deception, and it wasn't welcome. Firstly, data derived from such contacts were being recorded, not by a lunatic fringe, but by thousands of credible witnesses. Transcripts of alien contacts yielded common denominators regarding the information these mysterious entities were giving to harassed citizens. This information can be compiled into a theology that remains consistent throughout thousands of contact cases, and runs a remarkable parallel with classical demonology. The alien belief system inculcated into abductees completely supports New Age oriental teachings, denies Christianity and the deity of Jesus, and talks of a coming alien saviour/world leader who will bring peace and prosperity to mankind (to Christians the counterfeit/pseudo-Christ, the Antichrist, *ha-Satan*). Traditionally demons are quick to deny that we have any ultimate accountability for our actions – the serpent's hiss in the Garden. They tell us that we must realise the potential within so we can be as gods (*cf.* Gen 11:6). Notice the subtle counterfeiting: you can be a god in this life (Satan's message - Gen 3:5) instead of joint heirs ('gods') with Christ for eternity (Jesus' message – FG 10:34; Rev 20:4)

Many times during such contacts, alien entities have announced themselves as 'Ashtar', or as having come from the 'Ashtar Space Command'. They advise that we have strayed beyond the control bounds of our technology and that they are here to save us from destroying ourselves. They wish to ensure a smooth transition into the next plane of our human evolution so we can be as gods. The figure known to us as Jesus Christ has been misinterpreted by mankind. He was no different from any normal being except that he had mastered techniques we can all now draw upon so that a New Age or Dawn can begin to shine upon all humankind.

Researcher and author John Weldon, after many years of studying voluminous EBE evidence and files, makes this comment:

---

[268] EBE – Extra-biological entity

"How credible is it to think that literally thousands of genuine extraterrestrials would fly millions of light years simply to teach New Age philosophy, deny Christianity and support the occult? And why would the entities actually possess and inhabit people like demons do if they were really advanced extraterrestrials?"

Leading UFO publication *Flying Saucer Review* records that there has never been any evidence to support the supposition that these entities have come 'from outer space' (known as the Extraterrestrial Hypothesis – ETH). There is, on the other hand, compelling evidence that these creatures are 'extra-dimensional' and exist all around us in different dimensions or space planes. The Vatican, as well as other investigators and scientists, also ponder whether there exist portals or stargates on mountain-tops and other key locations around the Earth which serve as entry/exit points for hyperdimensional creatures. Of note are the numerous occasions in the Bible in which God forbids worship 'on the high places', yet key events in the scriptures occur on the summits of hills or mountains, such as the giving of the Law to Moses on Mt Horeb ('Sinai') in Exodus, the binding of Isaac on Mt Moriah, the Transfiguration, and so on. The Interdimensional Hypothesis (IDH), advanced by Vallée, Hynek and other ufologists, also seeks to explain how alien spacecraft have been viewed performing impossible manoeuvres at incredible speeds without disintegrating.

Brian Barclay and Bill Brumbaugh's *UFOs: The Hidden Truth* documentary explores some of the more widely-ignored spiritual connections surrounding the UFO conundrum. The authors build their case on the contemporary evidence, including some of the most exotic UFO footage available to date. The documentary explores the well-known cover-ups but delves further into unmasking the true identity of these entities. Barclay and Brumbaugh, together with leading research authors Dave Hunt and I D E Thomas, conclude that we are witnessing the coming of the dark gods.[269] Dave Hunt states:

---

[269] **Barclay, Brian & Bill Brumbaugh** *UFOs - The Hidden Truth,* a video documentary, PROACTIVE, 1627 W Main Street #213, Bozeman, MT 59715 USA

"In Close Encounters of the Third Kind – that first film that came out about UFOs – in the house that the mother and the little boy were living in, the toys begin running around and screws begin unscrewing themselves in the presence of UFOs. What the film was saying was, the same people who run UFOs run haunted houses. I would agree with that." [270]

Some Christian scholars surmise that God's violent destruction of Satan's exile base on Astra sent fragments hurtling into Mars and off into the solar system, blitzing Earth's canopy, the moon's surface and other planets beyond. Earth suffered the Flood – a combination of water derived from the collapsing canopy and the breaking open of the fountains of the deep. The Flood annihilated 100% of the Nephilim – the serpent's seed – initially accomplishing God's goal in terminating *ha-Satan's* hybrid programme, yet Gen 6:4 tells us that more creatures appeared **'after that'**, presumably as a result of further hyperdimensional sexual shenanigans between fallen angels and Earth women. Today Noah's Flood waters reside in the oceans, Earth's moon has been shotblasted, Mars endured major damage and a poleshift, and what's left of Astra forms the asteroid belt with which we're familiar today, whose debris periodically threatens Earth and appears, according to scripture, to have a prophetic role in the coming Great Tribulation.

Other researchers surmise that the enigmatic 'remains' at Cydonia may have a time-lock function intended by God; namely, that once technological development on Earth has reached the Space Age and man has the technology to visit Mars, the fate of Astra and the red planet will once again enter human consciousness, setting the stage for the mother of all delusions. 'Proof' will be presented for panspermia, namely that mankind in fact originated from the star-people. If this occurs, notice that man does not come up with this delusion, and nor does *ha-Satan. God does!*

And for this cause God shall send them strong delusion, that they should believe <u>the</u> lie [definite article in the Greek]; that they

---

[270] Ibid.

all might be damned who believed not the truth, but had pleasure in unrighteousness. (2 Thess 2:11-12)

The Vatican's in deep with extraterrestrial research, owning some advanced facilities at the University of Arizona's Mount Graham International Observatory in south-east Arizona. This usurped Apache holy site now hosts some of the most advanced optical equipment on the planet, including the Vatican Advanced Technology Telescope (VATT), the Submillimeter Telescope (SMT) and the most powerful viewing platform on Earth, the Large Binocular Telescope (LBT). NASA astronaut Gordon Cooper remarked in 2008:

"You want to know about UFO[s] and little green men? Contact the Vatican. They have an observatory out in Arizona, and that's what they are looking for." [271]

The Vatican has been at it for quite a while. The London *Daily Telegraph* reported in October 1992:

VATICAN SETS EVANGELICAL SIGHTS ON OUTER SPACE

The Roman Catholic Church is to team up with America's space agency to look for life in outer space and so spread the Gospel to extraterrestrials.

Jesuit priests who run the Vatican Observatory near Rome say they are joining forces with the US NASA agency to hunt for UFOs and signs of life on planets in solar systems similar to Earth's.

NASA's job will be to monitor for 'alien' communication signals; the Vatican, which has helped to build a new reflector telescope in Tucson, Arizona, would search for planets displaying conditions for life....

Should intelligent alien life be found, Fr. Coyne said, "the Church would be obliged to address the question of whether extraterrestrials might be brought into the fold and baptized." [272]

---

[271] Benford, T T "UFO, aliens and the Vatican: And why astronaut Gordon Cooper lied to me", *Yahoo Voices*, 11th June 2008: Per *Exo-Vaticana.*
[272] *Daily Telegraph*, 28th October 1992

In fact, the Church is ready for a lot more than that, say Putnam and Horn. They quote Dr Giuseppe Tanzella-Nitti, *Opus Dei* member and professor of theology at the University of the Holy Cross in Rome, as commenting:

"It seems important to note that a believer who is respectful of the requirements of scientific reasoning would not be obliged to renounce faith in God simply on the basis of the reception of new, unexpected information of a religious character from extraterrestrial civilizations. In the first place, human reason itself would suggest the need to submit this new 'religious content' coming from outside the Earth to an analysis of reasonableness and credibility (analogous to what we are accustomed to do when any religious content is proposed to us on Earth); once the trustworthiness of the information has been verified, the believer should try to reconcile such new information with the truth that he or she already knows and believes on the basis of the revelation of the One and Triune God, conducting a re-reading inclusive of the new data, similar to that which would be applied in an ordinary interreligious dialogue." [273]

Those familiar with the Vatican's baleful history will recognise the iron fist in the velvet glove. Jesus Himself gave His inner core of disciples several detailed briefings on the conditions prevalent on Earth immediately prior to His return. These discourses, recorded in scripture, are often mistaken for the same occasion, which they are not. These should be read *in context* in Matt 24/Mark 13 (Attendees: James, John, Peter and Andrew. Location: Mount of Olives) and Luke 17 & 21 (Attendees: Pharisees, the public and disciples: Location: the Temple (Luke 21:1). In the Olivet Discourse given to James, John, Peter and Andrew on the Mount of Olives, the LORD starts his end-times briefing with the words:

"Take heed that no man deceives you…" (Matt 24:4).

Then later:

"But as the days of Noah were, so shall also the coming of the Son of man be." (Matt 24:37)

In the Luke discourses, Yeshua states:

---

[273] **Tanzella-Nitti, Giuseppe** "Extraterrestrial Life", *Interdisciplinary Encyclopedia of religion and Science,* http://inters.org/extraterrestrial-life

"Take heed that ye be not deceived, for many shall come in My name, saying I am Christ [e.g. 'Jesus is LORD']; and the time draweth near: go ye not therefore after them. (Luke 21:8)

And: "And as it was in the days of Noah, so shall it be also in the days of the Son of man." (Luke 17:26)

And: "And there shall be signs in the sun, and in the moon, and in the stars; and upon the Earth distress of nations, with perplexity; the sea and the waves roaring; men's hearts failing them for fear, and for looking after those things which are coming on the Earth: for the powers of heaven shall be shaken." (Luke 21-25-26)

And: "Watch ye therefore, and pray always, that ye may be accounted worthy to escape all these things that shall come to pass, and to stand before the Son of man." (Luke 21:36)

The recurring themes running through these briefings are:

1) A time of great testing is coming upon the Earth (the Great Tribulation; 'the Time of Jacob's [Israel's] Trouble')

2) Deception will be the key problem, even for believers ('the elect') on Earth at that time

3) A phenomenon uniquely distinctive to Noah's day will again characterise the last days before Yeshua's return. This won't just be restricted to general wickedness, prevalent on Earth from the start. And it won't be another flood, since God promised never to visit another global inundation upon the planet (Gen 9:11)

4) Something will be coming upon the planet so frightening, men's hearts will fail them

5) There is a way you can escape what is coming. Be accounted worthy by Christ Himself.

Consider also that Yeshua could have explained *in plain language* precisely what was coming on the Earth *but chose not to,* merely dropping **'as it was in the days of Noah'** into the mix so 'the elect' would work it out with the help of His Spirit. God wants us to care enough to dig into His Word and put the pieces together – an exhortation repeated throughout the Bible. This is strongly suggestive of the same selection process we previously examined, namely that God is separating His chosen ('the elect') who care enough to study to show themselves approved from those who couldn't care less; who will ultimately become victims of a whole rack of deceptions in the days to come and harden their hearts to their predicament.

The Holy War is thus a spiritual war. It began with pride and sin found in the heart of the most incredible being God ever created. *Ha-Satan's* fall from God's grace infected mankind and a third of the angelic realm – a war which has splattered blood and misery down through history and will play out its denouement amid the jet exhaust, rap and neon of the 21st century in ways which will astonish. Meanwhile God has a people He chose before the foundation of the world whom He is calling out. These will know who they are, for they will respond to the call of His Spirit and Word. The rest won't.[274]

Mere Christian élitist dogma and superstition? We'll find out. Meanwhile, let's pick up Earth's story again in the days and years following Flood, for the clue to mankind's origins, as well as his present and future predicament, may already be written in stone across our planet, if we remove the blinders and comprehend what's before our very eyes.

---

[274] Eph 1:4-5; FG 6:44; 6:64-65; 2 Tim 2:19; 2 Thess 2:13; Rom 1:7; Isa 49:1,5; Jer 1:5; Gal 1:15; Acts 13:48

NEW BEGINNINGS
Back on a ruined Earth

And God remembered Noah and every living thing, and all the cattle that was with him in the Ark. And God made a wind to pass over the Earth and the waters assuaged. The fountains also of the deep and the windows of Heaven were stopped, and the rain from Heaven was restrained. And the waters returned from off the Earth continually, and after the end of the hundred and fifty days the waters were abated. And the Ark rested in the <u>seventh month, on the seventeenth day of the month, upon the mountains of Ararat.</u> (Gen 8:1-4)

The Jews today have two calendars – one civil and one religious. The original Genesis civil calendar commences in the month of Tishrei (in the autumn) with Rosh Hashanah – the Jewish New Year – which celebrates the creation of Adam and Eve. However, in Exodus 12:2, God later institutes the new religious calendar, and requires that it commence in the spring to commemorate when the Jews were brought out of Egypt. The first month of this new religious calendar is Abib, also known as Nisan. Therefore, the above **seventh month, on the seventeenth day of the month,** when Noah's Ark came to rest on the mountains of Ararat equates to the seventeenth day of the first month (Nisan) of the Jewish religious calendar, known as the Feast of Firstfruits. This feast day has the theme of 'resurrection by God's grace'. It's not only the day Noah's Ark comes to rest 'on the mountains of Ararat', it's also the exact day the Israelites cross the Red Sea, the same day Israel eats the firstfruits of the Promised Land (Josh 5:10-12), and the precise day the resurrection of Yeshua occurs following His crucifixion, **'the firstfruits of them that slept'** (1 Cor 15:20). These are four of many fulfilments of key events occurring on specific feast days set by YHWH, which we'll examine as we go.

How long were Noah and his family on the Ark?

"Noah entered the ark in the 600th year of his life, on the 17th day of the 2nd month (Gen 7:11-13). Noah left the ark on the 27th day of the 2nd month of the following year (Gen 8:14-15). Therefore, assuming a lunar calendar of 360 days, Noah was on the ark for approximately 370 days. Noah was told to go on the ark and in 7 days it would rain. So Noah was on the ark 7 days prior to the flood, adding to the 370, making it 377."[275]

It took a while for the waters to assuage. Noah kept sending out doves until the last one failed to return. I would imagine the ark smelt pretty fruity at this stage but they had done it, and all the animals survived too. Geologist John D Morris writes,

"Remember... that the land surface was fully saturated at the Flood's end, and a strong, prolonged wind would have helped dry it out. By sending out the ravens and the dove, Noah was testing to see how far this evaporation had progressed. Eventually, the face of the ground was dry (Genesis 8:13), but not yet able to support life. A month later was the Earth dried (v. 14) and Noah was able to free the animals.

"This evaporation was necessary on another front as well. Evaporating water removes significant heat from the system, and abundant heat was everywhere. Heat from the Earth's interior was introduced to the surface by the rising 'fountains of the great deep', probably boiling the oceans above the subterranean vents. Rapid lateral movements of the continents, as proposed by the best creationist model, would have generated immense heat from the friction involved. So too would the vertical uplift of the mountains, virtually all of which rose at this time as the down-warped sedimentary basins sought to regain isostatic equilibrium. No doubt Noah would have measured the average ocean temperature as quite higher than today's value." [276]

And it came to pass in the six hundredth and first year, in the first month, the first day of the month, the waters were dried up from off the Earth. And Noah removed the covering of the Ark and looked, and, behold, the face of the ground was dry. And in the second month, on the seven and twentieth day of the month, was the Earth dried.

And God spake unto Noah, saying, "Go forth out of the Ark, thou and thy wife and thy sons, and thy sons' wives with thee.

[275] http://wiki.answers.com/Q/How_long_was_noah_on_the_ark
[276] www.icr.org/article/3768/

Bring forth with thee every living thing that is with thee, of all flesh, both of fowl, and of cattle, and of every creeping thing that creepeth upon the Earth, that they may breed abundantly in the Earth and be fruitful and multiply upon the Earth." (Gen 8:13-17)

The first covenant

Noah frees the animals onto a barren, frightening landscape of hardened mud and thunderous skies. A somewhat chastened God declares that never again will He destroy mankind with water. He gives Noah a special sign to seal the covenant, employing something no doubt completely new to Noah's experience – a rainbow. This would not have been possible in the pre-Flood world if some sort of canopy existed to refract the sunlight.[277] If rainbows had routinely appeared before the Flood, why would God think it special enough as a pledge for such an important oath? Did Noah look up at the clouds with disappointment and mutter, "Oh, a rainbow"? In fact, was Noah even in the business of provoking God further after the terrifying, Earth-shattering apocalypse he had just survived? Probably not.

All over the world today you can see evidence of the Great Flood. I cover a number of examples in *Origins I*. God's stern action to destroy the world had the intended effect. The Nephilim were all dead, the seed of the serpent now extinct (Gen 3:15). *Ha-Satan's* attempt to corrupt the human genome to thwart the Seed of the woman had been brought to naught for now, and mankind could start anew, though Satan reboots the Nephilim programme (*cf.* Num 13:33) and more creatures appear as we'll find out later (Gen 6:4).

The traditional place for Noah's landing is 'on the mountains of Ararat', popularly believed to be near the confluence of the borders of Turkey, Armenia and Iran. Many an aspiring Indiana Jones (including Joanna Lumley!)[278] has departed on a quest for the Biblical boat, trekking off into what has become one of the most

---

[277] Day, Phillip, *Origins I – The Greatest Scientific Discovery*, op. cit.
[278] *ITV*, "Joanna Lumley - The Search For Noah's Ark", 23rd December 2012

politically charged and dangerous hotspots on Earth. The irony is, they may be looking in completely the wrong place.

The Ark found?

In the 5th September 1960 edition of *Life* magazine, an article on the U-2 spy plane photos reads as follows:

"While routinely examining aerial photos of his country, a Turkish army captain suddenly gaped at [a] picture. There, on a mountain 20 miles south of Mt. Ararat, the biblical landfall of Noah's Ark, was a boat-shaped form about 500 feet long. The captain passed on the word. Soon an expedition including American scientists set out for the site.

At 7,000 feet, in the midst of crevasses and landslide debris, the explorers found a clear, grassy area shaped like a ship and rimmed with steep, packed-earth sides. Its dimensions are close to those given in Genesis: 'The length of the ark shall be 300 cubits, the breadth of it 50 cubits, and the height of it 30 cubits,' that is, 450x75x45 feet. A quick two-day survey revealed no sign that the object was man-made. Yet a scientist in the group says, 'Nothing in nature could create such a symmetrical shape. A thorough excavation may be made another year to solve the mystery'."

A US nurse-anaesthetist named Ron Wyatt read that copy of *Life* and hastily embarked on a crusade, whose obsession would spawn one hundred trips to the Middle East until his death in 1999. Wyatt's claims to have found Noah's Ark have been largely discredited even by Christian groups, but the idea that there's something up at this particular location persists to this day.

www.arkonararat.com hosts a list of some who claimed to have found the Ark or came by unusual reports or pictures unexpectedly:

"275 BC – Berossus, reporting on the history of Babylonia, claims that pilgrims went up a mountain in Armenia to carve amulets from the petrified pitch that covers the Ark

30 BC - Hieronymous mentions remains of Noah's Ark

1st Century AD - Nicholas of Damascus mentions remains of Noah's Ark

50 AD - Josephus mentions remains of Noah's Ark 3 times

315? - 403 AD - Epiphanius reports that remains of the Ark are on a mountain in the Gordian range

349 - 407AD Chrysostom mentions remains of Noah's Ark

4th Century AD - Faustus of Byzantium reports the experiences of a bishop who travelled to the region of 'Gortouk' to see the Ark

560 - 636 AD - Isidore of Seville mentions remains of Noah's Ark

620 AD - According to Hussein El Macin of Baghdad, Roman Emperor Heraclius visits the remains of the Ark after conquering the Persian city of Themanin

1254 AD - Haithon refers to Mt. Ararat as the resting place of Noah's Ark

1255 AD - Guillaume of Ruysbroeck tells of the devout Jacob of Medzpin's adventure on Ararat, and his answered prayer to see the Ark

13th Century AD - Marco Polo mentions in his book *The Travels of Marco Polo* that the Ark was still resting on the summit of Mt. Ararat

1820 (?)AD - Explorer Claudius James Rich writes that one Aga Hussein has seen the remains of the Ark

1829 AD - Dr. Friedrich Parrot makes the first modern ascent of Greater Ararat. He visits the ancient St. James Monastery (also known as St. Jacob Monastery), that was destroyed in the 1840 eruption of Mt. Ararat

1854 AD - Haji Yearam and his father lead three British scientists up Ararat to the Ark remains

1878 AD - Viscount James Bryce climbs Ararat, as recounted in his book *Transcaucasia and Ararat*. He finds old hand-tooled timber on this treeless mountain

1883 AD - Turkish commissioners investigate severe Ararat avalanches and report seeing the preserved but battered Ark structure. Locals claimed the remains were visible for six years. (*Nieuwe Rotterdamsche Courant,* July 28, 1883; *Chicago Tribune,* August 10, 1883; *New York Herald,* August 10, 1883; *New York World,* August 13, 1883; *New York Times,* August 15, 1883; *The Watchtower,* September 1883)....[a testimony] considered the most complete and accurate account appeared in the *British Prophetic Messenger* in the summer of 1883

1887 AD - John Joseph, Prince of Nouri, Archbishop and Grand Apostolic Ambassador of Malabar, India and Persia, makes three attempts to climb Ararat. [There are claims of] a sighting near the saddle between the peaks. Suggests the Ark be sent to the Chicago World's Fair

1908(?) AD - George Hagopian climbs Ararat with his uncle and reports seeing and climbing onto the preserved Ark

1916-1917 AD - Czar Nicholas II sends an expedition of 150 men to map Ararat and document the Ark. Revolution erupts and evidence disappears

1936 AD - New Zealander Hardwidke Knight finds very old hand-tooled timbers high on Ararat

1942 AD - American soldier Ray Lubeck views Ark in a 30-120 second film clip on Midway Island in 1942

1943 AD - American soldier Ed Davis glimpses huge broken Ark sections in Ahora Gorge

1944 AD - American soldier Vince Will views Ark from plane on Mt. Ararat

1945 AD - American soldier *aka* Caleb views Ark from plane on Mt. Ararat

1946 AD - American soldier Charlie McCallen views Ark in a 30-60 second news reel in a movie theatre in Jackson, Tennessee

1948 AD - Farmer Shakru Arsent tells newspaper of farmer named Reshit seeing petrified remains of a ship-like structure high on Ararat

1953-1955 AD - William Todd, a photographer in Turkey, claims to have seen Noah's Ark many times while flying over Mt. Ararat

1956-1957 AD - Herb Knee views Ark in a 60-120 second news reel in a movie theatre in Winchester, Tennessee

1964 AD - Retired Air Force Master Sergeant E8 claims to see wood structure on Mt. Ararat

1968 AD - David Duckworth, a Smithsonian volunteer, says he saw Ark artefacts from Mt. Ararat

1969 -1970 AD - Lt. Col. Walter D. Hunter is shown photos of what allegedly is Noah's Ark

1992 - 1993 AD - Rolando Reyna watches a Saturday night newscast which shows film footage of Noah's Ark on Ararat in a Mexican City broadcast."[279]

A retired Air Force Master, Sergeant E8, who spent over 28 years in the Air Force and flew over 28,000 hours, believes he saw the Ark around 1964 on a flight out of Diyarbakir, Turkey. Arkonararat.com records:

"In the air, it was a beautiful day without clouds. He stated that after leaving Diyarbakir in a C-130 transport, they flew within 1/2 mile of Mount Ararat. The seven-member crew was talking about Mount Ararat on the radio. As they approached Ararat and circled around it, he guessed that they were flying at about 15,000 feet above sea level. Several of the crew including himself saw what looked like a dark-colored log sitting on the mountain at the edge of a drop-off and with a rising, light-colored area behind it. His eyes focused on this log and as the plane came closer, he said that it was obviously a man-made, cigar-shaped boat sitting high on the mountain. He estimated that the boat was 3/4 of the way up the mountain. He claimed that the boat was obviously man-made, had a smooth surface and looked like a flat barge.

When he was shown Elfred Lee's drawings of the Russian video which Ray Lubeck saw in WWII, the well-built Air Force Master Sergeant (now a supervisor for a California government agency) was visibly shaken and said that the picture is almost exactly what he saw, although from his angle and distance he did not notice a super-structure. He...guessed the flat boat (like a barge in the Northeast US) was 150 feet long by 20-25 feet wide. He said that the mountain and terrain was barren with no trees, so he could do nothing but guess at the dimensions.

Interestingly, at least two (if not more) crew members witnessed the man-made boat on the same flight. The other alleged eyewitnesses are still alive, he is in contact with them, and he is checking to see if

---

[279] www.noahsarksearch.com

they want to make a comment on what they saw. He also said that there is a chance they might have taken a photo of the alleged boat."[280]

Some say the Ark is resting on the mountains south of Greater and Lesser Ararat just down the valley from the ancient Turkish village of Kazan ('Village of Eight'). There is the Noah's Ark National Park Visitor's Centre on Google Earth.[281] The actual site of what some believe is the Ark is clearly seen to the south-east, labelled by Wikipedia as the Durupinar site. The length of the formation is 300 Egyptian cubits, which makes it the right size – two-thirds the length of the Titanic. Near Kazan village, twelve giant stones have been found with *curved* holes drilled through the tops. The larger the stone, the larger the hole. One stone weighs around 9,000 lbs. Some maintain that these are anchor (drogue) stones, similar to those much in evidence in the ancient world, used to give stability to a boat in a storm.[282] The reader will have to decide what, if anything, they are looking at.

There seems to be a lot of evidence. There's just one glitch with all this Ark stuff, however. *No hard evidence.* One minute we read of mere 'boat-shaped' earthworks, the next (if the previous reports are to be believed), a recognisable, flat, barge-like structure which, when viewed from 15,000 feet, appears man-made. Let's face it, there's either a boat up there or there isn't.

There's another problem. *The Bible doesn't put the Ark anywhere near 'Mount Ararat' in Turkey.* A closer look at Genesis 11:2 reveals that after the Flood, once the human population was well on its way again, the children of the Ark survivors journeyed *from the east* and found a plain in the land of Shinar (Mesopotamia – *lit.* 'land of two rivers' - Euphrates and Tigris), where they build Babylon and its infamous tower. Ararat in Turkey is *north* of Babylon, so the survivors would have to have headed *south.* It's a small discrepancy but it's a *remez* - a clue to something deeper. This being the case, a trusty map shows that, for the survivors of the

---

[280] www.arkonararat.com

[281] Visitors' centre is at 39 26 33.60 N, 44 14 00.67 E. 'Ark feature' is at 39 26 26.19 N, 44 14 05.49 E

[282] www.drdino.com

Flood to have come westward *from the east*, the Ark would need to have come to rest *in the mountains of Iran*. Interestingly, Marco Polo only named that Turkish mountain 'Ararat' based on his own belief that he had found something, and the name stuck because it was Marco Polo. But 'Ark evidence' has always been grandiose and exciting on the one hand, then thin, inconclusive and unsatisfying when you get down to the actual 'proof'. The impression is that people so badly want it to be up there that a 'daft' *from the east* in Genesis 11:2 passes them by with nary a blink.

Is it possible the Ark may still be found somewhere no-one has thought of looking? Is it possible the Ark may have a role to play in mankind's future? Dr Chuck Missler not only suggests that the Ark is in Iran, but that God may have meant for it to survive. He gleans this from an obscure detail in Genesis 6:14 illuminated by his own experience as a United States Naval Academy graduate. The passage states that the Ark was pitched *both within and without*. No shipbuilders did this. Missler believes that the only conceivable reason God instructed Noah to carry out this extra task may have been to permit the vessel to survive for a protracted period in the face of the elements. Welcome to another *remez*. We're back to **"It is the glory of God to conceal a thing, but the honour of kings is to search out a matter."** (Prov 25:2) For the latest on Ark research, you can consult the web references in this chapter and come to your own conclusions. Or get on a plane and go to Iran (good luck).

Starting anew

So Noah, his three sons, Japheth, Shem and Ham, and their wives disembark the Ark and set the animals free. Noah sacrifices some of the 'clean' animals to the LORD (he has seven pairs of each, so he won't run short), **And the LORD smelled a sweet savour; and the LORD said in his heart, "I will not again curse the ground any more for man's sake, though <u>the imagination of man's heart is evil from his youth;</u> neither will I again smite any more every thing living, as I have done."**

…And God blessed Noah and his sons and said unto them, "Be fruitful and multiply, and replenish the Earth. <u>And the fear of you and the dread of you shall be upon every beast of the</u>

Earth, and upon every fowl of the air, upon all that moveth upon the Earth, and upon all the fishes of the sea; into your hand are they delivered. Every moving thing that liveth shall be meat for you; even as the green herb have I given you all things. But flesh with the life thereof, which is the blood thereof, shall ye not eat." (Gen 8:21…9:4)

Contrary to some New Age environmentalist nonsense, wherein a wood louse has the same rights and worth on the planet as a human, God puts all creatures under the charge, care and dominion of man. And even more unpopular with the vegetarians: meat is now on the menu. This may be necessary to supply the extra protein required to survive in the new single-atmospheric-pressure environment.[283] We are told Noah immediately sets about tending the land. The scriptures do not reveal whether they lived out of the Ark for a few months while getting established, but we know they had tents (Gen 9:21). At some point – we don't know how long after – a crop of grapes is harvested to make wine, and Noah gets drop-down, drag-out drunk.

In the pre-Flood world, Noah knew how to make wine. We infer this because he knew how to make it afterwards (Gen 9:21). Interestingly, grape juice does not ferment under double atmospheric pressure, but does, as we know, in today's 14.7 lbs/sq. in. Did Noah make wine after the Flood and become intoxicated, unaware of the prevailing atmospheric conditions? Noah's inebriation seems unintentional. Then we have the following extraordinary incident:

And Noah began to be an husbandman [farmer] **and he planted a vineyard. And he drank of the wine and was drunken, and he was uncovered within his tent. And Ham, the father of Canaan, saw the nakedness of his father, and told his two brethren without.** (Gen 9:20-22)

Ham's big *faux pas*

When Noah finds out, he takes the serious step of cursing, not Ham, *but Ham's fourth son, Canaan*. His progeny shall be servants

---

[283] **Day, Phillip** *Origins I – The Greatest Scientific Discovery*, op. cit.

(slaves) in perpetuity. Noah also ranks all three sons interelationally by relaying the following:

"Cursed be Canaan; a servant of servants shall he be unto his brethren." And he said, "Blessed be the LORD God of Shem; and Canaan shall be his servant. God shall enlarge Japheth, and he shall dwell in the tents of Shem; and Canaan shall be his servant." (Gen 9:25-27)

Noah's sons, in order of birth, appear to be Japheth (Gen 10:21), Ham (the 'younger son' – Gen 9:24) and Shem.[284] According to blessing, however, they are ranked thus: Shem the favoured, followed by Japheth, then Canaan (Ham). Here are the questions: What did Ham actually do that is described as 'seeing his father's nakedness'? Was it something more than just 'seeing' that got Canaan's line punished? It would have to be something serious for his father to dole out such a judgment. And why to Canaan, the fourth-born and not Ham's heir, Cush, or for that matter, Ham's other children, Mizraim and Put? The Curse of Canaan has had scholars fretting and blushing for centuries, and more recently accusing one another of *racism*.

Ham's name comes from the Hebrew חָם meaning 'hot', 'burnt' or 'charred'. Was Ham black? Was he made black as a result of his father's curse? See where this is going? It gets worse. Wikipedia reports:

"The curse seems unusually severe for merely observing Noah unclothed. An explanation sometimes offered notes that the phrase 'expose father's nakedness' is used several times elsewhere in the Pentateuch as a euphemism for having sexual relations with one's mother, suggesting a different crime."[285]

---

[284] This is deduced from the chronologies given in Gen 10 and 1 Chron 1, wherein the descendants are listed commencing with the senior son. Genesis 5:32 states that Noah was 500 years old and he begot Shem, Ham and Japheth. Genesis 7:11-13 states that 100 years later Noah and his family entered the Ark. Genesis 11:10 states that Shem was 100 years old (2 years after the Flood) when he fathered Arphaxad. These verses seem to indicate that Shem was not the eldest. In scripture, however, Noah's sons are almost always listed as Shem, Ham and Japheth.

[285] http://en.wikipedia.org/wiki/Curse_of_Ham

It certainly does. Incest. **And the man that lieth with his father's wife hath uncovered his father's nakedness....** (Lev 20:11). And Leviticus 18:7-8 states: **The nakedness of thy father, or the nakedness of thy mother, shalt thou not uncover: she is thy mother; thou shalt not uncover her nakedness. The nakedness of thy father's wife shalt thou not uncover: it is thy father's nakedness.**

In the context of the Leviticus passages above, Habbakuk gives the following warning against getting your neighbour drunk so you can seduce his wife: **Woe unto him that giveth his neighbour drink, that puttest thy bottle to him, and makest him drunken also, that thou mayest look on their nakedness!** (Hab 2:15; *cf:* Lev 18:20)

Three interpretations to Ham's sin have therefore been offered over the years:

1) Ham sodomised his father
2) Ham castrated his father, preventing him from having a fourth son. Thus Canaan, Ham's fourth son, is cursed in revenge
3) Ham raped his mother, *fathering Canaan*

Bob Deffinbaugh provides one tactful solution:

"I am impressed with the way in which Moses reported this incident, with a minimum of details and description. To have written any more would have been to perpetuate the sin of Ham. Hollywood would have taken us inside the tent in wide-screen technicolor. Moses leaves us outside with Shem and Japheth."[286]

That may be so, Bob, but the Holy Spirit has seen fit to put this sordid business into the scriptures, so God wants us to know what happened. Let's do a little digging.

All about Canaan

With due deference to the tact Moses brings to the text, the aforementioned Leviticus passages do seem firm on describing the crime of incest. It would have to be something this bad for Noah to

---

[286] http://bible.org/seriespage/nakedness-noah-and-cursing-canaan-genesis-918-1032

pronounce such a curse. Did Ham have sexual relations with his mother, producing Canaan? This is intriguingly alluded to *twice in five verses*. In the first passage below, the sons of Noah are listed, and then a strange, incongruous, pointed statement is stuck in, explaining that it's Ham who's the father of Canaan (i.e. not Noah!). Given the context, the only explanation that makes sense is that Moses is discreetly setting the record straight by telling the reader, "Ham is the father of Canaan, not Noah!" Why mention Ham's *fourth son* at all unless the purpose is relevant to the preceding statement?

And the sons of Noah, that went forth of the Ark, were Shem and Ham and Japheth. <u>And Ham is the father of Canaan</u>. (Gen 9:18)

In Hebrew, the 'And' before Ham can be the aversive conjunction 'But'. Five verses later, it happens again:

And Ham, <u>the father of Canaan</u>, saw the nakedness of his father, and told his two brethren without. (Gen 9:22)

Why mention Ham's *fourth son again* out of context unless Ham's fatherhood of Canaan *is* the salient issue? What does Canaan have to do with the price of potatoes unless the hapless boy is intrinsic to the story? Moses may have been responding to claims by the Canaanites of his day that they were all fathered by Noah.

Let's look at the verses again, which now make more sense:

And the sons of Noah that went forth of the Ark were Shem, and Ham and Japheth. <u>But</u> [aversive conjunction] **Ham is the father of Canaan. These are the <u>three</u> sons of Noah** [OK? There are only *three!*]**, and of them was the whole Earth overspread.**

And Noah began to be an husbandman [farmer]**, and he planted a vineyard. And he drank of the wine and was drunken, and he was uncovered within his tent.**

And Ham, <u>the father of Canaan</u>, saw the nakedness of his father [i.e. committed incest with his mother]**, and told his two brethren without. And Shem and Japheth took a garment, and laid it upon both their shoulders, and went backward and covered the nakedness of their father** [i.e. their mother]**; and their faces were backward, and they saw not their father's nakedness.**

273

And Noah awoke from his wine, and knew what his younger son had done unto him. And he said, 'Cursed be Canaan; a servant of servants shall he be unto his brethren.' (Gen 9:18-25)

Ham seems unabashed about immediately reporting his abominable act to his brothers. Ham had lived the previous 100 years of his life in the godless, sexually hedonistic pre-Flood world, where such acts of incest were doubtless common. Cursed from birth, Canaan would have grown up quickly learning, with Ham for a father, that you may as well be hanged for a sheep as a lamb.

So, says Bob Enyart, Canaan had his grandmother for a mother, his grandfather for an uncle, his mother for a great aunt, his father for a cousin, and, worst of all, his brother for a father (half-brother, that is):

"This account, at the very beginning of the repopulation of the Earth, also helps to explain the world's ubiquitous taboo of incest between parent and child, found by anthropologists to exist in virtually every known age and in virtually every known culture. The lesson was a harsh one to learn. Canaan was cursed inherently by being conceived through incest. The law of reaping and sowing inexorably applies to the children of fallen men. A father's alcoholism punishes his child, not by fiat from God (nor Noah) but by the cause and effect that children suffer under bad parenting, an unavoidable part of man's fallen existence until God ends this phase of human history. So incest set the background for centuries of conflict between Noah's Hamitic descendants, especially those through Canaan, and the descendants of Shem, the Semites, especially the Jews, to whom God would promise the land of the Canaanites." [287]

It isn't necessary to get into the arguments abounding on the Internet over the business of Ham either being black or being 'blackened for his sins', and his progeny cursed and demoted to slaves. Even if Ham were the father of the black races, Ham wasn't the one cursed but Canaan. The story is thus about the origin of Canaan, who he is, and the sexually dysfunctional progeny he propagates, which go on to become Israel's arch enemy in the time

---

[287] http://kgov.com/why-was-canaan-cursed

of Joshua, committing the most appalling acts of sexual perversion and child sacrifice.

Of course, *ha-Satan* is lurking behind all of this. Following this event, Noah pronounces the curses and blessings on his brood:

"Cursed be Canaan; a servant of servants shall he be unto his brethren." And he said, "Blessed be the LORD God of Shem; and Canaan shall be his servant. God shall enlarge Japheth, and he shall dwell in the tents of Shem; and Canaan shall be his servant." (Gen 9:25-27)

This verse gives Satan all the information he needs to narrow his gunsights now to Shem's line for the 'scarlet thread' – the line through which God will provide mankind with the Seed of the woman, the redemptive Messiah. The names of Noah's sons are interesting validations of Noah's prophecy: 'Blessed be the LORD God of Shem' (Gen 9:25). Shem's name שֵׁם means 'name', 'fame', 'reputation'. Notice the blessing of Japheth, whose name יֶפֶת means 'may he enlarge, expand': **'God shall enlarge Japheth, and he shall dwell in the tents of Shem...'** (Gen 9:27). In other words, Japheth's destiny is to be entwined with Shem's, not independent.

The rebellion reprised

Noah farmed. As his sons multiplied their issue and the population increased, the tribes trekked *from the east* (where the Ark came to rest) into 'Shinar' and found a plain in which to settle, in what is assumed to be the once fertile Mesopotamian valleys of modern-day Iraq. We are told all men spoke one language. The table of nations list in Genesis 10 shows that the entire Middle East is eventually settled by Noah's descendants. Noah himself lives a further three hundred and fifty years after the Flood, and ends his days at an impressive nine hundred and fifty years of age. The Bible says that Noah was the father of civilisation, and if you calculate the timelines, you discover that Noah dies fifty-eight years *after* an idol-worshiping Iraqi named Abram was born to the south-east around Ur of the Chaldees, the tenth generation from Noah and the 20th generation from Adam.

So Eden was consumed in the Flood. The next time we find the Tree of Life, it has been taken to Heaven so no-one on Earth is becoming immortal any time soon (Rev 22:2,14). The ecology comes to life soon after the Flood, and doubtless around campfires on balmy nights anger smoulders in some quarters against a jealous God who wickedly drowned the legendary Old Ones and wiped paradise off the face of the Earth.

It's evident from scripture that the Holy War against God's authority, which began in the days of Enos prior to the Flood, breaks out again in the years after Noah's sons, Shem, Japheth and Ham, begin repopulating the Earth. More wicked angels come down from the sky to reprise their business with the daughters of men (Gen 6:4 – **'and also after that…'**). The drive of those opposing God's rule is to set about eradicating all known truth about God, and liberate man into doing what is right in his own eyes (Gen 3:4-5 - **"Ye shall be as gods…"**)

Many hearts must have romanticised the Adamic world that was no more. Anger and fear would have turned towards a 'diabolical' God who had murdered virtually all mankind and left the survivors struggling for their lives on a strange new planet of alien landscapes and amazing new geological features.

It wasn't that people didn't believe in YHWH in those early days following the Flood. They knew perfectly well that He existed, for mankind had been interacting with the angelic realm freely prior to the disaster (Gen 6:1-8). The evidence for God's recently spent anger could be seen in every newly formed mountain, in the severely curtailed human lifespans, and in the very starting over of civilisation anew (Psa 104:5-9). Yet God knows even the Flood won't change man's heart:

"I will never again curse the ground for man's sake, <u>although the imagination of man's heart is evil from his youth</u>. Nor will I again destroy every living thing as I have done." (Gen 8:21)

God recognises that while man breathes, wickedness will abound on Earth, which is now the domain of *ha-Satan* and the third of the angelic realm who followed him in his revolt. Satan lost his own 'children' (seed) in the Flood. He's out to rebuild his legions. He's out for a reckoning.

THE MEGALITHIC ERA

"It has become appallingly obvious that our technology has exceeded our humanity." – Donald Ripley, from the movie *Powder*

The first rule of research: open your eyes and see what is. All that stands before you, which you can physically handle, exists. This 'what is' demands explanation in a sane society, and is the basis for all science, which is the examination of available evidence in the pursuit of knowledge. Why am I pushing this? Because all over the world we have extensive evidence of Flood damage, an overview of which we've examined in *Origins I*, which many scientists and the public continue to ignore because its existence does not fit the preconceived bias they were taught concerning what supposedly happened in Earth's pre-history. The fact is, we know very little about history in general – just snapshots drawn from such documentation as remains, and from the archaeological record, which is often selectively interpreted.

For instance, all over the world there exist huge monuments whose origins and construction cannot be explained under our current interpretive paradigm. Known as megaliths, these astonishing structures exhibit no flood damage, indicating that they are post-Flood, yet have been constructed using methods and technologies that elude us today. They exist. You can touch them and stick your fingers into some pretty amazing holes. Orthodox academia, so fierce in policing its monopoly on 'historical truth', has conspicuously failed to explain what these monuments are, what their purpose is, who built them, or even how. Some of the earliest surviving written accounts talk of advanced beings as the architects, who had access to sophisticated technologies not known to those who followed them. In his *Giants, Flood Myths and Megalithic Structures*, author Patrick C Chouinard covers the astonishing legacy left by... who exactly? [288]

The spectacular construction projects coming up in a minute provoke a very different explanation from man's accepted history.

---

[288] www.grahamhancock.com/forum/ChouinardP1.php

For this reason they have been deliberately played down and trivialised to maintain the uniformitarian view of Earth's past.

BAALBEK, LEBANON: The largest dressed stones on Earth can be found at the Temple of Jupiter complex at Baalbek in the Beqaa Valley in Lebanon.[289] The Stone of the Pregnant Woman weighs an estimated *1,000 tons.* Nearby, there is a partially quarried stone that is even larger – an estimated *1,242 tons.* It has been calculated that to lift the Stone of the Pregnant Woman would take the equivalent of 21 modern, heavy-lift cranes. The idea that this stone and others like it could have been manhandled into position using rollers and hoists is risible.

PUMAPUNKU, BOLIVIA: This temple complex is situated on a high plateau in the Andes and comprises huge, dressed stones that have not only been precisely *drilled with complex shapes,* but *machined* for some specific purpose.[290] The two largest stones, weighing 131 and 85 tons, were cut from a red sandstone quarry six miles away near Lake Titicaca, then transported up a steep incline to the temple plateau. Traditional archaeology dates the site to 200 BC, yet how could a supposedly peasant people have pulled off an engineering feat employing complex logistics, transport capabilities and mathematics *we're not even capable of today?* Wikipedia, usually quick to scoff at 'conspiracy theories', is equally baffled:

"In assembling the walls of Pumapunku, each stone was finely cut to interlock with the surrounding stones and the blocks fit together like a puzzle, forming load-bearing joints without the use of mortar. One common engineering technique involves cutting the top of the lower stone at a certain angle, and placing another stone on top of it which was cut at the same angle. The precision with which these angles have been utilized to create flush joints is indicative of a highly sophisticated knowledge of stone-cutting and a thorough understanding of descriptive geometry. Many of the joints are so precise that not even a razor blade will fit between the stones. Much of the masonry is characterized by accurately cut rectilinear blocks of

---

[289] Google Earth: 34°0'25"N 36°12'14"E
[290] Google Earth: 16°33'42.59"S 68°40'48.09"W

278

such uniformity that they could be interchanged for one another while maintaining a level surface and even joints. The blocks were so precisely cut as to suggest the possibility of prefabrication and mass production, technologies far in advance of the Tiwanaku's Incan successors hundreds of years later." [291]

OLLANTAYTAMBO, PERU: The ruins of this ancient city fortress are located in the Sacred Valley of the Incas 9,000 feet above sea level.[292] Believed by mainstream archaeology to have been constructed in the mid 15th century AD by the Inca emperor Pachacuti, other researchers see in Ollantaytambo the recurring theme witnessed elsewhere of baffling high technology employed by supposedly primitive ancients with no technology gradient.

Features at Ollantaytambo include the construction of aquaducts and irrigation systems which still function today. Six huge red granite blocks weighing 50 tons each have been cut from the source quarry, transported across a plain, over a river, then up the Ollantaytambo mountain to the highest point, where they have been dressed and fitted together in the Wall of the Six Monoliths with such breathtaking precision, not even a human hair can be inserted in the joints. There exists no conventional means for elevating such weight even today. Instead, researchers posit some sort of anti-gravity technology. Such is the joint design that the monoliths can ride the frequent earthquakes of the region without damage. Who goes to such astonishing effort, how did they do it, and for what purpose? Modern engineers are baffled. To accomplish this feat today would require major changes to the mountainside, a road put in, and use of equipment and technologies simply not available to the ancients – or so we are told.

Elsewhere at the site, stone blocks at Ollantaytambo have been fused together with some kind of high-energy vitrification tool to provide a unique, permanent bond for the fortress walls. No evidence remains of how the ancients were able to provide such an

---

[291] http://en.wikipedia.org/wiki/Puma_Punku
[292] Google Earth: 13°15'22.60"S 72°15'40"W

intense heat-source to accomplish what is left to us today. Ollantaytambo is a fortress. *To protect whom from what?*

Not far away at the Temple of the Condor, the same vitrification process can be observed at the Wall of Living Rock, from which huge, cube-shaped slabs of adesite have been excised from the mountain with astonishing precision, leaving behind a scratch-free surface as smooth as a bathroom mirror. Orthodox historians maintain the pretence that this was all done with Stone or Bronze Age tools, yet these can't cut adesite.

To illustrate just how phenomenonal and other-worldly these structures are, consider that mankind's toughest lifting equipment is required to construct the skyscrapers, factories, bridges and other features of our modern infrastructure. Our most powerful hydraulic hoists struggle with weights over 5 tons, yet thousands of years ago, all over the world, temples and other monuments were constructed using massive blocks of quarried stone, many in excess of 100 tons, which were precisely cut out of solid rock, dressed, transported for miles, then lifted and set in place with an accuracy we could not hope to match today.

Today's uniformitarian wisdom would have it that these stones were cut by ancient man using hammers, chisels and copper wire, then transported and installed, sometimes hundreds of feet up mountains without the benefit of pully systems or the wheel. An absurd notion. Many researchers draw the obvious conclusion: that these ancient civilisations had access to specialist technologies whose nature and origin are unknown to us today. So the next questions you ask are: Who gave these to man, and why?

TEOTIHUACAN, MEXICO: This ancient meso-American city is located 30 miles north-east of Mexico City on a plain.[293] Thought to have been built around 100 BC and abandoned in the 7th or 8th centuries AD, the city probably housed 125,000 – 150,000 inhabitants at its zenith. Scientists are struck by a number of strange features at Teotihuacan. It has a modern metropolis feel with ceremonial architecture and the arrow-straight Street of the Dead. Its construction employs the same mathematical features as

---

[293] Google Earth: 19°41'33"N 98°50'37.68"W

the Great Pyramid and other pyramids at Giza. The Pyramid of the Sun at Teotihuacan has approximately the same base measurements as the Khufu pyramid at Giza (750 ft square), and is exactly half as high. The base perimeter of the Great Pyramid is 2π x its height whereas the Pyramid of the Sun base perimeter is 4π x its height. Π, the universal relationship of the circumference of a circle to its diameter, is traditionally believed by experts not to have been known at this time.

The layout of the city at Teotihuacan resembles a modern circuit board comprising two large processors represented by the Pyramids of the Sun and Moon. The configuration of the two largest pyramids with the smaller third pyramid, slightly offset, reminds of the constellation of Orion, and is precisely the configuration one finds with the three pyramids at Giza. Coincidence?

The whole city is impregnated with sheets of the silicate mineral mica, the nearest source of which is thousands of miles away in Brazil. Someone went to a lot of trouble to get the mica to Mexico. Since the mica is embedded in the construction materials at Teotihuacan and mostly not visible, its use was intended to be functional not aesthetic. A subterranean chamber of mica crystals has been discovered, leading researchers to surmise that the chamber itself may have housed some sort of power source. Mica is well known as an electrical insulator. It's also able to withstand tremendous temperatures as well as radiation, yet remain stable. It was used by NASA on the tiles of the Space Shuttle to withstand the tremendous heat generated by the spacecraft's re-entry into Earth's atmosphere.

Was Teotihuacan some sort of city-wide power generator for an unknown technology, wherein the impregnated mica not only insulated the inhabitants from tremendous heat, but also protected them from radiation? Was Teotihuacan some sort of spaceship docking facility, as the ancient astronaut theorists surmise? Though these themes are hinted at in films such as *Indiana Jones and the Temple of the Crystal Skull*, researchers can come up with no other theory to explain the existence of mica painstakingly installed throughout the complex, other than that this technical information, along with the intricate layout of the city, was given to the inhabitants by some outside, advanced civilisation. Interestingly, the earliest legends of Teotihuacan reveal that the city was built by gods who came down from the sky.

There are many other examples of monolithic architecture at Vijayanagara, India, Easter Island, Stonehenge and Avebury in England, Gigal Rephaim in Israel, and on and on. Close study of the heiroglyphs carved into the red granite of obelisks at Karnak, Egypt reveal that these were fashioned *with a rotating machine tool.* Examine the photos on Google for yourself. Hand-carving could never have achieved such precision.

The ancient astronaut hypothesis favoured by the likes of Erich von Däniken, Zecharia Sitchin, Robert Temple and David Icke is the explanation generally favoured by the engaged, secular public. Wiki gives it the usual brush-off:

"Ancient astronauts or ancient aliens, also known as paleocontact hypothesis, is a pseudo-scientific theory that states intelligent extraterrestrial beings have visited Earth in antiquity or prehistory and made contact with humans. Proponents suggest that this contact influenced the development of human cultures, technologies, and religions. A common claim is that deities from most, if not all, religions are actually extraterrestrials, and their advanced technologies were wrongly understood by primitive men as evidence of their divine status." [294]

Today there are popular alien religions such as Theosophy, Scientology, Nation of Islam, The Urantia Book, Heaven's Gate and Raëlism, branches of which hold that mankind has been constantly visited by benevolent, higher-intelligence, morally superior extraterrestrials from other planets who have imparted esoteric, advanced technologies to mankind for our physical and spiritual development.

Notice how well entrenched the Extraterrestrial Hypothesis (ETH) is in the public psyche today thanks to countless movies, books and TV programmes. The tendency too, regardless of movies such as *Independence Day* and *The Day the Earth Stood Still,* is that

---

[294] http://en.wikipedia.org/wiki/Ancient_astronauts

such beings are benevolent and have our best interests at heart. It is the researched position of the *Origins* series, however, that while such exo-entities are most likely the source of this knowledge and expertise, the evidence is overwhelming that they are a) not *extraterrestrial* but *hyperdimensional* and b) absolutely not working for mankind's rosy future but intent on executing a future global deception upon the human race. The megalithic structures which appeared after the Flood seem intricately connected to the ET/giant/Nephilim lore of the ancients. Horn and Putnam write:

"Mythology involving Watchers, fallen angels and giants as builders of some of these mysterious sites is repeated in legends around the world. These stories are consistent with Sumerian and Hebrew accounts of the Great Flood and of subsequent destruction of giant Nephilim, whose history of human sacrifices parallel those found on Mount Hermon.

A most dynamic question then arises concerning whether those megalithic builders known as Watchers would have also built similar structures on other planets, which perhaps were under their jurisdiction before the great war between God and Lucifer.... This also brings up a second hypothetical question: If edifices on Earth were built to mirror those on these angel planets, what was their purpose? Could it have been somehow to create a binding or 'unholy symmetry' between the fallen angels and man's sphere?"[295]

Giza - The Great Pyramid (GP)

Majestic they stand, overawing the windswept desert. Most people focus on the three pyramids on the Giza plateau, constructed of blocks of stone weighing 2-3 tons, yet the Giza complex also features temples fashioned from blocks of stone, some of which weigh 100 tons, and a few at 200 tons. These stones have astonished visitors for millennia, not least present-day author Robert Bauval, who remarks on History Channel's *Ancient Aliens* series:

"Let me tell you what a 100-ton block is. If you take a hundred family cars and you squeeze them together, you get one of these

---

[295] Putnam and Horn, *Exo-Vaticana*, op. cit., p.471

blocks. First of all, let alone how they moved these blocks is why would they want to use hundred-ton blocks? It simply doesn't make sense." There's no reason for them to want to build out of granite blocks the size of a semi truck. It's like, 'Okay, let's do something, but let's do it as difficult as we could possibly do it.' The reason why I am convinced that sophisticated technology was utilized in these ancient rocks is because, if we go to a stone quarry today and look at the scope of machinery required to accomplish similar things, those machines are huge."[296]

For ancient man the Egyptian pyramids must have evoked emotions of utter awe and humility. Today these icons still mystify with their strange dimensions and other-worldly properties. The Great Pyramid (GP) is the ultimate megalith. It fascinated Napoleon, who spent a night locked in its bowels, emerging the following day with tales of 'strange experiences'. The same questions surface:

1. Who built the pyramids?
2. How did they build them?
3. When and why?

Archaeologists have formed theories, written lots of books and I've read many of them. Wikipedia provides the orthodox position:

"The Great Pyramid of Giza, also called Khufu's Pyramid or the Pyramid of Khufu, and Pyramid of Cheops, is the oldest and largest of the three pyramids in the Giza Necropolis bordering what is now Cairo, Egypt, and is the only remaining member of the Seven Wonders of the Ancient World. It is believed the pyramid was built as a tomb for Fourth dynasty Egyptian King Khufu (Cheops in Greek) and constructed over a 20-year period concluding around 2560 BC. The Great Pyramid was the tallest man-made structure in the world for over 3,800 years. Originally the Great Pyramid was covered by casing stones that formed a smooth outer surface, and what is seen today is the underlying core structure. Some of the casing stones that once covered the structure can still be seen around the base. There have been varying scientific and alternative theories regarding the

---

Great Pyramid's construction techniques. Most accepted construction theories are based on the idea that it was built by moving huge stones from a quarry and dragging and lifting them into place. There are three known chambers inside the Great Pyramid. The lowest chamber is cut into the bedrock upon which the pyramid was built, and was unfinished. The so-called Queen's Chamber and King's Chamber are higher up within the pyramid structure."[297]

Not what it seems

One hundred and thirty-eight pyramids have been discovered across Egypt to date. Pyramids, of course, are associated with the land of the pharaohs, but in fact Sudan has more – 220 still standing. Delve a little deeper and the Great Pyramid (GP), one of three which make up the Giza Necropolis, is in all ways of an entirely different class to the others. As with the other megaliths, it was built by an advanced civilisation using accuracy and construction techniques unknown to us today. The GP was not intended as a monument to the dead like others which would follow. All the other pyramids are used as tombs with the burial chambers *underneath* the structure. The GP is not a tomb but has chambers *inside*.

No hieroglyphics have been found on the Great Pyramid's walls, nor inscriptions to any Egyptian pharaoh. Scientists are baffled as to how the GP came to be constructed on a pi (π) ratio, the universal relationship of the circumference of a circle to its diameter. Nineteenth century Egyptologist Sir John Herschel and Professor Charles Piazzi Smyth, mathematician and Royal Astronomer of Scotland, found that if the perimeter of the GP's base was divided by twice its height, the result was 3.141, or the math constant pi. Yet π was not recognised in history until the Greek era, almost two thousand years after the generally accepted date of the GP's construction. Smyth noticed another intriguing fact. The Pyramid's location was on the longest latitude and longest longitude line of dry land, *placing the construction at the precise geographical centre of the Earth.*

---

[297] www.wikipedia.org

Next, the Great Pyramid is empty except for one object: a lidless polished red granite coffer located in the King's Chamber. Did someone go to all the trouble to build a pyramid, which doubtless cost the lives of thousands (if you subscribe to the current theories), just to showcase an unmarked stone box? Yet not just any stone box. There are what appear to be intriguing Biblical connections. Scientists have calculated that the dimensions of this container are such that the Ark of the Covenant can fit into it 'hand in glove'. The coffer is also the exact volume of God's brass laver, originally placed as part of the holy furniture in the mobile Tabernacle of Moses so priests could bathe prior to serving God. Fifty times the volume of the GP's coffer (50 = Jubilee) gives you the precise volume of the King's Chamber of the Great Pyramid and the 'Molten Sea', the huge brass bath the priests would ceremonially bathe in before serving the LORD in Solomon's Temple. Just coincidence?

God's box

Moviegoers recall *Raiders of the Lost Ark,* which introduced many to the Ark of the Covenant, the portable acacia-wood, gold-overlaid container built by Moses to hold the stone tablets of the Ten Commandments. According to the Bible, the Shekhinah Glory of God was said to dwell between the cherubim on the Ark [298] until a permanent temple was later built in Solomon's time to house it. The Ark of the Covenant represented the awesome power of the Invisible Mighty One of Israel. God gave the dimensions and construction plans to Moses who built it. Once complete, any army carrying the Ark into battle emerged victorious. Those who peeked inside were utterly consumed. In the case of the men of Beth Shamesh, the men of a whole township perished on one occasion alone (1 Sam 6:19).[299] The Philistines seized the Ark in battle, only to send it hastily back to the Jews after a rather unpleasant

---

[298] 1 Sam 4:4; 2 Sam 6:2; 2 Kings 19:15, etc.
[299] There are issues with how the number of casualties in this verse has been translated. See *Origins 3 – The Predicament of Man.*

affliction began heaping itself up their backsides, and rats invaded their homes and cities.

Here's the problem: The Great Pyramid coffer was supposedly constructed around 2623 BC, *before* the generally accepted date of the Flood among creationists, during the reign of Pharaoh Khufu, and precisely crafted to accept the Ark of the Covenant, *the dimensions of which were not revealed to Moses by God for another 1,300 years.* So who knew the dimensions of the Ark 1,300 years before Moses got them from God?

Archaeologists can reconcile neither the coffer conundrum nor the π factor. Come to think of it, the dating of the various pharaonic dynasties is a complete mess in Egyptology. There are no markings on the Pyramid. There is growing doubt the GP was ever built in Khufu's era or any other Egyptian reign for that matter. No Pharaoh has resisted the temptation to smother even minor structures with hieroglyphics and adornments, once built. This has not been done with the most awesome man-made structure on Earth. Further, the intricate design and unbelievably accurate cutting and placing of the enormous slabs suggest far superior technologies at work. The great pyramidologist Sir William Flinders Petrie concluded that the extraordinary pyramid builders must have used enormous jewel-tipped saws, mechanical lathes, and a type of toughened tubular drill to create the evidence left to us today.

We do not find any other structures of Khufu's era demonstrating anywhere close to the same level of technology, which implies that these technologies were not known in Khufu's time. These early kings, enduing the mysterious GP with a heady mysticism, seemed to have used the original as a template for making subsequent and far less impressive counterfeits for themselves.

Other-worldly dimensions

Another anomaly was discovered in 1940. The sides of the GP appear slightly concave, an effect that cannot be seen by an observer on the ground. JP Petrie explains:

"This concavity divides each of the apparent four sides in half, creating a very special and unusual eight-sided pyramid; and it is executed to such an extraordinary degree of precision as to enter the realm of the uncanny. For, viewed from any ground position or distance, this concavity is quite invisible to the naked eye. The hollowing-in can be noticed only from the air, and only at certain times of the day. This explains why virtually every available photograph of the Great Pyramid does not show the hollowing-in phenomenon, and why the concavity was never discovered until the age of aviation. It was discovered quite by accident in 1940 when a British Air Force pilot, P Groves, was flying over the pyramid. He happened to notice the concavity and captured it in the now-famous photograph."[300]

The direct measure of the GP base is 365.242 sacred cubits, the precise number of days in the solar year. Two other measurements for the circumference give us the sidereal year and anomalistic year. 10 million sacred cubits gives us radius of the Earth from the centre to the North Pole, accurate to hundredths of a mile. If you take 25 pyramid inches to the cubit, the polar diameter of the Earth comprises exactly 500 million of them. How did the builders of the GP know this information, or is it all just coincidence?

The Great Pyramid could never be built with the same precision or to the same dimensions today. It comprises 900 million cubic feet of masonry and is 90 times the volume of the Chicago Sears Tower. The GP is the equivalent of a 40-storey structure built across seven city blocks so precisely that there is less than 1/10th of an inch error in its level across the 13-acre base. 2.5 million blocks were used in the original construction, weighing from 2 to 70 tons each. The resultant edifice is large enough to hold St Paul's Cathedral, St Paul's Basilica, the cathedrals at Florence and Milan and still have room to spare. The cornerstones of the pyramid rest on heat-compensating ball and socket mechanisms sunk eight inches into a solid rock base. The outside of the pyramid was originally covered with 144,000 blocks of brilliant white polished

[300] **Petrie, JP** *The Egyptian Pyramids: A Comprehensive, Illustrated Reference,* McFarland & Company, 2006, p.65

limestone casing blocks, the precise number of sealed Jewish witnesses Christ will have in the Great Tribulation (Rev 7:4). Imagine blocks measuring 5 feet x 8 feet x 12 feet, cut remotely and transported to the site. The masonry workmanship is accurate to 1/100th of an inch across 75 inches. These blocks have been so precisely joined together that the spaces between them are less than 1/50th of an inch, making the separation tolerances more minute than the tiles on the Space Shuttle. The door to the GP was so well constructed and jointed that it remained undiscovered from the outside for centuries.[301]

Mysticalblaze.com describes other interesting facts:

"There are 36,525 Pyramid inches in the perimeter of the Great Pyramid - the exact number of days in 100 years

The measurement of a straight line of the base of the pyramid corner to corner converted to the Mean Tropical Year in days is exactly correct at 365.242

The length of the sides of the triangle converted is 365.256 days - the exact length of the Earth's solar revolution in days

The length of the sides of the pyramid, if it had a capstone, converts to the exact orbital revolution of the Earth in days - 365.259

Half the length of the diagonal of the base x 10^6 reveals the distance of the Earth from the sun

The average height of Earth's land mass above sea level is the exact height of the Great Pyramid [454.5 feet high].

...The Great Pyramid is aligned almost perfectly north/south, with only 3 arc minutes of variation, a feat that no structure in our modern world has even come close to approaching.[302] As such it works as a giant sundial, accurately marking the solstices and equinoxes each year. It sits on a foundation that is over 13 acres in area and is almost perfectly level, only varying in height by 1/2 inch over the entire surface - another feat that we cannot duplicate today despite modern technology. It sits in the exact center of land mass of the Earth at 30 degrees north and 31 degrees east, and is also believed

---

[301] Dimensions and statistics compiled from research undertaken by Richard Noone and Kent Hovind.

[302] Not even the Paris Observatory is aligned as accurately, having a variance of around 6 arc minutes.

to be precisely at the center of gravity of the Earth. Though at first glance these findings may seem coincidental, all other factors considered, this was probably a very conscious placement by the builders."[303]

A Godly connection?

There are interesting Biblical parallels contained within the GP's construction. The Ark of the Covenant and its coffer are significant because the former is a representation of God's true Ark which remains in Heaven (Rev 11:19). Prior to Moses receiving the dimensions from God to construct a replica of the heavenly Ark, the latter's vital statistics would have been known only to four entities: The Father, the Son, the Holy Spirit and one other - the only cherub ever 'anointed' by God, the only 'high priest' angel ever allowed into the holiest regions of Heaven (**'You walked back and forth in the midst of fiery stones...'**) - the rebellious angel with no name, *ha-Satan* (Eze 28:14-15, NKJV). We can deduce this because the Ark in Heaven is the Holy of Holies, even as it resided only in the Holy of Holies in the Mosaic tabernacle on Earth, and later the temple of King Solomon.

The pyramid's passageways comprise a broad path that leads to a pit. Some surmise that this represents the predicament of man – destruction. There is a narrow way that leads up to the King's Chamber (life) (Matt 7:13-14). The Descending Passage masonry is accurate to 1/50th of an inch within the first 150 ft, an unbelievable feat. The next 200 ft is bored through bedrock and accurate to ¼ inch in 350 ft, something engineers could not accomplish today even with a laser drill.

There are 153 steps along the narrow way which seem to match the 153 fishes gathered in FG 21:11, believed also by some to symbolise the final ingathering of the world's nations at Christ's coming. The King's Chamber is located at the 50th row of construction blocks, 50 symbolising the Jubilee every 50 years when all the slaves in Israel were set free and leased land reverted to the owner (Lev 25:11ff.). Above the 50th level, the quality of the pyramid's construction declines markedly. The cornerstone of the

---

[303] www.mysticalblaze.com/PlacesPyramidsDimensions.htm

pyramid is missing, symbolising Christ, the rejected chief cornerstone (Dan 2:45; Psa 118:22; Matt 21:42; Mark 12:10). The five sides to the cornerstone, and thus the GP itself, some say, may be representative of the Biblical number for grace.

Isaiah writes of God's Day: **In that day shall there be an altar to the LORD in the midst of the land of Egypt, and a pillar at the border thereof to the LORD. And it shall be a sign and for a witness unto the LORD of Hosts in the Land of Egypt.** (Isa 19:19-20) The Great Pyramid was indeed located at the border of the Upper and Lower Kingdoms of Egypt at the time this verse was written. In fact, the name Gizeh in Arabic means 'border'. Today the construction resides 'in the midst of the Land of Egypt'. The original Hebrew used in this verse can be converted into numeric equivalents similar to the Greek language. Is it coincidence that the gametrical total for this Hebrew passage equals 5449, the precise height of the GP in inches?

The New Jerusalem?

Some surmise the Great Pyramid was constructed with other-worldly, alien expertise, perhaps knowledge available before the Flood when man was interacting directly with the angelic realm. There are further parallels with the description of God's heavenly city in the last book of the Bible, Revelation:

The city is laid out as a square; its length is as great as its breadth. And he measured the city with the reed: twelve thousand furlongs. Its length, breadth and height are equal. (Rev 21:16, NKJV)

The angel shows the apostle John the vision, takes a reed and measures the walls of the city. Its length, width and height are approximately 1,400 miles in each direction, making the New Jerusalem a little smaller than half the size of the United States of America. Why would God include the measurements of the city in His description at all? What shape is the city? Jack Heyford writes:

"The city is a perfect cube, a symbol of perfection..."[304]

---

[304] Heyford, Jack, *Spirit Filled Bible*, Nelson, 1991, p.1991

Other theologians agree the New Jerusalem is cuboid in shape, yet the dimensions could also hold Heaven to be a pyramid. A few verses later we learn: **But I saw no temple in it, for the LORD God Almighty and the Lamb are its temple. The city had no need of the sun or of the moon to shine in it, for the glory of God illuminated it. The Lamb is its light.** (Rev 21:22-23, NKJV)

The New Jerusalem is either a cube or pyramid. If a pyramid, Jesus illuminates the city with His glory, presumably from above, in his role as the Light of the world (FG 8:12; 9:5). Jesus is described as the stone rejected by the builders, who became the chief cornerstone (capstone) (Matt 21:42; Psa 118:22-23). Zechariah 4:7 (NKJV) states: **Who are you, O great mountain? Before Zerubbabel you shall become a plain! And he shall bring forth the capstone with shouts of "Grace, grace to it!"** Here Christ is again identified as the capstone.

The Great Pyramid lacks a capstone. Is counterfeiting underway? We're learning that *ha-Satan* is the counterfeiter of all God's ways. These days pyramids abound in the occult, and removed capstones and Satan's all-seeing eye pervade Masonry, can be found on the reverse side of the US one-dollar bill, are beamed from the top of the pyramidal Luxor Hotel in Las Vegas, and pyramids are used by many companies in their corporate logos.[305] Some propose that an attempt by *ha-Satan*, the false light, is underway to **be like the Most High** (Isa 14:14). Certainly some high-level politicians view this subject seriously enough to have considered some quite impressive pageantry. Robert Bauval enlightens:

"Amid accusation of 'Zionist' plots and 'Masonic' skullduggery, the Egyptian government is half-minded to cancel the placing of a golden capstone on top of the Great Pyramid on the eve of the new millennium. It all began, strangely enough, in Paris in May 1998 when, after a golden capstone was ceremoniously placed on top of the Egyptian obelisk which stands at the Place de la Concorde, the Egyptian Minister of Culture, Farouk Hosni, announced that a similar

---

[305] e.g. AOL, Alcan, the old Fidelity Investments logo, SunTrust, Delta Airlines, the US Federal Emergency Management Agency (FEMA).

ceremony would take place at the Great Pyramid of Giza at midnight on the 31st December 1999....

A high profile group in Washington DC calling itself The Millennium Society, with members such as ex-White House official, Edward McNally, and a list of guests including Ronald Reagan, Mikhail Gorbachev, Deng Xiaoping, Bill Clinton, Bruce Springsteen, Elizabeth Taylor and Nelson Mandela apparently will attend the World Millennium Charity Celebration, the 'Celebration of Civilisation' to welcome the Year 2000 at the Great Pyramid of Cheops and 23 satellite locations on New Year's Eve 1999. The Great Pyramid of Giza, Egypt, will be the cornerstone site of the World Millennium Celebration, and sanctioned events will be held at selected locations around the world. These celebrations will be linked to create a round-the-globe, round-the-clock welcome to the Year 2000."[306]

Due to fears of terrorist attacks, however, the ceremony was cancelled. GizaPyramid.com writes:

"No one has been able to explain why the Great Pyramid would have been built without a capstone. This is an interesting story associated with a visit to the top of the great pyramid. Many tourists have climbed to the top, which is not an easy journey. One such person was Sir William Siemens, a British inventor. He climbed to the top with his Arab guides. One of his guides called attention to the fact that when he raised his hand with outspread fingers, he would hear an acute ringing noise. Siemens raised his index finger and felt a distinct prickling sensation. He also received an electric shock when he tried to drink from a bottle of wine that he had brought with him. Being a scientist, Siemens than moistened a newspaper and wrapped it around the wine bottle to convert it into a Leyden jar (an early form of a capacitor). When he held it above his head, it became charged with electricity. Sparks then were emitted from the bottle. One of the Arab guides got frightened and thought Siemens was up to some witchcraft and attempted to seize Siemens' companion. When Siemens noticed this, he pointed the bottle towards the Arab and gave him such a shock that it knocked the Arab to the ground almost rendering him unconscious. When he recovered, he took off down the pyramid

---

[306] www.theforbiddenknowledge.com/hardtruth/golden_capstone.htm

shouting loudly. What kind of natural phenomena on the top of the Great Pyramid could produce such an electrostatic effect?" [307]

Some researchers again make the connection between ancient beliefs in 'holy high places', mountain tops, entry/exit stargates, and contacts with ETs, demons, and other entities inhabiting parallel dimensions. More down-to-Earth scientists are mystified by the sheer logistics required to cut and dress the multi-ton stones so accurately and lift them into place. Andrew Collins is one among many who suggests a type of sound technology employing vibratory resonance was used by 'the Ancients' to cut and lift large blocks of stone. In the 19th century, American John Ernst Worrell Keely pioneered apparatus that was able to shatter granite and perform other strange feats using sympathetic vibratory resonance. Collins also recounts the strange tale of a Swedish Dr Jarl who was invited to Tibet to watch monks lifting huge blocks of stone up a cliff-side using the sound of trumpets and other instruments which created a focused sonic platform.[308] Was this what happened at Jericho?

What is the secret?

The Great Pyramid is conspicuously post-Flood. Despite contrary assertions, the GP exhibits no water damage. The Sphinx is a different matter, though no credible scientist contends the monument endured the apocalyptic upheaval that was Noah's Flood:

"The Great Sphinx of Giza is made from megaliths. A megalith is a large stone which has been used to construct a structure or monument either alone or with other stones without the use of mortar or cement. The megaliths used to build the great monument of Giza are estimated to weigh 200 tons apiece, the smallest weighing 50 tons and built from megaliths fashioned from a single stone of rock. The

---

[307] www.gizapyramid.com/gip2.htm
[308] **Collins, Andrew** *Gods of Eden,* Headline, 1998, pp.78-86

294

body of the monument has been subjected to considerable water damage."[309]

The notion that these monuments could have survived the Flood may be discounted. According to the evidence, the Flood rearranged huge land features, carved canyons and trenches and built mountains. When sand is removed from between the Sphinx's paws, the space refills, indicating that these conditions did not exist when the Sphinx was built. Astounding technology was required to heft its 200-ton blocks into place, each of which was hewn from a single slab of stone.

The Sahara Desert to the west gives evidence of a huge, land-bound lake that once existed, which has since dried and desertified – an aftermath of the Flood's recession. Sahara Desert is about 4,000 years old, based on the desertification rate, according to the Potsdam Institute for Climate Impact Research.[310] Some maintain that the Giza complex was started in the century following the Flood (2200 – 2300 BC). Mizraim (King Menes), son of Ham, grandson of Noah, founded the nation of Egypt and became the father of the Pharaonic dynasties and, intriguingly, the Philistines. Whether Mizraim had other-worldly help can only be surmised by some extraordinary hieroglyphs found on monuments throughout the ancient empire. Real or fake? You be the judge.[311] Mizraim would have been familiar with all the pre-Flood stories of fallen angels, demigods and giants from his father. The question is, did he participate with the Watchers in person, as evidenced by the pantheon of gods and goddesses comprising the Egyptian religion thereafter?

Conclusion

Upon reviewing the volumes that have been written about the Great Pyramid, it seems that all suborn the fabulous monument to their own cause. Some say this is its greatest feat. It demands to be

---

[309] http://www.king-tut.org.uk
[310] Geophysical Research Papers, Germany, 15th July 1999
[311] Google images of the helicopter hieroglyphs.

studied and wondered at – a god-like attribute. But which God? William Fix summarises in his *Pyramid Odyssey*:

"...Men are capable of perceiving the Pyramid in an astonishing number of ways. Some have thought the Pyramid was an astronomic and astrological observatory. Some have thought it functioned as the equivalent of a theodolite for surveyors in ancient times.... Some think it performed as a giant sundial.... Some think it records the mathematics and science of a civilization which vanished.... Some think it is a huge water pump. Others have thought it was filled with fabulous treasures.... One early investigator came away convinced it was the remains of a huge volcano. Another thought the pyramids were Joseph's granaries. Some thought they were heathen idols which should be destroyed. Some believe the Pyramid captures powerful cosmic energies... Some think it is a tomb. Some think it is a Bible in stone with prophecies built into the scheme of its internal passages... Some think it was a mammoth public works project which consolidated the position of the pharaoh and the unity of the nation. Some think it was built by beings from outer space. Some say it was a temple of initiation. Some hold that it was an instrument of science. Some believe it is an altar of Guild built through direct Divine Revelation. And today, judging by the uses to which it has been put, some apparently think it is an outhouse."[312]

In our quest to get to the bottom of one of Earth's greatest mysteries – the Megalithic Era – we can yield to what we know. Astounding structures exist on Earth which have no rational explanations for their construction or origins, yet they demand to be explained. They are built using astonishing technology, the like of which we cannot hope to match today. Built into their architecture are ratios, constants and Earth/astronomic data that confound the experts; that could not have been known by the ancients according to the currently accepted frames of historic reference. Could the answer be found in a further megalithic structure we have yet to examine?

Welcome to a unique building, which dominated the minds of the post-Flood peoples, consolidated the power of the first world

---

[312] **Fix, William** *Pyramid Odyssey*, Smithmark Pub., 1978

dictator, and whose very construction provoked a response from beyond spacetime in what has to be one of the most bizarre and extraordinary episodes in all pre-history.

NIMROD AND BABYLON

If artificial structures were discovered on another planet such as Mars, which replicated those still standing on Earth, would you lose your religion? Would you gain a new one? What conclusions would the world peoples draw? What should we be making of the Megalith enigma? And, most strikingly, why did this extraordinary building bonanza abruptly cease and the sites fall into disuse as the centuries passed? Could another famous monolithic structure we've not yet examined hold the key?

Shortly after the Flood, trouble comes. Ham's firstborn is Cush, who has a son, Nimrod, who is thought to have become the first 'world leader' of civilisation. He has been identified with the hero Gilgamesh in early literature and is described in the Bible thus:

And Cush begat Nimrod: he began to be a mighty one in the Earth. He was a mighty hunter before the LORD: wherefore it is said, Even as Nimrod the mighty hunter before the LORD. (Gen 10:8-9).

Historians have traced a 'Ninus, son of Bel', to be Nimrod, son of Cush. Much early mythology centres around a lost leafy paradise populated by giants and men who lived over 900 years (Atlantis, etc.). Stories of half-man/half-beast entities abound, popularised later in Roman and Greek mythology, reflective of the Nephilim of the pre-Flood era. The Bible states that this abomination continues after the Flood (Gen 6:4), resulting in more problems for God's 'pure' line, down which will eventually come the 'Seed of the woman' and the virgin birth, providing mankind's Redeemer and Satan's defeat. Christian Answers writes:

"After the Flood, Noah had a talented but evil great-grandson named Nimrod, who rebelled greatly against God. The Bible says that he was 'a mighty one'. Jewish tradition indicates that Nimrod was a tyrant 'who made all of the people rebellious against God'. It is evident from history that Nimrod was not only a political leader but also the lead priest of a form of occultic worship.

Nimrod built and organized major cities. The Bible notes that these included Babel, Asshur, Nineveh and Calah (Genesis 10:10-12).

If you know anything about ancient history, the mention of these places may send shivers up your spine. For these were cities of almost unimaginable practices and perversion.

When Nimrod eventually died, the Babylonian mystery religion in which he figured prominently continued on. His wife Queen Semiramis saw to that. Once he was dead, she deified him as the sun-god. In various cultures he later became known as Baal, the Great Life Giver, the god of fire, Baalim [many Baals], Bel, Molech, etc."[313]

No-one was recording history yet, or if they were, the writings have not survived. Nimrod proves an elusive but ubiquitous shadow. The 1st century Jewish chronicler Flavius Josephus, who had access to documentation no longer extant, writes:

"...it was Nimrod who excited them to such an affront and contempt of God. He was the grandson of Ham, the son of Noah – a bold man, and of great strength of hand. He persuaded them not to ascribe it to God, as if it were, through His means they were happy, but to believe that it was their own courage which procured that happiness. He also gradually changed the government into tyranny, seeing no other way of turning men from the fear of God, but to bring them into a constant dependence upon his own power.

He also said he would be revenged on God if He should have a mind to drown the world again; for that he would build a tower too high for the waters to be able to reach! And that he would avenge himself on God for destroying their forefathers!"[314]

This is the view held in the ex-Biblical *Epic of Gilgamesh*, compiled around 2000 BC – one of the earliest surviving writings, installed on twelve clay tablets belonging to the 7th century BC Assyrian king, Ashurbanipal. Most commentaries on this early period speak of the 'fear of God's wrath' driving the majority into rebellion against Heaven. Satan is working through Cush and Nimrod at this stage. There's the great emphasis on immortality. There's the reversal of good and evil – a trademark wile of the Devil (Isa 5:20-23). So we get the 'bad' God Yahweh (YHWH)

---

[313] http://www.christiananswers.net/q-eden/edn-t020.html
[314] **Josephus, Flavius** *Antiquities,* I.4.2

versus the 'redeemer' Nimrod, who will get God off the backs of the people and exact revenge for Eden.

Some churchmen today actually regard Nimrod as some sort of patriarch because of Bible translations. Archaeologist Dr David P Livingston is appalled:

"Our English translation of the Hebrew of Genesis 10:8-10 is weak. The author of this passage of Scripture will not call Gilgamesh by his name and honor him, but is going to call him by a derisive name, what he really is — a rebel ['Nimrod']. Therefore we should translate Genesis 10:8-10 to read: Cush begat Nimrod; he began to be a tyrant in the Earth. He was a tyrannical hunter in opposition to the LORD. Thus it is said, 'Nimrod the tyrannical opponent of YHWH.'"[315]

Author and researcher Thomas Horn has another take on Nimrod from the aforementioned verse: **And Cush begat Nimrod: he began to be a mighty one in the Earth.** (Gen 10:8).

"Three sections in this unprecedented verse indicate something very peculiar happened to Nimrod. First, note where the text says, "he began to be." In Hebrew, this is *chalal,* which means 'to become profaned, defiled, polluted, or desecrated ritually, sexually or genetically'. Second, this verse tells us exactly what Nimrod began to be as he changed genetically—'a mighty one' (*gibbowr, gibborim*), one of the offspring of Nephilim. As Annette Yoshiko Reed says in the Cambridge University book, *Fallen Angels and the History of Judaism and Christianity,* "The Nephilim of Genesis 6:4 are always... grouped together with the *gibborim* as the progeny of the Watchers and human women." And the third part of this text says the change to Nimrod started while he was on "Earth." Therefore, in modern language, this text could accurately be translated to say: "And Nimrod began to change genetically, becoming a *gibborim,* the offspring of Watchers on Earth." [316]

[315] http://www.christiananswers.net/dictionary/nimrod.html
[316] http://www.newswithviews.com/Horn/thomas155.htm#_ftn1

Semiramis – the whore queen

We can't know for sure whether Nimrod was genetically 'jacked' other than he is described as impressive, a mighty one, *ha-gibbor*, and is credited with the founding of four cities on the Shinar plain: Babel (Babylon), Erech (Enoch), Accad and Calneh. Then he heads north into Assyria where he founds Nineveh, Rehoboth, Caleh and Resen. The legend goes that at some point, the fierce warrior becomes smitten with a beautiful tavern whore named Semiramis whom he marries. Semiramis, seeing a way out of her dismal profession, proceeds to mythologise her husband as god and redeemer of oppressed mankind, and Nimrod comes to be so regarded in many legends.

Alexander Hislop, a Church of Scotland minister, wrote extensively on this subject in his controversial *The Two Babylons*. In discussing Hislop's work, Wikipedia reports:

"According to Hislop, Semiramis was an exceedingly beautiful woman who gave birth to a son named Tammuz, was instrumental as the queen and wife of Nimrod, the founder of Babylon, and its religion, complete with a pseudo-Virgin Birth. This he [Hislop] called a foreshadowing of the birth of Christ, prompted by Satan. Later, Nimrod was killed, and Semiramis, pregnant with his child, claimed the child was Nimrod reborn.

Hislop claimed that the cult and worship of Semiramis spread globally, her name changing with the culture. In Egypt she was Isis, in Greece and Rome she was Venus and Diana, Athena and a host of other names, but was always prayed to and central to the faith which was based on Babylonian mystery religion."[317]

In other words, all pagan religions begin at Babylon and fan out across the world, taking with them a distorted, re-worked theology of what happened before and after the Flood. Hislop goes on to accuse the Roman Catholic Church of an un-Biblical fixation with the Virgin Mary, whose 'deification', he contends, is a re-invention of the Semiramis heresy. Stormy nostrums indeed back in the mid-1800s, when Catholics and Protestants were still

---

[317] http://en.wikipedia.org/wiki/Alexander_Hislop

banging heads; but historians widely agree that a particular form of goddess worship did take hold across early Mesopotamia, as evidenced by the names of the counterfeit Trinity: Osiris (Nimrod), Isis (Semiramis) and Horus (Nimrod/Tammuz); and that Nimrod and Semiramis, in their various forms and titles, were in the thick of it, egged on by Cush. The heresy involved convocations with fallen angels and demons ('Wise Ones', 'Ascended Ones', 'Nephilim', 'The Ancients', etc.), rebellion against God, 'cutting the cords of heaven' and getting God off the backs of the people (the Atlas myth), gross sexual sins and the sacrificing of infants, and the 'Seed of the woman' programme promoting a fake virgin birth involving Tammuz (a reborn Nimrod) as the counterfeit redeemer.

The Tower of Babel

Around 2184 BC in Shinar, modern-day Iraq, efforts are made to build a city and megalith, this time a vast tower. This is in direct disobedience to God's command for Noah's descendants to disperse and repopulate the Earth after the Flood:

And the whole Earth was of one language and of one speech. And it came to pass, as they journeyed from the east, that they found a plain in the land of Shinar and they dwelt there. And they said one to another, "Go to, let us make brick and burn them throughly." And they had brick for stone, and slime had they for mortar.

And they said, "Go to, let us build us a city and a tower, whose top may reach unto Heaven, and let us make us a name lest we be scattered abroad upon the face of the whole Earth." (Gen 11:1-4)

More rebellion against God, and the smart money has Cush and Nimrod into this project up to their necks. Most conservative scholars point out that these were not stupid people trying to build a literal tower to Heaven to challenge God, but that the city and tower must have had marked spiritual dynamics which offended God, lost to posterity. For my part, there's a little more to this building project than at first meets the eye.

And the LORD said, "Behold, the people is one, and they have all one language; and this they begin to do: and now

302

<u>nothing will be restrained from them which they have imagined to do</u>. Go to, let <u>Us</u> go down, and there confound their language, that they may not understand one another's speech."

So the LORD scattered them abroad from thence upon the face of all the Earth, and they left off to build the city. Therefore is the name of it called Babel, because the LORD did there confound the language of all the Earth: and from thence did the LORD scatter them abroad upon the face of all the Earth. (Gen 11:6-9)

Once again we see the 'Us' of the triune Godhead (*cf.* Matt 28:18-20). The LORD states that man can achieve anything he sets his mind to, which, while a blessing if done in God's name (*cf:* Matt 7:8; 21:21-22; FG 16:23-24), produces extreme danger if guided by 'another spirit'. By confusing the language so no-one can understand another, God saves mankind from the downward pull of his own corrupt nature. It's a temporary reprieve but illustrates God moving actively within His Creation to further His eternal purpose. How arrogant do you have to be before God intervenes in your life personally?

Babel (Babylon) is a major theme throughout the Message System. Babel בָּבֶל comes from the verb בלבל (*bilbel*) 'to confuse', i.e. 'babble', but etymologists believe this is wordplay on an earlier Akkadian meaning of 'gateway of God'. In scripture, 'Babylon' not only represents the actual historical city (the remains of which are in modern-day Iraq),[318] but also a foreshadowing of *ha-Satan's* antichrist religious system in Revelation and man's doomed pride in his own greatness in Dan 4:28-33. The Bible describes a Holy War between two cities, Jerusalem and Babylon, good versus evil, man versus God, holiness versus profanity, Spirit versus the flesh.

Just as man gets on his feet after the Flood and starts building, God wrecks it all again. *Why?* What's so special about this city and its tower? The answer is straightforward. On two occasions God instructs Noah's descendants to be fruitful, multiply and replenish the Earth (Gen 8:17; 9:1). Noah's descendants decide to defy God and build a city and a tower instead **'to make us a name lest we be scattered abroad on the face of the whole Earth.'** (Gen 11:4)

---

[318] Google Earth, 32 32 36.05 N, 44 25 00.30 E

Disobedience always brings judgment. God's actions result in scattering the population across the face of the Earth as ordered. S A Cranfill believes,

"The spiritual actions of the whole Earth in Gen. 11 strongly suggests... that the vast majority of Noah's descendants chafed under the godly leadership of Noah and Shem and looked instead to the proud and ambitious Cush [Ham's firstborn]." [319]

Interestingly, as with Noah and the Flood, there are stories all over the world that seem to agree on this strange event:

Greek Account: "When all men were of one language, some of them built a high tower as if they would thereby ascend up to heaven, but the Gods sent storms of wind and overthrew the tower and gave everyone his peculiar language, and for this reason it was that the city was called Babylon."

Sumerian Account: "Then Enki, the LORD of abundance (whose commands are trustworthy), the LORD of wisdom, who understands the land; the leader of the Gods, endowed with wisdom, the LORD of Eridu changed the speech in their mouths, contention into it, into the speech of man that (until now) had been one."

Mexican Account: "And as men were thereafter multiplying they constructed a very high and strong Zacualli (a very high tower) in order to protect themselves when again the second world should be destroyed. At the crucial moment their languages were changed, and as they did not understand one another, they went to different parts of the world."

Polynesian Account: "But the God in anger chased the builders away, broke down the building and changed their language, so that they spoke diverse tongues."

Crow Indian Account: "Then little Coyote did something bad. He suggested to Old Man that he give the people different languages so they would misunderstand each other and use their weapons in wars.... Old Man did what little Coyote said and the people had different languages and made war on each other." [320]

---

[319] Cranfill, S A, *They Came From Babel*, op. cit. p.71
[320] www.relijournal.com

Some believe the Etemenanki ziggurat (now a ruin) might have been the tower in question, though its estimated height (90 m) would hardly make it a skyscraper.[321] Why was the Tower of Babel a threat? If the ziggurat was intended to stop a second soaking, surely building it on the highest mountain possible rather than the plains of Shinar would have been the smarter bet. Babel is transparently lame as a direct, physical challenge to God. Allen Ross thinks Babel's threat came from its focal point for worship against God, or more specifically in honour to 'false gods' such as Satan and his Nephilim/Anakim.[322] Drs. Emil Gaveluk and Immanuel Velikovsky believe the tower could even have been some sort of transmission centre, or a spacecraft docking port to entice the Watchers to 'come down' and resume their pre-Flood carnal activities (i.e. Babel - 'gateway of the gods'). Once again the possibility arises that high places are what you use if you wish to access hyperdimensions or entice other beings onto the Earth. Cranfill refers to later Babylonian literature which seems to indicate 'the gods' had a hand in building the tower which, if such were fallen gods, would have provoked God beyond measure.

We've seen some of the megaliths have extraordinary architecture conducive to alien technology, such as the mica at Teotihuacan. Is there a link between what is thought to exist on Mars and a later attempt to replicate this colonisation on Earth? Was Mars some sort of alien/angel base obliterated by God, the remains of which NASA's rovers are sifting through even as you read this? Was Babel a continuation of the 'God versus Satan' Holy War being played out on a renewed Earth in the years following the Flood? We'll examine further.

Utter confusion

Suzanne Hayes writes:

"The loss of speech [at Babel] may have been a divine retribution or possibly a natural disaster - interpreted as an act of God. An article

---

[321] http://en.wikipedia.org/wiki/Etemenanki.
Google Earth, 32 32 11 N, 44 25 15 E
[322] **Ross, Allen P** "Genesis", *The Bible Knowledge Commentary,* vol.1, p.38

was published in the *Telegraph* in May 2008 which described how Roger Highfield, the *Telegraph's* Science Editor, participated in an experiment in which the speech area of his brain was temporarily disabled by a process of 'transcranial magnetic stimulation'. The area of the brain identified to be responsible for speech, speech tone and recognition is named after the man who discovered it - Broca's area.

The introduction of a magnetic force effectively turned off the ability to communicate - albeit on a temporary basis. Is it feasible therefore to consider that a large scale electro-magnetic emission or blast from the tower of Babel could have affected the speech centre of those around the tower on a permanent basis?" [323]

Though legends and myths on Babel abound, quite a few take it seriously to this day, including the European Union. In the 1990's, the EU Commission saw fit to sanction a poster stylising Peter Brueghel's 1563 painting of the Tower of Babel. The EU caption reads, "Europe. Many tongues. One voice," and has 12 yellow pentagrams (inverted stars as in Satanism) orbiting the structure. Just so we don't miss the point, there's a modern crane on top of the tower, symbolising the ongoing rebuilding of the EU as Babel.

On the front page of an edition of the German magazine *Der Spiegel*, there's a picture of 'the woman riding the beast', only this gal's wearing a swimsuit and holding the EU flag as she rides Europa the bull. The woman riding the beast is right out of Revelation 17. To say she's not 'a good person' is putting it mildly:

So he carried me away in the Spirit into the wilderness, <u>and I saw a woman sit upon a scarlet-coloured beast, full of names of blasphemy</u>, having seven heads and ten horns. And the woman was arrayed in purple and scarlet colour, and decked with gold and precious stones and pearls, having a golden cup in her hand full of abominations and filthiness of her fornication. And upon her forehead was a name written, MYSTERY, BABYLON THE GREAT, THE MOTHER OF HARLOTS AND ABOMINATIONS OF THE EARTH. And I saw the woman drunken with the blood of the saints, and with the blood of the martyrs of Jesus: and

---

[323] www.world-mysteries.com/newgw/gw_shayes_1.htm

when I saw her, I wondered with great amazement. (Rev 17:3-6, NKJV)

The woman riding the beast is Semiramis, but her transmogrification into someone else will be another astonishment to the reader, to be unveiled as we go. Meanwhile, one version of the 2 euro coin has the same woman (Semiramis) riding the beast. Another poster proclaims "ECU [the euro] – the way of the future." Incongruously, there's a fetching Semiramis once again astride the pagan white bull of Europa with the twelve stars surrounding, which is counterfeit imagery of the woman (symbolising Israel) and the twelve stars (tribes) described in Revelation 12:

And there appeared a great wonder in heaven; a woman clothed with the sun, and the moon under her feet, and upon her head a crown of twelve stars [twelve tribes of Israel]. **And she being with child cried, travailing in birth, and pained to be delivered. And there appeared another wonder in heaven; and behold a great red dragon, having seven heads and ten horns, and seven crowns upon his heads. And his tail drew the third part of the stars of heaven, and did cast them to the Earth** [angels cast out]. **And the dragon** [Satan] **stood before the woman** [Israel] **which was ready to be delivered, for to devour her child** [Yeshua, the Seed of the woman] **as soon as it was born. And she brought forth a man child who was to rule all nations with a rod of iron** [Yeshua *ha-Mashiach*]: **and her child was caught up unto God and to His throne** [ascension]. (Rev 12:1-6)

Aymon de Albatrus writes:

"It is hard to escape the notion that the second Babylon is now being rebuilt in Europe, and those who would follow Nimrod have now succeeded in building a parliament building in Strasbourg, France, whose centrepiece is an enormous replica of the unfinished tower of Babel. Indeed the building is commonly referred to as 'The Tower of Eurobabel'."[324]

---

[324] www.albatrus.org

Dr David R Reagan writes:

"Another demonic biblical symbol being used in conjunction with the European Union is the one from Revelation 17 where a great harlot is depicted riding a beast. For some strange and unknown reason this symbol is being used to represent the EU. For example, when Britain issued a stamp to commemorate the first European Parliament elections in 1979, the picture on the stamp depicted a woman riding a beast.

According to the Rev. Dr. Ian Paisley, a Northern Ireland Protestant minister and member of the European Parliament, the woman on a beast is now the official picture of the EU. He points out that the multi-million dollar new parliament building in Brussels, Belgium, contains a dome with a colossal painting, three times life size, of a woman riding a beast.

In Strasbourg, France, the rival parliamentary building (the one with the Tower of Babel) features a mural of a naked woman riding a beast. Likewise, the new Brussels headquarters of the Council of Europe contains a bronze statue of a woman riding a beast, and the beast is depicted riding on waves, just as in Revelation 17." [325]

While some may not take the Bible seriously, the people behind the European Union certainly do, but not in a way Auntie Hilda would have approved.[326]

Peleg – the Earth divided

And then, further action. With classic Biblical understatement, Genesis 10:25 records: **And unto Eber were born two sons: the name of one was Peleg; <u>for in his days was the Earth divided</u>. And his brother's name was Joktan.**

Peleg is singled out for special mention in the table of nations in Genesis 10. His brother, for some reason, is also mentioned.[327] Peleg

---

[325] www.raptureready.com/featured/reagan/dr43.html

[326] The EU Parliament building in Strasbourg is modelled on the Tower of Babel. Google Earth, 48 35 51.02 N, 7 46 06.82 E. The EU Parliament building in Brussels can be found at 50 50 18.17 N, 4 22 34.43 E. The allegation that seat number 666 in both parliaments is left empty for the Antichrist, alas, is an urban myth. (http://uk.answers.yahoo.com/question/index?qid=20110430130819AAghrUs)

is born 100 years after the Flood and lives to be 239, a considerably shorter lifespan than his father and grandfather enjoyed, who lived to 464 and 433 respectively. After Peleg, the lifespans reduce further, eventually down to 120, once again giving credence to the reduced atmospheric pressure scenario.

What does it mean that in Peleg's time the Earth 'was divided'? Peleg was one of Shem's grandsons and thus of the S(h)emitic line. Much speculation has gone into what such a division of the Earth might entail. Some believe it merely alludes to the dividing and scattering of Earth's population as a result of the language judgment at Babel. Others maintain that Peleg and Babel were contemporary, an assertion denied by the timelines given in scripture. Rick Lanser explains:

"Those who allege that the division in Peleg's day was that of Babel overlook the glaring inconsistency that the Babel event affected the *second* generation of the descendants of Japheth. Genesis 10:5 notes that from the sons of Javan, son of Japheth, **the coastlands of the nations were separated into their lands, every one according to his language....** (NASB). Simply put, language differences impacted Japheth's grandchildren, and since there was a universal language until Babel, we can connect the Babel event to this time. But we must jump three generations forward to the fifth generation of Semites before we come to Peleg's division. Accounting for long human lifespans at the time, plus a general equivalence in the timing of the generations following Noah's three sons (all childless while aboard the Ark), this means approximately 200 years separate the Babel and Peleg divisions. Thus, we must conclude they are NOT the same, and that one division is of languages, and the second, later one is of the Earth itself

---

[327] Joktan's name means 'little', 'insignificant'. There is some extra-Biblical speculation that Joktan's 13 sons went on to father the Sinitic peoples of China and east Asia, taking with them the original language of the pre-Flood era, unaffected by the chaos at Babel. Others aver that the boys populated the south Arabian peninsula, as two tribes in that region carry the same name as two of Joktan's sons, **Sheba and Havilah**. Josephus and Hippolytus place Joktan's descendants in the Indus region.

- of the primeval single landmass. They cannot be one and the same event."[328]

Lanser also points out that elsewhere in the Bible, the Hebrew etymological inference of Peleg's name suggests a physical (water) separation/canalling rather than semantic division of the races. Also, for Peleg to have been named specifically for this event (inferred in Gen 10:25), this 'dividing' must have initiated prior to Peleg's birth.

"It does not make sense that his parents would have waited until little Peleg was five years old - assuming Schroeder's reading of Ussher is correct - before naming him, and there is no evidence in the biblical text that allows us to conclude that Peleg was renamed, after the fashion of Abram > Abraham and Jacob > Israel, sometime later in life. This naming consideration strikes a logical blow at the Babel dispersion occurring five years after Peleg's birth. Further, it was pointed out to me that the Hebrew grammar, which uses the perfect form of *palag* in Gen. 10:25, refers to the event of dividing rather than the state of being divided. This does not appear to conflict with the division event being an ongoing one, initiated sometime before Peleg was born but continuing throughout his lifetime. The separation of the landmasses was not a one-time, 'state' event, but a continuing process of increasingly greater separation of land sections with associated infilling of the new low places by the sea. It began as a sort of natural 'canalization', and over time far exceeded that limited scale. We can see a similar process taking place even today in the Afar Triangle region of Africa." [329]

We can reasonably expect some dramatic settling of the Earth's crust following a global disaster on the scale of the Flood. The general speculation is that further geological upheavals followed, most probably the sinking/canalling of land-bridges producing the dividing of continents, approaching what we are familiar with today. It's also conceivable that the legends of lost civilisations

---

[328] www.biblearchaeology.org/post/2006/05/of-peleg-and-pangaea.aspx
[329] Ibid.

310

could also stem from a series of macro events in the days of Peleg, perhaps even triggered by another Mars fly-by:

'BRITAIN'S ATLANTIS' FOUND AT BOTTOM OF NORTH SEA - A HUGE UNDERSEA WORLD SWALLOWED BY THE SEA IN 6500 BC

'Britain's Atlantis' - a hidden underwater world swallowed by the North Sea - has been discovered by divers working with science teams from the University of St Andrews.

Doggerland, a huge area of dry land that stretched from Scotland to Denmark was slowly submerged by water between 18,000 BC and 5,500 BC.

Divers from oil companies have found remains of a 'drowned world' with a population of tens of thousands - which might once have been the 'real heartland' of Europe.

A team of climatologists, archaeologists and geophysicists has now mapped the area using new data from oil companies - and revealed the full extent of a 'lost land' once roamed by mammoths.[330]

Did the Earth's surface literally divide and regions sink, allowing the influx of water to divide up the land? Was this what happened to the humans and animals in Australia? Were the Straits of Gibraltar overflowed by the Atlantic into the Mediterranean? Did this also happen to the Gulf of Mexico?

Underground cities have been found around the world in Egypt, Cabo de San Antonio, Cuba and Mahabalipuram. Was Atlantis another, existing a few hundred years after the Flood until the sea overran it? An examination of ocean floors reveals the extent to which continental shelves link landmasses with a 30/50-foot variance. Did the geologic upheaval or 'canalling' in Peleg's day release further water from the fountains of the deep?

Dr John Morris has written extensively on the scientific anomalies which point to an expected, continuous stabilisation of the Earth's surface in the centuries following Noah's deliverance. Other observers maintain that such a migration of races is entirely plausible given the logistics:

---

[330] *Daily Mail*, 3rd July 2012

"If you calculate the distance from eastern Turkey to the tip of Australia and divide it by 100 years, you will find that both man and beast would only have to migrate less than 80 miles a year (0.21 miles a day) in order to reach Australia; less than 55 miles a year (0.15 miles a day) to reach North America via the Bearing Straits; and less than 48 miles a year (0.13 miles a day) if a land bridge (or possibly an ice bridge) existed across the northern polar regions. Those average daily distance requirements are much less than most people walk each day in their normal routines."[331]

Rick Lanser writes:

"The concept that biblical Pangaea existed until the time of Peleg provides a satisfying framework for understanding several mysteries of early Earth history. For one thing, it allows for a few hundred years of relatively easy human migration following Babel to widely separated places, without resorting to hypothetical land bridges or sophisticated ocean navigation knowledge by the first few generations following the Flood. (Such knowledge does not seem likely to have been possessed by the early, land-locked inhabitants of Mesopotamia.) A satisfying answer is also given to the question of how marsupials could find a home in Australia following the Flood - they just walked there! Isolated continents and impassibly high mountains did not exist at that early time, only developing in succeeding centuries as continued post-Flood Earth turmoil and the Ice Age wrought geological change on a grand scale. The resulting geographical isolation led, via inbreeding and selective pressures imposed by different environments, to the development of the various races of human beings, as well as providing safe havens from predators for various types of vulnerable animals, like the Dodo birds." [332]

Language differences notwithstanding, if God wanted the races divided, something major would have to have happened to force someone like Cush to admit defeat and flee south into Africa, with which he would thereafter be associated. Gaines R Johnson writes:

---

[331] http://www.kjvbible.org/peleg.html
[332] www.biblearchaeology.org/post/2006/05/of-peleg-and-pangaea.aspx

"After examining the Hebrew meanings, a more plausible alternative interpretation would be that it describes an earth-splitting event such as a valley opening in the ground and filling with water. That could have happened anywhere along the Dead Sea Rift zone.... and may have been associated with a delayed adjustment of the Earth's plates in response to the rapid subsidence of the sea floors by the Flood. In theory, when the weight of the waters of the Flood forced the sea floors downward to fill the void beneath, strain would have developed between the oceanic and continental portions of the crustal plates. Consequently, tectonic pressures were redistributed. About 100 years later, the strain and pressure redistribution may have caused the Earth's crust rapidly to rent in weaker places, much like a piece of ridged plastic which can be stretched and deformed. It will eventually snap if the strain remains constant. An abrupt change in sea levels could possibly accompany such an event."[333]

Development of the races

It also need not be a tortuous exercise to account for the characteristics distinguishing the races of humans we see today around the world. After Babel, the people scattered, each with his own language group. We have enough problems in Britain these days getting people of disparate languages to work together; imagine the effects of the Babel judgment. It's worth reiterating Rick Lanser's earlier comment about the timing of Babel in relation to the subsequent canalling judgment, which occurred during Peleg's lifetime:

"Those who allege that the division in Peleg's day was that of Babel overlook the glaring inconsistency that the Babel event affected the *second* generation of the descendants of Japheth. Genesis 10:5 notes that from the sons of Javan, son of Japheth, **the coastlands of the nations were separated into their lands, every one according to his language....** (NASB). Simply put, language differences impacted Japheth's grandchildren, and since there was a universal language until Babel, we can connect the Babel event to this time. But we must jump three generations forward to the fifth generation of Semites before we come to Peleg's division. Accounting for long human lifespans at the

---

[333] www.kjvbible.org/peleg.html

time, plus a general equivalence in the timing of the generations following Noah's three sons (all childless while aboard the Ark), ***this means approximately 200 years separate the Babel and Peleg divisions***. Thus, we must conclude they are NOT the same, and that one division is of languages, and the second, later one is of the Earth itself - of the primeval single landmass. They cannot be one and the same event."[334]

Which means everyone had plenty of time to spread out and hoof it out to the furthest reaches before being 'cut off' by the 'canalling'. Three factors are required to account for variance in racial distinguishing features, e.g. skin colour, facial characteristics, hair colour, height, and so on:

1) Isolated communities interbreeding
2) The nature and latitude of the environment
3) The food supply

Inherent in any racial group are genes conducive to a variety of skin types and other distinguishing features; this is known today in genetics and recognised in Noah's children, as we saw earlier with Ham. Answers in Genesis writes:

"The world environment had been dramatically changed by the Flood. As the groups dispersed, they were going to areas which offered them new and different climates and diets. Studies on the relationship between skin color and health in a given environment, suggest the following origin of racial colors. After Babel, those who went to colder climates who had darker skin, would probably suffer Vitamin D deficiencies such as rickets. The skin produces Vitamin D from sunlight. The person with darker skin is worse off in a cold region since there is less sunlight, and since he is more sunlight-resistant, he can produce less Vitamin D. The colder environment, both through sunlight and the available diet, would tend to favor those with fairer skins. Dark skinned people would be therefore less healthy and tend to have fewer children. Gradually the number of black people in any group that went to a cold region would dwindle. From that point on the remaining population was a "white" race.

---

[334] www.biblearchaeology.org/post/2006/05/of-peleg-and-pangaea.aspx

Likewise, those who went to brighter, hotter regions, and had darker skins would survive more easily (i.e. get less skin cancer, etc.) and hence be selected for. In this case, the whiter persons would dwindle from the population and a "black" race would result. It is interesting to note that if a pure white European is married to a pure black Negro, the offspring are an intermediate brown called mulatto. If two mulattos are married, the offspring can be any of 9 colors, from pure white to pure black."[335]

The peppered moth experiment is cited when proof of evolution is called for. Wikipedia provides the standard excursion, which has a familiar echo to the foregoing:

"The evolution of the peppered moth over the last two hundred years has been studied in detail. Originally, the vast majority of peppered moths had light coloration, which effectively camouflaged them against the light-colored trees and lichens upon which they rested. However, due to widespread pollution during the Industrial Revolution in England, many of the lichens died out, and the trees which peppered moths rested on became blackened by soot, causing most of the light-colored moths, or typica, to die off due to predation. At the same time, the dark-colored, or melanic moths, *carbonaria,* flourished because of their ability to hide on the darkened trees."[336]

Actually, as covered in *Origins I,* this is not evidence of evolution but natural selection. For what it's worth, this 'example of evolution' was disproved decades ago since peppered moths do not hang out on tree-trunks but up in the foliage. However, the example does shed light on how environment can quickly amend population demographics.

"After the 'new languages' arrived, man would tend to live and marry only with those who reinforced his language grouping and adhered to the culture he accepted. Each of these groups would have represented a 'gene pool' (certain number of inheritable characteristics) which now was isolated from all other gene pools. Within each of these groups, marriage only between those in the

---

[335] www.answersingenesis.org/articles/cm/v3/n3/origin-of-human-races
[336] http://en.wikipedia.org/wiki/Peppered_moth

group would tend to enhance those physical traits the individuals regarded as 'desired', e.g. size or skin color or intellect, and bring out any common oddities in the gene pool that previously would have been masked by continual intermarriage. It is easy to imagine how persons possessing genes for 'pygmy' size could be persecuted into leaving their ancestral society and seeking refuge from their society in a previously unoccupied and secluded habitat.

Further evidence for this common cultural and physical ancestry is supplied by a study of the stories which each group has in common, such as the large number of flood legends." [337]

And what of the Stone Age? Creation scientists believe there were no knuckle-dragging, half-ape/half-human beasts hanging out in caves. 'Neanderthal' artefacts were tools and weapons fashioned by the early survivors of the Flood, or by those fleeing persecution by others, or banished by communities for crimes, misdemeanours or failing to toe the party line. From the early days, a banishment like Cain's was not necessarily a death sentence. Separated from your community, condemned to wander and fend for yourself, you would kill animals for food, avoid beasts that could hurt you, and survive among the caverns and crags. And doubtless also lament your fate through the expression of rock art or scratched petroglyphs of humans and animals on the stone walls of your cave.

The end of Nimrod

So what happened to Nimrod and Semiramis? Here you enter a murky world of legends, myths and fanciful bedtime stories – the very aim, some scholars suspect, Semiramis intended. The Bible is silent on their fate. Legend holds that the couple remained defiant in Babylon on the eastern bank of the Euphrates, but God's powers could not be matched. The tower was never finished, its use stymied. Some say it was destroyed by God's divine wind (Spirit) at the time of the Babel judgment; others that it remained for some time as a symbol of neglect and failure.

---

[337] www.answersingenesis.org/articles/cm/v3/n3/origin-of-human-races

According to Alexander Hislop, Nimrod's continued rebellion against God finally provokes Noah's son, Shem to act. Because of Shem's great standing as one of the eight Flood survivors, he is feared and respected even by those who hate him. Shem persuades the Mizraic (Egyptian) authorities to act and Nimrod is arrested, put on trial before 30 judges and condemned to death. A further court rules that he should be denied burial. Nimrod is thus executed (we're not told how) and his body hacked into fourteen pieces, each taken to a different city in the empire to warn of the fate awaiting apostates.

Semiramis now has a problem. Pregnant through harlotry, she finds herself with no consort, a swollen belly, an undimmed fury against the God-botherers who murdered her husband, and but one option remaining. She sets out across the empire and recovers all her husband's pieces bar one – Nimrod's penis. Semiramis wastes no time confirming rumours that her child was conceived from 'the Seed of the woman', thus 'realising' the prophecy in Genesis 3:15. Institutionalising herself as chief goddess and her cult as 'a mystery', she keeps her activities secret and her end is unknown. Hislop maintains her Babylonian cult survived to underpin almost every religion that spread out across the world in the centuries that followed. Many featured phallic worship through sexual abominations (worship of the 'Seed'), crimes against children such as child sacrifice/abortion (to thwart the true Seed), phallic/relic worship (obelisks, 'bits' of Nimrod's body), worship of the sun (Lucifer), mystery religion, goddess worship (Madonna), and reincarnation/resurrection (Nimrod reborn as the golden child, Tammuz).

Like the Flood stories, elements of this cult abound to this day. Edith Starr Miller (Lady Queenborough) conducts a study in *The Occult Theocracy*. Alexander Hislop's efforts are exhaustive in *The Two Babylons*. Seventh Day Adventist co-founder Ellen Gould White's 1888 book, *The Great Controversy*, explains on the back cover:

"The title of this book refers to a great cosmic war that erupted in the universe thousands of years ago and has raged ever since. Few people alive today realize that this Earth is the primary battle zone of

317

that war. And fewer still know why the war is being fought and how and when it will end…." [338]

Christianity, Judaism, Kabbalah, Mormonism, Islam, Buddhism, Hinduism and a thousand faiths in between bear the scars of this war. The gods of Rome starred in it, as did the gods of ancient Greece. From Baal to Moloch (Heb: *melech* – 'king'), from Huang-ti of China to Quetzalcoatl of the Aztecs, the Semiramis 'truth' is still manifest. In Egyptian mythology, Shem becomes Seth or Set, the bad one who kills Osiris (Nimrod) and then cuts his body into 14 pieces, which Isis eventually recovers except for the penis. Cranfill summarises the Holy War:

"The significance of the lost phallus, of course, has to do with 'the Seed'. There is another Egyptian story which says that Set (Seth) lost his own testicles in his fight with Horus. The true Seed of the woman is Christ while the seed of the serpent is the Antichrist (Gen 3:15). The theme of history from the Garden to the Cross is Satan's determination to destroy the Seed (child) of the woman. From the beginning of paganism, this theme would lead humans into 'child devouring' or child sacrifice (Rev 12:4; Eze 16:21; 23:37)." [339]

Woe unto them that call evil good, and good evil; that put darkness for light, and light for darkness; that put bitter for sweet, and sweet for bitter! (Isa 5:20). Shem becomes the evil one and Nimrod the righteous sacrifice 'for whom the world weeps'. Counterfeiting becomes *ha-Satan's* central theme in the war against God. [340] From Greece to Rome, from Egypt to India, from Buddhism to the American Indians and Australian Aborigines, from abortion to UFOs to gay rights to online porn, elements of the rebellion, like the Flood, surface again and again. The Holy War is also a tale of two cities: Jerusalem, the spirit; Babylon, the flesh. Jerusalem the city of God; Babylon the city of Satan. Both cities are used literally and figuratively throughout the Message System, woven in with the other central themes of the ages: the woman riding the beast;

---

[338] **White, E G** *The Great Controversy,* Advent Books, 2003
[339] Cranfill S A, *They Came From Babel,* op. cit. p.89
[340] 2 Cor 4:3-4; 11:3-4; 11:14-15

the whore of Babylon; the woman and the child; child slaughter (outside the womb and within); sexual crimes against children; symbols of rebirth such as firs, eggs and pine-cones; those tattoos and goatee beards (Lev 19:27-28); the fish (Noah) reborn from the water (Jonah) and commencing repopulation (*ish-Nu* (Vishnu) – lit. the people of Noah); aliens coming to Earth to seed mankind; serpents; all-seeing eyes; pyramids; half-man/half gods; the zodiac; the true Trinity, Father, Son and Holy Spirit; the blasphemous trinity, Osiris, Isis, Horus; or later, Satan, the Antichrist and False Prophet; the trinity triangle (666); the trinity trefoil (666); baptismal cleansing of sin and rebirth by water (the Flood). And above all, *mystery.*

Symbology

Ellen Gould White presents research on how Semiramis's spiritual rebellion has infiltrated our modern world:

Serpent: The winged serpent in Egypt is ubiquitous as the soul of the departed (Tutankhamun's throne in Cairo). The Mayan serpent sun god Quetzacoatl. In ancient Rome, the serpent (Satan) carries the soul to heaven. In Viking lore, it is found on the prows of the longships carrying the lithsmen into battle. Lord Nrsimhadeva in India has a fan of serpents behind his head. Serpents abound in Catholic architecture. The serpent dragon is found on the papal crest in the Vatican. The top of the crosier a bishop holds in Christianity is curled into a serpent. Athena, the Greek god of war, holds the serpent.

The Trident represents the blasphemous trinity found in ancient Rome held by Poseidon/Neptune. It's a fertility symbol in Hinduism. It's on the cross at the high altar in St Paul's Cathedral in London. The trident protrudes from the head of the boy child held in the arms of the Madonna in Catholic art.

The Cornu: Two fingers extended in the horns of the Devil is featured on the statue of Apollo in the London Museum; the hand of Buddha; pre-Christian votive hands are found on statues in temples; on the statue of Jupiter, which has been renamed 'St Peter' in the Vatican; *Star Trek's* Vulcan hand sign also involves the cornu, a hand-gesture flashed around by everyone from Britney Spears to Spiderman to Barack Obama to the Pope![341]

The sun Disk/Wheel/Orb represents 'Lucifer', 'lightbearer', god of the sun. We see the sun-disk behind the heads of saints in Christian art. It is represented in the Catholic wafer (host) which is worshiped. The disk is behind the heads of the Japanese gods of happiness; the golden halo behind Krishna (*ish-Nu* – *lit.* 'people of Noah'); behind the head of a Hindu deity in the Gamet Museum, Paris; the face of Apollo, the Greek sun-god, replete with serpents and horns in the Pergamum Museum in East Berlin; an orb representing the sun is held in the hands of Isis (Semiramis); Hercules (Greece); Mithra, the Persian sun-god; a golden Christ is found with an orb in his hand. A solar wheel is depicted in the religious art of gods in India, Assyria, Thailand, of all places in Notre Dame Cathedral in Paris, and at the Jesuit monastery of St Ignatius Loyola in Spain. The largest sun-wheel of all makes up the entire Court of St Peter at the Vatican complex in Rome.

Pine cones: symbol of fertility/fecundity; found in Mexico; India; on Osiris the solar god of Egypt; in Assyria; held on the staff of Bacchus, the ancient god of drunkenness and revelry; mounted on the Pope's staff. The largest pine cone of all is found in the Court of the Pine Cone at the Vatican, Rome.

The Fish-God: symbolising man's triumph over God's judgment in the Flood; Oannes (Noah) is the Babylonian god with a fish's head. Vishnu (*ish-Nu* – *lit.* 'people of Noah') the Hindu god has a fish's head. Neptune/Poseidon is half-man/half-fish, and the ruler of the underworld (sea). Assyrian pagan priests wear half-man/half-fish regalia. Isis from Egypt is depicted as a fish. The pagan god Dagon is depicted with a fish helmet.[342] Cybele, the

---

[341] For an example of humans doing things without any clue, watch the cornu hand-sign compilation at http://youtu.be/oTG-B2d4fZk

[342] The Assyrians of Nineveh worshiped Dagon, the fish god. When the Jewish prophet Jonah was instructed by God to go to Nineveh to seek the empire's repentance, he balked, went the other way and was swallowed by a big fish (whale). He was puked up on a beach three days later (resurrected after three days, he was probably dead inside the fish). Jonah's skin would doubtless have been bleached by the stomach juices of the fish while inside. When Jonah finally makes it to Nineveh, he gives his message to the Assyrians without interest, viz:

Syrian goddess, wears a fish helmet. And Protestant and Catholic bishops are famous for wearing the mitre, which is a fish helmet.

The All-Seeing Eye: The eye of Horus, or Satan, is depicted on the US dollar bill, staring out of the pyramid capstone. Hathor is the eye of Osiris. The Masonic triangle (666) is encircled by a snake with the all-seeing eye in the middle. The evil eye is found within the eight-spoked sun-wheel and triangle at the apex of the dome in the Catholic cathedral at Santiago de Compostela in Spain.[343]

Cranfill summarizes:

"Control is exercised best by the 'knowledgeable few' over the 'ignorant masses'. What is confusing to many is that, throughout history, more often than not these 'knowledgeable few' have thought they were doing the right thing and working for the greater good. We have seen from a certain human point of view, Nimrod was a hero, a benefactor, and an enlightener of mankind. Manley Hall explains that the doctrines of the 'ageless' mysteries 'lead to the good of mankind', and that secret societies are the custodians of the highest cultural concepts.... Opposition drove the enlightened ones underground, to secrecy, but this necessity brought no 'decline' in the 'plan or purpose' of the initiates, who have always been dedicated to, and appealed to, 'the rational soul of the world'." [344]

Trickery to get you worshiping the wrong god. The Designer condemns the Anti-Human's attempts at every turn to violate His holy sovereignty, despoil man and lead him into error. In fact, so incensed does the Holy One become wherever He finds the work of Semiramis, the rivers of the Middle East run red in Old Testament blood with the slaughters rained down on the guilty. By the last days, we are told, all the kings of the Earth will have committed fornication with the Whore of Babylon (Rev 17:1-2), and though God exhorts his faithful to **"Come out of her, my people, that ye be not partakers of her sins, and that ye receive not of her**

"Forty days and you're getting yours." Incredibly Nineveh repents before YHWH from the king down! After all, this prophet was swallowed by Dagon and was puked back to life!

[343] White, E G, *The Great Controversy,* op. cit., p.289 ff.

[344] Cranfill S A, *They Came From Babel,* op. cit.

plagues" (Rev 18:4), only a remnant heeds the warning. The whole world is seduced by The Lie (Rom 1:25; 2 Thess 2:11). Only the remnant will preserve the ancient line of Noah and all known truth about God, and these, along with the Jews, will bear the brunt of Satan's wrath in the coming days of Antichrist and his False Prophet on Earth during the Great Tribulation.

Back in Nimrod's day a keen paradox was felt. For all the evil practised, the wicked were still aware that God did the creating. His handiwork was seen in every newborn's cry, every dog, every tree, every bird and bumble bee. The gulf separating the deeds of man from those of God are infinite. Incomprehensible. But God restrains. God kills. God is judgmental. God is against liberty and the true freedom of man. Yet deep down everyone knows God makes the warthog and dusts the powder on a butterfly's wing, while Nimrod can't even find his own penis.

ABRAHAM, FRIEND OF GOD

"Whatever the LORD pleases He does, in Heaven and in Earth, in the seas and in all deep places." (Psa 135:6, NKJV)

"A faith that can't be tested can't be trusted." – **Warren Wiersbe**

By some estimates, Nimrod was born within fifty years of the Flood and executed around 2020 BC. A few decades later, a descendant of Shem named Terah (*lit.* 'wanderer', 'delayer', loiterer') moves his family from southern Mesopotamia with the view to settling in Canaan. The trouble is, they never get there. So begins the incredible story of Abraham (born 'Abram'), the ancient patriarch to today's three leading monotheistic religions – Judaism, Christianity and Islam.

All sorts of conjectures and legends have arisen that Nimrod and Abram were contemporaries or even rivals; that Terah made idols for Nimrod and moved to Haran to do so. For our purposes here, let's stick with the Message System which reveals a further, unusual perspective you won't pick up unless you study the patriarchs' lifespans. From these we learn that:

a) **Abram knew (of) Shem, son of Noah, for 150 years** (the Bible doesn't actually state whether they met). In fact, Shem outlived Abram!

b) Shem was contemporary with Methuselah for 98 years.

c) Methuselah knew Adam for 243 years.

Which means that Abram is only three conversations/generations removed from Adam, and almost certainly knew Shem and, I believe it is reasonable to infer, *learnt from him*. God kept Shem alive for *502 years after the Flood* to educate successive generations on the lessons learned from the pre-Flood world: God's judgment and subsequent mercy portrayed through Noah and the other Flood survivors, what Methuselah was like, and what he had to say about Adam and Eve. In Shem we have all known truth about God preserved, and also a detailed remembrance of what the pre-Flood world was like, who the personages were, and how it all went wrong. This is important to understand because of what follows.

The LORD's call

In my childhood Sunday school class, Abraham was presented to me as a remote figure I had nothing in common with; full of faith (whatever that meant); a shaggy-haired, scraggly-bearded, sandal-wearing old-timer who shuffled around with a big staff doing everything God told him to do. He almost killed his son Isaac by sacrificing him, which was quite interesting but not half as interesting as David killing Goliath later and chopping his head off with a huge sword. Oh, and Abraham had something to do with the destruction of a wicked place called Sodom (cue titters around the class behind little pink hands). But who was Abraham? Can we get closer to the real man, hang some flesh and bone on him, decipher his character and the role he plays in the Holy War? Abraham does have some surprising weaknesses but he learns from them, and this alone will bring him closer to all of us. Let's do some digging.

I've read a huge amount of research material penned by authors who think they know what happened in pre-history, but I'm going to lean on the epistemological integrity of the Message System's Author by assuming that everything God wants us to know about Abraham He's put in the Bible. The first thing you notice is that Abraham's early life, as described, is a bit of a puzzle. For a start, he is born <u>Abram</u> ('my father is exalted') in a place with the great name of Ur of the Chaldees.[345] In modern parlance, Abram is an Iraqi, raised the eldest son of an idol-worshiping pagan named Terah (Josh 24:2). Abram's youngest brother, Haran, dies early on and leaves behind a son named Lot ('veil', covering'). Thereafter, Lot is taken under Abram's wing when father Terah moves the family.

---

[345] Ur is located at Google Earth, 30 57 45 N, 46 6 11 E near Nasiriyah, Dhi Qar Province, southern Iraq. It falls within the security perimeter of Imam Ali Air Base, formerly Camp Adder of the US Armed Forces. A ziggurat survives in what used to be the ancient city, dating back to the early Bronze Age (21st century BC). Abraham would have been very familiar with it.

That's the background. Not much need be said about the city of Ur's idolatry and evil practices at that time. It had a large ziggurat – a 'high place' – which survives to this day, on top of which stood a pagan temple, wherein every perverted practice you can imagine (and a few you cannot) was carried out to the gods' (*ha-Satan's*) delight. At the time, the area was under the control and influence of the powerful Elamite (proto-Persian) empire to the east (modern-day, south-western Iran). Suffice to say that young Abram is not raised in the most stable, holy or auspicious of environments, and there is nothing remarkable to separate him from thousands of similar pagan children other than that the Creator of the Universe *chooses him*. We sense from the text that Abram disagrees with his father's idol-worshiping tendencies from an early age, and this causes problems later on.

Abram is contacted by God and told to pack up, leave his family, and trek to the land of Canaan (modern-day Israel). There's a detail argued over incessantly here by scholars and expositors. Namely, that not just Abram, *but the whole family* up-sticks and quits their home town of Ur with the view to going westward to Canaan, but somehow ends up in Haran 600 miles to the north-west. It doesn't sound like a big deal but there is a *remez* here if we dig for it, so here's my spade.

The scriptures read as follows:

And Terah lived seventy years, and begat Abram, Nahor and Haran. Now these are the generations of Terah: Terah begat Abram, Nahor and Haran, and Haran begat Lot.

And Haran died before his father Terah <u>in the land of his nativity, in Ur of the Chaldees.</u>

And Abram and Nahor took them wives: the name of Abram's wife was Sarai; and the name of Nahor's wife, Milcah, the daughter of Haran, the father of Milcah, and the father of Iscah. But Sarai was barren; she had no child.

And Terah took Abram his son, and Lot the son of Haran his son's son, and Sarai his daughter in law, his son Abram's wife, <u>and they went forth with them from Ur of the Chaldees, to go into the land of Canaan;</u> and they came unto Haran and dwelt there.

And the days of Terah were two hundred and five years: and Terah died in Haran. (Gen 11:26-27)

From this we understand that:

1) Terah has three kids, of which Abram is the eldest.
2) Terah is 70 years old when he has Abram.
3) Haran, Abram's youngest brother, has a son named Lot.
4) Haran dies before his father in his 'native land' <u>which, the Holy Spirit sees fit to emphasise,</u> is Ur of the Chaldees.
5) The family leaves at Terah's insistence with the intent of going to Canaan (which is to the west), but ends up going north-west on a major 600-mile detour to Haran. The reason is unknown.
6) Terah stays in Haran until he dies at the ripe old age of 205.

No problems so far, except that the very next bit states:

Now the LORD <u>had</u> said unto Abram, "Get thee out of thy country, and from thy kindred, and from thy father's house, unto a land that I will shew thee [Canaan/Israel]. And I will make of thee a great nation, and I will bless thee, and make thy name great; and thou shalt be a blessing. And I will bless them that bless thee, and I will curse him that curseth thee: and in thee shall all families of the Earth be blessed." (Gen 12:1-3)

The LORD's call to Abram is placed here at Gen 12:1 right after describing the family's move to Haran, so the casual reader is forgiven for thinking that Abram gets the call to go to Canaan while living with the family in Haran, perhaps even after his father Terah dies (Acts 7:2-4). Much is made of this by some expositors, and even atheists gleefully point out a contradiction in the text, which by now you are learning is a *remez* – God's way of saying 'get your spade and dig here!'

- Even though the LORD's call is placed after the mention of the family moving to Haran and Terah's subsequent death there, the passage is consistent with Abram receiving the call personally years before in Ur since the text actually states: **Now the LORD <u>had</u> said unto Abram....**
- Furthermore, we are told the LORD's call is to Abram personally and not to Terah

- In fact, God wants Abram to leave not only the land of his birth ('**...thy country...**') but also his parental family ('**...thy kindred...**' which presumably includes his pushy Dad) and his father's house, and proceed directly westward to the land of Canaan, do not pass Go, do not collect £200.
- *Abram disobeys and doesn't do this!* Instead, probably after discussing the LORD's call with his idol-worshiping father, the latter agrees to sell up and leave Ur with the family, ostensibly with the intent of going to Canaan, but ends up hopping on a boat and going 500 miles up the Euphrates, then hoofing it 100 miles north to Haran instead.
- Examine any Biblical map to discover that is Haran[346] is not 'on the way to Canaan' by any stretch of the imagination, as some scholars would have it.

Peter Fast writes:

"Why Haran? Why did Terah stop there? In Genesis 11:31 it definitively states *"...and they went out with them from Ur of the Chaldeans to go to the land of Canaan; and they came to Haran and dwelt there."* Now, if one examines a map, Haran definitely is not Canaan. But why did Terah stop? Well, lets take a glimpse at what Haran was like in those days and perhaps we will find our key.

First, Haran was a caravan city, it was politically stable and flourishing. These are all very good reasons to stop, but I think the final one may be the hidden key, and that is Haran's chief god was Nanna the god of the moon. Why is this so important? Well, Nanna or Sin was also the chief god of Ur, where Terah had just left. Joshua 24:2 says, And Joshua said to all the people, **"Thus says the LORD God of Israel: 'Your fathers, including Terah, the father of Abraham and the father of Nahor, dwelt on the other side of the River in old times; and they served other gods.'"**

Thus, it is possible Terah found a new home in Haran, and wanted to stay because that was a city that honored and worshiped a god he would have revered all his life, Nanna the moon god. So, essentially we get a familiar religious scene, a good economy, and a

---

[346] Haran is identified with modern-day Harran in Turkey, Google Earth, 36 52 39 N, 39 2 2 E

location which is safe. Although we can not know for sure why, these could still very well be clues as to why Terah chose to live in Haran."[347]

Indeed, ancient Haran was the place to be in Abram's time, reckons Wiki:

"By the 19th Century BCE, Harran was established as a merchant outpost due to its ideal location. The community, well established before then, was situated along a trade route between the Mediterranean and the plains of the middle Tigris. It lay directly on the road from Antioch eastward to Nisibis and Nineveh. The [river] could be followed down to... Babylon. The fourth century Roman historian Ammianus Marcellinus (325/330–after 391) said, "From there (Harran), two different royal highways lead to Persia: the one on the left through Adiabene and over the Tigris; the one on the right, through Assyria and across the Euphrates." Not only did Harran have easy access to both the Assyrian and Babylonian roads, but also to north road to the Euphrates that provided easy access to Malatiyah and Asia Minor.

According to Roman authors such as Pliny the Elder, even through the classical period, Harran maintained an important position in the economic life of northern Mesopotamia."[348]

Who cares? Why all the mystery? Why can't the Bible lay out the motives of its players barefaced for all to see so we can move on? Because God wants us to care enough to dig. Abram finally makes the move from Haran and it's described thus:

So Abram departed, as the LORD had spoken unto him; and Lot went with him: and Abram was seventy and five years old when he departed out of Haran.

And Abram took Sarai his wife, and Lot his brother's son, and all their substance that they had gathered, and the souls that they had gotten in Haran; and they went forth to go into the land of Canaan, and into the land of Canaan they came. (Gen 12:4-5)

From this we surmise that:

---

[347] http://peterjfast.com/2012/05/14/abraham-from-ur-to-haran/
[348] http://en.wikipedia.org/wiki/Harran

1. Terah is 145 years old when Abram leaves him in Haran (*cf.* Gen 11:26,32; 12:4)
2. Terah survives a further 60 years *after* Abram departs before dying aged 205
3. Which means that Terah's death is <u>not</u> the reason Abram leaves Haran for Canaan, Abram's faith is: (**So Abram departed, <u>as the LORD had spoken to him</u>...**) Lazy expositors just assume Abram departs after his father dies without properly reading the text
4. Abram and Sarai are very wealthy citizens by the time they quit Haran. Lot's not doing badly either
5. Notice the quaintly phrased **and they went forth to go into the land of Canaan, <u>and into the land of Canaan they came.</u>** In other words, they leave for Canaan (again), only this time, strewth, they get there! (*cf.* Gen 11:31)

So we may conclude between the lines that Terah is a powerful patriarch who overawes his family and demands that they strive, do well and look up to him.[349] Terah worships 'other gods' and this does not sit well with Abram.[350] When Abram tells his father at Ur he's going to take his wife and move to Canaan to answer the LORD's call, Terah doesn't release him, probably makes excuses, and Abram is bulldozed into agreeing that the whole family move to Canaan. Only they don't, they go up-river to Haran instead. In effect, *Abram doesn't do what God tells him to do!* Terah lives up to his name of 'wanderer', 'delayer', 'loiterer' by holding Abram back, so you could argue that Terah is a type of Satan, holding back the faithful. Then again, if Abram really wanted to go to Canaan, he could have but he didn't. You'll also notice that the text goes out of

---

[349] Terah names his sons Abram ('my father is exalted'), Nahor ('hoarse', 'dry', 'hot'), Haran ('mountain-climber', 'achiever')

[350] Jewish tradition has a colourful legend for Terah: "Terah was a wicked, idolatrous priest who manufactured idols. In Jewish tradition, Abram is considered to be the eldest of three sons who was opposed to his father's idol shop. After Abram smashed his father's idols and chased customers away, Terah brought his unruly son before Nimrod, who threw him into a fiery furnace, yet Abram miraculously escaped. The Zohar says that when God saved Abram from the furnace, Terah repented." – Wikipedia, 'Terah'

its way not to make as big a deal of Abram's disobedience as I'm doing! Why? Because God has promised the faithful that he will be merciful in their iniquities and remember their sins no more (Isa 43:25; Jer 31:34; Heb 8:12). So Abram's sin is not in the surface text, but you'll find it if you dig.

I find this fascinating. This is not about gloating or showing Abram up. We can identify with Abram because he's flesh and blood like us, has family problems, makes mistakes, bad calls and fouls up like us, yet he's later inducted into the 'Hall of Faith' for his belief in the LORD (Heb 11:8-12), which is counted to him for righteousness (Gen 15:6; Rom 4:3). So God remembers his sin no more. Why? Because Abram tries and keeps trying. That should give each of us great hope. God loves a tryer. Abram is later described by the Creator Himself as 'the friend of God' (Isa 41:8; 2 Chron 20:7; Jam 2:23)

I agree with Peter Fast that the move to Haran on Terah's part probably has a religious motive linked to Terah's worship of the moon god, Sin (later 'al-ilah', i.e. 'the deity', Islam's 'Allah').[351] Haran is a centre for such veneration so becomes the natural home to such a man. Terah expects much from his family, especially obedience. The family does well in Haran but finally Abram is forced to leave. Does God jog his memory with another calling? The LORD's call at Gen 12:1 is strategically placed between the call in Ur and Abram's departure from Haran.

To the mystic, Terah ('wanderer', 'delayer', 'loiterer') represents one in the flesh who seeks a greater truth to life but in completely the wrong direction; who sets off in search of enlightenment but falls short, fails to overcome his 'other gods' fixation, delays the true called (Abram) from carrying out his mission, and does not make it to the Promised Land. By contrast, Abram overcomes his family's idolatrous hold on him (his name can now be interpreted 'my Father is exalted'), breaks free of ha-Satan's hindrance, and pushes on to the prize. His tenacity is accounted to him for faith in Heb 11:8-10.

---

[351] http://www.biblebelievers.org.au/moongod.htm; http://www.answering-islam.org/Resources/Morey/allah.html, etc.

Atheists and liberal theologians point to Acts 7:2-4 as an obvious error of scripture. Here in the New Testament, a recently converted Christian named Stephen has the audacity to lecture the supreme Jewish religious council, the Sanhedrin, on Old Testament scripture. Stephen is actually on trial for his life for blasphemy, but during his defence he appears to draw upon Jewish sources no longer extant by giving a number of details during his impassioned plea which are not contained in the OT. For our purposes, he proclaims that "...**the God of glory appeared unto our father Abraham when he was in Mesopotamia, before he dwelt in Charran** [Haran]**, and said unto him, 'Get thee out of thy country, and from thy kindred, and come into the land which I shall shew thee.' Then came he out of the land of the Chaldeans and dwelt in Charran: and from thence, when his father was dead, He removed him into this land, wherein ye now dwell.**" (Acts 7:2-4)

So, on the one hand, Stephen corroborates the fact that Abram got the LORD's call in Ur, then seems to state that Abram only proceeded to Canaan from Haran *after his father Terah dies*. The problem is, as atheists gleefully remonstrate, you can't reconcile Abram leaving Haran for Canaan at 75 (which Gen 12:4 states was his age at that moment), with Abram's supposed departure upon his father's death at 205, when Abram would have been 135! All sorts of strictures have been applied by scholars to make these verses fit. They don't fit.

It's a *remez!* Get digging!

Firstly, that's not what Stephen says. Did you notice the capital 'H' I underlined in the previous Bible passage? In the King James Authorised Version, Stephen actually says this: "**Then came he** [Abram] **out of the land of the Chaldeans** [Ur] **and dwelt in Charran** [Haran]**. And from thence, when his father** [Terah] **was dead, he** [Abram] **removed him** [Terah's body] **into this land** [Canaan/Israel]**, wherein ye now dwell.**"

Don't be put off by the erroneous capital 'H' you'll find in most Bible translations, a translational inference which completely changes the meaning to an erroneous... **And from thence, when his father** [Terah] **was dead, _H_e** [God?] **removed him** [Abram??] **into this land** [Canaan/Israel]**, wherein ye now dwell.**" Which

331

implies Abram only left Haran when his father died. Because of Gen 11:26, you can't have Terah dying at 205 and Abram 75 years old upon leaving Haran. Sorry.

So, how to reconcile? Simple. Terah is born. 70 years later, Abraham is born (Gen 11:26). 75 years after that, when Terah is 145, Abraham leaves Haran for Canaan (Gen 12:4). Abraham dwells in the Canaan region for 60 years, at which point Terah dies miles away in Haran aged 205 (Gen 11:32). When Terah dies and Abraham fails to return to Haran to claim his father's (extensive) inheritance, Abram renounces any claim he has to the old land and can now only rely on the LORD's promise in Canaan. *That's faith!*

The only explanation that fits is what the King James actually states; that Abraham had Terah's body removed from Haran and taken to Canaan for burial.[352] Although Terah didn't make it to Canaan and inherit due to his failure to overcome idolatry, in a sense he finally did 'come home' and now rests in the Promised Land. Read Acts 7:5 in the King James and come to your own conclusions.

In God's plan, Abram's new nation, which comes to be known as *yahudim* (*lit.* 'Those who praise Yah!'), is to be a living witness for God and an example to the pagan peoples of the blessings bestowed upon a nation which walks in the ways of the Creator. In God's plan, the descendants of Abram will father the Kinsman-Redeemer, the **Seed of the woman** (Gen 3:15), who will reverse the sin brought into the world through Adam's line and reconcile the world once more to God (Rom 5:18). The prerequisite for believers representing YHWH in this covenant is that they should live a life that is pleasing to God (i.e. be obedient and must overcome sin),[353] and in return He will bless them, cause them to flourish in this life, and reward them with an eternal inheritance. Part of the covenant between God and Abram will also account for, and punish disobedience through national and personal acts of discipline. Notice God's four, clear-cut 'I will' statements in the preceding 'call

---

[352] Moses would do the same with Joseph's bones almost five centuries later (Exo 13:19) and bury their ancestor at Shechem (Josh 24:32).

[353] Heb 11:6; Gen 4:7; Matt 3:8-10; 1 Pet 3:10-11, 13; Acts 26:20; Dan 4:27; Psa 34:14; Luke 13:3,5; Rom 12:21; 2 Pet 3:9; Rev 2:26; Eph 5:1

of Abraham' (Gen 12:1-3); these are *everlasting* and *unconditional* to Abram and his descendants. God will later repeat this covenant with Abram in Genesis 22:15-18, on this occasion *swearing an oath by/on Himself* - the most solemn indication that God will not change His mind *ever* (Gen 22:16-17; *cf.* Heb 6:13-18). This covenant is also reconfirmed to Isaac and Jacob, Abraham's descendants, in Genesis 26:2-5. Do you think God means it? Iran, Hezbollah, Hamas, the 'Islamic State' (IS), PLO, EU and the UN certainly don't.

'Going down to Egypt'

And Abram took Sarai his wife, and Lot his brother's son, and all their substance that they had gathered, and the souls that they had gotten in Haran; and they went forth to go into the land of Canaan; and into the land of Canaan they came.

And Abram passed through the land unto the place of Shechem,[354] unto the plain of Moreh. And the Canaanite was then in the land.

And the LORD appeared unto Abram, and said, "Unto thy seed will I give this land." And there built he [Abram] an altar unto the LORD, <u>who appeared unto him</u>.

And he removed from thence unto a mountain on the east of Bethel and pitched his tent, having Bethel on the west, and Ai [*pron.* 'ay-eye'] on the east: and there he built an altar unto the LORD, and called upon the name of the LORD.

And Abram journeyed, going on still toward the south. (Gen 12:5-9)

Abram is always building altars to the LORD wherever he goes. That the world greeting Abram is not as secure as Haran any more is putting it mildly (Gen 15:16). Chedorlaomer, king of the Elamite empire (originating in south-western Iran), is the military overlord exacting tribute from vassal city-states in eastern Canaan, especially around the Jordan. The natives are not happy. There's also a famine on. Canaan is a dangerous, lawless, nasty place that's losing the fear of God among men (Rom 3:18). It's also running out of food.

---

[354] Google Earth, 32 12 11 N, 35 18 40 E

In the spiritual realm, *ha-Satan* now has information on God's plan to father mankind's Redeemer through Abram's line, and manoeuvres to hound the patriarch. This latest intelligence on the Scarlet Thread means Satan now has advanced knowledge that the descendants of Abram will be going into bondage for 400 years[355] - ample time to slaughter God's people while they are under a foreign yoke and defenceless. And should that not work, *ha-Satan* knows he has 400 years to plan the destruction of God's people when they return to the Land from their far-flung bondage.

Though Abram is wealthy and possessed of a not inconsiderable private army of his own (Gen 14:13-15), the Hebrew chieftain must employ guile on various occasions to protect his own life and that of his stunning wife Sarai ('princess') as they travel.[356] Heading south into Egypt to find food, he informs those he comes across that Sarai is his sister to avoid being killed, and causing Sarai to be abducted for a steamier fate. By posing as her brother, any potential suitor will need to treat with him. Far from being a lie, the gorgeous Sarai is in fact Abram's half-sister.[357] Even in the court of the recently established Egyptian monarchy under Menes, Abram has to pull this ruse to protect himself and his wife from harm (Gen 12: 10-20). They very nearly come unstuck.

'Going down to Egypt' is also a spiritual type [Babylon too] to describe the righteous descending into 'the world system and its fleshly values', relying on the world for help, rather than pursuing the upward path of faith in the battle of flesh versus spirit. It's all part of your Earth training programme to prepare you for eternity. By contrast, men 'go up to Jerusalem' in the scriptures. Later, the prophet Isaiah remarks:

---

[355] God ensures the identity of the host nation remains secret so *ha-Satan* can't gain an advanced foothold (Gen 15:13-16).

[356] *cf.* Gen 12:11-13; 20:2-13; see also Gen 26:7-9

[357] According to Gen 20:12, Sarai is the daughter of Terah by another wife, making her Abram's half-sister. Two thousand years after the Creation, there is still no significant genetic load, so proximity marriages are not yet prohibited on health grounds. This will change by the time the LORD gives the Law to Moses. It is also recently understood by scholars that wives could be elevated to 'sister' status in the culture of Haran as a form of deep respect. This would not have been recognised by those far to the south in Egypt.

"Woe to them that go down to Egypt for help; and stay on horses, and trust in chariots, because they are many; and in horsemen, because they are very strong; but they look not unto the Holy One of Israel, neither seek the LORD!" (Isa 31:1)

If food is a major problem for Abram and his expansive entourage in Canaan, what other avenues are open to him? It's all well and good to witter, "Oh, he should have trusted in the LORD to provide and remained where he was!" but most of us are so well fed, we've never had to contend with the frightening prospect of not knowing where our next meal is coming from. Abram has serious commitments and some extensive dependants. Such matters always look different when the problem is yours. Warren Wiersbe comments:

"When circumstances become difficult and you are in the furnace of testing, remain where God has put you until He tells you to move. Faith moves in the direction of peace and hope, but unbelief moves in the direction of restlessness and fear. (Isa 28:16). In times of testing, the important question is not, "How can I get out of this?" but, "What can I get out of this?' (*cf.* Jam 1:1-12)

God alone is in control of circumstances. You are safer in a famine in His will than in a palace out of His will…. Abram failed the test of circumstances and turned from the will of God." [358]

Abram knows the lush Nile valley will provide food for everyone, so off he goes. Fleshly problems start almost immediately. Wiersbe muses that you know when you move from an attitude of faith to reliance on the world's system when…

1) You start scheming according to man's wisdom instead of trusting God
2) You move from confidence to fear
3) You move from caring for others to caring for yourself
4) You bring judgment on others instead of blessing. [359]

And it came to pass, that, when Abram was come into Egypt, the Egyptians beheld the woman [Sarai] that she was very fair.

---

[358] Wiersbe, W, *The Wiersbe Bible Commentary,* op. cit., p.61
[359] Ibid.

The princes also of Pharaoh saw her, and commended her before Pharaoh, and the woman was taken into Pharaoh's house.

And he entreated Abram well for her sake: and he had sheep, and oxen, and he-asses, and menservants, and maidservants, and she-asses, and camels. (Gen 12:14-16)

Abram finds himself having to deceive those he comes across to protect Sarai and himself. He becomes fearful for his own safety. His lack of faith and precipitous action will bring judgment upon Pharaoh's household. In fairness to Abram, it was common in the wicked cultures of the day for a husband to be killed and the wife taken as trophy, hence Abram's subterfuge. It says something of the quality of Sarai's beauty that word soon reaches, not just the street, not just halfway up the social ladder, but all the way to the very capstone of the Egyptian political pyramid – to Pharaoh himself.

Pharaoh makes a play for Sarai in all ignorance, believing her fair game as Abram's sister, and adds her to his harem. Abram is well looked after with gifts and hospitality as 'the brother' with whom Pharaoh must treat to obtain 'the sister'. The situation is potentially life-threatening for both Abram and Sarai – a predicament only God can resolve to keep His 'you-will-father-a-great-nation' promise to Abram. Great plagues strike Pharaoh's household (Gen 12:17). Horrified at being duped when he finds out who Sarai really is, Pharaoh confronts Abram:

"What is this that thou hast done unto me? Why didst thou not tell me that she was thy wife? Why saidst thou, 'She is my sister' so I might have taken her to me to wife? Now therefore behold thy wife, take her and go thy way!" (Gen 12:18-19)

He could equally have Abram taken out and killed, but Pharaoh probably suspects the Plague-Sending God would destroy him also. So he commands his men to send Abram, Sarai and their entourage on their way, not only with their own possessions; not only with the aforesaid sumptuous gifts of flocks and herds for Sarai's chastity, but even more loot to buy their concord, silence and avoid further celestial bother (Gen 13:1-2; *cf.* 24:35; 26:14). It's a narrow escape for Abram. His scheming almost cost the life of his beloved Sarai.

It is likely that Hagar is chosen as a handmaiden by Sarai during this sojourn in Egypt (Gen 16:1), so the problems for Abram and his descendants are only just beginning. See what 'going down to Egypt' gets you? The world's system. Nimrod's system. *Ha-Satan's* system. Note the pattern between Abram's Egyptian adventure and the Jews' future visit and escape in the times of Joseph and Moses:

1. There is a famine in Canaan
2. God's people decide to 'go down to Egypt' to get food
3. Things go horribly wrong
4. God intervenes to extricate His people
5. Great plagues are brought upon Pharaoh's house to persuade him to let God's people go
6. God's people are released and take great spoil of the Egyptians
7. They are delivered by God back to Canaan

So here we have Abram, in effect, acting out the future in advance, playing out a microcosm of what will happen to his descendants in the future 430-year period of Egyptian plenty and bondage. And that won't be all. There will be chance enough for the patriarch to act out a further prophecy for his nation's future, only this time one so unexpected and surprising it will thrust even Egypt, that bounteous Land of the sun-god (*ha-Satan*), into the shade.

A fond farewell

Abram and his entourage return to Canaan where food is still scarce and the social cohesion of the region ever fragile. One can't help wondering what the patriarch must be making of the land of his future inheritance, gazing around at the sexual abominations and casual violence abounding. Just how bad things have got in certain areas will become clear in a little while.

And Abram went up out of Egypt, he, and his wife, and all that he had, and Lot with him, into the South.[360] **And Abram was**

---

[360] Actually, they go *north* out of Egypt into the *south* of Canaan –lit. *negeb*. 'south'. The desert scrub region of southern Israel is known today as 'the Negev', with its administrative capital at Beersheba.

very rich in cattle, in silver and in gold. And he went on his journey from the south even to Bethel, unto the place where his tent had been at the beginning, between Bethel and Ai,[361] unto the place of the altar, which he had made there at the first. And there Abram called on the name of the LORD.

And Lot also, which went with Abram, had flocks, and herds and tents. (Gen 13:1-5)

There are constant references to Abram's great wealth throughout his story, and Lot hasn't done badly either. But this presents the challenge of procuring sufficient pasture for the animals without upsetting the natives, though fighting first breaks out between the herdsmen of Abram and Lot. How do you think this looks to the Canaanites? When believers fight among themselves it brings shame on the testimony of the LORD; i.e. "If believing in God means I've got to become someone like you, forget it!" The situation becomes so volatile, Abram summons Lot for a site meeting:

"**Let there be no strife, I pray thee, between me and thee, and between my herdmen and thy herdmen, for we are brethren. Is not the whole land before thee? Separate thyself, I pray thee, from me. If thou wilt take the left hand, then I will go to the right; or if thou depart to the right hand, then I will go to the left.**"

And Lot lifted up his eyes and beheld all the plain of Jordan, that it was well watered everywhere, before the LORD destroyed Sodom and Gomorrah, even as the garden of the LORD [i.e. Eden], **like the land of Egypt, as thou comest unto Zoar.**[362]

Then Lot chose for himself all the plain of Jordan; and Lot journeyed east, and they separated themselves the one from the other. Abram dwelled in the land of Canaan, and Lot dwelled in the cities of the plain, and pitched his tent toward Sodom. But

---

[361] Bethel ('House of God') is modern-day Beitin (Google Earth, 31 55 42.02 N, 35 14 17.41 E). Ai is just to the east at 31 55 01 N, 35 15 40 E. The 'mountain' in between might be the promontory found at 31 55 13.19 N, 35 14 58.58 E, just off the road. Bethel will actually be named by Abram's grandson Jacob when he stops the night at this location, fleeing from Esau, and has his famous 'Jacob's Ladder' dream (Gen 28:10-19).

[362] Google Earth, 31 02 49 N, 35 30 09 E

the men of Sodom were wicked and sinners before the LORD exceedingly. (Gen 13:8-13)

Notice Abram's generosity: 'Lot, you have first choice, I'll go second'. This is the relaxed munificence of a man who has come up from Egypt and once again trusts in his LORD's promises. It doesn't bother Abram which way Lot goes, because his own future is in the LORD's hands, and God will decide Lot's choice in any case. The nephew, alas, has left his heart in Egypt (Jam 4:4), seduced by the fertile southern Jordan valley, which reminds Lot of Egypt and the old stories of Eden's bounty.[363] Everything Abram and Lot received in Egypt causes them trouble, says Warren Wiersbe:

"Because of their great wealth, Abram and Lot could not live together and had to separate. (Gen 13:5-6). Hagar, the Egyptian maid-servant, brought division and sorrow into the home (Gen 16). Having had the taste of Egypt (the world), Lot started measuring everything by what he saw there (Gen 13:10-11), and this led to his downfall and the ruin of his family. There are no benefits from disobedience." [364]

Peace descends as herdsmen on both sides realise they are going to be free of each other. Abram kisses Lot in poignant farewell. The two kinsmen have been together and close for decades, originating from the oasis of Ur, then to the prosperous years in Haran, then their adventures through Canaan to Egypt and back. It is reasonable to suppose such *adieus* now are accompanied by tearful pledges that each shall come to the other's aid should emergencies arise. Notice the phrase, [Lot] **pitched his tent towards Sodom**, revealing where his true heart lies.

God has been watching Lot, sees which way Abram's nephew is heading spiritually, and so engineers the split. Chuck Missler makes the point that the path into disobedience happens in small

---

[363] Note also the underlined, editorial comment in the above passage, to the effect that the region was well watered everywhere (i.e. green and lush), but not after God's finished with it over Sodom and Gomorrah. This demonstrates that the cataclysm which will overtake the Vale of Siddim has permanent, natural consequences.

[364] Wiersbe, W, *The Wiersbe Bible Commentary*, op. cit., p.61

steps - a process that leads us away from God's path onto the hot and ready alternative. 2 Peter 2:7-8 tells us Lot was righteous but was later vexed by the filthy goings-on in dystopian Sodom. Yet no-one twisted Lot's arm to move there. Lot is a model of the carnal believer, believing in God, yet pulled this way and that by the world and his flesh, one boot firmly planted in each camp.

Missler's small steps to carnality will be seen throughout the *Origins* series. Throughout the ages, believers have been mocked and criticised by the heathen for the slightest slip, yet all are in the same boat. It's the Holy War between our flesh and the spirit; between the mortal and the immortal parts. God wants to know whether we care enough for Him to discipline ourselves for the purpose of eternal godliness, or not be bothered. Take the story of David and Bathsheba. In reading their tale in 2 Sam 11, one can be forgiven for thinking that David's glimpse of Bathsheba luxuriating in her rooftop bath is the very first time he ever set eyes on her. In fact, Bathsheba's husband is Uriah the Hittite, one of David's mighty men who fought with David throughout the latter's difficult exile from Saul's kingdom through to David's accession as king of all Israel. Uriah stayed the course and supported David throughout the hard years, so in recognition of his faithful service, Uriah's house is placed that close to the king's own palace in Jerusalem that you can spit from one roof to the next. David is not only aware of Bathsheba, *she is a family friend,* making the subsequent betrayal all the more heinous. Crimson Thread writes:

"To piece the story together, it is important to know just who Bathsheba was. From the story in 2 Sam 11, we know she was the wife of Uriah the Hittite. Of equal importance, she was the daughter of Eliam (2 Sam 11:3) and the granddaughter of Ahithophel (2 Sam 23:34).

A close reading of 2 Sam 23 reveals that both Uriah and Eliam were members of David's mighty men. It appears that they had been with David beginning with his time in the wilderness and formed the core of his force during his rise to the throne. Placed in this context, David's behavior was especially vile. He betrayed and killed a man who had been close to him and loyal for many years.

Bathsheba's grandfather was Ahithophel who was David's counselor (1 Chr 27:34) Ahithophel never forgave David for his behavior with his granddaughter and her husband. When Absalom siezed power and drove his father [David] out of Jerusalem, Ahithophel stayed behind and became chief advisor to the rebellion (2 Sam 15:30-31). It was he who advised Absalom to sleep with David's concubines (2 Sam 16:20-23).

Her pedigree casts Bathsheba's bathing on her roof into a different light. It is certain that she and David had known each other for years and that Bathsheba had grown up in the royal court. In other words, the bathing incident smells as much of enticement as it does of chance."[365]

In other words, a woman might take a bath on an open city rooftop if they are hoping a king might chance by on the royal parapet yonder. Bathsheba does not put up a fight when summoned to the king's palace. In the Holy War, the path to unrighteousness always consists of Missler's small steps. It's a process, and we'll see it with Lot and many others. And we'll see it with each of us.

Back to Abram and Lot. Notice the LORD does not engage with Abram in the serious business of His covenant *until the fleshly, wavering Lot has departed.*

And the LORD said unto Abram, <u>after that Lot was separated from him</u>, "<u>Lift up now thine eyes</u>[366] and look from the place where thou art northward, and southward, and eastward, and westward. For all the land which thou seest, to thee will I give it, and to thy seed <u>forever</u>. And I will make thy seed as the dust of the earth, so that if a man can number the dust of the earth, then shall thy seed also be numbered.

"Arise, walk through the land in the length of it and in the breadth of it, for I will give it unto thee."

---

[365] http://crimsonthread.org/articles/bathsheba

[366] Here is that key phrase which always signifies a major plot development. When someone 'lifts up their eyes' in the Bible, we are to do likewise!

Then Abram removed his tent, and came [south] and dwelt in the plain of Mamre,[367] **which is in Hebron, and built there an altar unto the LORD**. (Gen 13:14-18)

As if to commiserate with His friend at the parting, yet drag Abram's thoughts back on-mission, God reiterates His promise that the Land will be Abram's. All this talk of 'seed' surely causes Satan to prick up his ears, confirming that the Scarlet Thread and Seed of the woman will come down through Abram's line (Gen 3:15). After the invitation for a tour, the patriarch breaks camp and leads his entourage south to the place of Mamre, just outside modern-day Hebron. Here he builds another altar. This location in later times will become the site of a famous pagan fair (caravanserai) at the intersection of two major roads, as well as a place of pilgrimage for Jews and Christians due to a forthcoming, spectacular event soon to happen to Abram.

The battle of the nine kings

Some time passes. Abram puts down roots at Mamre and allies himself with the natives. Portions of Canaan are under the vassalage of the Elamite empire at this time (*orig.* southwest Persia, capital at Susa).[368] For twelve years, the various Canaanite city-states have been paying tribute to the Elamite king, Chedorlaomer. By the thirteenth year, they've had enough and stop paying. The following year, Chedorlaomer rounds up his Mesopotamian allies and heads south through Transjordan, attacking cities as he goes. Three of the targets comprise the Nephilim tribes of the Rephaim, Zamzummim and Emim – those giant creature-peoples whose spooky origins go back to Genesis 6 (*cf.* Gen 6:4, **and also afterward**). The five Cities of the Plain, including Sodom and Gomorrah, throw in together and confront Chedorlaomer's forces in the Vale of Siddim south of the Dead Sea: five kings against the empire's four.

---

[367] Google Earth, 31 33 23.53 N, 35 6 19.21 E
[368] Google Earth, 32 11 21.19 N, 48 15 28.03 E

And the vale of Siddim <u>was full of tarpits</u>; and the kings of Sodom and Gomorrah fled and some fell there, and they that remained fled to the mountains.

And they [the Elamites] took all the goods of Sodom and Gomorrah, and all their victuals, and went their way. And they took Lot, Abram's brother's son, who dwelt in Sodom, and his goods, and departed. (Gen 14:10-12)

Abram's nephew, now an inhabitant of some note in Sodom, becomes a prisoner-of-war. When Abram gets to hear of it, he doesn't hesitate on behalf of his kinsman. He recruits his Canaanite allies Mamre, Aner and Eschol, then mobilises a small army of his own retainers – 318 in total, and leads them off on a special forces raid north. It says something of both Abram and the times in which he lives that a) such servants are battle-trained and ready for trouble, b) Abram is wealthy enough to have such a private force on retention, and c) they think nothing of going after a vastly superior force, trusting in the LORD to deliver them. Now we see Abram the warlord, wielding significant military power and faith in his own right.

Abram tracks Chedorlaomer 120 miles into northern Canaan and falls upon his camp at night in a pincer attack. In the confusion of the rout, some of Abram's men recover the stolen goods and captives, including Lot, while Abram and the rest pursue Chedorlaomer and his other kings as far as Hobah, north of Damascus. All four kings are slaughtered, according to the King James rendition of Gen 14:17. An impressed King Bera of Sodom awaits Abram in the King's Valley,[369] and congratulates him upon his return.

"Give me the persons, and take the goods to thyself."

And Abram said to the king of Sodom, "I have lift up mine hand unto the LORD, the most high God, the possessor of Heaven and Earth, that I will not take from a thread even to a shoe-latchet, and that I will not take anything that is thine, lest thou shouldest say, 'I have made Abram rich', save only that

---

[369] Scholars speculate that the site of this meeting might be the Kidron Valley, the vale between the Mount Moriah ridge system (the later location of the Temple) and the Mount of Olives in today's Jerusalem.

which the young men have eaten, and the portion of the men which went with me, Aner, Eshcol, and Mamre; let them take their portion." (Gen 14:21-24)

The time you really foul things up is right after a victory, yet notice Abram's humility. He will not enrich himself as a result of a victory given to him by the LORD. (In the centuries to come, Gideon will not be so wise - Judg 8:23-27). Neither will Abram enrich himself with Sodom's wealth the way Lot has. Note that God has demonstrated to Sodom's population that He can and has saved them, but they go back to their city and evil ways – the same bunch, in fact, who will attempt unspeakable perversions against the LORD's own and meet with a fiery end. Consider also that while Lot may have bemoaned his capture by Chedorlaomer and the loss of his possessions, this was God pulling him out of Sodom (a model of the unregenerate world). With his wealth restored to him, Lot could have got the hint and moved on to somewhere else, or even returned to make his peace with Abram. Lot does neither. Back to Sodom he goes. How many of us do the same after being bailed out of a tight spot? We assure God we'll do things differently in the future, and then go right back to how we were. Welcome to the Holy War of man's inherent sin nature (Jer 17:9). There are none righteous, no not one (Psa 14:1-3; Isa 53:6).

A strange type

As a result of Abram's victory, we are introduced to a strange character, the mysterious king of Salem (later Jerusalem), named Melchizedek. This is a title, not a name, and means 'my king is righteous' or 'king of righteousness'. Melchizedek is described as both a king and 'priest of the Most High God'. He exits Salem with bread and wine to bless both Abram and God for delivering Abram's enemies into his hand (Gen 14:18-20). If the King's Valley is indeed the Kidron Valley, as some suspect, then Melchizedek's bread and wine ritual is conducted not even a mile from where Yeshua will hold His Last Supper with bread and wine 18 centuries later. Jack Heyford comments:

"Abram's seemingly routine encounter with the regional king of Salem is revealed centuries later as being an encounter with an

344

antetype of Jesus Christ in His role as Priest (Psa 110:4; Heb 7:1-10). 'Melchizedek' means 'My King is Righteous', and he greets Abram with a royal banquet (bread and wine). Uniquely occupying the offices of king and priest, he worships God Most High (somewhat of a rarity in the area at that time). Prior to any legal requirement, Abram responds to his office, generosity and blessing by giving him a tithe [tenth] of all the spoils gathered in the recent war." [370]

This tells us that tithing was around prior to the establishment of Judaism proper under the Mosaic Law. The bread and wine is a model for Christ's sacrament, and scholars make the point that since the later Levitical priesthood derives from the loins of Abram (Heb 7:9-10), and Abram gives tithes to Melchizedek, the Levitical priesthood is subservient to the eternal order of Melchizedek from which the Messiah springs (*cf.* Psa 110:4; Heb 5,6,7). There is an intriguing link between this strange king of Salem and the New Testament. Chuck Missler points out that there are only three entities described in the Bible as both priest and king:

1. Melchizedek (Gen 14:18)
2. *Yeshua ha-Mashiach* (Jesus Christ) (Zech 6:13)
3. Church believers, or the 'Body of Christ', as they come to be known (Rev 1:6; 5:10)

This has led some to surmise that Melchizedek is a type of Christ, while others go further to suggest that he is an OT theophany (pre-incarnate appearance) of Yeshua Himself, since the king's lineage and death go unrecorded (Heb 7:3). The writer of Hebrews states that Melchizedek is a man, but makes the point that an eternal priesthood is required since the Levites proved earthly and corrupt, necessitating extensive ceremonial purification prior to serving the LORD. The truth, I suspect, is as the book of Hebrews states; that Melchizedek is a similitude (model) of Christ of the eternal order of priests and kings who will serve the Lamb and Father in Heaven (Heb 7:15-17; Rev 5:8-10). Melchizedek's lineage and eventual death have been edited out of the text by the

---

[370] Heyford, Jack, *The Spirit-Filled Bible,* op. cit. p.26

Holy Spirit to set up this model for Christ as the ultimate 'King of Righteousness'.[371]

So Abram is learning his lessons. After the victory over Chedorlaomer granted to him by the LORD, he is met by two kings at Jerusalem, the king of Sodom ('burning') and the king of Salem ('peace'). One represents the flesh, the other the spirit. Abram turns away from the King of Burning (Sodom, *ha-Satan*) and receives bread and wine from the King of Righteousness (Salem, 'peace') and grants him tithes of the battle spoil (a tenth). Nice model.

The cutting of the covenant

After these things, the word of the LORD came unto Abram in a vision, saying, "Fear not, Abram: I am thy shield, and thy exceeding great reward."

And Abram said, "LORD God, what wilt thou give me, seeing I go childless, and the steward of my house is this Eliezer of Damascus?"

And Abram said, "Behold, to me thou hast given no seed: and, lo, one born in my house is mine heir."

And, behold, the word of the LORD came unto him, saying, "This shall not be thine heir, but he that shall come forth out of thine own bowels shall be thine heir." (Gen 15:1-4)

Abram is around 85 years old at this point, and Sarai 75. On a human level, they won't be having children, but Abram is learning to trust God and interpret his own predicament through the LORD's eyes. Do we do the same when we are in a fix? That Sarai has been barren all this time is, of course, both known and engineered by the LORD for a specific purpose, namely, that any child born to Sarai at this stage will be divinely appointed and special.

We are introduced here to Eliezer of Damascus, depicted as Abram's 'steward'. This is a lazy, ethnocentric KJV translation

---

[371] There will also be *ha-Satan's* counterfeit 'Lord of Righteousness' named Adonizedek, an Amorite king of Jerusalem who later leads a coalition of five Canaanite armies to resist Joshua's Israeli invasion. These five kings are trounced at Gibeon, defeated by the supernatural intervention of hailstones at Beth-horon, then dragged out of a cave of refuge at Makkedah and executed by Joshua.

conjuring a grovelling, indentured servant. In fact, according to the custom of the day, Eliezer is Abram's right-hand man, probably his business partner, a longstanding, close and trusted friend, professional confidante, and, in the absence of an heir from the wealthy sheikh's loins, heir-designate to Abram's prodigious estate. Eliezer means 'God is my help/comfort' or 'comforter' (Exo 18:4), a name also given to the Holy Spirit (FG 14:16, 26; 15:26; 16:7).

And [the LORD] **brought** [Abram] **forth abroad, and said, "Look now toward Heaven and tell the stars, if thou be able to number them." And He said unto him, "So shall thy seed be."**

And [Abram] **believed in the LORD, and He counted it to him for righteousness.**

And He **said unto him, "I am the LORD that brought thee out of Ur of the Chaldees, to give thee this land to inherit it."**

And [Abram] **said, "Lord GOD, whereby shall I know that I shall inherit it?"**

And He **said unto him, "Take me an heifer of three years old, and a she-goat of three years old, and a ram of three years old, and a turtledove, and a young pigeon."**

And [Abram] **took unto the LORD all these and divided them in the midst, and laid each piece one against another: but the birds he did not divide. And when the fowls came down upon the carcases, Abram drove them away.** (Gen 15:5-11)

Since Abram's original calling in Ur, the LORD has promised Abram repeatedly that He will make him the father of a great nation. In Abram shall all the families of the Earth be blessed (Gen 12:1-4). God reconfirmed this to Abram at Shechem after he left his father's house in Haran and entered Canaan (Gen 12:6-7). After Abram returned to Canaan from Egypt and re-camped at Bethel, he and Lot parted after strife among the herdsmen. God used this opportunity again to reiterate the promise (Gen 13:14-17). Then there's the campaign against Chedorlaomer, after which Abram is fêted by Bera of Sodom for his victory and blessed by Melchizedek for God's favour. So Abram's getting the message now. He knows that to be the father of a great nation he must have at least one son, yet in trying to 'help God' get His programme off the ground, Abram will receive a stern lesson both he and the world will not forget in a hurry. *Beware lest you 'help' God.* It usually turns out badly.

But for now the time has come formally to seal the covenant with Abram. The LORD has the patriarch set up a covenant ritual. In those days, when two men sealed a covenant, an offering was arranged and cut into two parts. Both parties then passed between the pieces in a figure-of-eight movement while repeating the terms of the agreement (from which we get 'cutting a deal'). Notice what God does in this case. He has Abram take a heifer, a she-goat, a ram, a turtle dove and young pigeon. The animals are killed and the mammals divided into pieces but the birds are not divided. Note the Holy Spirit sees fit to mention that during the procedure birds - in this case carrion creatures, symbols of evil – come down attempting to get at the sacrificial meat, but Abram shoos them off – a type of spiritual opposition to what's about to happen. Then God does something strange.

And when the sun was going down, a deep sleep fell upon Abram; and, lo, <u>an horror of great darkness fell upon him</u>.

And [God] said unto Abram, "Know of a surety that thy seed shall be a stranger in a land that is not theirs, and shall serve them; and they shall afflict them four hundred years. And also that nation, whom they shall serve, will I judge: and afterward shall they come out with great substance. And thou shalt go to thy fathers in peace; thou shalt be buried in a good old age. But in the fourth generation they shall come hither again, for the iniquity of the Amorites is not yet full." (Gen 15:12-16)

As the sun sets and the world grows dark, God puts Abram into a deep sleep, surrounds him with horror and great darkness, and shows him what will become of his descendants. Once the sun is down, God sets His seal to the covenant and passes between the pieces *alone*. In Hebrew this covenant has come to be known as *Brit bein HaBetarim* – 'the covenant between the parts'.

And it came to pass that, when the sun went down and it was dark, behold a smoking furnace and a burning lamp passed between those pieces. In the same day the LORD made a covenant with Abram, saying, "Unto thy seed have I given this land, <u>from the river of Egypt unto the great river, the river</u>

Euphrates..." (Gen 15:17-18) and repeats the terms of the agreement.

It is worth reading Genesis 15:1-21 to get the full import and context of the passage. God lists out other tribal areas which will be given to the descendants of Abram. The following important points should be noted about this covenant:

> It is *unilateral*. God seals the covenant Himself while Abram is asleep, thereby granting the descendants of Abram the stewardship of the Land *unconditionally*. Abram will have no say in the matter – indeed he can do nothing of his own part

> The LORD makes this covenant with Abram *and no other (nation)*

> The LORD makes this covenant with a human *and no other creature*

> The LORD makes this covenant with a human on Planet Earth, *and not with any creature of any other planet* (this becomes important later)

> The Land given belongs to God

> The bequest is *everlasting* (confirmed Gen 17:1-8)

> The extent of the bequest is from the Nile to the Euphrates! (Gen 15:18).

> God will provide Abram with a true heir (Isaac) via his wife Sarai, whose descendants will be as numerous as the visible stars in the heavens (Gen 15:4-5)

> God declares that He has accomplished this in the past tense! (Gen 17:5)

> God prophesies that these true descendants of Abram shall be in bondage to another nation for 400 years (Gen 15:13-14)

> God will judge that nation and His people will be brought out of servitude with great substance (Gen 15:14)

> In the spiritual realm, *ha-Satan* latches on to the word 'seed' and now knows Abram's lineage is the target now to thwart the eventual birth of the **Seed of the woman** (Gen 3:15)

This is the very covenant being challenged in the Middle East today by non-Jews and especially by the descendants of Ishmael. Note that the land currently held by modern Israel is a fraction of the covenant bequest. The rest given by the LORD to Abram and his descendants is currently under foreign occupation by Egypt, Jordan and the 'Palestinian' (Philistine/Edomite) peoples. God's bequest to Abram also includes lands from modern-day Saudi Arabia, Oman, Yemen, Turkey, Iraq, Syria, Lebanon, Kuwait and the UAE. Events in the future are prophesied to bring God's unconditional and everlasting promises to Israel into line after the Crazy Days, when Yeshua sets up His Millennial Kingdom. In the spiritual realm, *ha-Satan* is doing everything possible to encourage Israel's modern-day neighbours to dispossess the Jews and wipe them out.

God's everlasting covenant is subsequently confirmed to Abram when he is 99 years of age (Gen 17:1-8), at which point the stipulation of circumcision is added. The covenant is then reiterated to Abram's descendants Isaac (Gen 26:1-5) and Jacob (Gen 28:13-15), and *remains in force to this day.* Those who bless the Jews will be blessed, and those who curse them will be cursed. A summary of the covenant is given in Deuteronomy in Moses's day. Here the contract now has conditions insofar as the forthcoming nation of Israel's possession of the Land is concerned:

"I call Heaven and Earth to record this day against you, that I have set before you life and death, blessing and cursing. Therefore choose life, that both thou and thy seed may live. <u>That thou mayest love the LORD thy God, and that thou mayest obey His voice, and that thou mayest cleave unto Him: for He is thy life and the length of thy days</u>: that thou mayest dwell in the land which the LORD sware unto thy fathers, to Abraham, to Isaac, and to Jacob, to give them." (Deut 30:19-20)

The history of God's people will be tumultuous, in no small part due to their disobedience of the above resulting in subsequent removals from the Land. As we shall see, the fate of the Jews and the Land are so inextricably linked to their obedience or apostasy that you can literally set your watch by it. From the beginning, the literalness of God's covenant becomes apparent.

Hagar and Ishmael

Now Sarai, Abram's wife, bare him no children. And she had a handmaid, an Egyptian, whose name was Hagar.

And Sarai said unto Abram, "Behold now, the LORD hath restrained me from bearing. I pray thee, go in unto my maid. It may be that I may obtain children by her."

And Abram hearkened to the voice of Sarai. (Gen 16:1-2)

By this time, Abram and Sarai are getting edgy that the 'father of many nations' hasn't yet had a son. To be childless in this culture is considered a curse upon a woman. Sarai thus devises a fleshly strategy to help God accomplish His Will. *This is never a good idea:* a) when it is God's intention to arrange a miracle birth to past-it parents for His glory and b) when Sarai's strategy involves the heathen maid Hagar, whom they recruited when they 'went down to Egypt' ('into the world', physically and spiritually). It is unlikely that God is going to be happy and Abram too has his reservations but hearkens to Sarai in much the same way Adam hearkened to Eve in Gen 3:17, which didn't turn out to be such a great idea either.

Sarai's reasoning is not bankrupt on a human level. "**Behold now, the LORD hath restrained me from bearing.**" What else can she do? If Abram's going to have an heir other than his business partner, Eliezer, it will have to be by another woman – actually a common custom in those days, especially using maids. The mistake is in not trusting the LORD to do something extraordinary on their behalf, which God is going to do anyway for His glory to set Abram's seed apart. Patience to let God act in His own time is the sign of a mature faith. Both Abram and Sarai fail this test. If God closed up Sarai's womb but now says He's going to provide Abram with an heir, God's got the problem, not Sarai. Later, by Gen 22, God will set Abram a further faith test, which this time he will pass with flying colours.

And Sarai, Abram's wife, took Hagar her maid the Egyptian, after Abram had dwelt ten years in the land of Canaan, and gave her to her husband Abram to be his wife [Abram's just 86 at this point – Gen 16:16]. **And he went in unto Hagar and she conceived.**

And when she saw that she had conceived, her mistress was despised in her eyes.

And Sarai said unto Abram, "My wrong be upon thee. I have given my maid into thy bosom, and when she saw that she had conceived, I was despised in her eyes. The LORD judge between me and thee."

But Abram said unto Sarai, "Behold, thy maid is in thy hand. Do to her as it pleaseth thee." And when Sarai dealt hardly with her, she [Hagar] fled from her face.

And the angel of the LORD found [Hagar] by a fountain of water in the wilderness, by the fountain in the way to Shur. (Gen 16:3-7)

The blame game starts, again with echoes of Adam and Eve. Sarai says, "It's your fault, Abram." Abram's retort is probably "You talked me into it!" and on his knees that night: "Dear LORD, *the woman made me do it!*" (*cf.* Gen 3:12). No-one has the high ground in this matter. Hagar flees into the desert, the child within her, and is met by the Angel of the LORD by the fountain in the wilderness, later named Beer Lahai Roi ('the well of the One who lives and sees me'). Chuck Missler writes:

"The Angel of the LORD found the maidservant in the desert at a spring beside the road to Shur (*cf.* Gen 25:18) on the way to her homeland, Egypt. When she reached Shur (the wall), she paused before crossing the border. Here the Egyptians maintained a wall or strong line of forts to protect Egypt from invaders from the east. It is mentioned in Egyptian records as early as 2000 BC."[372]

This is the first mention in the Bible of the enigmatic Angel of the LORD. Unlike other angels, the Angel of the LORD has some unusual characteristics which provoke a *remez*:

> He is identified with YHWH and speaks in the first person of God [373]
> Yet at other times is distinct from the LORD [374]

---

[372] **Missler, Chuck** *Genesis* notes, www.khouse.org
[373] Gen 16:13; 22:11-12; 31:11,13; 48:16; Judg 6:11,16,22; 13:22-23; Zech 3:1-2
[374] 2 Sam 24:16; Zech 1:12

➢ Yet, since no-one has seen or heard the Father at any time (as we'll find out in a minute), scholars speculate that the Angel of the LORD is a pre-incarnate theophany of Yeshua (Jesus). The clue to this is that the Angel is the same as God yet distinct [375]

➢ Another clue is that the Angel meets Hagar by a fountain of water in the wilderness. Yeshua is closely connected with the fountains of living water theme originating in the OT and proclaimed by Jesus in the NT [376]

Notice the way in which the Designer speaks to Hagar:

And He said, "Hagar, <u>Sarai's maid</u>, whence camest thou? And whither wilt thou go?"

And she said, "I flee from the face of my mistress Sarai."

And the Angel of the LORD said unto her, "Return to thy mistress and submit thyself under her hands."

And the Angel of the LORD said unto her, "<u>I will</u> multiply thy seed exceedingly, that it shall not be numbered for multitude."

And the Angel of the LORD said unto her, "Behold, thou art with child and shalt bear a son, and shalt call his name Ishmael, because the LORD hath heard thy affliction. And he will be a wild man [*per'-reh*, Strongs H6501, *lit.* 'a wild donkey'/'wild ass of a man']**; his hand will be against <u>every</u> man, and <u>every</u> man's hand against him; and he shall dwell in the presence of all his brethren."** (Gen 16:8-12)

Some interesting insights here:

➢ The Creator of the Universe is not seeking information here, He seeks to have Hagar give a summary of her own predicament

➢ Notice the Creator does not acknowledge Hagar as Abram's wife but 'Sarai's maid'. Hagar's child will be born outside the covenant relationship and will not inherit. **Whatsoever is not of faith is sin** (Rom 14:23). Later, God will refer to Abram as having only one son (*cf.* Gen 21:10; 22:2; Gal 4:22-31)

➢ Which means that the descendants of Ishmael have no right or title to the Land in perpetuity

---

[375] *cf.* Gen 18:1-2; 19:1; Num 22:22; Judg 2:1-4; 5:23; Zech 12:8

[376] FG 4:6-26; 7:37-39; Psa 36:9; Prov 13:14; 14:27; Isa 12:3; 44:3; 49:10; Jer 2:13; 17:13; 31:12; Rev 21:6

- The Angel speaks in the LORD's first person singular: **I will multiply thy seed exceedingly....** Regular angels don't do this
- God names the child Ishmael ('God has heard'), which means Ishmael *will* play a role in God's plan. And since God intends to **multiply thy seed exceedingly, that it shall not be numbered for multitude,** Ishmael will play a lead role in the planet's future
- Notice it was in the LORD's power for Hagar not to become pregnant. Equally, He could have fixed it so that Ishmael had no sons. How many sons does Ishmael end up having? *Twelve!*
- Thus Abram will have two sons who will trigger a 4,000-year Holy War: Ishmael 'the child of the flesh' versus Isaac 'the child of the Spirit and covenant'
- Isaac in turn will have two sons, Esau and Jacob. Jacob will end up having twelve sons of his own, who will go on to father the twelve tribes of Israel
- Encyclopaedias state that Ishmael goes on to father the 'Arab' peoples. Perhaps more accurately, he is the progenitor of the non-Jewish Semitic peoples who later, from the 7th century AD onward, are drawn together under the banner of Islam
- On the face of the above verse, God is predicting that Ishmael will become a 'wild donkey of a man', the implication being that he will develop into a troublemaker who will create havoc (*cf.* Job 24:5), not only with those he comes across, *but among his own people*. While many Christian and Jewish ministries gleefully leap upon this description, citing the bellicose nature of modern Islam even against its own (e.g. the 1,400-year war between Sunni and Shi'ite), there are some sites which complain that this verse has been misinterpreted
- Ishmael will dwell in the presence of <u>all his brethren</u>, which will include the Jews
- God bothered to take on a visible body, come down and comfort a rejected heathen maid-servant, which tells us of His love for the abused, unbelieving, despised and downtrodden, as well as the unborn. YHWH made Hagar the mother of many nations

> Hagar is commanded by God to return to Sarai and Abram's household and submit to her mistress.

And Hagar bare Abram a son: and Abram called his son's name, which Hagar bare, Ishmael. And Abram was fourscore and six years old when Hagar bare Ishmael to Abram. (Gen 16:15-16)

There are some interesting details we can infer from these two verses. Hagar could easily have continued with her unborn child into Egypt and returned to the bosom of her family. She did not. She obeyed the LORD and returned to Abram and Sarai. This unexpected, surprise move lends credence to her testimony before Abram and Sarai that she met the Angel of the LORD at Beer Lahai Roi ('The God who sees and hears'). In turn, Sarai would likely have repented to God for abusing her servant, and Hagar would have apologised to her mistress for her arrogance and disdain. And Abram? Warren Wiersbe writes:

"Abram too had to submit to God. In this entire episode, Abram played a rather passive role. He let Sarai talk him into marrying Hagar, and he allowed Sarai to mistreat Hagar and drive her from the camp. Apparently Abram did not offer to help Hagar in any way (later he made up for that – (Gen 21:9ff). But when his son was born, Abram acknowledged him and obediently gave him the name that God had appointed." [377]

Those set apart

And when Abram was ninety years old and nine [i.e. 13 years later], **the LORD appeared to Abram and said unto him, "I am the <u>Almighty God</u>. Walk before Me and be thou perfect** [righteous]. **And I will make my covenant between Me and thee and will multiply thee exceedingly."**

And Abram fell on his face, and God talked with him, saying, "As for Me, behold, <u>My covenant is with thee</u> [not with anyone else!], **and thou shalt be a father of many nations. Neither shall thy name any more be called Abram** ['exalted father'], **but thy name shall be Abraham** ['father of many nations'], **for a father of many nations <u>have I made thee</u>** [past tense!]. **And I will make thee exceeding fruitful, and I will make nations of thee, and**

---

[377] Wiersbe, W, *The Wiersbe Bible Commentary*, op. cit., p.72

kings shall come out of thee. And I will establish My covenant between <u>Me and thee and thy seed</u> after thee in their generations <u>for an everlasting covenant</u>, to be a God unto thee, and to thy seed after thee. And I will give unto thee, and to thy seed after thee, the land wherein thou art a stranger, <u>all the land of Canaan, for an everlasting possession;</u>[378] and I will be their God." (Gen 17:1-8)

There are some great insights in the above passage:

➤ This is the first mention of a special title of God: *El Shaddai*, 'the Almighty'. It seems to be used by God to emphasise His omnipotence over man's frailty, not to denigrate but to provide assurance for those in trouble or great spiritual need.

➤ YHWH has made Abram and Sarai wait *thirteen years* since the birth of Ishmael before once again reiterating His covenant. Some believe the delay is to punish Abram and Sarai for their faithless dealings with Hagar. While certainly possible, it's also to emphasise *the uniqueness* of what is about to happen.

➤ Abram will father a people who, through a son born supernaturally to a mother well past child-bearing age, will have a matchless relationship with the Creator. They will be set aside as His people. Notice the Christian Church comes about the same way. God will ensure His Son, Yeshua, is born to a mother (Mary), a virgin, and those who follow Christ will have a matchless relationship with the Creator. They also will be set aside as His people. Two parallel programmes featuring two parallel peoples – the Christians and Jews – who have parallel origins and destinies, under the same God.

➤ While later under the Mosaic Law there are conditionals. i.e. if Abram's seed will obey God, they will be blessed (Deut 28:1-14); if they scorn His ways they will be cursed (Deut 28:15ff), *notice the Land grant is unconditional* (Gen 17:8): valid whether they are faithful or not, or whether they are removed from the Land or not.

---

[378] God's *eternal* bequest of the Land to the descendents of Abraham is still being disputed by Islam, George Galloway and millions of other anti-Semites worldwide.

➢ For those who are not God's people, if they bless Abram's line, they in turn shall be blessed. If they curse Abram and his descendants, they too shall be cursed (Gen 12:3). Once again, *this covenant remains in force to this day.* Who's cursing the Jews these days? Everyone I see on CNN and the BBC. At the end of the Great Tribulation, those survivors on Earth will be judged by Yeshua according to how they treated the Jews during the Crazy Days. The Oscar Schindlers who protected His people will be blessed, granted eternal life and allowed into the Millennial Kingdom, while those who betrayed, persecuted and gave over the Jews to death during the Trib will be thrown into the Lake of Fire (Matt 25:31-46). God is dead serious about punishing anti-Semitism.

➢ For his faithfulness, Abram becomes 'the friend of God' (2 Chron 20:7; Isa 41:8; Jam 2:23), with whom we can identify, since his life typifies the personal Holy War we all suffer between the flesh and the spirit. Abram will be an overcomer and thus a partaker in God's blessings. Lot will not.

Abram's story is more than just a legend of an old codger shuffling his way around the wilderness; it is reflective of God's central theme throughout the Bible: namely, that our temporary existence on Earth should be lived honestly, practising righteousness, faith, humility and patience with the goal of spiritual maturity (sanctification) through imitating God daily. Which means learning about the Designer's character – what He likes and does not like – so we know how to please Him.[379] This has eternal ramifications for each of us.

The carnal man/woman cares not. They mock and deny God, disdain His believers as 'self-righteous', holier-than-thou' and 'do-gooders'. These modern-day spiritual Canaanites live life in the flesh, condoning everything that God abhors. They bruit abroad perversions of every kind: the lauding of violence, the celebration and promotion of homosexuality, the wholesale slaughter of babies and worldwide promulgation of demonic entertainment. To God,

---

[379] Lev 11:44-45; 19:2; 20:7; 20:26; Mic 6:8; Zeph 2:3; Mal 3:16-18; Eph 6:6; Matt 5:13,16,20; 7:15-20; 28:18-20; 2 Chron 16:9; I John 2:29; 3:4-10; Phil 1:10-11; Eph 4:24; 5:1; 6:6; 1 Pet 4:1-2,19; Titus 1:16; Heb 12:14, etc.

who knows most won't repent, these are brute beasts fit only for the fire (2 Pet 2:12-22; Jude 10).

For those called to God's eternal purpose,[380] the Earth Programme is the temporary proving ground; on-the-job training under live-fire conditions with the LORD taking notes on how you do (Matt 12:36; 2 Cor 4:16-18). A believer's faith alone in God's sacrifice assures their salvation, but that's just the start, not the goal (Eph 2:8-10; Titus 3:4-8). The spiritual fruits we bear on Earth are even now being set towards our inheritance and rewards as partakers ('*metochoi*') in the LORD's forthcoming, thousand-year Millennial Kingdom (**'Thy Kingdom come, Thy will be done on Earth as it is in Heaven'** (Matt 6:10). Our salvation by faith assured, believers' works, for which we will be judged (1 Cor 3:11-15; 2 Cor 5:10), shall determine our careers and standing with Yeshua in eternity.[381] And, uncomfortable for some, not all of us shall be equal in the Eternal Kingdom. The Creator Himself states:

"Whosoever therefore shall break one of these least commandments, and shall teach men so, <u>he shall be called the least in the kingdom of Heaven</u>. But whosoever shall do and teach them, <u>the same shall be called great in the kingdom of Heaven</u>." (Matt 5:19; *cf.* Matt 19:28-30)

Britt Gillette clarifies:

"If everyone is equal in Heaven, then how can some be 'greatest' while others are 'least'? This is not a contradiction, but an indication of the true nature of Heaven. Whether our earthly deeds are deserving of gain or loss is completely dependent upon what we do in our earthly lives....

Jesus, knowing the nature of Heaven and the rewards that await us, discouraged us from becoming captives of this world and its fleeting pleasures. Instead, He encouraged us to focus on the accumulation of heavenly treasures:

"Don't store up treasures here on Earth, where moths eat them and rust destroys them, and where thieves break in and

---

[380] Eph 1:4-5; FG 6:44; 6:65; 2 Tim 2:19; 2 Thess 2:13; Rom 1:7; Isa 49:1,5; Jer 1:5; Gal 1:15; Acts 13:48

[381] Matt 18:23-35; 24:42-51; 25:14-30; Mark 8:34-38; Luke 12:1-12; 41-48; 19:11-27; Rom 8:17; Heb 6:9,10-12; 1 Cor 3:11-15; 2 Cor 5:10

steal. **Store your treasures in Heaven, where moths and rust cannot destroy, and thieves do not break in and steal. Wherever your treasure is, there the desires of your heart will also be."** (Matt 6:19-21, NLT)

Our treasures in Heaven are eternal. Why then do so many of us spend a lifetime hoarding earthly treasures – cars, houses, stocks and bonds – when each of us knows they are only temporary in nature? We can't take our earthly treasures to Heaven, but we can take our heavenly rewards. If any doubt persists as to how the treasures of Heaven compare to the treasures of this world, read what Paul has to say on the subject:

'That is what the Scriptures mean when they say, **No eye has seen, no ear has heard, and no mind has imagined what God has prepared for those who love him.** (1 Corinthians 2:9, NLT) [382]

There will be rewards for faithfulness, says Chuck Missler:

"Some will be entrusted with special privileges, some not (1 Cor 3:11-15). Some will reign with Christ, some not (2 Tim 2:12; Rev 3:21). Some will be rich, some poor (Luke 12:21,33;16:11). Some will have heavenly treasures of their own, some not (Lk 16:12).

Some will receive the crowns promised:

➤ The Crown of Life (Jam 1:12; Rev 2:10) for those who have suffered for His sake
➤ The Crown of Righteousness (2 Tim 4:8) for those who loved His appearing
➤ The Crown of Glory (1 Pet 5:4) for those who fed the flock
➤ The Crown Incorruptible (1 Cor 9:25) for those who press on steadfastly
➤ The Crown of Rejoicing (1 Thess 2:19) for those who win souls."[383]

Some blow their inheritance and rewards completely, though do not lose their 'sonship' or salvation. It's a major theme throughout our study of the Message System – ask Cain, ask Esau,

---

[382] http://www.raptureready.com/featured/gillette/bg21.html
[383] **Missler, Chuck** *Inheritance and Rewards* notes, www.khouse.org

ask Ishmael, Reuben, Moses, King Saul, the Prodigal Son and *millions of others* we'll come across. They started out with the promise *but did not overcome,* so they forfeited the Earthly inheritance God had in mind for them. Notice that all the blessings any will enjoy in this world or the next *originate from the covenant God makes with Abram in Gen 12, 15 and 17.*

God changes Abram's name to Abra<u>ha</u>m, inserting the Hebrew *heh,* representative of God's breath or Spirit (Gen 17:5). Thus Abram ('my father is exalted') becomes Abra<u>ha</u>m (God-breathed – now 'father of a multitude/many nations') as part of God's covenant with him, another pattern for the New Testament believer renouncing evil and receiving God's breath or Holy Spirit to indwell them. God states that He <u>has made</u> Abram a father of many nations (past tense), even though Isaac has not yet been born! From God's vantage outside of time, all this has already been accomplished. Sarai becomes Sara<u>h</u> with the addition of the same *heh* (Gen 17:15). Circumcision is introduced by God as a sign of the covenant to Abraham's descendants, and must be carried out on newborns on the eighth day - God's number of new beginnings. Dr Bert Thompson comments:

"In Genesis 17:12, God specifically directed Abraham to circumcise newborn males on the eighth day. Why the eighth day? If vitamin K is deficient, there will be a prothrombin deficiency and hemorrhaging may occur. Oddly, it is only on the fifth through the seventh days of the newborn male's life that vitamin K (produced by bacteria in the intestinal tract) is present in adequate quantities. Vitamin K, coupled with prothrombin, causes blood coagulation, which is important in any surgical procedure…. Obviously, then, if vitamin K is not produced in sufficient quantities until days five through seven, it would be wise to postpone any surgery until some time after that. But why did God specify day eight?

On the eighth day, the amount of prothrombin present actually is elevated above 100% of normal—<u>and is the only day in the male's life in which this will be the case under normal conditions</u>. If surgery is to be performed, day eight is the perfect day to do it. Vitamin K and prothrombin levels are at their peak."[384]

These medical details have only recently been recognised. How could Abraham have known this – or more precisely Moses, the likely author of the Genesis account? Dr Missler comments:

"Moses was schooled in all of 'The Wisdom of the Egyptians'... The Papyrus Ebers, 1332 B.C., states the following remedies: Embedded splinter? Apply worm's blood and ass's dung. Losing hair? Apply six fats (horse, hippopotamus, crocodile, cat, snake, ibex). Turning gray? Anoint with blood of black calf which has been boiled in oil or fat of rattlesnake. The well-stocked medicine cabinet included: lizard's blood, swine's teeth, putrid meat, moisture from pig's ears, milk goose grease, asses' hooves, animal fats, excreta from humans, donkeys, antelopes, dogs, cats, and flies)." [385]

Yet no trace of these abominations are to be found in the Torah. Studies also show that Jewesses have a much lower incidence of cervical cancer if they have intercourse with circumcised males, since this prohibits the retention of irritant material and micro-organisms thought to initiate the condition.[386] In his book, *None of These Diseases*, Dr S I McMillen writes,

"Abraham did not pick the eighth day after many centuries of trial-and-error experiments. Neither he nor any of his company from the ancient city of Ur in the Chaldees ever had been circumcised. It was a day picked by the Creator of vitamin K."[387]

Circumcision will confer no spiritual properties on Abraham or his descendants; an eight-day-old baby can have no clue to the significance of the action. Circumcision is already in existence in Abraham's day, but God employs the procedure as a special token/obligation of His covenant; a test of obedience with the parents to allow their male children to bear the covenant's mark.

---

[384] www.apologeticspress.org/articles/2204
[385] Missler, Chuck, *Genesis* notes, op. cit., p.195
[386] **Farmer, K H** *The Cancer Problem*, S. 85, 514, 889-891 (1963)
[387] **McMillen S I & David E Stern** *None of These Diseases, The Bible's Health Secrets for the 21st Century*, Fleming H Revell Co., 2000

And since the covenant is all about the special seed passing from one generation to the next, it is fitting that the covenant's mark is made in the flesh of that very organ of procreation.

And God said unto Abraham, "As for Sarai thy wife, thou shalt not call her name Sarai, but Sarah shall her name be. And I will bless her, and give thee a son also of her: yea, I will bless her, and she shall be a mother of nations; kings of people shall be of her."

Then Abraham fell upon his face, <u>and laughed</u>, and said in his heart, "Shall a child be born unto him that is an hundred years old? And shall Sarah, that is ninety years old, bear?"

And Abraham said unto God, "<u>O that Ishmael might live before thee!</u>"

And God said, "Sarah thy wife shall bear thee a son indeed; and thou shalt call his name Isaac ['he laughs']. And I will establish my covenant with him for an everlasting covenant, and with his seed after him. And as for Ishmael, I have heard thee. Behold, I have blessed him and will make him fruitful, and will multiply him exceedingly [and He does: Gen 25:12-16]; twelve princes shall he beget, and I will make him a great nation. <u>But my covenant will I establish with Isaac</u>, which Sarah shall bear unto thee at this set time in the next year."

And He left off talking with him, and God went up from Abraham.

And Abraham took Ishmael his son, and all that were born in his house, and all that were bought with his money, every male among the men of Abraham's house; and circumcised the flesh of their foreskin in the selfsame day, as God had said unto him. And Abraham was ninety years old and nine when he was circumcised in the flesh of his foreskin. And Ishmael his son was thirteen years old when he was circumcised in the flesh of his foreskin.

In the selfsame day was Abraham circumcised, and Ishmael his son. And all the men of his house, born in the house, and bought with money of the stranger, were circumcised with him. (Gen 17:15-27)

A singular visit

One day in the heat of noon, old Abraham is snoozing in the door to his tent by the terebinth trees at Mamre when he becomes aware of three men approaching. He's later given insight into recognising them as the LORD and two angels (Gen 18:1,13,17). Whoa, pause the tape! Welcome to another *remez* found inside an apparent contradiction. There are a group of verses in the Bible which declare that God <u>has</u> been seen by man, and another group which declare that no man can see or hear the Father or else they die. How to reconcile?

<u>'MAN HAS SEEN HIM'</u> VERSES

And when Abram was ninety years old and nine, <u>the LORD appeared to Abram</u> and said unto him, "I am the Almighty God. Walk before me and be thou perfect." (Gen 17:1)

<u>And the LORD appeared unto him</u> in the plains of Mamre: and he sat in the tent door in the heat of the day.... (Gen 18:1)

And God spake unto Moses, and said unto him, "I am the LORD. <u>And I appeared unto Abraham, unto Isaac, and unto Jacob</u>, by the name of God Almighty, but by my name YHWH was I not known to them. (Exo 6:2-3)

Then went up Moses, and Aaron, Nadab, and Abihu, and seventy of the elders of Israel. <u>And they saw the God of Israel</u>, and there was under His feet, as it were, a paved work of a sapphire stone, and, as it were, the body of Heaven in His clearness. And upon the nobles of the children of Israel He laid not His hand: <u>also they saw God</u>, and did eat and drink. (Exo 24:9-11)

And He said, "Hear now My words: If there be a prophet among you, I the LORD will make myself known unto him in a vision, and will speak unto him in a dream. My servant Moses is not so, who is faithful in all mine house. With him will I speak mouth to mouth, even apparently, and not in dark speeches; <u>and the similitude of the LORD shall he behold</u>: wherefore then were ye not afraid to speak against my servant Moses? (Num 12:6-8)

And he [Stephen] said, Men, brethren, and fathers, hearken; <u>The God of glory appeared unto our father Abraham</u>, when he was in Mesopotamia, before he dwelt in Charran [Haran], and

363

said unto him, "Get thee out of thy country, and from thy kindred, and come into the land which I shall shew thee." (Acts 7:2)

MAN HAS NOT SEEN HIM VERSES

And He [the LORD] said, "**Thou canst not see My face, for there shall no man see Me and live.** (Exo 33:20)

No man hath seen God at any time; the only begotten Son, which is in the bosom of the Father, He hath declared Him. (FG 1:18)

[Jesus speaks] "**And the Father himself, which hath sent Me, hath borne witness of Me. Ye have neither heard His voice at any time, nor seen His shape.**" (FG 5:37)

[Jesus speaks] "**Not that any man hath seen the Father, save he which is of God, he hath seen the Father.**" (FG 6:46)

[Paul speaks] "…**which in His times He shall shew, who is the blessed and only Potentate, the King of kings, and Lord of lords; who only hath immortality, dwelling in the light which no man can approach unto; whom no man hath seen, nor can see: to whom be honour and power everlasting. Amen.**" (1 Tim 6:15-16)

As usual, the atheists pop their champagne corks in celebration at another brazen mistake in the scriptures. "Honestly, how can God be so careless? And don't be getting God off the hook by saying that these were just dreams, visions, hallucinations or apparitions. It says they *saw/heard* God!"

The answer to the conundrum is that these OT patriarchs indeed saw and heard God, but in the form of the Son, never the Father (FG 1:18). The *remez* reveals that any human sensory perception of the LORD God of Israel is the Son in His pre-incarnate form at various points throughout the OT, or, when the Son is present and a voice speaks from Heaven, the Holy Spirit.[388] The *remez* describes the Trinity, much to the chagrin of those who have been erroneously taught that the Trinitarian nature of God is false. Daniel B Wallace Ph.D, a professor of New Testament Studies

---

[388] Compare FG 5:37 with Mark 1:11; FG 12:28; Luke 9:35. The 'Us' of Gen 1:26, Gen 11:7 and Psa 2 prefigure the triune God as Father, Son and Holy Spirit.

at Dallas Theological Seminary and one of the world's great experts on textual criticism and Biblical exegesis, puts the record straight:

"The Bible clearly contains these four truths: the Father is God, Jesus is God, the Holy Spirit is God, and there is only one God... And that's the Trinity." [389]

The second member of the Trinity is given a classic introduction at the start of the fourth gospel:

In the beginning was the Word, and the Word was with God, and the Word was God. <u>The same was in the beginning with God</u>. All things were made by Him [Yeshua], and without Him was not any thing made that was made. In Him was life, and the life was the light of men.... And the Word was made flesh and dwelt among us, (and we beheld His glory, the glory as of the only begotten of the Father,) full of grace and truth. (FG 1:1-4, 14)

Now, back to the story: One day in the heat of noon, old Abraham is dozing in the door to his tent at Mamre[390] when he becomes aware of three men approaching. He is later given insight into recognising them as God (Yeshua) and two angels (Gen 18:1,13,17). He's off his perch *in a jiffy* and *straightway* instructs Sarah *quickly* to knead meal and prepare cakes for their guests. Abraham washes his visitors' feet and sets them under the shade of a tree, then *scurries* off to select a suitable calf, kill it and have a servant *hastily* prepare and dress the meat. I've highlighted those words previously to emphasise that a) Abraham's a bit quicker off the mark for the LORD this time than he was in Ur, and b) he knows God does not come all the way from Heaven and take on human form with two angels for no good reason. So Sheikh Abraham treats his guests to a top-line, non-kosher meal of fatted calf, grain cakes, curds and milk while he stands humbly by, ministering to their needs. Jack Heyford comments:

---

[389] **Strobel, Lee** *The Case for the Real Jesus,* Zondervan, 2007, p.94
[390] The location of ancient Mamre is in northern Hebron at Google Earth, 31 33 32.74 N, 35 06 23.03 E. See http://en.wikipedia.org/wiki/Mamre

"This is typical Bedouin hospitality. Nothing is too good for a guest. It is still Bedouin custom in some areas for the host to stand while the visitors eat." [391]

Three measures of meal are mentioned, which is the fellowship offering. Again, the unwary pass this by when there's a nugget to be had. This is the same three measures of meal Jesus refers to in the NT:

Another parable spake He unto them; "The kingdom of heaven is like unto leaven, which a woman took, and hid in three measures of meal, till the whole was leavened." (Matt 13:33; Luke 13:21; *cf.* Rev 6:6). You miss the shocking inference of this brief parable unless you are Jewish, in which case surreptitiously corrupting the fellowship offering with a substance that is anathema to a Jew is considered beyond the pale – which, of course, the personage of Christ and His message were and still are to the children of Israel! [392]

And [the three visitors] **said unto** [Abraham]**, "Where is Sarah thy wife?"**

And he said, "Behold, in the tent."

And [the LORD] **said, "I will certainly return unto thee according to the time of life; and, lo, Sarah thy wife shall have a son."**

And Sarah heard it in the tent door, which was behind him. (Gen 18:9-10)

Sarah hears this from the tent and laughs inwardly. She is around 90 at this point and well past her best-before date. Yeshua asks Abraham why his wife mocks; can God not do anything? Spooked, Sarah denies laughing but Yeshua reproves her. *Yes, you*

---

[391] Heyford, Jack, *The Spirit Filled Bible,* op. cit., p.30

[392] Leaven (yeast) in the scriptures usually connotes sin, though is used in this parable's context to denote leaven's penetrating and converting properties. Adam Clarke writes: *"The kingdom of heaven is like unto leaven…. As the property of leaven is to change, or assimilate to its own nature the meal or dough with which it is mixed, so the property of the grace of Christ is to change the whole soul into its own likeness; and God intends that this principle should continue in the soul till all is leavened - till the whole bear the image of the heavenly, as it before bore the image of the earthly."* – Adam Clarke's *Commentary on the Bible*, Nelson, 1997

laughed. It's a faith test Abraham and Sarah have already failed with the illegitimate birth of Ishmael via Hagar. The fallout of that one will see millions murdered over the next 4,000 years into our modern age as Muslims, Christians and Jews contest the legitimacy of God's covenant with Abraham over the Land. Yet in this meeting, God's mind is on more immediate matters.

Holocaust by the Dead Sea

And the men rose up from thence and looked toward Sodom. And Abraham went with them to bring them on their way.

And the LORD said [to His angels], **"Shall I hide from Abraham that thing which I do, seeing that Abraham shall surely become a great and mighty nation, and all the nations of the earth shall be blessed in him? <u>For I know him</u>** [*cf.* FG 15:15], **that he will command his children and his household after him, <u>and they shall keep the way of the LORD, to do justice and judgment</u>** [be obedient]; **that the LORD may bring upon Abraham that which He hath spoken of him."** (Gen 18:16-19)

You read these four verses and carry on as normal, yet bound up in them is a foundational, Biblical truth. Namely, that because Abraham is God's friend, God's going to tell him what He intends to do about Sodom and Gomorrah (*cf.* Jam 2:23). Any friend of God will be told in advance what God is going to do. That's what the Message System is all about, and only God's friends are interested in reading and understanding it; the rest won't bother or will doze off after a few pages (the spirit of slumber - Rom 11:8). Consider Yeshua's statement in the 'upper room discourse'.

"<u>Ye are my friends</u>, if ye do whatsoever I command you. Henceforth I call you not servants, <u>for the servant knoweth not what his lord doeth</u>, but I have called you friends, for all things that I have heard of my Father I have made known unto you.

Ye have not chosen me, but I have chosen you, and ordained you [we are priests!], **that ye should go and bring forth fruit, and that your fruit should remain: that whatsoever ye shall ask of the Father in My name, He may give it you.** (FG 15:14-16)

Jesus cites His gift of precogniscence as evidence of who He really is (FG 14:29; 13:11)

Amos 3:7 states: **Surely the Lord GOD will do nothing but he revealeth his secret unto his servants the prophets.**

Albert Barnes writes:

"God revealed to Noah that He would bring the deluge, and to Abraham and Lot, that He would destroy the cities of the plain, and to Joseph the 7 years' famine in Egypt, and to Moses its plagues, and to Moses and Joshua all the chastisements of His people, and to Jonah the destruction of Nineveh, that they who heard of the coming punishment might either avoid it by repentance or, if they should despise it, might be more justly punished." [393]

Yeshua's warning to His disciples of Jerusalem's forthcoming destruction in Luke 19:41-44 enabled every Christian to flee the city during the lull in the Romans' siege in 70 AD when Vespasian returned to Rome upon Nero's death. The Jews remained in the city and were eventually slaughtered when hostilities recommenced.[394] The Bible is replete with examples of God giving His faithful the inside track to avoid their immolation. The apostle John is given the awesome Revelation of Jesus Christ to pass on to the world concerning the end times. In fact, this famous tome of the Apocalypse (*lit.* 'Unveiling') actually opens with:

The Revelation of Jesus Christ, which God gave unto Him [Jesus Christ], to <u>shew unto His servants things which must shortly come to pass</u>; and He sent and signified it by His angel unto His servant John (Rev 1:1).

How about Daniel, the beloved prophet (Dan 9:23), the disciple singled out by Yeshua in the Fourth Gospel – a gospel, incidentally, written by another beloved disciple (not John Zebedee!).[395] Daniel is given the rare privilege of being given perhaps the most astonishing prophecy of the entire scriptures foretelling THE PRECISE DAY *Mashiach* will come to announce His kingship (Dan

---

[393] **Barnes, Albert** *Barnes Notes on the Old and New Testaments,* Baker Books, 1982: Amos 3:7

[394] See *Origins 4 - Tetelestai*

[395] The revealing of the true author of the Fourth Gospel will surprise and astonish; a most striking and satisfying *remez* that opens up a whole new dimension to the NT.

9:24-27).[396] We are God's friends, so He will tell us what will happen via His Word. Apocalyptic privilege. A foreshadowing of God's unique attribute of prophecy.

Back to the story. After their meal Yeshua and the two angels are escorted by Abraham back to the road and they turn to look towards the Vale of Siddim.[397]

And the LORD said, "Because the cry of Sodom and Gomorrah is great and their sin is very grievous, I will go down now and see whether they have done altogether according to the cry of it, which is come unto Me. And if not, I will know." (Gen 18:20-21)

The two angels are sent off to the cities. Abraham has a fair idea of what God has in store; also that the Creator in His omniscience hardly need 'go down' and 'see for Himself' whether there wickedness be. An interesting discourse takes place, wherein Abraham attempts to intercede for the people of Sodom. Notice this is the second time the patriarch is stepping in to try to help Lot and the people of Sodom (*cf.* Gen 14:12-16).

"Wilt Thou also destroy the righteous with the wicked? Peradventure there be fifty righteous within the city [Sodom]**: wilt Thou also destroy and not spare the place for the fifty righteous that are therein? That be far from Thee to do after this manner, to slay the righteous with the wicked, and that the righteous should be as the wicked, that be far from Thee. Shall not the Judge of all the Earth do right?"** (Gen 18:23-25) Abraham probably gulps at that point, fearing he has overstepped the mark. And he knows to whom he is speaking – the One appointed to judge the Earth.[398]

And the LORD said, "If I find in Sodom fifty righteous within the city, then I will spare all the place for their sakes." (Gen 18:26)

---

[396] Daniel's Seventy Week prophecy is covered in detail in *Origins 4 – Tetelestai.*

[397] Traditional site is at Google Earth, 31 16 02.15 N, 35 28 06.86 E.

[398] The Old Testament YHWH and Daniel's 'son of man' are part of the same Godhead. Compare Rev 19: 11-16 with Isa 66:15-16. Also see FG 5:22-23,27; Dan 7:13-14; Acts 10:42; Acts 17:30-31; Rom 2:16; 2 Tim 4:1; Matt 16:27; 25: 31-34,41,46; 2 Thess 1:5-10; 2 Cor 5:10-11; Rev 2: 18-19,23

Abraham realises there aren't fifty righteous men in Sodom, so he takes another breath: **"Behold now, I have taken upon me to speak unto the LORD, which am but dust and ashes. Peradventure there shall lack five of the fifty righteous, wilt Thou destroy all the city for lack of five?"** (Gen 18:27-28)

God replies, **"If I find there forty and five, I will not destroy it."**

"Peradventure there should be forty found there?"

"I will not do it for the sake of forty."

"Let not the LORD be angry and I will speak; suppose thirty should be found there?"

"I will not do it if I find thirty there." (Gen 18:28-30)

And so on, down to ten. It's a tragi-comical moment, but the stakes could not be higher. We know how the story ends. The five cities of the Siddim Plain symbolise man's rebellion against God in the Holy War, driven by their sinful nature and the fallen realm. Both Abraham and God know they will not repent. In the end, reminiscent of the grace period God extended to man prior to the Flood, the two angels seek out Abraham's nephew, Lot, who lives in Sodom and has become one of the city councillors by this time (Gen 19:1).[399] These beings appear at Lot's door as ordinary men. Lot, realising who they are, hastily bundles them in, slams the door and bows low. In today's parlance, the conversation runs as follows:

Lot: "You are welcome here. Please wash and make yourselves at home for the night. I'll see you safely on your way in the morning."

Angels: "Thanks, but we'll spend the night in the street."

Lot: "I – wouldn't do that in this city if I were you."

Angels: "All right, we'll stay if you insist."

Lot washes their feet, as is the custom, makes them supper and the men sit down to eat. A little later, there's a commotion outside, and Lot discovers with sliding bowels a crowd has gathered in the street. Fists begin pounding on his door.

---

[399] Lot 'sat in the gate', which in ancient Hebrew meant he was one of the leaders of that city.

"Where are the men which came in to thee this night? Bring them out unto us, that we may know them carnally!" (Gen 19:5)

Which means exactly what you think it means. Lot's inward reaction to Sodom's finest clamouring to be the first to sodomise two of God's angels goes unrecorded. With courage, he steps out to confront the mob. **"I pray you, brethren, do not so wickedly! Behold now, I have two daughters which have not known man. Let me, I pray you, bring them out unto you, and do ye to them as is good in your eyes. Only unto these men do nothing, for therefore came they under the shadow of my roof."** (Gen 19:7-8)

Amazingly, Lot is prepared to sacrifice the virtue, perhaps even the lives of his own two virgin daughters rather than hand over the angels.[400] He appeals to Sodom's apparent tradition of not victimising travellers (Eze 16:49-50; Deut 10:18-19), but this cuts no ice with the mob.

"Stand back!" they cry. "You come here to live among us and act like our judge? We'll give you worse than them!"

At which point, Lot is grabbed by the angels and hauled back into the house. Before the crowd can vent its rage and batter down the portal, the angels smite the attackers outside with blindness and they stagger around, unable to find the door. Jack Heyford comments that the usual Hebrew word for blindness is not used here; instead, the construction suggests a brilliant flash inducing temporary blindness similar to that experienced by Saul of Tarsus on the road to Damascus.[401]

Sodom's fate is sealed. The angels tell Lot to prepare his household for departure. When Lot explains the situation to his sons-in-law, the lads think he's joking. From Gen 19:14 we infer that they remain behind and perish along with the city. Here we see the model again. Before God levels judgment as with the Flood, he tells his friends what He's about to do, then gets them out. His forbearance lasts only so long.

And when the morning arose, then the angels hastened Lot, saying, "Arise, take thy wife and thy two daughters which are

---

[400] Lot offers his virgin daughters to a fleshly mob, whereas Abraham will offer his son to the LORD.

[401] Heyford, Jack, *The Spirit-Filled Bible,* op. cit., p.32

here [no sons-in-law], **lest thou be consumed in the iniquity of the city. And while he lingered, the men** [angels] **laid hold upon his hand, and upon the hand of his wife, and upon the hand of his two daughters; the LORD being merciful unto him: and they brought him forth and set him without the city.**

And it came to pass, when they had brought them forth abroad, that they said, "Escape for thy life; look not behind thee, neither stay thou in all the plain; escape to the mountain, lest thou be consumed." (Gen 19:15-17)

Here are some terrific insights into how God judges and spares. In Gen 19:22, the angels sent to destroy Sodom and Gomorrah expressly state <u>that they cannot carry out their mission until Lot leaves</u>. God is prepared to spare the cities even if ten righteous people are found within. Which tells you something about how God deals with judgment. Alas, there are not ten righteous. Since Lot is judged righteous, removing him will clear the decks for action. This is also a model for the Flood, where the righteous were spared, albeit only eight. The righteous are not appointed to God's wrath (1 Thess 5:9), and this will be the model for the removal of God's believers in 'the Rapture'/*harpazo* prior to Daniel's Seventieth Week (seven years), which features the Great Tribulation commencing halfway through. Notice that this is the period in which God concludes His dealings with *Israel*, not the *Church*. (*cf.* Dan 9:27).[402]

Set fire to the rain

There were five Biblical 'cities of the plain'. The Vale of Siddim runs directly south from the forked southern tip of the Dead Sea. The names of the cities were Sodom, Gomorrah, Admah, Zeboiim and Bela (Zoar). Their precise locations are still a matter of debate though some interesting archaeology has come to light.

Then the LORD rained upon Sodom and upon Gomorrah brimstone and fire from the LORD out of Heaven. And He overthrew those cities, and all the plain, and all the inhabitants of the cities, and that which grew upon the ground. But [Lot's]

---

[402] The 'Rapture', 'end times', and Great Tribulation will be dealt with in detail in *Origins 5*.

wife looked back from behind him and she became a pillar of salt.[403] **And Abraham arose early in the morning to the place where he stood before the LORD. And he looked toward Sodom and Gomorrah, and toward all the land of the plain, and beheld, and, lo, the smoke of the country went up as the smoke of a furnace.** (Gen 19:24…28)

The destruction is thought to have consumed the entire plain. The archaeological hunt was on to find any remains which could shed light on the historicity of this momentous event. Our old friend Ron Wyatt – he of Noah's Ark fame – claimed to have found Sodom close to the south-western bank of the Dead Sea near the fortress mount of Masada. His wife compiled a video of what she claims are streets, city walls, unnatural anomalous features, a ziggurat, a sphinx-like outcrop and remains of cindered deposits which, when tested, were found to comprise 95% sulphur (brimstone).[404] *ChristianAnswers.Net* disagrees:

"The ruins of Sodom and Gomorrah have been discovered southeast of the Dead Sea. The modern names are Bab edh-Dhra,[405] thought to be Sodom, and Numeira,[406] thought to be Gomorrah. Both places were destroyed at the same time by an enormous conflagration. The destruction debris was about three feet thick. What brought about this awful calamity? Startling discoveries in the cemetery at Bab edh-Dhra revealed the cause. Archaeologists found that buildings used to bury the dead were burned by a fire that started on the roof….

There is ample evidence of subterranean deposits of a petroleum-based substance called bitumen, similar to asphalt, in the region south

---

[403] Sodom appears to have wielded a strange spell over its inhabitants. Lot was drawn to the dystopian city like a moth to a flame. Wiersbe remarks: "Instead of keeping his eyes on the heavenly city (Heb 11:10,14-16), Lot looked toward Sodom and began to walk by sight (Gen 13:10-11). Then he moved his tent near Sodom (Gen 13:12), and finally he moved into Sodom (Gen 14:12). Lot's location in the gate indicates that he was a man of some authority, for that was where official business was conducted (Ruth 4:1ff)." – (Wiersbe, W, *The Wiersbe Bible Commentary*, op. cit., p.78.) Lot's wife was so enamoured with the place, she could not resist one final look behind her (*cf.* Luke 17:32).

[404] http://uk.youtube.com/watch?v=lgQHQ992Wnw

[405] Google Earth, 31 15 14.14 N, 35 32 3.06 E

[406] At the mouth of Wadi Numeira, Google Earth, 31 07 53.72 N, 35 31 45.83 E

of the Dead Sea. Such material normally contains a high percentage of sulphur. It has been postulated by geologist Frederick Clapp that pressure from an earthquake could have caused the bitumen deposits to be forced out of the earth through a fault line. As it gushed out of the earth it could have been ignited by a spark or surface fire. It would then fall to earth as a burning, fiery mass.

It was only after Clapp formulated this theory that Sodom and Gomorrah were found. It turns out that the sites are located exactly on a fault line along the eastern side of a plain south of the Dead Sea, so Clapp's theory is plausible. There is some evidence for this scenario from the Bible itself. Abraham viewed the destruction from a vantage point west of the Dead Sea. The Bible records what Abraham saw: "He looked down toward Sodom and Gomorrah, toward all the land of the plain, and he saw dense smoke rising from the land, like smoke from a furnace." (Genesis 19:28) Dense smoke suggests smoke from a petroleum-based fire. Smoke rising like smoke from a furnace indicates a forced draft, such as would be expected from subterranean deposits being forced out of the ground under pressure."[407]

AccuracyInGenesis agrees:

"To date there has been located only evidence for two of the five Cities of the Plain, but they are proposing that the evidence is strong that the two most important cities of Sodom and Gomorrah have been found. That being the evidences found of destruction by fire at each site due to the layers of ash found in the digs by archaeologists. Bab edh-Dhra (Sodom) is the largest of the two sites, the 7-meter wide (23 feet) city wall enclosed 9-10 acres with gates located at the west and the northeast. The northeast gate had two flanking towers with massive stone and timber foundations, possibly the gate in which Lot sat (Genesis 19:1). Estimated population at the time of the destruction was between 600-1200. There was a large cemetery at Bab edh-Dhra and pottery evidence indicates that some of the residents of Numeira (Gomorrah) buried their dead in this cemetery. It appears that Numeria was in existence for only a short time, possibly less than 100 years. Paleobotany investigations indicated that a rich diversity of

---

[407] http://www.christiananswers.net/q-abr/abr-a007.html

crops were grown in the area including barley, wheat, grapes, figs, lentils, flax, chickpeas, peas, broad beans, dates and olives.

Concerning the cause of the destruction, they are proposing that it was the result of an earthquake that forced combustible material to the surface and into the atmosphere. Surveys have located bitumen, petroleum, natural gas and sulfur in the area. And to the east of the Dead Sea is a major fault line and these cities are located exactly on this fault line."[408]

Remarkably, the bitumen theory has some corroboration in the scriptures. Remember Gen 14:8-10, which described the Battle of Siddim, wherein the five kings of the plain attempted to cast off the Elamite empire and their Mesopotamian allies under King Chedorlaomer? The five kings of the plain lose the fight and many of their men are driven into the tarpits which pepper the vale.

Sexual shenanigans to blame?

Did Sodom and Gomorrah perish due to God's dim view of homosexuality (not to mention the attempted gang-rape of two of His angels)? Such notions appal gay rights groups today, who declare the episode was not about sodomy at all, but God's judgment on *inhospitality*. Metropolitan Community Churches writes:

"Now, during those days, if visitors came into a town to seek lodging, and were there and arrived after sunset, they were fair game to the townspeople. The townspeople could do whatever they wanted. Well in this case, they were angels who had come to Lot's home, and they were passing through, and the men came to have their way with the angels. Now, this isn't a case about how they were going to have sex with the people they perceived as men, but rather a case of hospitality. Were they there trying to make the people feel hospitable? Lot is saying that these are guests, these are foreigners, they are in my home; and he offers his daughters, which I've never been very fond of, because I think, "What are you doing?!" and it just talks about the value of women in that day. But Lot tries to get them to ignore them, but they still press on and they really want to get now

[408] http://www.accuracyingenesis.com/sodom.html

not only those two angels but they want to get the "companionship" of Lot as well, they want to have sex with Lot. So, it's about men, banding together in the town and going after people that have come into the town and having sex with them, and its not about the fact that they're men or women, its about the fact that they want to just abuse them; and it's a case of unfettered hospitality, they're not being hospitable to this group of people, and so, when we look at the Sodom passage, it's a passage about hospitality, and how to greet people who are coming into the city. So Sodom and Gomorrah has nothing to do with having sex men-to-men…. Sodom is destroyed because of its lack of hospitality, not because the men of the town wanted to have sex with angels." [409]

GotAnswers is having none of it:

"The men of Sodom and Gomorrah, thinking that the visiting angels were men, wanted to have sex with them. Those who attempt to explain away the biblical condemnations of homosexuality claim that the sin of Sodom and Gomorrah was inhospitality. While the men of Sodom and Gomorrah were certainly being inhospitable, that clearly was not all. The men of Sodom and Gomorrah desired to perform homosexual gang rape on the angels. Also, God never declared inhospitality to be an abomination to Him, while Leviticus 18:22 makes God's view of homosexuality clear: "Do not lie with a man as one lies with a woman; that is detestable."[410]

Jude, the brother of Jesus, gives some intriguing information: **"I will therefore put you in remembrance, though ye once knew this, how that the LORD, having saved the people out of the land of Egypt, afterward destroyed them that believed not. And the angels, which kept not their first estate, but left their own habitation, He hath reserved in everlasting chains under darkness unto the judgment of the great day. Even as Sodom and Gomorrah, and the cities about them in like manner, giving themselves over to fornication, <u>and going after strange flesh</u>, are set forth for an example, suffering the vengeance of eternal fire."** (Jude 5-7)

---

[409] http://www.mccchurch.org

[410] http://www.gotquestions.org/Sodom-and-Gomorrah.html

This passage infers that the sexual sins of Sodom and Gomorrah were similar to those of **the angels who did not keep their proper domain** in Genesis 6 (Nephilim/Anakim, etc), and that sex with **strange flesh** (aliens/demons) is particularly repugnant to God.

Hence the Flood.

Hence Sodom and Gomorrah.

God rescued Lot the first time from Sodom using Abraham's special forces raid on the camp of Chedorlaomer. The second time His angels had to take Lot by the hand and drag him out of Sodom. Wiersbe comments:

> "First, Lot lingered; then he argued; then he begged to be allowed to go his own way. Instead of being grateful for God's mercy and obeying his rescuers, Lot resisted and created trouble for them." [411]

While Abraham and Sarah, faithful to the Spirit, receive the wonderful news of an impending son and heir, Lot suffers the fate of the flesh, loses everything he owns in the fiery conflagration of Sodom, but is saved by God's grace for Abraham, 'yet as by fire' (1 Cor 3:15). His sons-in-law laughed at the warning and were torched along with the city, believing like fools today that God stays his judgment forever (Luke 17:26-30). They awoke that fateful morning with nothing out of the ordinary to warn them that this was their final day on Earth.

Too frightened to remain in any of towns surrounding the plain, Lot and his two daughters find refuge in a cave in the mountains. As realisation of their predicament sets in, it dawns on the two daughters that they have no hope of perpetuating Lot's seed now their husbands are dead. They come up with a baleful, eleventh-hour strategy:

And the firstborn said unto the younger, "Our father is old, and there is not a man in the Earth to come in unto us after the manner of all the Earth. Come, let us make our father drink wine and we will lie with him, that we may preserve seed of our father."

---

[411] Wiersbe, W, *The Wiersbe Bible Commentary*, op. cit., p.78

And they made their father drink wine that night: and the firstborn went in and lay with her father; and he perceived not when she lay down, nor when she arose.

And it came to pass on the morrow, that the firstborn said unto the younger, Behold, I lay last night with my father: let us make him drink wine this night also; and go thou in and lie with him, that we may preserve seed of our father."

And they made their father drink wine that night also: and the younger arose and lay with him; and he perceived not when she lay down, nor when she arose.

Thus were both the daughters of Lot with child by their father. (Gen 19:31-36)

It's a shoddy, sordid end to Lot and his family's descent into degradation and apostasy. From Ur of the Chaldees to Lot's prosperity in Haran, to his spiritual high with Abraham in Canaan, to his seduction by Egypt, to his move to Sodom, to losing everything he owned, to looking out of a cave's mouth now at the devastation God has wrought across the plain before him. It must certainly have seemed to Lot and his two daughters that they were the only survivors left on Earth.

In the Bible, losers seem to end up in caves (Josh 10:16-19; Rev 6:15-17), yet it never occurs to Lot's daughters to seek God's face in prayer, repent and ask for guidance for their clan for the future. God would have honoured their repentance and listened. Instead, incest is the only strategy they can come up with, and the penalty will be paid in heavy coin. The firstborn daughter bears a son and calls his name Moab ('through our father'). The younger's child is named Ben-Ammi ('son of my kin'). Both children will go on to father the Moabite and Ammonite nations, who will harry and vex Israel down through the perilous centuries to come, right into our own modern age.

ISAAC, SON OF LAUGHTER

Birth and controversy

One can only imagine Abraham, caught up in the terrifying, all-consuming judgment of Sodom and Gomorrah, adrift in a world of blessings and curses, of literal covenants and paybacks, cut foreskins, fire from Heaven, and smoke billowing up from the Earth. "Oh God, why me?" he must have thought a thousand times. And where was this great nation God promised him, through whom the Creator would rule for eternity? Sarah was barren and Abraham was pushing a hundred, so an heir to kick off the whole project was sporting long odds. It's hard to know what each of us would have done in Abraham's shoes. You can't run from God. Perhaps it was dawning on the patriarch by now that God didn't run from anything either.

"My thoughts are not your thoughts, nor are your ways My Ways," says the LORD. (Isa 55:8, NKJV) In fact, some of God's ways are downright bizarre. Killing every air-breathing creature on Earth except those God had shut up in a big box takes some beating. Confusing everyone's language at Babel. The whole Nimrod and Semiramis saga. Sodom and Gomorrah. Symbols, sacrifices and the shed blood of innocent animals to cover sins when you couldn't stop sinning. Birth, death. Snipped foreskins. The whole panoply of life. What was it for? Wherefore the struggle? Define the purpose. You couldn't dream up a weirder world if your afterlife depended on it. And it soon gets weirder.

The early cultures were fixated on offspring. Unlike today where it's all done by government, children were your means of support, sustenance, defence, continuity and destiny. Abraham is likely one of the richest sheikhs in the region at this point, but Sarah is childless, and in such a male-dominant culture, if the wife can't produce heirs, tongues wag and you very soon find someone who will. A young lad, Ishmael, already dwells in the tents of Abraham as testament to the patriarch's dip in faith thirteen years before on such matters, but things are about to change.

And the LORD visited Sarah as He had said, and the LORD did unto Sarah as He had spoken. For Sarah conceived and bare Abraham a son in his old age, at the set time of which God had spoken to him.

And Abraham called the name of his son that was born unto him, whom Sarah bare to him, Isaac [*lit.* 'laughter']. And Abraham circumcised his son Isaac, being eight days old, as God had commanded him. And Abraham was an hundred years old when his son Isaac was born unto him.

And Sarah said, "God hath made me to laugh, so that all that hear will laugh with me." (Gen 21:1-6)

It's hard to underestimate the effect Isaac's birth has on Sarah. Fêted, spoiled and loved by her husband, the secret 'what if' she harboured her whole life vanishes in the joys and laughter of newborn life. Little Isaac is weaned probably around three – some say five - and Abraham throws a great feast to celebrate.[412] Here we come across an enigmatic few verses:

And the child grew and was weaned: and Abraham made a great feast the [same] day that Isaac was weaned. And Sarah saw the son of Hagar the Egyptian [i.e. Ishmael], which she had born unto Abraham, <u>mocking</u>.

Wherefore she said unto Abraham, "Cast out this bondwoman and her son, for the son of this bondwoman shall not be heir with my son, even with Isaac."

And the thing was very grievous in Abraham's sight because of his son. (Gen 21:8-11)

---

[412] At what age Jewish children were weaned is disputed by scholars. Adam Clarke writes: "From the speech of the mother to her son in 2 Maccabees 7:27, it seems likely that among the Jews they were weaned when three years old: "O my son, have pity upon me that bare thee nine months in my womb, and gave thee suck three years, and nourished thee and brought thee up." And this is further strengthened by 2 Chronicles 31:16, where Hezekiah, in making provision for the Levites and priests, includes the children from three years old and upwards; which is a presumptive proof that previously to this age they were wholly dependent on the mother for their nourishment. Samuel appears to have been brought to the sanctuary when he was just weaned, and then he was capable of ministering before the LORD, 1 Samuel 1:22-28; and this certainly could not be before he was three years of age." - *Adam Clarke's Commentary on the Bible*, Nelson, 1997

What does Sarah see that gets her so enraged that she demands the immediate expulsion of Hagar and Ishmael (again)? It's hard to believe a little sibling mockery is the cause. The affair is such that Abraham himself is sorely distressed at the implications.

There are some translational issues here. In the Masoretic Text (600-900 AD), it simply says **Sarah saw the son of Hagar the Egyptian, whom she had born to Abraham, mocking**. The Greek Septuagint translation, put together around 275 BC, contains four extra words: **"with her son Isaac"**. So does the Latin Vulgate (400 AD ff).

The plot thickens when you examine the Hebrew word used in this case for 'mocking'/'scoffing' and compare it with its other uses elsewhere in the scriptures. The Hebrew root is מצחק, tsachaq, (Strongs H6711): which is translated **laugh, play, mock, make sport**. A few chapters later when Isaac is fully grown, we have the Bible's third 'passing-my-wife-off-as-my-sister-in-a-strange-land' incident (Gen 26:7ff). On this occasion Isaac uses his father's subterfuge and passes his wife Rebekah off to the Philistine monarch as his sister. Later, Isaac is spotted from a window by the king tsachaq-ing with Rebekah. Jack Heyford's NKJV translation makes it clear they are caressing/fondling in the manner of lovers. At any rate, the behaviour is sufficiently sexual in nature for the king immediately to deduce that they are man and wife, so he confronts Isaac (Gen 26:9). The same Hebrew word tsachaq is also used by Potiphar's wife to describe to her husband, the captain of the Pharaoh's guard, what she says Joseph tried to do to her. It's quite clear from the context of her accusation in Gen 39:17-18 that the purported action is sexual.

Did Sarah see an unforgivable act committed by Ishmael on her beloved child? The apostle Paul is clear that Ishmael was in someway persecuting his three-year-old brother, and makes a wider spiritual lesson out of the event (Gal 4:22-31). But why is the Masoretic Text, usually so authoritative and accurate, noticeably different from the Septuagint and Vulgate on this occasion? Google up "Did Ishmael sexually molest Isaac?" and come to your own conclusions. Since militant Islam was on the march from the 7th century AD onwards, were the Jews who compiled the Masoretic

Text covering themselves for fear of Muslim reprisals? Most Protestant translations of the scriptures these days are derived from the Masoretic Text, so their versions omit the extra four words **"with her son Isaac"**.

Whatever Sarah witnessed, that's it for Hagar and Ishmael in the tents of Abraham so far as she's concerned. She may also be clearing the decks for fear of what disinherited Ishmael may do to Isaac once Abraham is dead. It's a defining moment – the separating of Ishmael and Isaac – yet the two brothers evidently keep in contact since they both arrange their father's funeral seventy years later in the cave of Machpelah ('Cave of the Patriarchs') [413] (Gen 25:9)

And God said unto Abraham, "Let it not be grievous in thy sight because of the lad, and because of thy bondwoman; in all that Sarah hath said unto thee, hearken unto her voice, <u>for in Isaac shall thy seed be called</u>. And also of the son of the bondwoman will I make a nation, <u>because he is thy seed</u>." (Gen 21:12-13)

Satan's ears prick up. God is telling the patriarch once more that Isaac constitutes the line of the Scarlet Thread (**Seed of the woman** – Gen 3:15), but that Ishmael will be honoured and provided for because he is Abraham's son.

And Abraham rose up early in the morning and took bread and a bottle of water, and gave it unto Hagar, putting it on her shoulder, and the child, and sent her away. And she departed and wandered in the wilderness of Beersheba.

And the water was spent in the bottle and she cast the child under one of the shrubs. And she went, and sat her down over against him a good way off, as it were a bowshot: for she said, "Let me not see the death of the child." And she sat over against him, and lift up her voice and wept.

And God heard the voice of the lad; and the angel of God called to Hagar out of Heaven, and said unto her, "What aileth thee, Hagar? Fear not, for God hath heard the voice of the lad where he is. Arise, lift up the lad, and hold him in thine hand, for I will make him a great nation."

---

[413] Google Earth: 31° 31' 29.08" N, 35° 6' 38.62" E

And God opened her eyes and she saw a well of water; and she went, and filled the bottle with water, and gave the lad drink [*cf.* FG 7:37; Rev 22:17]. And God was with the lad; and he grew and dwelt in the wilderness and became an archer. And he dwelt in the wilderness of Paran [Arabia], and his mother took him a wife out of the land of Egypt. (Gen 21:14-21)

Rabbi Yacov Rambsel writes:

"Notice the name of Ishmael יִשְׁמָעֵאל, is encoded in **And God heard** וַיִּשְׁמַע אֱלֹהִים. The LORD had compassion on Hagar and her son and was completely aware of their dreadful situation. Years later, Hagar's son Ishmael became the father of twelve sons and a daughter, and most of their names are encoded within the first chapter of Genesis. We must remember that they also were of the natural seed of Abraham. The same Messiah who will bless Israel also will bless the offspring of Hagar." [414]

Josephus records:

"When the lad was grown up, he married a wife, by birth an Egyptian, whence the mother was herself derived originally. Of this wife were born to Ishmael twelve sons; Nabaioth, Kedar, Abdeel, Mabsam, Idumas, Masmaos, Masaos, Chodad, Theman, Jetur, Naphesus, Cadmas. These inhabited all the country from the Euphrates to the Red Sea, and called it Nabatene. They are an Arabian nation, and name their tribes from these, both because of their own virtue, and because of the dignity of Abraham their father." [415]

Today the sons of Ishmael are daily contesting the right of the sons of Isaac to the Land with increasing vehemence. This sets the stage for the incredible dramas to be played out in the 'last days', described in detail as we progress with the *Origins* series.

---

[414] Rambsel, Y, *The Genesis Factor*, op. cit. pp.62-62
[415] **Josephus** *Antiquities*, I.12.4

The Akedah

Isaac grows and flourishes, but then comes one of the most disturbing passages in the Bible. This event is known as the *Akedát Yitzḥák*, or 'The Binding of Isaac':

And it came to pass after these things, that God did tempt [actually 'test'] Abraham and said unto him, "Abraham!" And he said, "Behold, here I am." And He said, "Take now thy son, <u>thine only son Isaac</u>, whom thou <u>lovest</u>, and get thee into the land of Moriah, <u>and offer him there for a burnt offering upon one of the mountains which I will tell thee of</u>." (Gen 22: 1-2)

Several things to note here:

> ➤ This is the first mention of 'love' in the Bible, the love of a father for his only son (*cf.* FG 3:16)
>
> ➤ God is going to tempt (test) Abraham
>
> ➤ Notice God refers to Isaac as Abraham's *only son* with no mention of Ishmael, who appears to have been edited out of the score. Isaac is the son of the covenant, not Ishmael
>
> ➤ God wants Isaac to be sacrificed *as a burnt offering* (which belongs only to God – Lev 1:3) on a specific mountain in the land of Moriah which the Almighty will reveal

On the face of it, what a horrendous proposition for a loving father. Is God really condoning human sacrifice when it is specifically outlawed later in the Torah (Deut 18:10)? I thought God did not change (Mal 3:6)? Abraham has no problem with it – at least no protestations are recorded. Abraham is learning God's ways. God promised Abraham that the blessed nation would come through his son, Isaac – indeed God speaks about having already accomplished this in the past tense (Gen 17:5). So if God wants Isaac killed, God's the one with the problem, He'll have to resurrect Isaac (Heb 11:17-19). On the one hand, it seems a supreme test of faith. On the other, Abraham realises the Creator is up to something. Above all, Abraham has learned to be *obedient*, which is what God wants from each of us regardless. A yielding. An end to our participation in the Holy War against Him. And unlike the delay at Haran, Abraham gets on this one first thing the following morning and gets that famous saddle on his ass.

And Abraham rose up early in the morning and saddled his ass, and took two of his young men with him, and Isaac his son, and clave the wood for the burnt offering, and rose up, and went unto the place of which God had told him. [so four of them are going.]

Then on the third day Abraham lifted up his eyes[416] **and saw the place afar off. And Abraham said unto his young men, "Abide ye here with the ass; and I and the lad will go yonder and worship and come again to you."** [Is Abraham lying? He's going to kill the lad! Perhaps he knows it's just a test.] **And Abraham took the wood of the burnt offering and laid it upon Isaac his son, and he took the fire in his hand, and a knife, and they went both of them together** [*Heb. lit.* 'they both went in agreement'].

And Isaac spake unto Abraham his father, and said, "My father!" And he said, "Here am I, my son." And he said, "Behold the fire and the wood, but where is the lamb for a burnt offering?" And Abraham said, "My son, God will provide Himself a lamb for a burnt offering." So they went both of them together. [again, 'they both went in agreement']. (Gen 22: 3-8)

We've all heard the story but there are some intriguing details often missed:

Many assume Isaac was a toddler at the time, perhaps five to seven years old, but it's unlikely Abraham would have heaped all that wood upon a five-year-old. Others aver that Isaac was young enough not to argue about the strange events in which he was participating, yet old enough to carry the wood up the hill. In fact, scholarly opinion puts Isaac in his thirties at the time of the Akedah. This estimate of Isaac's age is derived from the information that Sarah is 91 years old when she gives birth to Isaac (Gen 17:17,21) and she dies aged 127 (Gen 23:1), making Isaac 36 at her death. Since Sarah's death is covered in the chapter

---

[416] There's that phrase again! Every time someone 'lifts up their eyes' in scripture and beholds something, pay attention! It's usually something momentous. On this occasion, in Hollywood script parlance, God's giving you an establishing shot of the most significant spot on the planet.

immediately following the Akedah, some scholars surmise that Isaac was at the very least in his early thirties. The 1st century AD Jewish historian Flavius Josephus puts him at 25.[417]

The text reveals something more extraordinary. *Isaac goes along with it all! They both go in agreement!* Let's dig further.

And they came to the place <u>which God had told him of</u> [i.e. God has a special place picked out]**; and Abraham built an altar there** [Abraham's always building altars] **and laid the wood in order, and bound Isaac his son, and laid him on the altar upon the wood. And Abraham stretched forth his hand and took the knife to slay his son.**

And the Angel of the LORD called unto him out of Heaven, and said, "Abraham, Abraham!" And he said, "Here am I." And He said, "Lay not thine hand upon the lad, neither do thou any thing unto him, for now I know that thou fearest God, seeing thou hast not withheld thy son, <u>thine only son from Me</u>." (Gen 22:9-12)

Let's hit the pause button to consider what Jewish scholars make of this whole episode. In a word, it baffles them. We see denial, twisting of scripture and all sorts of strictures employed by Hebrew sages down through the centuries in an attempt to get God out of a supposed 'human sacrifice/moral dungeon' scrape. Most Jewish scholars reconcile Gen 22 by believing God was merely testing Abraham's loyalty to see if he would kill his own son, but would never have allowed him to complete the act. But doesn't God know everything already? Clearly the Akedah was not done for the LORD's benefit.

Some Jews hold that Sarah died upon learning of the trauma of Isaac at Mount Moriah, and interpret Gen 23:2 to mean that Abraham comes to mourn for his dead wife directly from the dreadful business at Mount Moriah. They hold that this explains Isaac's apparent absence at his mother's funeral since he fled in terror after his father's abortive attempt to do him in.[418]

---

[417] Josephus, *Antiquities,* op. cit., I.13.2

[418] www.hebrew4christians.com/Scripture/Parashah/Summaries/Chayei_Sarah/ Akedah/akedah.html

Most Jews do not appreciate the astonishing model God is presenting here, so the whole purpose of the Akedah is strange to them and interpreted mystically along the lines of 'God moves in mysterious ways'. *Wikipedia* describes the Hebrew confusion thus:

"The early rabbinic midrash *Genesis Rabbah* imagines God as saying "I never considered telling Abraham to slaughter Isaac (using the Hebrew root letters for 'slaughter', not 'sacrifice')". Rabbi Yona Ibn Janach (Spain, 11th century) wrote that God demanded only a symbolic sacrifice. Rabbi Yosef Ibn Caspi (Spain, early 14th century) wrote that Abraham's 'imagination' led him astray, making him believe that he had been commanded to sacrifice his son. Ibn Caspi writes "How could God command such a revolting thing?" But according to Rabbi Joseph H. Hertz (Chief Rabbi of the British Empire), child sacrifice was actually "rife among the Semitic peoples", and suggests that "in that age, it was astounding that Abraham's God should have interposed *to prevent* the sacrifice, not that He should have asked for it." Hertz interprets the *Akedah* as demonstrating to the Jews that human sacrifice is abhorrent. "Unlike the cruel heathen deities, *it was the spiritual surrender alone that God required.*" [emphasis mine]. In Jeremiah 32:35, God states that the later Israelite practice of child sacrifice to the deity Molech "had [never] entered My mind that they should do this abomination"." [419]

In fact, God abhors human sacrifice (Deut 12.30-32) – always has done, always will – which is why He stayed the knife.[420] To believe that the Akedah is about human sacrifice is to miss the whole point of God's demonstration which, by its controversial nature, was designed to get posterity's attention. Abraham has sojourned in Canaan where the locals routinely carry out such abominations, yet God's halting of Isaac's immolation shouts "This is not acceptable to Me!" The above-mentioned Jeremiah passage actually has God lamenting, **"And they built the high places of Baal [*ha-Satan*], which are in the valley of the son of Hinnom, to**

---

[419] http://en.wikipedia.org/wiki/Akedah

[420] See also Lev 18:21; 20: 2-5; 2 Kings 16:3; 17:31; 21:6; 23:10; Deut 18:10; Eze 20:31. In each case the sacrifice referred is child sacrifice not general adult sacrifice, which was rare.

cause their sons and their daughters to pass through the fire unto Molech [*ha-Satan*]; which I commanded them not, neither came it into My mind that they should do this abomination, to cause Judah to sin." (Jer 32:35)

Islam is in a similar pickle over the Akedah. Muslims are taught that it was Ishmael not Isaac who acquiesced to being sacrificed, and when God saw Abraham was prepared to go through with it, stayed his hand. Isaac was later given to Abraham and Sarah as a reward for the patriarch's obedience. Wiki concludes:

"Muslims consider that visions experienced by prophets are revelations from God, and as such it was a divine order to Abraham. The entire episode of the sacrifice is regarded as a trial of God for Abraham and his son, and both are seen as having passed the test by submitting to God and showing their awareness that God is the Owner and Giver of all that we have and cherish, including life and offspring. The submission of Abraham and his son is celebrated and commemorated by Muslims on the days of Eid al-Adha. During the festival, those who can afford, and the ones in the pilgrimage, sacrifice a ram, cow, sheep or a camel. Part of the sacrifice meat is eaten by the household and any remaining is distributed to the neighbors and the needy. The festival marks the end of the Hajj pilgrimage to Mecca.

The well-known site of Marwah (Arabic مروة) may be identified with the biblical Moriah (Hebrew מוריה) in Gn 22:2, Marwah being the mount just outside the perimeter of the Kaaba. However, it should be noted that the Hebrew Bible identifies the Temple Mount in Jerusalem as Mount Moriah, as early as the First Temple period in the book of Second Chronicles chapter 3, around 1,700 years predating Islam's account." [421]

So what is this disturbing chapter really all about? You've probably gathered by now that Genesis 22 is one huge *remez*, a veritable glory, so let's sharpen the spade, examine the story in more detail, and see what we dig up.

Naturally God, being omniscient, knows in advance what Abraham will do in such a predicament, so He hardly need put

[421] http://en.wikipedia.org/wiki/Akedah

Abraham through the experience to learn some new information about His patriarch. *God cannot learn:* it's one of the constraints on His nature. He knows full well Abraham will go through with killing Isaac since Abraham knows by now that God will have to resurrect Isaac if He is to fulfil His promise that **'in Isaac shall thy seed be called'** (Gen 21:12). So Abraham is standing on God's promise that Abraham will father a great nation. Abraham has already worked out that it's God's problem long before he gets to Mount Moriah. Notice *Abraham's faith that Isaac will be resurrected* is the major point here and referred to by Paul in Hebrews:[422]

By faith Abraham, when he was tried, offered up Isaac: and he that had received the promises offered up his only begotten son, of whom it was said, 'That in Isaac shall thy seed be called'. Accounting that God was able to raise him up, even from the dead, from whence also he received him in a <u>figure</u> [i.e. in a figurative sense – a type/model]. (Heb 11:17-19)

Let's rewind the story and press play again:

And they came to the place <u>which God had told him of</u> [i.e. God has a special place picked out – that's a hint!]**; and Abraham built an altar there and laid the wood in order, and bound Isaac his son, and laid him on the altar upon the wood. And Abraham stretched forth his hand and took the knife to slay his son.**

And the Angel of the LORD called unto him out of Heaven, and said, "Abraham, Abraham!" And he said, "Here am I." And He said, "Lay not thine hand upon the lad, neither do thou any thing unto him, for now I know that thou fearest God, seeing thou hast not withheld thy son, <u>thine only son from Me.</u>"

And Abraham <u>lifted up his eyes</u> [again!] **and looked, and behold behind him a ram caught in a thicket by his horns. And Abraham went and took the ram, and offered him up for a <u>burnt offering in the stead of his son</u>. And Abraham called the name of**

---

[422] Commentators still maintain that the writer of Hebrews is unidentified, which is nonsense and sloppy researching. Paul's authorship is covered in *Origins 4 – Tetelstai*. Paul leaves clues in the text to his authorship for those close to him, but for political reasons wishes to remain anonymous to the Jews reading the epistle so their prejudice against him personally by this time for 'betraying Judaism and following Christ' will not prevent them from learning the truths he wants to impart.

that place YHWH Yireh, as it is said to this day: 'In the mount of the LORD it shall be seen'. (Gen 22:9-14)

What shall be seen?

The story is replete with insights:

> ➤ The party consists of four men and a donkey (ass)
> ➤ God will show them specifically the mount He has in mind. i.e. not just any old hill but one with abiding significance to the LORD
> ➤ When they get to the mount Abraham instructs his two servants to stay with the donkey while he and his son head up for the offering
> ➤ Abraham makes it clear to his servants *they will both be coming down again*
> ➤ When Isaac asks where the lamb is for the burnt offering, notice Abraham's response: **"God will provide <u>Himself</u> a lamb for the burnt offering."** It's a weighty, ambiguous choice of words, especially when you consider where they are climbing to. Murray McLellan enlightens:

"Mount Moriah is a mountain ridge that runs through Jerusalem. Mount Moriah is not a single peak but an elongated ridge that commences to rise at its southern end at the junction of the Kidron and Hinnom Valleys, at the original City of David – Jerusalem (elevation approximately 600 meters, or 1,968 feet). The ridge then climbs in elevation to a maximum of 777 meters (2,549 feet) just north-east of the present Damascus Gate of the Old City."[423]

When they reach the top, Abraham and Isaac are standing at the highest point in the area, elevation 777 metres(!) which, centuries later, will become the execution ground of Golgotha, 'the Place of the Skull'. Some commentators maintain that the episode occurred on what is now the Temple Mount, yet this is not the highest point of the Moriah ridge system. If Abraham and his son are in fact standing on what will later be Golgotha, 1,900 years later God will provide Himself a sacrificial Lamb without blemish on this very spot in the form of His only Son, Yeshua. Even more

---

[423] www.soundofgrace.com/v11/n6/themount_mm_116.htm

fascinating is that *it's the pre-incarnate form of Jesus speaking as God in the first-person of the Angel of the LORD,* who calls forth to stop Abraham from slaying his son.[424] This same Jesus will become the Lamb of God whose blood will be poured out for the redemption of mankind. Notice two other features:

1) Both Isaac and Jesus bear the means of their execution up the hill
2) Both go up the hill willingly in complete agreement with their fathers

Abraham knows he is acting out prophecy, which is why he names the place **YHWH Yireh, as it is said to this day: 'In the mount of the LORD it shall be seen'**. (Gen 22:9-14) *What shall be seen?*

God's own death for the redemption of mankind. It's hard to imagine Jewish rabbis conspiring to squirrel this story away in the Holy Torah with its incredible model of Yeshua as *Mashiach*. At the Jordan, John the Baptist will proclaim Jesus **"The Lamb of God which taketh away the sin of the world!"** (FG 1:29). 1,900 years after Abraham, another Father will offer His beloved only Son on Mount Moriah in precisely the same place for the sins of mankind. Isaac bears the wood (mentioned five times – the number of 'grace'), which is man's burden (sin), to his place of sacrifice just as *ha-Mashiach* will bear the burden of our iniquities and be punished in our place for them in the ultimate sin-offering. Notice Isaac does not die, a substitute dies in his stead (the ram). This is no child sacrifice, it's a model of God's sacrifice *for each of us*. Abraham knows he is acting out prophecy for the LORD, which is why he names the place prophetically, **'In the mount of the LORD it shall be seen'**. God acts out His redemptive plan in advance with Abraham's help to show the patriarch the shape of things to come.

An interesting question: What does Abraham think is going to happen? On the face of it, being asked by the Creator of the universe to sacrifice the beloved son for whom you've waited a

---

[424] The Angel of the LORD, a pre-incarnate Jesus Christ, also confronts Moses in the Burning Bush incident (*cf.* Exo 3:13-14; FG 8:56-58). We know the Angel of the LORD is no ordinary angel because this Angel speaks as God and receives worship as the LORD (Exo 3:6); regular angels do not (Rev 19:10).

lifetime has got to unnerve and frighten you witless. Yet such is Abraham's faith at this point that he knows beyond question that God must intervene and stop the offering or He will have to resurrect Isaac from the dead. Either way, Abraham's going through with the killing and Isaac will be coming back down that hill (*cf*: Gen 22:5). Paul sees this too, and in satisfyingly ambiguous language both implies Abraham knows the Akedah is a model, and that the patriarch does in fact receive his son back from the dead figuratively when he raises him off the altar after God's intervention (Heb 11:19).

There is an even deeper *sod* interpretation. Abraham and Sarah supernaturally received Isaac as a baby out of their bodies which were incapable of childbirth due to age. Isaac is thus a miracle birth, a type of Christ. At the point when the father raises the knife over his miracle son, Abraham has placed Isaac's life beyond his own reach and into God's hands in the same way Yeshua will do on the cross in the self-same spot (Luke 23:46). In other words, Isaac is dead to Abraham at the point when God intervenes. We must die to ourselves and place our eternal destiny in God's hands to live forever. That's the way God wants it – shall we argue with Him? And there is only one Saviour. The same Yeshua, who intervened as Angel of the LORD with Abraham and Isaac, said the following words to the Sanhedrin Pharisee, Nicodemus:

"For God so loved the world that He gave His only begotten Son, that whosoever believeth in Him should not perish but have everlasting life. For God sent not His Son into the world to condemn the world, but that the world through Him might be saved. He that believeth on Him is not condemned, but he that believeth not is condemned already, because he hath not believed in the name of the only begotten Son of God." (FG 3:16-18)

Heavy stuff, certainly. Deliberately. We're trying to learn about an Entity so far removed from human comprehension in His power and infinite ability, our only recourse is blindly to follow the Infinite Mind, a process known as faith. "But that's check-your-mind-in-at-the-door religion!" No, it's how we deal with what we can't possibly understand. We're to do as we're told, the same way my six-year-old daughter (sometimes) does, when I tell her to do something for her own good she doesn't yet understand. God wants us to fear not, stand still and watch what He's going to show us next (Exo 14:13).

What does God want out of the whole affair? To scare the heck out of Abraham and Isaac? Of course not. He could have done that in Beersheba. God wants us to *get it.* The Akedah is for our benefit, less so Abraham and Isaac's. It's a prefiguring of the *Mashiach's* sacrifice to come as well as a demonstration to the whole world of the type of trust each of us must have in the God of Abraham, Isaac and Jacob if we are to be delivered from death to life *for eternity.* Man has no capacity to imagine God's realm, nor the implications of His dimensionality, much less what eternity is all about. The Akedah is a rehearsal of God's ultimate act of redemption, and the chief theme of the entire Message System has God adopting the most bizarre mechanism of putting on public show His own death on a wooden cross on a hill in Canaan. The crucifixion is the most famous, the most publicised, and most excruciating[425] execution in history, and our acceptance or rejection of God's sacrifice will be the basis by which all mankind will be judged, whether they like it or not. Some will be redeemed, most will not (Matt 7:13-14).

Predictably this does not sit well with celebrity atheists like Dr Richard Dawkins. Richard considers himself a 'bright' – one of the most enlightened men on the planet, author of *The God Delusion* and thankful escapee from the abusive shackles of a mythical God. To him the Bible is wicked nonsense which can even harm schoolchildren. He has a very different view of the Akedah:

"A modern moralist cannot help but wonder how a child could ever recover from such psychological trauma. By the standards of modern morality, this disgraceful story is an example simultaneously of child abuse, bullying in two asymmetrical power relationships, and the first recorded use of the Nuremberg defence: "I was only obeying orders". Yet the legend is one of the great, foundational myths of all three monotheistic religions."[426]

---

[425] In fact, this is where we get the word 'excruciating' from. Latin *crux* = cross.
[426] **Dawkins, Richard** *The God Delusion,* Black Swan, 2007, p.274

And on the subject of God's sacrifice 1,900 years later on the same spot:

"The idea that God could only forgive our sins by having his son tortured to death as a scapegoat is surely, from an objective point of view, a deeply unpleasant idea. If God wanted to forgive us our sins, why didn't he just forgive them? Why did he have to have his son tortured?" [427]

The apostle Paul was having similar problems with the Jews and Greeks 2,000 years ago:

"For the preaching of the cross is <u>to them that perish</u> foolishness; but <u>unto us which are saved</u> it is the power of God. For it is written, 'I will destroy the wisdom of the wise, and will bring to nothing the understanding of the prudent'.

Where is the wise? Where is the scribe? Where is the disputer of this world? Hath not God made foolish the wisdom of this world? For after that, in the wisdom of God the world by wisdom knew not God, it pleased God by the foolishness of preaching to save them that believe. For the Jews require a sign and the Greeks seek after wisdom, but we preach Christ crucified, unto the Jews a stumbling-block, and unto the Greeks foolishness, <u>but unto them which are called</u>, both Jews and Greeks, Christ the power of God and the wisdom of God. Because the foolishness of God is wiser than men; and the weakness of God is stronger than men." (1 Cor 1:18-25)

Notice Paul highlights only two types of people: those who are destined to perish, and those who are already saved (**them which are called**). i.e. some get it, most won't. Dawkins makes sweeping criticisms of God yet cannot make a blade of grass from scratch, much less describe how such transcendent intricacies come about. Instead of revealing to us that He looks like Jim Caviezel, God reveals something far more earth-shattering in His Word. His Will. What He wants us to do. He reveals His character and a love for us that is so multi-dimensional, it bathes us even in the harshest of His acts. God's reality is so far beyond our comprehension that His will demands our humility before Him to stand still and do as we're

---

[427] **Dawkins, Richard,** Revelation TV interview with Howard Conder, March 2011

told. How many people are humble before the God of Abraham, Isaac and Jacob today? Not many. But they soon will be. The Crazy Days are coming.

Chuck Missler points out two further, enthralling details of the Akedah account, which confirm the Bible as an integrated message system. Firstly, if the 'sacrifice' of Isaac is carried out at Golgotha, it's not only outside the future city walls of Jerusalem, but also north of the future Temple complex which will stand on the threshing floor of Arunah. Levitical Law will demand that **"....he shall kill it on the side of the altar <u>northward</u> before the LORD: and the priests, Aaron's sons, shall sprinkle his blood round about upon the altar."** (Lev 1:11) God will not withhold his only Son (Rom 8:32) but will deliver him up for us all at Golgotha, which stands **'on the side of the altar northward before the LORD'** in relation to the Jerusalem Temple, fulfilling Levitical Law.

Secondly, after the drama on Mount Moriah, Isaac is edited out of the text by the Holy Spirit! We have no reason to suppose he does not come tripping down the hill with Dad to join the two bored servants and ass for the ride back to Beersheba, *yet Isaac is deliberately not mentioned again until he is united with his bride, Rebekah, two chapters later.* This again plays precisely to God's prophetic model of the crucifixion. Abraham is in the role of God the Father. Isaac is in the role of the miracle Son, Yeshua, the sacrificial Lamb. And in Genesis 24, an unnamed servant (in fact, Eliezer of Damascus, Abraham's business partner, whose name means 'Comforter'!) is in the role of the Holy Spirit, who goes unnamed as He never testifies of Himself (FG 16:13), to seek a bride for Isaac – Rebekah – who is in the role of the Bride of Christ, the Church.

Let's put it together. After His sacrifice, resurrection and ascension, Yeshua is no more seen until He is united with His Bride, the Church, at the *harpazo,* 'the Rapture', the snatching away of Christ's own for the marriage supper of the Lamb. Then He returns to Israel with His Bride at the Second Coming. Notice that from the time of Isaac's 'sacrifice and resurrection' at his father's hand on Mount Moriah, Isaac is no more seen until he is united with his bride, Rebekah, at the conclusion of Genesis 24.

The Akedah finishes up:

And the angel of the LORD called unto Abraham out of Heaven the second time, and said, "By myself have I sworn, saith the LORD, for because thou hast done this thing, and hast not withheld thy son, <u>thine only son</u> [once again, notice the emphasis. No Ishmael], **that in blessing I will bless thee, and in multiplying I will multiply thy seed as the stars of Heaven, and as the sand which is upon the sea shore; and thy seed shall possess the gate of his enemies. And in thy seed shall all the nations of the Earth be blessed** [i.e. have the chance of redemption], **because thou hast obeyed My voice."**

So Abraham returned unto his young men [no Isaac mentioned!]**, and they rose up and went together to Beersheba; and Abraham dwelt at Beersheba.** (Gen 22:15-19)

One princess lost, another gained

The beautiful Sarah dies at 127 years of age. Abraham is heartbroken. This timeless beauty is the first and only woman in the Hebrew scriptures whose age and death are recorded as a mark of respect. His princess gone, Abraham bargains for the cave of Machpelah at Hebron in true Bedouin fashion, eventually purchasing it from Ephron the Hittite along with an adjoining field. This is the only land Abraham will ever own. The Cave of the Patriarchs, today buried under the Ibrahimi Mosque, eventually becomes the resting place for Abraham, Isaac, Jacob and their three senior wives, Sarah, Rebekah and Leah, considered the patriarchs and matriarchs of the Hebrew race.

No further conversations are recorded between God and Abraham after the Akedah, which of course does not mean there weren't any. In Genesis 24, three years after Sarah's death,[428] Abraham takes it upon himself to arrange a bride for Isaac. Notice that Isaac is still edited out of the action though he's obviously still with his father at Beersheba. Now Abraham summons his most

---

[428] *cf.* Gen 17:17; 21:5; 25:20

senior servant, more than likely Eliezer of Damascus, his business partner, who governs the patriarch's affairs (*cf.* Gen 15:2; 24:2,10). Yet notice that this servant *goes deliberately unnamed throughout the entire narrative*, which turns out to be the longest chapter in the book of Genesis!

And Abraham said unto his eldest servant of his house, that ruled over all that he had, "Put, I pray thee, thy hand under my thigh. And I will make thee swear by the LORD, the God of Heaven, and the God of the Earth, <u>that thou shalt not take a wife unto my son of the daughters of the Canaanites</u>, among whom I dwell. But thou shalt go unto my country, and to my kindred, and take a wife unto my son Isaac."

And the servant said unto him, "Peradventure the woman will not be willing to follow me unto this land, must I needs bring thy son again unto the land from whence thou camest?"

And Abraham said unto him, "Beware that thou bring not my son thither again. The LORD God of Heaven, which took me from my father's house, and from the land of my kindred, and which spake unto me, and that sware unto me, saying, 'Unto thy seed will I give this land'; He shall send His angel before thee, and thou shalt take a wife unto my son from thence. And if the woman will not be willing to follow thee, then thou shalt be clear from this my oath: only bring not my son thither again."

And the servant put his hand under the thigh of Abraham his master and sware to him concerning that matter. (Gen 24:2-9)

Here we see Abraham swearing Eliezer into solemn agreement prior to the latter departing for Haran in Mesopotamia (*lit.* 'the land between the rivers') to seek a bride for Isaac among his kin. Notice Abraham's express instructions not to have Isaac a) leave Abraham and b) marry a Canaanite. The bloodline is to remain as pure as possible, with the selection made among Abraham's kin to avoid any chance of Nephilic pollution. Note also that neither Abraham nor Isaac go on the mission. Abraham is going to trust the LORD to make the selection.

Eliezer by this time is an old man (Gen 24:2) but totally devoted to Abraham, whom he calls 'my master' nineteen times in the ensuing narrative. He stoically puts together a train of ten camels and doubtless a sizeable armed escort from among

Abraham's hearthmen to protect the valuables accompanying him. It's a 450-mile journey to the region of Haran, a long way for an old man.

Two weeks later, the caravan arrives at the palmed gates of the Syrian city of Nahor (Aram Naharaim) near Haran.[429] Eliezer does not enter.

And he made his camels to kneel down without the city by a well of water at the time of the evening, even the time that women go out to draw water.

And he said, "O LORD God of my master Abraham, I pray Thee, send me good speed this day, and shew kindness unto my master Abraham. Behold, I stand here by the well of water, and the daughters of the men of the city come out to draw water. And let it come to pass that the damsel to whom I shall say, 'Let down thy pitcher, I pray thee, that I may drink'; and she shall say, 'Drink, and I will give thy camels drink also': let the same be she that Thou hast appointed for Thy servant Isaac; and thereby shall I know that Thou hast shewed kindness unto my master." (Gen 24:11-14)

Eliezer is putting out what comes to be known as 'a fleece'. In other words, "If someone says or does something specific, I will know your hand is in the matter, LORD." It's not advisable to test God in this fashion (Deut 6:16), though we'll see Gideon employing the technique in Judges 6:38-40 (*Origins 3 – The Predicament of Man*) to furnish proof that God is behind him in a difficult decision. Gideon has a weak faith and has to test God twice! The lesson for believers these days is that while the scriptures are given for our instruction and benefit so we can learn about such events, *what happens in the Bible is not necessarily what we should do.* i.e. if your wife fails to become pregnant, it's really not OK for you to 'go in unto' the hired help these days. Post-Pentecost, believers have both God's Word and His Spirit to guide us in making difficult decisions, and this is what faith is all about. And would we believe a supernatural sign even if one were given? (Luke 16:29-31) What about 'Doubting' Thomas? (FG 20:29)? Yeshua warns twice against

---

[429] Note the influence of Abraham's kin in the region. Nahor and Haran were the names of Abraham's brothers. Now we have cities named after them.

seeking after 'signs' in Matt 12:39 and 16:4. The Pharisees asked for a sign that Yeshua was the Messiah (Matt 12:38) immediately after witnessing Jesus performing miracles! In the end, a hard heart will reject even the greatest sign of all – Yeshua's Resurrection and the promise of forgiveness and our own resurrection to eternal life.

But Eliezer feels so led by the Spirit, having witnessed God's blessings on his master for decades. Accordingly, even *before* he's finished entreating God's favour(!), a gorgeous young girl comes out of the city with a pitcher on her shoulder to draw water. After she fills the container, Eliezer makes his approach:

"Please let me drink a little water from your pitcher."

Girl: "Drink, my lord."

As she lowers her pitcher to provide for the old man, Eliezer and his entourage doubtless make a great impression on the girl. Everyone looks rich and very well kiltered. There are ten camels laden with stuff. A contingent of Abraham's armed guard look on with interest at the beauty before them. The girl recognises that she is dealing with someone of singular importance.

Girl: "I will draw water for your camels also, until they have finished drinking."

The appearance of camels in these early texts cause some scholars like T E Peet a migraine, but they need not. Peet maintains that the beasts were not domesticated until several centuries after the patriarchal period, which is nonsense. Camels were as much a part of the post-Flood landscape as the other beasts which disembarked the Ark, and would have been domesticated quickly for their unique uses. Giant pre-Flood camels have been unearthed:

GIANT CAMEL FOSSILS FOUND IN SYRIA

"Archaeologists have discovered the 100,000-year-old fossilised remains of a previously unknown giant camel species in Syria: The bones of the dromedary were unearthed by a Swiss-Syrian team of researchers near the village of El Kowm in the central part of the country. The animal is thought to have been double the size of a modern-day camel…. Professor Le Tensorer, who has been excavating at the desert site in Kowm since 1999, said the first large bones were found some years ago but were only confirmed as belonging to a camel after more bones from several parts of the same animal were recently discovered. Between 2005 and 2006, more than 40 bone fragments of giant camels were found by the team." [430]

BibleGateway records:

"Critics have set aside the statement that Abraham had camels in Egypt as an error. But archaeological evidence, including some twenty objects ranging from the seventh century BC. to the period before 3000 BC, proves the authenticity of the Bible record concerning Abraham. It includes not only statuettes, plaques, rock carvings, and drawings representing camels, but also "camel bones, a camel skull, and a camel hair rope" (J. P. Free, Archaeology and Bible History). [431]

There is also the small matter of camels playing a central part in the narrative at hand. Modern, smaller camels drink huge amounts of water to store for desert treks, and can tank up on more than 95 litres (25 US gallons) of water in 10 minutes to rapidly relieve dehydrated tissues. [432] Watering ten of the larger, ancient kind to satiety is no trivial chore, and that's the whole point of the story. No camels, no story, Mr Peet! Eliezer stands patiently by while the girl performs her lengthy task with efficiency. Finally, when the camels have slurped and belched their last, Eliezer unstraps his saddlebags.

And it came to pass, as the camels had done drinking, that the man took a golden earring of half a shekel weight, and two bracelets for her hands of ten shekels weight of gold, and said, "Whose daughter art thou? Tell me, I pray thee. Is there room in thy father's house for us to lodge in?"

And she said unto him, "I am the daughter of Bethuel, the son of Milcah, which she bare unto Nahor." She said moreover unto him, "We have both straw and provender enough, and room to lodge in."

And the man bowed down his head and worshipped the LORD. (Gen 24:22-26)

---

[430] http://news.bbc.co.uk/1/hi/sci/tech/6035113.stm
[431] www.biblegateway.com/passage/?search=Genesis+12-15&version=AMP, notes on Gen 12:16
[432] *Encyclopaedia Britannica*, (fifteenth edition), 2:764, 1992

And so we meet Rebekah, granddaughter to Abraham's brother, Nahor, who made the trek with the family all those years ago from Ur of the Chaldees to Haran. Jack Heyford writes:

"Rebekah's name refers to 'tying or binding up', implying that her beauty was so great, it could literally captivate or fascinate men. She is introduced as a diligently industrious and beautifully sensitive girl. Her willingness to serve Eliezer and her readiness to draw water for all ten of the thirsty camels dramatize this. A lesson in the way God provides surprising rewards for servant-spirited souls is seen in what happened to Rebekah. Little did she know those camels were carrying untold gifts for her and her family." [433]

Rebekah runs home to tell her mother's household to prepare. Rebekah's brother is a sharp lad called Laban. When he hears what happened at the well, and when he personally examines the expensive nose ring and bracelets now adorning his sister's person, he's out of the gates to the man by the well in a flash. Laban, we'll discover later, has an eye for the loot. Also, as the prospective bride's brother, Laban's role will be to negotiate the contract, a role to which he will be eminently suited.

And he said, "Come in, thou blessed of the LORD. Wherefore standest thou without? For I have prepared the house and room for the camels."

And the man [still the unnamed Eliezer] **came into the house and he ungirded his camels, and gave straw and provender for the camels, and water to wash his feet, and the men's feet that were with him. And there was set meat before him to eat: but he said, "I will not eat until I have told mine errand."**

And [Laban] said, "Speak on."

And he said, "I am Abraham's servant. And the LORD hath blessed my master greatly, and he is become great. And He hath given him flocks and herds and silver and gold and menservants and maidservants and camels and asses. And Sarah, my master's wife, bare a son to my master when she was old, and unto him hath he given all that he hath. And my master made me swear, saying, 'Thou shalt not take a wife to my son of the daughters of

---

[433] Heyford, Jack, *The Spirit-Filled Bible*, op. cit., p.39

the Canaanites, in whose land I dwell, but thou shalt go unto my father's house, and to my kindred, and take a wife unto my son." (Gen 24:31-38)

BibleGateway writes:

"The characteristics of a model servant of God are pictured here: 1. He is dependable and trustworthy (Gen. 24:2); 2. He is a praying person (Gen. 24:12); 3. He is so in earnest that he refuses to eat before attending to his Master's business (Gen. 24:33); 4. He never speaks his own name but is always speaking about his Master (Gen. 24:35ff.); 5. He gives God all the glory (Gen. 24:48)." [434]

After days of fellowship between Eliezer and Rebekah's family, during which Abraham's servant blesses the household with sumptuous gifts, the time comes to depart. Rebekah's family asks her honestly: "Will you go with this man?"

And she answers, "I will go."

And they sent away Rebekah their sister, and her nurse, and Abraham's servant, and his men. And they blessed Rebekah and said unto her, "Thou art our sister, be thou the mother of thousands of millions, and let thy seed possess the gate of those which hate them."

And Rebekah arose, and her damsels, and they rode upon the camels and followed the man. And the servant took Rebekah and went his way.

And Isaac came from the way of the well Lahairoi [lit.** 'who liveth and seeth me' - Isaac's now back in the narrative!], for he dwelt in the south country [Beersheba in the 'Negev' (**lit.** south]. And Isaac went out to meditate in the field at the eventide. And <u>he lifted up his eyes</u> and saw, and, behold, the camels were coming. And Rebekah <u>lifted up her eyes</u>, and when she saw Isaac, she lighted off the camel.**

For she had said unto the servant, "What man is this that walketh in the field to meet us?"

And the servant had said, "It is my master."

Therefore she took a veil and covered herself.

And the [unnamed] servant told Isaac all things that he had done. And Isaac brought her into his mother Sarah's tent and took Rebekah, and she became his wife, and he loved her. And Isaac was comforted after his mother's death. (Gen 24:59-67)

BibleGateway again:

"This chapter is highly illustrative of God the Father, Who sends forth His Holy Spirit to win the consent of the individual soul to become the bride of His Son. Keep these resemblances constantly in mind as you read and see how the story unfolds. First meet the Father and note His concern about His Son's bride. Then get acquainted with the Holy Spirit's great, selfless heart, Whose one purpose is to win the girl for His Master's Son. Then meet the Son and note His tenderness as He claims His bride. The longest chapter in Genesis is devoted to this important story."[435]

<u>Which holds eternal implications for each of us.</u>

The romance of redemption

The entire story of scripture is about God's redemption of the Creation and those He has chosen from before the foundation of the world to rule with Him for eternity. Another foundational truth is that God has chosen to model our salvation on the classic Jewish wedding. Many believers unfamiliar with what this entails will recognise a surprising confluence with what they have already learned from New Testament soteriology (study of salvation). Let's run through the procedure.

1) Choose the spouse

Believers have been chosen by Christ as His bride from the foundation of the world.[436] Ancient Jewish marriages were almost always arranged by the parents, not only to allow 'the head to prevail over the heart' in terms of dispassionate choice, but also to secure purity of bloodline and ethnic cohesion.

---

[435] www.biblegateway.com, Gen 24:4 notes

[436] Eph 1:4-5; FG 6:44; 6:64-65; 2 Tim 2:19; 2 Thess 2:13; Rom 1:7; Isa 49:1,5; Jer 1:5; Gal 1:15; Acts 13:48

The process starts with the father of the groom selecting the bride. The choice was never left to the groom or bride! In the old days the father sent his favoured servant (the unnamed servant who never testifies of Himself – the Holy Spirit (FG 16:13) – Eliezer, 'the Comforter') to seek out a bride for his son, usually someone his son had never met. The servant would take the highest offer his master could afford, for instance, ten pieces of silver or gold, to 'purchase' the bride (*cf.* Luke 15:8).

If the bride's father was impressed and consented, the prospective bride would be asked if she was willing, which she mostly was since spinsters or childless wives were pitied and looked down upon, and marriage represented the chance to start early for children, and be blessed with a husband (provider) and a home of your own.

2) The betrothal (*erusin, kiddushin*)

Once the groom's father is satisfied as to choice of bride, the future bridegroom leaves his house to meet his prospective bride for the first time and the betrothal period begins. Compare this with Christ leaving Heaven to come to Earth the first time to meet His prospective bride, the Church (Eph 5:25-27)

A pledge (*tenaim*) is made by the groom with an object of value, such as a ring or money, and the bride price is paid (*mohar*). In Christ's case, the purchase price for His bride (the Church believer) is the shedding of His blood on the cross (1 Cor. 6:19-20; 1 Peter 1:18-19). The money is received by the bride's father, though part of the *mohar* is retained by the bride, who is extremely careful not to lose the coins since they will be worn in her bridal headdress.

The *ketubah* contract is then drawn up, signed by both parties, after which the bridegroom declares in full hearing of witnesses, "It is finished!" i.e. "Paid in full!" At this point, believers are betrothed to Yeshua *ha-Mashiach*, their salvation assured by the bride-price paid on the cross (Hos 2:19; 2 Co 11:2). *Notice the bride has no part to play in the payment of the bride price, the Father pays it.*

The first wedding cup is drunk, the *kiddushin* ('holy', 'sanctified'), the same communion cup drunk by Yeshua at the Last

Supper (Luke 22:20; 1 Cor 11:25). The groom gives a speech of promise, wherein he declares: "I have to go to prepare the *chuppah* (bridal chamber), a place for you at my father's house." (*cf.* FG 14:2-3; Matt. 24:36). While it took took six days for Him to accomplish the Creation, Yeshua has been preparing our *chuppah* for almost 2,000 years!

3) Preparing the *chuppah*

The bride is set apart and sanctified during the betrothal period. *The bride is the Father's gift to the Son.* John MacArthur writes:

"This is a staggering reality. In the mystery of the Trinity we see that there is an ineffable and eternal love between the Members of the Trinity. Jesus refers to it in His high-priestly prayer: "Father, I desire that they also, whom You have given Me, be with Me where I am, so that they may see My glory which You have given Me, *for You loved Me before the foundation of the world"* [FG 17:24, emphasis added].

"That love must find an expression. True love always seeks ways to give. And in a demonstration of His perfect love for His Son, the Father made a pledge to the Son. And what was that pledge? He promised the Son a redeemed people – justified, sanctified and glorified. He promised to bring the redeemed ones to glory, that they might dwell in the very place where Father and Son have dwelt since before time began – the very realm of God. And this collective body of called-out ones – a people for His name (Acts 15:14) from every tribe and people and tongue and nation (Rev. 13:7) – would form a living temple for the Holy Spirit (Eph. 2:21-22), becoming the very dwelling-place of God.

"That is the eternal promise the Father made to the Son. Why? As an expression of His love. The redeemed of humanity, then, are a gift from Father to Son." [437]

Christ's believers are set apart and must sanctify themselves in preparation for His Coming (Eph 5:25-27; 1 Cor 1:2; 6:11; Heb 10:10; 13:12). Will we be pure in thought, word and deed when the Bridegroom comes, or marred by the stains of this world? The

---

[437] http://www.gty.org/resources/articles/A352/Why-I-Love-the-Church-Part-3

bride wears a veil so others know she is consecrated. Chuck Missler writes:

"After this ceremony, the bride remained in her father's home to prepare for the day her groom would come back for her, marry her, and take her to his house or some special room he had built [*chuppah*]. Cohabitation was forbidden at this time and the bride had to remain a virgin, using this time to prepare for her marriage. In other words, the bride must make herself ready. This preparation meant making her own wedding gown, getting ready for her new role, transferring her allegiance from her father to her new husband... learning to love him, and setting her mind on how to please him." [438]

Malcolm Wood writes:

"During this period of separation, both bride and groom are busy. The bride gathers her wardrobe and prepares for her future in a new home with her bridegroom. She is always seen veiled to show she is set apart, consecrated, bought with a price. The groom, on the other hand needs to prepare the living accommodation for his bride in or near his father's house. This may require building and will certainly involve stocking the place for the seven-day honeymoon. At every stage of this preparation, the groom's father has to give his approval, and thus he becomes the one who really determines the date of the wedding." [439]

The length of the bridegroom's absence is deliberately indeterminate. He can come to get her at any time, day or night, but only after the bridegroom's father has determined adequate provision has been made for the bride. Notice the dynamic of <u>imminence</u> – very important. There is an expectation on the bride's part to be ready *at all times* to receive him, though the period could be one to two years. The bridegroom's witness, or 'best man', or 'friend of the bridegroom' (Holy Spirit) ensures the bride is kept watchful of the bridegroom's return during the sometimes lengthy betrothal period. Javier Valdivieso writes that the brief period

[438] **Missler, Chuck** *The Kingdom, Power and Glory,* King's High Way Ministries, Coeur d'Alene, ID, 2007, p.121
[439] http://projectissachar.com/wiki/romance-redemption

enjoyed by the groom and bride together at the betrothal before his departure is filled with joy and promises for the future, but also angst at what that future may bring:

"This tradition is kept even in our day. The groom went back to his father's house to build an addition to the existing dwelling, where he would receive his wife in about one or two years. In modern Israel you can see many additions that have been made for this purpose. The bride would then say, "Do not go," and the groom would respond, "It is better for you that I go but I will come back." "When?" she asked. And the groom would respond, "I do not know, nor the servant, only my father knows the day"." [440]

4) The wedding (*nissuin, chuppah, huppah,* 'the lifting away')

The bridegroom can, and often does show up at midnight for the nuptials! The bride has to have her lamp filled with oil and ready, and is usually attended by other virgins with their lamps also anticipating the bridegroom's return. The oil is symbolic of the Holy Spirit, the lamp or vessel represents the believer, so the picture is that God's Spirit will shine forth God's light from the human vessel if all goes well.

In ancient times the bridegroom comes as a thief in the night to steal his bride away to the place he has prepared for her (*cf.* 1 Thess 5:1-11). The first the bride knows of it is when she hears a shout, "The bridegroom has come!" and the blast of the *shofar*. In like manner, Yeshua has promised to return for His bride at any hour to take her to His Father's house. The *harpazo* or 'Rapture' (the snatching up of the bride like a thief in the night) will occur at any time, in the twinkling of an eye, accompanied by a shout, the voice of an archangel and the trumpet of God (1 Cor 15:51-52; 1 Thess 4:16-17).

The bride's virgin attendants fire up their lamps to light the way as the bride's father symbolically turns his head away and the beloved 'thief in the night' snatches up his daughter and steals her away to the place prepared for her.

---

[440] http://www.tasc-creationscience.org/content/ancient-jewish-wedding-missing-link-christianity-0#footnote1_wc1o3ei

The procession beats a path to the father of the bridegroom's house, lamps lighting the way, where the wedding ceremony takes place. The nuptials themselves are attended only by a few invited guests and the ceremony conducted under a canopy (*chuppah*), comprising four poles bearing a stretched sheet/cloth/prayer shawl over the heads of the participants, symbolising their new home. The bride is surrounded by her virgins, usually ten in number. After the ceremony makes them man and wife, the bride and groom enter the *chuppah* physically to consummate the marriage, after which the groom emerges to notify the best man that it is done. Seven days of celebration and great rejoicing follow, culminating in the sumptuous marriage feast, during which the second marriage cup is drunk (Yeshua may again drink of the fruit of the vine - Luke 22:17-18, 29-30; Rev. 19:7-8). The marriage feast is often held at a different location and this time many guests are invited.

There is a huge amount one could get into here concerning Israel's destiny as distinct from the Church's, the Rapture, the Second Coming, the rule of the Antichrist and False Prophet, Daniel's Seventieth Week, the Great Tribulation and so on. How about the parable of the wise and foolish virgins taught by Yeshua:

"Then shall the Kingdom of Heaven be likened unto ten virgins, which took their lamps and went forth to meet the bridegroom. And five of them were wise and five were foolish. They that were foolish took their lamps and took no oil with them, but the wise took oil in their vessels with their lamps.

While the bridegroom tarried, they all slumbered and slept. And at midnight there was a cry made, "Behold, the bridegroom cometh! Go ye out to meet him!"

Then all those virgins arose and trimmed their lamps. And the foolish said unto the wise, "Give us of your oil, for our lamps are gone out."

But the wise answered, saying, "Not so, lest there be not enough for us and you. But go ye rather to them that sell and buy for yourselves."

And while they went to buy, the bridegroom came; and they that were ready went in with him to the marriage, and the door was shut.

Afterward came also the other virgins, saying, "LORD, LORD, open to us."

But he answered and said, "Verily I say unto you, I know you not."

Watch therefore, for ye know neither the day nor the hour wherein the Son of man cometh." (Matt 25:1-13)

A disturbing parable with eternal implications.

The date of the bridegroom's return is only known by the bridegroom's father! (Mark 13:32)

We'll deal with all this later on, but let's set the style of the Jewish wedding in our minds, for it crops up from time to time in remarkable places. For now, join me in rejoicing for Isaac and his new bride, Rebekah, and indulge me with the opportunity to build the evidence over the *Origins* series to present the truly extraordinary picture that runs as a theme throughout the entire Message System, summarised by Yeshua during His ministry, which has overriding significance for us all. We should perhaps with sober meditation note the inclusion of the doctrine of imminence in the matter of the Jewish Wedding, namely, that on planet Earth the next item on God's agenda is for the Father of the Bridegroom to tell His Son to fetch His bride as soon as the fullness of the Gentiles has come in (Rom 11:25). This implies that there is a set number of believers, known only to the Father. Which is a call for all to get serious. For the bride to be prepared.

Isaac inherits

The scriptures mention that Abraham marries a concubine named Keturah (Gen 25:1-6; 1 Chron 1:32), with whom he has six sons. In view of Abraham's vitality, some scholars place this union prior to Sarah's death, which is possible. The six sons are mostly identified with the Arab/Bedouin peoples, though no 'Arab' of today can trace his heritage back to either Ishmael or Keturah since, unlike Isaac's Messianic lineage, there was no commandment to keep the bloodlines pure. Abraham wisely pays these sons off and sends them to the East away from Isaac, his heir, to prevent succession squabbles after his death.

Not much is mentioned about Isaac's character. He comes across as gentle, quiet, sensible and contemplative (Gen 24:63), no firebrand like his descendants to follow, or a trailblazer like his Dad, but there is one incident we'll examine, in which we learn something unusual about him. Though now an extremely wealthy man, Isaac realises that Rebekah is barren. He pleads with the LORD, and Rebekah finally conceives, but the pregnancy is not an easy one. Distressed at the struggles within her, Rebekah enquires of the LORD: "If all is well, why am I like this?"

And the LORD said unto her, "Two nations are in thy womb, and two manner of people shall be separated from thy bowels. And the one people shall be stronger than the other people, and the elder shall serve the younger [note this prophecy from the mouth of God Himself]**."**

And when her days to be delivered were fulfilled, behold, there were twins in her womb. And the first came out red, all over like an hairy garment; and they called his name Esau.

And after that came his brother out, and his hand took hold on Esau's heel; and his name was called Jacob: and Isaac was threescore years old when she bare them.

And the boys grew, and Esau was a cunning hunter, a man of the field; and Jacob was a plain man, dwelling in tents.

And Isaac loved Esau, because he did eat of his venison, but Rebekah loved Jacob. (Gen 25:23-28)

From the text we gather that:

> ➢ Abraham is 160 when the troublesome twins are born. He obviously comes to know them well and eventually dies when the boys are 15 [441]
>
> ➢ The two boys are very different in both appearance and temperament
>
> ➢ They fight for supremacy even in the womb!
>
> ➢ Once again, God ordains that the elder will serve the younger
>
> ➢ Esau comes out first, characterised by red hair and a ruddy complexion. He is named Esau עֵשָׂו which means

---

[441] Abraham is 100 years old when he fathers Isaac. Isaac is 60 when the twins are born. Abraham dies aged 175.

'hairy', 'rough'. He will be a straightforward, worldly man of the outdoors, a hunter and his father's favourite

➤ Jacob, by contrast, is Ya'akov יַעֲקֹב ('may God protect'). But the name also sounds like *aqeb* ('heel') and *aqab* ('watch from behind', 'overtake'), so the name connotes 'heel-catcher', 'sly', 'conniving' and 'deceiving', all epithets that will well apply to this extraordinary character. Jacob is a dweller in tents and his mother's favourite

➤ Parental favouritism becomes a major problem for this family and countless generations to follow. Two nations will indeed emerge from Rebekah's travail. Esau fathers the Edomites, identified by some prophecy scholars as closest to the modern-day Palestinians,[442] who will become the implacable enemy of Israel, the nation fathered by Jacob

Then Abraham dies. Upon his death, the patriarch leaves all that he owns to Isaac (Gen 25:5).

And these are the days of the years of Abraham's life which he lived, an hundred threescore and fifteen years [i.e. 175 years]. **Then Abraham gave up the ghost and died in a good old age, an old man and full of years, and was gathered to his people.**

And his sons Isaac and Ishmael buried him in the cave of Machpelah, in the field of Ephron the son of Zohar the Hittite, which is before Mamre; the field which Abraham purchased of the sons of Heth; there was Abraham buried, and Sarah his wife.

And it came to pass after the death of Abraham, that God blessed his son Isaac; and Isaac dwelt by the well Lahairoi. (Gen 25:7-11)

A troublesome stew

This is followed soon after by the famous confrontation between Esau and Jacob over the birthright:

And Jacob cooked a stew: and Esau came from the field and was faint. And Esau said to Jacob, "Feed me, I pray thee, with

---

[442] Eze 36:5; Oba 15-21; www.cuttingedge.org/News/n2095.cfm

that same red pottage, for I am faint." Therefore was his name called Edom.

And Jacob said, "Sell me this day thy birthright."

And Esau said, "Behold, I am at the point to die. What profit shall this birthright do to me?"

And Jacob said, "Swear to me this day." And [Esau] sware unto him, and he sold his birthright unto Jacob. Then Jacob gave Esau bread and pottage of lentils; and he did eat and drink, and rose up, and went his way. Thus Esau despised his birthright. (Gen 25:29-34)

Five verses with which we are all familiar. Some insights:

> The eldest son in this culture is entitled to a double portion of the inheritance and headship of the family (Deut 21:17). By despising this, Esau is scorning the covenant God made with his father and his descendants

> Jack Heyford writes: *"According to Hurrian custom (the area around Haran), a man could sell his birthright to his brother.... Jacob is obviously ruthless, but the focal point is Esau's lust for the present and tangible at any cost (Gen 25:34). The NT calls him a 'profane person' (Heb 12:16)."* [443]

> Esau's casual disrespect for God and his family's heritage will also be seen in his taking of pagan Canaanite wives to spite his father (Gen 26:34; 28:8-9)

> This is the start of the fulfilment of God's prophecy that the elder would serve the younger (Gen 25:23)

A famine comes upon the land and Isaac is compelled to consider a trip to Egypt to procure food as his father Abraham had done. God persuades Isaac not to 'go down to Egypt' with its attendant problems and reiterates His covenant:

"Go not down into Egypt; dwell in the land which I shall tell thee of. Sojourn in this land, and I will be with thee, and will bless thee; for unto thee, and unto thy seed, I will give all these countries, and I will perform the oath which I sware unto Abraham thy father. And I will make thy seed to multiply as the stars of Heaven, and will give unto thy seed all these countries; and in thy seed shall all the nations of the earth be blessed,

---

[443] Heyford, Jack, *The Spirit-Filled Bible,* op. cit., p.42

because Abraham obeyed My voice and kept My charge, My commandments, My statutes and My laws. (Gen 26:2-5)

So Isaac goes down to Gerar on the border of Philistia and Egypt. Due to the interest Rebekah's beauty provokes among the heathen, Isaac is forced to take a leaf out of Dad's book and pass Rebekah off as his sister. A similar situation is brought about when the King of the Philistines known as 'Abimelech' (a title, not a name) looks out of a window and espies Isaac and Rebekah caressing each other in a manner inappropriate between brother and sister.[444]

And Abimelech called Isaac and said, "Behold, of a surety she is thy wife. And how saidst thou, 'She is my sister?'"

And Isaac said unto him, "Because I said, 'Lest I die for her'."

And Abimelech said, "What is this thou hast done unto us? One of the people might lightly have lain with thy wife, and thou shouldest have brought guiltiness upon us."

And Abimelech charged all his people, saying, "He that toucheth this man or his wife shall surely be put to death." (Gen 26:9-11)

We now know from the Nuzi tablets (Mesopotamia) that a husband could legally elevate a favoured wife to the status of sisterhood as a mark of respect and additional protection. *Bible Archaeology* reports:

"Excavations were carried out at Nuzi by American teams from 1925 to 1933. The major find was more than 5,000 family and administrative archives spanning six generations, ca. 1450-1350 BC. They deal with the social, economic, religious and legal institutions of the Hurrians [around Haran].

"The tablets tell of practices similar to those in Genesis such as adoption for childless couples (Gen 15:2) children by proxy (Gen 16; 21:1), inheritance rights (Gen 25:29), marriage arrangements (Gen 28) and levirate marriage (Gen 38; Dt 25:5). They also demonstrate the significance of the deathbed blessing (Gn 27;48) and household gods

---

[444] This is the same verb used to describe what Ishmael was doing to three-year-old Isaac at a weaning feast held in the latter's honour (Gen 21:8-11). The Hebrew root is מצחק, *tsachaq*, (Strongs H6711): laugh, play, mock, make sport, caress, fondle

413

(Gen 31:14-30). Some Nuzi tablets, called 'tablets of sistership', reveal agreements in which a man adopted a woman as a sister. In the society of the Hurrians, a wife enjoyed both greater protection and a superior position when she also had the legal status of a sister. In such a case, two separate documents were drawn up, one for marriage and the other for sistership. This may explain why both Abraham (Gn 12:10; 20:1) and Isaac (Gn 26:7) said their wives were their sisters. It is possible that they had previously adopted them to give them higher status, in accordance with the custom of the day." [445]

It's also interesting that in a pagan Canaanite culture renowned for performing the most appalling acts in the name of religion (not least sexual rituals and child sacrifice), adultery should hold such terror and be punishable by burning (*cf.* Gen 38:24; Lev 21:9; Judg 15:6).

Abimelech treads cautiously because, like his eponymous predecessor with Abraham, he sees that the Creator is with the Hebrew (Gen 26:28). Isaac has become wealthy and powerful due to the LORD's blessing on his crops (Gen 26:12-14). Isaac's men have also progressively taken control of the region's water supplies by repairing the wells in the Negev originally built by Abraham. The Philistines are envious of, and detest Hebrew control of these water sources, and have been filling them in with dirt. As fast as they fill them in, Isaac's men dig them out and effect repairs. Abimelech decides the most prudent course is to make peace with Isaac to avoid further trouble (Gen 26:28-31). Isaac settles his family in the town of the seven wells, which he names Beersheba ('well of the oath', 'seven wells' - Gen 26:33). This will be Isaac's base of operations until his death.

The conspiracy against God
And then we come to one of the most famous stories about Jacob; well known but much misunderstood.

---

[445] www.biblearchaeology.org/post/2006/02/27/Great-Discoveries-in-Biblical-Archaeology-The-Nuzi-Tablets.aspx

And it came to pass that when Isaac was old and his eyes were dim, so that he could not see, he called Esau his eldest son, and said unto him, "My son."

And [Esau] said unto him, "Behold, here am I."

And [Isaac] said, "Behold now, I am old, I know not the day of my death. Now therefore take, I pray thee, thy weapons, thy quiver and thy bow, and go out to the field, and take me some venison, and make me savoury meat such as I love, and bring it to me that I may eat, that my soul may bless thee before I die." (Gen 27:1-4)

Four seemingly innocuous verses which carry a whole world of hurt. Firstly, this is not some casual goodwill gesture Isaac is bestowing upon his eldest. Jack Heyford explains the significance of what Isaac intends carrying out - the patriarchal blessing:

"To bless meant to transfer from father to eldest son the family's material property, aspirations and spiritual promises. Modelled after God's interaction with His people, the patriarchal concept of the blessing later becomes foundational in the transmission of emotional and spiritual vitality from generation to generation." [446]

The patriarchal blessing is in effect the execution of an oral will, conferring upon *the chosen son* the spiritual headship of the family, through whom God's blessings will flow, and a double portion of the inheritance. Usually the firstborn receives this, but we've already detected a pattern emerging; that God sometimes passes over the eldest in favour of the younger, especially when the elder is the son of the flesh and not the spirit.[447] In Isaac's case, it's all the more remarkable that the patriarch would consider defying God's promise that Jacob would inherit (Gen 25:23), and attempt to confer the blessing on his profane eldest (Heb 12:16).

Some surmise that Isaac is unaware that Esau sold his birthright years before to Jacob in the red pottage incident, yet not only do the scriptures not state this, Esau himself gives the game

---

[446] Heyford, Jack, *Spirit-Filled Bible*, op. cit., p.44

[447] Abel over Cain; Shem over Japheth; Isaac over Ishmael; now Jacob over Esau. Later Ephraim over Manasseh; Moses over Aaron, and David over all his elder brothers.

away in Gen 27:36, making it clear that Isaac already knows. How likely is it, in any case, that word of such a significant incident would *not* have done the rounds in an intimate household, especially this one?

The more you study this whole saga, the more deeply troubled and unhappy Isaac's household appears. For starters, the family is riven with parental favouritism: Isaac for Esau, Rebekah for Jacob. As for the twins, they trust each other about as far as they can throw a camel. Esau – emotional, dramatic, pugnacious (Gen 25:30,32; 27:34,38,41) – has already demonstrated to his father his ineligibility to inherit. He has married two pagan Canaanite women by this time and will add another to his household further to spite his parents.[448] Yet Isaac goes ahead with the patriarchal blessing for Esau anyway, *and in private.* Bob Deffinbaugh writes:

"Normally the blessing would have been given before the entire family because it was, in reality, an oral will which legally determined the disposition of all that the father possessed. Distribution of family wealth and headship would best be carried out in the presence of all who were concerned. Thus we later find Jacob giving his blessing in the presence of all his sons (Genesis 49)....

"From excavations at Nuzu in central Mesopotamia we learn that the oral blessing or will had legal validity and would stand up even in the courts. Nuzu tablet P56 mentions a lawsuit between three brothers, in which two of them contested the right of a third to marry a certain Zululishtar. The young man won his case by arguing that this marriage was provided for in his father's deathbed blessing." [449]

So we're left with the unsavoury conclusion that Isaac is pressing ahead with Esau's investiture in defiance of God, his wife and younger son, securing the conspiracy in private, *intending also to cut out Jacob altogether* (we're told there is no blessing left for Esau after Jacob receives it in his stead (Gen 27:33-38)). Isaac has full

---

[448] Gen 26:34-35; 28:6-9; *cf:* Gen 24:3; Deut 7:1-11; 1 Cor 7:39-40; 2 Cor 6:14-18
[449] http://bible.org/seriespage/working-devil-serving-lord-genesis-271-46#P2831_747821. **Vos, Howard** *Genesis and Archaeology,* Chicago: Moody Press, 1963, p.96. The information cited by Vos comes from Cyrus Gordon, "Biblical Customs and the Nuzu Tablets," *The Biblical Archaeologist,* February, 1940, p. 8.

authority as patriarch to award his blessing to whom he will. It must have given Jacob chills to realise the full import of his father's actions. Isaac cannot plead ignorance. He knows perfectly well what God said to Rebekah at the twins' birth - that Jacob would inherit. Don't you think Rebekah would have been the first to remind Isaac of any oversight? This was doubtless the reason for her favouritism toward her youngest in the first place, notwithstanding Jacob is presented as a gentler and more intelligent figure than Esau.

Isaac is portrayed as weak and presumptuous. His judgment is certainly wanting:

> ➢ He thinks he can break God's word
> ➢ He seriously underestimates his wife and younger son
> ➢ Though he thinks he's dying – hence the reason for conferring the blessing – Isaac will in fact survive a further 43 years to suffer the break-up of his family (Gen 35:28) [450]

Back to the story:

And it came to pass that when Isaac was old and his eyes were dim, so that he could not see, he called Esau his eldest son, and said unto him, "My son."

And [Esau] said unto him, "Behold, here am I."

And [Isaac] said, "Behold now, I am old, I know not the day of my death. Now therefore take, I pray thee, thy weapons, thy quiver and thy bow, and go out to the field, and take me some venison, and make me savoury meat such as I love, and bring it to me that I may eat, that my soul may bless thee before I die."

And Rebekah <u>heard</u> when Isaac spake to Esau his son. And Esau went to the field to hunt for venison and to bring it.

And Rebekah spake unto Jacob her son, saying, "Behold, I heard thy father speak unto Esau thy brother, saying, 'Bring me

---

[450] Harold Stigers draws on Genesis 47:9; 45:11; 41:26-27; 41:46; 30:22ff. and 29:18,27 to calculate that Jacob was 77 years old when he fled Canaan for Padan-Aram. If this is correct, Isaac would be 137 years old at the time of the incident since he was 60 years old when the twins were born (Gen 25:26). cf. **Stigers, Harold** A Commentary on Genesis, Zondevan, 1976, p.211. Isaac's half-brother Ishmael dies aged 137, so Isaac may reasonably feel that his own time is short, especially since the problems of old age are now upon him.

venison and make me savoury meat, that I may eat, and bless thee before the LORD before my death'. Now therefore, my son, obey my voice according to that which I command thee.

"Go now to the flock and fetch me from thence two good kids of the goats; and I will make them savoury meat for thy father such as he loveth. And thou shalt bring it to thy father that he may eat, and that he may bless thee before his death."

And Jacob said to Rebekah his mother, "Behold, Esau my brother is a hairy man and I am a smooth man. My father peradventure will feel me, and I shall seem to him as a deceiver; and I shall bring a curse upon me and not a blessing."

And his mother said unto him, "Upon me be thy curse, my son. Only obey my voice and go fetch me them." (Gen 27:1-13)

What happens next is something out of a pantomime sketch. Jacob dutifully fetches the two goat kids for his mother to make the counterfeit stew. (Isaac's not only almost blind at this point, we assume his palate is likewise incapacitated since Rebekah doesn't believe he will distinguish between goat meat and venison). Rebekah takes the choice clothes from Esau's wardrobe and gets Jacob dressed up....

And she put the skins of the kids of the goats upon his hands, and upon the smooth of his neck. And she gave the savoury meat and the bread, which she had prepared, into the hand of her son Jacob.

And he came unto his father, and said, "My father." And [Isaac] said, "Here am I. Who art thou, my son?"

And Jacob said unto his father, "I am Esau thy firstborn. I have done according as thou badest me. Arise, I pray thee, sit and eat of my venison, that thy soul may bless me." (Gen 27:16-19)

No-one's going to come out of this well. Up to now we've been impressed with Rebekah willingly leaving her father's house in Padan-Aram at the behest of a stranger (Eliezer, Abraham's seneschal) to make the trek south to Canaan to commit herself to a husband she had never met. Now we see a side to her we did not suspect.

The Hebrew root for the word translated **And Rebekah heard** (שמעת - Strongs H8085, *shama'*) implies that Rebekah was used to eavesdropping her husband's conversations. When we meet

418

Rebekah's brother Laban a little later, we'll get the full measure of this family's connivance. Expositors like Bob Deffinbaugh suggest some intriguing possibilities:

"In my estimation, such a plan could hardly have been something conceived on the spur of the moment. I tend to think that Rebekah had been thinking about this possibility for some time, and that many of the props were already in place for this theatrical production. How could she possibly have considered minute details such as the goatskin gloves and neck coverings in so short a time? And how, in a few moments time, could they have been fashioned so expertly so as to have fooled Isaac? Did she just happen to have Esau's garments at hand even though he was married and perhaps not living at home? Rebekah was too shrewd to leave these matters to chance or to last-minute accomplishment. I think this production had been staged far in advance of its performance." [451]

Has Rebekah thought things through?

- ➤ She feels strongly enough about the situation to go over her husband's head in an act of *über*-deceit, which tells us something of the state of the marriage
- ➤ We're surprised too that Rebekah seeks to force God's hand in fulfilling the prophecy that her favourite son Jacob would inherit (Gen 25:23)
- ➤ By executing this fraud, she's not only provoking God but also deceiving her own husband and firstborn son
- ➤ Does she believe the prophecy will come to pass *only* if she gives God a helping hand?
- ➤ God spoke to her directly at the birth of her twins. Believing that God needs any help from us is always dangerous territory
- ➤ Rebekah's actions now are reminiscent of Abraham taking Hagar to wife to provide himself a son. And they will end as badly
- ➤ Does Rebekah honestly think God won't punish her?

How about Isaac? Watch this:

---

[451] http://bible.org/seriespage/working-devil-serving-lord-genesis-271-46#P2831_747821

And Jacob said unto his father, "I am Esau thy firstborn; I have done according as thou badest me. Arise, I pray thee, sit and eat of my venison, that thy soul may bless me."

And Isaac said unto his son, "<u>How is it that thou hast found it so quickly, my son?</u>"

And [Jacob] said, "Because the LORD thy God brought it to me."

And Isaac said unto Jacob, "Come near, I pray thee, that I may feel thee, my son, <u>whether thou be my very son Esau or not.</u>"

And Jacob went near unto Isaac his father; and he felt him, and said, "<u>The voice is Jacob's voice but the hands are the hands of Esau.</u>"

And he discerned him not because his hands were hairy, as his brother Esau's hands, so he blessed him. And he said, "<u>Art thou my very son Esau?</u>"

And [Jacob] said, "I am."

And he said, "Bring it near to me, and I will eat of my son's venison, that my soul may bless thee." And he brought it near to him, and he did eat: and he brought him wine, and he drank.

And his father Isaac said unto him, "Come near now and kiss me, my son."

And he came near and kissed him: and he smelled the smell of his raiment, and blessed him, and said, "See, the smell of my son is as the smell of a field which the LORD hath blessed. Therefore God give thee of the dew of heaven, and the fatness of the earth, and plenty of corn and wine. Let people serve thee, and nations bow down to thee. Be lord over thy brethren, and let thy mother's sons bow down to thee. Cursed be every one that curseth thee, and blessed be he that blesseth thee." (Gen 27:19-29)

Notice how Isaac is deceived by all five of his senses:

> ➢ Firstly, *vision:* Isaac's almost blind, so he can't see what's going on. That's a major drawback for a conspirator. Isaac is deceived. Jacob feels no guilt

> ➢ It's reasonable to assume that Isaac never experienced identity confusion issues in his previous dealings with Esau. *Notice Isaac knows something is up.* He voices his suspicions *four times* (see underlined passages above)

➤ *Taste:* Apparently Isaac can't tell the difference between goat meat and venison, yet his sense of *smell* seems good enough to discern the taint of Esau's tunic. Isaac is deceived. Jacob feels no guilt

➤ What about Isaac's sense of *touch*? How do you convincingly drape kid skins on your hands and not have someone know the difference? Isaac is deceived. Jacob feels no guilt

➤ Though the scriptures state that Isaac does not recognize Jacob and the ruse works (Gen 27:23), Isaac's *hearing* hasn't deceived him, it's Jacob's voice before him (Gen 27:22), yet Jacob lies repeatedly in his father's hearing. Isaac is deceived. Jacob feels no guilt

➤ If Isaac has suspicions that Jacob's attempting to trick him, *why does he proceed with this most important blessing anyway?* He could quite easily have called for Rebekah or another servant to verify the identity of the man before him and expose the plot. He doesn't. Isaac is deceived. Jacob feels no guilt

➤ Notice how Isaac states out loud that he is feeling hairy hands and smelling an outdoorsy tunic, therefore it must be Esau. Is the patriarch trying to convince himself in some way?

➤ There's no indication that Isaac ever holds a later grudge against Rebekah or Jacob for fooling him out of Esau's blessing. Isaac realises God's prophecy has come to pass anyway. His acquiescence goes in his favour, unlike the path Esau will take

What do we learn about Jacob?

➤ He feels no guilt over taking part in the ruse, any more than he did when he purchased Esau's birthright years earlier. Jacob's only worry is not for anyone else, it's being found out and cursed instead of blessed (Gen 27:12)

➤ When Rebekah diverts any curse onto herself, that's alright with Jacob (Gen 27:13-14)

- Jacob starts with the first lie, **"I am Esau, your firstborn"** and other lies follow thick and fast:
- **"I have done just as you told me."**
- **"Sit and eat of my game."**
- Isaac: **"Are you really my son, Esau?"** Jacob: **"I am."**
- Then this one:
- Isaac: **"How is it that you have found it** [the game] **so quickly?"**
- Jacob: **"Because the LORD your God brought it to me."**
- Whoops. Implicating God in such a deception is asking for it, and Jacob will certainly get it

You know when you move from an attitude of faith to reliance on the world's system when…

- You start scheming according to man's wisdom instead of trusting God
- You move from confidence to fear
- You move from caring for others to caring for yourself
- You bring judgment on others instead of blessing
- And what about Esau?

And it came to pass, as soon as Isaac had made an end of blessing Jacob, and Jacob was yet scarce gone out from the presence of Isaac his father, that Esau his brother came in from his hunting.

And he also had made savoury meat, and brought it unto his father, and said unto his father, "Let my father arise, and eat of his son's venison, that thy soul may bless me."

And Isaac his father said unto him, "Who art thou?"

And he said, "I am thy son, thy firstborn Esau."

And Isaac trembled very exceedingly, and said, "Who? Where is he that hath taken venison and brought it me, and I have eaten of all before thou camest, and have blessed him? Yea, and he shall be blessed."

And when Esau heard the words of his father, he cried with a great and exceeding bitter cry, and said unto his father, "Bless me, even me also, O my father!"

And he said, "Thy brother came with subtlety and hath taken away thy blessing."

And [Esau] said, "Is not he rightly named Jacob? For he hath supplanted me these two times. He took away my birthright; and, behold, now he hath taken away my blessing." And he said, "Hast thou not reserved a blessing for me?"

And Isaac answered and said unto Esau, "Behold, I have made him thy lord, and all his brethren have I given to him for servants; and with corn and wine have I sustained him: and what shall I do now unto thee, my son?"

And Esau said unto his father, "Hast thou but one blessing, my father?" Bless me, even me also, O my father." And Esau lifted up his voice, and wept. (Gen 27:30-38)

Chuck Missler writes:

"So in a sense Rebekah and Jacob won, though they gained nothing that God would not have given them anyway; and they lost much. Their family life was destroyed, and each had to bear lonely hours of separation, disillusionment and regret. Rebekah would never see her favourite son again, and Jacob would have to face life without a father, mother or brother. Yet God would work through their conniving. Their activities only succeeded in doing what God's oracle had predicted. God's program will triumph, often in spite of human activities. Natural senses play a conspicuous part – especially the sense of taste in which Isaac prided himself, but which gave him the wrong answer. Jacob received a blessing from his father by hiding behind the name and wearing the garments of his father's beloved firstborn son. So do we!" [452]

And Esau hated Jacob because of the blessing wherewith his father blessed him: and Esau said in his heart, "The days of mourning for my father are at hand; then will I slay my brother Jacob."

And these words of Esau her elder son were told to Rebekah, and she sent and called Jacob her younger son, and said unto him, "Behold, thy brother Esau, as touching thee, doth comfort himself, purposing to kill thee. Now therefore, my son, obey my voice and arise, flee thou to Laban my brother to Haran, and tarry with him <u>a few days</u> until thy brother's fury turn away; until thy

---

[452] Missler, Chuck, *Genesis* notes, www.khouse.org

brother's anger turn away from thee <u>and he forget that which thou hast done to him</u>. **Then I will send and fetch thee from thence. Why should I be deprived also of you both in one day?"** (Gen 27:41-45)

Isaac is persuaded by Rebekah to sanction Jacob's trip the 450 miles north to Padan Aram (Haran) in Syria to Laban's household. This gets the two brothers out of each other's way and ensures Jacob avoids a Canaanite bride and marries within the dynasty. Rebekah thinks the separation will be temporary. In fact, she will never see her son Jacob again.

JACOB

Five hundred years after the Flood, the tribes and peoples have spread out across the Earth along with the animals. So have the Nephilim. Major changes to Earth's geography and ecology have been wrought by macro events both celestial and terrestrial. The Earth at the time of Jacob has divided into the geography we mostly recognise today but further erosion and silting occur, as we'll find out later, not to mention seismic activity, some of it severe.

Many of the dinosaurs have been hunted down for their meat and killed, but more than a few are still around and cause for celebration.[453] One of the oldest surviving artefacts on Earth is the slate palette from Heirakonopolis, which shows the triumph of the first king of a united Egypt with long-necked dragons.[454] Indian pictographs have been photographed in the Havasupai Canyon in Grand Canyon, which clearly depict a Tyrannosaurus along with a flying beast of some sort.[455] Rock art in northern Queensland reveals a startlingly clear, colour image of a Plesiosaur surrounded by Aborigines attempting to kill the creature because it has eaten one of their number. The victim is shown inside the dinosaur.[456]

The legacy of Semiramis and Nimrod has spawned a hundred sex and death cults and false religions across the Middle East and beyond; at their confluence Baphomet (goat) worship, sun and moon veneration, bull worship, calf worship, fertility rites of the most obscene order, gross crimes against children, and sexual sin. Nimrod's messy end, along with that of Sodom and Gomorrah, have proved a mere blip on the radar of heathen endeavour. Such

---

[453] Mosaics can be viewed at www.exchangedlife.com/Creation/dinosaurs.shtml. Noah would have brought dinosaur babies with him on-board the Ark, but once released, the post-Flood conditions of the planet would have made their continued existence fraught.

[454] **Pritchard, James B** *Ancient Near East in Pictures,* Princeton University Press, 1969, p.93

[455] **Hovind, K** Creation Seminar DVD, www.drdino.com

[456] *CEN Technical Journal,* Vol. 12, No. 3, 1998, p.345

divine action may only have served to promulgate the rebellion against YHWH in the belief that mankind was being victimised by a cruel Creator. Behind it all lurks the contentious 'King of Tyre', the 'prince of this world', 'the god of a thousand names', the horned taker of souls, heaven's 'wronged' avenging archangel with no name, the great counterfeiter, *ha-Satan* the adversary, the Devil who stirs men's hearts in a spiritual rebellion to challenge God, cut the cords to Heaven and **be like the Most High** (Psa 2:1-3; Isa 14:14).

Continued earthquakes as a result of the Flood doubtless keep everyone on their toes. Remembering the Flood, everyone is wary of Shem, the firstborn of Noah. One might even infer a holy awe by Earth's population of the one surviving human who inhabited the antediluvian 'paradise' and survived the Flood *by 503 years*. Shem, even in his own life, would have seen himself deified as the evil and troublemongering Set, and the irony would not have been lost on the long-suffering patriarch.

"Woe to those who call evil good and good evil; who put darkness for light, and light for darkness; who put bitter for sweet and sweet for bitter", laments Isaiah centuries later (Isa 5:20). Shem would have done all possible to ensure the survival of all known truth about God, and instructed his descendants to pass down the oral tradition from father to son in the most meticulous manner. A close examination of the lifespans given in the Bible reveals that Shem lived long enough to know Abraham, Isaac and Jacob and tell them about the Flood. God, as Master of all life, ensured Shem's survival for this very purpose.

Many a slip betwixt cup and lip

Research by Graham Phillips, Ian Wilson, Prof. James Tabor and others tracks the future centuries of the line of Abraham – the so-called Scarlet Thread – down which will come the Seed of the woman, who will redeem mankind and the Creation from the curse of the Fall (Gen 3:15).

As we've seen, Abraham's heir is Isaac, and Isaac in turn has two sons, Esau and Jacob. Esau is the son of the flesh who disdains his birthright enough to sell it for a mess of red pottage. Jacob is the son of the Spirit but a born conniver. The two siblings start fighting in the womb, and their descendants, the Jews and Arabs, are still at it today. You've got to wonder what the Creator makes of it all – a question whose answer in a moment may surprise you.

We left Jacob at the end of the last chapter heading out to his uncle Laban in Haran, fearful that his twin brother Esau would hunt him down and exact a terrible revenge for stealing both his father's blessing and the inheritance as the firstborn. The central lesson of the Holy War, of course, is that man repeatedly attempts to rig the deck of his own destiny by doing what he wants, rather than placing his trust in God to provide, thereby rejecting the all-important man-God relationship, the essential part of boot-camp training in preparation for our role in the ultimate reality: eternity. Which brings us back to the great paradox: We have free will to act as we please. I chose what to wear this morning... or did I? If God is God and all-powerful, then He must steer events anyway to accomplish His own will in our lives. Or does He? Were we created and just left to get on with it, or are we robots subject to subtle direction every step of the way?

We hear the phrase 'God's will', but what is that exactly? Is the Creator's will for you different from what He has in mind for me? What does the Message System have to say about the way in which God interacts with each of us? The answer is, we come across a number of 'God's wills' in the scriptures. Here they are:

1) THE CREATOR'S PERFECT/ SOVEREIGN/ULTIMATE WILL

God has a foreordained, overall plan and purpose for the Earth programme and after that the wider Creation for eternity. This is sometimes referred to by theologians as the Creator's sovereign or perfect will. In other words, God didn't just make everything and then head off to Magaluf to let us get on with it. Since He is the God of every process and has unlimited 'bandwidth', God's ultimate sovereignty over His Creation *decrees that He must permit everything,* however awful, to come to pass for some purposeful, higher end (Amos 3:6; Eph 1:11; Job 42:2). You simply can't have an all-powerful Creator not in control of every aspect of the game, not

427

even One who can be surprised at all by anything we do. As God is omniscient, omnipresent and omnipotent, He cannot learn or be surprised by anything, which is both highly comforting and frankly alarming.

"This understanding of His sovereign will does not imply that God causes everything to happen. Rather, it acknowledges that, because He is sovereign, He must at least permit or allow whatever happens to happen. This aspect of God's will acknowledges that, even when God passively permits things to happen, He must choose to permit them, because He always has the power and right to intervene. God can always decide either to permit or stop the actions and events of this world. Therefore, as He allows things to happen, He has 'willed' them in this sense of the word." [457]

Many people I speak to are upset that a supposed 'Good God' allowed evil in the first place. According to the Message System, He did not. He allowed man free will to choose his own path, and in so doing we brought evil upon ourselves. Did God know this was going to happen? Of course. You cannot have love without free will. And you cannot have love without the antithesis of love: indifference, hate. Dorothy Sayers comments:

"For whatever reason God chose to make man as he is – limited and suffering and subject to sorrows and death – He had the honesty and the courage to take His own medicine. Whatever game He is playing with His creation, He has kept His own rules and played fair. He can exact nothing from man that He has not exacted from Himself. He has Himself gone through the whole of human experience, from the trivial irritations of family life and the cramping restrictions of hard work and lack of money to the worst horrors of pain and humiliation, defeat, despair and death. When He was a man, He played the man. He was born in poverty and died in disgrace and thought it well worthwhile." [458]

The sovereignty of an omnipotent, perfect God is inviolate, cannot be abrogated, and nothing can happen beyond God's

---

[457] http://www.gotquestions.org/Gods-will.html#ixzz2qURPaFwr
[458] **Sayers Dorothy** *Creed or Chaos*, Harcourt Brace, New York: 1949, p.4

control. God cannot and will not change His mind about His sovereignty, nor retract the covenant promises He made to Israel and the wider world via His Word. God's perfect will is also central to His plan for believers under the New Testament, the offer of salvation and eternal life for each of us through the Word made flesh - His Son (Eph 1:3-6; Rom 11:1-2, 29)

2) GOD'S PRECEPTIVE/REVEALED WILL

The Creator has made clear to us His preceptive will in the principles/precepts laid down in His Word. So we learn a huge amount about what God desires for us and what He abhors by examining how He interacts with Biblical figures. He grants us the opportunity to take a ringside seat to study these aspects of His will in action and decide for ourselves how we will behave. For instance, it was not God's will for Lot and Abraham to fall out, nor for Lot to end up in Sodom. God respects man's free will and must therefore manoeuvre in accordance with the choices made by Abraham and Lot. In fact, God manoeuvred events so He could rescue Lot from Sodom *twice.* This cause-and-effect ballet is fascinating, and not just in connection with scriptural events. What about our own lives? What about the choices we have made? Can we remember those occasions when we were led off in a completely new direction as the result of a 'chance' event or encounter with someone? There are no chances in God's system (*cf.* Ruth 2:3).

God's preceptive will is that we should learn to be like Him, practise godliness, and merge our nature with His, since He wishes each of us to be as He is one day and rule with Him as joint heirs for eternity.[459] The end result? One will in the universe. His becomes ours. But we have free will to act in concordance with, or against these principles of God's revealed will. Will we choose God's way, or take a leaf out of Frank Sinatra's song-sheet and do it *My Way?*

---

[459] Psa 82:6; Isa 9:7; Dan 7:18-22, 27; Luke 19:17; FG 10:34; Acts 26:18; 1 Cor 6:2-3; 2 Tim 2:12; Heb 3:14; 1 John 3:2; Rom 8:17; Rev 20:6; 2:26

"In this sense, many people are seeking God's will when it is already obvious. You don't have to pray about living with your boyfriend; God has spoken." (Heb 13:4; 1 Cor 6:9-20). [460]

3) GOD'S PREFERENTIAL/DESIDERATIVE WILL

This represents what God desires to see happen. It is God's preferential will that all might be saved (2 Pet 3:9; 1 Tim 2:3-4), yet man can reject God of his own free will, so clearly not all will be saved, which means God does not get what He wants out of the programme. Many times in His ministry, Jesus makes known what the Father would have of each of us, representing the best plan for our lives (*cf.* Matt 18:12-14 and the parables).

4) GOD'S PERMISSIVE WILL

This is what God permits, *even though it is sin.* We actually would not get very far in life if God did not permit us to sin. We were born to sin with the nature of Adam, so if God were that intransigent, there would be blackened, charcoal remains of us up the Finchley Road as a result of getting fried at the slightest goof. Why does God permit sin? Because He wants to teach us the consequences of the incredible gift of free will, good and bad, and how we can harness the Creator's true power.

We return to the concept that *"God can always decide either to permit or stop the actions and events of this world. Therefore, as He allows things to happen, He has 'willed' them in this sense of the word."* [461] Consider that God had to 'permit' Cain to kill Abel for that act to go ahead. Notice God did not strike down Cain, nor did Cain go on to kill Adam's next son, Seth. Notice God permitted Ham to commit his sinful act in Noah's tent when He could have struck Ham down before the event. Conclusion: God did not breach Ham's free will, and He won't breach yours either. Instead, Ham and Canaan's lives headed in a new direction as a result of Ham's sin. God could have prevented the Fall of Adam and Eve, *but did not.* He could have prevented the sin of Sodom and its

---

[460] https://bible.org/question/can-you-help-me-understand-gods-perfect-will-versus-his-permissive-will
[461] http://www.gotquestions.org/Gods-will.html#ixzz2qURPaFwr

eventual destruction by writing "I've Got My Beady Eye on You, Rotters" in the skies above the Plain of Siddim. He did not. God's permissive will is how He interacts with the free will He has granted man, yet in all this He is always in control.

What is God's will? God's will is God's ways. I'm getting into this because as we enter Jacob's incredible life we will see these wills of God interacting in a remarkable fashion with Jacob's own, and from examining these events and motivations, we will clearly comprehend the implications of our own modern predicament, soon to be backdropped by the first of many 'game-changing' macro events due to stun our planet in the coming years.

Jacob in Haran

So we return to Jacob fleeing north from Beersheba towards Haran in Syria to escape the dark threats of his brother, Esau. Pulling off the road for the night near Luz, Jacob gets his head down and dreams of a ladder set up on the Earth whose top reaches into Heaven. He sees the angels of God ascending and descending, with God at the top intoning:

"I am the LORD God of Abraham thy [fore]father, and the God of Isaac: the land whereon thou liest, to thee will I give it, and to thy seed. And thy seed shall be as the dust of the earth, and thou shalt spread abroad to the west, and to the east, and to the north, and to the south. And in thee and in thy seed shall all the families of the Earth be blessed.

"And, behold, I am with thee, and will keep thee in all places whither thou goest, and will bring thee again into this land, for I will not leave thee, until I have done that which I have spoken to thee of." (Gen 28:13-15)

In his dream, Jacob shares God's reality. God is reiterating the covenant He swore to Abraham and Isaac. Jacob awakens, stunned by the experience:

"How awesome is this place! This is none other but the house of God, and this is the gate of Heaven!"

We get another hint of 'high places', suggesting that there may be certain places on Earth with special significance which act as 'stargates' between the Earth and the ethereal realms or hyperdimensions. We think back to Nimrod's tower at Babel, or Abraham and Isaac on Mount Moriah, and later we will encounter Mounts Horeb ('Sinai'), Nebo, Hermon and others – even Mount Graham in Arizona - which hold significance as the *Origins* story progresses.

In the morning, Jacob erects a pillar and names the place Bethel ('house of God'). It's the start of God dealing with Jacob to shape him up for his coming role as family patriarch, and also to compel him to endure some painful but instructive lessons on the rights of the firstborn after conniving and defrauding his brother.

Jacob presses on north alone – no other travelling companions are mentioned. Four hundred miles later as he approaches Haran, he comes upon a watering well used by local shepherds for their flocks. Jacob enquires whether anyone knows Laban, son of Nahor. Not only do the locals know him, they point out his daughter Rachel, who is approaching, even at that moment, to water her father's sheep at the well. (What are the chances that this is the same well where Eliezer met Rebekah?)

Rachel is a stunner and Jacob is love-struck. He introduces himself as her cousin, son of Rebekah, Laban's sister. Delighted, Rachel runs to tell her father of their visitor, and before you can say *mazal tov*, Jacob is brought into the family pile like the long lost kin that he is. He's introduced to all the family, which includes Rachel's elder sister, Leah, who is described as 'tender-eyed' and contrasted with Rachel's beauty and popularity (Gen 29:17).

Jacob stays all month enjoying Laban's hospitality. He helps out with chores and jobs around the farm, doubtless stealing wistful glances at the focus of his every attention – the comely Rachel; looks which do not pass unnoticed by the hawk-eyed Laban. Jacob is drawn aside one day:

"You are my kin. Shall you work for me for nothing? Tell me, what can I pay you?"

Laban has been thinking. The abrupt appearance of his nephew a month ago can only mean one thing. The lad's been sent up to find a wife - a re-run of the previous occasion when Abraham's servant, Eliezer, made the trek on his master's behalf on a similar errand for Isaac. It's not clear whether Laban ever gets to know that

Jacob is on the run from Esau under less than propitious circumstances. To Laban, Jacob's presence is eminently explainable and shows great potential for profit. And, judging by the wistful glances, Jacob doesn't look like he's in a hurry to be off.

Jacob replies, "I will serve you seven years in return for your daughter Rachel's hand in marriage."

Laban feigns surprise. Grins inwardly. "Better she marries you than any other man. You stay with me."

And Jacob served seven years for Rachel; and they seemed unto him but a few days, for the love he had to her. (Gen 29:20)

When the seven years are up, Jacob formally presses Laban for Rachel's hand in marriage. Laban organises a great feast for everyone in the neighbourhood, and the occasion is spent in great celebration. At the appointed time, the veiled bride is brought forward and Jacob retires with his new wife for the night to consummate the marriage.

The following morning, as Jacob rubs his eyes at the sunlight casting its shards through the shutters upon the bed, the awful truth sets in. The woman lying beside him is not the gorgeous Rachel, it's Leah - she of the 'tender eye'. Jacob is beside himself with fury. Leah was obviously put up to it and played along – she could quite easily have owned up before the deed was done instead of playing the deceiver. And no pork beans for guessing who dreamt up this whole bacchanalian mess of pottage. Jacob hunts down the guilty party.

"What is this thou hast done unto me? Did not I serve with thee for Rachel? Wherefore then hast thou beguiled me?"

And Laban said, "It must not be so done in our country, to give the younger before the firstborn. Fulfil her week, and we will give thee this also for the service which thou shalt serve with me yet seven other years." (Gen 29:25-27)

The deceiver has just been deceived, and doesn't relish the taste of his own medicine. God rubs it in by having Laban cite local custom in telling Jacob that the younger sibling does not take precedence over the elder! To make matters worse, Laban has no intention of relenting of his trickery, but remains serious in securing a further seven years' graft from Jacob for Rachel.

In the realm of conniving, Jacob has just met his match. Between a rock and a hard place, what choice does the son of Isaac have? Laban holds the power to make or break Jacob's heart. The luscious Rachel remains ever out of reach. Esau's still prowling around Canaan dreaming of sharp knives and viper-filled pits, so returning to Canaan is not an option; and certainly not with Leah; and certainly not without Rachel. Jacob grits his teeth and agrees to take Rachel to wife and complete a second seven-year term of service.

It's not all bad. With Leah comes one of Laban's handmaids, Zilpah; and with Rachel, another maid, Bilhah. As Jacob gets his new household in order, our attention is drawn to a single sentence: **And** [Jacob] **loved Rachel more than Leah** (Gen 29:30). What at first seems obvious harbours a sadder truth. Schemers tend to be slow forgivers and Jacob's going to make Leah pay. We have no further details on Leah's physical appearance, other than reading between the lines to surmise that Laban pulled this stunt to do the best he was able for his plain but eldest daughter. The sadder truth for Jacob? The destructive favouritism shown by his own parents during his own upbringing tore the family apart, and the same pattern will play out in Jacob's own family to lay the foundations for what has to be one of the most astonishing and heartfelt dramas in the Bible. But first, God's going to mix things up a little.

And when the LORD saw that Leah was hated, He opened her womb: but Rachel was barren. And Leah conceived and bare a son, and she called his name Reuben ['See, a son!']. **For she said, "Surely the LORD hath looked upon my affliction; now therefore my husband will love me."**

And she conceived again and bare a son; and said, "Because the LORD hath heard that I was hated, He hath therefore given me this son also." And she called his name Simeon ['Hearing'].

And she conceived again and bare a son; and said, "Now this time will my husband be joined unto me because I have born him three sons." Therefore was his name called Levi ['joined'; 'attached'].

And she conceived again and bare a son: and she said, "Now will I praise the LORD." Therefore she called his name Judah ['Yah be praised!']; and left off bearing. (Gen 29:31-35)

In naming her sons so, we gain an insight into Leah's isolation and misery caused by her lack of emotional acceptance by Jacob. Rachel's not faring too well either. While Leah bounces out four sons, one after the other, Rachel comes to the bitter realisation that there is no blessing in childbirth for her. In a culture, where barrenness is truly a curse, an alternative strategy is often employed: the same Sarah used to tragic effect years earlier.

And when Rachel saw that she bare Jacob no children, Rachel envied her sister and said unto Jacob, "Give me children or else I die."

And Jacob's anger was kindled against Rachel, and he said, "Am I in God's stead, who hath withheld from thee the fruit of the womb?"

And she said, "Behold my maid Bilhah, go in unto her; and she shall bear upon my knees that I may also have children by her."

And she gave him Bilhah her handmaid to wife: and Jacob went in unto her. And Bilhah conceived and bare Jacob a son.

And Rachel said, "God hath judged me, and hath also heard my voice, and hath given me a son." Therefore called she his name Dan ('judge'). (Gen 30:1-6)

The score is now 4-1. Rachel encourages Jacob and Bilhah again, and another son is born.

And Rachel said, "With great wrestlings have I wrestled with my sister, and I have prevailed." And she called his name Naphtali ('my wrestling'). (Gen 30:8)

We see the rivalry between the two wives surfacing again – all over Jacob's overt penchant for favouritism, 'inherited' from his parents, which landed him in so much hot water with Esau. Leah's been taking a rest from childbearing. Seeing the effectiveness of Rachel's strategy, Leah orders her own maid Zilphah into the fray. One can't help but picture a bed-weary Jacob gasping for a day off.

Zilpah, Leah's maid, bare Jacob a son. And Leah said, "A troop cometh!" and she called his name Gad ('a troop, 'invader'; also 'good fortune'). And Zilpah, Leah's maid, bare Jacob a second son. And Leah said, "Happy am I, for the daughters will call me blessed!" And she called his name Asher ('happy'). (Gen 30:10-13)

By this time Rachel is truly desperate. Leah has been barren for some time after Judah's birth so Rachel picks her moment. She spots Leah's eldest boy, Reuben, returning from the wheat harvest that summer with certain plants reputed to be potent aphrodisiacs. Scholars are divided over exactly what דודאים ('dudaim') may represent. The Latin Vulgate follows the Greek Septuagint translation in labelling them mandrakes. There may be some problems with this since mandrake roots contain alkaloid hypnotic and hallucinogenic chemicals known to induce delirium and even coma. Perhaps you slept with them under your pillow. The root sometimes grows into a bifurcated humanoid shape, giving rise to its early association with witchcraft and the supernatural. The *Journal of the Royal Society of Medicine* comments:

> "J K Rowling's *Harry Potter and the Chamber of Secrets* includes a scene in which the hero and his friends are in a greenhouse, taking instruction from Professor Sprout on the re-potting of mandrakes. To protect their hearing, the class is equipped with earmuffs." [462]

Occult enthusiasts smile at Rowling's 'ear-muff' allusion. Medieval superstition held that a demon inhabited the root and emitted a hideous shriek when the mandrake was ripped from the ground, hence the need to block your ears with traditional wax or… modern ear-muffs. In reality, medieval landowners were getting fed up with mandrakes being lifted from their fields at night, so the superstition probably had its roots in a cunning plan to safeguard a generous profit and ward off mandrake robbers.

Other scholars suggest that 'dudaim' could refer to ginseng, another root with purported fertility powers. Whatever the true nature of the plant, Rachel is desperate to lay hands on some.

Then Rachel said to Leah, "Give me, I pray thee, of thy son's mandrakes."

---

[462] *J R Soc Med.* 2003 March; 96(3): 144–147

And [Leah] said unto her, "Is it a small matter that thou hast taken my husband? And wouldest thou take away my son's mandrakes also?"

And Rachel said, "Therefore he shall lie with thee tonight for thy son's mandrakes." (Gen 30:14-15)

Some interesting dynamics here. Notice the wifely hierarchy. Leah acknowledges that Rachel is the preferred one. Rachel rubs it in by effectively stating, "Give me some of Reuben's mandrakes and I'll let you lie with Jacob tonight." We see by that statement the power Rachel has, even over her husband. Jacob will do as ordered. Beauty holds the whip hand. Leah takes the offer seriously:

And Jacob came out of the field in the evening, and Leah went out to meet him, and said, "Thou must come in unto me, for surely I have hired thee with my son's mandrakes." And he lay with her that night.

And God hearkened unto Leah, and she conceived and bare Jacob the fifth son.

And Leah said, "God hath given me my hire because I have given my maiden to my husband." And she called his name Issachar ('man of hire').

And Leah conceived again and bare Jacob the sixth son.

And Leah said, "God hath endued me with a good dowry. Now will my husband dwell with me because I have born him six sons." And she called his name Zebulun ('dwelling').

And afterwards she bare a daughter, and called her name Dinah ('judged'; 'vindicated'). (Gen 30:16-21)

You can imagine the anguish assailing Rachel at this point. There's no indication Leah was being cruel to her – she didn't need to be. The veritable army she had birthed attested to her fecundity. Yet in all this, Jacob loves Rachel more than Leah. Rachel has suffered gracefully, especially before the LORD in prayer, for God takes pity at this time and moves on Rachel's behalf:

And God remembered Rachel, and God hearkened to her, and opened her womb. And she conceived, and bare a son; and said, "God hath taken away my reproach." And she called his name Joseph; and said, "The LORD shall add to me another son." (Gen 30:22-24)

Rachel's son is destined to wow the world. She names him Joseph ('may YAHWEH increase/add') in expectation that God will bless her more. Joseph becomes the 11th of Jacob's sons. The question is, why would God deliberately put Rachel through this whole experience of barrenness? There is no earthly reason why Rachel would not be capable of bearing children, especially in view of her sister's fertility. As usual, the answer lies in a verse often passed over by the casual reader. Here it is: **And when the LORD saw that Leah was hated, He opened her womb: but Rachel was barren.** (Gen 29:31)

Study how that is phrased. Whose hatred of Leah provoked God to act? Jacob's. God has taken exception to Jacob's favouritism, a form of pride, *executed by the latter's free will.* It is evident from what follows that Jacob does not heed the lesson God has been demonstrating in the saga of his wives'/concubines' fertility, so God must later explain it to Jacob a little more clearly. We're not unsympathetic with the son of Isaac. Jacob is understandably angry at Leah for having pulled the marriage stunt in cahoots with her father. Yet years later, long after he has the woman of his dreams, *Jacob still nurses that grudge.* In so doing, he's forgetting that an omniscient God *must permit every act,* so in Jacob's continued anger we see not only immaturity and a lack of forgiveness, but also a marked lack of faith in the God he purports to trust. Though easy for us armchair expositors to wax lyrical on another's faults, the scriptures have been given by God for our instruction in righteousness (Rom 15:4; 2 Tim 3:16), which is the very nature of God Himself, so let us not flinch from asking what Jacob should have done upon discovering Laban's duplicity. Gone before his Maker perhaps with something like, "I'm not sure what the ultimate goal is here of being tricked by Laban and Leah, but I know You handle all things, Father, so I will wait on You to reveal what You want me to do. In the meantime, I forgive both of them and ask you to bless my marriage." Which, of course, God does anyway with the cohort of Leah's kids now tugging at Jacob's elbow. How about the following two New Testament verses, which confirm that God is running the special Earth programme, during which 'the called' are to be conformed to the image of His Son for an ulterior, eternal purpose:

And we know that all things work together for good to them that love God, to them who are the called according to His purpose. For whom He did foreknow, He also did predestinate to be conformed to the image of His Son, that He might be the firstborn among many brethren. (Rom 8:28-29).

Jacob and his family return to Canaan

By now Jacob's family is large by any standards: two wives, two concubines, eleven sons and a daughter. Chafing at length to be gone, Jacob approaches Laban:

"Give me my wives and my children, for whom I have served thee, and let me go: for thou knowest my service which I have done thee."

And Laban said unto him, "I pray thee, if I have found favour in thine eyes, tarry: for I have learned by experience that the LORD hath blessed me for thy sake." And he said, "Appoint me thy wages, and I will give it." (Gen 30:26-28)

On the spiritual side, Laban realises he's being blessed by God because of Jacob. On a more pragmatic level, Jacob and his family have enriched Laban with their years of hard work tending his flocks. No wonder Laban insists: "Name your price."

So Jacob proposes a deal; that all the spotted, speckled, and brown goats and sheep of Laban's flocks, at any time, should henceforth be his. Since these animals are the least valuable and desirable of the flocks, Laban sees no harm in it. The rest of the chapter seems to indicate that in the years that followed, Jacob performs strange breeding experiments in which he is able dramatically to boost the number of spotted, speckled, and brown animals. Laban gets upset and changes the goalposts. Often. The breeding programme always comes out in Jacob's favour, indicating divine intervention. So successful are Jacob's efforts, that Laban's sons murmur among themselves:

"Jacob hath taken away all that was our father's; and of that which was our father's hath he gotten all this glory."

And Jacob beheld the countenance of Laban, and, behold, it was not toward him as before. (Gen 31:1-2)

Jacob knows he has outstayed his welcome. The LORD confirms this, so Jacob summons Leah and Rachel and lays out the situation:

"I see your father's countenance, that it is not toward me as before; but the God of my father hath been with me. And ye know that with all my power I have served your father. And your father hath deceived me, and changed my wages ten times; but God suffered him not to hurt me. If he said thus, 'The speckled shall be thy wages', then all the cattle bare speckled. And if he said thus, 'The ringstraked shall be thy hire', then bare all the cattle ringstraked. Thus God hath taken away the cattle of your father and given them to me." (Gen 31:5-9)

Which, being women, Leah and Rachel would have worked out months before. With resignation, they reply, **"Is there yet any portion or inheritance for us in our father's house? Are we not counted of him strangers? For he hath sold us and hath quite devoured also our money. For all the riches which God hath taken from our father, that is ours, and our children's: now then, whatsoever God hath said unto thee, do."** (Gen 31:14-16)

Jacob hastily gets his family, belongings and flocks together, and they set out. Before they leave, Rachel also steals her father's *teraphim*. This word usually refers to pagan household gods, and they almost certainly were in Laban's case. Theologians endlessly debate the significance of Rachel's *teraphim* theft when she was supposed to have given herself over to Jacob's Hebrew Deity. In her award-winning essay on the subject, Susannah Rutherglen argues that the theft probably had little to do with the pagan, religious significance of the idols:

"…The narrator of Genesis 31 is not especially concerned that Rachel's involvement with the idols might be theologically questionable. It is interesting, then, that almost all interpretations of Rachel's story amount to attempts to whitewash the theologically suspect parts of her story…. In other words, Rachel, by sitting on the *teraphim* while she is menstruating, deliberately defiles them in order to make them unfit for worship: she saves Laban from his paganism.

This reading makes little inherent sense, since there is no need to defile something that is already quite unholy. More importantly, though, it makes little narrative sense. If Rachel found the idols offensive, why did she take such pains to find and to pack them during what must have been an extremely hasty preparation to go? Why did she enumerate them among her most essential household items, the things she would take away for a long journey from a place to which she would never return? And so on." [463]

In other words, Rachel, supposedly a genuine follower of YHWH (Gen 31:16), is not held to account by the Biblical narrator in placing great store by pagan, religious artefacts. Reasonably, this would imply that they had another function, and they did. We learn from Moshe Greenberg's detailed study of the Tablets of Nuzi that *teraphim* were also treated as title deeds to property – a legitimate proof of inheritance – not just as religious artefacts.[464] Both as civic title deeds and religious tradition, they would hold great value, reckons Jack Heyford:

"These *teraphim*, small figurines of the family gods, held great meaning for the heirs. According to the ancient law around Haran, the sons, particularly the eldest, had the privilege of inheriting the family 'gods' as well as all the property that went with them. Rachel stole them either to ridicule her father's religion, to lay claim to the inheritance, or to remain attached to her native religion." [465]

Even this explanation has its problems, says Susannah Rutherglen:

"Without interrogating the [Nuzi] cuneiform evidence (which Moshe Greenberg has done to quietly devastating effect), I want to suggest a set of reasons why this idea does not work within the narrative. First of all, the household gods were stolen, not bequeathed. Had Jacob shown up at Laban's funeral with the *teraphim* in hand, he

[463] **Rutherglen, S** *Rachel and the Household Gods,* Norton Scholar's Prize Winning Essay, 2002, http://books.wwnorton.com/books/aboutcontent.aspx?id=16915
[464] **Greenberg, Moshe** "Another Look at Rachel's Theft of the Teraphim", *The Journal of Biblical Literature* 81 (Spring 1962): 239-248.
[465] **Heyford, Jack** *Spirit-Filled Bible,* Thomas Nelson, 1991, p.51

would have received an arrest warrant, not an inheritance. The gods were stolen with little obvious prospect of gain and at great risk - a risk implied by the lengths to which Rachel went to hide them, and by Jacob's acknowledgment of the gravity of such a theft: 'Any one with whom you find your gods shall not live,' he assures Laban (Gen 31:32)." [466]

Consider this. If Rachel intended stealing the *teraphim* as a means to lay legal claim to Laban's estate (unlikely for Rutherglen's above reason), *would she even want to?* Her husband Jacob, for the few years prior to his separation from the House of Laban, had been simultaneously enriching himself and separating his own possessions from Laban's in the curious breeding experiments conducted with Laban's livestock. By all accounts, Jacob has become more wealthy than Laban at the time of his departure: a fact noted with grave misgiving by Laban's own sons (Gen 31:1). The importance both Laban and Jacob attach to the *teraphim* is emphasised by their over-reaction to the theft, yet the narrator of the text merely expounds the incident and does not explain its significance. This is a *remez* – a hint of something deeper. *Perhaps it does not require explaining.* Put yourself in Rachel's shoes. From her own knowledge of her father, what are the most important things in Laban's life? Money, possessions and kin. What do the *teraphim* represent? The legal ability to pass wealth onto your children and perpetuate the family's existence and fortunes.

The most likely explanation for the Rachel's *teraphim* heist, therefore, is in understanding Rachel's familiarity with her father's predisposition for dirty dealing, and her desire to manoeuvre accordingly to protect herself and her new family from any future threats from her father. *Teraphim* are of great religious and civic significance in Laban's culture (and Jacob would have known this), so the theft can be reasonably explained as Rachel arming herself with some bargaining power, should Laban do anything to stop Jacob and his family from fleeing. Rachel knows one thing for sure.

---

[466] **Rutheglen, S,** *Rachel and the Household Gods,* op. cit.

Father Laban will be very upset when he finds out. Which he doesn't for three days, because he's away with his sons, shearing.[467]

When he eventually learns the truth, Laban dissolves into fury, grabs a posse of his sons and kin, and sets off after Jacob. This is a heavily armed mob. Laban knows from previous conversations that Jacob's heart has been set on returning to his family seat in Canaan (Gen 30:25), so they take the road southwest. It takes the Syrians seven days to overhaul Jacob's caravan in the mountains of Gilead, by which time Laban's kin are spoiling for a fight. For years they have jealously watched Jacob defrauding their father, himself a known conniver, with one scheme or another, divesting the family of a significant portion of its stock and wealth. Now Jacob has cut loose and fled with their sisters and their father's *teraphim* after twenty years' service... *without saying a word?*

But Laban has a problem. God came to him in a dream one night during the pursuit, and the words are still rattling around in Laban's head: **"Be careful that you speak to Jacob neither good nor bad"**, which idiomatically in Hebrew translates, "See you don't make any threats against Jacob." Laban now has good cause to realise that there is a whole spiritual dimension to this; and is canny enough not to provoke Jacob's God, who so deftly outmanoeuvred him through Jacob over the years. Laban, like Jacob, is a poor loser, and this whole affair has proved a rank lesson in public humiliation for him around Haran and the surrounding region. When the two finally come face to face in the mountains, Laban restrains his men and plays the wronged father-in-law.

"What hast thou done, that thou hast stolen away unawares to me, and carried away my daughters, as captives taken with the sword? Wherefore didst thou flee away secretly and steal away

---

[467] The 'three days' period theme occurs frequently in the scriptures, and symbolically translates to a period of divine dealing and completion leading to a significant new beginning or chapter in the particular protagonist's life. 'Three' generally represents an announcement of something significant to follow. *cf.* Isa 6:3; Rev 4:8; the three sons of Noah who survived the Flood; the three days Jonah spent in the whale, which prefigured the three days and nights Yeshua would spend in the tomb before His resurrection; three disciples were taken onto the mount of transfiguration; the third person of the Trinity, the Holy Spirit.

from me; and didst not tell me, that I might have sent thee away with mirth, and with songs, with tabret, and with harp?

"And hast not suffered me to kiss my sons and my daughters? Thou hast now done foolishly in so doing. It is in the power of my hand to do you hurt. But the God of your father spake unto me last night, saying, 'Take thou heed that thou speak not to Jacob either good or bad'. And now, though thou wouldest needs be gone, because thou sore longedst after thy father's house, yet wherefore hast thou stolen my gods [*teraphim*]?" (Gen 31:26-30)

To his credit, Jacob actually comes clean about the real reason for his expeditious departure from Haran: **"Because I was afraid, for I said, 'Peradventure thou wouldest take by force thy daughters from me.'"** (Gen 31:31) As for Laban's missing idols, this is the first Jacob has heard of them. With the careless air of one with nothing to hide, he intones:

"With whomsoever thou findest thy gods, let him not live. Before our brethren, discern thou what is thine with me, and take it to thee." For Jacob knew not that Rachel had stolen them. (Gen 31:32)

Laban and his sons set about searching the tents of Jacob's family for his *teraphim*. If Jacob had known for one moment the danger in which he had just placed his beloved Rachel, his bowels would have turned to water. Instead he stands there, arms folded, face creased with outrage as Laban rifles through his tent, Leah's tent, the concubine's tents, and finally pushes into Rachel's.

Now Rachel had taken the images and put them in the camel's saddle and sat upon them. And Laban searched all the tent but found them not.

And she said to her father, "Let it not displease my lord that I cannot rise up before thee, for the custom of women is upon me." And he searched but found not the images. (Gen 31:34-35)

It's a clever ruse, carried out with ice-cold nerve in the face of heinous consequences, but Rachel also manages to insult her father's religion in the worst way by sitting on his idols during an implied period of menstruation (Lev 15:19-20). Laban emerges empty-handed to be confronted by a furious Jacob:

"So what is my trespass? What is my sin, that thou hast so hotly pursued after me? Whereas thou hast searched all my stuff, what hast thou found of all thy household stuff? Set it here before my brethren and thy brethren, that they may judge betwixt us both.

"This twenty years have I been with thee; thy ewes and thy she-goats have not cast [miscarried] their young, and the rams of thy flock have I not eaten. That which was torn of beasts I brought not unto thee; I bare the loss of it; of my hand didst thou require it, whether stolen by day, or stolen by night. Thus I was; in the day the drought consumed me, and the frost by night; and my sleep departed from mine eyes.

"Thus have I been twenty years in thy house; I served thee fourteen years for thy two daughters, and six years for thy cattle: and thou hast changed my wages ten times. Except the God of my father, the God of Abraham, and the fear of Isaac, had been with me, surely thou hadst sent me away now empty. God hath seen mine affliction and the labour of my hands, and rebuked thee last night." (Gen 31:36-42)

The final raw and sore confrontation: one which destroys any relationship left between the two men. Laban proposes a covenant between them, not only to keep the peace and ensure each party's future safety from the other, but also to demark a physical border so they will never have to meet or deal with each other again. Both sides heap up stones and find a rock to act as a pillar. The place comes to be known as Mizpah in Gilead.

And Laban said to Jacob, "Behold this heap, and behold this pillar, which I have cast betwixt me and thee. This heap be witness, and this pillar be witness, that I will not pass over this heap to thee, and that thou shalt not pass over this heap and this pillar unto me, for harm.

The God of Abraham, and the God of Nahor, the God of their father, judge betwixt us." And Jacob sware by the fear of his father Isaac.

Then Jacob offered sacrifice upon the mount, and called his brethren to eat bread: and they did eat bread, and tarried all night in the mount. And early in the morning Laban rose up and kissed

445

his [grand]sons and his daughters and blessed them. And Laban departed, and returned unto his place. (Gen 31:51-55)

What a relief Jacob must have experienced finally to be free. Such a palpable liberation from stress must also have extended to the resolution achieved by both connivers at their separation: an eschewing of violence in favour of a final, frosty border accommodation. There is no indication that Rachel ever told Jacob about the *teraphim* she had robbed from her father, or under what circumstances she had secreted them. Perhaps she wished to spare him the angst of the disaster that could have befallen her had Laban found them in her possession and held Jacob to his exhortation to kill the guilty party. Suffice to wonder whether Laban could actually have killed his beloved daughter under such circumstances, even to save face. We will never know, as Laban disappears henceforth from the scriptural record, though his legacy is to remain blood to Jacob: an eventuality by marriage from which they could never separate themselves. Laban thus has the distinction of becoming a forebear to the future nation of Israel via his daughter, Rachel, and even to the *Mashiach* Himself. Most commentators state that the stolen *teraphim* are a sideshow, a brief irrelevance to the Jacob and Rachel narrative, and they do not surface again. *Or do they? Remember the remez?*

Gunther Plaut writes:

"Here the theme of retribution may again be glimpsed. For while the Torah passes no explicit judgement on Rachel's behavior, its tragic consequences will all too soon become evident. The commentators who exculpate Rachel are therefore wide of the mark. Jacob's oath that whoever may be found with the *teraphim* should not remain alive (Gen. 31:32) is exacted not by Laban, as expected, but by God himself. Rachel dies in her next childbirth and is buried by the roadside (Gen, 35:16-20). She is the only Matriarch not interred in Machpelah, the gravesite of the other Matriarch and Patriarchs." [468]

God would prefer us not to swear oaths because of the consequences if we mess up (Matt 5:33-37; Jam 5:12), but if we do

---

[468] **Plaut, Gunther** *The Torah: A Modern Commentary,* Union of American Hebrew Congregations: New York, 1981, p.214

swear (oaths of office, etc.) the LORD takes the commitment extremely seriously and expects us to do the same (Exo 20:7; Deut 23:23; Num 30:2ff; Ecc 5:4). This is another theme that will have tragic consequences for key figures as we proceed, even among politicians and presidents down to our own modern age. It is an attribute of God's nature that He cannot lie or break His promises (Heb 6:17-18), and He doesn't expect us to either. In fact, God delights in making and keeping His promises to us, in stark contrast to the 'gods' of other religions (demons). God is jealous for His name, the perfection of His justice and righteousness, and for His unique reality as Creator of all to the exclusion of any other gods or religions from everlasting to everlasting. *God never argues for His existence, He declares it.*[469] Among the many promises God has made to man, the three towering commitments that ring throughout the Bible are:

1) Israel's permanence [470]
2) The *literal* second coming of *Mashiach* (Yeshua) to rule the Earth [471]
3) Eternal life to all who believe in YHWH through Jesus Christ [472]

Peace with Esau?

Travelling southwest from Haran towards Canaan with a lighter step now Laban is behind them, for Jacob and Rachel tragedy is yet future. Jacob encounters an angelic host on the way (Gen 32:1-2) – a briefly mentioned but intense experience which reassures Jacob in another matter that has been playing on his mind. There is still that dreaded, longstanding bad blood between himself and Esau to resolve. Determined to clear the path ahead of past woes, Jacob despatches messengers south into Edom to track

---

[469] Deut 4:35; 32:39; Isa 41:4; 43:10; 44:6-8; 45:5-8; FG 1:1-3; 1 Tim 2:5-6; Rev 1:8; 22:13

[470] Gen 12:1-3; 13:14; 15:18-21; 28:14-15; Deut 30:1-10; 2 Sam 7:10-13; Isa 9:7; Dan 2:44; Jer 31:31-34; Luke 1:32-33; Heb 8:6-13

[471] There are approximately 2,400 prophecies heralding this throughout the Bible. *cf.* Revelation, *passim*

[472] FG 3:16,36; 4:14; 10:28; 17:2-3; Rom 6:23; 1 Tim 1:16; 1 John 5:11,13,20

down his elder sibling. Witness the conciliatory tone Jacob decides to adopt in the message he has his servants convey:

"Thus shall ye speak unto my lord Esau; 'Thy servant Jacob saith thus, "I have sojourned with Laban, and stayed there until now: And I have oxen, and asses, flocks, and menservants, and womenservants: and I have sent to tell my lord, that I may find grace in thy sight." ' " (Gen 32:4-5)

The servants return some time later with news. His brother Esau will indeed be coming to meet Jacob for a reunion. And 400 roughnecks will be accompanying him.

The news fills Jacob with dread. He now faces a situation many of us have experienced all too well: a significant, unwelcome, even life-threatening confrontation, whose outcome is uncertain. What is the first thing Jacob does? In true Jacob fashion, he spreads the risk to his retinue and possessions!

Then Jacob was greatly afraid and distressed: and he divided the people that was with him, and the flocks, and herds, and the camels, into two bands; and said, "If Esau come to the one company, and smite it, then the other company which is left shall escape." (Gen 32:7-8)

And the second thing (which should have been the first)? Jacob petitions the LORD in his terror:

"O God of my father Abraham, and God of my father Isaac, the LORD which saidst unto me, 'Return unto thy country, and to thy kindred, and I will deal well with thee': I am not worthy of the least of all the mercies, and of all the truth, which Thou hast shewed unto thy servant [God keeps His servants informed!]**; for with my staff I passed over this Jordan; and now I am become two bands.**

"Deliver me, I pray thee, from the hand of my brother, from the hand of Esau: for I fear him, lest he will come and smite me, and the mother with the children. And Thou saidst, 'I will surely do thee good, and make thy seed as the sand of the sea, which cannot be numbered for multitude.' " (Gen 32: 9-12)

We can all identify times in the past (perhaps even the present) when we have been truly terrified. Our prayers in such a predicament tend to be refreshingly honest. If we come clean with God about our deepest fears, He'll come through for us. Jacob's own prayer is heartfelt, sincere and earnest. In typical Jacob 'lawyerly' fashion, however, notice how he holds the God of the universe to His covenant promise to bring him safely back to Canaan, and multiply his seed throughout the Earth (Gen 28:13-15). Which, of course, won't be happening if Esau and his roughnecks sharpen their swords and decide to settle old scores.

While on the one hand placing his trust in God to deliver him from his brother, Jacob still acts in the flesh by rigging the meeting to be irresistibly lucrative for Esau. He rounds up two hundred she-goats, twenty he-goats, two hundred ewes, twenty rams, thirty milch camels with their colts, forty kine, ten bulls, twenty she-asses and ten foals. He devises an elaborate plan with his servants to have this lot delivered to Esau in successive droves in advance of his own meeting:

"I will appease him with the present that goes before me, and afterward I shall see his face; perhaps he will accept me." (Gen 32:20)

You miss it unless you are looking for it. This is not complete faith in God to deliver him, this is the old Jacob. Is he really seeking a sincere, heartfelt reunion with his twin? No. The main aim of the forthcoming confrontation, as with the one with Laban, will be appeasement of an enemy and a truce to remove the threat. Jacob really has no intention of seeing Esau again after that, as we will find out. A heel-catching, chiselling deceiver comes to trust no-one, and this one is not even trusting God yet. God has been dealing with Esau's hard heart in the intervening 20 years. Jacob's will be another matter.

A holy struggle

That night, Jacob has an extraordinary experience, about which volumes have since been written:

And he arose that night and took his two wives, his two female servants, and his eleven sons, and crossed over the ford of Jabbok. He took them, sent them over the brook, and sent over what he had. Then Jacob was left alone; and a Man wrestled with him until the breaking of day.

Now when He saw that He did not prevail against him, He touched the socket of his hip; and the socket of Jacob's hip was out of joint as He wrestled with him. And He said, "Let Me go, for the day breaks."

But he said, "I will not let You go unless You bless me!"

So He said to him, "What is your name?"

He said, "Jacob."

And He said, "Your name shall no longer be called Jacob, but Israel; for you have struggled with God and with men, and have prevailed."

Then Jacob asked, saying, "Tell me Your name, I pray."

And He said, "Why is it that you ask about My name?" And He blessed him there.

So Jacob called the name of the place Peniel: "For I have seen God face to face, and my life is preserved." (Gen 32:22-30, NKJV)

What a bizarre incident. Think about it. Imagine *you* wrestling with a strange person *all* night. Most commentators acknowledge that this is a theophany – an encounter with God. It's actually another superb *remez* – a hint of something deeper. Idiomatically, Jacob is faced with a personal struggle (the process of the flesh wrestling with the Spirit - sanctification) before he can enter the land of promise (Canaan/rest). Recall that when Abraham received three guests at his tents at Mamre, he is later given insight into recognising them as God and two angels (Gen 18:1,13,17). It's worth reminding ourselves that there are a group of scriptures we examined in the Abraham chapter, which declare that God <u>has been seen by man</u>, and another group which declare that <u>no man can see or hear the Father</u> or else they die.

The answer to the conundrum is that these OT patriarchs indeed saw and heard God, but in the form of the Son, never the Father (FG 1:18). The *remez* reveals that any human sensory perception of the LORD God of Israel is the Son in His pre-incarnate form at various points throughout the OT, or, when the Son is present and a voice speaks from Heaven, the Holy Spirit.[473] The *remez* thus describes the Trinity, much to the chagrin of those

---

[473] Compare FG 5:37 with Mark 1:11; FG 12:28; Luke 9:35. The 'Us' of Gen 1:26, Gen 11:7 and Psa 2 prefigures the triune God as Father, Son and Holy Spirit.

who have been taught that the Trinitarian nature of God is false and not in the Bible. Daniel B Wallace Ph.D, a professor of New Testament Studies at Dallas Theological Seminary and one of the world's great experts on textual criticism and Biblical exegesis, reminds us:

"The Bible clearly contains these four truths: the Father is God, Jesus is God, the Holy Spirit is God, and there is only one God... And that's the Trinity." [474]

The second member of the Trinity is given a classic introduction at the start of the fourth gospel:

In the beginning was the Word, and the Word was with God, and the Word was God. <u>The same was in the beginning with God</u>. All things were made by Him [Yeshua], and without Him was not any thing made that was made. In Him was life, and the life was the light of men.... And the Word was made flesh and dwelt among us, (and we beheld His glory, the glory as of the only begotten of the Father,) full of grace and truth. (FG 1:1-4, 14)

Jacob has been wrestling with Yeshua Himself, and it's a watershed moment. Jack Heyford comments:

"This is one of the Bible's mysterious narratives. The Man is identified by Hosea as an angel (Hos 12:4) [the Angel of the LORD]. The importance of the narrative is Jacob's willingness to contend with God at his time of desperate need. He knows that God has willed to bless him, and he will settle for nothing less than his full inheritance (Gen 32:26). His contending tenacity causes him again to prevail.

The Man obviously knew Jacob's name. He was made to say it because of its meaning – 'Supplanter' or 'Deceiver'. He must acknowledge his weakness before he is transformed." [475]

In wrestling with Jacob, God is forcing the patriarch to transform himself from the fleshly Jacob into spiritual Israel (Gen 32:28). As Chuck Missler puts it, the good news is that if God can justify Jacob, He can justify any of us.[476] Though Jacob exhibits all-

[474] **Strobel, Lee** *The Case for the Real Jesus,* Zondervan, 2007, p.94
[475] Heyford, Jack, *Spirit-Filled Bible,* op. cit. p.54
[476] Missler, Chuck, *Genesis* commentary, www.khouse.org

too-human flaws of self-interest, self-preservation, one-upmanship, and chiselling the best deal he can get at the expense of others, his brazen tenacity to stay the course, even when beaten, commends him to God, who even has to resort to supernatural means to disentangle Himself from the encounter! (Gen 32:25). But Jacob *does* get what he wants: the confirmation from God of his birthright and blessing: the two bequests of which he defrauded his brother, Esau.

Changing names

So Jacob gets the new name, 'Israel', which is curiously ambiguous as to meaning. Expositors have variously rendered it: 'He strives with God, 'One who has prevailed with God', 'One who struggled with the divine angel', 'Persevere with God'. How about 'A princely wrestler with God'? God has ordained Jacob to be the line down which Earth's Saviour will come (so *ha-Satan* pricks up his ears), yet Israel's national history will be a constant wrestling match with God before the eyes of the world in the centuries to follow. The Jews will groan under their yoke as 'the chosen people' of an infallible, omnipotent Creator. When Yeshua sees that he cannot prevail in His struggles with Jacob at Jabbok, He touches him on the sinew of his thigh, resulting in a limp Jacob will suffer for the rest of his days (Gen 32:31). Special insights, selfless fellowship, and intimate moments with God do come at a price, for God's power is made perfect in weakness (Job 16:12; Isa 52:14; 2 Cor 12:7-9: Gal 4:13-15; 6:17).

The Biblical concept of names should be briefly raised here. Notice how certain people get a new name throughout the Message System: Abram becomes Abraham; Sarai becomes Sarah; Jacob becomes Israel; Saul becomes Paul; Simon becomes Peter. Notice that in Abram, Sarai and Saul's case, they are never again referred to by their old names. This is not true for Israel and Peter, who are sometimes called Jacob and Simon, even after the renaming event, when they are acting 'in the flesh' and do not overcome the world (*cf.* Luke 22:31; FG 21:15-19). Names have a great significance in the Bible. Notice how the greatest being Yeshua ever created was unnamed because of rebellion. No human knows the Devil's original name; he is only known by a title: *Ha-Satan* (the adversary).

Receiving a new name is strongly linked to the concept of sanctification; overcoming the flesh/world and engaging in a deeper, faithful relationship with the Creator. Sanctification is not *an event*, it is *a process* of spirit overcoming the flesh through faith:

(Jesus speaks): **He that overcometh, the same shall be clothed in white raiment; <u>and I will not blot out his name out of the Book of Life</u>,**[477] **but I will confess his name before my Father, and before his angels.** (Rev 3:5)

Notwithstanding in this rejoice not, that the spirits are subject unto you; but rather rejoice, <u>because your names are written in Heaven</u>. (Luke 10:20)

He that hath an ear, let him hear what the Spirit saith unto the churches; To him that overcometh will I give to eat of the hidden manna, and will give him a white stone, <u>and in the stone a new name written</u>, which no man knoweth saving he that receiveth it. (Rev 2:17)

The brothers meet

And Jacob <u>lifted up his eyes</u>, and looked, and, behold, Esau came, and with him four hundred men. And he divided the children unto Leah, and unto Rachel, and unto the two handmaids. And he put the handmaids and their children foremost, and Leah and her children after, and Rachel and Joseph hindermost. (Gen 33:1-2)

Hurtfully, Jacob ranks his wives, mistresses and children in reverse order of value to himself, just in case there's trouble. So the concubines Bilhah and Zilpah and their children, Dan, Naphtali, Gad and Asher, know they will be cut down first, should Esau and his roughnecks resolve to slaughter. Then goes Leah and her seven

---

[477] This verse implies that people's names *can* be blotted out of the Book of Life! How to reconcile with the concept of eternal security of the believer? In *Origins 4 - Tetelestai,* we will examine the concept of true and false believers: the wheat and the tares. For those wishing to do a little preliminary research, the following verses will be instructive: Exo 32:32-33; Psa 69:28; Matt 7:13-23; FG 15; Gal 5:22-24; 1 John 5:4-5; 2 Pet 2:20-22; Rev 2,3; 22:6-19

children: Reuben, Simeon, Levi, Judah, Issachar, Zebulun and Dinah. Finally, there's Rachel and Joseph at the back, the most precious of the bunch. It tells you something of Jacob's mindset in a tight spot, and I'm sure the ranking is not lost on the wives, concubines, and their children. Jacob has not purged himself of the destructive favouritism of his parents; the very reason why he's here to make peace with Esau now.

"And he [Jacob] passed over before them, and bowed himself to the ground seven times, until he came near to his brother. And Esau ran to meet him, and embraced him, and fell on his neck, and kissed him: and they wept.

And he [Esau] <u>lifted up his eyes</u>, and saw the women and the children; and said, "Who are those with thee?" And [Jacob] said, "The children which God hath graciously given thy servant." (Gen 33:1-5)

Jacob actually takes the lead, which demonstrates a change in character. Everyone in Jacob's retinue knows he is dreading the confrontation, yet he leads the procession anyway.

Takao Kiyohiro writes:

"The brother running to him came up to him, and a surprising thing happened. What Jacob saw there was not the figure of a brother crazed with anger and brandishing a sword. Esau welcomed him with opened arms, he hugged him, held his head, and kissed him. Esau was weeping. Jacob wept with him. So, reconciliation took place in a manner which far exceeded Jacob's thoughts on it….

In short, Esau's forgiveness was for Jacob but a reflection of God's forgiveness. Jacob saw in Esau's favour the grace of God. For Jacob, his being forgiven by Esau and his reconciliation having come to pass was also an event that happened between God and Jacob and not just something that happened between two people." [478]

Then the handmaidens came near, they and their children, and they bowed themselves. And Leah also with her children came near, and bowed themselves: and after came Joseph near and Rachel, and they bowed themselves.

---

[478] The Reconciliation Of Jacob And Esau, http://www.j-e-s-u-s.org/english/2004/e040905.htm

And [Esau] said, "What meanest thou by all this drove which I met?" And [Jacob] said, "These are to find grace in the sight of my lord."

And Esau said, "I have enough, my brother; keep that thou hast unto thyself."

And Jacob said, "Nay, I pray thee, if now I have found grace in thy sight, then receive my present at my hand: for therefore I have seen thy face, as though I had seen the face of God, and thou wast pleased with me. Take, I pray thee, my blessing that is brought to thee; because God hath dealt graciously with me, and because I have enough."

And [Jacob] urged him, **and** [Esau] <u>took it</u>. (Gen 33:6-11)

Chuck Missler comments:

"The acceptance of a gift is equivalent to the striking of a covenant of friendship. If your present is received by your superior, you may rely on his friendship; if it is declined you have everything to fear. It was on this ground that Jacob was so urgent in pressing Esau to accept his present. Esau took it and so gave Jacob an assurance of his complete reconciliation." [479]

But it's clear that two brothers trust each other only as far as they can swing a camel. Watch what happens next:

And [Esau] said, "Let us take our journey, and let us go, and I will go before thee."

And [Jacob] said unto him, "My lord knoweth that the children are tender, and the flocks and herds with young are with me: and if men should overdrive them one day, all the flock will die. Let my lord, I pray thee, pass over before his servant: and I will lead on softly, according as the cattle that goeth before me and the children be able to endure, <u>until I come unto my lord unto Seir</u>." [480]

And Esau said, "Let me now leave with thee some of the folk that are with me." [i.e. some roughnecks!]

And [Jacob] said: "What needeth it? Let me find grace in the sight of my lord."

---

[479] Missler, Chuck, *Genesis* notes, p.253
[480] More lies and deception. Jacob has no intention of doing this.

So Esau returned that day on his way unto Seir.

And Jacob journeyed to Succoth, and built him an house, and made booths [sheds] for his cattle: therefore the name of the place is called Succoth." (Gen 33:12-17)

God actually wants Jacob to return to the land of his kindred in Canaan, which would be Isaac's place at Mamre/Hebron (Gen 31:13; 35:27). But once again, Jacob follows his own will, which will have tragic consequences. It's not clear from the text, but instead of keeping his promise to follow Esau south into Seir (the land of Edom), Jacob reverses his course across the Brook Jabbok, collects the rest of his flocks and herds, then heads to Succoth where he builds a house and sheds for his cattle. He stays there awhile.[481] These are the actions of a man who has resolved to have nothing more to do with the brother he wronged other than to settle the threat of violence against himself and his family via a token reconciliation. Warren Wiersbe has Jacob pegged:

"Esau did the gracious thing and offered to accompany his brother south to his home in Mount Seir, but Jacob had no desire to spend more time with Esau than was necessary. Like his farewell with Laban, Jacob's meeting with Esau was a truce, not a true reconciliation. But Jacob gave the impression that his destination was indeed Mount Seir (v.14), and he offered every excuse he could think of to convince Esau to go before him and let him proceed at his own pace. The repetition of the phrase 'my lord' in this paragraph may indicate Jacob's respect and courtesy, but it also suggests that Jacob was grovelling again. One thing was sure: Jacob was deceiving again.

"Esau started back to Mount Seir, travelling south, while Jacob moved northwest to Succoth and then further on to Shechem. There's no record that Jacob ever visited his brother in Mount Seir. It's likely that after they met at Isaac's funeral, they never saw each other again. (Gen 35:27-29)" [482]

Trouble at Shechem

We're about to witness more of Jacob's selfish motives in what occurs when he crosses into Canaan with his retinue and arrives at

---

[481] Succoth is so named because Jacob built *sukkot* (booths, sheds) for his cattle.

[482] Wiersbe, W, *The Wiersbe Bible Commentary*, op. cit., p.111

Shechem, a small livestock town in the central highlands. Shechem is destined to play a defining role in Israel's history.[483] Situated on the main trading route that runs north/south through Canaan, it trades locally in olives, wheat, livestock and pottery. The powerbroker/prince of the region is Hamor the Hivite (*Hamor*, 'ass'), whom Jacob approaches with a view to purchasing a parcel of land to settle the family. He erects an altar there on the newly purchased possession and the family begins to settle down. This is in itself a problem, as we'll soon discover.

Jacob's daughter, Dinah, decides to go into Shechem to seek out the local gals and make friends. This is in direct contravention to the Hebrew custom of remaining separate from Canaanites, not because of race but because of idol-worship and spiritual uncleanliness.[484] It does not appear that Dinah has either a chaperone or permission from her mother, Leah, to make this foray. Mike Ford writes:

"It is difficult to pin down Dinah's age at this point, but she was probably thirteen or fourteen years old. Most commentators agree on this, though some think she was as old as her late teens. By following the timeline of Jacob's journey, service to Laban, and return to Canaan, the evidence points to a young girl of around thirteen. Some thirteen-year-old girls look and act like streetwalkers, yet other girls of that age still play with dolls." [485]

The Jewish historian Josephus states that there was a Hivite festival occurring at the time of this incident. Dinah may have felt comfortable enough with her neighbours to have gone into town

---

[483] Google Earth 32 12 11 N, 35 18 40 E

[484] Abraham did not want a Canaanite wife for Isaac (Gen 24:2-3), neither did Isaac wish one for Jacob (Gen 28:1). This would later be ratified in the Torah (Exo 34:11-16). In Deut 7:1-5, God marks out the Hivites, among other peoples, for extermination under Joshua due to their wickedness, idol-worship, and putative genetic contamination with the Nephilim. God wants to remove the possibility of spiritual corruption of the Jews by these peoples.

[485] **Ford, M** "The Rape of Dinah", http://www.cgg.org/index.cfm/fuseaction/Library.sr/CT/RA/k/1566/Rape-Dinah.htm

"to see the finery of the women of that country." [486] The visit is to end in disaster:

And when Shechem the son of Hamor the Hivite, prince of the country, saw her, he took her, and lay with her, and defiled her. And his soul clave unto Dinah the daughter of Jacob, and he loved the damsel, and spake kindly unto the damsel. (Gen 34:2-3)

Dinah is accosted by the son of Hamor, the youth Shechem (presumably named after his home town). Shechem pesters her, then takes Dinah off to violate her. It's rape, yet many expositors spend hours agonising over who was to blame, whether Dinah led Shechem on, if she should even have been out on her own, and so on. This is probably not the first occasion that Shechem has seen the lass. He is certainly smitten with inordinate affection (Col 3:5).

And Shechem spake unto his father Hamor, saying, "Get me this damsel to wife."

And Jacob heard that he had defiled Dinah his daughter: now his sons were with his cattle in the field: and Jacob held his peace until they were come. (Gen 34:2-5)

Notice the change in family dynamics. Jacob's only daughter has just been raped, yet Jacob waits for his boys to arrive. Would he have done the same had this been Rachel's daughter instead of Leah's?

Witness Shechem's character: **"Get me this damsel to wife!"** the language of a spoilt heir to a powerful father, who will indulge his every whim. Where is Dinah after the rape? Detained at Shechem's place (Gen 34:26). Is she a bargaining chip? Does she stay willingly? Is this an exciting, teenage sexual adventure to her? Perhaps a chance to hit back at the misogynistic attitudes of her stifling, male-dominated family? Expositors' quills have furiously scribbled throughout the ages.

One senses a weariness in Hamor as he wends his way out to Jacob's tents, dysfunctional brat in tow, in an attempt to settle the business. Rest assured that father and son would not have gone alone, certainly in view of the rape, the detaining of the girl, and the strength of Jacob's clan. Though Canaanites are a rough bunch, Hamor and Shechem become uneasy as they are surrounded by the

---

[486] **Josephus** *Antiquities,* 1:21:1

hostile sons of Jacob, the elder in their twenties, recently returned from the fields after learning the worst.

... and the men were grieved, and they were very wroth, because he had wrought folly in Israel in lying with Jacob's daughter; which thing ought not to be done.

And Hamor communed with them, saying, "The soul of my son Shechem longeth for your daughter: I pray you give her him to wife. And make ye marriages with us, and give your daughters unto us, and take our daughters unto you. And ye shall dwell with us: and the land shall be before you; dwell and trade ye therein, and get you possessions therein."

And Shechem said unto her father and unto her brethren, "Let me find grace in your eyes, and what ye shall say unto me I will give. Ask me never so much dowry and gift, and I will give according as ye shall say unto me: but give me the damsel to wife." (Gen 34:7-12)

There are some interesting dynamics here that don't sink in when you first read the story. Shechem does not apologise, but he does offer a hint of remorse for the heinous act: **"Let me find grace in your eyes, and what ye shall say unto me I will give."** However rough and ready, Shechem is clearly struck by the girl and wants to make amends to gain her, no matter the cost. The fact that Dinah is currently ensconced in Shechem's house and has not been returned to her family infuriates her siblings further. Dinah's rape is socially fatal within the clan. Their sister is left now with no prospect of a valid Hebrew marriage in the future. Theirs is a cold anger, and again we see the subtle shift in the power-structure within Jacob's family. Jacob previously waits for his sons to come in from the field (Gen 34:5). Now the patriarch of the family does not answer Hamor and Shechem, the sons do:

And the sons of Jacob answered Shechem and Hamor his father deceitfully, and said, because he had defiled Dinah their sister: And they said unto them, "We cannot do this thing, to give our sister to one that is uncircumcised; for that were a reproach unto us. But in this will we consent unto you: If ye will be as we be, that every male of you be circumcised; then will we give our daughters unto you, and we will take your daughters to us, and we will dwell with you, and we will become one people. But if

ye will not hearken unto us, to be circumcised; then will we take our daughter, and we will be gone."

And their words pleased Hamor, and Shechem, Hamor's son. (Gen 34:13-18)

Shechem is too smitten by the girl to sense the danger he is in. Hamor is blind to the trap also, engrossed as he is with the ulterior motive to his plan, to which the Holy Spirit gives us an ear when prince and heir explain the proposal later to the men of Shechem:

"These men are peaceable with us; therefore let them dwell in the land, and trade therein; for the land, behold, it is large enough for them; let us take their daughters to us for wives, and let us give them our daughters. Only herein will the men consent unto us for to dwell with us, to be one people, if every male among us be circumcised, as they are circumcised. Shall not their cattle and their substance and every beast of theirs be ours? Only let us consent unto them, and they will dwell with us." (Gen 34:21-23)

Jacob's wealth is very conspicuous to the Canaanites; they want it for themselves. Hamor and the men of Shechem deem it a light bargain to have their foreskins snipped in return for the chance to enrich themselves – perhaps even to dispose of Jacob and his clan when the time is right. It will prove a fatal accord.

And unto Hamor and unto Shechem his son hearkened all that went out of the gate of his city; and every male was circumcised, all that went out of the gate of his city.

And it came to pass on the third day, when they were sore, that two of the sons of Jacob, Simeon and Levi, Dinah's brethren, took each man his sword, and came upon the city boldly, and slew all the males. And they slew Hamor and Shechem his son with the edge of the sword, and took Dinah out of Shechem's house, and went out. The sons of Jacob came upon the slain, and spoiled the city, because they had defiled their sister. They took their sheep, and their oxen, and their asses, and that which was in the city, and that which was in the field, and all their wealth, and all their little ones, and their wives took they captive, and spoiled even all that was in the house. (Gen 34:24-29)

Simeon and Levi are the henchmen: sons two and three; Dinah's direct siblings via Leah. They say the apple never falls far

460

from the tree. In setting up the deceitful contract with Hamor and Shechem, all Jacob's sons are proving the measure of their father in deceit. The death squad raid on Shechem will shape their characters for the incredible dramas that will play out in their near future. Though Genesis 34:27 seems to imply that all Jacob's sons take part in the sacking of Shechem, Joseph is still a child at this time. What is Jacob's reaction to the town's immolation?

And Jacob said to Simeon and Levi, "Ye have troubled me to make me to stink among the inhabitants of the land, among the Canaanites and the Perizzites: and I being few in number, they shall gather themselves together against me, and slay me; and I shall be destroyed, I and my house." (Gen 34:30)

He forgoes rebuking his boys for the sin of wholesale murder, plunder and the kidnapping of Shechem's wives and children. Jacob's first concern is that Simeon and Levi's special forces raid has put his own safety at risk, not to mention the security of his family and all their possessions. Jacob's in the flesh once again, unwilling to put faith in God's promise of protection over his house (Gen 28:15). As for Simeon and Levi, their wicked act, though not rebuked for the curse to God that it is, will ultimately cost them their father's deathbed blessing (Gen 49:5-7).

No-one comes out of this story well. Not Dinah, nor Leah, her mother; nor Jacob; nor Hamor and Shechem; and especially not Simeon and Levi, the murderers, nor the rest of Jacob's plundering clan. And why is that? Why are there losers all round in this sordid tale? *Because Jacob had no business settling in Shechem in the first place.* God had called him back to the family seat at Hebron. There are echoes here of Abraham's detour northwest to Haran when he had been specifically instructed by God to head west into Canaan. The conclusion? Disobedience to God produces lasting, baleful results. God evidently had his own grudge against Hamor and his Hivites, and uses the incident provoked by Dinah to dish out lessons to everyone. The only piece of good news is that Rachel is pregnant once more. We hear no more of Leah, who predeceases Jacob some time later and is buried at Machpelah (Gen 49:31). While Jacob's boys feature prominently in the next chapters of God's story, and go on to father the tribes of Israel, Dinah too disappears from the record. We are not told what becomes of Jacob's hapless daughter. Did she eventually marry anyone? Was her life ruined as a result her ill-judged trip into town? 'It could be that the purpose of a life is only to serve as a warning to others' runs the proverb. God intended for the Hebrews to be a people set apart for His purposes. Explicit warnings had been given not to intermarry or procreate with the Canaanite peoples. Like Lot, Dinah made the mistake of courting a harsh and unforgiving world, and was doubtless forever changed by the experience.

Jacob returns home

And God said unto Jacob, "Arise, go up to Bethel, and dwell there: and make there an altar unto God, that appeared unto thee when thou fleddest from the face of Esau thy brother."

Then Jacob said unto his household, and to all that were with him, "Put away the strange gods that are among you, and be clean, and change your garments: and let us arise, and go up to Bethel; and I will make there an altar unto God, who answered me in the day of my distress, and was with me in the way which I went."

And they gave unto Jacob all the strange gods which were in their hand, and all their earrings which were in their ears; and Jacob hid them under the oak which was by Shechem. And they journeyed: and the terror of God was upon the cities that were round about them, and they did not pursue after the sons of Jacob. (Gen 35:1-5)

Syrian paganism still infects Jacob's family. The patriarch takes stock of the spiritual degradation of his clan, commendably takes action to remedy same, then takes them south. Though bad news rides a swift camel, and the other cities in the region soon receive word of Shechem's grisly fate, the Canaanites make Jacob no bother, for the fear of the LORD is upon them.

Jacob builds an altar to the LORD at Bethel, where he had experienced the 'ladder to Heaven' incident on his outbound journey. Rebekah's nurse, Deborah, who has accompanied Jacob throughout his years of exile, dies here and is buried under a terebinth tree. God appears to Jacob in this place again to bless him and reaffirm His covenant promise:

And God said unto him, "Thy name is Jacob: thy name shall not be called any more Jacob, but Israel shall be thy name." And he called his name Israel.

And God said unto him, "I am God Almighty [*El Shaddai*: the All-Sufficient One]**: be fruitful and multiply; a nation and a company of nations shall be of thee, and kings shall come out of thy loins; And the land which I gave Abraham and Isaac, to thee I will give it, and to thy seed after thee will I give the land."**

And God went up from him in the place where He talked with him. (Gen 35:10-13)

For reasons not given, the journey continues south past Hebron, the home of Jacob's father, Isaac, and on to Ephrath, later known as Bethlehem. Rachel is in labour by this time. Problems with the birth set in immediately.

And they journeyed from Bethel; and there was but a little way to come to Ephrath: and Rachel travailed, and she had hard labour. And it came to pass, when she was in hard labour, that the midwife said unto her, "Fear not; thou shalt have this son also."

And it came to pass, as her soul was in departing, (for she died) that she called his name Ben-Oni ['son of my sorrow']**: but his father called him Benjamin** ['son of my right hand']**.**

And Rachel died, and was buried in the way to Ephrath, which is Bethlehem. And Jacob set a pillar upon her grave: that is the pillar of Rachel's grave unto this day. (Gen 35: 16-20)

Rachel's roadside grave is recorded as still existing in Saul's lifetime (1 Sam 10:2), though the authenticity of the traditional site, which hosts the Bilal bin Rabah mosque, is disputed. Their reactions to Rachel's death are not recorded, but the tragedy would have hit Jacob and Joseph hard. Rachel was the love of Jacob's life, and Joseph was his most favoured son. Such favouritism has already been the cause of much trauma in Jacob's life thus far, and is a fault the patriarch appears ill-inclined to remedy. But God will use the evil fruit of Jacob's partiality for good. And while Rachel's life could well have been shortened due to Jacob's rash oath to Laban in the matter of the *teraphim*, God intends to bless Joseph the *wunderkind* with one of the most meteoric rises to glory ever recorded in history, and give him a double portion of his father's inheritance. It's a story which has captured the hearts of a thousand generations, and there are some astonishing insights we can glean into God's character, His will, the human condition, and the extraordinary way in which the Creator chooses to save the wealthiest pagan nation on Earth from certain destruction, as an object lesson into His grace and mercy.

JOSEPH

Most people know of the story of Joseph: how a precocious teenager with his 'coat of many colours' landed himself in trouble with his jealous brothers; was sold into slavery and hauled off to Egypt; was fitted up by the predatory wife of his master; thrown into prison; then released to experience what has to be the most bizarre ascent to political glory you've ever heard of. Just a legend or fanciful tale? Let's examine the story with fresh eyes and encounter some amazing insights that are not widely known. Warren Wiersbe introduces us to one of the Old Testament's great heroes:

"The history of Joseph can be read on at least three different levels. If we read it simply as literature, we discover a fascinating story involving a doting father, a pampered son, some jealous brothers, a conniving wife, and an international food crisis. It's no wonder that for centuries creative artists have turned to this story for inspiration. In 1742, Henry Fielding patterned the hero of Joseph Andrews after the biblical Joseph, and the next year, Handel produced his *oratorio, Joseph*. Over a period of sixteen years, the German novelist Thomas Mann wrote four novels based on the life of Joseph. In our own day, we have the rock cantata *Joseph and the Amazing Technicolor Dreamcoat* and its song, *Any Dream Will Do*." [487]

You will recall that Joseph is the 11th son of Jacob and his favourite boy, born when Jacob was 91 years of age.[488] Joseph's mother was Rachel, daughter of Laban, who tragically died in childbirth producing Jacob's 12th and final son, Benjamin. By the time Jacob finally returns to the family seat at Mamre (Hebron) in

---

[487] Wiersbe, W, *The Wiersbe Bible Commentary,* op. cit., p.116

[488] "If Jacob was 130 years old when he went to Egypt (Gen 47:9) and Joseph was 39 (Gen 41:46 [30 years old], plus seven years of plenty and two years of famine [Gen 45:11]), then Jacob was 91 when Joseph was born." - Wiersbe, W, *The Wiersbe Bible Commentary,* op. cit., p.116, note 6

Canaan after his twenty-year Syrian exile, he is 108 years old, and his father Isaac is a venerable 168 years of age.[489]

So what? What possible relevance could a 3,800-year-old story have in our own modern age? Aside from the homiletic benefit of learning of the Creator's character, we are about to learn how to trust Him when we enter dark times and all seems hopeless. Life seems comfortable enough for most people now, but few have any idea how drastically the world will change in the coming years. God intends us to learn a range of eternal truths relevant to this future by studying His interaction with the Old and New Testament characters who have been there before us.[490] Remember, this education is not some four-year course to garner a faceless job in the city until we retire, this is boot camp to prepare us for the Eternal Kingdom! A lot of these characters we are learning about will be there as your eternal companions. And the one figure who is the fulcrum of all history, who overawes eternity and any chance of a hopeful future for each of us, is the One whom Joseph is modelled on in the coming chapter. Arthur W Pink cites 100 ways in which Joseph is a type of Christ: Joseph is a shepherd; he opposes evil; he is hated by his brethren; and he foretells his own future sovereignty, eventually rising to sit at the right hand of the ruler of the known world. We'll examine many more intriguing parallels as we proceed.

Of course, the stories we are studying are homilies, yet since the Creator Himself is the Word made flesh (FG 1:1-3,14), we find ourselves examining a transcendent literary phenomenon in the Bible, the hyperdimensional implications of which are transmuted into our modern age. We observe the characters struggling with their moral and physical dilemmas (the Holy War); making decisions - sometimes right, sometimes wrong. But, unlike the story of Jacob, we will discover far deeper themes underpinning

---

[489] "If Joseph was 17 when he was taken to Egypt (Gen 37:2), then Jacob would have been in Canaan 11 years and was 108 years old. His father would have been 168 years old (Gen 25:26), and therefore still alive when Joseph was sold. Isaac would have died 12 years later, one year before Joseph was elevated to being the second ruler in Egypt." - Wiersbe, W, *The Wiersbe Bible Commentary*, ibid.
[490] Rom 15:4; 1 Cor 10:6,11-12; 2 Tim 3:16

the Joseph narrative that enable us to get to the heart of the education the Creator desires for each of us.

So let's set the scene. God has a people picked out, which He desires to be kept separate from the evils of the world to be a witness of His glory. Man has been given the incredible gift of free will to choose his own path, for it is only by free will that true love can be known. God's intent is for us to harmonise our wills with His, to produce a single will in the universe. This conformity has to come from us voluntarily via our own will; he cannot and will not force us to do this. It's a remarkable and singular restriction the Creator of the universe has placed upon His own actions. Was God the cause of World War 1? No, man was. Could He have stopped it? Of course, *but He didn't*. The Earth programme is a free arena, wherein the participants exercise full volition, but choices always have consequences, for which each person will ultimately be held accountable. Mankind hates any accountability which compels him to confront his own degenerate nature. Ask Levi and Simeon, who butchered the men of Shechem.

Trouble in the family

Ask Reuben. Shortly after Rachel's death, a brief verse records that Jacob's eldest son takes his father's concubine, Rachel's maid Bilhah, and lies with her. We are told that **Israel** [Jacob] **heard about it** (Gen 35:22). What at first glance appears to be a rash and hurtful exhibition of lust is in fact the first act of a hostile takeover in that culture. Later in Jewish history, a general named Abner will be accused by the weak king Ishbosheth, son of King Saul, of lying with one of his father's concubines in an attempt to usurp Ishbosheth's power before the people. Concubines are considered kingly property, passed from father to son, and messing with the patriarchal/royal harem is serious business. In so doing, the perpetrator is assuming the rights of a king in defiance of the reigning monarch, thereby committing treason. Ishbosheth may have been weak and fearful of his 'uncle' Abner who put him into power, but the evidence against Abner was apparently compelling enough for Ishbosheth to say something. So he did. And Abner went toxic (2 Sam 3:7-11).

King David's unruly son, Absalom, commits a similar act when his father flees Jerusalem in the face of his son's rebellion. David leaves behind ten concubines to mind the house, whom Absalom rapes in a tent on the roof of said dwelling in full view of the people. He is counselled to do this by Ahithophel, former advisor to King David and grandfather of the famous Bathsheba,[491] whom David took from her lawful husband, Uriah the Hittite (2 Sam 15:16; 16:22; 20:3).

Reuben's attempt to become patriarch of the family by such sordid means is doomed to failure, and he will ultimately lose the double-portion of his birthright as firstborn, which Jacob later transfers to Joseph and his sons (Gen 48; *cf.* 49:3-4; 1 Chron 5:1). Not an auspicious start, then, to the sons of Jacob who will go on to populate the future nation of Israel. The first three of Jacob's sons – Reuben, Simeon and Levi – have thus far all been disgraced. The fourth son, Judah, will become the line down which the Messianic 'scarlet thread' will run, culminating in the birth of the Creator on Earth – Jesus Christ. In Genesis 49:10, Jacob will give an astonishing prophecy over this son, Judah, which foretells not only the birth of *Mashiach*, but the unique time in which this momentous event will occur.

Joseph: naïve dreamer?

The first time we are properly introduced to Jacob's 11th son, the ingenuous Joseph, he appears to be telling tales on his elder brothers:

And Jacob dwelt in the land wherein his father was a stranger, in the land of Canaan. These are the generations of Jacob. Joseph, being seventeen years old, was feeding the flock with his brethren; and the lad was with the sons of Bilhah, and with the sons of Zilpah, his father's wives: and Joseph brought unto his father their evil report.

<u>Now Israel loved Joseph more than all his children,</u> because he was the son of his old age: and he made him a coat of many colours. <u>And when his brethren saw that their father loved him</u>

---

[491] Compare 2 Sam 11:3 with 2 Sam 23:34

more than all his brethren, they hated him, and could not speak peaceably unto him. (Gen 37:1-4)

You'd think by now that Jacob would have learned the lesson of the dangers of favouritism. You would be wrong. Notwithstanding Joseph and his mother had been publicly placed above his other siblings in the 'protection ranking' prior to the encounter with Esau and his 400 henchmen, a thousand words, looks and gestures since – every little act and nuance of speech – would have betrayed a father's partiality for a single son. Much has been made of the 'coat of many colours', which may just be fanciful 1611 King James for a seamless jacket or 'long, sleeved coat': a literal translation of the Hebrew phrase. Scholars are generally in agreement that full-sleeved coats were expensive and rare in that culture, and only within the purview of the well-to-do (*cf.* 2 Sam 13:18). Whatever the true nature of Joseph's coat, the text intends to convey to us that it was unique; valued; envied; the gift of a doting father to a favoured, 17-year-old son.

Whilst tempted to conclude that the kid has it coming (running off to tell his father of every mischief stirred up by his wayward kin), we should perhaps credit Jacob with knowing the true nature of his brood by now. These were the men who took part in the brutal slaughter and sacking of Shechem because of Dinah's violation. These were the men who kidnapped the surviving women and children of that city and enslaved them. After that, the eldest, Reuben, committed fornication with one of his father's wives to unseat Jacob as patriarch. It's fair to assume that Jacob probably has the measure of his sons by now, and there will be more evidence for this as we get into what happens to Joseph.

And Joseph dreamed a dream, and he told it his brethren: and they hated him yet the more. And he said unto them, "Hear, I pray you, this dream which I have dreamed: For, behold, we were binding sheaves in the field, and, lo, my sheaf arose, and also stood upright; and, behold, your sheaves stood round about, and made obeisance to my sheaf."

And his brethren said to him, "Shalt thou indeed reign over us? Or shalt thou indeed have dominion over us?" And they hated him yet the more for his dreams, and for his words. (Gen 37:5-8)

Clearly, Joseph isn't stupid; naïve, perhaps, but not daft. While some expositors scratch their heads that the lad could be so innocent and candid (given his siblings' penchant for violence), I believe we are witnessing a character trait in Joseph with which his father is already familiar: one which will set him apart on a number of occasions in the future to propel him on his meteoric rise to fame. Joseph is without malice. He is a good person who calls it how it is. He is immune to practising the violence and cynicism of his age. He has no ulterior agenda other than to serve. He is completely trustworthy.

There are close parallels between these attributes of Joseph and those of Jesus:

- Joseph has his father's love and trust
- He has a simple, reliable opposition to evil
- He is a shepherd (*cf.* Gen 37:2; Psa 23)
- He is hated because of his words (Gen 37:4,5,8; FG 7:7; 8:40)
- He foretells his future sovereignty (Gen 37:7,9; Matt 26:64; 2 Pet 3:4; Rev 12:1.5)
- He is envied and hated by his brethren (Gen 37:4; Psa 69; FG 1:11)
- He is sent forth by his father (Gen 37:13; 1 John 4:10; Heb 10:7)
- He does the will of his father
- He has a distinctive vestment which is envied and taken by his enemies (Gen 37:3; Judg 5:30; Psa 22:18; Matt 27:35; FG 19:23)

Joseph has a further dream (the two-dream paradigm will run throughout his story). This time his vision even upsets his father:

And [Joseph] dreamed yet another dream, and told it his brethren, and said, "Behold, I have dreamed a dream more; and, behold, the sun and the moon and the eleven stars made obeisance to me."

And he told it to his father, and to his brethren: and his father rebuked him, and said unto him, "What is this dream that thou hast dreamed? Shall I and thy mother and thy brethren indeed come to bow down ourselves to thee to the earth?"

And his brethren envied him; but his father observed the saying. (Gen 37:9-11)

Here are three verses which hold some terrific insights. The sun, moon and stars idiom crops up again in the book of Revelation in connection with the end times:

And there appeared a great wonder in heaven; a woman clothed with the sun, and the moon under her feet, and upon her head a crown of twelve stars: And she being with child cried, travailing in birth, and pained to be delivered.

And there appeared another wonder in heaven; and behold a great red dragon, having seven heads and ten horns, and seven crowns upon his heads. And his tail drew the third part of the stars of heaven, and did cast them to the earth:[492] **and the dragon stood before the woman which was ready to be delivered, for to devour her child as soon as it was born.**

And she brought forth a man child, who was to rule all nations with a rod of iron: and her child was caught up unto God, and to his throne.[493] **And the woman fled into the wilderness, where she hath a place prepared of God, that they should feed her there a thousand two hundred and threescore days.** (Rev 12:1-6)

Readers and scholars have argued for centuries over who this woman is in Revelation's cryptic imagery. Is the woman the Church, being persecuted in the horror of the end times under Antichrist? Will the faithful Church really be put through the terrors of the Tribulation, as many people believe today?

If this woman is the Church, rues Chuck Missler, then she's in trouble because she's pregnant rather than a virgin bride – the icon of the faithful Church (*cf.* Eph 5:22-32).[494] In fact, Jacob interprets the Revelation idiom for us in Joseph's dream: The woman represents the nation of Israel with her twelve tribes (sons) being

---

[492] Most scholars interpret this as a third of the angelic realm following Satan, the dragon, in his revolt.

[493] This passage was also interpreted by G H Pember to be a reference to the *harpazo* (Rapture).

[494] **Missler, Chuck** *Genesis* audio commentary, www.khouse.org. For a fuller explanation of 'the Bride of Christ', see http://www.sacred-texts.com/chr/tbr/tbr082.htm

persecuted by the dragon (*ha-Satan*). The man child is Yeshua, born out of Israel to rule the nations with a rod of iron with David, His prince, in the coming Millennial Kingdom. The Trib is even referred to by the prophet Jeremiah as 'the time of Jacob's trouble' (Jer 30:7).

Those post-Tribulation-Rapture believers already burying their baked beans in the backwoods and arming themselves with AK-47s for what they see as a coming showdown with the Antichrist's New World Order Beast System need to do further research on their ecclesiology. In Revelation 2 and 3, Christ's letters to the seven churches reveal that one church (Philadelphia) *will be spared from the very time of the Tribulation* (Rev 3:10) because of her faithfulness and perseverance. Another church, Thyatira, is told by Yeshua that its members will be put through the Great Tribulation *unless* they repent of their deeds. Which, of course, implies that if they *do* repent, they won't endure the most dreadful three-and-a-half years the world will have ever seen (Rev 2:22-23). As we proceed in the *Origins* series, we will find out God's purpose for the Great Tribulation: who will be put through it, and who won't.[495]

Back to Joseph and his second dream. Although Jacob is ticked off with the import of his son's 'sun, moon and stars' dream, that the whole family will bow down before Joseph, notice that *he observes the saying.* Jacob himself is not inexperienced with dreams and visions, and a small part of him files away the incident, doubtless wondering whether his son's visions, like his own, are from the LORD and of prophetic import.

The family plot against Joseph

And his brethren went to feed their father's flock in Shechem. And Israel said unto Joseph, "Do not thy brethren feed the flock in Shechem? Come, and I will send thee unto them." And [Joseph] said to him, "Here am I."

---

[495] *cf.* Dan 12:1; Hos 5:15; Zech 13:7-9

And [Israel/Jacob] **said to him, "Go, I pray thee, see whether it be well with thy brethren, and well with the flocks; and bring me word again."**

So he sent him out of the vale of Hebron, and [Joseph] **came to Shechem.** (Gen 37:12-14)

Amazing to relate, the ten eldest sons of Jacob have brazenly returned to the very town they once sacked over the rape of Dinah, whose male citizens they murdered. Here they feed their sheep! Reading between the lines, there is probably some local ill-feeling or fear towards them, for when Joseph arrives at Shechem, his brothers are nowhere to be found.

And a certain man found [Joseph]**, and, behold, he was wandering in the field: and the man asked him, saying, "What seekest thou?"**

And he said, "I seek my brethren: tell me, I pray thee, where they feed their flocks."

And the man said, "They are departed hence; for I heard them say, 'Let us go to Dothan.' " And Joseph went after his brethren, and found them in Dothan.

And when they saw him afar off, even before he came near unto them, they conspired against him to slay him. And they said one to another, "Behold, this dreamer cometh. Come now therefore, and let us slay him, and cast him into some pit, and we will say, 'Some evil beast hath devoured him': and we shall see what will become of his dreams."

And Reuben heard it, and he delivered him out of their hands; and said, "Let us not kill him." And Reuben said unto them, "Shed no blood, but cast him into this pit that is in the wilderness, and lay no hand upon him"; that he might rid him out of their hands, to deliver him to his father again. (Gen 37:15-22)

There are two more parallels here between Joseph and Jesus:

- He came unto his own, but his own received him not (FG 1:11)
- He is conspired against (Matt 12:14)

Once more, the true nature of these wastrels is revealed. The initial idea among the brothers is to kill Joseph. This is too much for the eldest, Reuben, whose plan is to dump him in an empty cistern (probably one of many small reservoirs common across the parched land), then take him out later and pack him off home to Father, saving his life. He appears to get his way.

And it came to pass, when Joseph was come unto his brethren, that they stript Joseph out of his coat, his coat of many colours that was on him; And they took him, and cast him into a pit: and the pit was empty, there was no water in it.

And they sat down to eat bread: <u>and they lifted up their eyes</u> **and looked, and, behold, a company of Ishmeelites came from Gilead with their camels bearing spicery and balm and myrrh, going to carry it down to Egypt.**

And Judah said unto his brethren, "<u>What profit is it if we slay our brother, and conceal his blood?</u> **[i.e. "What do we get out of it?"] Come, and let us sell him to the Ishmeelites, and let not our hand be upon him;** <u>for he is our brother and our flesh</u>.**" And his brethren were content.**

Then there passed by Midianites merchantmen; and they drew and lifted up Joseph out of the pit, and sold Joseph to the Ishmeelites for twenty pieces of silver: and they brought Joseph into Egypt. (Gen 37:23-28)

Some insights here:

- Can you beat Judah? "There's no point in killing him. Let's sell him to the Ishmeelites and make some money! Let our hand not be upon him. After all, he *is* our brother and our flesh!" They were just talking about *killing* him a little while before!

- Joseph is insulted and stripped. *So was Yeshua* (Matt 27:27-28; FG 19:23)

- Joseph is cast into a pit with no water. *So was Yeshua* (Zech 9:9-11; Matt 12:40)

- Joseph is lifted out of the pit. *So was Yeshua* (1 Cor 15)

- His wicked brethren heard Joseph's cries and saw his distress, yet did nothing (Gen 42:21); *The same with Yeshua* (Matt 27:42-43, 46-47)

- Joseph was betrayed/sold down the road by Judah for 20 pieces of silver (Gen 37:28); *Yeshua was betrayed/sold down the road by Judas for 30 pieces of silver* (Matt 26:14-16)

474

- Three guesses who the main culprits among the brothers are. Judah we know. The others are doubtless Simeon and Levi, regarded by their father as the cruellest of the bunch (Gen 49:5-7) - partners in crime over the Shechem slaughter
- It appears from the text that Joseph was in the pit but a short while, yet some expositors think he may have been in there for three days, crying out (Gen 42:21). Was this the reason Joseph later has his brothers jailed in Egypt for three days (Gen 42:17), then releases them to return to Canaan, all except Simeon, whom he keeps in jail (Gen 42:24)?

And Reuben returned unto the pit; and, behold, Joseph was not in the pit; and he rent his clothes. And he returned unto his brethren, and said, "The child is not; and I, whither shall I go?"

And they took Joseph's coat, and killed a kid of the goats, and dipped the coat in the blood; and they sent the coat of many colours, and they brought it to their father; and said, "This have we found: know now whether it be thy son's coat or no."

And [Jacob] knew it, and said, "It is my son's coat; an evil beast hath devoured him; Joseph is without doubt rent in pieces."

And Jacob rent his clothes, and put sackcloth upon his loins, and mourned for his son many days. And all his sons and all his daughters rose up to comfort him; but he refused to be comforted; and he said, "For I will go down into the grave unto my son mourning." Thus his father wept for him.

And the Midianites sold [Joseph] into Egypt unto Potiphar, an officer of Pharaoh's, and captain of the guard. (Gen 37:29-36)

Reuben was apparently away on an errand. He returns to find Joseph gone from the pit. The others fill him in on their transaction with the Ishmeelites, and doubtless grease Reuben's palm with his two-piece cut of the blood money. A plan is then hatched to take Joseph's distinctive coat, daub it in the blood of a killed kid (goat), and present it to their father as evidence that Joseph has met some beastly end.

It says a lot about these rascals that they would put their father through such needless pain, but isn't that the model of us with our own heavenly Father? (Eph 4:30) There is another intriguing parallel between Joseph and Yeshua: Joseph's brothers have sinned, but they choose to bring the blood before the father to get themselves off the hook with a 'sin offering' created by the death and blood of an innocent (the goat-kid)! (*cf.* Heb 9:12). Notice also: just as Jacob himself used clothing to deceive his father Isaac to obtain the favoured son's blessing, so now Jacob is being deceived by clothing over the fate of *his* most favoured son.

Jacob is absolutely traumatised when presented with his son's distinctive vestment. This is his most beloved son, born to him by the love of his life, Rachel.

"My son's tunic!" the old man wails. "A wild beast has devoured him! Joseph has been torn to pieces!" No doubt the brothers give each other knowing winks behind their father's back, fumbling the silver in their pockets. This is sibling rivalry with a hard edge on hurt, yet, as we shall see, **all things work together for good to them that love God, to them who are the called according to His purpose.** (Rom 8:28).

The new life in Egypt

And Joseph was brought down to Egypt; and Potiphar, an officer of Pharaoh, captain of the guard, <u>an Egyptian</u>, bought him of the hands of the Ishmeelites, which had brought him down thither.

And the LORD was with Joseph, and he was a prosperous man; and he was in the house of his master <u>the Egyptian</u>. And his master saw that the LORD was with him, and that the LORD made all that he did to prosper in his hand. And Joseph found grace in his sight, and he served him: and he made him overseer over his house, and all that he had he put into his hand.

And it came to pass from the time that he had made him overseer in his house, and over all that he had, that the LORD blessed the Egyptian's house for Joseph's sake; and the blessing of the LORD was upon all that he had in the house, and in the field.

And he left all that he had in Joseph's hand; and he knew not ought he had, save the bread which he did eat. And Joseph was a goodly person, and well favoured. (Gen 39:1-6)

Joseph becomes a servant to one Potiphar (*poti-phar:* 'devoted to Pharaoh'), an 'officer' of Pharaoh, captain of the guard. It doesn't take long for Potiphar to realise that this particular slave under his control is markedly different. For a start, he's extremely well presented and intelligent. Moreover, Potiphar senses a trustworthiness in Joseph early on which is not betrayed. Before you know it, Joseph is placed in charge of Potiphar's household and the LORD begins blessing Potiphar on Joseph's account.

Potiphar is described as an 'officer' of Pharaoh. The Hebrew word for officer is סריס (*sariys*), which can be translated 'one who is castrated'; 'a eunuch', as well as 'officer' or 'minister of state'. Clearly Potiphar isn't a eunuch in the true sense of the word since he has a wife whom we will shortly encounter. Thus *sariys* is viewed by scholars as a title, a job description in Potiphar's case, which places Potiphar in charge of the state police – 'chief of the executioners' – in any event, a position of extreme importance under Pharaoh's personal control. Potiphar has *beaucoup* clout. But all is not as it seems.

I have underlined the same word twice in the Bible passage above. Have another look. The Holy Spirit has seen fit to mention TWICE that Potiphar is an Egyptian. Why bother? Of course he's an Egyptian! This is Egypt, and this guy is an officer of Pharaoh, who is... Egyptian! Two mentions of anything in the Bible means that God wants us to take careful note of what we're being told (*cf.* Gen 41:32). A double mention is the LORD's emphasis. Joseph has two dreams. An Egyptian Potiphar is a *remez* – a hint of something deeper.

Many with an interest in Egyptology have been frustrated at the difficulty in setting the Biblical Joseph in real history; the Moses Pharaoh too. Yet if Moses wrote the Torah texts, he would have known his pharaohs firsthand - he was apparently raised by the daughter of one of them - *yet he never names them*. Researcher Ian Wilson wants to know why. Later in the Bible, Pharaoh Necho (II) is named under different circumstances by a different writer (2 Chron 35:20).

Professor Donald Redford, in his *A Study of the Biblical Story of Joseph,* makes the case that certain apparent anomalies in the scriptures argue that such early stories reflect a view from the 8th Century BC at the earliest. For instance, the name 'Potiphar' is not traced in any Egyptian records until this time. Egyptians are very fond of carving all their animals in their art, and yet camels, such as those told in the Joseph story, are not depicted by them until the 700s BC. Later, in the story of Moses, we see different names used for God's mountain - Mount Horeb and Mount Sinai. Why two different names, asks Graham Phillips. Redford also draws our attention to an oath made by Joseph in Genesis 42:16: **"By the life of the Pharaoh..."** He argues that this oath did not exist in this form until much later.

Other scholars have remarked that the authorship of the Torah (first five books), usually attributed to Moses, may in fact have been compiled by several authors due to style variations, and committed to writing much later than originally thought.[496] They hasten to add that this does not infer the texts are corrupted or error-filled, or that Moses did not contribute at all - he did (Exo 17:14; 24:4, 7; 34:27). A later authorship for some Exodus sections, they maintain, could account 'for the discrepancies', and probably the most notable non-sequitur of all: namely, why not a single positive identification of a Joseph- or Moses-era pharaoh is made anywhere in the narrative.[497]

My take on this? Moses wrote the Torah. There were camels around in the Middle East long before 700s BC [498] – they were on the Ark! Redford and others are wrong on a number of accounts, which we'll examine as we go. Besides, if this *is* God's Word, and it is, *then He intended it that way*. We're going to find out soon that there is a high probability that the Pharaoh Joseph encounters in a minute *is not even Egyptian, nor is the dynasty ruling Egypt at that time 'Egyptian'*, hence the contrast with Potiphar. More on this in a minute. Back to Joseph's drama in Potiphar's house.

And it came to pass after these things, that his master's wife cast her eyes upon Joseph; and she said, "Lie with me."

But he refused, and said unto his master's wife, "Behold, my master wotteth not [knows not] what is with me in the house, and

---

[496] **Wilson, Ian** *The Exodus Enigma,* Book Club Associates, 1986

[497] **Phillips, Graham** *Act of God,* Pan, 1998, p.177

[498] http://www.biblearchaeology.org/post/2014/02/17/the-date-of-camel-domestication-in-the-ancient-near-east.aspx#Article

he hath committed all that he hath to my hand [i.e. 'My master is trusting me with everything.']. **There is none greater in this house than I. Neither hath he kept back any thing from me but thee, because thou art his wife. How then can I do this great wickedness <u>and sin against God</u>?"**

And it came to pass, as she spake to Joseph day by day, that he hearkened not unto her, to lie by her, or to be with her. And it came to pass about this time, that Joseph went into the house to do his business; and there was none of the men of the house there within. And she caught him by his garment, saying, "Lie with me". And he left his garment in her hand, and fled, and got him out.

And it came to pass, when she saw that he had left his garment in her hand, and was fled forth, that she called unto the men of her house, and spake unto them, saying, "See, he hath brought in an Hebrew unto us to mock us; he came in unto me to lie with me, and I cried with a loud voice. And it came to pass, when he heard that I lifted up my voice and cried, that he left his garment with me, and fled, and got him out."

And she laid up his garment by her, until his lord came home.

And she spake unto him according to these words, saying, "The Hebrew servant, which thou hast brought unto us, came in unto me to mock me. And it came to pass, as I lifted up my voice and cried, that he left his garment with me, and fled out."

And it came to pass, when his master heard the words of his wife, which she spake unto him, saying, "After this manner did thy servant to me," that his wrath was kindled. And Joseph's master took him, and put him into the prison, a place where the king's prisoners were bound: and he was there in the prison. (Gen 39:7-20)

Joseph is 'a goodly person and well favoured' (Gen 39:6). The New King James (NKJV) translates it as 'handsome in form and appearance'. Joseph's a catch. Potiphar's wife comes across as unhappy, brooding about the house and bored with life. She craves some action but Joseph will disappoint her, though she works on him day by day to break down his resolve so he will succumb to her charms.

And that's a clue to Potiphar's wife, reckons Heather Farrell:

"As I have studied the story of Potiphar's wife, the less I think that she was the promiscuous sexual predator that she is often made out to be. What I see is a bored, lonely, rich woman whose life was not everything she had dreamed it would be. Perhaps her marriage with Potiphar was unhappy, perhaps she lacked intellectual stimulation. Perhaps she was far from home and family. Perhaps she felt unwanted or undervalued. Perhaps Potiphar really was a eunuch and she lacked intimacy and the possibility for children.

"There are hundreds of reasons why she began - perhaps even unknowingly - to 'cast her eyes' around in search of something else. It just so happened that her eyes fell upon Joseph: young, handsome, talented, honest, smart, loyal, and blessed by the LORD. One can only imagine that she must have compared him to Potiphar and saw in Joseph all the things she felt her marriage and life were lacking.

"I think that when you closely study the story of Potiphar's wife and Joseph it becomes apparent that her desire and passion for Joseph was something that was built over time. I don't think she saw Joseph and a few days later was chasing him around trying to get him into bed with her. No, the story suggests that she and Joseph knew each other well and that she had allowed an emotional intimacy to build between them; way before she ever asked Joseph to be with her." [499]

Other expositors remark that Joseph is sensitive to her feelings on the first rebuttal, patiently giving his reasons for refusing her; which position is at odds with the common view that Joseph is attempting to repel a sex-mad cougar in a confined space. The two apparently know each other well enough for Potiphar's wife to know, and therefore appreciate, his moral beliefs and the importance of his obedience to God. Yet it is not enough. She cannot accept Joseph's rejection of her. Has Potiphar rejected her too by this time, or did their love just grow cold, if it ever existed in the first place? In the end, Joseph has no choice but to flee. The thin line between love and hate is breached when emotional intimacy is sold short (*cf.* 2 Sam 13:10-16). Now she wants to hurt Joseph as

---

[499] **Farrell, Heather** *Potiphar's Wife,*
http://www.womeninthescriptures.com/2012/11/potiphars-wife.html

much as he's just hurt her. Potiphar is given a full briefing by his wife of 'wicked Joseph' upon his return (the household staff have already been told). Joseph's position and further employment are untenable.

Joseph is thrown into prison – a frankly baffling sentence considering the severity of the crime. As chief of the executioners, Potiphar could have responded in the most cruel fashion to the object of his wife's salacious accusations: head chopped off; hands lopped off, body gibbeted on a tree; worse. We're told in Gen 39:19 that Potiphar, upon hearing the nature of his wife's accusations, flies into a rage. *It doesn't say against whom.* The assumption is always that he's furious with Joseph for having betrayed his trust and molested his wife, yet Joseph's prison sentence is, by any standards, bizarrely compassionate given the crime against such a senior minister. The conclusion one may draw is that Potiphar has long taken the measure of his wife for who she is, but has to make a public show to save professional face and avoid humiliating his family. For Joseph to have been awarded such a powerful role in Potiphar's life evinces a respect between the two men which would only have been possible through a close friendship and trust. It is clear to me that Potiphar's anger is directed towards his wife for having allowed her lust to rob him not only of a singular and most excellent steward, but a valued friend.

There are more of Arthur W Pink's parallels here between Joseph and Jesus Christ:

- Joseph becomes a servant. *So does Yeshua* (Phil 2:6-7)
- Joseph prospers as a servant due to the LORD's hand. *So does Mashiach* (Psa 1:3; Isa 52:13; 53:10)
- Joseph's master is very pleased with him. *The same with Yeshua* (FG 8:29)
- Joseph is a goodly person, well favoured. *So is Yeshua* (Matt 27:54)
- Joseph is sorely tempted, yet does not sin. *The same with Yeshua* (Luke 4)
- Joseph is falsely accused. *So is Jesus* (Matt 26:59-60)
- Joseph offers no defence against false accusations. *The same with Jesus* (Isa 53:7; Mark 15:3-5)

- Joseph is punished without any evidence being presented to substantiate his guilt. *So is Yeshua* (FG 18:38)
- Joseph suffers, though he is innocent. *So does Yeshua* (FG 18:38)
- Joseph suffers at the hands of the Gentiles (Egypt – a model for 'the world'). *So does Jesus* (Acts 4:26-27; *cf.* Psa 2:1-4)

Joseph's prison time

We feel for Joseph. Nothing in his life is going right. He lost his mother; was loathed and betrayed by his brothers; thrown into a pit; sold into slavery; transported out of his own land to Egypt; was falsely accused of molesting his new master's wife. Now he faces the business end of a foreign prison. Yet any protestations by the luckless Joseph towards his ruin *go unrecorded!* Why? Because Joseph knows the unseen hand of the LORD is behind all things (Rom 8:28-29). This robust faith will shortly be put to the test.

But the LORD was with Joseph, and shewed him mercy, and gave him favour in the sight of the keeper of the prison. And the keeper of the prison committed to Joseph's hand all the prisoners that were in the prison; and whatsoever they did there, he was the doer of it. The keeper of the prison looked not to any thing that was under his hand; because the LORD was with him, and that which he did, the LORD made it to prosper. (Gen 39:21-23)

This is now the third time that Joseph has been granted a deep trust by a peer in adverse circumstances: firstly from his father (despite the hostility shown to Joseph by his siblings); then Potiphar (despite the adverse condition of Joseph's slavery); now the keeper of the prison, who perceives the same intrinsic trustworthiness to Joseph which the others noticed. There is an intriguing detail in the following passage:

And it came to pass after these things, that the butler of the king of Egypt and his baker had offended their lord the king of Egypt. And Pharaoh was wroth against two of his officers, against the chief of the butlers, and against the chief of the bakers. And he put them in ward in the house of the captain of the guard, into the prison, the place where Joseph was bound.

And the captain of the guard charged Joseph with them, and he
served them: and they continued a season in ward. (Gen 40:1-4)

Who is the captain of the guard? Potiphar! (Gen 39:1). Most
expositors miss this. Potiphar is *still* trusting Joseph – even in the
face of his wife's accusations – firstly by allowing the keeper of the
prison to delegate responsibility for all the prisoners to Joseph, and
now personally requesting that Joseph look after two of Pharaoh's
recently disgraced officers: the king's personal cupbearer ('butler'),
and the chief of the bakers. (Note the intriguing echo of the
mystical bread and wine model).

**And they dreamed a dream both of them, each man his
dream in one night, each man according to the interpretation of
his dream, the butler and the baker of the king of Egypt, which
were bound in the prison.**

**And Joseph came in unto them in the morning, and looked
upon them, and, behold, they were sad. And he asked Pharaoh's
officers that were with him in the ward of his lord's house**
[Potiphar again!], **saying, "Wherefore look ye so sadly today?"**

**And they said unto him, "We have dreamed a dream, and
there is no interpreter of it."**

**And Joseph said unto them, "Do not interpretations belong
to God? Tell me them, I pray you."**

**And the chief butler told his dream to Joseph, and said to
him, "In my dream, behold, a vine was before me; and in the vine
were three branches: and it was as though it budded, and her
blossoms shot forth; and the clusters thereof brought forth ripe
grapes: And Pharaoh's cup was in my hand: and I took the
grapes, and pressed them into Pharaoh's cup, and I gave the cup
into Pharaoh's hand."**

**And Joseph said unto him, "This is the interpretation of it:
The three branches are three days: Yet within three days shall
Pharaoh lift up thine head and restore thee unto thy place: and
thou shalt deliver Pharaoh's cup into his hand, after the former
manner when thou wast his butler.**

**"But think on me when it shall be well with thee, and shew
kindness, I pray thee, unto me, and make mention of me unto
Pharaoh, and bring me out of this house: For indeed I was stolen**

away out of the land of the Hebrews: and here also have I done nothing that they should put me into the dungeon.

When the chief baker saw that the interpretation was good, he said unto Joseph, "I also was in my dream, and, behold, I had three white baskets on my head: And in the uppermost basket there was of all manner of bakemeats for Pharaoh; and the birds did eat them out of the basket upon my head."

And Joseph answered and said, "This is the interpretation thereof: The three baskets are three days: Yet within three days shall Pharaoh lift up thy head from off thee, and shall hang thee on a tree; and the birds shall eat thy flesh from off thee."

And it came to pass the third day, which was Pharaoh's birthday, that he made a feast unto all his servants: and he lifted up the head of the chief butler and of the chief baker among his servants. And he restored the chief butler unto his butlership again; and he gave the cup into Pharaoh's hand: But he hanged the chief baker: as Joseph had interpreted to them.

Yet did not the chief butler remember Joseph, but forgat him. (Gen 40:5-23)

More of Arthur W Pink's parallels between Joseph and Jesus spring to mind:

- Joseph was numbered among the transgressors – two in particular. *So was Jesus* (Isa 53:12; Matt 27:38)
- Joseph was the means of blessing to one, and condemnation to the other (hung on a tree). *So was Jesus with the two thieves at the crucifixion* (Luke 23:39-43)
- Joseph was given prophecies directly from God. *So was Jesus* (FG 12:49)
- These prophecies came true both for Joseph and for Yeshua. (Matt 5:18)
- Joseph wanted to be remembered. *So did Jesus* (Luke 22:19)

After Joseph's first two dreams, whose interpretations were ill-received by his family, God sends a further two dreams, this time to the butler and baker in Potiphar's gaol. Once again, when God says something twice, we should pay attention (Gen 41:32). We aren't told how long Joseph was behind bars before the butler and baker had their dreams, but evidently some years have passed.[500] Not only are these dreams interpreted by Joseph with God's help, they are fulfilled quickly and dramatically with the reinstatement of the butler and execution of the baker. If Joseph thought the butler would be grateful and immediately remember him once out of prison, he was mistaken.

The rise to glory

And it came to pass at the end of two full years, that Pharaoh dreamed: and, behold, he stood by the river. And, behold, there came up out of the river seven well favoured kine [cows] and fat-fleshed; and they fed in a meadow. And, behold, seven other kine came up after them out of the river, ill-favoured and lean-fleshed; and stood by the other kine upon the brink of the river. And the ill-favoured and leanfleshed kine did eat up the seven well favoured and fat kine. So Pharaoh awoke.

And he slept and dreamed the second time: and, behold, seven ears of corn came up upon one stalk, rank and good. And, behold, seven thin ears and blasted with the east wind sprung up after them. And the seven thin ears devoured the seven rank and full ears. And Pharaoh awoke, and, behold, it was a dream.

And it came to pass in the morning that his spirit was troubled; and he sent and called for all the magicians of Egypt, and all the wise men thereof: and Pharaoh told them his dream; but there was none that could interpret them unto Pharaoh.

Then spake the chief butler unto Pharaoh, saying, "I do remember my faults this day: Pharaoh was wroth [angry] with his servants, and put me in ward in the captain of the guard's house, both me and the chief baker: And we dreamed a dream in one night, I and he; we dreamed each man according to the interpretation of his dream. And there was there with us a young man, an Hebrew, servant to the captain of the guard; and we told him, and he interpreted to us our dreams; to each man according to his dream he did interpret. And it came to pass, as he

---

[500] Joseph is seventeen when he goes down to Egypt, and is thirty by the time he interprets Pharaoh's dreams (Gen 37:2; 41:46).

interpreted to us, so it was; me he restored unto mine office, and him he hanged."

Then Pharaoh sent and called Joseph, and they brought him hastily out of the dungeon: and he shaved himself, and changed his raiment, and came in unto Pharaoh.

And Pharaoh said unto Joseph, "I have dreamed a dream, and there is none that can interpret it: and I have heard say of thee, that thou canst understand a dream to interpret it."

And Joseph answered Pharaoh, saying, "It is not in me: God shall give Pharaoh an answer of peace." (Gen 41:1-16)

Pharaoh explains the details of his two dreams and ends by telling Joseph that none of his wise men have the slightest clue what they mean. That's a first. What soothsayers ever resist the temptation to pontificate on anything, unless there are penalties if their predictions don't come true! (*cf.* Dan 2:1-13). Notice that Joseph explains to Pharaoh that God is the interpreter of the king's dreams, not Joseph (*cf.* Dan 2:27-28). God is to get the glory for the dreams, their interpretation, and what will follow for the nation of Egypt.

And Joseph said unto Pharaoh, "The dream of Pharaoh is one: God hath shewed Pharaoh what he is about to do. The seven good kine are seven years; and the seven good ears are seven years: the dream is one.

"And the seven thin and ill-favoured kine that came up after them are seven years; and the seven empty ears blasted with the east wind shall be seven years of famine. This is the thing which I have spoken unto Pharaoh: What God is about to do he sheweth unto Pharaoh. Behold, there come seven years of great plenty throughout all the land of Egypt: And there shall arise after them seven years of famine; and all the plenty shall be forgotten in the land of Egypt; and the famine shall consume the land; And the plenty shall not be known in the land by reason of that famine following; for it shall be very grievous. And for that the dream was doubled unto Pharaoh twice; <u>it is because the thing is established by God</u>, and God will shortly bring it to pass.

"Now therefore let Pharaoh look out a man discreet and wise, and set him over the land of Egypt. Let Pharaoh do this, and let him appoint officers over the land, and take up the fifth part of the land of Egypt in the seven plenteous years. And let them gather all the food of those good years that come, and lay up corn under the hand of Pharaoh, and let them keep food in the cities. And that food shall be for store to the land against the seven years of famine, which shall be in the land of Egypt; that the land perish not through the famine."

And the thing was good in the eyes of Pharaoh, and in the eyes of all his servants.

And Pharaoh said unto his servants, "Can we find such a one as this? A man in whom the Spirit of God is?"

And Pharaoh said unto Joseph, "<u>Forasmuch as God hath shewed thee all this</u>, there is none so discreet and wise as thou art: Thou shalt be over my house, and according unto thy word shall all my people be ruled: only in the throne will I be greater than thou."

And Pharaoh said unto Joseph, "See, I have set thee over all the land of Egypt."

And Pharaoh took off his ring from his hand, and put it upon Joseph's hand, and arrayed him in vestures of fine linen, and put a gold chain about his neck; And he made him to ride in the second chariot which he had; and they cried before him, "Bow the knee!" And [Pharaoh] made [Joseph] ruler over all the land of Egypt.

And Pharaoh said unto Joseph, "I am Pharaoh, and without thee shall no man lift up his hand or foot in all the land of Egypt." And Pharaoh called Joseph's name Zaphnathpaaneah ['a revealer of secrets']; and he gave him to wife Asenath the daughter of Potipherah priest of On. And Joseph went out over all the land of Egypt.

And Joseph was thirty years old when he stood before Pharaoh king of Egypt. And Joseph went out from the presence of Pharaoh, and went throughout all the land of Egypt. (Gen 41:25-46)

After listening to the king's descriptions, Joseph explains that Pharaoh's two visions foretell of seven years of plenty in Egypt, followed by seven years of famine. Pharaoh is impressed and decides to make Joseph grand vizier (e.g. 'prime minister', 'vice president') over the entire country in order to oversee the storage of food during the good years in readiness for the famine; and presumably to 'take the can back', should the famine not happen! It's not beyond the bounds of possibility that Potiphar, as chief of Pharaoh's bodyguard, could have had a word in the king's ear about Joseph's quality as a governor. What Potiphar's wife now makes of it all, alas, goes unrecorded.

A fine 'coat of many colours' may have landed him in deep trouble in the past, but Joseph's elevation to high office now earns him an astonishing wardrobe to underscore his meteoric change of status. Vestments of the finest linen; a weighty gold chain around his neck; the king's ring gleaming on his finger; and Joseph's own personal, top-of-the-line, chauffeur-driven war-chariot drawn by the finest, 'blinged-out' horses in the land.

More of A W Pink's parallels emerge between Joseph and Jesus Christ:

- Joseph is a revealer of secrets. *So is Yeshua* (FG 12:49)
- Joseph warns of danger, and urges provisions and preparation. *So does Yeshua* (Matt 24 & 25)
- Joseph is exalted over all Egypt (a model of the world). *So is Yeshua* (1 Pet 3:22; Rev 5 & 20)
- Joseph overcomes and sits on another's throne. *So does Yeshua* (Rev 3:21)
- Joseph is given vestments and insignia worthy of a saviour. *So is Yeshua* (Acts 5:31; Heb 2:9; Rev 1:13)
- Joseph receives a new name. *So does Yeshua* (Phil 2:9; Matt 1:21; Rev 3:12)
- Joseph receives a Gentile wife. *So does Yeshua* (Eph 5:22-32; Rev 19:7-8)
- Joseph is thirty years old when he begins his real work. *So is Yeshua* (Luke 3:23)

Some find Joseph's story embarrassingly implausible, while others angrily denounce the gullible who believe its historicity. That it's a cracking tale is not in doubt. Joseph's life is quintessential Disney 'rags to riches', full of moral signposts, and told with an invincible script. Joseph's place is secure as one of literature's great, principled protagonists, from humble slave to second-in-command of the world's most powerful country (not bad for a dreamer). But honestly: we're supposed to accept this as *actual history?*

Absolutely.

And Pharaoh giving over governorship of *his entire country* to a foreign slave who's provided some fanciful interpretations to two royal dreams as yet unfilled? Connect yourself to the oxygen, people!

Actually, yes. The Bible expects us to take it on trust as actual history.

Come on! What *real* king would be mad enough to act in such a fashion? What if Joseph is proved wrong? How foolish would Pharaoh look then as the whole world gazed on?

The 'Shepherd Kings'

I mentioned earlier that all is not what it seems with the Joseph story. The dating of the various Egyptian Pharaonic dynasties by regular historians is well known to be a mess. There is wide variance even among Christian and Jewish scholars in deciding the identity of the Joseph- or Moses-era Pharaoh. In fact, the more you get into reconciling the chronologies of Egypt and their corresponding Hebrew protagonists according to the current wisdom, the bigger the pickle you find yourself in. This has caused some scholars to re-think the whole approach, while others have cast up their hands and denied Jacob and his sons ever went to Egypt in the first place for an extended period.

This capitulation cannot be maintained in view of the evidence. For instance, those who deny Israel spent any time in Egypt need to explain why there are a significant number of Egyptian names in the genealogies of the Levites. Examples are Moses, Assir, Pashhur, Hophni, Phenehas, and Merari. Moreover, details of life and customs in Egypt cited in the Bible appear genuine and consistent with a protracted Israeli sojourn in Egypt. We'll examine examples as we proceed. But I'm interested in the re-thinkers. When faced with a mess, stand back and look at the whole era to see if you've missed something obvious. The stories of Joseph, Moses, the Exodus and the Canaan invasion, if true, would be so extraordinary in their historical impact that if they really happened, some imprint of these events on discovered, secular history and the archaeological record would surely be knowable. And here's where we enter some really fascinating territory.

In his book, *Act of God*, Graham Phillips recounts that a few decades before Joseph (around 1800 BC) and a thousand kilometres to the north-east, another drama has been playing out in the archaeological record. The Babylonians attack and sack a Mesopotamian city named Mari (modern-day Tell Hariri, Syria). The tribes of the Mari and their vassal states flee the Chaldean invaders and migrate south-west into Canaan. During their exodus, the Mari co-mingle with the Semite peoples of Canaan, and soon a powerful alliance is formed with considerable military muscle. The Mari exodus eventually ends up on the fertile plains of northern Egypt. These nomadic peoples bring with them mobile resources as yet unknown to the Egyptians, such as the war-horse, which make these *Hikau khasut*, or 'rulers of the desert highlands', a formidable enemy. Abraham, Isaac and Jacob would have been very familiar with them among the Canaanite peoples. The Hyksos, or 'Shepherd Kings', as they have mistakenly come to be known,[501] are also skilled in advanced fortification techniques, greatly improved battle-axes, the deadly compound bow, and the latest in moving platforms from which to fire it - the sleek and manoeuvrable war-chariot.[502]

The Hyksos must have been a worrying development for the Egyptians. We only know of their existence from the 4th century BC Graeco-Egyptian historian, Manetho. Almost none of Manetho's works are still extant, but his non-surviving works are quoted at some length by the 1st century AD Jewish chronicler, Flavius Josephus, and we have most of his. Some historians have taken Josephus at Manetho's word that there is a bloody Hyksos invasion of northern Egypt, in which the weakened Pharaonic dynasty is routed and sent packing south to Thebes. However, the

---

[501] Josephus famously mistranslated the Greek word as 'shepherd kings'. Egyptians named them *hega-khase*: 'rulers of foreign lands', and did their best to expunge all memory of them after driving them out of Lower Egypt centuries later.
[502] **Phillips, Graham** *Act of God*, Pan, 1998, pp.190-193

archaeological evidence appears to indicate that the Hyksos tribes gradually settle in the region of the Nile Delta and build up a rival population base, which finally gains control of Lower Egypt.

Phillips' research reveals a text currently displayed in the Brooklyn Museum dating from the reign of Sobekhotep III (13th dynasty), which depicts 79 household servants for the Pharaoh, of which 45 appear to be Hyksos, identifiable through their tell-tale Semite appearance and dress. This factor seems to indicate a protracted assimilation of the Hyksos rather than outright confrontation, though there must have been 'incidents'.[503] Clearly Hyksos would not be in the majority serving in the king's household if they were an invading force. What is clear from the recovered history of Lower (northern) Egypt during the Hyksos period (15th dynasty), Phillips maintains, is that these new foreign leaders viewed and styled themselves as pharaohs when they eventually seized power, and were viewed by their own as such. Traditional Egyptian pharaohs were to be admired and worshiped, and the Hyksos rulers were well up for adoration and worship. The true Egyptian faction was banished south to Thebes, where they muttered and plotted revenge on the Hyksos for the next two centuries.

The scriptural evidence indicates that Potiphar himself is an Egyptian, or maybe Hyksos settled long enough to be termed 'an Egyptian'. As previously indicated, the Holy Spirit sees fit *twice* to repeat that Potiphar is an Egyptian. As we know by now, the Holy Spirit never does anything for no reason. It's a *remez*. One's tempted to ask, "Why bother mentioning that detail? Potiphar's obviously an Egyptian because he's in Egypt, and he's been given a position of great authority (captain of Pharaoh's bodyguard) by Pharaoh himself, so obviously Potiphar's an Egyptian!" Then you ask, "OK, we're told twice that Potiphar's an Egyptian… *as opposed to what?*"

We also read that Potiphar is familiar in some way with the Hebrew God: **"And Joseph was brought down to Egypt; and Potiphar, an officer of Pharaoh, captain of the guard, <u>an Egyptian</u>,**

---

[503] Ibid, p.192

bought him of the hands of the Ishmeelites, which had brought him down thither. And the LORD was with Joseph and he was a prosperous man; and he was in the house of his master <u>the Egyptian</u>. And his master [i.e. Potiphar] <u>saw that the LORD was with him and that the LORD made all that he did to prosper in his hand</u>." (Gen 39:1-3)

Phillips wonders whether Potiphar is a naturalised Hyksos. As scripture does not record a migration of Hebrews to Egypt prior to Joseph, it is unlikely that Potiphar, a native in Egypt, would have had any prior knowledge of the Hebrew Deity or even care, and yet he appears to be familiar with Him. After Joseph interprets Pharaoh's dreams, the king releases him from prison and makes him vizier over Egypt. Genesis 41:38-40 reads: **And Pharaoh said unto his servants, "Can we find such a one as this, <u>a man in whom the Spirit of God is</u>?" And Pharaoh said unto Joseph, "<u>Forasmuch as God hath shewed thee all this</u>, there is none so discreet and wise as thou art: Thou shalt be over my house, and according unto thy word shall all my people be ruled: only in the throne will I be greater than thou."** (Gen 41:38-40)

It's an extraordinary, revealing detail. Here Pharaoh, in addition to Potiphar, recognises the Holy Spirit at work in Joseph's life! This is not the language of a pagan, polytheistic king with a god for every day of the year, chief among them all the god Re. Notice Pharaoh does not say 'your God', just 'God'. If Pharaoh is Hyksos, Phillips contends, he would have firsthand knowledge of the Hebrew Deity (the Hyksos were part-Canaanite), and would have no qualms about promoting a Hebrew (even a recent jailbird) to an exalted post, so the theory is at least feasible. On the other hand, if Pharaoh is an Egyptian who has been worshipping Re and the Egyptian pantheon with no prior knowledge of YHWH, he has just committed an act of unprecedented insanity in the eyes of his people. He has promoted a foreign convict to prime minister on the basis of a fanciful interpretation of a royal dream yet to be realised.[504]

As we'll shortly discover, Joseph's Pharaoh is also so friendly to Joseph's family that he invites his new Hebrew vizier to find

---

[504] Phillips, Graham, *Act of God,* op. cit., "The Children of Israel"

suitable herdsmen from among his own family to tend the royal herds! (Gen 47:6) To Phillips this is a problem. Even a cursory examination of Pharaonic religion will reveal that bulls and calves were sacred to the king, often regarded as divine incarnations. How credible is it that an Egyptian monarch would have done such a thing? What is more remarkable, if this pharaoh is a true Egyptian, says Phillips, is that his people apparently have no problem with 'an alien criminal' being promoted over their heads and receiving orders to bow down before him (Gen 41:43). In other words, *we are told the 'Egyptian' people go along with it all*. None of this is explainable if the pharaoh in question is an Egyptian, says Phillips. All of it is if he is Hyksos. One of the last 16th dynasty pharaohs, by the way, is Yakob-aam, a name of distinctly Hebrew origin.[505]

The retaking of the north

Phillips' reasoning is therefore logical that Joseph's pharaoh could be a sympathetic Hyksos, the leader of an affiliation of Canaanite and Mesopotamian tribes which migrated southwest and became powerful enough to rival the true pharaohs in northern (Upper) Egypt. In Egyptology this era is known as the Second Intermediate Period (15th – 17th dynasties), in which scholars generally recognise that the Egyptians are not in control of Lower (northern) Egypt because of the Hyksos.

To the south ('Upper Egypt'), the true Egyptian princes lick their wounds in Thebes for about two centuries. The Thebans are not idle during this period. They breed horses and copy the Hyksos compound bow and chariot before embarking on a series of campaigns to re-take the north.[506] Seqenenre II is the first 17th dynasty Theban king to revolt against the north, probably, according to the following inscription, due to punitive Hyksos taxation. His attack fails and Seqenenre is evidently hacked to death. His mummified body was discovered in 1881 displaying

[505] **Clayton, P A** *Chronicle of the Pharaohs,* London, 1994
[506] **Phillips, Graham,** *Act of God,* op. cit., p.196; **Yadin, Y** *The Art of Warfare in Biblical Lands in the Light of Archaeological Discovery,* London: 1963

sword-wounds to the head and neck.[507] Egyptologist and weapons expert Gary Shaw concludes, after a close study of the king's wounds:

"…that the most likely cause of Seqenenre's death is ceremonial execution at the hands of an enemy commander, following a Theban defeat on the battlefield." [508]

His son and successor Pharaoh Kamose launches a full-on, furious assault against the northern 'Asiatics' who just murdered his father. Kamose's frustration as a true Egyptian is evident in an inscription on the Carnarvon Tablet I:

"Let me understand what this strength of mine is for! [One] prince is in Avaris [the Hyksos capital in the Nile Delta], another is in Ethiopia,[509] and [here] I sit associated with an Asiatic [Hyksos] and a Negro! Each man has his slice of this Egypt, dividing up the land with me…. No man can settle down when despoiled by the taxes of the Asiatics. I will grapple with him, that I may rip open his belly! My wish is to save Egypt and to smite the Asiatic!"

Kamose holds his own against his enemy's superior strength and finally Ahmose overcomes the Hyksos dynasty, unites Egypt once more, and becomes the first 18th dynasty pharaoh to rule over a unified Egypt (c. 1570 BC). After reunification, we see successive Egyptian pharaohs doing all possible to expunge the memory of the 15th dynasty Hyksos pharaohs in what was evidently regarded as a shameful period in Egyptian history. The Hyksos kings do not appear in any surviving kings' lists. We only know of them through the Egyptian priest and chronicler, Manetho, via the Jewish writer, Josephus, and through fragments of extant *stelae* and inscriptions on tombs. This retaking of the north by the Theban princes to re-establish the true Egyptian line will also account for

---

[507] **Wilson, Ian** *The Exodus Enigma*, London, 1985, p.73

[508] **Shaw, Garry J** "The Death of King Seqenenre Tao", *Journal of the American Research Center in Egypt*, 2009, p.45

[509] Egypt's Nubian (Ethiopian) province to the south takes full advantage of the Hyksos usurping the north to revolt and crush the Theben princes in between. However, after Ahmose I sacks Avaris, he sails southward to Khenti-hen-nefer to destroy the Nubian nomads.

two important details of the Biblical sojourn of Israel in Egypt: firstly, why we don't know the identity of the Joseph-era pharaoh (he was excised from the record by his successors), and secondly, why there later arose a pharaoh 'who knew Joseph not', and began the oppression of the Israelites.

Joseph and the famine

And Joseph was thirty years old when he stood before Pharaoh, king of Egypt. And Joseph went out from the presence of Pharaoh, and went throughout all the land of Egypt.

And in the seven plenteous years the earth brought forth by handfuls. And [Joseph] gathered up all the food of the seven years, which were in the land of Egypt, and laid up the food in the cities: the food of the field, which was round about every city, laid he up in the same. And Joseph gathered corn as the sand of the sea, very much, until he left numbering; for it was without number.

And unto Joseph were born two sons before the years of famine came, which Asenath the daughter of Potipherah priest of On bare unto him. And Joseph called the name of the firstborn Manasseh ['forgetting']: "For God," said he, "hath made me forget all my toil, and all my father's house."

And the name of the second called he Ephraim ['twice fruitful']: "For God hath caused me to be fruitful in the land of my affliction." (Gen 41:46-52)

These two children will become important a little later when Jacob adopts them as his own. They will each effectively become a 'half-tribe' of Joseph, giving Joseph a double portion of the family inheritance, which should have gone to the disgraced Reuben.

And the seven years of plenteousness, that was in the land of Egypt, were ended. And the seven years of dearth began to come, according as Joseph had said: and the dearth was in all lands; but in all the land of Egypt there was bread.

And when all the land of Egypt was famished, the people cried to Pharaoh for bread: and Pharaoh said unto all the Egyptians, "Go unto Joseph; what he saith to you, do."

And the famine was over all the face of the earth: And Joseph opened all the storehouses, and sold unto the Egyptians; and the

famine waxed sore in the land of Egypt. And all countries came into Egypt to Joseph for to buy corn; because that the famine was so sore in all lands. (Gen 41:53-57)

One is given to wondering what on Earth Potiphar and his wife make of Joseph now; or even what grace Joseph extended to the pair who had been the cause of so many long years of imprisonment. Knowing Joseph, I imagine he showed them grace to honour God, which would have impressed them no end (Matt 5:16).

Notice that Joseph does not give away the food, he sells it to the people! And God gets the credit for saving Egypt ('the world') from the deadly consequences of the worst famine in living memory. Joseph's long years of testing and preparation in prison are at an end. God now honours Joseph's trust and gripe-free endurance by:

1) Giving Pharaoh two dreams
2) Reminding the butler about Joseph, who then tells Pharaoh about Joseph's dream-interpretation skills
3) Having Pharaoh summon Joseph
4) Causing Pharaoh to be impressed enough by Joseph to choose him as the man who will save Egypt
5) Causing word of Egypt's plenty to travel to other lands....

Now when Jacob saw that there was corn in Egypt, Jacob said unto his sons, "Why do ye look one upon another?" And he said, "Behold, I have heard that there is corn in Egypt: get you down thither and buy for us from thence; that we may live and not die."

And Joseph's ten brethren went down to buy corn in Egypt. But Benjamin, Joseph's brother, Jacob sent not with his brethren; for he said, "Lest peradventure mischief befall him." (Gen 42:1-4)

Jacob appears to express surprise at his sons' reluctance to procure food for the clan. While their father is certainly not yet privy to the circumstances surrounding his beloved Joseph's fate, the brothers certainly are. Egypt is not only a bizarre, pagan place worshiping demon gods and prone to enslaving strangers, it's where the brother they betrayed ended up and doubtless perished

(Gen 42:13). Some commentators wonder why the ten of them go. The answer is threefold:

1)   Jacob's clan has grown to an extensive community of at least seventy kin, plus slaves on top, so the sheer bulk of food required necessitates special arrangements for manpower, beast and cartage

2)   Travel at the time is dangerous, so there is safety in numbers

3)   A father knows his sons, so it's likely that Jacob harbours painful suspicions of what might have befallen Joseph years before. Jacob is not about to release Benjamin - his second most favourite son by Rachel – to be the next target of a lethal sibling jealousy (Gen 42:38). Sons who can wipe out Shechem are famously capable of anything

And the sons of Israel came to buy corn among those that came: for the famine was in the land of Canaan. And Joseph was the governor over the land, <u>and he it was that sold to all the people of the land</u>: and Joseph's brethren came, and bowed down themselves before him with their faces to the earth.

And Joseph saw his brethren, and he knew them, but made himself strange unto them, and spake roughly unto them; and he said unto them, "Whence come ye?" And they said, "From the land of Canaan to buy food."

And Joseph knew his brethren, but they knew not him. (Gen 42:5-8)

Warren Wiersbe remarks:

"As second ruler of the land, Joseph certainly didn't participate in each individual grain transaction because he had many important things to do. Furthermore, the food supply was stored in several cities (Gen 41:46-49), and Joseph had commissioners assisting him (Gen 41:34-36). [Yet], in the providence of God, Joseph was on hand when his ten brothers arrived to buy grain, and he recognised them....

"Certainly a man who could interpret the dreams of others could interpret his own dreams. Joseph must have concluded that the famine would bring his brothers to Egypt, and that meant he would have to confront them with their sins against him and their father. He wanted his own heart to be clean and right before God so that he could be a blessing to them just as he'd been a blessing wherever God had placed him." [510]

Some commentators regard Joseph's harsh attitude toward his brothers to be at odds with the Christ-like grace he extends to others, but God has some refining to do with Jacob's unruly bunch, and He's going to use Joseph to effect the change.

The ten brothers are already partially fulfilling Joseph's dreams by bowing down before him now, but here we come across a surprising non-sequitur. Remember that Joseph's original 'sun, moon and stars' dream was interpreted by Jacob to mean that there would be eleven 'stars' (brothers) *plus Mum and Dad* who would bow down before Joseph. Wait... wasn't Rachel dead by this time? There are two possibilities. Either Rachel was still alive at the time Joseph had these dreams at the age of 17, which means that chapters 35 and 37 are probably anachronistic, or that Leah is somehow implied. Akanimo Uwan believes that:

"...Benjamin was born after Joseph was sold. The dreams he had were prophetic occurrences of what would transpire in his life in future. So, when he had those dreams and his father asked him if he, his mother and the rest would bow to him, that is a clue that Rachel was still alive and Benjamin wasn't yet born." [511]

And since Rachel died giving birth to Benjamin, this means that Jacob must have realised, in his interpretation of Joseph's 'sun, moon and stars' dream, that he would have another child at some point (the eleventh star). Those expositors who assume Rachel died before Joseph dreamed, (therefore making Benjamin an infant at the time Joseph was sold), rationalise that Leah would have become the adoptive mother of Benjamin after Rachel's death in childbirth, and that this is the mother referred to by Jacob. But that's not what Jacob actually says in the interpretation. Let's look at the passage again:

---

[510] Wiersbe, W, *The Wiersbe Bible Commentary,* op. cit., pp.124, 125

[511] http://blog.markhamanderson.com/josephs-visions-dont-add-up/

And [Joseph] dreamed yet another dream, and told it his brethren, and said, "Behold, I have dreamed a dream more; and, behold, <u>the sun and the moon and the eleven stars made obeisance to me.</u>"

And he told it to his father, and to his brethren: and his father rebuked him, and said unto him, "What is this dream that thou hast dreamed? <u>Shall I and THY MOTHER and thy brethren indeed come to bow down ourselves to thee to the earth?</u>"

And his brethren envied him; <u>but his father observed the saying.</u> (Gen 37:9-11)

Who was Joseph's mother? Rachel! Puts it all in a completely different light, doesn't it? Jacob's interpretation of Joseph's dream would make no sense if Rachel had died a few years before, so it seems likely that Rachel was still alive when Joseph had the dream, and was probably pregnant, hence Jacob not having a problem with 'eleven stars' when he only had ten at that point! *There is no verse that I am aware of which indicates that Joseph knew Benjamin was in existence prior to his experience in Egypt.* Rachel was likely still alive when he was sold into Egypt, which means Benjamin was not yet born. This will also account for some interesting aspects to the story when it hots up in a minute. Let's continue with the narrative.

The brothers bow down before this mighty Egyptian ruler. They miss the irony of this, not knowing who he is. Joseph is dressed as an Egyptian, made up like an Egyptian ruler, speaking Egyptian, and communicating with his brothers through an interpreter. Which sets the stage for all sorts of interesting mischief.

And Joseph remembered the dreams which he dreamed of them, and said unto them, "Ye are spies; to see the nakedness of the land ye are come!"

And they said unto him, "Nay, my lord, but to buy food are thy servants come. We are all one man's sons; we are true men, thy servants are no spies."

And he said unto them, "Nay, but to see the nakedness of the land ye are come!"

And they said, "Thy servants are twelve brethren, the sons of one man in the land of Canaan; and, behold, the youngest is this day with our father, and one is not."

And Joseph said unto them, "That is it that I spake unto you, saying, 'Ye are spies'. Hereby ye shall be proved: By the life of Pharaoh ye shall not go forth hence, except your youngest brother come hither. Send one of you, and let him fetch your brother, and ye shall be kept in prison, that your words may be proved, whether there be any truth in you: or else by the life of Pharaoh, surely ye are spies!"

And he put them all together into ward three days. (Gen 42:9-17)

This last verse leads some commentators to surmise that Joseph endured the pit/cistern for three days after being cast into it by his brothers at Dothan prior to being sold to the Ishmeelites (Gen 37:23-28). In the Bible, 'three days' signifies the lead-up to something momentous about to be performed by God.

We will see that the news that there is another brother makes a deep impression on Joseph, especially if Rachel was still alive and pregnant at the time Joseph went missing. Unwittingly, the brothers give the roll-call of kin: "...**twelve brethren, the sons of one man in the land of Canaan; and, behold, the youngest is this day with our father, and one is not.**" Joseph will know by this news that he is believed dead. That his mother and father would have grieved terribly. The shock and trauma of losing her son could even have unsettled Rachel's pregnancy to deadly effect. There are more clues that this might have been the case as we proceed.

Joseph's harshness to strangers would not be unusual. In his capacity as Pharaoh's vizier, Joseph is required to examine newcomers to the land. Egypt is the only land with food in the midst of dire and straitened times. Desperate men will take desperate measures to feed their families. Who knows who might be staking out the nation with a view to a kill?

And Joseph said unto them the third day," This do, and live; <u>for I fear God</u>: If ye be true men, let one of your brethren be bound in the house of your prison: go ye, carry corn for the famine of your houses: <u>But bring your youngest brother unto me; so shall your words be verified, and ye shall not die</u>." And they did so.

And they said one to another, "We are verily guilty concerning our brother, in that we saw the anguish of his soul, when he besought us, and we would not hear; therefore is this distress come upon us."

And Reuben answered them, saying, "Spake I not unto you, saying, 'Do not sin against the child'; and ye would not hear? Therefore, behold, also his blood is required."

And they knew not that Joseph understood them; for he spake unto them by an interpreter. (Gen 42:18-23)

Once again, we see Joseph's emphasis on meeting his brother. The brother he never knew? It's interesting that, unbidden, the brothers sense that the reason for their current calamitous predicament is what they did to Joseph. True guilt is corrosive and stays with the guilty until they repent. Joseph's artful use of the phrase "… for I fear God" should have raised suspicions (Egypt under the Hyksos is still pantheistic!), but the mention of their Creator only convicts the brothers further. God requires an accounting of the shedding of blood, and the brothers – especially Reuben, Simeon and Levi – know it (Gen 9:5-6; 42:22). This hint of repentance is the first step to their rehabilitation: an admission of wrongdoing not only to each other, but to God, and unwittingly to Joseph, the one they wronged, whom they believe to be long dead.

And [Joseph] turned himself about from them, and wept; and returned to them again, and communed with them, and took from them Simeon, and bound him before their eyes. (Gen 42:24)

Not often remarked upon is another clue the brothers miss that all may not be as it seems. They claim four times to be 'true men', so this Egyptian ruler gives them the chance to prove themselves by returning home to bring back Benjamin. Yet how would the Egyptian ruler even know the person they might return with is Benjamin and not a changeling? Joseph deliberately sets a test not even he can verify! Isn't the true test of a man to see him in a situation he would rather not have you see him in? Simeon is chosen by Joseph for a hostage as the cruellest of the bunch (Gen 49:5-7). Joseph knows the brothers must eventually return to Egypt, if not to rescue Simeon, then to replenish their food stocks. And with them must come the beloved Benjamin.

Then Joseph commanded to fill their sacks with corn, and to restore every man's money into his sack, and to give them provision for the way: and thus did he unto them. And they laded their asses with the corn, and departed thence.

And as one of them opened his sack to give his ass provender in the inn, he espied his money; for, behold, it was in his sack's mouth.

And he said unto his brethren, "My money is restored; and, lo, it is even in my sack!" And their heart failed them, and they were afraid, saying one to another, "What is this that God hath done unto us?"

And they came unto Jacob their father unto the land of Canaan, and told him all that befell unto them; saying, "The man, who is the lord of the land, spake roughly to us, and took us for spies of the country. And we said unto him, 'We are true men; we are no spies: We be twelve brethren, sons of our father; one is not, and the youngest is this day with our father in the land of Canaan.'

"And the man, the lord of the country, said unto us, 'Hereby shall I know that ye are true men; leave one of your brethren here with me, and take food for the famine of your households, and be gone: And bring your youngest brother unto me: then shall I know that ye are no spies, but that ye are true men: so will I deliver you your brother, and ye shall traffick in the land.' "

And it came to pass as they emptied their sacks, that, behold, every man's bundle of money was in his sack: and when both they and their father saw the bundles of money, they were afraid.

And Jacob their father said unto them, "<u>Me have ye bereaved of my children</u>: Joseph is not, and Simeon is not, and ye will take Benjamin away: all these things are against me."

And Reuben spake unto his father, saying, "Slay my two sons, if I bring him not to thee: deliver him into my hand, and I will bring him to thee again."

And [Jacob] said, "My son shall not go down with you; for his brother is dead, and he is left alone: if mischief befall him by the way in which ye go, then shall ye bring down my gray hairs with sorrow to the grave." (Gen 42:25-38)

Jacob refuses to let Benjamin go, putting the family into a deadlock. Consider that it's been seventeen years since Joseph was sold into Egypt. If Benjamin was born prior to Joseph's abduction, he would now be, say, 20 or older, and very much his own man in that culture ("Forget it, Father, I'm off!"). That Jacob is still highly protective of the lad suggests circumstantially that Benjamin may be younger than seventeen; thus still under his father's direct guidance, and therefore not known to Joseph, *nor by name.*

While the brothers are now painfully aware that this whole nightmare is God's punishment for what they did to Joseph, Jacob must be wondering at the cause for so much misery. His are the words of the defeated. Over the coming weeks, the family will glumly finish up the food they purchased before being compelled to confront Egypt ('the world') again. Meanwhile, Simeon is doing time in Egypt. It's quite revealing that there seems to be no sense of urgency within the family to alleviate Simeon's predicament!

And the famine was sore in the land. And it came to pass, when they had eaten up the corn which they had brought out of Egypt, their father said unto them, "Go again, buy us a little food."

And Judah spake unto him, saying, "The man did solemnly protest unto us, saying, 'Ye shall not see my face, except your brother be with you.' If thou wilt send our brother with us, we will go down and buy thee food: But if thou wilt not send him, we will not go down: for the man said unto us, 'Ye shall not see my face, except your brother be with you.' "

And Israel said, "Wherefore dealt ye so ill with me, as to tell the man whether ye had yet a brother?"

And they said, "The man asked us straitly of our state, and of our kindred, saying, 'Is your father yet alive? Have ye another brother?' And we told him according to the tenor of these words. Could we certainly know that he would say, 'Bring your brother down?' "

And Judah said unto Israel his father, "Send the lad with me, and we will arise and go; that we may live and not die, both we, and thou, and also our little ones. I will be surety for him; of my hand shalt thou require him: if I bring him not unto thee, and set him before thee, then let me bear the blame forever. For except

we had lingered, surely now we had returned this second time." (Gen 43:1-10)

Jacob's desperation is vented by an exasperated, "Why did you have to tell that Egyptian you had another brother?" Judah steps to the fore and breaks the deadlock. He shows his father that they have little choice because the alternative is death by starvation. All they have done by inaction is to prolong the agony. Notice that Judah was the one who came up with the original plan to sell Joseph into slavery. Now he will have to persuade his father to release Benjamin into his care so the family can purchase more food and recover Simeon. Judah will shine in the coming days, to his credit. As Jacob's fourth son, his progeny will become the royal/Messianic line, after Reuben, Simeon and Levi blew their inheritance through their previous, appalling behaviour.[512]

Jacob sees no other way out, just as Joseph must have predicted:

And their father Israel[513] said unto them, "If it must be so now, do this; take of the best fruits in the land in your vessels, and carry down the man a present, a little balm, and a little honey, spices, and myrrh, nuts, and almonds. And take double money in your hand; and the money that was brought again in the mouth of your sacks, carry it again in your hand; peradventure it was an oversight. Take also your brother, and arise, go again unto the man. And God Almighty give you mercy before the man, that he may send away your other brother, and Benjamin. If I be bereaved of my children, I am bereaved." (Gen 43:11-14)

Curiously, it seems the family is not 'on the bread line' if they have such extras to send down as gifts to Joseph! Jacob's last statement is resigned and very Jewish: **"If I be bereaved of my children, I am bereaved."** You can almost imagine him casting his hands up in the air.

---

[512] Reuben bedded one of his father's concubines. Simeon and Levi were responsible for the slaughter of the Shechemites after the rape of their sister, Dinah.

[513] Jacob is referred to in scripture by his new name 'Israel', when he is acting in the spirit. Most of the time, though, he's just 'Jacob'.

And the men took that present, and they took double money in their hand, and Benjamin; and rose up, and went down to Egypt, and stood before Joseph.

And when Joseph saw Benjamin with them, he said to the ruler of his house, "Bring these men home, and slay, and make ready; for these men shall dine with me at noon."

And the man did as Joseph bade; and the man brought the men into Joseph's house.

And the men were afraid, because they were brought into Joseph's house; and they said, "Because of the money that was returned in our sacks at the first time are we brought in; that he may seek occasion against us, and fall upon us, and take us for bondmen, and our asses."

And they came near to the steward of Joseph's house, and they communed with him at the door of the house, and said, "O sir, we came indeed down at the first time to buy food. And it came to pass, when we came to the inn, that we opened our sacks, and, behold, every man's money was in the mouth of his sack, our money in full weight: and we have brought it again in our hand. And other money have we brought down in our hands to buy food: we cannot tell who put our money in our sacks."

And [the steward] said, "Peace be to you, fear not: Your God, and the God of your father, hath given you treasure in your sacks: I had your money." And he brought Simeon out unto them.

And the man brought the men into Joseph's house, and gave them water, and they washed their feet; and he gave their asses provender. And they made ready the present for Joseph's coming at noon: for they heard that they should eat bread there.

And when Joseph came home, they brought him the present which was in their hand into the house, and bowed themselves to him to the earth. And he asked them of their welfare, and said, "Is your father well, the old man of whom ye spake? Is he yet alive?"

And they answered, "Thy servant our father is in good health, he is yet alive." And they bowed down their heads and made obeisance.

And [Joseph] **lifted up his eyes and saw his brother Benjamin, his mother's son, and said, "Is this your younger brother, of whom ye spake unto me?" And** [Joseph] **said, "God be gracious unto thee, my son."**

And Joseph made haste; for his bowels did yearn upon his brother: and he sought where to weep; and he entered into his chamber, and wept there. (Gen 43:15-30)

Some great points to note:

- Joseph is finally face-to-face with his beloved brother, Benjamin. The experience is so intense that Joseph has to remove himself from their presence to weep, lest he cause suspicion among his brothers
- Joseph can only guess that it is Benjamin. Even if Benjamin had been born prior to his abduction (unlikely), he would not have recognised him as a young man. Perhaps there is a detectable, familial likeness as a direct brother. After all, Leah was plain, Rachel was stunning. The true Benjamin would be as handsome and pleasing as Joseph
- Jacob's sons are gaining some solid lessons in humility. Previously the big fish in a little pond up in Canaan, the burly sons of a wealthy landowner; now they are outmatched and outclassed in Egypt
- Joseph deliberately puts them into an environment (his sumptuous house) to make them feel uncomfortable and out of their depth
- Joseph appears to have coached his steward in the ways of the Hebrew God
- Simeon is finally brought out of prison, doubtless chastised by the experience. It's been a number of months
- Joseph's brothers bow down again before him, partially fulfilling Joseph's dream. This time there are eleven stars, but no mother or father as yet

And [Joseph] **washed his face, and went out, and refrained himself, and said, "Set on bread."**

And they set on for him by himself, and for them by themselves, and for the Egyptians, which did eat with him, by

themselves: because the Egyptians might not eat bread with the Hebrews; for that is an abomination unto the Egyptians.

And they sat before him, the firstborn according to his birthright, and the youngest according to his youth: and the men marvelled one at another.

And he took and sent messes [servings] unto them from before him: but Benjamin's mess was five times so much as any of theirs. And they drank, and were merry with him. (Gen 43:31-34)

This 'high-born Egyptian official' ranks the brothers in their correct order of age at their table! Again, this is to create uncertainty and unease. Then Benjamin gets a favoured portion. Gradually the brothers relax and begin enjoying themselves, realising they are not under threat.

But Joseph and God are not through with these ruffians yet. If God is going to use these boys to father his forthcoming great nation, there must be further testing, and a display of genuine repentance. This is precisely the experience each of us currently undergoes during our own 'Earth programme'. God wants to build an eternal dynasty *with us* (Rev 2:26), so we require testing and refining in the fire of trials. We must overcome evil by doing good if we wish to abide forever. God needs overcomers for his forthcoming forever kingdom, not the overtaken.[514] This is the process underway with the brothers now.

And [Joseph] commanded the steward of his house, saying, "Fill the men's sacks with food, as much as they can carry, and put every man's money in his sack's mouth. And put my cup, the silver cup, in the sack's mouth of the youngest, and his corn money."

And [the steward] did according to the word that Joseph had spoken. (Gen 44:1-2)

This is called entrapment. Joseph's steward must be really enjoying himself by now.

---

[514] Gen 4:7; Psa 34:14; Psa 37:27; Dan 4:27; Matt 3:8-10; Luke 13:3,5; Acts 26:20; Rom 12:21; Eph 5:1; Titus 1:16; 1 Pet 3:10-12; 2 Pet 3:9; Rev 2:26

As soon as the morning was light, the men were sent away, they and their asses. And when they were gone out of the city, and not yet far off, Joseph said unto his steward:

"Up, follow after the men; and when thou dost overtake them, say unto them, 'Wherefore have ye rewarded evil for good? Is not this it in which my lord drinketh, and whereby indeed he divineth? Ye have done evil in so doing.' "

And [the steward] overtook them, and he spake unto them these same words. And they said unto him, "Wherefore saith my lord these words? God forbid that thy servants should do according to this thing. Behold, the money, which we found in our sacks' mouths, we brought again unto thee out of the land of Canaan. How then should we steal out of thy lord's house silver or gold? With whomsoever of thy servants it be found, both let him die. And we also will be my lord's bondmen." (Gen 44:3-9)

The steward would have taken armed guards with him. The effect of the brothers' apprehension on the road by the Egyptian ruler's personal seneschal is keen and shocking to the Hebrews, especially when accused of such a crime. The brothers' reaction echoes their father's own when Jacob was confronted decades before by another family member, Laban, who accused his family of stealing the *teraphim*:

Jacob: **"With whomsoever thou findest thy gods, let him not live!"** (Gen 31:32)

Jacob's sons: **"With whomsoever of thy servants it be found, both let him die!"** (Gen 44:9)

Definitely the sons of the father.

And [the steward] said, **"Now also let it be according unto your words. He with whom it is found shall be my servant; and ye shall be blameless."**

Then they speedily took down every man his sack to the ground, and opened every man his sack. And [the steward] searched, and began at the eldest, and left at the youngest [another shock to the brothers!]: and the cup was found in Benjamin's sack.

Then they rent their clothes, and laded every man his ass, and returned to the city.

And Judah and his brethren came to Joseph's house; for he was yet there: and they fell before him on the ground.

And Joseph said unto them, "What deed is this that ye have done? Know ye not that such a man as I can certainly divine?" (Gen 44:10-15)

That last statement is layered in irony. Joseph plays every inch the Egyptian ruler, and can indeed divine, but not in the heathen fashion via spells, cups and trinkets, but by the invisible Mighty One of Israel. There is more grovelling of the brothers before him, fulfilling the prophecy.

And then we have Judah. Realising they have been caught *in flagrante delicto*, and knowing that Benjamin shall not now be taking the road home to their grieving father, Judah makes one of the most impassioned pleas for clemency in the entire Bible. Notice in what follows that he does not dodge their putative guilt, but appeals to Joseph's humanity. This is a far cry from the Judah of thirteen year before, standing over the pit, looking down at Joseph, wondering how much he can flog him for. Now it's Judah on his knees, game over, staring up at Joseph for mercy:

And Judah said, "What shall we say unto my lord? What shall we speak? Or how shall we clear ourselves? God hath found out the iniquity of thy servants: behold, we are my lord's servants, both we, and he also with whom the cup is found."

And [Joseph] said, "God forbid that I should do so: but the man in whose hand the cup is found, he shall be my servant; and as for you, get you up in peace unto your father." [515]

Then Judah came near unto him, and said, "Oh my lord, let thy servant, I pray thee, speak a word in my lord's ears, and let not thine anger burn against thy servant: for thou art even as Pharaoh.

"My lord asked his servants, saying, 'Have ye a father, or a brother?' And we said unto my lord, 'We have a father, an old man, and a child of his old age, a little one; and his brother is dead, and he alone is left of his mother, and his father loveth him.'

---

[515] Joseph manoeuvres his brothers into the predicament of having to explain the loss of another son (Benjamin) to a grieving father, only this time for real.

"And thou saidst unto thy servants, 'Bring him down unto me, that I may set mine eyes upon him.'

"And we said unto my lord, 'The lad cannot leave his father: for if he should leave his father, his father would die.'

"And thou saidst unto thy servants, 'Except your youngest brother come down with you, ye shall see my face no more.'

"And it came to pass when we came up unto thy servant my father, we told him the words of my lord. And our father said, 'Go again, and buy us a little food.'

"And we said, 'We cannot go down: if our youngest brother be with us, then will we go down: for we may not see the man's face, except our youngest brother be with us.'

"And thy servant my father said unto us, 'Ye know that my wife bare me two sons. And the one went out from me, and I said, "Surely he is torn in pieces"; and I saw him not since. And if ye take this also from me, and mischief befall him, ye shall bring down my gray hairs with sorrow to the grave.'

"Now therefore when I come to thy servant my father, and the lad be not with us; seeing that his life is bound up in the lad's life; it shall come to pass, when he seeth that the lad is not with us, that he will die: and thy servants shall bring down the gray hairs of thy servant our father with sorrow to the grave. For thy servant became surety for the lad unto my father, saying, 'If I bring him not unto thee, then I shall bear the blame to my father forever.'

"Now therefore, I pray thee, let thy servant abide instead of the lad a bondman to my lord; and let the lad go up with his brethren. For how shall I go up to my father, and the lad be not with me? Lest peradventure I see the evil that shall come on my father." (Gen 44:16-34)

What an amazing petition. Joseph must have breathed a sigh of relief when he sat through this one. Judah and his brothers are now discerning good from evil and taking a stand, truly knowing now the implications of the loss of a loved one (Heb 5:13-14). Chuck Missler comments:

"Joseph's master-stroke: He tested their concern for Benjamin in order to get them to recognize their evil. If they had no compassion for this second son of Rachel, then they would have no part in the fulfilment of the promises. God could start over again and make Joseph into a great nation if the others proved unworthy. The test involved the men's silver in their sacks (as had been done on the first return trip), and placing Joseph's own silver cup in Benjamin's sack, and then pursuing them to arrest Benjamin.

"When the steward caught up with them and accused them of theft, he deliberately created tension among them by opening the sack of the oldest first and ending with the youngest. He knew, of course, that the silver cup was in Benjamin's sack. The sudden threat to Benjamin was like a sword thrust through their hearts (*cf.* Solomon's plan, 1 Kings 3:16-28). All the conditions were present for another betrayal when Benjamin was accused. Yet this time their response shows how well the chastening had done its work. They tore their clothes in grief, a response which they had earlier caused their father to make over Joseph's loss (Gen 37:34)....

"Judah's intercession was remarkable, one of the sublime utterances of Literature.... The spirit of self-sacrifice, once so foreign to Judah, shone forth with rare beauty. By his references to his father's suffering, Judah revealed himself as one now keenly aware of sacred values and relationships." [516]

Joseph reveals himself to his brothers

Then Joseph could not refrain himself before all them that stood by him; and he cried, "Cause every man to go out from me!" And there stood no man with him, while Joseph made himself known unto his brethren. And he wept aloud: and the Egyptians and the house of Pharaoh heard.

And Joseph said unto his brethren, "I am Joseph. Doth my father yet live?" And his brethren could not answer him; <u>for they were troubled at his presence.</u>

And Joseph said unto his brethren, "Come near to me, I pray you." And they came near. And he said, "I am Joseph your brother, whom ye sold into Egypt. Now therefore be not grieved, nor angry with yourselves, that ye sold me hither: for God did send me before you to preserve life. For these two years hath the

---

[516] Missler, Chuck, *Genesis* notes, op. cit., pp.286-287

511

famine been in the land: and yet there are five years, in the which there shall neither be earing nor harvest.

"And God sent me before you to preserve you a posterity in the earth, and to save your lives by a great deliverance. So now it was not you that sent me hither, but God: and he hath made me a father to Pharaoh, and lord of all his house, and a ruler throughout all the land of Egypt." (Gen 45:1-7)

Considering all that Joseph has suffered at the hands of those before him now, *what an extraordinary perspective.* Joseph's faith is one of the cardinal lessons of this young man's life. If God is in charge of EVERYTHING – and He is - *then God has done it that way for a reason.* Think about that nugget when applied to your own or anyone else's life. Bad, even horrendous things happen to good people, and have done so throughout history: the victimisation of God's Jewish people from the start; Christians fed to lions; the 70 AD wholesale slaughter of the Jewish population of Jerusalem; medieval martyrs burnt alive for their faith; the Nazi holocaust; atrocities visited upon God's people even in our modern age. Why does our Creator permit it? At no time during his enforced servitude is any complaining recorded from Joseph. Many times during his years of captivity he must have wondered about the adverse events of his life; the end-game and even the purpose of it; what would become of him; a yearning no different from a million others awaiting a cruel and undeserved fate at the hands of their tormentors. Yet Joseph's astonishing faith holds that it's God's problem. All will work out well in the end for those who love God, for those who are the called according to His purpose (Rom 8:28-29). Notice that Joseph, unlike his forefathers, has never had the benefit of direct contact with YHWH; only through dreams, yet he is always aware that God is working away behind the scenes to accomplish His purposes. If Egypt is a model for the harsh and unforgiving world, then Joseph has certainly overcome the world by his patience and faith.

"Haste ye, and go up to my father, and say unto him, 'Thus saith thy son Joseph, "God hath made me lord of all Egypt: come down unto me, tarry not: And thou shalt dwell in the land of Goshen, and thou shalt be near unto me, thou, and thy children, and thy children's children, and thy flocks, and thy herds, and all that thou hast: And there will I nourish thee; for yet there are five years of famine; lest thou, and thy household, and all that thou hast, come to poverty." '

"And, behold, your eyes see, and the eyes of my brother Benjamin, that it is my mouth that speaketh unto you. And ye shall tell my father of all my glory in Egypt, and of all that ye have seen; and ye shall haste and bring down my father hither."

And he fell upon his brother Benjamin's neck, and wept; and Benjamin wept upon his neck. Moreover he kissed all his brethren, and wept upon them: and after that his brethren talked with him. (Gen 45:1-15)

More of Arthur W Pink's parallels between Joseph and Jesus come to mind:

- Joseph proves a wonderful counsellor. *So does Yeshua* (Matt 7:28; 13:54; FG 7:46; Col 2:3)
- Joseph is given a Gentile bride. *So is Yeshua* (Rev 19:7-8)
- Joseph's marriage is arranged by the king. *So is Yeshua's* (Matt 22:2)
- Joseph is given a new name. *So is Yeshua* (Matt 1:21; Phil 2:9, 10; Rev 3:12)
- Joseph is 30 years old when he commences his real work. *So is Yeshua* (Gen 41:46; Luke 3:23)
- Joseph's work on the king's behalf involves plenty of activity and travelling. *So does Yeshua's* (Matt 4:23; 9:35)
- Joseph is unrecognised by his brethren. *So was Jesus* (FG 1:11)
- Joseph made himself known to his brethren the second time. *So will Jesus* (after Israel rejects Him the first time) (Isa 65:1; Hos 5:15; Acts 7:13)
- Joseph extends an incredible grace to those who wronged him. *So does Yeshua* (Zech 13:1; Isa 54:7, 8; Luke 23:34)
- Joseph's brethren are confounded at his presence. *So are Yeshua's* (Zech 12:10; FG 20:28)
- Joseph is a man of tremendous compassion in adverse circumstances (weeps seven times). *So is Yeshua* (*cf.* Luke 23:32-43; FG 11:35)

- Joseph becomes the saviour of Egypt ('the world'). *So does Yeshua* (FG 3:16)

Throughout the Joseph story, we are once more struck by the extraordinary character of the protagonist. David Pawson elucidates:

"The remarkable thing is that nothing said about Joseph is bad…. Abraham, Isaac and Jacob certainly had their weaknesses and sins. Not one word of criticism is levelled at Joseph. The worst thing he did was to be a bit tactless and tell his brothers about his dream of future greatness, but there is no trace whatever of a wrong attitude or reaction in Joseph's character. His reactions as he sinks down the social ladder are first-class: there is no trace of resentment, no complaining, no questioning of God, no sense of injustice that he should finish up in prison, on death row in Pharaoh's jail…. Even at rock bottom languishing in jail, his concern seems to have been primarily to help others as he seeks to comfort Pharaoh's cup-bearer and baker. Joseph is a man who seems to have no concern for himself, but a deep concern for everyone else." [517]

Joseph's circumstances and life hardly fit our own, yet how many times do we whine and moan at our predicaments with scant regard for the big picture? Unbelievers are rocked hither and thither on what they believe are the random tides of an ultimately pointless life, but for those of us who do trust God, *are we really trusting Him, no matter the predicament?* We like the Joseph story, especially how it all comes right in the end, but do we pause to consider how hard it must have been for Joseph in those dark years of uncertainty? As Pawson says, not one word of complaint is recorded. Daniel and Jesus are the only other personages in the Bible about whom that can be said. The clear message of the Joseph story is that, however hard it may be, we are to emulate this behaviour as a demonstration of our faith in God and His bigger picture. This is part of our training in the Earth programme to prepare us properly for service in the Eternal Kingdom. Daily we will be given further opportunities to practise this extraordinary behaviour as trials and tribulations come our way. Will we

---

[517] **Pawson, David** *Unlocking the Bible,* HarperCollins, 2007, p.92

overcome the world, even as Joseph has done? Do we even care enough to? [518]

Jacob comes to Egypt

And the fame thereof was heard in Pharaoh's house, saying, "Joseph's brethren are come!" And it pleased Pharaoh well, and his servants.

And Pharaoh said unto Joseph, "Say unto thy brethren, 'This do ye; lade your beasts, and go, get you unto the land of Canaan. And take your father and your households, and come unto me: and I will give you the good of the land of Egypt, and ye shall eat the fat of the land. Now thou art commanded, this do ye; take you wagons out of the land of Egypt for your little ones, and for your wives, and bring your father, and come. Also regard not your stuff; for the good of all the land of Egypt is yours.' "

And the children of Israel did so: and Joseph gave them wagons, according to the commandment of Pharaoh, and gave them provision for the way. To all of them he gave each man changes of raiment; but to Benjamin he gave three hundred pieces of silver, and five changes of raiment. And to his father he sent after this manner; ten asses laden with the good things of Egypt, and ten she-asses laden with corn and bread and meat for his father by the way.

So he sent his brethren away, and they departed: and he said unto them, "See that ye fall not out by the way [i.e. "No arguing on the way home!"- Joseph knows his brothers!]."

And they went up out of Egypt, and came into the land of Canaan unto Jacob their father, and told him, saying, "Joseph is yet alive, and he is governor over all the land of Egypt." And Jacob's heart fainted, for he believed them not.

And they told him all the words of Joseph, which he had said unto them: and when he saw the wagons which Joseph had sent to carry him, the spirit of Jacob their father revived. And Israel said, "It is enough; Joseph my son is yet alive: I will go and see him before I die."

---

[518] Gen 4:7; Psa 34:14; Psa 37:27; Dan 4:27; Matt 3:8-10; Luke 13:3,5; Acts 26:20; Rom 12:21; Gal 5:24; Eph 5:1; Titus 1:16; 1 Pet 3:10; 2 Pet 3:9; Rev 2:26

And Israel took his journey with all that he had, and came to Beersheba, and offered sacrifices unto the God of his father Isaac. And God spake unto Israel in the visions of the night, and said, "Jacob, Jacob." And he said, "Here am I."

And he said, "I am God, the God of thy father: fear not to go down into Egypt; for I will there make of thee a great nation. I will go down with thee into Egypt; and I will also surely bring thee up again: and Joseph shall put his hand upon thine eyes."

And Jacob rose up from Beersheba: and the sons of Israel carried Jacob their father, and their little ones, and their wives, in the wagons which Pharaoh had sent to carry him. And they took their cattle, and their goods, which they had gotten in the land of Canaan, and came into Egypt, Jacob, and all his seed with him: His sons, and his sons' sons with him, his daughters, and his sons' daughters, and all his seed brought he with him into Egypt. (Gen 45:16 - 46:7)

God tells Jacob that Joseph will close his eyes when he dies, a cause of considerable comfort to the old man. God also reiterates His covenant promise to make of Jacob a great nation.

And [Jacob] sent Judah before him unto Joseph, to direct his face unto Goshen; and they came into the land of Goshen. And Joseph made ready his chariot, and went up to meet Israel his father, to Goshen, and presented himself unto him; and he fell on his neck, and wept on his neck a good while.

And Israel said unto Joseph, "Now let me die, since I have seen thy face, because thou art yet alive." (Gen 46:28-30) [519]

Seventy Hebrews come down to Egypt (Gen 46:27). Experts estimate that this population grows to around two million in the ensuing centuries leading up to the Exodus. The curtain will shortly come down over Israel's story in Egypt as we end this volume, but will rise again in *Origins 3* to reveal a very different, later Egypt, with a multitude of Jews enduring harsh bondage under a pharaoh 'who knew Joseph not' (Exo 1:8).

---

[519] Faint echoes here of the NT seer, Simeon, who is told by the Holy Spirit that he shall not see death until he has seen Jesus. Well worth reading Luke 2:25-35 to get the parallel with Jacob and Joseph now.

And while on the subject, let us wonder for a moment at the sheer magnificence of this Joseph-era pharaoh, not often remarked upon. An example of grace in his own right, this ruler is not only uncommonly magnanimous, he goes out of his way to allow Joseph to invite the entire family down to Egypt with a view to settling there, giving them the prime choice of land in the Delta around Goshen. Could there be an ulterior motive? Some have suggested that if this ruler is a Hyksos king styling himself as an Egyptian pharaoh, he will be ever aware that the true displaced Egyptian dynasty south at Thebes will at some point attempt to regain control over Lower Egypt. Therefore all help might be required, especially if accompanied by provable, awesome Deity.

Efforts have been made to identify this pharaoh, whose name has been lost to history. The Holy Spirit could quite easily have had Moses name him, yet has chosen not to. Rather, God wishes to follow his common duplex pattern throughout the Bible, on this occasion to contrast a good pharaoh (Joseph-era) with the forthcoming antitype who will oppose Moses. But the real emphasis in Joseph's story is his model for God's Son, Yeshua *ha-Mashiach*, Jesus Christ, our Creator and Saviour, the future Judge and King of Planet Earth for a thousand years in the Millennial Kingdom, and our God forever, before whom *every* knee shall bow (Phil 2:9-11), yes, even the ones that don't want to.

To Joseph, the honour he now enjoys as vizier is only thanks to God's outworking of His will. Staring into his father's beloved, frail face now, Joseph must have wondered many times during the harsh years whether he would ever see the old man again. Imagine his joy now in being able to take his father and brothers to meet Pharaoh and present them formally before the court. But not without giving the entire family a pep talk first before ushering them into the royal presence:

And Joseph said unto his brethren, and unto his father's house, "I will go up, and shew Pharaoh, and say unto him, 'My brethren, and my father's house, which were in the land of Canaan, are come unto me; And the men are shepherds, for their trade hath been to feed cattle; and they have brought their flocks, and their herds, and all that they have.'

"And it shall come to pass, when Pharaoh shall call you, and shall say, 'What is your occupation?' That ye shall say, 'Thy servants' trade hath been about cattle from our youth even until now, both we, and also our fathers', that ye may dwell in the land of Goshen; <u>for every shepherd is an abomination unto the Egyptians</u>."

Then Joseph came and told Pharaoh, and said, "My father and my brethren, and their flocks, and their herds, and all that they have, are come out of the land of Canaan; and, behold, they are in the land of Goshen."

And he took some of his brethren, even five men, and presented them unto Pharaoh.

And Pharaoh said unto his brethren, "What is your occupation?"

And they said unto Pharaoh, "<u>Thy servants are shepherds</u>, both we, and also our fathers."

They said moreover unto Pharaoh, "For to sojourn in the land are we come; for thy servants have no pasture for their flocks; for the famine is sore in the land of Canaan: now therefore, we pray thee, let thy servants dwell in the land of Goshen."

And Pharaoh spake unto Joseph, saying, "Thy father and thy brethren are come unto thee: The land of Egypt is before thee; in the best of the land make thy father and brethren to dwell; in the land of Goshen let them dwell: and if thou knowest any men of activity among them, <u>then make them rulers over my cattle</u>."

And Joseph brought in Jacob his father, and set him before Pharaoh: and Jacob blessed Pharaoh. And Pharaoh said unto Jacob, "How old art thou?"

And Jacob said unto Pharaoh, "The days of the years of my pilgrimage are an hundred and thirty years: few and evil have the days of the years of my life been, <u>and have not attained unto the days of the years of the life of my fathers in the days of their pilgrimage</u>."

And Jacob blessed Pharaoh, and went out from before Pharaoh.

And Joseph placed his father and his brethren, and gave them a possession in the land of Egypt, in the best of the land, in the land of Rameses, as Pharaoh had commanded. And Joseph

nourished his father, and his brethren, and all his father's household, with bread, according to their families. (Gen 46:28 - 47:12)

Some points to note:

- Joseph's brothers soon recover their recalcitrant nature. Having been warned by Joseph not to mention to Pharaoh that they are shepherds, they do exactly that, going on to assert that they have come to Egypt to survive the famine; and by the way, the choice cut of the land would be appreciated! (Goshen)
- Pharaoh is quite happy for Joseph's kin to ranch his cattle! This would be unthinkable under a true Egyptian pharaoh, who would not only hold all Canaanites in utter contempt (especially shepherds), but view his cows as holy, only to be tended by selected priests
- Jacob laments that his longevity will not be as his forebears – a passing allusion to the lifespans progressively shortening after the Flood
- Jacob blesses Pharaoh, a sure contrast to the pharaoh who will follow centuries later to curse and afflict the Israelites

Chuck Missler writes:

"JACOB AND JOSEPH COMPARED: Both begin with the father being deceived and the brothers being treacherous (Gen 27; 37); both include a 20-year period of separation, with the younger brother in a foreign land. Jacob (31:38); Joseph—13 years in Potiphar's house and prison from age 17 to age 30 (37:2; 41:46); after 7 years of abundance his brothers came to Egypt, (41:53-54; 42:1-2); both conclude with a reunion and reconciliation of the brothers (33:1-15; 45:1-15)." [520]

All's well that ends well

And so the story ends for now for Joseph and his family, who settle into their new lands in Goshen under Pharaoh's patronage. Joseph sets about tending to the urgent business of adjudicating the people's needs during the famine, and has a remarkable plan for

---

[520] Missler, Chuck, *Genesis* notes, op. cit. p.288

enriching Egypt. As the famine progresses, people begin running out of money, having spent it all on the food which the state has sold them. So Joseph accepts the people's livestock in exchange for victuals. When the horses, cattle, flocks and donkeys all run out, Joseph begins sequestering the people's lands in return for their continued sustenance. It's all done with grace, but by the time the famine has run its seven-year course, Pharaoh ends up owning Egypt, which has now become a land of tenant farmers.

And Joseph bought all the land of Egypt for Pharaoh; for the Egyptians sold every man his field, because the famine prevailed over them: so the land became Pharaoh's. And as for the people, he removed them to cities from one end of the borders of Egypt even to the other end thereof. Only the land of the priests bought he not; for the priests had a portion assigned them of Pharaoh, and did eat their portion which Pharaoh gave them: wherefore they sold not their lands.

Then Joseph said unto the people, "Behold, I have bought you this day and your land for Pharaoh: lo, here is seed for you, and ye shall sow the land. And it shall come to pass in the increase, that ye shall give the fifth part unto Pharaoh, and four parts shall be your own, for seed of the field, and for your food, and for them of your households, and for food for your little ones."

And they said, "Thou hast saved our lives: let us find grace in the sight of my lord, and we will be Pharaoh's servants."

And Joseph made it a law over the land of Egypt unto this day, that Pharaoh should have the fifth part; except the land of the priests only, which became not Pharaoh's.

And Israel dwelt in the land of Egypt, in the country of Goshen; and they had possessions therein, and grew, and multiplied exceedingly. And Jacob lived in the land of Egypt seventeen years: so the whole age of Jacob was an hundred forty and seven years. (Gen 47:20-28)

Centralised government; income tax at 20%, and food on the table for everyone. But the population is now in bondage to Pharaoh, though their tax rate is under half that of today's USA!

Jacob's final days

Jacob survives a further 17 years. He has elicited a promise from Joseph that he will be buried in the family plot in the cave of Machpelah in Hebron, Canaan. One of the last acts the patriarch carries out is formally to adopt Joseph's two sons, Manasseh and Ephraim. Interestingly, he passes over Manasseh, the firstborn, and places his right hand on Ephraim's head instead. This upsets Joseph, who thinks the old man is undergoing a senior moment:

And Joseph said unto his father, "Not so, my father: for this is the firstborn; put thy right hand upon his head."

And his father refused, and said, "I know it, my son, I know it: he also shall become a people, and he also shall be great: but truly his younger brother shall be greater than he, and his seed shall become a multitude of nations."

And he blessed them that day, saying, "In thee shall Israel bless, saying, 'God make thee as Ephraim and as Manasseh': and he set Ephraim before Manasseh (Gen 48:18-20).

There has been a clear pattern from the start of the elder often being passed over for the younger: Abel over Cain; Shem over Japheth; Isaac over Ishmael; Jacob over Esau; now Ephraim over Manasseh; later, Moses over Aaron, and David over all his elder brothers. God indeed gives a special blessing to the firstborn, but in the case of the heir's default, He reserves His sovereign right to reallocate His favours. Only God knows the end from the beginning, and He must have communicated His desires to Jacob in the matter of these blessings for Ephraim and Manasseh.

In so doing, Israel grants Joseph a double portion of the family inheritance in line with the privileges of the firstborn. As Jacob's son, Joseph will father one of the tribes of the future nation of Israel, but this tribe of Joseph will comprise two tribes within it: Ephraim and Manasseh.

On his deathbed, Jacob prophesies over each of his sons in short cryptic verses, some of which are extraordinary. We'll keep these for *Origins 3 – The Predicament of Man*, as they become important in Israel's subsequent history. After finishing, Jacob draws up his feet into the bed, gives up the ghost, and is gathered unto his people. It's the end of one era and the start of another. Joseph approaches Pharaoh:

"My father made me swear, saying, 'Lo, I die: in my grave which I have digged for me in the land of Canaan, there shalt thou bury me.' Now therefore let me go up, I pray thee, and bury my father, and I will come again."

And Pharaoh said, "Go up, and bury thy father, according as he made thee swear."

And Joseph went up to bury his father: and with him went up all the servants of Pharaoh, the elders of his house, and all the elders of the land of Egypt, And all the house of Joseph, and his brethren, and his father's house: only their little ones, and their flocks, and their herds, they left in the land of Goshen.

And there went up with him both chariots and horsemen: and it was a very great company. And they came to the threshing-floor of Atad, which is beyond Jordan, and there they mourned with a great and very sore lamentation: and he made a mourning for his father seven days.

And when the inhabitants of the land, the Canaanites, saw the mourning in the floor of Atad, they said, "This is a grievous mourning to the Egyptians": wherefore the name of it was called Abelmizraim, which is beyond Jordan.

And his sons did unto him according as he commanded them. For his sons carried him into the land of Canaan, and buried him in the cave of the field of Machpelah, which Abraham bought with the field for a possession of a burying-place of Ephron the Hittite, before Mamre.

And Joseph returned into Egypt, he, and his brethren, and all that went up with him to bury his father, after he had buried his father. (Gen 50:5-14)

It's the first time Joseph has been out of Egypt since he was sold as a slave there years before. It must have been a moving time for him to revisit the land of his youth, even under such circumstances, yet Joseph is by now thoroughly Egyptianised. Contrasted with Egypt, Canaan is a mess after the ravages of the famine. The experience of being among the violent Baal-worshiping Amorites too must have caused Joseph to yearn for a return to the lovely Asenath and his children in Egypt, which of course he does. But there's a problem upon his return:

And when Joseph's brethren saw that their father was dead, they said, "Joseph will peradventure hate us, and will certainly requite us all the evil which we did unto him." And they sent a messenger unto Joseph, saying, "Thy father did command before he died, saying, 'So shall ye say unto Joseph, "Forgive, I pray thee now, the trespass of thy brethren, and their sin; for they did unto thee evil": and now, we pray thee, forgive the trespass of the servants of the God of thy father.' "

And Joseph wept when they spake unto him. And his brethren also went and fell down before his face; and they said, "Behold, we be thy servants."

And Joseph said unto them, "Fear not: for am I in the place of God? But as for you, ye thought evil against me; but God meant it unto good, to bring to pass, as it is this day, to save much people alive. Now therefore fear ye not: I will nourish you, and your little ones."

And he comforted them, and spake kindly unto them. (Gen 50:15-21)

And there's Joseph for you. All for the others, and his own interests in God's hands.

POSTSCRIPT

Joseph dies at the grand old age of 110; admittedly not long by patriarch standards, but a fair innings compared with today. He lives long enough to see Ephraim's children to the third generation, and the grandchildren of Manasseh are also brought up on Joseph's knee. The book of Genesis, which began with the Shekinah Glory at the Creation, closes with Joseph's coffin in Egypt, and a promise that his bones would be taken back to Canaan one day and laid to rest by his descendants in the land of God's promise.

It's a suitable spot to put down my pen and consider the astonishing journey we've taken so far. I'm struck by extraordinary thoughts. As I look out of my study window, my garden grows before my eyes. I'm aware of all the detail, the intricacies; pears on that tree; apples on the other one by the gate; roses growing up to stare through my window; total order. How downright improbable that it all came about *from an explosion*. And the fact that everything is *just there* isn't enough. *What sustains it?* Am I mad for asking? I certainly look mad. Am I deluded or *inspired?*

Atheists complain that if there were a God, why wouldn't He skywrite messages to us so there's no doubt? Christian author Mark Eastman states that God could certainly rip a hole in the sky once a month, stick his head through and boom, "Hello humans! I'm God and you're not!" *but He doesn't.* Therefore, if He exists but doesn't wish to make Himself known in sky-ripping, tea-leaves or Ouija, the obvious conclusion is that *He wants us to search for Him*. This is the selection method God intends us to use to prove that we care enough about Him to know more. And where better to search for the Creator than in His Word, the written manifestation of His Deity (FG 1:1-3)?

When asked what he might say if he ran into the Almighty after he died, Richard Dawkins quotes atheist Bertrand Russell:

"Sir, why did You take such pains to hide Yourself?" [521]

---

[521] Stein, Ben, *Expelled – No Intelligence Allowed*, DVD, available at www.credence.org, op. cit.

524

Hide Himself?! He showed up one time as a man, performing miracles, and you didn't believe Him then! Yet Richard has certainly read enough of the Old Testament to fuel his outrage at Joshua's genocide of certain Canaanite tribes (dealt with in *Origins 3 – The Predicament of Man*). But is the Designer really hidden for those who want to find Him? Up until recently, there was a Bible in every hotel bedroom drawer. It's the bestselling book of all time, indicating that numerous people have loved God enough to read what He has to say and ponder it. The Bible answers the question of 'God hiding' in somewhat sterner terms:

"For the wrath of God is revealed from Heaven against all ungodliness and unrighteousness of men, who hold the truth in unrighteousness. <u>Because that which may be known of God is manifest in them, for God hath shewed it unto them. For the invisible things of Him from the creation of the world</u> [Greek: <u>*kosmos*</u>] <u>**are clearly seen, being understood by the things that are made, even his eternal power and Godhead, so that they are without excuse.**</u>

Because that, when they knew God, they glorified Him not as God, neither were thankful, but became vain in their imaginations, and their foolish heart was darkened.

<u>**Professing themselves to be wise, they became fools**</u>**, and changed the glory of the incorruptible God into an image made like to corruptible man, and to birds, and four-footed beasts and creeping things** [e.g. monkeys, 'missing links' and amoebas!]. **Wherefore God also gave them up to uncleanness through the lusts of their own hearts, to dishonour their own bodies between themselves. Who changed the truth of God into a lie, and worshipped and served the creature more than the Creator, who is blessed for ever. Amen."** (Rom 1:18-25)

"Or speak to the Earth, and it shall teach thee: and the fishes of the sea shall declare unto thee. Who knoweth not in all these that the hand of the LORD hath wrought this?" (Job 12:8-9)

I'm intrigued by how SETI scientists blow millions of dollars trying to find intelligent life in the universe, or search the radio waves for some sort of intelligent ET message, positively *yearning* to take the champagne off ice and shout from the rooftops, "We are not alone!" And yet, when faced with irrefutable proof of the extraterrestrial message system they've had all along in their hotel bedroom drawer, highlighting in kaleidoscopic detail the Author who made them and everything else, they are disbelieving; hostile; they don't like what He tells them. It's a sovereignty thing. The serpent's hiss in the Garden. To be like the Most High. To play at being God. Man puffed up with his own achievements to do what he likes with his free will. *I did it My Way.* The downward pull of human nature. The original sin. Pride.

A person's refusal to defer to a transcendent power greater than themselves will always be down to pride; the inability to admit that they aren't in charge; that there's accountability at the end of a life; that He's God and they're not. It's just easier to pretend He doesn't exist. To reject the stark proofs for the Bible's unique and transcendent pedigree – this extraordinary compilation of 66 books written by 40 authors – on the face of it seems an act of wilful stupidity in view of the evidence (Psa 14:1). An 'expert' rejecting the Bible's authenticity *is certainly not scientific behaviour*, it is a wilful act of prejudice. Yet almost all the people I have come across, who vociferously denounce the Bible as 'God's Word', when pushed, admit that they have never studied it, nor come across any of the analyses covered in this book. Those who do try to read parts of it put it down a few minutes later and go off in search of something more interesting. Why? In the absence of God's Spirit, the Bible (the Son) has no form or comeliness that they should desire it (Isa 53:1-5). You can be 'religious' and still not get it because the Spirit of God is not in you. Centuries later, Yeshua will be surrounded by hostile, disbelieving *religious* Scribes and Pharisees seeking to kill Him for His claim to be the Creator. They don't get who He is because the Spirit is not in them either. This is what Jesus says to them:

"Search the scriptures; for in them ye think ye have eternal life: <u>and they are they which testify of Me</u>. And ye will not come to Me, that ye might have life. I receive not honour from men. But I know you, <u>that ye have not the love of God in you</u>. I am come in My Father's name, and ye receive Me not. If another shall come in his own name, him ye will receive. <u>How can ye</u>

believe, which receive honour one of another, and seek not the honour that cometh from God only?" (FG 5:39-44)

If you've made it to these final pages, the chances are you're a truth-seeker and God's Spirit is tugging at you. And don't for one moment think the reason for this is down to my imperfect efforts to stumble through explanations for eternal concepts. You will have noticed that a sizeable chunk of this journey has been quoting and reviewing scripture – the Word Himself made flesh – so thankfully those parts of *Origins 2* are God-breathed and inspired even if the rest isn't.

You will also have noticed something else. The Bible is not really about the Creation. God spends a few chapters in Genesis and a few others elsewhere to describe how He brought all things into being. (Notice God doesn't 'make a case' for Creation, He just declares it). *The rest of the Bible is given over to the redemption of mankind.* That's you and I in the Holy War. You will also have noticed that there is a selection process underway. Tomorrow is promised to no man, so everyone is on the clock with our toes hanging over the edge of eternity. God wants each of us to seek Him, make our peace in the Holy War, and in so doing have our eternal passports stamped 'Not Guilty' *before* the Judgment. God desires a relationship with you, not bovine, check-your-mind-in-at-the-door, cyborg servitude. There are hundreds of verses in the Message System given over to this. Here is a sample:

"I love them that love Me; and those that seek Me early shall find Me." (Prov 8:17)

Jesus: **"Ask, and it shall be given you; seek, and ye shall find; knock, and it shall be opened unto you: For every one that asketh receiveth; and he that seeketh findeth; and to him that knocketh it shall be opened."** (Matt 7:7-8)

The LORD is good unto them that wait for Him, to the soul that seeketh Him. (Lam 3:25)

Seek ye the LORD while He may be found, call ye upon Him while He is near: Let the wicked forsake his way, and the unrighteous man his thoughts: and let him return unto the LORD, and He will have mercy upon him; and to our God, for He will abundantly pardon. "For my thoughts are not your thoughts, neither are your ways My ways," saith the LORD. "For as the

heavens are higher than the Earth, so are My ways higher than your ways, and My thoughts than your thoughts." (Isa 55:6-9)

Jesus: "But seek ye first the kingdom of God, and His righteousness; and all these things shall be added unto you." (Matt 6:33)

"And ye shall seek Me and find Me, when ye shall search for Me with all your heart." (Jer 29:13)

But without faith it is impossible to please Him: for he that cometh to God must believe that He is [exists], and that He is a rewarder of them that diligently seek Him. (Heb 11:6)

How relevant is all this? At the time of writing, the Islamic State is butchering and raping its way across Iraq to secure its new 'caliphate', in the belief that their god will reward them with the highest state of paradise for this abominable behaviour. American photographer James Foley has just been beheaded on film by what sounds like a British jihadist. Hamas and Israel are bombing each other in the usual, relentless war of rockets and tit-for-tat shootings. Israel's right to exist is being fashionably questioned by left-wing *chatterati* around the world, like British 'Respect' MP George Galloway, who has just proclaimed his Bradford constituency 'an Israel-free zone', stating that his comments cannot be viewed by the police as racist since Israel is not a race.[522] I am reminded of God's promise to Abraham:

"And I will bless them that bless thee, and curse him that curseth thee: and in thee shall all families of the earth be blessed." (Gen 12:3)

Doesn't sound like George gets the blessing. The Holy War rages today as it ever did. As parts of the world descend once more into violence and anarchy, God gives each believer a simple remedy. Notice that it's not about persuading the wicked to repentance, it's about believers in Him cleaning up their own act!

"If My people, which are called by My name, shall humble themselves, and pray, and seek My face, and turn from their wicked ways; then will I hear from heaven, and will forgive their sin, and will heal their land. Now Mine eyes shall be open, and

---

[522] *Daily Mail*, "I won't be silenced, says Galloway", 20th August 2014

Mine ears attend unto the prayer that is made in this place." (2 Chron 7:14-15)

What God wants is our surrender in the Holy War.
While He yet may be found.

THE END

Books in the *Origins* series

Origins 1 – The Greatest Scientific Discovery (2009)
Origins 2 – Holy War (2014)
Origins 3 – The Predicament of Man (2015)
Origins 4 – Tetelestai (2015/2016)
Origins 5 – Parousia (2017)

INDEX

533

N

O

P

ABOUT THE AUTHOR

Phillip Day was born in England in 1960. He was educated at the leading British education establishments Selwyn and Charterhouse, and throughout his 20s had a successful entrepreneurial career founding businesses in sales and marketing. With a firm grounding in business and the ways of the media, Phillip's research career began after he became interested in wars going on in the realms of health, politics and the information sciences over  issues that were being deliberately misreported to the public. He is founder and chief executive of the Campaign for Truth in Medicine, a global citizen's health advocacy movement.

His research into human origins reflects the same dedication Phillip has previously brought to the subjects of public health and disease, which have resulted in fourteen books exposing numerous examples of the establishment's entrenched scientific error and brazen profiteering to society's cost. Today, Phillip Day's speaking schedule takes him all over the world, lecturing on the subject of entrenched scientific error, health, disease and wellness.

Phillip Day heads the publishing and research organisation Credence and lives in Kent, England. He is married to Samantha and they have a daughter, Anna.